# GOVERNMENT AND POLITICS IN THE LONE STAR STATE

## *THEORY AND PRACTICE*

**L. TUCKER GIBSON, JR.**
*Trinity University*

**CLAY ROBISON**
*Houston Chronicle*

Prentice Hall, Englewood Cliffs, New Jersey 07632

*Library of Congress Cataloging-in-Publication Data*

GIBSON, L. TUCKER
Government and politics in the Lone Star State: theory and
practice / L. TUCKER GIBSON, JR., CLAY ROBISON.
p. cm.
Includes bibliographical references and index.
ISBN 0-13-912791-7
1. Texas—Politics and government—1951- I. Robison, Clay.
II. Title.
JK4816.G53    1993
320.9764—dc20        92-26851

Acquisitions Editor: *Julie Berrisford*
Editorial/production supervision and interior design: *Joanne Riker*
Cover design: *Joe DiDomenico*
Prepress buyer: *Kelly Behr*
Manufacturing buyer: *Mary Ann Gloriande*

Printed in the United States of America

10 9 8 7 6 5 4 3 2 1

ISBN 0-13-912791-7

Prentice-Hall International (UK) Limited, *London*
Prentice-Hall of Australia Pty. Limited, *Sydney*
Prentice-Hall Canada Inc., *Toronto*
Prentice-Hall Hispanoamericana, S.A., *Mexico*
Prentice-Hall of India Private Limited, *New Delhi*
Prentice-Hall of Japan, Inc., *Tokyo*
Simon & Schuster Asia Pte. Ltd., *Singapore*
Editora Prentice-Hall do Brasil, Ltda., *Rio de Janeiro*

To Roxanne and Taylor, my wife and daughter, for their love, patience and inspiration and to the memory of my mother, Louise, a caring person whom we all miss.

*Clay Robison*


To Dorothy, my wife and best friend, for her patience and encouragement during the long months when my attention was consumed by this project.

*L. Tucker Gibson, Jr.*

# CONTENTS

**12** LOCAL GOVERNMENTS IN TEXAS:  CITIES, TOWNS, COUNTIES, AND SPECIAL DISTRICTS  *371*

**13** CONTEMPORARY PUBLIC POLICY ISSUES IN TEXAS  *418*

GLOSSARY  *453*

INDEX  *463*

# PREFACE

There is no way around it. Often discussed but seldom praised, government plays a major role in molding the quality of our lives. Such vital, everyday basics as the purity of the air we breathe, the water we drink, and the food we eat are determined by levels of governmental action or inaction. So are the safety of our streets and neighborhoods and the quality of our schools. Governmental regulatory practices set the price we pay for telephone service, and tax policies help determine how much we pay for gasoline, clothes, jewelry, and most other commodities. Government even tells us we must wear seatbelts and motorcycle helmets.

To understand government and how its laws and policies affect us, we have to understand the principles upon which it is based and know something of the theories behind political behavior. But government is more than a set of principles and theories. Government is alive. It is people, bending and changing the rules to meet changing conditions.

The subject of this book is Texas government and its relationship to the people it serves and to the federal and local governments that form the American political system. In the following chapters, we will attempt not only to outline the principles and theories upon which state government is built, but also to discuss their practical applications and misapplications in anecdotal material drawn from actual events.

We will present a great deal of information about the structure and functions of political and governmental institutions so as to provide the reader with the basic data and tools necessary to understand how these institutions are supposed to work. And we will weave through this material our assessments of how these institutions really work, because theory and reality often are not the same. Our purpose is not to train you to be a political scientist, but to assist you in a lifelong journey in civic education, whereby you can develop the concepts, skills, and behaviors necessary to make political and governmental institutions more responsive to your needs and interests.

One of the authors is a journalist who has covered Texas government and politics for more than 20 years. He crafts his arguments from the perspective of one who has seen both the best and the worst of public officials. Having made the observation of political behavior a lifelong vocation, he brings to our analysis a healthy skepticism of what those in public life say they are doing and insight into what they have actually done. His job has been to tell the story, and as you cover the different chapters in this book, we suggest that you ask, "What is the story here?"

The second author is a political scientist trained in the theories and concepts that apply to the study of state and local politics. His contribution to this enterprise is to provide a theoretical perspective on the subject matter that he has been teaching for more than 25 years. He also brings a perspective of 20 years of campaign consulting, redistricting of local governmental bodies and public opinion research for both the public and private sectors. Several chapters will reflect a more theoretical approach than others. This was done to introduce the reader to concepts and a vocabulary that have become part of the general discussion and debates of government and politics.

We are concerned with the normative, or value, issues of government, and we have some rather strong opinions as to what governments and public officials should or should not do. At times, these opinions are likely to be imbedded in our discussion. We have not attempted to gloss over controversial issues, and there are implicit values in the very nature of our approach and the assumptions upon which we have built our discussion and analysis. When you encounter these assumptions and values, we invite you to question them. In the process, you will begin to develop a better understanding of your own value system as well as those values held by others.

## ACKNOWLEDGMENTS

Numerous individuals provided information and assistance that was crucial in the preparation of this book. The authors particularly would like to thank Ann Arnold, executive director of the Texas Association of Broadcasters and a former member of the Capitol press corps; Bo Byers, retired Austin bureau chief of the *Houston Chronicle*; political consultant George Christian; Lawrence Olsen, executive vice president of the Texas Good Roads/Transportation Association; state Representative D.R. "Tom" Uher; the staff of the Legislative Reference Library, especially Sally Reynolds and Nancy Moreno; Andy Welch and other members of the State Comptroller's information services staff; Kathy Staat and other Senate Media Services staffers, and John Bender of former House Speaker Gib Lewis' staff.

Mary Ann Jacko spent hours poring over the mechanical details of each draft and provided invaluable comments on style and format.

Despite our illegible handwriting and our limited wordprocessing skills, Susie Dubose and Jane Wagenfuehr patiently and enthusiastically assisted us in getting this manuscript into final form. Three Trinity University student assistants— Melissa Fernandez, Kristen Giddens, and Michelle Lew—graciously undertook numerous assignments throughout this project.

A special note of appreciation to our colleagues, at the *Houston Chronicle* and Trinity University, for their comments, collegiality, and encouragement.

Trinity University provided Tucker Gibson with a leave of absence during the fall of 1991, and this time was critical to the completion of the project.

The production personnel of Prentice Hall, especially Joanne Riker and Edie Riker, were most helpful in transforming our manuscript into a finished product.

Karen Horton, Dolores Mars, and Julie Berrisford of Prentice Hall assisted us through many of the initial hurdles we faced as we developed this project, and we appreciate their confidence, direction, and support.

# 1

# THE SOCIAL AND ECONOMIC MILIEU OF TEXAS POLITICS

I'm from Texas.
What country are you from?
*Bumper sticker seen on a car in San Antonio*

Texans sincerely believe that all other Americans are envious of them.
*J.B. Priestley*[1]

Where else but in the Lone Star State is it considered socially acceptable to toss cow chips and eat chili at the same time? Where else would a Hollywood producer claim to be amazed at finding a quality symphony concert rather than tumbleweeds and six-shooters?[2] And where else would most residents apparently not be offended?

Where else could a wealthy poultry producer pass out $10,000 checks to state lawmakers on the Senate floor and not be prosecuted? Where else would a multimillionaire oilman saddle up in the middle of the space age and try to ride horseback into the Governor's Mansion? And where else would he come within a neck of being elected?

Texas still has a rugged, bigger-than-life mystique that both angers and amuses many non-Texans, but it hardly offers immunity from a host of nagging, down-to-earth problems confronting most states on the threshold of the 21st century. While most of the problems aren't new, they have become increasingly important for Texas as it adjusts to a changing economy and a changing political landscape.

To many Texans, government is almost an abstract institution, an anonymous bureaucracy represented by some famous names in the headlines and familiar faces on the 6 o'clock news. Many distrust government, a sentiment that traditionally has been strong in Texas, and hope it interferes with their lives as little as possible. But, like most Americans, Texans also assume there will be potable water flowing through their kitchen taps, streets and highways to drive their cars on, public schools to send their children to, parks for family outings, and police officers to help protect their lives and property.

Obviously, we all have a stake in what government does because government has a daily impact on us, our livelihoods, and our quality of life. We pay taxes for a multitude of programs and services and would like to feel that the benefits we receive are worth what we are paying. The only time many people get excited or concerned about government, however, is when it fails to meet their demands or expectations. Many individuals, moreover, know little about their state and local governments—the governments directly responsible for essential daily services. Such indifference and ignorance can be harmful to the people's interests, particularly at a time like now, when Texas is in a critical period of change that will determine what kind of state it will be for years to come and, consequently, how well or how poorly the public's needs will be met.

Like many other states, Texas recently experienced a tumultuous decade of economic boom and bust. High oil and natural gas prices had put the Texas economy in overdrive during the 1970s and early 1980s, but world energy prices plummeted in the mid-1980s, precipitating a major recession. Texas also was battered by numerous bank and savings and loan failures, and many of the state's major financial institutions were reorganized. The real estate industry likewise went bust in the 1980s, and the rate of foreclosures on buildings and raw property escalated. There was little new commercial or housing construction in the final years of the decade, and many support industries also were forced into bankruptcy. In both the public and private sectors, questions were raised as to what went wrong and why. And it didn't take long for people to begin to point accusatory fingers at each other.

Throughout the ordeal, however, the Texas Legislature was able to keep state offices open, while several other states with budgetary problems were forced to temporarily suspend some public services. Texas survived its crisis, but major problems still persist, and how state leaders address them will go a long way toward determining the quality of life for all Texans well into the next century.

Continued population growth, a painful economic transformation, a political realignment, and an expanding influence of racial and ethnic minorities pose tremendous challenges to the resources, capabilities, and the very structure of Texas government. Crime, poverty, an inadequate public education system, and the traumatic loss of a healthy energy revenue base have strained the existing tax system and the patience of taxpayers. While wealthy school districts try to protect the quality of their educational programs in the wake of a court order that may force them to share revenue with their poor neighbors, property owners throughout the state threaten to revolt over soaring school taxes. The state is in the midst of an unprecedented prison construction program, but there still isn't enough space to accommodate all the convicts that judges and juries are sending to prison. Murderers and rapists, consequently, are still being returned to the streets too early, and many Texas citizens live in fear. The lingering effects of the 1980s recession and the influx of immigrants from Mexico have added to the strain on social services that always have been stingily funded in Texas. And the state's growth has worsened environmental problems that affect the health and well-being of everyone.

These problems and issues are ingredients of politics, the subject of this book. Politics is fundamentally about conflict between competing interests and the way a society resolves it, or decides "who gets what, when, and how."[3] Government is the system that we have developed to structure conflict, develop an orderly and stable process by which competing interests can be expressed, and, finally, decide who will benefit and who will pay the bill.

In recent years, we have watched some societies and their political systems disintegrate because they have been unable to resolve fundamental economic, social, and cultural conflicts. War, violence, and terror have been experienced by many nations around the world, and Americans, who have been blessed with a relatively stable political system since 1865, often have difficulty understanding why these societies have been unable to resolve the fundamental issues confronting them in an orderly process. But one should never assume that the stability and the orderliness of our government and its decision-making processes are assured in the future. Indeed, some observers would suggest that the levels of urban violence in the United States are indicative of a growing inability of our institutions to deal with fundamental conflicts. The continued ability of our political system to institutionalize conflict is one of the big questions that we must consider as we focus our attention on state government.

As we begin our analysis, we ask why Texans and their public officials make the political choices they do. Why, for example, do expenditures for public education rank low (29th in the nation) in comparison to other states? How do we account for Texas' highly regressive tax system? Why are Texans so willing to fund the construction of highways and roads while letting the state rank 49th out of the 50 states in expenditures for public welfare?[4]

These policy questions are directly linked to a variety of questions that should be raised about governmental institutions and the political system. Texas functions under a state constitution that most scholars agree is obsolete, and, yet, when Texans had an opportunity to adopt a modern constitution, they refused to do so. Why are they content to continue to amend the present charter on a piecemeal basis? Why, until recently, was Texas a one-party Democratic state? How does one explain a long legacy of racial discrimination, and what factors have forced changes in the relationships among the state's ethnic and racial groups? Does a small group of powerful individuals make the primary policy decisions of the state, or are there various centers of competing power? Many argue that special interests dominate state and local government, subordinating the public interest. Is this true? After the bitter 1990 gubernatorial primaries and general election, it was argued that political campaigns were dirtier than ever. Does the historical evidence support this conclusion?

It is difficult to imagine that one or more of these issues does not affect each one of us personally, because we have an investment in what our politicians and governments do. We pay the costs, even though we may not receive the benefits of specific policy decisions. The actions and decisions of governmental leaders can have an immediate and direct effect on our lives, and from time to time, those holding positions of institutional power have made decisions that have cost the rest of us dearly. One merely needs to turn to the disastrous performances of the savings and loans and banks in Texas and the failure of both the state and federal governments to regulate the financial industry.

Each generation has to address fundamental questions of the role of government, the relationship of the people to that government, good public policy, and what can be done to make government more responsive and responsible. When one hears or reads of many of the contemporary policy debates, there is a real sense of *déjà vu*, or that we have seen these problems and issues before. Funding of public education, a major problem in the 1990s, for example, also was an issue in the Texas revolution of 1836, the Reconstruction era after the Civil War, and throughout much of the state's history. There are some new issues, such as the regulation of genetic engineering, the changing international economy, and the health and social problems posed by AIDS. But many of the issues that we will discuss throughout this book are enduring issues of government and politics.

There have been, however, fundamental changes in the social, economic, and political structure of the state over the past generation, and such changes often require new solutions to old problems. Funding public education in the days of the one-room schoolhouse was one thing. Funding today's educational system in a way that provides equity among the state's 1,050 school districts is an entirely different matter.

The demographics, or population characteristics, of the state have changed dramatically since the 1940s when Texas was still predominantly rural. Texas is now an urban state with urban problems. With 17 million residents, it is the third most populous state and has the potential, by the turn of the century, of having the second largest population. Its ethnic and racial composition has changed, and it is also now home to a large number of individuals who were born and reared in other areas of the country and have a limited sense of Texas history and politics. While oil and natural gas are still important to the state's economy, economic diversification is the dominant theme promoted by business leaders, government officials, and economists.

These changes are placing heavy demands on the basic governmental institutions of the state, and there is increasing evidence that many of these institutions are incapable of responding adequately. As Texans face the prospects of the 1990s and the 21st century, in which change will be further accelerated, there will be increased attention to modernizing and adapting government to these new realities.

The remainder of this chapter will introduce you to the people of Texas, the views they have of themselves, the political subcultures, and the state's economy.

We refer to these factors generally as the political environment, a concept developed by political scientist David Easton to refer to the milieu, or context, in which political institutions function.[5] We have chosen what we regard to be the most significant components of the political environment of Texas, but there are other factors that could be incorporated into this discussion.

## THE MYTHS OF TEXAS' POLITICAL CULTURE

While most Texans have only a cursory knowledge of the state's governmental institutions, its political history and contemporary public policy, they do have views—often ill-defined—of the state, its people, and its culture. There are key elements of these views, shared by millions of Texans, that some scholars have defined as **political myths**.

In recent years, serious scholarship has focused on myths as ways to assess the views people have of their common historical and cultural experiences. A myth can be regarded as a "mode of truth ... that codifies and preserves moral and spiritual values" for a particular culture or society.[6] Myths are stories, narratives, or phrases that are used to describe past events, explain their significance to successive generations, and provide an interpretive overview and understanding of a society. Myths provide a world picture or, in our case, a picture of the state of Texas. The relevance of a myth depends, in part, on the degree to which it approximates events it is describing.

Texas has produced its own myth of origin which continues to be a powerful statement about the political system and the social order on which it is based.[7] For many Texans, the battle of the Alamo clearly serves to identify the common experiences of independence and the creation of a separate, unique political order.[8] No other state was a republic prior to joining the Union, and several scholars argue that independence and "going at it alone" from 1836 to 1845 resulted in a cultural experience that distinguishes the Texas political system from those of other states. A whole set of heroes came out of the formative period of Texas history, including many who fought and died at the Alamo or secured Texas independence on the San Jacinto battlefield. Texas school children are introduced to these heroes at a very early age with field trips or "pilgrimages" to the Alamo in San Antonio and visits to the San Jacinto monument in Houston.

The Texas mythology also includes the Texas Ranger and the cowboy. There is considerable lore of the invincible, enduring ranger defeating overwhelming odds. And newspapers and dime novels in the 19th century introduced readers throughout the United States to the cowboy, who often was portrayed as an honest, hardworking individual wrestling with the harsh Texas environment. The cowboy's rugged individualism, with strong connotations of self-help, symbolizes a political culture in Texas that places little premium on government as a solution to political or economic problems.[9] It is the kind of **individualism** that continues to be exploited by political candidates in campaign ads and by the legislature in stingy appropriations for welfare and other public assistance programs.

The frontier to which the Texas Ranger and the cowboy belong is part of a cultural myth of limited government and unlimited personal opportunity. The frontier in the Texas experience also perpetuates the myths of "land as wilderness and land as garden."[10] These emphasize a need to dominate, control, and subdue the land, and they shape many of the contemporary attitudes toward land use in Texas.

The Texas myths, however, have been primarily the myths of the white, Anglo population and have little relevance to the cultural and historical experiences of many African-American and Hispanic Texans. From the 1840s to the mid-1960s, these latter groups were excluded from full participation in Texas politics and the state's economic and social life. To many Hispanics, for example, the Texas Ranger is not a hero, but a symbol of ruthless suppression.

Over the past 20 years, African-Americans and Hispanics have made significant gains politically and economically. Minority populations are expected to continue to increase at a faster rate than Anglos, and there is a real possibility that the Hispanic and African-American populations will comprise a majority of the state's population after the first quarter of the 21st century. As this occurs, Hispanic and African-American historical figures are likely to be incorporated into the common mythology of the state, and some components of the mythology will be redefined. This may already have begun to occur. For example, African-Americans in Texas have been successful, after several years of trying, in getting the legislature to make Martin Luther King, Jr.'s birthday a state holiday.

## THE POLITICAL CULTURE OF TEXAS

There is general support among all the states for the institutional and legal arrangements that have developed in the United States, including personal liberties, equality, rule of law, and limitations on governments. But there are differences between the states and even between regions within individual states. Texas is a highly diverse state. There are racial and ethnic differences from one region to another, as will be discussed later, and there are differences in political attitudes and behavior.

The concept of **political culture** helps us compare some of the latter differences. Political culture has been defined as "the set of attitudes, beliefs, and sentiments which give order and meaning to a political process and which provide the underlying assumptions and rules that govern behavior in the political system."[11] The political culture of the nation or state includes fundamental beliefs about the proper role of government, the relationship of the government to its citizens, and who should govern.[12] These are complex attitudes and behaviors rooted in the historical experience of the nation, shaped by the groups that immigrated to the United States and carried them across the continent.

One of the foremost authorities on the American political culture, Daniel Elazar, believes that three political subcultures, or views, have emerged over time in the United States: the individualistic, the moralistic, and the traditionalistic. Sometimes, they complement each other, while at other times they produce conflict.[13]

## The Individualistic Subculture

The individualistic political view holds that politics and government function as a marketplace. Government does not have to be concerned with creating a good or moral society but exists for strictly "utilitarian reasons, to handle those functions demanded by the people it is created to serve."[14] Government should be limited and its intervention in the private activities of its citizens kept to a minimum. The primary function of government is to assure the stability of a society so that individuals can pursue their own interests. In this view, politics is not a high calling but is like any other business venture where skill and talent prevail and the individual has some anticipation of economic and social benefits. Politics is often perceived by the general public to be a dirty business that should be left to those willing to soil their hands. This tradition may well contribute to political corruption, and members of the electorate who share this view may not be concerned when governmental corruption is revealed. New policy initiatives are more likely than not to be initiated by groups or individuals other than public officials.[15]

## The Moralistic Subculture

The moralistic subculture regards politics as one of the "great activities of man in his search for the good society." [16] Politics, it believes, is the pursuit of the common good. Unlike the attitude expressed in the individualistic subculture that governments are to be limited, the moralistic subculture considers government a positive instrument with a responsibility to promote the general welfare.[17] Politics, therefore, is not to be left to the few but is a responsibility of every individual. Politics is a duty and possibly a high calling. This cultural tradition has a strong sense of service. It requires a high standard for those holding public office and believes public office is not to be used for personal gain. Politics may be organized around political parties, but this tradition has produced nonpartisanship where party labels and organizations are eliminated or play a reduced role.[18] This tradition produces a large number of "amateur" or "nonprofessional" political activists and officeholders and has little toleration for political corruption. From the moralistic perspective, governments should actively intervene in the social and economic lives of their citizens. Public policy initiatives can come from officeholders as well as from those outside the formal governmental structure.[19]

## The Traditionalistic Subculture

The traditionalistic political subculture holds that there is a hierarchical arrangement to the political order. This serves to limit the power and influence of the general public, while allocating authority to a few individuals who comprise a self-perpetuating elite. The elite may enact policy that benefits the general public, but that is secondary to its interests and objectives. Public policy reflects the interests of those who exercise influence and control, and the benefits of public policy go disproportionately to the elites. Family and social relationships form the basis for maintaining this elite structure. There is no emphasis on mass political participation in a traditionalistic subculture, and in many regions of the country where such patterns existed, there were systematic efforts to reduce or eliminate the participation of the general public. While political parties may exist in such a subculture, they have only minimal importance. Many of the states characterized by the traditionalistic subculture were southern states where two-party politics were replaced by factionalism within the Democratic Party.[20]

The historical origins of these three subcultures can be explained, in part, by the early settlement patterns of the United States and by the cultural differences among the groups of people who initially settled the eastern seaboard. The New England colonists, influenced by Puritan and congregational religious groups, spawned the moralistic subculture. Settlers with entrepreneurial concerns and individualistic attitudes tended to locate in the mid-Atlantic states, while the initial settlement of the South was dominated by elites who aspired, in part, to recreate a semifeudal society.

As expansion toward the frontiers progressed, there were identifiable migration patterns from the initial three settlement regions. Texas was settled by individuals holding primarily the individualistic and traditionalistic views of a political system, and the blending of these two views, along with the historical experience of the Republic and the frontier, have contributed to the distinct characteristics of the Texas political culture.[21]

These two cultural traditions have shaped Texans' views of the role of government, who should govern, and what constitutes good public policy. Given the characteristics of these two traditions, one might well conclude, as have many scholars, that Texas politics are conservative, designed to minimize the role of government, hostile toward taxes—especially those that are allocated toward social services—and potentially manipulated by the few for their narrow advantages.

Some scholars have reservations about the concept of political subcultures because it is a complex theory that is difficult to test. Their reservations are legitimate, but we know of no other single theory that presents such a rich historical perspective on the relationship of settlement patterns in the state and the evolution of political attitudes and behavior.

## THE PEOPLE OF TEXAS

The politics and government of Texas can be understood, in part, from the perspective of the people living in the state. What follows in this section is a descriptive analysis of a select number of demographic, or population, characteristics of Texans. In subsequent chapters, we will examine the relationship of race, ethnicity, and other demographic characteristics to partisan behavior, public opinion, institutional power, and public policy.

## Native Americans

There are only three small Indian tribes (Alabama-Coushatta, Tigua, and Kickapoo) living on reservations in Texas, and the Native American population is less than one-half of one percent of the state's total population. Unlike those in Oklahoma, New Mexico, and Arizona, the Native American population in Texas has little influence on governmental institutions, politics or public policy. By contrast, the 19th century history of Texas included numerous conflicts between the Native American, Hispanic, and Anglo populations. As the European populations expanded to lands traditionally claimed by various Indian tribes, conflict ensued, and the Indian population was eventually eliminated or displaced to other states.

Interestingly enough, though, the Indian legacy remains with the state's name. The word Texas came from Tejas, which means "friends" or "allies." As Spanish explorers and missionaries moved across Texas, they confronted a Native American confederacy, the Hasinai. It is to this particular Indian group that they applied the term, and eventually, the name became the permanent name of the region and then the state.[22]

In 1989, the Texas Department of Highways and Public Transportation proposed changing the state's vehicle license plates to include the phrase, "The Friendship State." The public reaction, however, was immediate and generally hostile, and the proposal was quickly dropped. Some Texans apparently found the phrase incompatible with the state's rugged frontier image. The irony, though, is that the common nomenclature for the state, which means friendship, is used almost every day by these same people.

## The Hispanic Population

In the 18th and 19th centuries, neither Spain nor Mexico was very successful in convincing Hispanics to settle in the Tejas territory of Mexico. The Spanish regarded it as a border province with relatively little value except as a strategic buffer between Spanish colonies and those held by the British and the French. By the time Mexico declared its independence from Spain in 1821, the total Texas population under Spanish control was estimated to be approximately 5,000 people. And with the rapid expansion of Anglo-American immigration to Texas in the 1820s and 1830s, Hispanics became a small minority of the population.[23]

Some Hispanics were part of the Texas independence movement from Mexico, and after independence in 1836, men such as José Antonio Navarro and Juan Seguin were part of the Republic's political establishment. But except for the region along the Mexican border, the declining Hispanic population resulted in a reduced political and economic role for that ethnic group. There was even an effort in the constitutional convention of 1845 to strip Hispanics of the right to vote. The attempt failed, but it was an early indication of Anglo hostility toward the Hispanic population.[24]

By 1887, the Hispanic population had declined to approximately four percent of the state's population. In 1930, it was 12 percent and was concentrated in the border counties from Brownsville to El Paso (Table 1-1). There were modest increases in the Hispanic population until it reached 18 percent of the state's population in 1970, after which it has grown at a more rapid rate. By 1990, it had reached 25 percent, spurred along by immigration from Mexico and other Latin American countries, as well as higher birth rates among Hispanic than among Anglo women.

Except for the Asian population, which is still considerably smaller, the Hispanic population now is growing at a significantly higher rate than other populations in Texas. In addition to their traditional concentrations in the Rio Grande Valley and South Central Texas, large Hispanic populations are found in most metropolitan areas.

Hispanics will continue to increase at a higher rate than most other populations, and by 2000, the Hispanic population is projected to be 30 percent of the state's total. This growth already has been translated into significant political power and influence. Two Hispanics have been elected to statewide office. And with successful redistricting and legal challenges to city and county electoral systems, Hispanics now hold a significant number of local elected offices in areas where they are concentrated. By 1991, according to a report by the National Association of Latino Elected and Appointed Officials, Texas had approximately 2,000 Hispanic elected officials, the highest number of any state.[25]

The regions of the state where Hispanics were concentrated (South and South Central Texas) before their more widespread migration to cities were

**TABLE 1-1**   Ethnic and Racial Composition of Texas 1860–2000

| Year | Total Population | % Anglo | % African American | % Hispanic | % Other |
|------|-----------------|---------|--------------------|-----------|---------|
| 1860 | 604,215 | 63.2 | 30.3 | 6.5 | – |
| 1930 | 5,824,715 | 73.3 | 14.7 | 12.0 | – |
| 1950 | 7,711,194 | 74.3 | 12.7 | 13.0 | – |
| 1960 | 9,579,677 | 72.6 | 12.4 | 15.0 | – |
| 1970 | 11,196,730 | 69.1 | 12.5 | 18.4 | – |
| 1980 | 14,228,383 | 65.6 | 12.0 | 21.0 | 1.4 |
| 1990 | 16,986,510 | 60.3 | 11.9 | 25.5 | 2.3 |
| 2000 | 20,200,000* | 55.5 | 12.2 | 28.9 | 3.4 |

*Population projected to the year 2000.

Data for Asian and other populations not tabulated by the Bureau of the Census prior to 1980. Spanish total for 1970 based on "Persons of Spanish language or surname."

Sources: Terry G. Jordan with John L. Bean, Jr., and William M. Holmes, *Texas: A Geography* (Boulder: Westview Press, 1984), pp. 81,83; U. S. Census, 1869–1990; Office of the Governor, Texas 2000 Commission, *Texas Past and Future: A Survey*; Texas Comptroller of Public Accounts, *It's Texas: Here's Why.*

considered part of the traditionalistic subculture, where power was reserved for the few. Extreme poverty, low levels of education, and local economies based on agriculture contributed to the development of political systems dominated by a few Anglos who often considered Hispanics second class citizens. Hispanics' increasing political clout, however, has produced major governmental changes in those regions.


## The African-American Population

There were African-Americans in Texas during the colonization period, but the modern story of African-American settlement did not begin until after independence in 1836. When Texas was part of Mexico, Mexican law restricted slavery within the territory, and this minimized efforts on the part of southern Anglos to import slaves to Texas. During the period of the Republic and prior to the Civil War, there was a significant increase in the African-American population. At the time of the Civil War, 30 percent of the state's residents were African-American, but that percentage declined after the war. By 1960, it had leveled off to 12 percent, the same level counted in 1990 (Table 1-1).

There is a large concentration of African-Americans in East Texas, primarily because of the original settlement of that area by southerners who brought slaves with them. African-Americans also are concentrated in the urban areas of Dallas, Fort Worth, Austin, and Houston. There are few African-Americans living in the western counties or in the counties along the border with Mexico. The increased number of African-American state legislators, city council members, county commissioners, and school board trustees representing urban communities is an indication of the political power of the African-American population in selected areas, but only one African-American has been elected to statewide office in Texas.

While the number of African-Americans born in Texas increased, there was a net loss of African-Americans migrating from the state from 1940-1970 because of racial discrimination and limited economic opportunities for them in Texas. During that period, significant numbers of African-Americans from Texas and other southern states moved to the upper Midwest and the Northeast. Between 1970 and 1980, however, about 115,000 more African-Americans moved back into Texas than those who left, a pattern that also has been observed in many other southern states.[26] If this trend continues, it will help expand political influence for African-Americans across Texas.

The whites who migrated to Texas from the lower southern states brought with them the dominant values of the traditionalistic political subculture. African-Americans were incorporated into this subculture, and although African-Americans were freed after the Civil War, continued political and economic discrimination into the 1960s made it virtually impossible to change the dominant values of the eastern part of Texas. As was true in South Texas, the politics of East Texas were arranged to serve the interests of the white elites.

## The Anglo Population

In the vernacular of Texas politics, the white population is referred to as the "Anglo" population, although there is no census designation for such a group. The term is used to refer to Jews, Irish, Poles, and just about any other individual who is designated by the Bureau of the Census as a "non-Hispanic white."

Scholars have identified two early distinct patterns of Anglo migration into Texas from other states. These early patterns as well as population movements through much of the late 19th and early 20th centuries largely explain the regional locations of the state's two dominant political subcultures.

Beginning in 1815, the first Anglos moving to Texas were from Tennessee, Kentucky, Arkansas, and North Carolina. These settlers came from the upper South, a region significantly influenced by the individualistic subculture of limited government. The earliest settlement was primarily in what is now Northeast Texas in the Red River Valley. After Mexican independence from Spain, there was a second wave of immigration from the upper South. Few of the early colonists were plantation slaveholders from the lower South.

After Texas independence, slavery was legalized, and settlers from the lower South arrived. By the outbreak of the Civil War, Anglos who had moved to Texas from the lower South were roughly equal in number to those from the upper South. Arrivals from the slaveholding lower South initially settled in southeastern Texas near Louisiana, but soon they also began to move northward and westward.

These two groups had settled in distinct areas of the state. If one were to draw a line between Texarkana and San Antonio, most of those settling north and west of this line would be from the upper South and heavily influenced by the individualistic subculture, which favors limited government. Those settling south and east of the line would be from the lower southern states and shaped by the traditionalistic subculture, which holds that governmental power should be reserved for a handful of select people.

This pattern of immigration and settlement continued after the Civil War. It was primarily those populations from the upper South who pushed westward to the Panhandle and West Texas. This expansion introduced the western part of the state to the cultural experience of those who resisted any notion that government existed to solve all of society's ills. And to this day, West Texas is still one of the most politically conservative areas of the state.[27]

In 1860, Anglos comprised approximately 63 percent of Texas' population (Table 1-1). The Anglo population increased until it reached 74 percent in 1950. But the stabilization of the African-American population percentage and the increase in the Hispanic population had reduced the Anglo share to 60 percent in 1990. It is projected that Anglos will account for only 56 percent of the Texas population by the year 2000.

The Anglo population, as is true for Hispanics and African-Americans, is diverse. Exhibits in the Institute of Texan Cultures in San Antonio remind one of that fact. Towns throughout Texas are identified with immigrants of national origin other than Anglo-Saxon, and these national groups brought with them a rich heritage. Castroville, for example, is identified with the Alsatians; New Braunfels and Fredericksburg, the Germans; Panna Maria, the Poles; West and Halletsville, the Czechs.

## The Asian Population

In 1980, Asian-Texans comprised .8 percent of the state's population, but by 1990 the figure had grown to 1.9 percent. This rapid increase parallels national trends. Changes in immigration policy and the dislocation of Asians due to war and political persecution have resulted in larger numbers of Asian immigrants entering the United States and Texas since the 1970s. In Texas, for example, groups of Vietnamese relocated in fishing towns at various points along the Texas coast, and by the early 1980s they owned a large part of the fishing and shrimping fleet.

## POLITICS, RACE, AND ETHNICITY

Today, there are few people who go running around the state wearing Ku Klux Klan robes and marching in support of white supremacy. The state's law restricting African-Americans from voting in party primaries was declared unconstitutional in the 1940s, and many of the restrictive laws that were intended to reduce political participation by African-Americans and Hispanics have been eliminated. The federal Voting Rights Act also has helped open up state and local electoral systems to minorities. While there is still evidence of employment discrimination, federal and state laws have given minorities greater access to jobs, and restrictive codes prohibiting a specific group of people from buying residential property have been declared unconstitutional.

Nonetheless, racial and ethnic issues are implicit in many contemporary political and policy issues. Throughout the debates on restructuring the school finance system, the protagonists were identified as the rich and poor school districts of the state. But, in large part, the terms rich and poor were alternative terms for nonminority and minority school systems. By 1991, minority children accounted for a majority of the enrollment in Texas public schools. There have been bitter debates about reapportionment of political districts to increase Hispanic and African-American representation. And while there are many poor Anglos throughout the state, the disproportionately high poverty rates among minority groups often transform debates about social services into issues of race or ethnicity.

Forty years ago, V.O. Key, a Texan and scholar of American politics, concluded that Texas politics was moving from issues of race to issues of class and economics. He argued that voters in Texas "divide along class lines in accord with their class interests as related to liberal and conservative candidates."[28] In part, he was correct in that unabashed racial bigotry and public demagoguery are no longer acceptable. In part, though, he was incorrect and much too optimistic. If the state divides on economic issues, this division often puts the majority of Anglos on one side and the majority of Hispanics and African-Americans on the other.[29]

In the chapter on local government, we will address the issue of polarized voting among ethnic and racial groups. In many state and local elections, there is evidence of significant voting along ethnic lines. When an African-American and an Anglo candidate run against each other, Anglo voters are likely to vote for the Anglo candidate, and African-American voters are likely to vote for the African-American candidate. A similar pattern emerges in races between Anglos and Hispanics.

Race and ethnic issues emerge in jury selection, employment patterns, enrollment and dropout rates in public schools, contracts with state and local governments, and expenditures for public health and social service programs. These and other issues demonstrate the necessity for understanding the racial and ethnic composition of the state. The future of the state also is tied directly to the ability of public and private institutions to address the issues that divide racial and ethnic groups.

## POPULATION GROWTH AND THE CHANGING FACE OF TEXAS POLITICS

Over the past 50 years, the Texas population has increased at rates much higher than the national average. From 1940 to 1950, the number of Texans increased by 20 percent. During the next decade, the population grew by 25 percent. Between 1960 and 1970, the population growth rate dropped to 17 percent, but increased to 27 percent during the 1970s. From 1980 to 1990, the state's population increased by 19 percent.[30] With the completion of the 1990 census, the population of Texas was 16,986,510, an increase of 2.7 million people in 10 years. Texas is now the third most populous state, and is projected to rank second in population by 2000.

There has been a shift of the nation's population from the Northeast and the Midwest to the southern and western states. This shift from the frostbelt to the sunbelt was identified by demographers (those who study populations) more than 20 years ago. The pattern clearly continued in the past decade and is likely to continue through the next 10 years. As a partial result of these migration patterns, Texas gained three additional seats in the U.S. Congress after the 1990 census.

The birth rates in Texas explain part of the population increases, but migration from other states also has been a significant factor in Texas' recent growth. For each of the censuses from 1940 to 1970, in-migration accounted for less than 10 percent of the growth rate.[31] Between 1970 and 1980, in-migration accounted for 58.35 percent of the total growth.[32] Since 1980, in-migration contributed to the state's population growth but at a lower rate than in the previous decade.

This pattern has contributed to the restructuring of the traditional, Democratic one-party political system in Texas into a two-party system. One recent study concluded, "The influx of residents from outside of Texas is having a profound influence on the relative party strengths of the Democratic and Republican parties, with Republican being the clear beneficiary of this important demographic trend."[33]

An earlier study concluded that the largest number of new immigrants to Texas came from the four adjacent states. But Texas, especially its urban areas, is attractive to individuals from New York, Ohio, Delaware, Illinois, Connecticut, Virginia, Michigan, Pennsylvania, Indiana, New Jersey, and Maryland.[34] Many of these states have strong Republican parties, and we would expect a large number of people moving from these states to Texas to have Republican loyalties. Party realignment will be more fully addressed in the chapter on political parties.

The arrival of more people has increased demands on all levels of government in Texas, and there will be even more demands for energy, water, waste disposal, housing, public education, roads, and transportation in the future. Some communities may be limited in their ability to provide services and absorb additional population. San Antonio, for example, is projected to run out of landfill space in the next three or four years. Environmental laws make it very difficult to obtain new licenses for garbage and waste disposal, and without these additional facilities, new population growth cannot be serviced.

## The Census Undercount

The 1990 census was challenged by several states, cities, and minority groups for undercounting the populations of some states, particularly their minority residents. While admitting that such an undercount had occurred, Secretary of Commerce Robert Mosbacher said the Bureau of the Census would not adjust its figures because of methodological problems with such adjustments.

It has been estimated that about 600,000 persons were not counted in Texas, and the effects of such an undercount are significant. It may have cost Texas an extra seat in Congress, and it likely cost minorities some additional seats in the Texas Legislature, which based its redrawing of House and Senate district boundaries on the official census figures. And, according to Texas Attorney General Dan Morales, who sued the federal government over the issue, the undercount could cost the state approximately $1 billion in federal funds during the 1990s because the state's share of federal funds for a variety of programs is largely based on population.

## The Size and Geographic Diversity of Texas

Texas is a big state. Covering 267,339 square miles, it is second only to Alaska in terms of total land mass. While Texans appear to have adjusted to long distances—we don't seem to mind driving 50 miles for a night out—visitors from out-of-state often are overwhelmed by Texas' size and diversity. The distance from Texarkana in Northeast Texas to El Paso in far West Texas is about 800 miles, and a person living in Texarkana is closer to Chicago than to El Paso. Brownsville in far South Texas is closer to Mexico City than it is to Texline in the Texas Panhandle.[35] Many would argue that perceptions of size have helped shape political attitudes and concepts, and Texas' size obviously has affected state policy. Roads and highways, for example, historically have received a significant—and some would argue a disproportionate—

share of the state's budget. Economic development in such a large, diverse state required a commitment to highway construction, and roads were regarded as essential to the development of an integrated economy.

V.O. Key argued that the great distances in Texas were politically important because they made it difficult for a politician to develop a personal following, such as was the case in many southern states. Size and distance deterred the development of a statewide political machine similar to those that developed in Virginia and Louisiana in the 1920s and 1930s. Texas' size works against the organizational strategies and continued negotiations necessary to sustain a political machine. While there have been regional or local political machines, such as the now-defunct Parr machine in South Texas, none of these was extended statewide.

Size also contributes to the high costs of political campaigns. Candidates in the 1990 gubernatorial campaign spent more than $50 million to communicate with and mobilize Texas voters. There are 20 separate media markets in the state, and the costs for communicating with the voters is likely to increase. In several of the following chapters, the question of the state's size will be related to political campaigns, the mass media and political behavior.[36]

If Texas were still an independent nation, it would be the 37th largest in geographic area. The state has one-twelfth of the total coastline of the United States. It has 23 million acres of forest and more than 4,790 square miles of lakes and streams.

A traveler driving across Texas is struck by the diversity in topography, climate, and vegetation. The state's "landforms range from offshore bars and barrier beaches to formidable mountains, from rugged canyons, gorges, and badlands to totally flat plains."[37] The western part of the state is dry and semiarid, while the east is humid and subtropical, producing extremes in precipitation.[38] South Texas often enjoys a tropical winter, while North Texas experiences cold winters with snowfall.[39] The growing seasons in the south are virtually year round, while those in the north are approximately 180 days. East Texas is characterized by its piney woods, while semiarid South Texas has its brush country.

Geography shaped historical migration and land use in Texas and, while we are capable of partially compensating for climate and geography through modern technology, geography continues to shape the economies and population patterns of the state.

## Population Concentrations

Texas is a metropolitan state with most Texans living in central cities and the surrounding cities, towns, and counties. These urban areas are classified as metropolitan statistical areas (MSA), primary metropolitan statistical areas (PMSA), and consolidated metropolitan statistical areas (CMSA). In 1980, some 53 of the state's 254 counties, which accounted for 79.5 percent of the state's population, were included in 28 of these areas (Table 1-2).[40] By 1990, these areas included 81.6 percent of the population.

**TABLE 1–2** Population in the Metropolitan Statistical Areas of Texas 1980 and 1990

| Metropolitan Statistical Area | 1980 | 1990 | Percentage Change |
|---|---|---|---|
| Abilene | 110,932 | 119,655 | 7.86 |
| Amarillo | 173,699 | 187,547 | 7.97 |
| Austin | 536,688 | 781,572 | 45.63 |
| Beaumont-Port Arthur | 375,497 | 361,226 | –3.80 |
| Brazoria | 169,587 | 191,707 | 13.04 |
| Brownsville-Harlingen | 209,727 | 260,120 | 24.03 |
| Bryan-College Station | 93,588 | 121,862 | 30.21 |
| Corpus Christi | 326,228 | 349,894 | 7.25 |
| Dallas | 1,957,378 | 2,553,362 | 30.45 |
| El Paso | 479,899 | 591,610 | 23.28 |
| Fort Worth-Arlington | 973,138 | 1,332,053 | 36.88 |
| Galveston-Texas City | 195,940 | 217,399 | 10.95 |
| Houston | 2,735,766 | 3,301,937 | 20.70 |
| Killeen-Temple | 214,656 | 255,301 | 18.93 |
| Laredo | 99,258 | 133,239 | 34.24 |
| Longview-Marshall | 151,752 | 162,431 | 7.04 |
| Lubbock | 211,651 | 222,636 | 5.19 |
| McAllen-Edinburg-Mission | 283,229 | 383,545 | 35.42 |
| Midland | 82,636 | 106,611 | 29.01 |
| Odessa | 115,374 | 118,934 | 3.09 |
| San Angelo | 84,784 | 98,458 | 16.13 |
| San Antonio | 1,071,954 | 1,302,099 | 21.47 |
| Sherman-Denison | 89,796 | 95,021 | 5.82 |
| Texarkana | 75,301 | 81,665 | 8.45 |
| Tyler | 128,366 | 151,309 | 17.87 |
| Victoria | 68,807 | 74,361 | 8.07 |
| Waco | 170,795 | 189,123 | 10.76 |
| Wichita Falls | 121,082 | 122,378 | 1.07 |

Sources: U.S. Bureau of the Census, *1990 Census of Population and Housing; 1980 Census of Population and Housing.*

**Urbanization** and suburban sprawl now characterize Texas' settlement patterns, and suburban areas extend beyond county boundaries in many regions of the state (Figure 1-1). There are areas that are taking on the characteristics of an urban corridor or megalopolis, patterns of urbanization found in other areas of the country. Residents of these areas often encounter problems that cut across political jurisdictions, and local governments sometimes find it difficult to resolve them. In a later discussion of local government, we will assess some of the problems that result from jurisdictional conflict and overlap and argue that forms of local government developed in the late 19th century and early 20th century are insufficient to deal with these problems.

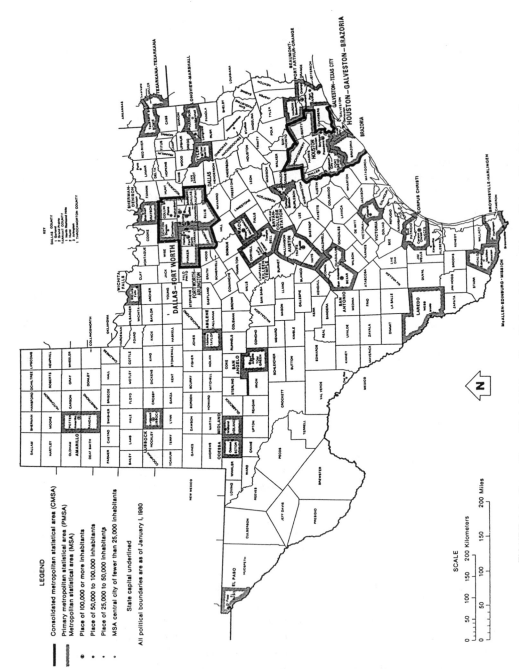

**FIGURE 1-1** Texas Consolidated Metropolitan Statistical Areas, Primary Metropolitan Statistical Areas, and Metropolitan Statistical Areas (U.S. Bureau of the Census)

Population density refers to the number of people per square mile in a specific political jurisdiction. The greater the number of people living in close proximity, the greater the number of problems that emerge as people disagree on the use of land and resources. Complex social and economic relationships produce increased demands for government regulation, controls, and intervention. There are marked differences in the population and density of Texas' 254 counties. Loving County in West Texas has a population of about 100 persons living in an area of 671 square miles. The most populous county is Harris County (Houston) with a population of more than 2.8 million persons living in 1,734 square miles. The problems and issues that Loving County faces are significantly different from those faced by Harris County. Yet, both counties function with the same form of government that was created by the constitution of 1876.

## Urban-Rural Distribution of the Texas Population

Despite the frontier image that it still conveys to many outsiders, Texas is now an urban state and has been for the past 40 years. Although it was a rural state during the first 100 years of its history, approximately 80 percent of its population now resides in areas classified by the Bureau of the Census as urban (Table 1-3).

There are, of course, clear differences in the size, racial and ethnic composition, and economies of Texas' cities, and issues and governmental problems vary significantly from community to community. Some cities are affluent, while others are experiencing declining economies and a reduction in public services. Some cities

**TABLE 1–3**  Urban-Rural Population of Texas 1850–1990

| Year | Urban | | Rural | | Total |
|---|---|---|---|---|---|
| 1850 | 4 % | (7,665) | 96 % | (204,927) | 212,592 |
| 1860 | 4 | (26,615) | 96 | (577,600) | 604,215 |
| 1870 | 7 | (54,521) | 93 | (764,058) | 818,579 |
| 1880 | 9 | (146,795) | 91 | (1,444,954) | 1,591,749 |
| 1890 | 16 | (359,511) | 84 | (1,886,016) | 2,245,527 |
| 1900 | 17 | (520,759) | 83 | (2,527,951) | 3,048,710 |
| 1910 | 24 | (938,104) | 76 | (2,958,438) | 3,896,542 |
| 1920 | 32 | (1,512,689) | 68 | (3,150,539) | 4,663,228 |
| 1930 | 41 | (2,389,348) | 59 | (3,435,367) | 5,824,715 |
| 1940 | 45 | (2,911,389) | 55 | (3,503,435) | 6,414,824 |
| 1950 | 63 | (4,838,050) | 37 | (2,873,134) | 7,711,194 |
| 1960 | 75 | (7,187,470) | 25 | (2,392,207) | 9,579,677 |
| 1970 | 80 | (8,922,211) | 20 | (2,274,519) | 11,196,730 |
| 1980 | 80 | (11,333,017) | 20 | (2,896,174) | 14,229,191 |
| 1990 | 80 | (13,634,517) | 20 | (3,351,993) | 16,986,510 |

Sources: U.S. Censuses, 1850–1990

**TABLE 1–4**  Ten Largest Texas Cities

| City | 1990 | 1980 | 1960 | 1940 | 1920 | 1900 |
|------|------|------|------|------|------|------|
| Houston | 1,630,553 | 1,595,138 | 838,219 | 384,514 | 138,276 | 44,633 |
| Dallas | 1,006,877 | 904,078 | 679,684 | 294,734 | 158,976 | 42,638 |
| San Antonio | 935,933 | 785,880 | 587,718 | 253,854 | 161,379 | 53,321 |
| El Paso | 515,342 | 425,259 | 276,687 | 96,810 | 77,560 | 15,906 |
| Austin | 465,622 | 345,496 | 186,545 | 87,960 | 34,876 | 22,258 |
| Fort Worth | 447,619 | 385,164 | 356,268 | 177,662 | 106,482 | 26,688 |
| Arlington | 261,721 | 160,113 | 44,775 | 4,240 | 3,031 | 1,079 |
| Corpus Christi | 257,453 | 231,999 | 167,690 | 57,301 | 10,522 | 4,703 |
| Lubbock | 186,206 | 173,979 | 128,691 | 31,853 | 4,051 | -0- |
| Garland | 180,650 | 138,857 | 38,501 | 2,233 | 1,421 | 819 |

Sources: U.S. Census, *Selected Population and Housing Characteristics, 1990*. From the 1990 Census Summary Tape File 1A(STF1A), Texas and Texas Counties; U.S. Censuses, 1900–1980.

have witnessed significant population gains in the past 10 years, while others have lost residents (Table 1-4).

To a great extent, Texas politics has been divided along urban-rural lines. Redistricting battles and other legislative issues are evidence of these conflicts. Until recently, the Texas Legislature was dominated by rural lawmakers, many of whom were often insensitive to urban needs. Many of urban Texas' problems also are exacerbated by constitutional restrictions written when Texas was still a rural state.

Three of the 10 largest cities in the United States, based on the 1990 census, are in Texas. And like urban areas throughout the United States, Texas' largest cities are increasingly populated by minorities. This has been the result of higher birth rates of minority populations, urban migration patterns and what is often referred to as "white flight" from the cities to suburban areas. Five of Texas' 10 largest cities (Houston, Dallas, San Antonio, El Paso, and Corpus Christi) now have a "majority minority" population. These minority populations include Hispanics, African-Americans and Asians—groups that don't always constitute a cohesive block of interests. As minority growth continues in the 1990s, there will be potential areas of conflict among these groups, a topic which we also will address in the chapter on local government.

## Income and Income Distribution

There is a wide disparity in the distribution of income and wealth across the state. *Texas Monthly* published its 1991 list of the 100 richest people in Texas and concluded that the Texas rich are getting richer "while most Texans continue to battle the slump."[41] To make the magazine's list, an individual had to have assets of $130 million, and these 100 individuals had combined net assets of $36.7 billion. The list included 21 women, but it was comprised primarily of WASP (white, Anglo-Saxon, Protestant) males. While the list included many individuals whose wealth was linked to oil and real estate, those with ties to new businesses and industries, especially in the high-tech sector, experienced significant gains.[42]

The per capita income (total income divided by the population) for the United States was $17,592 in 1989. It was $15,512 in Texas, or 88 percent of the national average (Table 1-5). From 1985 to 1989, the state's per capita income has decreased in relationship to the national average, demonstrating the recent weakness of the Texas economy.

There are significant numbers of Texans living in severe poverty. Seven of the 20 poorest counties in the nation are located in Texas. These are border area counties (Starr, Maverick, Dimmit, Zavala, Willacy, Zapata, and Hidalgo) with large Hispanic populations and unemployment rates that are twice the state average. In each of these counties, the per capita income was less than 50 percent of the national average. The per capita income in Starr County in 1989 was $4,548, or 26 percent of the national average.

In 1989, the poverty level guidelines used in Texas to establish eligibility for many federal and state programs was $12,000 for a family of four. For one person, the figure was $5,980 and an additional $2,040 was allowed for each additional family member.[43] According to a census by the Texas Department of Human Services, approximately 18 percent of the state's population fell below the poverty level. The impact of poverty was felt disproportionately by children younger than 18, persons older than 65, Hispanics, African-Americans, and those living in one-parent households.[44]

In late 1991, the Department of Agriculture published the rather startling information that one of every 10 persons in the United States was enrolled in the food stamp program. By contrast, approximately two of every 10 persons living in South Texas counties were recipients of food stamps, including more than 30 percent of the residents of most border counties.[45]

Financial resources can be translated into political power and influence, and these limited economic data indicate that some Texans have enormous resources in relationship to other groups. Partisan alignment and public policy issues are shaped by these factors.

**TABLE 1-5**   Average Personal Income for the U.S. and Texas 1984-1989

| Per Capita Personal Income | 1984 | 1985 | 1986 | 1987 | 1988 | 1989 |
|---|---|---|---|---|---|---|
| U.S. | 13,116 | 13,899 | 14,597 | 15,425 | 16,510 | 17,592 |
| Texas | 12,781 | 13,472 | 13,489 | 13,736 | 14,590 | 15,512 |
| Texas Percent of national average | 97% | 97% | 92% | 89% | 88% | 88% |

Source: U.S. Department of Commerce, Bureau of Economic Analysis, *Local Area Personal Income, 1984-1989*, Vol. 5, Tables 1, 5.

## Education and Literacy

During this last decade of the 20th century, public education along with health care, taxes, the environment, and economic development will dominate state politics. Litigation has forced the legislature to struggle with radical changes in the funding of public education, and education will be a primary factor in determining the success of the state's efforts to compete in a new global economy.

Over the next decade, 75 percent of the new jobs created in Texas will be in service industries. Most of these jobs will require increased reading, writing, and math skills, and high school dropouts will find fewer and fewer employment opportunities. While it was estimated that approximately 22 percent of the jobs in the United States required a college education in the mid-1980s, some experts project that 50 percent of the jobs created in the next decade will require college educations.[46] There is no question that Texas faces a crisis in public education, and our ability to resolve it will directly affect the financial well-being of large segments of the state's population.

There are wide disparities in the educational levels of the three primary ethnic/racial groups in the state. In the 1980 census, approximately 70 percent of the Anglo population 25 years of age and older had completed high school, but only 53 percent of the African-American population and 36 percent of Hispanics. In the same year, only 9 percent of African-American adults and only 6 percent of Hispanic adults reported that they had completed college, while 20 percent of Anglo adults had college degrees.

In a national survey conducted by the Bureau of the Census in 1989 (Table 1-6), all three groups indicated an increase in the number of years of completed education for persons 25 years old and older.

But members of the two dominant minority populations continue to have substantially lower educational levels than other Texans. Education not only helps determine a person's employment potential, it also affects his or her political participation. Individuals with high educational levels are much more likely to be informed about politics and participate in the political process than those less educated.

**TABLE 1–6** Texas and United States Educational Attainment by Race and Ethnicity 1989 (for Population Age 25 and Older)

|  | Texas | | United States | |
|---|---|---|---|---|
|  | High School* | College* | High School* | College* |
| African-American | 69.8% | 10.9% | 64.6% | 11.8% |
| White | 74.9 | 22.9 | 78.4 | 21.8 |
| Hispanic | 45.2 | 8.3 | 50.9 | 9.9 |
| Total | 74.3 | 21.7 | 76.9 | 21.1 |

*Completed 4 or more years.

Source: U.S. Bureau of the Census, Unpublished data from the March, 1989 *Current Population Survey*, Report P–20, No. 451.

## THE ECONOMY OF TEXAS

Politics, government, and economics are inextricably linked. An economy that is robust and expanding provides far more options to government policymakers than an economy in recession. A healthy tax base is dependent on an expanding economy, and when the economy goes through periods of recession, state and local governments are confronted with the harsh realities of having to increase taxes or cut back on public services, usually at a time when more members of the public are in need of governmental assistance.[47]

In 1986, Texas had a gross state product of $300 billion. By comparison, the gross national product of the United States that year was $4.2 trillion, the GNP of the Soviet Union was $2 trillion, and the GNP of Japan was $1.5 trillion. The economy of Texas was third among the 50 states, following California and New York.[48]

At the beginning of the 1980s, Texas had experienced a sustained period of growth, and it was able to adopt new policies and expand existing services with only minimal tax increases. By 1991, the state had experienced a decade of economic boom and busts, and the legislature had been forced to tighten up on public services and impose a series of significant tax increases.

Historically, the health of the Texas economy has been linked to oil and natural gas. In 1981, for example, 27 percent of the state's economy was tied to energy-related industries. The decade started with rapid increases in the world price of oil, and there was an economic boom throughout the financial, construction, and manufacturing sectors of the state's economy.

But the Texas economy does not operate in a vacuum, and a series of national and international events soon began producing major problems. Beginning in 1982, there was a disastrous slide in the value of the Mexican peso, which had a direct negative impact on the economies of the cities and counties on the Mexican border. In 1983, a severe drought in West Texas and a harsh freeze in South Texas damaged crops, including the Texas citrus industry. World oil prices began to drop in 1981, and by 1982, serious unemployment problems began to appear in the Gulf Coast and Plains regions of the state. In 1984 and 1985, the economic news coming out of Texas was mixed. Some regions of the state, such as the Dallas-Fort Worth Metroplex and the Central Corridor (San Antonio-Austin-Waco-Bryan-College Station), continued to show expansion with construction one of the primary economic generators. But Houston and other energy-centered areas continued to suffer.[49]

Then, economic disaster struck Texas in 1986, with a 60 percent drop in the price of oil and corresponding reductions in the price of natural gas. Drilling activity in the state plummeted and was followed by a loss of 84,000 energy-related jobs. The problem was compounded by the fact that there also was a worldwide slump in the electronics industry. These events hurt the construction and real estate sectors of the economy and, in turn, manufacturing and retail trade. For 16 straight months in 1986 and 1987, the state's employment dropped with an estimated loss of 233,000 jobs.[50]

These economic reversals had a subsequent disastrous effect on Texas' banks and savings and loans. "In 1987 and 1988, more Texas financial institutions failed than at any other time since the Great Depression," the state comptroller's office reported. And the pattern of bank failures continued through 1990.[51] The federal government developed a plan to bail out institutions that were covered by federal deposit insurance. But as the magnitude of the problem became clearer, there was a bitter debate over its causes. The issues were rather complex, but there was a lot of blame to be shared, including the deregulation of the savings and loan and banking industries, inadequate government scrutiny of banking practices, a frenzy of speculation with questionable or unsecured loans, and outright fraud and malfeasance.[52]

The effects of these economic reversals were felt throughout Texas as the state and local governments suffered declines in revenues. With falling property values, local governments that depend on the property tax were particularly vulnerable. The legislature convened in special session in 1986 to pass an $875 million tax bill and cut the state budget by about $580 million in an attempt to "patch up" the widening holes in projected state revenues. In 1987, the legislature, mandated by the constitution to a "pay as you go" system of government and denied the powers of deficit financing, enacted a $5.6 billion tax bill, including an increase in the sales tax, a regressive tax that most adversely affects low income people.[53]

By 1988, slow but modest growth was being experienced in most of the economic subregions of the state. Oil and natural gas, while still important to the economy, were being replaced as the driving force in economic expansion. Increased manufacturing, in particular, was responsible for the incremental recovery the state experienced through 1991.[54] Because of the significant changes that occurred in the Texas economy during the 1980s, a number of economists argue that the state is now less vulnerable to the volatility of the energy industry.

Texas has experienced **economic diversification**. The state has shifted from its overreliance on energy to manufacturing, services, and trade with foreign countries. The largest growth sector has been in service industries, which run the gamut from low-paying restaurant workers to high-salaried medical and legal professionals. In 1988, there were 28 separate industries that generated more than 5,000 jobs each in Texas. Twenty-three of these were some type of service industry.[55] Based on current projections, 1.5 million jobs will be added to the Texas economy in the 1990s. No new jobs are projected for the mining sector, which includes the oil and natural gas industry, but manufacturing is projected to produce 224,000 jobs, and the construction industry will generate 113,000 jobs. Eighty percent of the job growth will be in these sectors of the economy: services (466,200 jobs), trade (354,400), government (192,700), transportation and public utilities (96,200), and finance, insurance, and real estate (94,800).[56]

A second notable change has been an emerging shift to high-tech industries. Many economic and political leaders argue that the state's future must be directly tied to these developing industries, and the state and many cities have developed aggressive recruitment programs that include economic development bonds and tax abatements. Evidence of this commitment to high technology was the state's successful effort in 1988 to snare the Department of Energy's Superconducting Supercollider, a major research facility that will be located near Waxahachie.

The term, high-tech, is generally used to describe business activities that produce new technology based on highly sophisticated computer applications. Companies that make semiconductors, microprocessors, computer hardware, and software clearly fall into this category, and so do companies that produce telecommunications devices, fiber optics, aerospace guidance systems, and some medical instruments.[57] These industries have been joined by new biotechnology industries that are involved in producing new medicines, vaccines, and genetic engineering of plants and animals. Houston and Dallas have emerged as centers for biotechnology with some development also occurring in San Antonio, Austin, and Fort Worth.[58]

There also is an emergence of what is often referred to as the **globalization** of the Texas and the U.S. economy. Throughout the 1980s, world oil prices directly affected Texas, and Texans were made keenly aware of their increased interdependence on the world economy. But this development is much more complex. Foreign investment in Texas business has become increasingly more common. Cities throughout Texas are developing sister-city relationships with cities around the world, and part of this activity is generated by economic considerations. The maquiladora program and the proposed free trade agreement between the United States and Mexico have already produced changes in the economic relationships between those two countries, and there are projections for increased economic interdependence for North America.

## Economic Regions of Texas

The economic diversity of Texas has been described in terms of six distinct economic regions, each of which has its own characteristics and economic base (Figure 1-2). General descriptions of the state's economy obscure the marked differences in these regions, and it is important to understand that economic growth or decline varies among them. One region may be undergoing rapid growth while another may be experiencing a recession.

The Plains Economic Region includes 98 counties and the cities of Amarillo, Lubbock, Wichita Falls, Midland, Abilene, Odessa, and San Angelo. Historically, this area has been dominated by agriculture and oil, but its economy has become more diversified over the past 30 years. Manufacturing has increased, particularly the production of fabricated metals, oil field machinery and defense-related transportation equipment, and food processing. Growth in service industries, particularly education, health, and telecommunications, also has been significant. There also has been growth in agribusiness, and the development of biotechnology applications in agriculture are expected to further stimulate this region's economy. The growth potential of this area is particularly dependent on water, and the primary source of water for the region is the Ogallala Aquifer.[59]

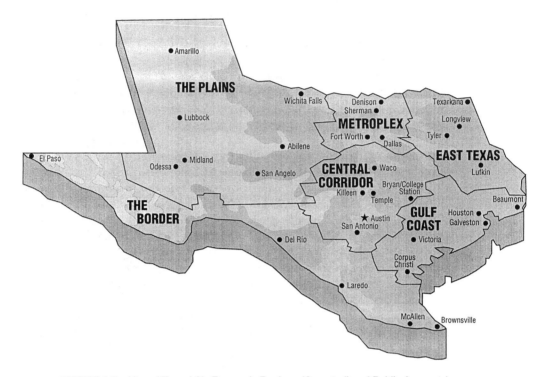

**FIGURE 1-2**   Map of Texas' Six Economic Regions (Comptroller of Public Accounts)

The Dallas-Fort Worth metropolitan area and adjacent counties make up the Metroplex Economic Region, which continues to be a major finance center with the location of regional offices of the Federal Reserve Bank and the Federal Home Loan Bank. The region also has a manufacturing sector dominated by high-tech and defense-related industries, with the latter facing potentially significant changes in the wake of national arms reduction policies. The Superconducting Supercollider will be located in this region. This area also is the trade center for the Southwest. The Dallas Market Center is the world's largest wholesale trade complex, serving buyers from around the globe.

Energy, agriculture and timber production have historically been important to the East Texas Economic Region, comprised of 35 counties and the cities of Longview, Marshall, Tyler, and Texarkana. Economic growth has been tied to forest product industries, the fabrication of metals and oil field machinery, food processing, manufacturing, printing, and publishing.

The 32-county Gulf Coast Economic Region is dominated by the petrochemical industry. Houston, Beaumont, and Corpus Christi comprise approximately 62 percent of the U.S. petrochemical capacity. As home to the Johnson Space Center, this region also has an important role in the aerospace industry. The

Texas Medical Center, the world's largest medical complex, is located in Houston, an important city in the development of the biotechnology industry. This region's excellent port facilities include the Port of Houston. The Formosa Plastics project in Calhoun County will be one of the largest ethylene plants ever built if it wins the approval of state and federal environmental agencies, and there are a number of other industries that plan new projects in this region.[60] Formosa Plastics and the petrochemical industry also pose significant environmental problems and raise serious policy questions about balancing economic and environmental considerations. (See Chapter 13.)

The Central Corridor Economic Region straddles Interstate 35 and is anchored by Waco and San Antonio. It also includes Bryan and College Station. Institutions of higher learning, including the state's two largest universities—the University of Texas at Austin and Texas A&M University—play a dominant role in the economy of this 39-county area. Military bases and government also are significant parts of the economy, which could be adversely affected by cutbacks in defense expenditures. There is an expanding emphasis on high tech and biotechnology with major research programs located at the various universities in this region. Tourism also is a growth industry in the Central Corridor.

The Border Economic Region includes 30 counties stretching from Brownsville to El Paso. Its economy is linked to that of Mexico, with which Texas shares 1,250 miles of border. Recent changes in Mexico's economic policies and the move to develop a free trade agreement could significantly change the economy of this region, the state's poorest. The changes were initiated, in part, by the creation of maquiladoras, or plants located in Mexico that assemble products from parts imported from the United States. Agriculture and trade have historically been important to this region, and there has been a continued expansion of agribusiness in the Lower Rio Grande Valley. An enormous two-way movement of people across the border has helped generate tourism and retail trade activities. But in recent years, the counties along the border have had the highest unemployment rates in Texas, and the region's per capita income is the lowest in the state.


### SUMMARY AND CONCLUSIONS

**1.** Texas has witnessed significant demographic and economic changes in the last four decades, and these changes have subsequently been reflected in a transformation of state politics, governmental institutions, and public policy.

**2.** Texans, in part, explain and understand themselves in terms of political myths which serve to provide generalized views of the state, its common historical experience, and views of the people and its institutions. These myths have been defined primarily in terms of the Anglo population, but with the increased demographic diversification of the state, these views are likely to be redefined through the collective experiences of the expanding minority populations.

**3.** The political culture includes fundamental beliefs Texans hold about the proper role of government, the relationship of the government to its citizens, and who should govern. The two traditions that have characterized much of the state's political history are the individualistic and the traditionalistic subcultures. These traditions are explained, in part, by the settlement patterns of the state, but more importantly, they provide insight into the traditionally conservative politics and public policies of the state, the dominant role of an elite structure during much of the state's history, and a long tradition of limiting participation among minority groups.

**4.** Demographically, Texas is a highly diverse state, but more importantly, the state's population continues to undergo major changes. The state continues to experience a high overall rate of growth, but the most significant increases have been among the Hispanic and Asian populations. Based on current estimates, the state will have a "majority minority" population in the first quarter of the 21st century. These changes in demography, in some measure, explain the changes in the Texas party system.

**5.** Politics in the state are largely shaped by the ethnic and racial composition of the population. As the minority population has increased as a proportion of the total population, there has been an increase in the number of minority elected officials at all levels of state and local government. And many of the policy concerns of the minority populations are now being addressed by governments across the state.

**6.** Despite the size and land area of the state and a sense of "wide open spaces," eight out of ten Texans live in urban areas located in 53 of the 254 counties. Several of these areas now constitute urban corridors. As the state moves into the 21st century, urban problems are taking on more importance.

**7.** There are wide disparities in wealth and income levels across the state, and the inequities in wealth and resources are directly related to ethnicity and race.

**8.** There are wide disparities in educational levels across the state, and both the African-American and Hispanic populations, in comparison with the Anglo population, report a larger proportion of high school dropouts and fewer college graduates. Literacy and the development of a technologically competent work force are directly related to the state's ability to compete in the global economy.

**9.** The 1980s began with an economic boom, but during most of the decade, the state was plagued with significant economic problems, including a decline in oil prices and massive losses in the banking, savings and loan, and real estate industries. By the end of the decade, there were indications of economic diversification with the expansion of high-tech and other service industries. Moreover, the end of the decade demonstrated that Texas, with large amounts of imports and exports, was becoming increasingly integrated into the global economy.

**10.** Texas has a highly diverse economy and six distinct economic regions, which have had marked contrasts in performance. While the state has faced a volatile period, economic diversity has minimized the effects of its economic downturns.

## KEY TERMS

Political myths
Individualism
Political culture
Individualistic subculture
Moralistic subculture

Traditionalistic subculture
Urbanization
Population density
Economic diversification
Globalization of the economy

## FURTHER READING

Bellah, Robert N., *The Broken Covenant: American Civil Religion in Time of Trial*. New York: Seabury Press, 1975.

Buenger, Walter L., and Robert A. Calvert, eds., *Texas Through Time: Evolving Interpretations*. College Station: Texas A&M University Press, 1991.

Calvert, Robert A., and Arnoldo DeLeon, *The History of Texas*. Arlington Heights, Ill.: Harlan Davidson, 1990.

Chilton, Stephen, "Defining Political Culture," *Western Political Quarterly*, 41 (September 1988), pp. 419-445.

Dunn, Charles W., *Religion in American Politics*. Washington, D.C.: Congressional Quarterly Press Inc., 1989.

Elazar, Daniel, *American Federalism: A View from the States*. New York: Thomas Y. Crowell, 1966.

Fehrenbach, T. R, *Lone Star: A History of Texas and the Texans*. New York: Macmillian, 1968.

Fitzpatrick, Jody L., and Rodney E. Hero, "Political Culture and Political Characteristics of the American States: A Consideration of Some Old and New Questions," *Western Political Quarterly*, 41 (March 1988), pp. 145-153.

Jordan, Terry G., with John L. Bean, Jr., and William M. Holmes, *Texas: A Geography*. Boulder: Westview Press, 1984.

McComb, David G., *Texas: A Modern History*. Austin: University of Texas Press, 1989.

Montejano, David, *Anglos and Mexicans in the Making of Texas, 1836-1986*. Austin: University of Texas Press, 1987.

O'Conner, Robert F., editor, *Texas Myths*. College Station: Texas A&M University Press, 1986.

Reichley, A. James, *Religion in American Public Life*. Washington, D.C.: The Brookings Institution, 1985.

Richardson, Rupert, Ernest Wallace, and Adrian N. Anderson, *Texas: The Lone Star State*. 5th ed. Englewood Cliffs, N.J.: Prentice Hall, 1988.

## ENDNOTES

1. J.B. Priestly: Jacquetta Hawkes, *Journey Down a Rainbow* (New York: Harper & Brothers, 1955), p. 26. Used by permission of the University of Chicago Press.
2. *Dallas Morning News*, Sept. 25, 1991.
3. Harold Lasswell, *Who Gets What, When, How* (New York: Meridian Books, Inc., 1958).
4. Texas Comptroller of Public Accounts *Fiscal Notes*, (June 1989), p. 6.
5. David Easton, *A Framework for Political Analysis* (Englewood Cliffs: Prentice-Hall, Inc., 1965), chap. 5.
6. Louise Cowan, "Myth in the Modern World," in *Texas Myths*, ed. Robert F. O'Conner (College Station: Texas A&M University Press, 1986), p. 4.
7. Ibid., p. 14. For an excellent analysis of the concept of the "myth of origin" as integrated into the American mythology, see Robert N. Bellah, *The Broken Covenant: American Civil Religion in Time of Trial* (New York: The Seabury Press, 1975).
8. Ibid., p. 14.
9. T.R. Fehrenbach, "Texas Mythology: Now and Forever," in *Texas Myths*, pp. 210-217.
10. Robin Doughty, "From Wilderness to Garden: Conquering the Texas Landscape," in *Texas Myths*, p. 105.

11. Lucian W. Pye, "Political Culture," *International Encyclopedia of the Social Sciences*, Vol. 12 (New York: Macmillan, 1968), p. 218.

12. Ellen M. Dran, Robert B. Albritton and Mikel Wyckoff, "Surrogate Versus Direct Measures of Political Culture: Explaining Participation and Policy Attitudes in Illinois," *Publius* 21 (Spring 1991), p. 17.

13. Daniel Elazar, *American Federalism: A View from the States* (New York: Thomas Y. Crowell, 1966), p. 86.

14. Ibid., p. 86.

15. Ibid., pp. 86-89.

16. Ibid., p. 90.

17. Ibid., p. 90.

18. Ibid., p. 91.

19. Ibid., p. 92.

20. Ibid., pp. 92-94.

21. Ibid., pp. 97, 102, 108.

22. Rupert N. Richardson, Ernest Wallace and Adrian Anderson, *Texas: The Lone Star State*, 5th ed. (Englewood Cliffs: Prentice Hall, 1988), p. 1.

23. Terry G. Jordan with John L. Bean, Jr., and William M. Holmes, *Texas: A Geography* (Boulder: Westview Press, 1984), pp. 79-86.

24. David Montejano, *Anglos and Mexicans in the Making of Texas, 1836-1986* (Austin: University of Texas Press, 1987), p. 38.

25. *San Antonio Express News*, September 19, 1991, p. 10A.

26. R.L. Skrabanch and Steve H. Murdock, "The Black Population of Texas," *Texas Business Review*, 56 (May-June 1982), p. 144.

27. Jordan, et al, *Texas*, pp. 71-77.

28. V.O. Key, *Southern Politics in State and Nation* (New York: Vintage Books, 1949), p. 261.

29. For an excellent analysis of Key's projections for political change in Texas, see Chandler Davidson, *Race and Class in Texas Politics* (Princeton: Princeton University Press, 1990).

30. Office of the Governor, Texas 2000 Commission, *Texas Trends*, p. 5.

31. Ibid., p. 9

32. Office of the Governor, Texas 2000 Commission, *Texas Past and Future: A Survey*, p. 6.

33. James A. Dyer, Arnold Vedlitz, and David B. Hill, "New Voters, Switchers, and Political Party Realignment in Texas," *Western Political Quarterly*, 41 (March 1988), p. 159.

34. David A. Plane, "Where do New Texans Come From" *Texas Business Review*, 56 (November-December 1982), p. 291.

35. Richardson, et al, *Texas: The Lone Star State,*. p. 2.

36. V.O. Key, *Southern Politics in State and Nation*, p. 260.

37. Jordan, et al., *Texas*, p. 7.

38. Ibid., pp. 18-21.

39. Ibid., p. 21.

40. Office of the Governor, Texas 2000 Commission, *Texas Past and Future: A Survey*, p. 18.

41. *Texas Monthly*, 19 (September, 1991) p. 114.

42. Ibid., p. 114.

43. Texas Department of Human Services, *1989 Special Texas Census: Summary of Selected Findings*, August 1, 1990, p. 10.

44. Ibid., pp. 7-11.

45. *San Antonio Express News*, November 10, 1991, p. 23A.

46. Texas Comptroller of Public Accounts, *Fiscal Notes*, (March 1991), p. 10.

47. For an expanded analysis of the Texas economy and the dominate role played by larger corporations, see James W. Lamare, *Texas Politics: Economics, Power and Policy*, 4th ed. (St. Paul: West Publishing Company, 1991), chap. 2.

48. Texas Comptroller of Public Accounts, *It's Texas: Here's Why*, 1989, pp. 9-10.

49. Texas Comptroller of Public Accounts, *Fiscal Notes* (December, 1990), pp. 6-7.

50. Ibid., pp. 6-7.

51. Texas Comptroller of Public Accounts, *Fiscal Notes* (March 1989), p. 3.

52. Ibid., p. 3.

53. Texas Comptroller of Public Accounts, *Fiscal Notes* (December 1990), p. 7.

54. Texas Comptroller of Public Accounts, *Fiscal Notes* (February 1989), p. 1.

55. Texas Comptroller of Public Accounts, *Fiscal Notes* (April 1989), p. 2.
56. Texas Comptroller of Public Accounts, *Fiscal Notes* (February 1990), p. 1.
57. Harry Hurt, "Birth of a New Frontier," *Texas Monthly* (April 1984), pp. 130-135.
58. Texas Comptroller of Public Accounts, *Fiscal Notes* (April 1990), pp. 1-8.
59. Texas Comptroller of Public Accounts, *Its Texas: Here's Why*, pp. 15-30.
60. Texas Comptroller of Public Accounts, *Fiscal Notes* (February 1989), p. 6.

# 2

# THE TEXAS CONSTITUTION

> People like to be remembered in the Texas Constitution; but unfortunately, not all people are remembered equally, and the sum of those special interests protected does not necessarily add up to the general or public interest.
>
> *Janice May*[1]

Bogged down with statutory detail and an antigovernment bias from the post-Reconstruction era in which it was written, the Texas Constitution is more a textbook example of what a constitution shouldn't be than what one should resemble. State government functions despite its constitutional shackles: a weak chief executive; an outdated, part-time legislature; a poorly organized judiciary and a series of dedicated funds that limit the state's budgetary options. The constitution has been amended many times since its adoption in 1876. But a total rewrite, which many scholars and politicians alike agree is overdue, has been elusive, thanks to numerous special interests who find security in the present document: from holders of obsolete offices to beneficiaries of dedicated funds and bureaucrats who fear change.

Constitutions are more than the formal frameworks that define the structure, authority, and responsibilities of governmental institutions. They also reflect fundamental political, economic, and power relationships as determined by the culture, values, and interests of the people who create them and the events of the period in which they were written.[2]

Texas has had seven constitutions, and understanding that legacy is critical to understanding contemporary Texas politics and public policy. The first constitution was adopted in 1827, when the state was still part of Mexico. The second was drafted when Texas declared its independence from Mexico in 1836 and became a Republic, and a third was adopted in 1845 when the state joined the Union. A fourth

was written when Texas joined the Confederacy in 1861, and a fifth was
en the state rejoined the union in 1866. The sixth constitution was
1869 to satisfy the Radical Reconstructionists' opposition to the 1866
1, and the seventh constitution was adopted in 1876 after the termination
ruction policies.

ritten at the close of the darkest period in Texas history, a period of
ad governmental corruption and repression, the Constitution of 1876, with
erous piecemeal amendments, still shapes the governmental responsibilities
olitical power within the state.

## TIONALISM

### ons of a Constitution

constitution defines the principles of a society and states or suggests what political
objectives that society is attempting to achieve. It outlines the specific institutions
that these people will use to achieve their objectives, defines who can participate in
collective decisions and who can hold public office. It also defines the relationship
between those people who govern and those who are governed and sets limits on
what each group can and cannot do. Because of the stability of the American political
system and a general commitment to the rule of law, we often overlook the fact that
constitutions also reflect the way that a society structures conflict through its
institutional arrangement.[3]

### The Texas Constitution in a Comparative Perspective

Constitutions do not lend themselves to easy reading. The formal, legal language
often obscures the general objectives of the document and its relevance to contemporary issues of political power and public policy. But Texans, as are people
throughout the United States, are strong supporters of constitutional law. While
many people may not know much about the specifics of their state constitution,
there is a near reverence for the "fundamental law" of the state. That—plus the
influence of special interest groups happy with the status quo—explains why Texas
is still governed under a cumbersome document drafted more than 100 years ago.

Scholarly experts believe constitutions should be brief and explicit and
include general principles rather than specific legislative provisions. In other words,
they should provide a basic framework for government and leave the details to be
imposed in statutory law. Secondly, experts say, constitutions should make direct
grants of authority to specific institutions, so as to increase the responsiveness and
the accountability of individuals elected or appointed to public office. Scholars also
believe that constitutions should provide for orderly change, but should not be
written in such a restrictive fashion that they require continual modifications to meet
contemporary needs.[4]

Amended only 27 times since its adoption in 1789, the U.S. Constitution is a concise, 7,000-word document that outlines broad, basic principles of authority and governance. No one would argue that the government of the 1990s is comparable to that of 1789, but the flexibility of the U.S. Constitution makes it as relevant now as it was in the 18th century. It is often spoken of as "a living charter or document" that doesn't have to be continually amended to meet society's ever changing needs and conditions. Its reinterpretations by the courts, the Congress, and the president have produced an expansion of powers and responsibilities within the framework of the original language of the document.

By contrast, the Texas Constitution is an unwieldy, restrictive, 62,000-plus word document that has been on a life-support system—the piecemeal amendment process—for most of its lifetime (Table 2-1). It is less a set of basic governmental principles than it is a compilation of detailed statutory language reflecting the distrust of government that was widespread in Texas when it was written. The constitutional experiences of Texas parallel those of many southern states that have had multiple constitutions in the post-Civil War era. The southern states, Texas included, are the only group of states to formally acknowledge the supremacy of the U.S. Constitution, a requirement to satisfy the demands of Radical Reconstructionists after the former Confederate states were readmitted to the Union. The Texas Constitution attempts to diffuse political power among many different institutions. As drafted in 1876, it also included provisions related to elections, civil rights, and apportionment that were later invalidated by the U.S. Supreme Court. Those early provisions were efforts to limit the power of minority groups to fully participate in state government.[5]

## THE CONSTITUTIONAL LEGACY

Each of Texas' seven constitutions was written in a distinct historical setting. And while there are significant differences among these documents, each contributed to the state and local governments that we know today.

### Constitution of Coahuila y Tejas (1827)

Sparsely populated Texas was part of Mexico when that country secured its independence from Spain in 1821, about the same time that Stephen F. Austin and others initiated Anglo colonization of Texas. Initially, Anglo Texans appeared to be willing to be incorporated into the Mexican political system as long as there was limited intrusion of the Mexican government into their daily affairs. In 1824, the new Republic of Mexico adopted a constitution for a federal system of government that recognized Texas as a single state with Coahuila, its neighbor south of the Rio Grande. Saltillo, Mexico, was the state capital.

Each state was authorized to develop a constitution, and the state constitution for Coahuila y Tejas was completed in 1827. This document provided for a unicameral congress of 12 deputies, including two from Texas, elected by the

**TABLE 2–1**   State Constitutions (as of January 1, 1990)

| State | Number of Constitutions | Estimated Date of Current Constitutions | Estimated Number of Words | Amendments Submitted to Voters | Adopted |
|---|---|---|---|---|---|
| Alabama | 6 | 1901 | 174,000 | 726 | 513 |
| Alaska | 1 | 1959 | 13,000 | 31 | 22 |
| Arizona | 1 | 1912 | 28,876 | 198 | 109 |
| Arkansas | 5 | 1874 | 40,720 | 164 | 76 |
| California | 2 | 1879 | 33,350 | 781 | 471 |
| Colorado | 1 | 1876 | 45,679 | 239 | 115 |
| Connecticut | 4 | 1965 | 9,564 | 26 | 25 |
| Delaware | 4 | 1897 | 19,000 | ** | 119 |
| Florida | 6 | 1969 | 25,100 | 79 | 53 |
| Georgia | 10 | 1983 | 25,000 | 35 | 24 |
| Hawaii | 1 | 1959 | 17,453 | 93 | 82 |
| Idaho | 1 | 1890 | 21,500 | 187 | 107 |
| Illinois | 4 | 1971 | 13,200 | 11 | 6 |
| Indiana | 2 | 1851 | 9,377 | 70 | 38 |
| Iowa | 2 | 1857 | 12,500 | 51 | 48 |
| Kansas | 1 | 1861 | 11,865 | 115 | 87 |
| Kentucky | 4 | 1891 | 23,500 | 58 | 29 |
| Louisiana | 11 | 1975 | 51,448 | 51 | 27 |
| Maine | 1 | 1820 | 13,500 | 186 | 157 |
| Maryland | 4 | 1867 | 41,349 | 233 | 200 |
| Massachusetts | 1 | 1780 | 36,690 | 143 | 116 |
| Michigan | 4 | 1964 | 20,000 | 47 | 16 |
| Minnesota | 1 | 1858 | 9,500 | 206 | 112 |
| Mississippi | 4 | 1890 | 24,000 | 133 | 102 |
| Missouri | 4 | 1945 | 42,000 | 115 | 74 |
| Montana | 2 | 1973 | 11,866 | 25 | 15 |
| Nebraska | 2 | 1875 | 20,048 | 283 | 189 |
| Nevada | 1 | 1864 | 20,770 | 175 | 108 |
| New Hampshire | 2 | 1784 | 9,200 | 274 | 142 |
| New Jersey | 3 | 1948 | 17,086 | 52 | 39 |
| New Mexico | 1 | 1912 | 27,200 | 231 | 120 |
| New York | 4 | 1895 | 80,000 | 274 | 207 |
| North Carolina | 3 | 1971 | 11,000 | 34 | 27 |
| North Dakota | 1 | 1889 | 20,564 | 222 | 125 |
| Ohio | 2 | 1851 | 36,900 | 245 | 145 |
| Oklahoma | 1 | 1907 | 68,800 | 274 | 133 |
| Oregon | 1 | 1859 | 26,090 | 367 | 188 |
| Pennsylvania | 5 | 1968 | 21,675 | 25 | 19 |
| Rhode Island | 2 | 1843 | 19,026 | 99 | 53 |
| South Carolina | 7 | 1896 | 22,500 | 647 | 463 |
| South Dakota | 1 | 1889 | 23,300 | 185 | 97 |
| Tennessee | 3 | 1870 | 15,300 | 55 | 32 |
| Texas | 5* | 1876 | 62,000 | 483 | 326 |
| Utah | 1 | 1896 | 11,000 | 126 | 77 |
| Vermont | 3 | 1793 | 6,600 | 208 | 50 |
| Virginia | 6 | 1971 | 18,500 | 23 | 20 |
| Washington | 1 | 1889 | 29,400 | 153 | 86 |
| West Virginia | 2 | 1872 | 25,600 | 107 | 62 |
| Wisconsin | 1 | 1848 | 13,500 | 168 | 124 |
| Wyoming | 1 | 1890 | 31,800 | 97 | 57 |

*Texas has functioned under five constitutions since the state joined the union in 1845. Prior to membership in the union, Texas operated under a Mexican constitution and the constitution of the Republic.
**Proposed amendments are not submitted to voters in Delaware.
Source: © 1992 The Council of State Governments. Reprinted with permission from *The Book of the States.*

people. Most of the legislators were from the more populous and Spanish-speaking Coahuila, and the laws were published in Spanish, which few Texas colonists understood. The executive department included a governor and a vice governor. The governor enforced the law, led the state militia, and granted pardons. The constitution made Catholicism the state religion, although that requirement wasn't enforced among Texas' Anglo settlers. Additionally, Anglo Texans were not subject to military service, taxes, or custom duties. In effect, Texas served as a buffer between Mexico and various Indian tribes and the United States.

But with increased Anglo immigration and the perceived threat of U.S. imperial or expansionary policies, Mexico soon attempted to extend its control over Texas. This extension of authority reinforced existing cultural differences between the Anglo and Spanish populations and would eventually lead to revolution by Anglo Texans.[6]

This formative period produced some enduring contributions to the Texas constitutional tradition. Elements of the Mexican legal system are still to be found in property and land laws, water laws and water rights and community property laws. One justification for the revolution of 1836 was the failure of the Mexican national government to provide for sufficient funding of public education. But while there were expectations of funding by the central government, a "concept of local control over school development was firmly established."[7] This has been a continuing constitutional question and is central to the current issue of funding of public education.

## The Constitution of the Republic of Texas (1836)

The late 1820s and the early 1830s witnessed increased immigration from the United States into the territory of Texas and, with it, heightened tension and conflict between the Anglo settlers and the Mexican government. Mexico had every right as a nation to enforce its laws on the citizens who resided within its borders. But efforts to impose national authority within Texas produced conflicts between cultures, legal traditions, and economic interests that resulted in open rebellion by the colonists.

At the same time, Mexico also was embroiled in its own internal dissension. It struggled to stabilize its own political system but didn't have the legacy and social and political institutions to assure a successful democratic system. In many respects, the events in Texas were a footnote to the power politics in Mexico, and had the autonomy of Texas that was provided for under the Mexican Constitution of 1824 been maintained, the history of this region might well have been different.

Increased internal conflict among competing Mexican interests resulted in the seizure of power by the popular general, Antonio Lopez de Santa Anna Perez de Lebron. Santa Anna began to systematically suspend the powers of the Mexican Congress and local governments, and in October 1835, the national Constitution of 1824 was voided. Mexico adopted a new constitution organized around the principle of a unitary state with power centralized in the national congress and the presidency. The principle of federalism, which divided power and authority between the national government and the states, was repudiated. This major change intensified conflict between the national government and the Mexican states. Texas was not the only area of Mexico where the principles of federalism were highly regarded, and while Texas was eventually successful in establishing its autonomy, several other Mexican states were subjected to harsh military retaliation.

As the Mexican government under Santa Anna attempted to regain control over Texas, colonists who initially supported the national government and those who expressed ambivalence were only slowly converted to the cause of independence. Stephen F. Austin had consistently supported the position that Texas was a Mexican state, and he represented a large part of the Anglo population living in Texas. But when Mexican troops finally moved across the Rio Grande into Texas in the fall of 1835, Austin sent out a call for resistance.

The numerous special interests that later were to obstruct the course of constitutional development in Texas were missing at the small settlement of Washington-on-the-Brazos in 1836. The 59 male colonists who convened to declare Texas' independence from Mexico on March 2 and to adopt a constitution for the new republic two weeks later had two overriding interests: the preservation of their fledgling nation and the preservation of their own lives. By the time they had completed their work, the Alamo had fallen to a large Mexican army under Santa Anna, only 150 miles away, and a second Mexican force also was north of the Rio Grande. Accordingly, the constitution writers wasted little time on speechmaking.

And, consequently, the constitution adopted on March 16, 1836, wasn't cluttered with the details that still weaken the present document. It drew heavily from the U.S. Constitution and, since 44 of the 59 delegates were from the South, from the constitutions of several southern states. The document created an elected bicameral congress and provided for an elected president. Members of the clergy were prohibited from serving as president or in congress, and there was no official, state-preferred religion. Slavery was legal, but importation of slaves from any country other than the United States was illegal. And free Negroes had to have congress' permission to leave Texas.

Approximately six weeks after the disastrous defeat at the Alamo, the Texas army, under the command of Sam Houston, defeated Santa Anna's army at the Battle of San Jacinto on April 21, 1836. The war of independence had been relatively short and involved limited casualties, but the problems of creating a stable, political system under the new constitution were formidable. There was no viable government in place, no money for paying the costs of government and no party system.[8] And, although defeated, Mexico did not relinquish its claims to Texas and was to demonstrate in subsequent actions that it wanted to regain this lost territory. Nevertheless, the "transition from colony to constitutional republic was accomplished quickly and with a minimum of disorganization."[9]

Independence and national autonomy during the period from 1836 to 1845 contributed significantly to the development of a sense of historical uniqueness among Texans. While the effects on the state's political psyche may be difficult to measure, the "Lone Star" experience has been kept alive through school history texts, the celebration of key events, and the development of a mythology of the independence period.

## The Constitution of 1845

During the independence movement and immediately thereafter, there were overtures to the United States to annex Texas, but they were initially blocked by the issue of slavery and its relationship to economic and regional influence in U.S. politics. Increased immigration to Texas in the late 1830s and early 1840s, more interest among Texans in joining the Union, and expansionist policies of the U.S. government stepped up pressures for annexation. It was a major issue in the U.S. presidential campaign of 1844, and the election of James K. Polk accelerated the move toward Texas' admission to the United States in 1845.

The annexation bill approved by the U.S. Congress included a compromise on the slavery issue, which allowed slavery to continue in Texas.[10] Racial issues that emerged from this period continue to shape contemporary politics and public policy in the state. Texas still struggles with voting rights issues, the inequities in funding of public education and higher education, and the mal-distribution of economic resources that directly affect the quality of life for many minority groups across the state.

The terms of Texas' admission into the Union also provided that Texas could divide itself into as many as five states, a provision long since forgotten by most people until state Representative David Swinford, a Republican from Dumas, made such a proposal in 1991. The idea attracted some newspaper headlines and some interest in the Panhandle, which is geographically isolated from most of Texas, but wasn't given serious consideration by Swinford's colleagues.

The state constitution drafted to allow Texas' annexation was about twice as long as the Constitution of 1836. It borrowed not only from its predecessor but also from the constitutions of other southern states.

It created an elected legislature that met biennially and included a House of Representatives and a Senate. It provided for an elected governor and an elected lieutenant governor and empowered the governor to appoint a secretary of state, attorney general, and state judges, subject to Senate confirmation. The legislature chose a comptroller, treasurer, and land commissioner. But in 1850, Texas voters amended the constitution to make most state offices elective. In this respect, Texas was following a national pattern of fragmenting the powers of the executive branch of state government. Today, Texas still has a plural executive system under which practically all statewide officeholders are elected independently of the governor, a system that contrasts sharply with the appointive cabinet system of executive government enjoyed by the president of the United States.

The 1845 constitution protected private homesteads from foreclosure, guaranteed separate property rights for married women, and established a permanent fund for the support of public schools, all provisions that exist in the present constitution. The 1845 charter also recognized slavery, prohibited anyone who had ever participated in a duel from holding public office, and prohibited state-chartered banks. This constitution "worked so well that after several intervening constitutions, the people of Texas recopied it almost in toto as the Constitution of 1876."[11]

The prohibition against state-chartered banks apparently stemmed from the American financial panic of 1837 and subsequent depression, which affected the Republic of Texas and which was largely blamed on banks. In an 1983 column in the *Dallas Morning News*, Mike Kingston, editor of the *Texas Almanac*, cited a bit of Texas lore that holds that, in a deathbed plea, Andrew Jackson, a strong enemy of banks as president, urged the drafters of the 1845 constitution to outlaw banks. Kingston called Jackson, a mentor of early Texas leader and hero Sam Houston, "the godfather of Texas whose opinion carried weight with the emerging state's leadership."[12] Deathbed plea or not, most subsequent constitutions also prohibited state-chartered banks in Texas. They were legalized after a constitutional amendment in 1904.

## The Civil War Constitution (1861)

When Texas seceded from the Union in 1861, just before the outbreak of the Civil War, the state constitution was again revised. Although most of the provisions of the 1845 document were retained, significant changes were made in line with Texas' new membership in the Confederacy. Public officials were required to pledge their support of the Confederate constitution, greater protection was given to slavery, and the freeing of slaves was prohibited.

Any semblance of a two-party system was destroyed by the issues of slavery and secession during the 1850s, and state politics were dominated by personalities and factions. Factionalism within the Democratic party persisted for more than 100 years until the emergence of a two-party system in the 1980s.

The Civil War era also contributed to a legacy of states' rights, which was to persist well into the next century and spark an extended struggle for desegregation. Theoretically, the constitutional issue of the Civil War was whether or not a state, once having joined the Union, could leave the Union. The southern states subscribed to a confederal view of the national government, and it was their position that a state could withdraw, or secede. While the northern victory dispelled this interpretation, Texas, along with other southern states, found ways to thwart national policy through the 1960s. Their efforts were based, in part, on their continued arguments of states' rights.

## The Constitution of 1866

After the war, Texas government was subject to national control through, first, a military government and then a provisional government headed by A. J. Hamilton, a former U.S. congressman who had remained loyal to the Union. These were dark days for Texans. While the state had witnessed relatively few battles and had not suffered from scorched earth tactics used by Union generals, the economy was, nevertheless, in disarray. Many Texas families also had lost loved ones, and many surviving Confederate veterans had been wounded physically or psychologically. While the national government developed policies to assist the newly freed slaves, these policies were never fully funded and were halfheartedly, and often dishonestly, carried out. And the presence of an occupation army further exacerbated conflict and shaped subsequent political attitudes.

The reconstruction plan initiated by President Lincoln but never fully implemented envisioned a rapid return to civilian government for the southern states and their quick reintegration as equals in the national political system. Requirements were modest: the abolition of slavery, the repudiation of the secession ordinance of 1861, and the repudiation of all debts and obligations incurred under the Confederacy.[13]

Texas voters once again revised their constitution. A constitutional convention called by provisional Governor Hamilton revived the constitution of 1845 and amended it to include the stipulations required by the national government. But while slavery was eliminated and the freed slaves were given the right to hold property and were accorded legal rights before a jury, no African-American could testify in any court case involving whites. And African-Americans were denied the right to vote.[14] The new constitution was adopted in June of 1866, a new government was elected, and on Aug. 20, 1866, President Andrew Johnson "declared the rebellion in Texas at an end."[15]

In short order, though, the mild reconstruction policies of Johnson were replaced by the severe policies of the Radical Reconstructionists who captured control of Congress in 1866. The new Texas constitution was invalidated by Congress, which passed, over the president's veto, the Reconstruction Acts that established military governments throughout the South. The civilian government initiated by the state constitution of 1866 was shortlived, and Texas functioned for two years under a reinstituted military government.

The motives of the **Radical Reconstructionists** are left to the analysis of others, but this period had an enduring impact on Texas constitutional law and politics. In a broad sense, it prolonged the full reintegration of Texas into the national political system, and in specific terms, it transformed the constitutional tradition of Texas to one of hostility and suspicion toward government.

## The Constitution of Reconstruction (1869)

The Reconstruction Acts required a Texas constitution that would grant Negro suffrage and include other provisions acceptable to Congress. A Republican slate of delegates to a new constitutional convention produced a new charter that was published in 1869. It didn't reflect the majority Texas sentiment of the time, but it conformed to Republican wishes. Centralizing more powers in state government while weakening local government, it gave the governor a four-year term and the power to appoint other top state officials, including members of the judiciary. It provided for annual legislative sessions, gave African-Americans the right to vote and, for the first time, provided for a centralized, statewide system of public schools. Texans were unhappy enough with their new constitution, but the widespread abuses of the document that followed under the oppressive and corrupt administration of Radical Republican **Governor E.J. Davis** were factors that, in a few years, were to place shackles on state government that are still in place today.

In the election of 1869, the first under the new constitution, the military governor certified that Davis, a former Union Army officer, beat Conservative Republican A.J. Hamilton by 39,901 to 39,092 votes. This was allowed despite widespread and flagrant incidents of voter fraud, which also were ignored by President Ulysses S. Grant and Congress. A radical majority in the new Texas Legislature then approved a series of authoritarian—and, in some respects, unconstitutional—laws proposed by Davis. They gave the governor the power to declare martial law and suspend the laws in any county and created a state police force under the governor's control that could deprive citizens of constitutional protections. The governor also was empowered to appoint mayors, district attorneys, and hundreds of other local officials. Another law that designated newspapers as official printers of state documents, in effect, put much of the press under government control.

All in all, Davis exercised some of the most repressive powers ever imposed on United States citizens. And Texans responded, first in 1872, when they elected a Democratic majority to the legislature, which abolished the state police and repealed other oppressive laws, and again in 1873, when they elected a Confederate veteran, Democrat Richard Coke, governor by more than a 2-1 margin over Davis. Like the Radical Republicans in the previous gubernatorial election, the Democrats were not above abusing the democratic process and, once again, voting fraud was rampant.

"What seems to have happened is that the carpetbaggers had taught the Texans how. Democrat politicos bluntly indicated that power would be won depending on who outfrauded whom. No practice was ignored....There was terror, intimidation, and some murders on both sides," wrote historian T. R. Fehrenbach.[16]

Despite the election outcome, Davis initially refused to leave office and appealed to President Grant for federal troops to help him retain power. Grant refused, but the city of Austin was divided into two armed camps of Coke and Davis supporters for several tense days in January 1874. Davis finally gave up after the Texas militia turned against him and marched on the capitol. Bloodshed was avoided, Reconstruction was ending, and the constitution of 1869 was doomed.

## The Constitution of 1876: Retrenchment and Reform

The restored Democratic majority promptly took steps to assemble a new constitutional convention, which convened in Austin on Sept. 6, 1875. The delegates were all men. Most were products of a rural and frontier South and, still smarting from Reconstruction abuses, they considered government a necessary evil that had to be heavily restricted. Many, however, had previous governmental experience. Initially,

75 Democrats and 15 Republicans were elected delegates, but one Republican resigned after only limited service and was replaced by a Democrat.[17]

The vast majority of the delegates were white, and there is some disagreement over how many African-Americans served in the convention. Some historians say there were six. According to one account, however, six African-Americans were elected but one resigned after only one day of service and was replaced in a special election by a white delegate. All of the African-American delegates were Republicans.[18]

Only four of the delegates were native Texans. Most had immigrated to Texas from other southern states, including 19—the largest single group—from Tennessee, which one author called the "breeding ground" of Texas delegates. Their average age was 45. The oldest was 68, the youngest, 23.[19] Eleven of the delegates had been members of previous constitutional conventions in Texas, but there is disagreement over whether any had participated in drafting the Reconstruction Constitution of 1869. In any event, the influences of the 1869 constitution were negative, not positive.

At least 30 of the delegates had served in the Texas Legislature, two others had served in the Tennessee and Mississippi legislatures, two had represented Texas in the U.S. Congress and two others had represented Texas in the Confederate Congress. Delegates also included a former attorney general, a former lieutenant governor, and a former secretary of state of Texas, and at least eight delegates had judicial experience. Many delegates had been high ranking Confederate military officers. One, John H. Reagan, had been postmaster general of the Confederacy.[20] Reagan later would become a U.S. senator from Texas and would serve as the first chairman of the Texas Railroad Commission.

Another delegate who epitomized the independent, frontier spirit of the time was John S. "Rip" Ford, a native of South Carolina who had come to Texas in 1836 as a physician. He also became a lawyer, journalist, state senator, mayor of Austin, and Texas Ranger captain. In 1874, he was a leader of the militia that marched on the capitol and forced E.J. Davis to relinquish the governor's office to his elected successor. Ford had been a secessionist delegate to the 1861 convention and during the Civil War had commanded a makeshift cavalry regiment that fought Union soldiers along the Texas-Mexico border.[21]

According to one account, delegates to the 1875 convention included 33 lawyers, 28 farmers, three physicians, three merchants, two teachers, two editors, and one minister. At least 11 other delegates were part-time farmers who also pursued other occupations.[22] Other historians have come up with slightly different breakdowns, but all agree that the influence of agricultural interests was substantial in the writing of the new Texas charter.

About half the delegates were members of the Society of the Patrons of Husbandry, or the Grange. An organization formed to improve the lot of farmers, the Grange became politically active in the wake of national scandals involving abuses by big business and government. The Grange started organizing in Texas in

1873, and its influence was directly felt in constitutional provisions limiting taxes and governmental expenditures and restricting banks, railroads, and other corporations.

When they got down to work, the delegates didn't try to produce a document that would be lauded as a model of constitutional perfection or mistaken for a literary masterpiece. They faced the reality of addressing serious, pressing problems, an immediate crisis that didn't encourage debate over the finer points of academic or political theory or produce any prophetic visions of the next century.

The Civil War, Reconstruction, and the Radical Republican administration had plunged the state into economic ruin and the state government into deep debt, despite the heavy taxation of Texas citizens, particularly property owners. The bottom had fallen out of land prices, a disaster for what was still an agricultural state. Governmental corruption had been pervasive under the Davis administration, and the dictatorial powers that Davis had exercised, particularly the abuses of his hated state police, had left deep scars. Moreover, the national political scene under President Grant's two administrations from 1869-1877 also had been plagued by corruption and scandal.

The framers of the new constitution reacted accordingly. In seeking to restore control of their state government to the people and restore economic stability, they fashioned what was essentially an antigovernment charter. Centralization was replaced with more local control, strict limits were placed on taxation, and short leashes were put on the legislature, the courts, and especially the governor.[23]

Texas' traditional agricultural interests, which had been called upon to finance industrial development and new social services during Reconstruction, were once again protected from onerous governmental intrusion and taxation. The retrenchment and reform embodied in the new charter soon would hamper the state's commercial and economic development. But the post-Reconstruction Texans applauded the multitude of restrictive details that the new constitution carried. They ratified the new document in February 1876 by a vote of 136,606 to 56,052.

## GENERAL PRINCIPLES OF THE TEXAS CONSTITUTION

A relatively short preamble and the first two sections of the Bill of Rights express the underlying organizational principle of the Constitution of 1876. It was a social compact, formed by free men (no women participated in its drafting), in which "all political power is inherent in the people,...founded on their authority, and instituted for their preservation."[24] These brief sections are based on the concepts of **popular sovereignty** and **compact theory**, both of which were part of a legacy of constitutional law in the United States. While the language articulates the noble aspirations of a free and just society, it was limited in scope and application. Women and minorities were initially denied full citizenship rights. And while women gained the right to vote in 1920, it has taken years for African-Americans and Hispanics to receive the full protection implicit in these statements.

A second major principle is **limited government**. The Bill of Rights and other provisions throughout the constitution place limits on governmental authority and power. The constitution spells out the traditional rights of religious freedom, procedural due process of law, and other rights of the citizen in relation to the government.

A third major principle is that of **separation of powers**. Unlike the U.S. Constitution, where this principle emerges through powers defined in the three articles related to the Congress, the president, and the judiciary, Article II of the Texas Constitution specifically provides for it.

The Constitution of 1876 created three branches of government—legislative, executive, and judicial—and provided for a system of checks and balances that assured that no single branch would dominate the others. This principle originated with the United States Constitution because its drafters were concerned with the so-called "mischief of factions." They feared that groups or special interests would be able to capture governmental institutions and pursue policies that were not in the national interest. So institutional power was fragmented to guard against that potential problem. In some respects, this was an issue of even greater concern among the framers of the Texas Constitution. Their reactions to the highly centralized authority and abuses of the Davis administration produced institutional arrangements that took the separation of powers principle to its extreme.

Lawmaking authority is vested in an elected legislature that includes a 150-member House of Representatives and a 31-member Senate and meets in regular sessions in odd-numbered years and in special sessions of limited scope and duration when called by the governor. The 65 sections of Article III are excessively detailed in the powers granted and the restrictions imposed on the legislature.

An elected governor shares authority over the executive branch with several other independently elected, statewide officeholders. The governor can veto bills approved by the legislature, and it requires a two-thirds vote of the House and the Senate to override a veto.

Members of the judiciary also are elected—from justices of the peace with limited jurisdiction at the county level to the highest statewide appellate courts. This reflects the strong sentiment of post-Reconstruction Texans for an independent judiciary and is a major difference from the federal government, where judges are appointed by the president. Also unlike the federal system, where the U.S. Supreme Court is the court of last resort in both civil and criminal appeals, Texas has two courts of last resort. The Texas Supreme Court has jurisdiction over civil matters, and the Texas Court of Criminal Appeals reviews criminal cases. While this provision was not included in the constitution originally adopted in 1876, it was added in 1891 by a constitutional amendment.

## WEAKNESSES AND CRITICISMS OF THE CONSTITUTION OF 1876

While the general public spends little time debating constitutions and their effects, public officials, scholars and those who write and comment about politics and public policy spend a great deal of time on the subject. And critics have raised many questions about the Texas Constitution.

Many experts believe that it excessively fragmented governmental authority and responsibility, particularly in the executive branch. The fundamental law of the state created a plural executive arrangement under which most other statewide officeholders, including the lieutenant governor, the attorney general, the comptroller, and the treasurer, are elected independently of the governor and answer directly to the people in the performance of their duties.

While there is a natural disposition for the public to look to the governor to establish policy priorities, the governor doesn't have control over the other elected state executives and shares both authority and responsibility for policy with those individuals. Former Republican Governor Bill Clements, for example, found himself sharing executive responsibilities with Democrats who sharply disagreed with his priorities and frequently acted to block them. And even if the governor is of the same party as these other elected officials, differences in personality, political philosophy, and policy objectives can produce tension and sometimes deadlock.

The governor's power has been further diffused by the creation over the years of numerous boards and commissions that set policy for executive agencies not headed by elected officials. Although the governor appoints most of those board members, they serve staggered six-year terms, which are longer than a governor's term. And a newly elected governor—who can't fire a predecessor's appointees— usually has to wait through most of his or her first term to gain a majority of appointees to most of the boards. Democratic Governor Ann Richards expressed considerable frustration at holdover appointees of Republican Governor Bill Clements after she took office in January 1991. Later that year, she asked the legislature to take the power to appoint the executive directors who run the day-to-day operations of the agencies from the boards and give it to the governor, but she was given that authority over only a few agencies.

Fragmented authority and responsibilities also are found in county governments, which are administrative agents of the state (see Chapter 12). Various elected county officials often clash over public policy, producing inefficiencies or failing to meet public needs. And just as the voters are faced with a long ballot for statewide offices, they also must choose among a long, often confusing list of county officers as well. Since a long ballot may discourage many people from voting, this obstacle also may serve to reduce public accountability, an end result that the framers of the Constitution of 1876 certainly never intended.

The constitution created a low-paid, part-time legislature to ensure the election of citizen lawmakers who would be sensitive to the needs of their constituents, not of professional politicians who would live off the taxpayers. Unwittingly, however, the constitution writers also produced a lawmaking body easily influenced by special interest groups. And the strict limitations placed on the legislature's operations, functions, and powers were to slow its ability to meet the increasingly complex needs of a growing, modern Texas.

In 1971, voters approved a constitutional change to lengthen the terms of the governor and other executive officeholders from two to four years. This change gives the governor more time to develop public policies with the prospect of seeing these policies implemented. But voters repeatedly have rejected proposals to provide for regular, annual legislative sessions. And the level of legislative pay remains among the lowest in the country.

The Texas Constitution also created a judiciary of locally elected judges, including justice of the peace, county, and district courts. While there are appeal procedures, these elected judges derive a great deal of autonomy, power, and influence from the fact that they obtain their offices from local constituencies. Another example of decentralization is the public school system. The centralized school system authorized under the Constitution of 1869 was abolished and local authorities were given the responsibility of supervising public education.

While articulating a general commitment to democracy and individual rights, the constitution initially retarded democratic development in Texas.[25] As did many of the other southern states, Texas developed restrictive laws on voter participation. It levied a poll tax, which reduced the voting of minorities and poor whites, until 1966, when an amendment to the U.S.Constitution prohibited its use. It took federal court intervention to eliminate a system where African-Americans were systematically excluded from voting in the Democratic primary, which, in a one-party state, was where elections were decided. The elimination of significant numbers of individuals from participating in elections helped perpetuate the one-party political system that was to persist for approximately 100 years.[26]

The Texas Constitution also is burdened with excessive detail. While few individuals are disposed to read the 62,000-plus word document, a person casually perusing it will find references to the schools that comprise the Texas A&M University System; the division of counties of certain size into justice of the peace precincts; the operation of hospital districts in Ochiltree, Castro, Hansford, and Hopkins counties, and expenditures for relocation or replacement of sanitary sewer laterals on private property. The U.S. Constitution, which has only approximately 7,000 words, outlines broad governmental powers and leaves the details for implementing them to legislation enacted by Congress. But the Texas Constitution often spells out the authority and power of a governmental agency in specific detail. Most experts would argue that many constitutional articles are of a legislative nature and have no business in a constitution.[27] Excessive detail, though, defines and restricts, and this has been a continued legacy of the framers of the 1876 document.

Consequently, there are obsolete provisions in the constitution. Article 6, which defines suffrage, or the right to participate in the election process, prohibits anyone younger than 21 from voting. But that age limitation has been superseded by the 26th Amendment to the U.S. Constitution, which extended the franchise to persons 18 years of age or older. There have been some efforts to "clean up" the constitution by eliminating such deadwood—fifty-six obsolete provisions were removed in 1969, but the problem persists.[28]

Another important criticism of the constitution focuses on the amendments and the amendment process. At the beginning of the chapter, a table was presented comparing the Texas Constitution to the constitutions of the other states. Alabama has had more constitutional amendments than any other state, but Texas ranks fourth with 339 amendments from 1876 through 1991. Again, for comparative purposes, the U.S. Constitution has been amended only 27 times since 1789, and 10 of those amendments were adopted as the Bill of Rights immediately after the government organized. The numerous restrictions and prohibitions in the Texas Constitution require extensive, if not excessive, amendments to enable state government to adapt to social, economic, and political changes.

Studies suggest that proposed amendments pertaining to the basic structure of state government, such as public finance and tax exemptions for specific groups, have had less success with the voters than constitutional amendments related to public education, welfare, and health care.[29]

## CONSTITUTIONAL CHANGE AND ADAPTATION

Many Texans may still share the independent, frontier spirit that had little use for government in 1876. But their needs are more complex now and can't readily be met by a government with limited flexibility to adjust to changing conditions. Population growth and urbanization have created environmental problems and conflicts over land use that remain unresolved. A confusing collection of special, dedicated funds makes it difficult for the legislature to streamline the state budgetary process and adjust priorities for spending. And a part-time legislature, many experts believe, is incapable of timely addressing the myriad issues confronting the third most populous state on the eve of the 21st century.

Although the drafters filled the constitution with a multitude of restrictive provisions, they also provided a relatively easy method of amending it. The piecemeal amendment process has enabled state government to meet some of the changing needs of its citizens, but it also has added thousands of words to the document.

Proposed constitutional amendments can be submitted only by the legislature. Approval by two-thirds of the House and the Senate puts them on the ballot, where adoption requires a majority vote. While voters had approved 339 amendments through 1991, they had rejected 160 others. There have been only 28 years since the present charter was ratified in 1876 in which voters haven't been asked to change it. The first amendment was adopted on Sept. 2, 1879. A record 25 amendments were on the Nov. 3, 1987, ballot. Seventeen were adopted, and eight were defeated. There also were two binding referenda on the 1987 ballot, placed there by the legislature to give the voters the final say on whether parimutuel betting should be legalized and the State Board of Education should be elected or appointed.

Some amendments are of major statewide importance, but many have affected only a single county or a handful of counties or have been offered simply to rid the constitution of obsolete language.

Unlike voters in many other states, Texas citizens can't force the placement of constitutional amendments or binding referenda on the ballot because Texas doesn't have initiative and referendum. On taking office in January 1979 as Texas' first Republican governor since Reconstruction, Governor Bill Clements made the adoption of initiative and referendum a priority. But the process couldn't be provided without a constitutional amendment, and the Democrat-controlled legislature, which didn't want to give up such a significant policy prerogative to the electorate, ignored him.

The legislature not only decides which amendments go to the voters, it also determines the caption language that will be placed on the ballot to describe a proposal. Since the entire text of an amendment isn't printed on the ballot, the caption takes on increased importance—and, in some cases, controversy. Opponents of some major amendments have accused lawmakers of deliberately trying to sneak proposals past the electorate with misleading or inadequate ballot captions.

In 1989, the legislature proposed an amendment that would have more than tripled the $7,200 annual salary paid to lawmakers. It also would have removed the electorate's control over future raises by tying legislative pay to a percentage of the governor's salary, which is set by the legislature. But the wording on the ballot simply said: "The constitutional amendment to limit the salary of the lieutenant governor and the speaker of the House of Representatives to not more than one-half of the governor's salary and to limit the salary of a member of the legislature to not more than one-fourth of the governor's salary." Opponents of the proposal argued that the use of the word "limit" was an attempt to mislead voters into thinking the amendment could mean a pay reduction. In reality, the governor's salary, which had been freed from constitutional restraints in 1955, was then about $90,000 and usually was increased by the legislature each biennium. The voters, however, apparently weren't too confused. They rejected the amendment by a wide margin in an election that had been preceded by media reports of numerous free trips and thousands of dollars in political contributions that lawmakers accepted from lobbyists and special interest groups.

The constitution also provides for revision by constitutional convention, which the legislature can call with the approval of the electorate. Delegates to such a convention have to be elected and their terms subject to voter approval. In 1919, voters overwhelmingly rejected a proposal for a constitutional convention.[30] There were subsequent efforts, including an attempt by Governor John Connally in 1967, to initiate reforms using a constitutional convention, but they also were defeated.[31] Connally's efforts, however, did result in adoption of the "clean up" amendment in 1969 to remove many obsolete provisions from the constitution, and it laid the groundwork for a constitutional convention in 1974.

The 1974 convention, the only ever held under the present 1876 charter, ended in failure. Its delegates were the 181 members of the legislature.

## The Constitutional Reform Efforts of 1971 to 1975

The **Constitutional Convention of 1974** had its beginning in 1971, when state Representative Nelson Wolff of San Antonio and several other freshman legislators won the leadership's backing for a full-scale revision effort. In 1972, voters approved the necessary constitutional amendment, which specified that the convention would be comprised of House members and senators elected the same year.

Voters also approved a huge turnover in the statehouse, in the wake of the Sharpstown stock fraud scandal and court-ordered, single-member House districts in metropolitan counties (see Chapter 8). Ironically, the legislative leaders who initially had supported the revision effort in 1971 would not be around to see it through. House Speaker Gus Mutscher was convicted of bribery in the Sharpstown scandal and forced out of office, and Lieutenant Governor Ben Barnes lost a 1972 race for governor.

In 1973, the Legislature created a 37-member Constitutional Revision Commission to hold public hearings around the state and make recommendations to the convention. Members of the commission, chaired by former Texas Supreme Court Chief Justice Robert W. Calvert, were appointed by Governor Dolph Briscoe and other top state officials.

The constitutional convention, or "con-con," as it came to be called by legislators and members of the media, convened on January 8, 1974. House Speaker Price Daniel, Jr. was elected president, and Lieutenant Governor Bill Hobby, in an address to delegates, offered a prophetic warning: "The special interests of today will be replaced by new and different special interests tomorrow, and any attempt to draft a constitution to serve such interests would be futile and also dishonorable."[32]

Hobby's plea was largely ignored. Special interests dominated the convention, which finally adjourned in bitter failure on July 30, failing by three votes to get the two-thirds vote necessary to send a new constitution to Texas voters for ratification.

The crucial fight was over a business-backed attempt to lock the state's right-to-work law, which prohibits union membership as a condition of employment, into the constitution, an effort bitterly fought by organized labor. The gallery in the House of Representatives chamber, which served as the convention hall, was packed with labor representatives and other spectators when the final vote was taken, about a half hour before the convention's midnight adjournment deadline. Daniel held the electronic voting board open for 28 minutes, hoping three delegates could be persuaded to switch their votes, but time ran out. Tension and emotions were running so high that, at one point, state Representative Jim Mattox of Dallas, who later would become attorney general, challenged Daniel's delay in announcing the vote and publicly called the convention president a "liar."[33]

But while the right-to-work dispute took the brunt of the blame for the convention's failure, there also were other factors working against the revision effort.

One was Governor Briscoe's refusal to exercise any significant leadership on behalf of a new state charter. Except for opposing proposals that he thought would further weaken the authority of the governor, he provided little input to the convention and didn't attempt to twist delegates' arms to get enough votes to send the document to the electorate. Louisiana voters had approved a new state constitution in 1974, and Governor Edwin Edwards' strong support had been considered instrumental. Gubernatorial leadership in other states also appears to have been critical to successful constitutional conventions.

Another major obstacle was the convention's makeup. Texas, unlike most other states, chose to use the 181 members of the legislature to comprise its constitutional convention. Soon after the convention began its work, many of them were facing re-election campaigns in the party primaries.

Additionally, a minority of legislators didn't want a new constitution and attempted to delay or obstruct the convention's work at every opportunity. In frustration, President Daniel called them "cockroaches." Most legislators, even those who wanted a new constitution, reacted to their own political fears and ambitions. They were very susceptible to the influence of special interests, far more susceptible than most private-citizen delegates likely would have been. And special interests were legion at the convention. In addition to various business and professional groups and organized labor, many county officeholders whose jobs—protected by the constitution of 1876—were suddenly in jeopardy put pressure on the delegates.

Some county judges lobbied against a proposal to streamline the judiciary because they feared it would relieve them of judicial duties. Under the present constitution, county judges are primarily administrative officers and don't have to be lawyers, but they do have limited judicial responsibilities. So persistent was their lobbying that Daniel referred to some of them as a "wrecking crew." Representative DeWitt Hale of Corpus Christi, chairman of the Committee on the Judiciary, was "disgusted because a handful of judges could be so disruptive to the convention."[34]

Influential regents, lobbyists, and alumni of the University of Texas and Texas A&M University systems guarded the Permanent University Fund, their rich constitutional endowment. And highway lobbyists, backed by thousands of contractors and business people from throughout the state, fought any attempt to raid the highway trust fund, the constitutional provision that dedicates three-fourths of the revenue from the state gasoline tax to highway projects.

Delegates tried to walk a tight rope over the emotionally charged issue of gambling. They yielded to the wishes of charitable and fraternal organizations and tentatively approved a provision to allow bingo and raffles to be conducted for charity, receiving some public ridicule for giving constitutional status to a game of chance. But delegates voted to maintain the general constitutional prohibition against lotteries. In a strong letter to Robert W. Calvert, the chairman of the Constitutional Revision Commission, Baylor University President Abner McCall had warned of considerable public opposition to any new constitution that legalized gambling: "The commission may adopt proposals to make the machinery of Texas government more efficient, but many of us will not trade a little more efficiency for a greater danger of corruption of government by state sponsored gambling."[35]

But, in the end, the crucial fight was over right-to-work. Reflecting the sentiment of many other business groups, the Greater San Antonio Chamber of Commerce told convention delegates that such a guarantee against forced union membership should be in the constitution, even though it had been a state law since 1947 and was in no danger of being repealed. Right-to-work, the chamber wrote, "is considered by many to be so fundamental in nature as to require Constitutional protection."[36] The Texas AFL-CIO disagreed. Business was politically stronger than organized labor in Texas, but the two-thirds vote that was necessary to put a new constitution on the ballot was too high an obstacle.

During its next regular session in 1975, the legislature, with the strong support of House Speaker Bill Clayton and Lieutenant Governor Bill Hobby, resurrected the constitutional revision effort. Lawmakers voted to present to Texans the basic document that the convention had barely rejected the previous summer in the form of eight separate constitutional amendments. The first three articles dealing with the separation of powers and the legislative and executive branches were combined into one ballot proposition. Each of the remaining seven propositions was a separate article, each to be independently approved or rejected by the voters. The most controversial issues that the 1974 convention had debated, such as right-to-work, were excluded. The streamlined amendments would have considerably shortened the constitution and provided some major changes, including annual legislative sessions, a unified judicial system, more flexibility in county government and the possibility of budgetary powers for the governor. It was a much more flexible, modern constitution than the 1876 document and had cost several million tax dollars and countless hours to produce. But voters rejected all eight propositions on Nov. 4, 1975, some by margins of more than 2-1.

The legislature's Sharpstown scandal of 1971 and the Watergate scandal that had forced the resignation of a president in 1974 had raised Texans' distrust of government, and the proposed new constitution had been drafted by state officials, not by private citizens.

Nelson Wolff, who years later would be elected mayor of San Antonio, also had noted an earlier, general lack of citizen interest in the work of the constitutional convention. In his book, *Challenge of Change,* he wrote: "The constitutional revision effort in Texas had attempted to use every means known to get citizen participation in the process. A toll-free telephone had been set up for the convention. Committees of the convention met at night and on weekends to provide working people an opportunity to testify. We provided to the best of our ability optimum conditions for testimony. Yet many people avoided participation in the revision process."[37] Most people are not attentive to the details and nuances of constitutional revisions, and it is a difficult task translating these complexities into arguments that make sense to the average voter.[38] There is some evidence to suggest that the advocates of constitutional reform were ineffective in their public relations campaign. The voter distrust and apathy played right into the hands of numerous special interests who didn't want to give up the protections that the old constitution afforded them.

Efforts to enact these proposals were further thwarted by Governor Dolph Briscoe. While he had never taken an active role in the revision effort, three weeks before the 1975 election, he openly opposed the eight propositions and suggested that the existing constitution had served the state well and would continue to be adequate for the future.[39]

## Further Piecemeal Reforms

So it was back to piecemeal constitutional changes. One hundred eighteen amendments were approved by Texas voters between 1975 and 1991, and twenty-five were rejected.

One of the more significant constitutional changes adopted since the 1974 convention was an amendment to give the governor and legislative leaders authority to deal with budgetary emergencies between legislative sessions. The provision was approved in November 1985 after similar proposals were rejected by voters in 1980 and 1981. Under the amendment and a related statute, money can be transferred between programs and agencies without the necessity of the governor calling the legislature into an emergency special session. The governor proposes transfers to the 10 legislative leaders on the Legislative Budget Board (LBB), including the lieutenant governor and the speaker, and the LBB can reject or modify the governor's proposal. The process has been used numerous times. Without it, Governor Bill Clements would have had to call a weary legislature into a fifth special session in 1990 to keep critical programs operating at the deficit-plagued Department of Human Services. Lawmakers already had been through four special sessions that year to try to comply with a state court order for school finance reform.

Constitutional amendments also have been approved to abolish obsolete offices, such as treasurer and surveyor, in some counties. But voters in the smallest county can't abolish their office of county surveyor without voters in every other county also being asked to vote on the issue. What's more, the ballots cast in the large metropolitan counties will decide the fate of most constitutional amendments, even one affecting only a single, small rural county.

## Constitutional Provisions, Interest Groups, and Elites

Only a small percentage of registered voters, often less than 20 percent, normally participate in elections when constitutional amendments are the only issues on the ballot (Table 2-2). When constitutional amendments are submitted to the voters during gubernatorial or presidential elections, the turnout is much higher; but in many instances, the proponents of constitutional amendments make calculated decisions to submit amendments to Texas voters in special elections when the turnout will be much lower. This results in a relative handful of Texans ultimately

TABLE 2–2   Turnout for Constitutional Amendments 1951–1972, 1976–1991

| Type of Election | Percent of Registered Voters Voting | |
| --- | --- | --- |
| | 1951–1972 | 1976–1991 |
| Special Elections* | 16% | 16% |
| General Elections in Off-Years | 39 | 47 |
| General Elections (Presidential) | 51 | 67 |

*Only Constitutional Amendments on the ballot

Sources: Janice May, *Amending the Texas Constitution, 1951–1972;* Secretary of State, Elections Division.

deciding on fundamental changes in government. And that enhances the influence of special interests over the process.

A constitution functions within the context of a complex political system, and interest groups, which historically have been strong in Texas, work diligently to protect their concerns and objectives. Interest groups develop strategies to get provisions into the constitution that benefit them or to keep provisions out of the constitution that they fear would hurt them. Since most amendments represent non-partisan issues, a well-financed public relations campaign is likely to produce public support for an amendment.[40]

Interest groups are able to kill many proposed constitutional changes in the legislature, where the two-thirds vote requirement works to their advantage. Only a small fraction of constitutional amendments proposed by legislators get put on the ballot. Those that do almost invariably have the support of one or more special interest groups, who often finance publicity campaigns to promote the propositions to the voters. Few amendments attract organized opposition, but sometimes organization isn't necessary to derail an amendment, as was the case with the legislative pay raise proposal in 1989.

The amendment, which also would have removed voters' control over legislative pay, was endorsed by the League of Women Voters, the Texas Chamber of Commerce, and a host of consumer and public interest groups, including Common Cause, the Texas Consumer Association, the Texas Women's Political Caucus, the Gray Panthers, and the Christian Life Commission of the Southern Baptist Convention. The groups backed the proposal as a good government measure that would encourage more qualified people to seek legislative office and reduce the dependence of lawmakers on political contributions. (At the same time, most public and special interest groups are reluctant to oppose any legislative pay raise for fear of antagonizing lawmakers and reducing their influence with the legislature. It would be akin to biting the hand that feeds them.) But despite such support and the fact there was only minimal organized opposition, the pay raise was overwhelmingly defeated as was a related proposition that would have boosted expense allowances for legislators. This was only the latest of periodic pay raise proposals to be rejected by Texas voters. The last raise they approved was in 1975, when legislative compensation was increased from $4,800 a year to $7,200.

Many of the recent constitutional changes have reflected a pro-industry and economic development push that contrasts sharply with the anti-business sentiment of the original constitutional framers. Recent amendments also have helped build up a public bonded indebtedness that the 19th century writers would have been unable to comprehend. Texas was rural then. It is now the country's third most populous state, is largely urban, and is working to diversify and rebuild its economy in the wake of the disastrous oil and real estate busts of the 1980s. Business turned to state government for tax breaks and other economic incentives and found receptive ears in the legislature and the governor's office. Nine of the record 25 amendments on the November 1987 ballot were actively promoted as an economic development package by the Build Texas Committee, a bipartisan group of business and civic leaders.

Three of the amendments proposed an expansion of the infrastructure of governmental services so crucial to attracting industries and enhancing the quality of life of their employees. Those propositions called for hundreds of millions of dollars in tax-backed general obligation bonds for new state prisons, mental health and mental retardation facilities, water reservoirs, flood control projects, and loans to local governments to finance jails, parks, convention centers, and other public works projects. Other amendments in the "Build Texas" package called for direct benefits to industries through special tax breaks and state loans and grants for economic diversification. Still another amendment proposed $500 million in tax-backed bonds to convince the federal government that Texas was ready to help build the Superconducting Supercollider, a highly sought particle accelerator and coveted research facility that eventually was awarded to Texas. It was viewed as a major economic boost with strong spinoff potential for realtors and other business people.

Governor Bill Clements, a Republican, and Lieutenant Governor Bill Hobby, a Democrat, were among state officials endorsing the "Build Texas" package. Hobby claimed the bonds would help Texas meet federal court orders for new prisons and mental health facilities and directly or indirectly create more than 50,000 jobs.

But then-Comptroller Bob Bullock and Attorney General Jim Mattox, both Democrats, raised warning flags. Bullock said the voters' decision on the bonds "could mark a departure in the method of paying for state government." During the previous three years, Texas had added $940 million more in general obligation bonds than it had retired. Up to that point, the general obligation bonds had been self-supporting for such purposes as financing water reservoirs, student loans and land purchases by veterans. These programs had used the credit of the state to borrow money at low interest rates and then lend the money to individuals or local governments, which repaid the debts. The state had to pay them off only in the event of a default.

The new water bonds—the latest in a series periodically approved by voters—as well as those bonds proposed for local public works projects also would be self-supporting. But $1 billion in bonds proposed for prisons, mental health facilities, and the supercollider would have to be serviced with general revenue and eventually would cost taxpayers millions of dollars more, Bullock warned. These proposed bonds bent state government's pay-as-you-go principle.

Voters approved the bonds for water projects, prisons, mental health and mental retardation facilities, and the supercollider. But they rejected the public works bonds for local governments. Voters approved an *ad valorem* tax exemption for mobile offshore oil and gas drilling equipment stored in coastal counties. Supporters said the tax break would encourage companies to store their unused rigs in Texas, rather than some other coastal state, and provide some maintenance jobs. They also approved an amendment to authorize loans and grants of state money for economic development and diversification. But they rejected a proposition to issue $125 million in bonds to provide venture capital for small businesses and agricultural production. They also rejected an amendment for a so-called "freeport" tax exemption for goods used in manufacturing that were stored in Texas for only a limited period.

The venture capital and freeport proposals were so important to the business community that it convinced the legislature to put similar amendments on the 1989 ballot, and voters approved them the second time around. The bonds for venture capital were scaled back to $75 million. And the freeport amendment had a much more appealing ballot caption than it had in 1987. The 1987 caption had simply identified the proposal as a constitutional amendment "relating to the exemption from ad valorem taxation of certain tangible personal property temporarily located within the state." The successful 1989 caption began, "The constitutional amendment promoting economic growth, job creation and fair tax treatment for Texans who export goods...." The amendment didn't require local governments to grant the exemption, and many didn't initially because of the millions of dollars of revenue it would have cost them.

In 1991, voters put the state even further in debt by approving a $1.1 billion bond issue for more prisons and mental health and mental retardation facilities.

From an elitist perspective (see Chapter 4), it has been argued that the Texas Constitution serves the interests of a small number of individuals who control dominant institutions in the state. This argument suggests that the severe constraints built into the constitution limit the policy options of state government and have historically thwarted the efforts of larger public interest groups to restructure or improve the tax system, education policy, social services, health care, and other policies that would benefit low- and middle-income Texans. Power is so fragmented that these groups have had to turn to the courts to force change. This same argument, incidentally, has often been made about the United States Constitution.

If this interpretation is accurate, it is ironic that the Texas constitutional framers of 1876 directed much of their wrath against railroads, banks, and other institutions that we would designate as elitist. The tumultuous last quarter of the 19th century witnessed high levels of class and economic conflict with the emergence of the Greenbacks and the Populists who articulated the interests of the lower income groups. But monied business interests eventually were able to use the state constitution and subsequent legislation to reestablish their dominance over Texas government. While the elite structure of the state has changed since 1876, some scholars would argue that there has been a gradual transfer of power and control to new elites, who continue to exercise enormous influence over public policy.

### Change through Court Interpretation

There is some evidence that Texas courts are now prepared to play a more expansive role in the interpretation of the constitution and, in turn, effect major changes in state policy. The best-known example is the *Edgewood* v. *Kirby* school finance case, in which the courts invalidated the system of funding public education and ordered the legislature to provide more equity in tax resources among the state's 1,000-plus school districts, even at the expense of local tax increases in some districts. Wide disparities in spending on students between rich and poor districts—the result of wide disparities in local property values—violated the state constitution's requirement for an "efficient" system of public schools, the Texas Supreme Court ruled.

## CONSTITUTIONAL RESTRAINTS AND THE ABILITY TO GOVERN

The non-partisan League of Women Voters of Texas has been a long-suffering advocate of a total rewrite of the state constitution. Nevertheless, before each constitutional amendments election, it normally announces which propositions it endorses for the sake of good government and which it opposes. But league leaders lost their patience in 1987 with the placement of the record 25 amendments and two binding referenda on the same ballot. They announced they would neither support nor oppose any amendment that year. Instead, they urged voters to examine the propositions carefully and to complain to their legislators about the length of the ballot. "Enough is enough. Let us work together to halt this ridiculous system of running the government by means of the constitution," the league said. But without a new constitution, the only way state government can prepare for the challenges of the 21st century under a highly restrictive constitution written in the 19th is to continue this pattern of "amendomania."[41]

### Prospects for Future Change

Experts are able to quickly point out the many weaknesses and flaws of the Texas Constitution. But attempts at wholesale revision have not been successful. Numerous piecemeal changes have been made, but they have not addressed the fundamental criticisms of the charter. What is to be made of all this?

First, Texas has a long history of suspicion of government, and this tradition continues. Most people fear governmental abuses and excesses more than they feel concern about government's inability to quickly and efficiently respond to the needs of its citizens. In the vernacular of the layperson, "If it ain't broke, don't fix it." And it is not clear that the layperson regards the constitution to be "broke."

Secondly, there are many groups and interests that benefit from the existing constitution and have demonstrated a collective resolve to minimize change.

Finally, most Texans give little thought to changing the constitution because they are ill-prepared to deal with the complexities of the document. And there are enormous problems educating and motivating the public to the need for constitutional revision.

### SUMMARY AND CONCLUSIONS

**1.** In addition to defining the formal institutional structure of governments, constitutions reflect the primary values and political objectives of a state. The constitution defines the relationships between those who govern and the general population, and ultimately the constitution structures political power within the state. Governments do not have unlimited power and authority, and a constitution provides basic protection for the citizen from excesses and abuses of those who hold power.

**2.** Texas, like most other states, has functioned under a series of constitutions, and each is appropriately understood from the perspective of the events of the period in which it was adopted. Moreover, each of Texas' seven constitutions has contributed to the constitutional legacy of the state.

**3.** Texas currently operates under a constitution that was adopted at the end of the Civil War and the Radical Reconstruction era, and the events of that period left an enduring legacy of suspicion of government, limited government, and fragmented governmental institutions.

**4.** The 1876 Constitution was predicated on the theory that governmental excesses could be minimized by carefully defining what governments could or could not do.

**5.** While the constitutional framers were primarily concerned with governmental power, they failed to understand that the institutions they created would ultimately allow major economic interests within the state to control and dominate the policymaking institutions, often to the detriment of the lower socio-economic groups within the state.

**6.** What the delegates to the Constitutional Convention of 1875 regarded to be the strengths of the constitution—fragmented authority, detailed limitation on the power and authority of governmental institutions, and decentralization—have served to limit the ability of state and local governments to effectively adapt to economic and demographic changes. The perceived solutions to many of the problems of 1875 have compounded problems of state and local governments in the 1990s.

**7.** A series of efforts to overhaul and reform the state's constitution have failed. Consequently, the state has been forced to pursue a strategy of amending the constitution on a piecemeal basis. This has produced some success in modernizing the charter, but many structural problems of state government require major institutional changes that cannot be resolved through this amendment process.

**8.** A large segment of the Texas population that reflects the values of the state's conservative political culture continues to be suspicious of far-reaching constitutional changes. Moreover, constitutions and the debates that surround them are complex, and most people give little attention to these issues. Consequently, it is much easier to mobilize public opinion against rather than for wholesale change.

**9.** Over the years, a variety of businesses and groups have attempted to protect their interests through constitutional amendments. But the same groups usually oppose any proposed changes that threaten their influence, power, or benefits. Consequently, the interests of small segments of the state's population usually prevail over the interests of the majority.

## KEY TERMS

Constitution of Coahuila y Tejas
Constitution of the Republic
Constitution of 1845
Civil War Constitution
Constitution of 1866
Radical Reconstructionists
Reconstruction Constitution
Governor E. J. Davis

The Grange
Constitution of 1876
Popular sovereignty
Compact theory
Limited government
Separation of powers
Constitutional Convention of 1974

## FURTHER READING

Braden, George D., et al., *The Constitution of the State of Texas: An Annotated and Comparative Analysis*. 2 vols. Austin: Texas Advisory Commission on Intergovernmental Relations, 1977.

Braden, George D., *Citizens Guide to the Texas Constitution*. Austin: Texas Advisory Commission on Intergovernmental Relations and The Institute for Urban Studies, University of Houston, 1972.

Bruff, Harold H., "Separation of Powers Under the Texas Constitution," *Texas Law Review*, 68 (June 1990), 1337-1367.

Cnudde, Charles F., and Robert. E. Crew, Jr., *Constitutional Democracy in Texas*. St. Paul: West Publishing Company, 1989.

Harrington, James C., "Free Speech, Press, and Assembly Liberties Under the Texas Bill of Rights," *Texas Law Review*, 68 (June 1990), 1435-1467.

Lutz, Donald S., "The Texas Constitution," in *Perspectives on American and Texas Politics: A Collection of Essays*, eds. Donald S. Lutz and Kent L. Tedin. Dubuque, Iowa: Kendall/Hunt, 1987.

Mauer, John Walker, "State Constitutions in a Time of Crisis: The Case of the Texas Constitution of 1876," *Texas Law Review*, 68 (June 1990), 1615-1647.

May, Janice C., *The Texas Constitution Revision Experience in the 70s*. Austin: Sterling Swift, 1975.

McKay, Seth Shepard, *Debates in the Texas Constitutional Convention of 1875*. Austin: University of Texas Press, 1930.

McKay, Seth Shepard, *Seven Decades of the Texas Constitution of 1876*. Lubbock: Texas Tech College, 1943.

Watts, Mikal, and Brad Rockwell, "The Original Intent of the Educational Article of the Texas Constitution." *St. Mary's Law Journal*, 21 (1990), pp. 771-821.

Wolff, Nelson, *Challenge of Change*. San Antonio: The Naylor Co., 1975.

## ENDNOTES

1. Janice May, "Constitutional Revision in Texas," in Richard H. Kraemer and Philip W. Barnes, eds., *Texas: Readings in Politics, Government and Public Policy* (San Francisco: Chandler Publishing Company, 1971), p.317. Used by permission of HarperCollins Publishers.

2. Daniel Elazar, "The Principles and Traditions Underlying American State Constitutions," *Publius*, 12 (Winter 1982), p. 23.

3. Donald S. Lutz, "The Purposes of American State Constitutions," *Publius* 12 (Winter 1982), pp. 31-36.

4. David Saffell, *State Politics* (Reading, Mass.: Addison-Wesley Publishing Company, 1984), pp. 23-24.

5. Elazar, "Principles and Traditions Underlying American State Constitutions," pp. 20-21.

6. T.R. Fehrenbach, *Lone Star: A History of Texas and the Texans* (New York: The Macmillan Company, 1968), p. 152-173.

7. Richard Gambitta, Robert A. Milne, and Carol R. Davis, "The Politics of Unequal Educational Opportunity," in *The Politics of San Antonio*, ed. David R. Johnson, John A. Booth, and Richard J. Harris (Lincoln: University of Nebraska Press, 1983), p. 135.

8. Joe B. Frantz, *Texas: A Bicentennial History* (New York: W.W. Norton & Company, Inc., 1976), p. 73.

9. Ibid., p. 76.

10. Fehrenbach, *Lone Star*, p. 265.

11. Frantz, *Texas*, p. 92.

12. *Dallas Morning News*, April 7, 1983.

13. Fehrenbach, *Texas*, p. 396.

14. Ibid., pp. 398-399.

15. Ibid., p. 401.

16. Ibid., p. 429.

17. J.E. Ericson, "The Delegates to the Convention of 1875: A Reappraisal," *Southwestern Historical Quarterly*, 67 (July 1963), p. 22.

18. Ibid., p. 23.

19. Ibid., p. 23.

20. Ibid., pp. 25-26.

21. Fehrenbach, *Texas*, pp. 374, 431, 434.

22. Ericson, "The Delegates to the Convention of 1875: A Reappraisal," pp. 24-25.

23. Fehrenbach, *Texas*, p. 435.

24. *Texas Constitution*, Article 1, Sections 2 and 3.

25. Janice May, "Constitutional Revision in Texas," p. 82.

26. Ibid., p. 82.

27. David Berman, *State and Local Politics*, 6th ed. (Dubuque: Wm. C. Brown Publishers, 1991), p. 61.

28. May, "Constitutional Revision in Texas," p. 313.

29. Janice May, *Amending the Texas Constitution, 1951-1972* (Austin, Texas Advisory Commission on Intergovernmental Relations, 1972), p. 20.

30. John E. Bebout, "The Problem of the Texas Constitution," in *The Texas Constitution: Problems and Prospects for Revision*, p. 9.

31. Ibid., p. 11.

32. *Houston Chronicle*, Jan. 8, 1974.

33. *Houston Chronicle*, July 31, 1974.

34. Nelson Wolff, *Challenge of Change* (San Antonio: The Naylor Co., 1975), p. 170.

35. *Houston Chronicle*, Sept. 20, 1973.
36. Greater San Antonio Chamber of Commerce, "Position Statements to Constitutional Convention Delegates," January 1974, pp. 1-2.
37. Wolff, *Challenge of Change*, pp. 45-46.
38. Bebout, "The Problem of the Texas Constitution," pp. 45-46.
39. *Houston Chronicle*, Oct. 15, 1975.
40. Lewis A. Froman, Jr., "Some Effects of Interest Group Strength in State Politics," *American Political Science Review*, 60 (December 1966), pp. 952-963.
41. "California's Constitutional Amendomania," *Stanford Law Review*, 1 (1949), pp. 279-288.

# 3

# INTERGOVERNMENTAL RELATIONSHIPS

The question of the relation of the States to the Federal Government is the cardinal question of our constitutional system.

*Woodrow Wilson*[1]

If you live in a large metropolitan area of Texas, it is likely that you are subject to the jurisdiction of as many as 10 or more different governments or taxing authorities. A person living within the corporate limits of San Antonio, for example, is subject to the laws, regulations, and/or taxes of the federal government, the state of Texas, Bexar County, the city of San Antonio, the Alamo Community College District, one of 16 independent school districts, the Edwards Underground Water District, the San Antonio River Authority, the Bexar County Hospital District, and a public transportation authority.

There are more than 83,000 governmental units in the United States with approximately 500,000 persons serving on their governing bodies. According to a 1987 census of governments (Table 3-1), Texas had more than 4,400 individual governments, including 254 counties, 1,156 municipalities, and approximately 3,000 school districts and other single-purpose districts.

The jurisdictional structure of governments in this country is extremely complex and confusing, and people are often frustrated when they try to identify the government which has the authority or responsibility to address a specific need or concern. Governments share many responsibilities, and it is quite possible for an individual to get caught between agencies of different governments.

These diverse arrangements are primarily the result of our interest in limiting the powers of government and our disdain for strong centralized authority.

**TABLE 3–1**   Governments in the United States and Texas 1987

|                      | U.S.   | Texas  |
| -------------------- | ------ | ------ |
| U.S. Government      | 1      | 1      |
| State Government     | 50     | 1      |
| Counties             | 3,042  | 254    |
| Municipalities       | 19,200 | 1,156  |
| Townships and Towns  | 16,691 | –      |
| School Districts     | 14,721 | 1,113  |
| Special Districts    | 29,532 | *1,892 |
| Total                | 83,237 | 4,417  |

*850 of these special districts have property-based taxing authority

Sources: U.S. Department of Commerce, Bureau of the Census, *1987 Census of Governments*,
   Vol.. 1., No. 1.

The enormous size of the country and the great distances between cities also contributed to the proliferation of smaller governmental units, as did regional differences in economics and political cultures.

## STRUCTURING REGIONAL AND NATIONAL INTERESTS

Governments around the world are struggling to find ways of accommodating local and regional interests with national interests. As countries of the former Soviet Bloc attempted to integrate diverse racial, cultural, and ethnic groups within a single political system, they confronted many of the same issues that the United States faced during its formative period. There are three fundamental systems—unitary, confederal, and federal—for designing the relationship of the central government to its constituent parts.

There are countries, democratic as well as authoritarian, where ultimate authority or power is vested in a national or central government. Under such a **unitary system**, local or regional governments are created by the national government and have only the power and authority granted to them by the national government.

A **confederation** is based on the principle that each component government is sovereign in its own right, and the powers of the national government are limited to those powers delegated to it by the member governments. The United States experimented with a confederal system prior to the adoption of the present Constitution in 1789, and the southern states used the confederal principle during the Civil War. There are inherent weaknesses in such a system, including the ability of member governments to nullify the acts of the national government and withdraw from the relationship.

Delegates to the U.S. constitutional convention of 1787 rejected the confederal principle in favor of **federalism**, which balances the power and sovereignty of the state governments with that of the national government. Both the states and the national government derive their authority directly from the people, and the states have considerable latitude and autonomy within their areas of defined power and responsibility. In many respects, federalism is a middle ground between a confederal system and a unitary system of government.

The unitary principle, however, determines the relationship between state and local governments under the Texas Constitution and state laws. Counties, cities, and special districts have only those powers granted them by the state. There is no such thing as the sovereignty of local governments in Texas. Local governments are primarily administrative subdivisions of the state. The prevailing constitutional theory regarding local governments in the United States, which has been incorporated into Texas law, was articulated in the Dillon Rule, which held that if a state could create local governments, it could also destroy or eliminate them.[2] Political considerations, however, usually preclude the elimination of local governments, which we will discuss in more detail in Chapter 12.

## DEFINING FEDERALISM

While the U.S. Constitution outlines federalism in broad terms, it does not clearly specify the governmental relationships that should be established. For more than 200 years, scholars, politicians, judges, and bureaucrats not only have been debating the complexities of the federal system, they also have been trying to figure out how to define federalism.[3] One scholar has identified 267 concepts relating to the term.[4] And the problem is compounded by the fact that the relationships among federal, state, and local governments have changed over the past two centuries.

### Federal-State Relationships

We tend to think of federalism as a division of power between the states and the national government, and we look to the Constitution to specify the powers and responsibilities of each. But the Constitution is vague on these points, and "all efforts to define the distribution of authority among governments have been unsuccessful."[5] The structure and operation of our federal system of government confuses many individuals. It is a system of many shared functions and responsibilities that often make it difficult to identify a single person or institution as having the ultimate responsibility for addressing a specific issue or problem.

Ambiguous constitutional provisions have helped produce jurisdictional conflicts throughout the nation's history. We even fought a war among ourselves to determine what the powers and authority of the states and national government were. And while the Civil War resolved the issue that a state could not withdraw from the federal union, a large number of other questions continue to be debated. These ambiguities and changes in political and economic conditions make the relationships among governments subject to further change in the future.

The enumerated or **delegated powers** of the national government are outlined primarily in Article I, Section 8 of the Constitution. They include the powers to tax, to borrow and coin money, to declare war, and to regulate interstate and foreign commerce.

The first 17 paragraphs of Section 8 are rather specific, apparently because the constitutional framers, who were apprehensive of potential abuses, intended to limit the powers of the national government. But they did not close the door to unforeseen events. They further provided in paragraph 18 of Section 8 that Congress shall have the power "to make all Laws which shall be necessary and proper for carrying into Execution the foregoing Powers..."[6] This clause, often referred to as the "elastic clause," provides the basis for the **implied powers**, which have been used to justify the subsequent expansion of the federal government's powers.

To further compound the jurisdictional question, Article VI states that the U.S. Constitution and the laws made in pursuance "shall be the supreme Law of the Land."[7] This **supremacy clause** suggests that when a conflict develops between the powers of the states and the national government, the federal law prevails.

But the Constitution also provides that the states shall have certain powers. The Tenth Amendment, adopted in 1789 by Congress and ratified by the states in 1791, was intended to address the concerns of state governments. This **reserved powers** clause states, "The powers not delegated to the United States by the Constitution, nor prohibited by it to the States, are reserved to the States respectively or to the people."[8] Although the Constitution does not spell out the authority of the states and their subdivisions in detail, the states have assumed a formidable array of powers and responsibilities. Most official actions affecting our daily lives are taken by state or local governments. The police, regulatory, and taxing powers of the state affect us daily. And more than 90 percent of all litigation takes place in state or local courts, not in federal courts.

There also are certain constitutional guarantees to the states. Texas is assured a republican form of government, protection against invasion and domestic violence, and the power to maintain a militia. If a person is accused of a federal crime in Texas, the trial is to be held in Texas. Texas cannot be divided into another state without its permission and is assured two members of the U.S. Senate and membership in the U.S. House of Representatives based on its population in relation to the other states. After the 1990 census, Texas had 30 House members. The state also has a role in ratifying amendments to the U.S. Constitution and controls many aspects of federal elections.[9]

Nevertheless, the U.S. Constitution's language lends itself to controversy and interpretation, and, over the years, Congress and the courts have attempted to resolve conflicts over powers and jurisdiction. In many instances, the Supreme Court has played an instrumental role in redefining the relationships between the states and the federal government.

Reflecting its drafters' concern about governmental excesses, the Constitution also limits the powers of both the states and the national government. These prohibitions, or **denied powers**, are interspersed throughout the document and are enumerated, in particular, in the Bill of Rights. The original intent of the Bill of Rights was to limit the powers of the national government. But since the Civil War, the federal courts have gradually incorporated the Bill of Rights into the 14th Amendment, which was intended to restrict the powers of the state governments. This expansion of the Bill of Rights to the states has been described as the nationalization of the Bill of Rights.

## Relationships Among the States

The federal system is not limited to the relationships of the states to the national government (vertical federalism). It also includes the relationships of the states to each other (horizontal federalism). Many of these constitutional-legal obligations were included in the Articles of Confederation, which established the first system of national government. Conflict as well as cooperation among the states during that period provided the rationale for defining the obligations and responsibilities of the states to each other.

The Constitution states, "Full Faith and Credit shall be given in each State to the public Acts, Records, and judicial Proceedings of every other state."[10] To eliminate chaos and to stimulate cooperation, this **full faith and credit** clause assures that official governmental actions of one state are accepted by other states. A marriage in Texas is recognized as legal in other states. So are business contracts. This also means that a person cannot flee to another state to avoid an adverse court judgment.

As a person travels from one state to another, the Constitution entitles that person to the **privileges and immunities** of the states where he or she is going. A person can acquire property in another state, establish residency and eventually citizenship, and be assured of access to the legal system of that state. But there are certain exceptions that have been established by court interpretation. States, for example, can charge non-residents higher college tuition or higher fees for hunting and fishing licenses.

The Constitution also provides for the return of a person accused of a crime. If a person who has been charged with manslaughter in Texas attempts to avoid trial by fleeing to Oklahoma, he or she can be returned to Texas by a process called interstate **extradition**. States routinely handle hundreds of these cases each year. Once the accused has been located, the state seeking the individual will request that the second state arrest and return him. The governor is responsible for granting extradition requests.

Until fairly recently, governors used an 1861 court decision to maintain that they had the discretion to refuse another state's extradition request.[11] This was the prevailing view for 125 years until Puerto Rico challenged the discretionary powers of the governor in an 1987 case.[12] The Supreme Court held that the "duty to extradite is mandatory, and the federal courts are available to enforce that duty."[13]

The Constitution writers also anticipated the need for structuring more formal, long-term, cooperative relationships among the states. Article I, Section 10 allows the states, with the approval of Congress, to enter into interstate compacts. There were approximately 50 of these compacts in the 1960s, but they had decreased to fewer than 10 by the 1980s.[14] Texas now belongs to several **interstate compacts**, including the Interstate Oil and Gas Compact, the Interstate Mining Compact, and is negotiating with several other states to form the Low Level Radioactive Waste Compact.

In addition to these interstate compacts, joint action and collaboration among the states has included the enactment of uniform state laws, reciprocal or contingent legislation, and interstate administrative cooperation. These agreements and joint efforts permit the states to work together in dealing with common issues or problems, such as water pollution, drug abuse, radioactive waste, economic development, and higher education; and there are many indications to suggest the expanded use of these resources. To achieve what Morton Grodzins, an authority on American federalism termed "federalism without Washington," the states have organized a number of cooperative organizations such as the Council of State Governments and a variety of organizations of state elected officials.[15]

While cooperation is desired, states often find themselves involved in disagreements that only lawsuits can resolve. Boundary disputes, control or use of water resources, and licensing fees that affect interstate shipping are among issues that are litigated in the federal judiciary, where the Supreme Court has original jurisdiction in all "controversies between two or more states."[16]

## Alternative Views of Federalism

The constitutional-legal descriptions of federalism can leave one with the idea that the federal, state, and local levels of government are autonomous and function independently. Grodzins has argued that this perspective, which is inaccurate, was analogous to a layer cake theory of intergovernmental relations.

Grodzins suggested that intergovernmental relations can be more accurately symbolized by a marble cake. Rather than possessing distinct and separate powers and responsibilities, governments have shared responsibilities. In describing federalism, Grodzins wrote:

> Whenever you slice through it (the marble cake) you reveal an inseparable mixture of differently colored ingredients. There is no neat horizontal stratification. Vertical and diagonal lines almost obliterate the horizontal ones, and in some places there are unexpected whirls and imperceptible merging of colors, so that it is difficult to tell where one ends and the other begins. So it is with federal, state and local responsibilities in the chaotic marble cake of American Government.[17]

Public functions are not neatly divided among the different levels of government. In virtually every area of public policy, governments coordinate, collaborate, and cooperate to meet shared goals and objectives. This view reflects, in large measure, governmental relationships associated with cooperative federalism, which we will discuss later in this chapter.

A third metaphor, the picket fence theory of federalism, builds, in part, on Grodzins' notions of shared powers and responsibilities but focuses on specific policy areas that cut across each level of government (Figure 3-1). This metaphor

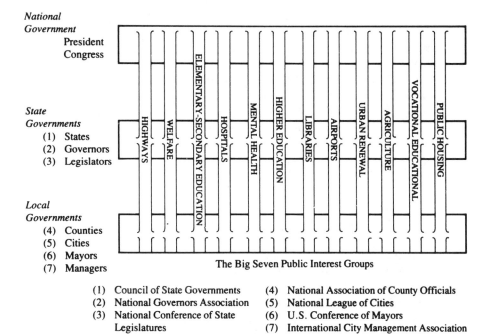

National
Government
    President
    Congress

State
Governments
    (1)  States
    (2)  Governors
    (3)  Legislators

Local
Governments
    (4)  Counties
    (5)  Cities
    (6)  Mayors
    (7)  Managers

The Big Seven Public Interest Groups

| (1) | Council of State Governments | (4) | National Association of County Officials |
| (2) | National Governors Association | (5) | National League of Cities |
| (3) | National Conference of State Legislatures | (6) | U.S. Conference of Mayors |
| | | (7) | International City Management Association |

**FIGURE 3-1**   Picket Fence Federalism: A Schematic Representation.   (Deil S. Wright, *Understanding Intergovernmental Relations*, 2nd ed. Monterey, California:  Brooks/Cole Publishing Company, 1982.)

suggests that we look at a specific function (highways, education, welfare), identify the primary participants at each level of government, and map out their patterns of interaction. While the diagram is an oversimplification, it does permit us to assess the policymaking processes in addition to institutional relationships.[18]

As might be expected, the complexity of federalism has generated much discussion about how to best describe and assess the relationships among governments. The problem, of course, is compounded by the fact that governmental relationships change over time with changes in the political parties, presidents, prevailing economic and social conditions and general expectations and demands of governments.

## CHANGING PATTERNS IN FEDERAL RELATIONSHIPS

### Dual Federalism

In both theory and practice, federal relationships from 1790 to the 1930s usually are defined in terms of dual federalism. Both the national and state governments were continually engaged in legal and policy issues that attempted to define the lines of demarcation between their respective powers. There was a continued saga of "sorting out roles and specifying clear boundaries."[19] Conflicts usually were resolved through court cases and statutory laws, but the federal-state issues centering on the economics of slavery erupted into the Civil War. The dual federalism of this era was marked by adversarial, if not antagonistic, relationships at various levels of government.

One of the first instances when the U.S. Supreme Court addressed the issue of state-federal relationships was in the case of *McCulloch* v. *Maryland.* The state of Maryland had levied a tax on the Baltimore branch of the Bank of the United States. McCulloch, the bank's cashier, refused to pay the tax, thus precipitating a lawsuit. The case raised a fundamental issue regarding federalism. Did the national government have the power to create a bank, which, in fact, would compete with state banks? The Supreme Court, then headed by Chief Justice John Marshall, an advocate of central power, ruled that the implied powers clause of the Constitution, linked to the delegated or enumerated powers, gave the federal government this authority.

A second issue was whether a state could tax the branch bank, an institution of the national government. The court again ruled in favor of the U.S. Government. It held that the states do not have the power to tax the national government because, if this were to be permitted, the states could destroy national institutions and federal laws would be subordinate to those of the states, thus undermining the supremacy clause of the Constitution. Hundreds of federal-state issues have been litigated in the federal courts since that case. Along with political and economic changes, these cases have been central to redefining federal-state relationships over the past 200 years, although the principles outlined in McCulloch remain intact.

## Cooperative Federalism

The economic hardships produced by the Great Depression of the 1930s resulted in demands for a greater role of the federal government in domestic policy. States and cities simply were unable to provide many basic services or address the personal needs of large segments of the population who were unemployed. The states did not have the economic resources to deal with problems that extended beyond their borders, and many lacked the political or institutional will to implement new policies. Moreover, the increased economic interdependency of the states and the national scope of economic problems were compelling arguments for federal intervention. While there were precedents for greater federal-state cooperation prior to the 1930s, the New Deal expanded dramatically the role of the federal government in relationship to the states and local governments.[20] V.O. Key, who wrote extensively on state government, summarizes the extent of these changes:

> The federal government underwent a radical transformation after...1932. It had been a remote authority with a limited range of activity. It operated the postal system, improved rivers and harbors, maintained armed forces on a scale fearsome only to banana republics, and performed other functions of which the average citizen was hardly aware. Within a brief time, it became an institution that affected intimately the lives and fortunes of most, if not all, citizens.[21]

Those supporting the development of **cooperative federalism** rejected the notions of dual federalism where each level of government had virtual or exclusive authority in select areas of domestic policy. The commerce and the supremacy clauses of the Constitution were used to support an expanded role of the federal government. Many of the new programs engaged local, state, and federal policymakers in cooperative efforts from program development to program implementation. Cooperative federalism assures that all three levels of government share the responsibility for domestic programs "by making the larger governments primarily responsible for raising revenues and setting standards, and the smaller ones primarily responsible for administering the programs."[22]

Over the past 50 years, the federal government has used various devices to shape and implement domestic programs, but the primary vehicle has been the **categorical grant-in-aid**. There are more than 400 of these grant programs, through which approximately 80 percent of federal aid to states and local governments is allocated. Money allocated under a specific program can be spent only for that purpose or category. Federal laws also include specific standards or requirements that recipients must meet, such as prohibitions against racial or sex discrimination or prohibitions against non-union pay scales.

There are two types of categorical grants. The first is the project grant that requires a state or local government to apply for a grant with the appropriate federal agency and compete against other governments for the grant dollars. The money is awarded on the basis of the merits of an application. The second type of categorical grant is the formula grant. As the name implies, federal funds are allocated to states and local governments on the basis of a prescribed formula. These formulas vary from program to program but might include income or poverty levels of a state's residents, population totals or rural characteristics. Congress determines the formulas for specific programs, and the federal dollars are then distributed on the basis of the statutory criteria. Many of these federal grants require **matching funds** from the governments that receive the money. The percentage of costs borne by the federal government varies from program to program, with the state or local governments picking up the balance. One reason for requiring such matches is to encourage state and local governments to have a strong commitment to the funded program and its policy objectives.

The domestic programs initiated by President John F. Kennedy (1961-1963) and subsequently expanded by President Lyndon B. Johnson in the Great Society programs resulted in a dramatic expansion of the federal government's role to virtually every area of domestic policy. The number of identifiable grant programs increased in eight years from 132 to 379; federal funding for grant programs more than trebled within 10 years, and the federal share of state and local budgets increased from 17 percent in 1960 to 23 percent in 1970. Many of these programs targeted specific populations for assistance and were intended to redistribute resources primarily to lower income groups. Moreover, there were several federal programs that virtually bypassed state governments and went directly to local governments, thus eroding the legal relationship of local governments to the states.[23]

When Richard Nixon was elected president in 1968, he, like many other conservatives, criticized the expanded role of the federal government and advocated a reversion of program responsibilities to the states. As grant programs had evolved, various groups and individuals—or stakeholders—had developed vested interests in maintaining them. Members of Congress viewed many of these programs as "pork" for the folks back home, and administrators at all levels of government justified their jobs and their agencies' existence on the basis of these programs.

## New Federalism

The **"new federalism"** of President Nixon (1969-1974) was designed to "rationalize the intergovernmental system by restructuring the roles and responsibilities of governments at all levels."[24] At the same time, Nixon wanted to reduce the role of the federal government and largely decentralize federal programs. His strategy included four key components. The first was management reforms to expedite and coordinate the grant application process. Secondly, many of the overlapping or related categorical grants would be consolidated into a few large **block grants**. State and local governments would have greater discretion over the use of these grants, and excessive paperwork required for grant applications would be eliminated. Nixon's third component was general **revenue sharing** that would either replace or supplement the existing categorical grants. States and local governments were to receive these federal funds with virtually "no strings attached." They could be used for any purpose determined by the recipient government. Finally, Nixon advocated a restructuring of the nation's welfare system. He unsuccessfully proposed replacing Aid to Families with Dependent Children (AFDC), the existing grant program, with the Family Assistance Plan, a federal income payment based on family size.[25]

After almost six years of program initiatives and changes that were supposed to increase state and local powers, Nixon produced results that appeared to be just the opposite. Many believe that "Nixon left behind what was probably a more centralized federal system than the one he inherited."[26] Federal expenditures for many domestic programs had increased dramatically, and the regulatory powers of the federal government had been expanded.

In terms of public rhetoric, President Ronald Reagan (1981-1989) publicly expressed a commitment to the reduction of federal programs, especially welfare programs, and the revitalization of the power of state and local governments. His position was somewhat of a departure from that of Nixon, and while he used some of the same tactics and resources, he clearly had a different agenda. Reagan was particularly critical of welfare assistance and, beginning with his 1981 legislative agenda, attempted to reduce federal support for social programs and eliminate categorical grants through their consolidation into block grants. In 1981, Reagan "convinced Congress to consolidate seventy-six categorical grant-in-aid programs and a block grant program into nine new or reconstituted block grants."[27] He attempted to consolidate additional grant programs during subsequent congressional sessions but had little success.

Reagan also opposed revenue sharing, which the federal government ended in 1986. The program was attacked for contributing to the federal budget deficit, funding governments that did not need the money, funding programs of questionable merit, and producing a reliance on revenue sharing dollars for the operating budgets of many governments.

Reagan's attack on the social services and his efforts to reduce federal funding of these programs were particularly harsh on state and local governments that had taken on many of the responsibilities for the administration and implementation of public assistance. One strategy initiated by the Reagan administration in 1982 was to turn back welfare (Aid to Families with Dependent Children) and the foodstamp programs to the states in return for the federal government assuming responsibility for the Medicaid program, which provided health care for many low-income individuals. While this proposal was rejected by Congress, Reagan, as well as his successor, George Bush, attempted on numerous occasions to return programs to state governments.[28]

The story is still out on the impact of Reagan's administration on the federal system. On the one hand, some believe that Reagan, primarily through executive orders and administrative initiatives, increased the discretionary authority of the states. On the other hand, while Reagan spoke of dual federalism, returning authority to the states and limiting the national government, his "New Federalism was a general philosophy favoring a smaller federal role but not necessarily a larger state and local role in the governance system."[29]

The "new federalism" of both Reagan and Nixon masked the "silent revolution" in federal relationships. As conservatives, both might have been expected to attack the expanded role of the federal government, and both articulated such positions. In fact, though, federal **preemptions** and **mandates** that reduced states' control over programs while raising the states' costs of providing services were increased during both administrations. During the nation's 200-year history, Congress has enacted approximately 350 statutes that preempted the authority or powers of state and local governments. Some 190, or more than half, have been enacted since 1969 (Table 3-2 on page 72).[30] Many of these preemptive restrictions were adopted with Reagan's approval and appear to reflect Reagan's commitment to marketplace economics and a reduced role for all governments.[31]

Based on constitutional law, statutory law or federal regulations, states or local governments can be mandated "to undertake a specific activity or provide a service meeting minimum national standards."[32] All during the 1980s, while decentralization and return of power to the states had been major themes of the Reagan administration, Congress enacted numerous statutes that imposed additional mandates and regulations on the states.[33]

While President Bush was perceived to be sensitive to state and local problems during the first years of his administration, there was little significant change from the policies and actions of his predecessor. The federal deficit and the

**Table 3-2** Federal Preemption Statutes, 1981-1988*

---

**Civil Rights**

Voting Rights Act Amendments of 1982
Migrant and Seasonal Agricultural Worker Protection Act of 1983
Older American Act Amendments of 1984
Age Discrimination in Employment Amendments of 1986
Electronic Communications Privacy Act of 1986
Uniformed and Overseas Citizens Absentee Voting Act of 1986
Alaska Native Claims Settlement Act Amendments of 1987
Employee Polygraph Protection Act of 1988
Fair Housing Amendments Act of 1988
Family Support Act of 1988

**Commerce**

Product Liability Risk Retention Act of 1981
Bus Regulatory Reform Act of 1982
Debt Collection Act of 1982
Federal Seed Act Amendments of 1982
Surface Transportation Assistance Act of 1982
Motor Vehicle Width Regulations of 1983
Cable Communications Policy Act of 1984
Counterfeit Access Device and Computer Fraud and Abuse Act of 1984
Local Government Antitrust Act of 1984
Longshoremen's and Harbor Workers' Compensation Act Amendments of 1984
Motor Vehicle Theft Law Enforcement Act of 1984
Patent Law Amendments Act of 1984
Shipping Act of 1984
Fair Labor Standards Amendments of 1985
Food Security Act of 1985
Computer Fraud and Abuse Act of 1986
Department of Transportation and Related Agencies Appropriation Act of 1986
False Claims Amendments Act of 1986
Federal Fire Prevention Appropriation/Daylight Savings Time Extension Act of 1986
Futures Trading Act of 1986
Liability Risk Retention Act of 1981
Abandoned Shipwreck Act of 1987
Competitive Equality Banking Act of 1987
National Appliance Energy Conservation Act of 1987
Poultry Producers Financial Protection Act of 1987
Prescription Drug Marketing Act of 1987
Alcoholic Beverage Labeling Act of 1988
Fair Credit and Charge Card Disclosure Act of 1988
Federal Energy Management Improvement Act of 1988
Trademark Law Revision Act of 1988
Worker Adjustment and Retraining Notification Act of 1988

**Environment**

Marine Mammal Protection Act Amendments of 1981
Endangered Species Act Amendments of 1982
Atlantic Striped Bass Conservation Act of 1984
Marine Sanctuaries Amendments of 1984
Pacific Salmon Treaty Act of 1985
Atlantic Striped Bass Conservation Act Amendments of 1986
Surface Mining Control and Reclamation Act Amendments of 1986
Marine Plastic Pollution Research and Control Act of 1987
Water Quality Act of 1987
Degradable Plastic Ring Carriers Act of 1988

**Table 3-2** (continued)

---

(Environment continued)
Federal Hazardous Substances Act Amendments of 1988
Federal Insecticide, Fungicide, and Rodenticide Act Amendments of 1988
Medical Waste Tracking Act of 1988
Ocean Dumping Ban Act of 1988
Rio Chama Wild and Scenic River, New Mexico, Act of 1988
Shore Protection Act of 1988
United States Public Vessel Medical Waste Anti-Dumping Act of 1988

**Finance**

Garn-St. Germain Depository Institutions Act of 1982
Tax Equity and Fiscal Responsibility Act of 1982
Tax Reform Act of 1984
Tax Reform Act of 1986

**Health**

National Organ Transplant Act of 1984
Virus, Serum, and Toxin Act Amendments of 1985
Asbestos Hazard Emergency Response Act of 1986
Comprehensive Smokeless Tobacco Health Education Act of 1986
Protection and Advocacy for Mentally III Individuals Act of 1986
Safe Drinking Water Act Amendments of 1986
Anti-Drug Abuse Act of 1988
Child Protection and Obscenity Enforcement Act of 1988
Indoor Radon Abatement Act of 1988
Lead-Based Paint Poisoning Prevention Act Amendments of 1988
Organ Transplant Amendments of 1988

**Immigration**

Immigration Reform and Control Act of 1986
Refugee Assistance Extension Act of 1986

**Safety**

Motor Vehicle Safety and Cost Savings Authorization Act of 1982
Nuclear Waste Policy Act of 1982
Vessel Safety Standards Act of 1983
Coast Guard Authorization Act of 1984
Hazardous and Solid Waste Amendments of 1984
Maritime Safety Act of 1984
Motor Carrier Safety Act of 1984
Tandem Truck Safety Act of 1984
Low-Level Radioactive Waste Policy Amendments Act of 1985
Commercial Motor Vehicle Safety Act of 1986
Emergency Planning and Community Right-to-Know Act of 1986
Hazard Emergency Response Act of 1986
Federal Hazardous Substances Act Amendments of 1988
Rail Safety Improvement Act of 1988
Toxic Substances Control Act Amendments of 1988
Truck and Bus Safety and Regulatory Reform Act of 1988
Uranium Mill Tailings Remedial Action Amendments of 1988

---

*Many preemption statutes affect more than one functional area, but have been listed only under the major functional area.

Source: Joseph F. Zimmerman, "Federal Preemption Under Reagan's New Federalism," *Publius: The Journal of Federalism*, 21 (Winter 1991), pp. 13-14

agreements to cap federal expenditures provided no prospects for additional financial assistance to the states. Ironically, the federal government in 1991 was expected to "add more to its debt than all 50 states are raising and spending for all their programs."[34] Congress, with the approval of President Bush, continued to impose mandates that added to the financial burdens of state and local governments while preempting more and more authority over programs from the states.[35]

In 1990, for example, Congress passed the Americans with Disabilities Act. In addition to its general prohibition of discrimination against persons with disabilities, the act required that all "fixed-route public transportation systems be made accessible to the handicapped" by equipping all new buses and transit facilities with wheelchair lifts and other equipment. It is estimated that several hundred million dollars will eventually be expended to meet these requirements, and most of the cost will be incurred by local governments.[36] During 1990, Congress also passed three other major pieces of legislation (the Clean Air Act Amendments, the Education of the Handicapped Act Amendments, and the Fiscal 1991 Budget Reconciliation Act), which imposed additional requirements on the states and local governments.

With the costs of medical care soaring, many states, including Texas, vociferously complained in 1991 about new federal guidelines for Medicaid, which would shift more of the burden for supporting the joint state-federal health care program to the states.

Just as states decry the buck-passing effects of federal mandates, similar complaints are heard from local governments about state programs, a topic to be discussed in Chapter 12.[37]

## The Role of the Supreme Court in Defining Federalism

In a 1985 Texas case, *Garcia* v. *San Antonio Metropolitan Transit Authority*, the U.S. Supreme Court held 5-4 that states could not claim immunity from federal regulation over functions that have been defined as "integral" or "traditional."[38] This case, which involved municipal employees and their coverage by the Fair Labor Standards Act, had far-reaching implications for federal-state relationships.[39] In the extreme, the case suggested that Congress, not the courts interpreting the Constitution, would define federalism. The case also suggested that there were no "discrete limitations on the objects of federal authority" other than those provisions of the Constitution that give the states a role in the selection of the president and members of Congress. If the position of this case prevails, some scholars believe it will eliminate any remaining autonomy of the states.[40]

## THE IMPACT OF FEDERALISM ON STATE FINANCES

State government as well as many of the larger cities in Texas have full-time staffs dedicated to getting additional federal dollars under existing and proposed grant programs. The Texas Office of State-Federal Relations, headed by Jane Hickie, has a staff of 20 people divided between Washington and Austin with an annual budget of approximately $1 million. Texas, like every other state, lobbies the federal government for additional programs, changes in programs, relief from mandates and preemptions and adjustments in the funding formulas that often adversely affect the state.[41]

Several studies indicate that Texas has received a smaller return on its tax dollars through federal grants than other states (Figure 3-2). The state comptroller's office reviewed many of the federal grant programs and determined that in several instances the funding formulas developed by Congress may have had an adverse effect on Texas' share of federal dollars. The state planned to attempt to obtain more equitable formulas as Congress amended or reauthorized these grant programs.[42]

Some state agencies and local governments apparently also have difficulty mastering the complexities of the grant application process. As indicated earlier, many federal programs are awarded on the basis of competitive applications. Available programs must be identified through publications such as the *Federal Register*, and policymakers supported by staff must submit the appropriate applications in a timely manner. Many small cities across Texas may have only a handful of

**Figure 3-2**   Disparities in Federal Grants to the States.  (Bob Bullock, Texas Comptroller of Public Accounts, *Dollars We Deserve: How Texas is Short-changed on Our Fair Share of Federal Money*, March 1990.)

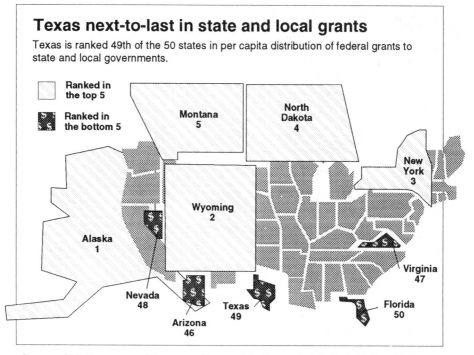

Sources:  U.S. Department of Commerce, Bureau of the Census; Bob Bullock, *Dollars We Deserve: How Texas is Short-Changed on Our Fair Share of Federal Money*, March, 1990

employees performing everything from garbage collection to tax collection. While federal grants are available, these communities may not have the skills or resources to apply for them, while other communities may be disinterested. The state is organized into regional councils of government, which can assist local governments in the art of grantsmanship. While there are some counties, cities, school districts, and special districts that are very aggressive and successful, there is a great disparity among local governments in winning grants.

As a consequence of agency performance audits conducted by the comptroller's office in 1991, state agencies are now required to look at their specific programs and aggressively pursue relevant federal grants. To this end, the Office of State-Federal Relations functions as a coordinating agency to help identify grant programs, inform agencies of grant availability, assist in the writing of grant applications and monitor agency activities in pursuing grants.[43]

Texas' 1990 budget included approximately $6 billion in federal funds, 64 percent of which was tied to state matching funds. Human services (Table 3-3), which include a wide range of social services for millions of low-income Texans, received $3 billion, or approximately 50 percent of all federal funds. Transportation, which was primarily highway construction, received $1 billion, or 17 percent. Education programs received 16 percent of the federal funds, and health services accounted for 7 percent. Total state spending for 1990 was approximately $23 billion, with federal funds comprising 24.9 percent of the total.

## REACTIONS TO THE EXPANDED ROLE OF THE FEDERAL GOVERNMENT

Some state agencies and communities across Texas have resisted taking federal dollars because of the "strings attached" to the grant programs. Upon accepting

TABLE 3–3   Federal Revenue by Agency, Year Ended August 31, 1990

|                                         | 1990            |
| --------------------------------------- | --------------- |
| Department of Human Services            | $2,695,560,522  |
| Dept. of Highways/Public Transportation | 1,032,552,571   |
| Texas Education Agency                  | 948,217,867     |
| Texas Department of Commerce            | 315,159,115     |
| Texas Department of Health              | 231,475,752     |
| Texas Employment Commission             | 155,240,788     |
| Texas Rehabilitation Commission         | 131,507,176     |
| Texas HHS Coordinating Council          | 66,693,800      |
| Texas Dept. of MHMR                     | 53,039,773      |
| All Other Agencies                      | 300,820,338     |
| Total All Agencies                      | $5,930,267,702  |

Source: Bob Bullock, Texas Comptroller of Public Accounts, *Texas Annual Cash Report*, Volume I, 1990.

money from the federal government, a recipient is obligated to comply with the statutory regulations covering its use. This is something like a "carrot and stick," whereby state and local governments receive funding in exchange for compliance with regulations that reflect the agenda of the national government.

Regulations tied to a specific grant can cross over to a totally different policy arena, thus further coercing states and local governments to comply with federal policy objectives. For example, the Texas Legislature raised the minimum legal drinking age from 18 to 21 in 1986. While there were groups in the state that had lobbied for this older drinking age, a major impetus for the change came from federal legislation that linked the drinking age to federal grants for road construction. Texas could have refused to adopt the age change, but the state would have lost 10 percent of its federal highway dollars after 1988. Federal law also makes a similar link between highway speed limits and federal highway construction funds.

Many of the federal assistance programs were designed to redistribute resources from the wealthier segments of the population to lower income groups. Philosophically, there are people across the state who disagree with this practice. Moreover, redistribution of resources is linked in Texas to issues of race and ethnicity because minority groups constitute a disproportionate segment of the state's low-income population. There have been political leaders who resisted federal grant programs for fear that funding projects would enhance the political position of minority groups.

Federal grants have been criticized and resisted by some groups and officeholders in Texas on the grounds that they force governments to rearrange their priorities. The funds for specific programs may not meet the primary needs of a state or community, but it is very difficult for most public officeholders to pass up these available dollars.

Some suggest the increased use of fiscal federalism (federal grants linked to preemptions and mandates) has produced a mindset that the federal government should assume more responsibility for domestic programs, both in terms of program development and funding.[44] They fear that federal dominance undermines the creative capacity of states and local governments to deal with many local and regional problems. But the federal deficit has produced a retrenchment in federal initiatives, resulting in a greater emphasis on regulatory policy rather than innovation.

## TRANSNATIONAL REGIONALISM

To this point, we have argued that governmental relationships in the United States have become more complex and interdependent since the New Deal, although there have been recent attempts to reverse that development. For Texas, intergovernmental relationships are even more complex because it shares a 1,248-mile border with Mexico and what transpires on one side of the border affects the other. Common problems and interests bond the two neighbors—Texas was even part of Mexico prior to the state's independence in 1836—and from every indication, these relationships will take on greater importance in the future.

Many Mexicans have considered U.S. policy toward Mexico imperialistic. As has been the case with several other Latin American countries, Mexico, fearing American dominance, has had a historic distrust of the United States and relationships have often been strained. The United States fought a war with Mexico in 1845, and on numerous occasions, American troops have entered Mexican territory. Suspicion and apprehension of U.S. policy objectives resulted in Mexican policies on trade, commerce, and foreign ownership of property that were designed to insulate the country from excessive foreign influence and domination.

Nevertheless, the interests of the two countries are inextricably bound by geopolitical factors, economics, and demographics. One Mexican author has compared the interdependence of the two countries to Siamese twins "warning that if one becomes gangrenous, the other twin will also be afflicted."[45]

Negotiations on a free-trade agreement in 1991 marked a significant change in the relationship of the two countries. They were precipitated, in part, by world economics and the emergence of regional trading zones. But the administration of Mexican President Carlos Salinas de Gortari also was reacting to the failure of Mexico's economic policies of the 1980s and a fear of economic isolation. The end of the Cold war, a reduction in Central American conflicts, and internal population pressures also were factors.[46]

The convergence of interests of the United States and Mexico resulted in "fast track" negotiations to reduce tariffs and increase trade between the two countries. By most estimates, future free-trade policies will increase trade between the two neighbors, strengthen existing economic ties, and create new ones. Texas, in particular, can expect some economic changes. There also will be further integration of "Mexican workers into the U.S. economy through employment in their own country in both American and Mexican companies geared to the U.S. market."[47]

Local governments, chambers of commerce, professional and trade associations, and individual companies throughout Texas generally endorsed this development of a transnational economic system, and cities are competing to position themselves to take advantage of these changes. But as more attention is given to the potential effects of the proposed free-trade agreement, it is becoming clear that its benefits will not be distributed uniformly. The regions that would benefit the most in terms of new manufacturing jobs are those with the greatest value-added production (chemicals, electronic machinery). Urban areas projected to gain are the Dallas-Fort Worth area and Houston.[48]

There also are those on both sides of the border who argue that these free-trade policies will adversely affect their respective countries. Labor unions in the United States are particularly concerned that cheap labor costs in Mexico will result in a further exodus of jobs from the United States. Some manufacturers argue that labor and capital costs in Mexico will threaten their American markets. In Mexico, there is a concern that American corporations will dominate and reduce Mexico's control over its own economy.[49]

These trade negotiations with Mexico are part of a broader policy to create a North American Free Trade Agreement which would be expanded to include

Canada. Such an agreement would be formidable because the United States, Mexico, and Canada combined have 355 million consumers and a $5.5 trillion gross national product, approximately the same as Western Europe's GNP.[50]

## Trade Patterns Between Texas and Mexico

The United States and Texas clearly profit from Mexico's prosperity. In 1986, U.S. exports to Mexico were $12.4 billion, and in 1990 had increased to $28.4 billion. Mexico is the United States' third largest trading partner. In 1989, some 82 percent of U.S. exports to Mexico and 72 percent of the imports from Mexico were manufactured goods.[51] Exports to Mexico directly contribute to hundreds of thousands of jobs in the United States.[52] It has been estimated that for each $1 billion of exports, an additional 22,000 jobs are created north of the border.[53]

Texas' exports to Mexico increased from $8.24 billion in 1988 to $9.75 billion in 1989 and $11.71 billion in 1990. In 1989, exports to Mexico accounted for 31.5 percent of the total exports from Texas.[54] That same year, more than $8 billion in U.S. exports went through Laredo and another $2 billion worth went through Brownsville, providing a much-needed boost to the economies of those border cities.

Imports to the United States from Mexico totaled $30.2 billion in 1990. Approximately 15 percent was oil, more than 60 percent were manufactured goods, and approximately 8 percent were agricultural products.[55] Texas cities along the border as well as Corpus Christi and Houston are the ports of entry for Mexican products, and the volume of trade moving through Texas cities and along Texas highways is impressive. Numerous local initiatives are now taking place as cities and counties attempt to stimulate economic growth and development linked to international trade.

There have been cooperative efforts between the United States and Mexico for years. Texas created a Good Neighbor Commission, now defunct, to encourage public and private initiatives which would improve relations with Mexico. Other groups and organizations attempted cooperative efforts for such projects as the Amistad Dam, disaster relief, health and welfare programs, conservation efforts, and highway improvements to promote trade and tourism.[56]

## The Illegal Immigration Issue

Population growth in Texas has always been affected by migration from other states and foreign countries. But the proximity of Texas to Mexico has put the state in the center of a long-running dispute over the illegal immigration of large numbers of Mexicans and other Latin Americans. In 1990, there were an estimated 1.5 million to 3 million people, mostly from Mexico and Central America, living in the United States illegally.[57] Many of these illegal immigrants enter through Texas and continue on to other areas of the country, but many others remain in the state. Officials can only estimate the numbers because these immigrants don't provide a great deal of information about themselves through surveys or other forms of data collection where their anonymity might be compromised.

The failure of the Mexican economy and the attraction of employment opportunities north of the border have been major reasons for this migration, although political instability and persecutions in Central America also have been significant factors in recent years. Significant portions of the Texas and American economies have been built on the availability of cheap, low-skilled Mexican labor. Many agricultural producers in Texas and a number of other states have depended for years on the Mexicans who were willing to cross the border for seasonal work. Janitorial and cleaning services, clothing manufacturers, restaurants, and many construction businesses also have hired thousands of the illegal, or undocumented, immigrants.[58] Many also have been hired in Texas as domestic, household workers.

The hiring of illegal workers was widely practiced under a double standard that made the workers subject to sanctions—primarily deportation—if they were caught but didn't punish the Americans who hired them. Various federal immigration laws since the 1880s placed restrictions on immigration, making it illegal to enter the United States without following specific procedures. But until the enactment of a major immigration reform law in 1986, it was not illegal to hire undocumented workers.[59]

Illegal immigration increases the strain on governmental services and poses sticky political and policy questions for the state and the nation. Children of illegal immigrants represent a heavy financial burden for many school districts and taxpayers along the border, raising controversy over whether they should be allowed to attend public schools. Undocumented aliens also increase the demand for health care and other public assistance programs, while some citizens, particularly unskilled workers, view the illegal arrivals as a threat to their jobs and standard of living.[60] There also is controversy over the counting of the illegal immigrants in the U.S. Census for the purpose of determining political representation. These are only some of the issues that divide the Texas electorate over the status of illegal aliens. Across Texas, there is a common complaint that the citizens of the state carry the burden for the failure of the federal government, which has authority over immigration, to develop policies to stem the illegal flow.

After illegal immigration seemed to accelerate in the 1980s, Congress enacted the Immigration Reform and Control Act (IRCA) of 1986.[61] It imposed fines on employers who hired illegal aliens and provided jail sentences for flagrant violators. Potential employees had to provide documentation, and employers had to verify their citizenship. Minority civil rights groups were concerned that employers would use this new law to discriminate against American citizens of Latin descent, although the statute prohibited such practices.

The new law also provided a means for giving legal status, or amnesty, to hundreds of thousands of illegal immigrants who had moved to the United States prior to January 1, 1982. And to meet the needs of agricultural producers, it provided for temporary resident status of agricultural workers who could satisfy specific residency requirements.[62]

It is questionable whether this reform law has stemmed the tide of illegal immigration. Throughout the Southwest, thousands of illegal aliens are still being arrested and detained before being returned home, and the movement of Mexican workers into Texas and the United States remains a sticky issue. The Bush administration insisted that the immigration issue be excluded from the negotiations over the free-trade agreement.[63] The maquiladora program initiated by Mexico in the late 1960s resulted in the growth of an export-assembly industry designed, in part, to provide employment for Mexican nationals in Mexico and reduce immigration to the United States. There has been a noticeable migration from the interior of Mexico to the northern border between Texas and Mexico, where the maquiladora plants are located. But migration to the United States did not slow significantly.[64]

While it has been suggested that a free-trade agreement will stem illegal immigration to the United States from Mexico, there are indications that it may well have the reverse effect. The economies of Mexico and the United States are functioning at different levels of development, and experiences in other parts of the world suggest that the development of strong economic relations encourages the movement of workers from poorer to wealthier nations.[65] While President Bush has attempted to detach immigration from free-trade discussions, we can expect Mexico to attempt to link the two issues. And the many Hispanic groups unhappy with the 1986 immigration law can be expected to continue working to change it.

## Maquiladoras

Mexico's movement toward a closer economic relationship with the United States is part of a long-term pattern of changes. The maquiladora program was initiated under Mexico's Border Industrialization Program (BIP) in 1964 to boost employment, foreign exchange, and industrial development. It also was designed to transfer technology to Mexico, help train workers, and develop managerial skills among Mexican nationals.[66] The original concept was to develop twin plants, one in the United States and one in Mexico, under a single management.[67] A U.S. plant would manufacture parts, and its Mexican counterpart would assemble them into a product, which, in turn, would be sent back to the United States for further processing or for shipping to customers.[68] Parts shipped into Mexico would not be subject to the normal tariffs, and the tax imposed on the assembled product sent back to the United States would be minimal.[69] In 1984, Mexico changed its laws to permit U.S. and other foreign firms to establish these relationships throughout Mexico, rather than just on the border, and to permit 100 percent foreign ownership of the assembly plants in Mexico. The latter step was a radical departure from previous Mexican law, which prohibited such foreign ownership.[70]

The maquiladora program has not resulted in the construction of a significant number of manufacturing plants on the Texas side of the border because American companies have used existing plants throughout the United States to produce parts to be assembled in Mexico. Nevertheless, Texas' border counties have benefited economically. In 1987, there were 104 maquiladora plants operating in Mexico from Matamoras (across the border from Brownsville) to Nuevo Laredo (across from Laredo). These plants employed 60,000 people on the Mexican side of the border and provided an estimated 10,000 support jobs in transportation, warehousing, and other services in Texas.[71]

With Mexico's membership (since 1986) in the international General Agreement on Trade and Tariffs (or GATT) and the possibility of a North American Free Trade Agreement, the maquiladora program will likely be expanded. There is American opposition to the program from organized labor, which argues that the maquiladoras drain jobs from the United States. But U.S. businesses, encouraged by the federal government, are expected to expand this economic interdependence between the two countries. American businesses have complained for years that they cannot compete against the cheap foreign labor costs of world manufacturers, and this program provides their own source of inexpensive labor. Numerous experts anticipate that the Texas economy would directly benefit from a further expansion of the maquiladora program.

## Common Borders, Common Problems

To anyone living on the border, the economic interdependence of the United States and Mexico is evident on a daily basis. Thousands of pedestrians, cars, and trucks move across the international bridges, to and from the commercial centers on both sides of the Rio Grande. When the Mexican economy suffered a precipitous decline in 1982, the peso devaluation severely disrupted the Texas border economy. Unemployment skyrocketed in the counties along the border, and a considerable number of U.S. businesses in the area eventually failed. These border counties historically have been poor, and Mexico's economic problems exacerbated their problems.

While a great deal of the effort toward improving relations between the United States and Mexico has focused on potential economic benefits, other complex problems confronting both countries also merit attention.

One is health care. Many of the public health facilities on the U.S. side of the border report that Mexican women will come across the border to give birth to their children in American facilities. The object is to give their children the option of U.S. citizenship and access to American educational opportunities.[72] This practice has the effect of creating a "binational family," but it also increases the burden on public hospitals—and taxpayers—in Texas.

Increased industrialization and population concentrations along the border also increase environmental problems. U.S. anti-pollution laws and enforcement have been much more stringent than those of Mexico, but air and water pollution generated in Mexico does not stop at the border. And a country, such as Mexico, that is under enormous pressure to industrialize rapidly is less likely to be concerned with environmental issues. Furthermore, U.S. efforts to impose its environmental standards on Mexico could be interpreted as another American effort to dominate the country.[73]

Some American companies, meanwhile, have been accused of poor environmental practices at their plants in Mexico, practices that would subject the companies to fines in the United States but which are largely ignored by Mexican authorities.

Regional interdependence, while perhaps not recognized by most people on both sides of the border, has taken on greater importance in the press and academic, business, and labor communities in the United States. Transnational public policies seem to be emerging, creating a range of legal issues that must still be resolved, including products liability, insurance, copyrights, and patents. The governors of Mexican and U.S. border states have their own association, the Border Governors Conference, which meets regularly to discuss such issues as free trade, the environment, education, and tourism. Recent Texas governors have supported efforts to improve relations with Mexico, and Texas state agencies have been given increased authority to work in cooperative efforts with Mexican officials.[74]

Another indication of a transnational commitment was the announcement of cooperative efforts between Mexico and the United States to create a "sister sanctuary" in Mexico to Big Bend National Park and establish the world's largest international preserve. Big Bend National Park has 800,000 acres, and there is an adjacent state park of 250,000 acres on the Texas side of the Rio Grande. The new plans called for the development of a park as big as 1 million acres in Sierra del Carmen in the adjacent Mexican state of Coahuila.[75]

## SUMMARY AND CONCLUSIONS

**1.** Texans are subject to the jurisdiction and taxing authority of a variety of different governments. This complex structure of federalism is often confusing, and the overlapping authority and responsibilities of these various governments often create problems for citizens.

**2.** There are alternatives for structuring the relationships between a national government and its states, and the United States has experimented with confederation and federalism. In contrast, the relationship of states to local governments is based on the unitary principle.

**3.** While the U.S. Constitution provides the broad outline of federal-state relationships, the language of the various constitutional provisions is sufficiently ambiguous to result in multiple interpretations. Over the course of the nation's history, federal-state relationships have been subject to redefinition, and recent actions by Congress, the president, and the courts speak to the continued changes.

**4.** In addition to the vertical relationships of federalism (states and the national government), the U.S. Constitution defines the obligations states have to each other (horizontal federalism). Issues and problems facing states do not stop at their borders, and states have joined numerous cooperative efforts to address these common problems. As the states have become increasingly interdependent, cooperative efforts to deal with pollution, water resources, crime, and a host of other issues have taken on more importance.

**5.** A number of recent presidents have criticized the national government's accumulation of power over domestic policies and have articulated a commitment to returning power and responsibility for domestic programs to the states. The New Federalism, which included efforts to restructure the federal grant programs, was justified in these terms.

**6.** While there has been a great deal of political rhetoric over the excessive use of federal powers and the dilution of state powers, recent policies supported by presidents and Congress have expanded the role of the federal government in domestic policy. Over the past 20 years, there have been numerous laws enacted by the federal government that preempt state authority or mandate state governments and their political subdivisions to carry out provisions of federal legislation. In many instances, federal mandates have been imposed on the states without sufficient funding, thus adding to the fiscal crisis facing state and local governments.

**7.** The federal government has the constitutional authority to define the relationships between the U.S. and Mexico. But Texas shares a 1,250-mile border with Mexico, and with the increasing economic, social, and political interdependence between Mexico and Texas, it is appropriate to define these relationships in terms of transnational regionalism.

**8.** The economy of Texas has become inextricably linked to the economies of the Mexican border states. Over the past 20 years, the Mexican government has successfully implemented the maquiladora program, and under the administration of President Carlos Salinas de Gortari, Mexico has joined the General Agreement on Trade and Tariffs, thus expanding trade potential between the United States and Mexico. Successful negotiations of a North American Free Trade Agreement will further expand U.S. trade with Mexico and have an immediate impact on the Texas economy.

**9.** Texas attracts a large number of illegal immigrants from Mexico as well as other Latin American countries. They place additional pressures on the state's economy and the state's ability to provide adequate health care, social services, and education. Federal legislation in the 1980s attempted to stem the tide of illegal immigration, but despite the punitive measures incorporated into the federal law, there is considerable disagreement over whether illegal immigration has been reduced. A free trade agreement with greater movement across the border between the United States and Mexico is likely to increase these population pressures on Texas.

**10.** Environmental, economic, and health care issues are not constrained by the border between Texas and Mexico, and such transregional problems as pollution demonstrate the necessity for governments and businesses on both sides of the border to collaborate on developing solutions. But many American environmentalist groups have alleged that U.S. corporations will ship their dirty industries to Mexico to avoid U.S. regulations.

## KEY TERMS

Unitary system
Confederation
Federalism
Delegated powers
Implied powers
Supremacy clause
Reserved powers
Denied powers
Full faith and credit
Privileges and immunities
Extradition

Interstate compacts
Cooperative federalism
Categorical grant-in-aid
Matching funds
Block grants
Revenue sharing
Preemptions
Mandates
New federalism
Transnational regionalism

## FURTHER READINGS

Break, George, *Financing Government in a Federal System.* Washington, D.C.: Brookings Institution, 1980.

Bullock, Bob, Texas Comptroller of Public Accounts, *Dollars We Deserve*, Vol. 1-5. Austin: Comptroller of Public Accounts, 1990.

Center for the Study of Federalism, *Publius.* This journal is an excellent source of information on a wide variety of topics centered on federalism and federal relationships.

Goldwin, Robert A., ed., *A Nation of States*, 2nd ed. Chicago: Rand McNally College Publishing Company, 1974.

Graves, W. Brooke, *American Intergovernmental Relations: Their Origins, Historical Development and Current Status.* New York: Scribner, 1964.

Grodzins, Morton, *The American System*, edited by Daniel J. Elazar. Chicago: Rand McNally & Company, 1966.

Henig, Jeffrey R., *Public Policy and Federalism.* New York: St. Martin's Press, 1985.

Langley, Lester D., *MexAmerica: Two Countries, One Future.* New York: Crown Publishers, 1988.

Martin, Roscoe C. *The Cities and the Federal System.* New York: Atherton Press, 1965.

Martinez, Oscar J. *Troublesome Border.* Tucson: University of Arizona Press, 1988.

Metz, Leon C., *Border: The U.S.-Mexico Line.* El Paso, Tex.: Mangan Books, 1989.

Weintraub, Sidney, *A Marriage of Convenience: Relations Between Mexico and the United States.* New York: Oxford University Press, 1990.

Wright, Deil S., *Understanding Intergovernmental Relations*, 2nd ed. Monterey, Cal.: Brooks/Cole Publishing Company, 1982.

## ENDNOTES

1. Woodrow Wilson, *Constitutional Government in the United States*, (New York: © Columbia University Press, 1921), p. 173. Reprinted by permission from the publisher.
2. For a discussion of the Dillon Rule, see Anwar Syed, *The Political Theory of American Local Government* (New York: Random House, 1966), Chapter 3.
3. Thomas J. Anton, *American Federalism and Public Policy* (New York: Random House, 1989), p. 3.
4. See William H. Stewart, "Metaphors, Models, and the Development of Federal Theory," *Publius* 12:5-24. and William H. Stewart, *Concepts of Federalism* (Lanham, Md. Center for the Study of Federalism and University Press of America, 1984).
5. Anton, *American Federalism and Public Policy*, p. 19.
6. *U.S. Constitution*, Article 1, Section 8, Paragraph 18.
7. *U.S. Constitution*, Article 6.
8. *U.S. Constitution*, Amendment X.
9. For an excellent summary of the guarantees to and limitations on state governments defined by the U.S. Constitution, see Thomas Dye, *American Federalism* (Lexington, Ky.:D.C. Heath and Company, 1990), pp. 9-11.

10. *U.S. Constitution*, Article IV, Section 1.
11. *Commonwealth of Kentucky v. Denison, Governor*, 65 U.S. (24 How.) 66 (1861).
12. *Puerto Rico v. Branstad*, 483 U.S. 219 (1987).
13. Kenyon Bunch and Richard J. Hardy, "Continuity or Change in Interstate Extradition? Assessing *Puerto Rico v. Branstad*," *Publius* 21 (Winter 1991), p. 59.
14. Keon S. Chi, "Interstate Cooperation: Resurgence of Multistate Regionalism," *The Journal of State Government* 63 (July -September 1990), p. 59.
15. Morton Grodzins, *The American System*, edited by Daniel J. Elazar (Chicago: Rand McNally & Company, 1966), pp. 151 - 153.
16. *U.S. Constitution*, Article III, Section 2.
17. Morton Grodzins and Daniel Elazar, "Centralization and Decentralization in the American Federal System," in , *A Nation of States*, 2nd ed., ed.Robert A. Goldwin, (Chicago: Rand McNally College Publishing Company, 1974), p. 4.
18. Diel S. Wright, *Understanding Intergovernmental Relations*, 2nd ed., (Monterey, California: Brooks/Cole Publishing Company, 1982), pp. 60-68.
19. Ibid., p. 46.
20. Timothy Conlan with an introduction by Samuel H. Beer, *New Federalism* (Washington, D.C.: The Brookings Institute, 1988), p. 5.
21. V.O. Key, *The Responsible Electorate* (Cambridge, Harvard University Press, 1966), p. 31.
22. Daniel J. Elazar, *American Federalism: A View From the States*, 2nd ed., (New York: Harper and Row Publishers, 1972), p. 47.
23. Conlon, *New Federalism*, p. 6.
24. Ibid., p. 3.
25. Ibid., pp. 3, 19-30, 77-81.
26. Ibid., p. 90.
27. Joseph F. Zimmerman, "Federal Preemption Under Reagan's New Federalism," *Publius* 21 (Winter 1991), p. 11.
28. Michael A. Pagano, Ann O'M. Bowman and John Kincaid, "The State of American Federalism," *Publius* 21 (Summer 1991), p. 1.
29. Zimmerman, "Federal Preemption Under Reagan's New Federalism," p. 26.
30. Robert B. Hawkins, "Pre-Emption: The Dramatic Rise of Federal Supremacy," *The Journal of State Government* 63 (January - March 1990), p. 10.
31. Zimmerman, "Federal Preemption Under Reagan's New Federalism," p. 26.
32. Ibid. p. 27.
33. Timothy J. Colon, "And the Beat Goes On: Intergovernmental Mandates and Preemption in an Era of Deregulation," *Publius*, 21 (Summer 1991),p. 52.
34. David Broder, "Double Whammy socks State, Local Government," *San Antonio Express News*, November 19, 1991, p. 10A.
35. Pagano, et al., "The State of American Federalism, 1990-1991," p. 1.
36. Conlan, "And the Beat Goes On," pp. 44-46.
37. Susan A. MacManus, "'Mad' about Mandates: The Issue of Who Should Pay for What Resurfaces in the 1990s", *Publius* 21 (Summer 1991), pp. 59-75.
38. *Garcia v. San Antonio Metropolitan Transit Authority*, 105 S. Ct. 1005.
39. Anton, *American Federalism and Public Policy*, pp. 14-16.
40. Dye, *American Federalism: Competition Among Governments*, pp. 8-12.
41. Texas Comptroller of Public Accounts, *Dollars We Deserve*, March, 1990
42. Ibid.
43. Telephone interview with Tara Russell, Office of State-Federal Relations, Austin, Texas, November 22, 1991.
44. Robert B. Hawkins, The Dramatic Rise of Federal Supremacy, *The Journal of State Government*, 63 (January - March 1990), p. 12.
45. M. Delal Baer, "North American Free Trade," *Foreign Affairs*, 70 (Fall 1991), p. 138.
46. Ibid., pp. 132-149.
47. Saskia Sasssen, "Free Trade and Immigration," *Hemisphere* 3 (Winter/Spring 1991) p. 2.
48. Chandler Stolp and Jon Hockenyos, Free Trade Over Texas, *San Antonio Light*, September 15, 1991, p. E-1.
49. Sassen, "Free Trade and Immigration," p. 16.
50. Bruce Stokes, "Yukon to Yucatan," *National Journal*, 39 (September 29, 1990), pp. 2324-2328.

51. Ingrid Mohn, "U.S. - Mexico Free Trade Agreement Means Greater Mutual Prosperity," *Business America* (October 8, 1990), p. 5.
52. Baer, "North American Free Trade," p. 139.
53. Mohn, "U.S.-Mexico Free Trade Agreement Means Greater Mutual Prosperity," p. 3.
54. John McGray, McRay Research, San Antonio, TX 1991.
55. Congressional Research Service, *North American Free Trade Agreement: Issues for Congress*, March 25, 1991, p. 14.
56. International Graduate Planning Program, School of Architecture and Division of Extension, the University of Texas, *Investigation into the effects and Potentials of: Programa Nacional Fronterizo* (Austin, Texas 1967), p. 7.
57. "Sweeping Changes Abroad Confound U.S. Policy," *Congressional Quarterly*, 48 (February 24, 1990), pp. 592.
58. James F. Pearce and Jefferey W. Gunter, "Illegal Immigration from Mexico: Effects on the Texas Economy," *Federal Reserve Bank of Dallas Economic Review* (September, 1985), p. 4.
59. Robert W. Gardner and Leon F. Bouvier, "The United States," in William J. Serow, Charles B. Nam, David F. Sly, and Robert H. Weller, editors, *Handbook on International Migration* (New York: Greenwood Press, 1990), p. 342.
60. Pearce and Gunther, "Illegal Immigration from Mexico: Effects on the Texas Economy," p. 2.
61. Gardner and Bouvier, "The United States," p. 342.
62. "Congress Clears Overhaul of Immigration Law," *Congressional Quarterly Almanac, 1986* (Washington, D.C.: Congressional Quarterly, Inc., 1987), pp. 61-67.
63. Sassen, "Free Trade and Immigration," p. 2.
64. Ibid.
65. Ibid.
66. Joan B. Anderson, "Maquiladoras and Border Industrialization: Impact on Economic Development in Mexico," *Journal of Borderland Studies*, V (Spring, 1990), p. 5.
67. Michael Patrick, "Maquiladora and South Texas Border Economic Development," *Journal of Borderland Studies*, IV (Spring 1989) p. 90.
68. Ibid
69. Martin E. Rosenfeld, "Mexico's In Bond Export Industries and U.S. Legislation: Conflictive Issues," *Journal of Borderland Studies*, V (Spring 1990), p. 57.
70 Ibid., p. 47.
71. Patrick, "Maquiladoras and South Texas Border Economic Development," p. 90.
72. Joan Anderson and Martin de la Rosa, "Economic Survival Strategies of Poor Families on the Mexican Border," *Journal of Borderland Studies*, VI (Spring, 1991), p. 51.
73. Howard G. Applegate, C. Richard Bath and Jeffery T. Trannon, "BiNational Emissions Trading in an International Air Shed: The Case of El Paso, Texas and Ciudad Juarez," *Journal of Borderland Studies*, IV (Fall 1989) pp. 1-25.
74. *San Antonio Express-News*, February 18, 1991, p. 1-A.
75. *San Antonio Express-News*, August 25, 1991, p. 1-A.

# 4

# INTEREST GROUPS
# AND POWER
# IN TEXAS POLITICS

In America there is no limit to freedom of association for political ends.

*Alexis de Tocqueville*[1]

I think it was a very interesting study in how government works.

*Lt. Governor Bob Bullock commenting on the crucial role that
lobbyists played in getting a tax increase passed in 1991.*[2]

The legislature's back was almost to the wall. It was late summer, a new state budget had to be balanced by Sept. 1, and the House had just dismantled a critical tax bill. So Lt. Governor Bullock, the Senate's presiding officer, took over and supervised the drafting of a new revenue measure—a laundry list of tax and fee increases—by a small group of legislators and staff. As is often the case with major pieces of legislation, the new bill was negotiated in private with little information passed on to other legislators, the press, or the general public.

Then more than 60 lobbyists, including some who had helped scuttle the House tax bill only a few days earlier, were summoned to the lieutenant governor's office, where Bullock twisted arms, urging the lobbyists to support the new tax package and help sell it to the House. And the goal wasn't a simple majority vote. The bill had to be approved by a two-thirds vote in both the House and the Senate in order to become law immediately. Approval by fewer than two-thirds of lawmakers would delay the effective date of the bill for three months and cost state government millions of dollars in lost revenue. Such a wide margin seemed particularly unlikely in the House, where it would require 100 votes. But Bullock gave some of the lobbyists—including those representing the cigarette, highway construction, hotel, and insurance industries—an extra incentive to get behind the package. If the measure went into immediate effect, several contingency tax increases affecting their clients wouldn't be needed and wouldn't be implemented.

The lobby put on a full court press. In a matter of hours, hundreds of telephone calls were placed to influential constituents in state representatives' home districts. The Texas Medical Association, relieved that this bill didn't place physicians' services under the sales tax and fearful that the next tax bill might, helped finance a phone bank that targeted school officials throughout the state who had a lot to lose if the legislature failed to enact a new budget on time. The school board members and superintendents, in turn, contacted their individual legislators. Other interest groups followed similar constituent mobilization strategies. When the vote came, the House initially approved the tax bill 80-67, a clear majority but not enough to put the measure into immediate effect and spare the contingency taxes. After a motion was made to reconsider the vote, a second ballot netted 99 votes, still one short of the number necessary. Then House Speaker Gib Lewis held the vote open until Representative Keith Oakley, a Democrat from Terrell, changed his "no" vote to "aye." Lobbyists cheered in the gallery and happily slapped Oakley on the back when he left the chamber. Representative Al Price, a Democrat from Beaumont, complained, "What we have before us is proof positive that the people elect us, but the lobbyists instruct us."[3]

Or, as others would observe, it was business as usual for the Texas Legislature. No tax bill—or virtually any other proposal—is approved by the legislature without the involvement of interest groups whose lobbyists are Capitol fixtures. The enactment of public policy in Texas, as is true in other states, reflects the complex relationships among interest groups, elected public officials, and those who administer the laws.

To many Texans, lobbying is an unsavory business conjuring up images of manipulation, greed, or bribery, where the interests of a few take precedence over the general interests or needs of the state. Sensing this underlying disdain, political candidates often claim to be running against "the special interests" and promise to be responsive to all the people rather than to a few well-financed business, trade, or union groups. While it is not clear what impact these kinds of campaign promises have on elections—and most successful candidates freely accept campaign contributions from interest groups—many Texans, along with Americans nationwide, feel that government is dominated by a few big interests looking out for themselves rather than benefiting all of the people. The National Election Surveys conducted by the University of Michigan since 1964 indicate a clear pattern of increased public distrust of government. In 1964, 28 percent of those surveyed felt that government was run by a few big interests, but during most of the years since 1974, more than 60 percent of Americans expressed this sentiment.[4]

In Texas alone, special interest groups spend millions of dollars a year trying to elect favored candidates or influence the outcome of governmental decisions. Such expenditures always have raised ethical questions about purchasing undue influence on policymakers and are a continuing source of controversy.

## INTEREST GROUPS DEFINED

Theorists have spent considerable effort distinguishing interest groups from other social organizations, and, while definitional issues remain, an **interest group** may be defined as "an organized collection of individuals who are bound together by shared attitudes or concerns and who make demands on political institutions in order to realize goals which they are unable to achieve on their own."[5] Members of an interest group share common interests or goals, organize to pursue those goals collectively because they cannot achieve them individually and focus some of their efforts on influencing governmental decisions.[6] These characteristics, particularly the political and policy objectives of the interest group, distinguish these groups from the various other organizations in Texas.

We do not know exactly how many groups or organizations there are in the United States or even Texas. Nationally, the *Encyclopedia of Associations* has identified more than 22,000 national, nonprofit organizations. Comparing these totals with earlier estimates, it is clear that there has been an "explosion" of organizational and group activity over the past 30 years.[7] Across the country at the state and local level, it has been estimated that there are 200,000 different groups or organizations.[8] We have no comprehensive directory of groups or organizations in Texas, but a casual review of the list of associations and organizations in metropolitan phone books leads to the conclusion that there are thousands. Some have long histories and a durable presence in the policy processes, while others are formed to address a specific need, interest, or problem and disappear after a relatively short period. While most groups or organizations have the potential to participate in the policymaking processes, many will not. In the attempt to define the pressure group system in Texas, we place considerable emphasis on those groups that can be identified as continuous active players.

Most groups and organizations are not formed for political purposes. One scholar has suggested that only 10 percent of the people participate in organizations active in the pressure group system.[9] People usually don't join a chess club or a fraternal order, for example, to have an impact on public policy. And participation in church-related activities is based primarily, if not exclusively for most people, on spiritual or personal needs, although church groups can become involved in the political process. Some churches, for example, have been very active in the debate against abortion.

We also should distinguish between categorical groups and interest or pressure groups. Women collectively constitute a categorical grouping of the female population; and senior citizens, African-Americans and Hispanics also comprise categorical groups. While these often are spoken of as groups of people with similar political objectives, individuals within each hold a wide diversity of interests, concerns, and goals. An interest group is a segment of the population that organizes for specific purposes and objectives in the policymaking process. The Bexar County Women's Political Caucus, for example, is an interest group representing a segment of the females in Bexar County.

## Group Membership

It has been estimated, nevertheless, that 75 percent of the American people belong to some type of organization. Church membership is clearly the single largest category with approximately 42 percent of the total, but Americans join a wide array of civic, sports, service, fraternal, hobby, economic, and professional groups and organizations. Close to 50 percent of the country's population reported membership in two or more groups.[10]

Americans are clearly a "nation of joiners," and on first glance, it would appear that the overwhelming majority of Americans have potential access to the policymaking process by way of their membership in groups or organizations. Closer inspection, however, raises serious questions as to the distribution of political power and resources in this country and state. A general perception that the policy playing field is tilted to benefit some groups or interests to the exclusion of others has some validity.[11] And if parts of the population have limited potential to affect the decisions of government, this raises serious questions about the very nature of a democratic society as well as the role of groups within this political structure.

Those who study organizations generally agree that persons with higher incomes, better educations, higher status occupations, and higher standards of living are more likely than other people to belong to groups.[12] Historically, men have joined at a higher rate than women; older people join at higher rates than younger people; Anglos are more likely to be members than are Hispanics or African-Americans; and people with established community ties are more likely to participate. Not only do these people join more groups, but they are more likely to be active participants. These findings suggest that there is a class bias in the interest group system in Texas in that people from higher socioeconomic classes are more easily organized and are likely to maintain their support for these organizations.[13] Lower socioeconomic groups, minorities, and diffused constituencies, such as consumers, find it very difficult to compete on an equal footing with business, industrial, and professional groups, who also can better afford lobbying expenses and the financial contributions to political campaigns that usually guarantee access to officeholders.

## Why People Join Interest Groups

Individuals join groups and organizations for a variety of reasons, which may change over time. People derive a number of personal and material benefits from joining interest groups.[14] A teacher, for example, may join the Texas State Teachers Association because it lobbies for higher teacher salaries, better fringe benefits and working conditions, and general educational issues. But TSTA also offers its members publications, insurance programs, potential legal assistance, discounts for travel, and valuable professional information.

People also realize social or what is often referred to as solidary benefits from joining groups. Membership and participation provide them with a sense of personal identification with larger organizations and institutions that are likely to be more visible and potentially effective in the policy-making process than an individual would be acting alone.[15] They may believe their personal status and prestige also are enhanced by group membership.[16]

And, finally, there is the personal satisfaction or sense of purpose that a person receives from belonging to a group that he or she believes has a worthwhile cause or objective. There are people who join groups to try to make the world a better place.[17] One motivation for joining such groups as Common Cause or the League of Women Voters, for example, may be a commitment to improving the election system in Texas. For many people, reform of the election system provides broad, but intangible, benefits that go well beyond the group or organization.

## INTEREST GROUPS, PLURALISM, AND DEMOCRATIC THEORY

The issue of interest groups and political power in American politics has been debated since the Constitutional Convention of 1787. Writing in the *Federalist Papers* at a time when there were no political parties or interest groups as we know today, James Madison argued that it was inevitable that people would organize into groups, or "factions," and attempt to impose their will on others and use governments for their specific purposes. Madison also recognized two basic problems: there was a potential for the majority to tyrannize or impose its will on others, and a potential for the majority, in its pursuit of narrow self-interests, to harm the long-term interests of society as a whole.[18]

The cure for this **mischief of factions** was both institutional and socioeconomic. If the number of factions or groups increased, there would be greater competition and less likelihood that any one group could dominate the policymaking process. Competitors would have to find compromises. And institutional power would be fragmented among three branches of government and a federal system, where powers would be further divided between the national government and the states.

Drawing in part on this tradition established by Madison, David Truman, an American political scientist, argued in his classic study, *The Governmental Process*, that American politics can be understood primarily in terms of the way groups interact with each other.[19] Expanding on Truman's theories, other scholars have attempted to develop a general understanding of politics using groups as the primary unit of analysis. These scholars often are referred to as pluralists and their theories, **pluralism**. While there are differences in emphasis among the pluralists, they have established some general characteristics of a pluralistic society:

- Groups are the primary actors in the policy-making process, and in addition to providing the individual with political resources, they serve to link the individual to governmental institutions.
- Politics is basically group interaction, where groups come into conflict with each other over the limited resources of society, and public policy is ultimately the resolution of group conflict and differences.

- There are so many groups that no one group can dominate the political process. While there is not absolute equity in the distribution of resources among groups and interests, a group always has the potential to influence policy. If a group does not exist to address a particular concern or problem, it can easily be organized.
- While most people do not actively participate in the policy-making process, they have access to the process through the leaders of the groups of which they are members. And there are numerous leadership opportunities within groups for individuals who want active roles.
- Most group leaders are committed to democratic values, and while the essential conflict in the American political system centers on them, competition makes them responsive to their members at large and serves to check or constrain their actions.[20]

Pluralism is appealing because it gives credence to our general views of a democratic society and offers potential solutions, or at least hope, for those people who are excluded from full political participation or benefits.

One can find evidence in Texas to support the pluralist view. There are thousands of different groups organized on a statewide or community level. Hundreds of lobbyists are registered in Austin to represent a wide diversity of economic, social, civic, and cultural organizations. A growing state population and a diversifying economy have significantly increased the number of interest groups over the past three decades.

David Truman has suggested that there are periods, or waves, in American political history in which there are rapid proliferations of groups in response to economic, social, or political change.[21] To compensate for imbalances in the political system, additional groups will be organized and attempt to reestablish an equilibrium.

The severe economic problems of the 1980s, coupled with problems of public school funding, environmental protection, medical care for low-income Texans, and other pressing issues, have generated additional interest groups. Social movements, including those focusing on the interests of Hispanics, African-Americans, women, and gays, have produced even more local and statewide organizations. And the policy positions of some groups have spurred the development of opposing groups which was evident, for example, in the water disputes in the central Texas region of the Edwards Aquifer. Still other groups have emerged to protect existing interests or the status quo when threatened by change, and government policies and regulations have resulted in the formation of new groups.[22]

With the elimination of the most severe discriminatory practices, minority Texans also have experienced significant economic, social, and political gains. In addition to having increased access to mainstream groups, minorities have organized their own professional and economic organizations. It is not uncommon to find Hispanic chambers of commerce or African-American bar associations in many Texas cities.

Advocates of pluralism may use the above arguments and examples to suggest that the evolving pattern of state politics confirms their view. While not denying the deficiencies of earlier periods when large segments of the population were excluded from effective participation in the electoral or policy-making processes, they would argue that the political system is open and accessible to new groups and organizations. They would argue that more groups are participating in the political process today and that those holding public office are responsive to the needs and interests of a greater diversity of Texans than ever before.

## THE ELITIST ALTERNATIVE

There are political scientists, however, who insist that the pluralist theories simply do not describe the realities of power and policymaking in Texas or the nation at large. Many scholars criticize the research methods and findings of the pluralists and suggest that the pluralists have not given sufficient attention to the fact that a few individuals control enormous resources. While there are thousands of groups, they are not equal in political resources nor can they equally translate their interests or demands into public policy.

**Elitism** is the view that political power and the ability to influence the most important policy decisions are held by a few individuals who derive power from their leadership positions in large institutions. From the elitist perspective, power is not an individual commodity or resource but is an attribute of social organizations.[23] The elitist urges that careful attention be given to the resources of groups and their relationships to large institutions. For many elitists, power is often equated with economic resources.

They also believe that the existence of elites within any society is inevitable. Robert Michels, a European social scientist writing during the first part of this century, argued that any organization, no matter how structured, will eventually produce an "oligarchy," or rule by a few individuals. Michels' **iron rule of oligarchy** was applicable to any organization and was a universal law applied to all social systems.[24]

Beginning with C. Wright Mills in his book, *The Power Elite*, elite theory has produced many proponents among American scholars.[25] There has been a rigorous intellectual debate between elitist and pluralist theorists, and while many of the theoretical and methodological issues have been unresolved, a number of generalizations can be derived from the elitist school of thought:

- Power is held by a few individuals and is derived from their positions in large institutions. In addition to economic institutions, these include the government, the mass media, and civic organizations.
- Historically, political elites constituted a homogeneous group drawn primarily from the upper and upper-middle classes. They were older, well-educated, primarily white, Anglo-Saxon males.
- While there is competition among elites and the institutions they represent, there is considerable consensus and cohesion among elites on primary values, interests, and the rules of the game.
- Elites are linked by a complex network of interlocking memberships on the governing bodies of corporations, financial institutions, foundations, and civic and cultural organizations.

- Policy decisions are made by a few individuals and primarily reflect the interests of the dominant institutions. The interests of the dominant elites are not necessarily opposed to those of other classes of society.
- The vast majority of the population are passive spectators to the policymaking process. Voting has been the primary means by which the masses can participate in governmental decisions, but other than selecting governmental officials, elections have limited effects on policy decisions.[26]

A number of students of Texas government and politics have argued from this elitist perspective. George Norris Green, writing about the period from 1938 to 1957, postulated that since 1939, "Texas has been governed by conservatives, collectively dubbed **the Establishment.**"[27] The Texas Establishment was a "loosely knit plutocracy comprised mostly of Anglo businessmen, oilmen, bankers and lawyers" that emerged in the late 1930s, in part, as a response to the liberal policies of the New Deal.[28] They were extremely conservative, producing a "virulent" strain of conservatism marked by "Texanism" and "super-Americanism."[29]

The "traditionalistic-individualistic" political culture was especially conducive to the dominance of the conservative establishment, which had little interest in the needs of the lower socioeconomic groups within the state. The exclusion of minorities from participation in elections and low rates of voter turnout resulted in the election of public officials who were sympathetic to the views of the conservative elites. And public opinion was manipulated by "unprincipled public relations men" and "the rise of reactionary newspapers."[30]

In a more recent study of Texas politics, Chandler Davidson argues that there is a group of Texans, extraordinarily wealthy or linked to large corporations, who constitute "an upper class in the precise meaning of the term: a social group whose common background and effective control of wealth bring them together politically."[31] While warning against a hasty conclusion that an upper class is a ruling class, Davidson uses many of the methodological tools of the elitists to identify Texans with great personal and institutional resources. Resources are primarily economic, but the analysis includes generalizations about shared values, group cohesiveness and interlocking relationships.[32] Nevertheless, the upper class has enormous political power. When united on specific policy objectives, its members usually have prevailed against "their liberal enemies concentrated in the working class."[33] Moreover, the institutional arrangements of the state's economic and political structure work to produce upper class unity that contributes to their successes in public policy.[34]

As might be expected, the sharply contrasting views of political power in Texas have produced an ongoing debate. To a large extent, the issue of who really rules has not been resolved because of insufficient data to support one position over the other. There also is evidence suggesting that power relationships change over time. Historically, Texas government and public policy were dominated by an "upper class" or a conservative "Establishment." But with the enormous social and economic changes that have taken place over the past 20 years, we may well be moving from an elitist system to some variation of pluralism.

## HYPERPLURALISM, POLICY SUBSYSTEMS, AND SINGLE-ISSUE INTEREST GROUPS

Some would argue that the rapid expansion of interest groups in Texas and the nation has produced a system of **hyperpluralism**. In effect, hyperpluralism is the interest group system out of control.[35] Historically, political stability was achieved by competition and bargaining among interest groups. Public policy was developed that had some degree of coherence and reflected shared views of the general interest.

But as groups proliferate, there is a potential for the policy process to degenerate into a series of subsystems. This problem has been compounded by the notion that the demands of all interest groups are legitimate and governments should attempt to respond to as many groups as possible. This theory of interest group liberalism is developed at length by Theodore Lowi in *The End of Liberalism*.[36]

Governments respond to the demands of various groups by enacting laws and regulations or appropriating funds for specific purposes. In many cases, additional agencies may be created within the executive branch of government to carry out the new laws or policies. Legislative committees and subcommittees also may be given oversight authority over new programs. Eventually, the interactions among the interest groups, the administrative agencies and the legislative committees produce permanent relationships that have been described as the **iron triangles of government** (see Chapter 13).

Lowi's concerns about the excesses of pluralism may be valid. There are state agencies such as the Funeral Services Commission, the Texas Board of Examiners in the Fitting and Dispensing of Hearing Aids, and the Natural Fibers and Food Protein Commission, to name but a few, which are very closely tied to the groups or industries they regulate. In some cases, an interest group will even lobby for a dedicated source of funding for its programs, thus assuring it will benefit from a specific tax or taxes year after year, regardless of other state needs.

Hyperpluralism can lead to deadlock. As each group expands its demands on government, there is a high probability that some interests or groups will be neglected. Established groups with significant financial and organizational resources are able to block changes in public policies that would adversely affect them. This can serve to almost immobilize government and maintain the status quo, despite pressing needs for change.

In recent years, a number of scholars have identified another threat to the stability of the political system—**single-issue groups**. These are highly ideological groups that attempt to push on the public agenda a single issue or cause without regard for the views or attitudes of other groups. These groups often are reluctant to compromise and often engage in tactics and strategies designed to extract concessions upon threat of policy deadlock. The National Rifle Association, for example, is single-minded in its opposition to any efforts to regulate or control guns. Some of the groups involved in the abortion issue also demonstrate similar characteristics. Their definition of an issue leaves no grounds for accommodation or compromise.

## RESOURCES OF INTEREST GROUPS

Some interest groups, of course, are extremely powerful and exercise considerable influence over the formation of public policy, while others are ineffectual and weak. The differences can be explained by a number of factors.

One is the size of a group, the number of members and voters it can potentially influence. There are numerous teachers and educational groups within the state, for example, representing a significant number of individuals. The promise of support or the threat of retaliation by such groups will be assessed by a legislator as he or she decides to support or oppose the groups' policy proposals. As will be discussed later in this chapter, individual educational groups don't always agree on legislation, but their numbers are difficult to ignore. Teachers who had been instrumental in the 1982 election of Governor Mark White withdrew that support in 1986 in dispute over some of White's education reform steps, and the loss of that support contributed to his defeat.

The size of a group alone, however, does not guarantee power or influence. A large group internally divided with no clear policy focus is less likely to be successful than a smaller group with a fixed goal. Major factors in a group's success are its cohesiveness and the ability of its leaders to mobilize its membership in support of stated policy objectives.

Another key factor is the distribution of a group's membership across the state. A group concentrated in one geographic area has less potential impact on the election of a large number of legislators than does a group with members distributed across the state. Organized labor, long maligned in Texas politics, has its greatest strength in the Houston-Beaumont areas. On the other hand, teachers and trial lawyers are plentiful throughout the state and have the potential to affect more local and district elections.

A group's power also is determined by its economic resources, or wealth. Groups that represent low-income people have critical problems in raising the dollars necessary to mount effective lobbying campaigns or to support political candidates of their choosing. By contrast, organizations representing large corporations or high-income professional groups are in a much better position to solicit and collect funds and purchase access to policymakers with major campaign contributions and lobbying expenditures.

A group's influence is also affected by its reputation. A major function of interest groups is to provide information to policymakers, and the reliability and accuracy of this information are critical. If a group lies, unduly distorts information, or is less than forthright in its dealings with other actors in the policymaking process, its reputation can be irreparably damaged.[37]

The leadership of a group and its permanent staff also contribute to its success. Leadership styles vary, and successful leadership is "situational."[38] As policy issues develop, a competent staff will conduct research, provide position papers, draft specific proposals, contact key decision-makers and the press, maintain communication with the membership, and develop public relations strategies to mobilize the membership to bring pressure on policymakers.

## THE DOMINANT INTEREST GROUPS IN TEXAS

Throughout much of this century, state government was dominated by the large corporations and banks, the oil companies and the agricultural interests that backed the conservative Democratic officeholders who had a stranglehold on the legislature, the courts and the executive branch.[39] Big business still carries a lot of weight in Austin and can purchase a lot of influence with major political contributions. That's why, for example, Lt. Governor Bob Bullock enlisted the lobby's help in getting the 1991 tax bill passed. And state officials who want to build public support for new policy proposals usually solicit the support of the business community first.

But beginning in the 1970s, influence began to be more diffused. The trial lawyers became active political players and contributors. The emergence of single-member districts (see Chapter 8), which increased the numbers of minorities, Republicans and liberal Democrats elected to the legislature and helped break the conservative Democratic lease on the statehouse, increased the influence of consumer, environmental and other public advocacy groups. And organized labor, which had been shut out by the corporate establishment, found some common interests with the trial lawyers and the consumer groups and attempted to open some doors. The decline of oil and gas production and the emergence of high-tech service industries as major contributors to the state's economy also served to diffuse the business lobby into more competing factions.

Two studies, conducted more than 20 years apart, placed Texas among states with strong pressure group systems.[40] Powerful pressure groups usually evolve in states with weak political parties, which characterized Texas during most of this century.[41] During the many years that Texas was classified as a one-party state, the Republican party posed no serious challenge to the Democratic monopoly, and the Democratic party was marked by intense factionalism. Although the conservative Democratic wing generally dominated state politics through the 1970s, interest groups often played a greater role in the policymaking process than did the party. Subsequent Republican growth has changed Texas' party system (see Chapter 6), but interest groups remain strong in the state and, for practical purposes, comprise a "fourth branch" of state government.

### Business

The diverse business interests in Texas organize in three basic ways to influence the policymaking process. There are a number of broad-based associations that represent business and industry in general. These include the Texas Association of Business, the Texas Chamber of Commerce, and the Texas Association of Taxpayers. Their overall goal is to maintain and improve upon a favorable business climate. In recent years, these groups have spent a lot of time and money fighting trial lawyers on business liability and so-called "tort reform" issues (see below). They also have worked to reform the state's business tax structure but have not reached agreement on the need or advisability of a state income tax.

The business community also organizes through trade associations that represent and seek to advance the interests of specific industries. Some of the more visible and active associations are the Texas Bankers Association, the Wholesale Beer Distributors of Texas, the Texas Motor Transportation Association, the Texas Independent Producers & Royalty Owners Association, the Texas Chemical Council, the Texas Automobile Dealers Association, the Texas Restaurant Association, the Association of Fire & Casualty Companies in Texas, and the Associated General Contractors of Texas. The contractors' group has two branches, including one to which most highway contractors belong. Many highway contractors also belong to the Texas Good Roads/Transportation Association, which lobbies for highway construction funding. This group, which is quite effective in Austin, also includes representatives of other businesses and individuals interested in the maintenance of a strong highway network.

As a third option, many individual companies retain their own lobbyists to represent them before the legislature and administrative agencies. A lobbyist may be a salaried employee of the company he or she represents or may be a professional, freelance lobbyist, or "hired gun," who is retained by several clients. Some wealthy individuals, such as billionaire computer magnate Ross Perot of Dallas, even hire their own lobbyists.

Although most business groups band together against organized labor, consumer advocates and trial lawyers on major political and philosophical issues (such as how to compensate injured workers or how much liability should be imposed on a manufacturer or a retailer when a faulty product injures someone), the business lobby is far from monolithic. The free enterprise system has seen to that. There are numerous issues on which different business groups or trade associations differ. In 1991, for example, the Texas Association of Taxpayers, which includes executives of some of the largest corporations doing business in Texas, became the first business group to openly endorse a state income tax as a means of replacing the inequitable corporate franchise tax and reducing property taxes. But the Texas Association of Business came out against an income tax because, the group feared, it would encourage excessive state spending. And, of course, there are issues on which competing businesses within the same industry line up on opposite sides, sometimes to the extent of major, open warfare. A "full lobby employment" fight occurred in 1987 in a hotly contested dispute between AT&T and its competitors over legislation affecting the regulation of long distance telephone service within Texas. About 20 "hired guns," including a former land commissioner, a former House speaker, and several other former legislators, were hired by the various phone companies in an intense lobbying effort that cost an estimated $2 million to $3 million.[42]

For many years, the interest groups associated with oil and natural gas played a dominant role among the business and industry lobbies. At one time, oil and gas accounted for 30 percent of the state's economic output. But in recent years, this contribution has declined to approximately 15 percent, and the oil and gas lobby, though still effective, now has to work with political leaders who are focused on economic diversification.

Other sources of traditional political power in Texas—the banking, savings and loan, and real estate industries—also were at the center of Texas' collapsed economy in the 1980s. And longtime consumer discontent with the insurance industry found a heroine in Governor Ann Richards, who took office in 1991 with a vow to toughen the state's regulation of insurance. That doesn't mean that lobbyists for those groups have found the doors of influence and power slammed in their faces in Austin. Quite the contrary. But, stung by the recession, activist trial lawyers and a heightened public interest in consumerism and environmental protection, business in general has frequently found itself in a troubled political posture in recent years.

Despite these changes, political consultant George Christian reported that most legislation hostile to general business interests was either defeated or "watered down" by lawmakers in 1991. Business, however, lost major battles on priority legislation that it supported in its continuing war against the trial lawyers.[43]

## Trial Lawyers

Trial, or plaintiffs', lawyers make their livings representing injured persons in lawsuits against defendants believed to be responsible, or liable, for the injuries. They are compensated with a share of the damages awarded their clients by a court or negotiated in a settlement with the defendant or his insurance company. A defendant can be a doctor accused of malpractice in the handling of an individual's care, a manufacturer accused of making a faulty product that caused an injury, a city whose truck was involved in an auto accident, an employer whose worker suffered an injury on the job, or just about any legal entity deemed responsible for causing harm to someone. Trial lawyers, individually and through their political action committee, Lawyers Involved for Texas, or LIFT, have contributed millions of dollars to judicial, legislative, and other selected candidates since the 1970s, when they became a major political factor in Texas. In the early 1980s, they succeeded in electing several Texas Supreme Court justices who shared their viewpoint, and the court issued major, precedent-setting opinions making it easier for plaintiffs to win large damage awards. The business and medical community retaliated by boosting their own political contributions and lobbying effort and, by 1990, had succeeded in tipping the Supreme Court's philosophical scale back to its traditional business-oriented viewpoint (see Chapter 11).

But the war over tort law, as it is called, continues to rage, and one of the fronts is in the legislature. While the business lobby does well in the more conservative House, trial lawyers have had the upper hand in the Senate in recent years, thanks to Senate rules that allow one-third of its members, or only 11 senators, to block any piece of legislation. And since the trial lawyers now are primarily playing defense against business efforts to change liability laws to make it more difficult for plaintiffs to sue or win large judgments, they have concentrated on killing House-passed bills in the Senate. The business lobby in 1987 won some tort changes and in 1989, with the strong backing of Governor Bill Clements, got a law passed to overhaul the state's system for compensating workers injured on the job. But it took a regular legislative session and two special sessions before sponsors of the workers' compensation changes succeeded in breaking the trial lawyers' bloc in the Senate.

The trial lawyers lost several legislative races in 1990, including their effort to unseat veteran Democratic Senator Chet Brooks of Pasadena, one of three key senators who had broken ranks with them over workers' compensation. But they retained a strong Senate bloc against business the following year. George Christian, a consultant for the business side of the tort war, indicated that the 1991 regular session was probably the best the Texas Trial Lawyers Association (TTLA) had ever had, thanks not only to the restrictive Senate rules but also to the Senate Economic Development Committee, which fatally stalled action on several business-backed bills approved by the House. Significantly, the economic development panel was chaired by a trial lawyer, Senator Temple Dickson, a Democrat from Sweetwater. "Since it nearly always plays defense, TTLA puts business in the position of laying siege to an almost impregnable castle," Christian wrote in a session post-mortem for the Texas Chamber of Commerce.[44]

The trial lawyer bloc in the Senate, however, was threatened by a redistricting plan ordered by a federal court that jeopardized the re-election prospects of some incumbent Democrats in 1992 and increased the likelihood of more business-oriented Republicans being elected to the Senate.

## Education

In the past several years, educational interests have been very visible in the policymaking process in Austin, and higher education lobbying has been particularly effective. The changing global economy has enhanced the role of higher education in developing the state's future. Most parents—and there are many in the legislature—see the futures of their own children tied to educational progress. Even though detractors periodically accuse state-supported universities and medical schools of extravagantly spending non-tax revenue on entertainment and office furnishings, most legislators are reluctant to cut tax dollars to the schools and be branded as antieducation.

Most university regents, chancellors, and presidents also are well-connected politically. And they have the capability—through the use of donations and other non-tax funds—to hire a well-paid cadre of legislative liaisons. Officially, they are called vice chancellors for governmental relations or vice chancellors for state affairs or special assistants, not lobbyists, because technically it is illegal for officials on the state payroll to try to influence legislation. But these are lobbyists. They provide information to legislators on pending issues affecting their employers and have entertained lawmakers with lunches, dinners and rounds of golf. Non-tax funds are used to supplement their salaries and expense accounts. In 1991, the *Fort Worth Star-Telegram* counted at least 22 legislative liaisons on university payrolls with salaries and expenses from September 1990 through July 1991 exceeding $1.6 million. Four of the liaisons were paid more than the governor's $93,532 salary that year.[45]

Another effective lobbying source for universities, particularly the larger ones, are the armies of alumni, many of them politically influential, ready to make phone calls or write letters on behalf of their alma maters when the need arises. The business community also is a strong supporter of higher education.

Meanwhile, the struggle for equity and equality in public elementary and secondary education in Texas, which remained a major issue in the 1990s, has been complicated by more than two dozen groups representing various—and often conflicting—interests within the educational community. There are at least four different teachers associations, one for school boards, a separate lobby group for school administrators, and still others for elementary school principals and secondary school principals. Separate groups also have been formed for urban school districts, suburban districts, rural districts, and districts with large numbers of special needs students. Many of the associations are well-financed, and some indirectly receive taxpayer money through dues paid by member school districts. Virtually all the groups have paid lobbyists, and while all claim to support educational quality, their primary goals are to protect the specific interests of their members.

"Obviously, from time to time there are going to be differences," Johnny Veselka, executive director of the Texas Association of School Administrators, told the *Houston Chronicle*. "Obviously, there are some issues that are management oriented. In those instances, it might become management versus labor. We might not agree with teachers."[46] Legislators often found themselves in the middle of warring factions, and some lawmakers reacted angrily during the difficult deliberations over school finance reform. "I have had it up to here with these special interest groups operating at taxpayer expense, sending hundreds of lobbyists to Austin," said Senator Carl Parker, a Port Arthur Democrat who chaired the Senate Education Committee. "They're not looking out for the children of Texas, not one bit. They're looking out for their little wasteful, personal bailiwick."[47]

## Public Interest Groups

Most of the **public interest groups** represented in Austin are concerned primarily with protecting consumers and the environment from big business, promoting stronger ethical standards for public officials, and increasing funding for health and human services programs for the poor, the elderly, the young, and the disabled. Many have full-time lobbyists, but grass-roots, volunteer efforts are crucial to their success. Among the most active are Common Cause, the Sierra Club, Consumers

Union, the Texas Consumers Association, the Gray Panthers, the Children's Defense Fund, Americans Disabled for Attendant Programs Today (or ADAPT), and Public Citizen, a Texas affiliate of the national public interest group founded by consumer advocate Ralph Nader. People First is an umbrella organization of groups seeking more health and human services funding from the legislature, which spends less than most other states on such programs. Although public interest lobbyists concentrate most of their attention on the legislature, some consumer groups also are active before state regulatory agencies, particularly the Public Utility Commission, which sets telephone and electric rates for millions of Texans.

Among the more militant groups is ADAPT, which staged two highly visible demonstrations by wheelchair-bound Texans during 1991—an overnight occupation of the governor's reception room and a wheelchair parade up Congress Avenue to the Capitol—to demand more money for community-based facilities and attendant services for the disabled.[48]

Tom "Smitty" Smith, longtime director of Public Citizen's Texas office, operated on a shoestring budget that allowed him to pay only one additional staffer—a part-time clerk. He had no money for entertaining lawmakers—"I've been taken to lunch by legislators five times as much as they have taken me." And he had no political action committee through which to funnel campaign contributions to legislative candidates. But he believed he and a cadre of mostly young volunteers were getting their message across and the legislature was becoming more responsive to consumer and environmental concerns. He concluded, "Maybe it's because the public is becoming more articulate."[49]

But most public interest advocates, like almost everyone else who enjoys any lobbying success, practice the art of compromise, sometimes to the point of swallowing a pretty big pill.

The Sierra Club supported both Governor Ann Richards and Lt. Governor Bob Bullock in the 1990 political races, and both Democrats ran on strong environmental platforms. But right after taking office, Bullock appointed Senator Bill Sims, a conservative Democrat from San Angelo who was viewed as environmentally insensitive, to chair the key Senate Natural Resources Committee. And Richards named her biggest campaign contributor, Walter Umphrey, a Beaumont attorney and stockholder in a hazardous waste disposal company with a poor environmental record, to the Parks and Wildlife Commission (see Chapter 9). The Sierra Club and other environmentalists only mildly protested both appointments. No one representing any environmental group testified against Umphrey at his Senate confirmation hearing. Had the appointment been made by Richards' Republican predecessor, Bill Clements, environmentalists likely would have been lined up two or three deep to testify against him. In this case, environmentalists chose not to embarrass their choice for governor—or embarrass themselves over her first choice for an environmentally sensitive position, after their support obviously had taken a back seat to a major campaign contributor.

## Minorities

The advent of single-member, urban legislative districts in the 1970s significantly increased the number of African-American and Hispanic lawmakers and strengthened the influence of minority interest groups. These groups often have found that the courthouse can still be a shorter route to success than the statehouse, but the legislature has become more and more attentive to their voices.

The League of United Latin American Citizens (or LULAC) and the Mexican American Legal Defense and Educational Fund (MALDEF) are two of the better known Hispanic organizations, while the National Association for the Advancement of Colored People (NAACP) is a leader in promoting and protecting the interests of African-Americans. In recent years, the Industrial Areas Foundation, a collection of well-organized, church-supported community groups, also has become a strong and effective voice for low-income minorities. It will be discussed in more detail later in this chapter.

Founded in 1929 to bring Hispanics into the American mainstream, LULAC is the oldest and largest Hispanic organization in the United States and continues to be particularly influential in such causes as education and election reform in Texas. It was a plaintiff in a major federal lawsuit to replace the countywide system of electing state trial judges in the largest Texas cities with single-member districts so as to boost the election of minorities to the bench (see Chapter 11).

By the late 1980s, however, some older members had begun to feel that the organization was becoming too much a part of the establishment and was losing the fire that had won major victories in the past. "With 6,000 councils worldwide, LULAC now looks and acts like a corporation. LULAC is slick, polished and professional. LULAC members seeking national office, for example, videotaped campaign speeches and sponsored receptions with open bars," wrote *Dallas Morning News* reporter Gilbert Bailon in describing LULAC's 1988 national convention in Dallas. And former LULAC national president Tony Bonilla, an attorney from Corpus Christi, didn't particularly like what he saw. "Our interest now is self-promotion and self-interest rather than service for the economically distressed. There has been no call to battle," he said. The group's political influence, however, was convincingly demonstrated by the fact that three presidential candidates, including George Bush, addressed the same convention, which was held only a few weeks before the national Democratic and Republican nominating conventions.[50]

More recently, LULAC's ranks also have been wracked by bitter dissension over its national leadership. In 1990, Las Vegas businessman Jose Velez, whose lineage is Nicaraguan and Puerto Rican, became the first non-Mexican-American elected to LULAC's top office. He won with the help of newly admitted chapters, or councils, from northern California that were largely Filipino-American, the first predominantly non-Hispanic chapters ever admitted to LULAC. Longtime LULAC member Sylvia Hernandez Maddox of Austin told the *Austin American-Statesman* soon after Velez's election that the new president's style was "unsettling to those of us who have devoted most of our lives to the cause of LULAC: fighting discrimination and promoting educational opportunities. The impression that is left is that Velez does not share the same deep concerns for those traditional Hispanic issues that we Mexicanos in Texas have."[51]

The Mexican American Legal Defense and Educational Fund, which was formed in San Antonio in 1968, fights in the courtroom for the civil rights of Hispanics. In its first case, MALDEF challenged the method of selecting grand juries in South Texas, where Hispanics were excluded from the process. It also has fought numerous battles over the drawing of political boundaries for governmental bodies but is probably best known for its success in the lengthy litigation over public school finance. MALDEF represented the property poor school districts who were plaintiffs in the *Edgewood* v. *Kirby* case that won a unanimous, landmark Texas Supreme Court order in 1989 for a more equitable distribution of education aid between rich and poor districts and legislative attempts to overhaul the school finance system (see Chapter 13).

The National Association for the Advancement of Colored People has worked hard to increase employment opportunities for African-Americans with state agencies, particularly in higher paying administrative jobs. In the late 1980s, it filed job discrimination complaints with the federal government against the State Department of Highways and Public Transportation and the Department of Public Safety, two of state government's worst offenders in minority hiring and promotion practices. Publicity and pressure generated by the NAACP doubtlessly contributed to the DPS decision in 1988 to promote the first African-American trooper, at least in this century, to the elite Texas Rangers crime-fighting force. Lee Roy Young, Jr., a 14-year DPS veteran, became a Ranger on Sept. 1. A second African-American Ranger, Earl Ray Pearson, was named the next year. The DPS also began work on a new affirmative action plan and developed racial sensitivity training.

Responding to the NAACP's concerns, a federal transportation investigator ruled in 1991 that the highway department discriminated against minorities and women in hiring and promotion practices and threatened to withhold $900 million in federal highway funds if improvements weren't made. The highway department soon announced major policy changes, including a decision to consider—for the first time in its 74-year history—applicants from outside the agency for top-level administrative posts. It also promised to step up efforts to recruit minorities and award highway contracts to minority-owned businesses. The department also appointed the first African-American, Edwin M. Sims, an 11-year veteran of the agency, to a high level administrative position, director of the occupational safety division.

After Governor Ann Richards took office in 1991, promising to open up a "New Texas" to more opportunities for minorities in state government, Gary Bledsoe, president of the NAACP's Austin branch, wrote to her to complain of the Alcoholic Beverage Commission's failure to hire many African-Americans. Bledsoe accused the agency of harboring a "bubba kind of mentality."[52] Richards asked the agency, which also had a shortage of female employees, to submit to her a revised affirmative action program to correct the deficiencies. Later in the year, the longtime head of the agency unexpectedly announced his retirement amid allegations of unfair commission treatment of minority businesses and sexual harassment of female employees of the agency.

## Labor

Organized labor traditionally has taken a back seat to business in Texas, a strong "right-to-work" state in which union membership can't be required as a condition of employment. Antilabor sentiment ran particularly high in the 1940s and 1950s at the height of the conservative Democratic establishment's control of Texas politics, and labor-baiting campaigns in which unions were portrayed as evil, communist sympathizers were not uncommon then.[53] There are pockets of strong labor influence in Texas, including the southeast part of the state, where thousands of petrochemical workers are unionized. And unions can provide strong grass-roots support for political candidates through endorsement cards, phone banks and other get-out-the-vote efforts. Two of labor's major victories in Texas politics include the election in 1957 of liberal Democrat Ralph Yarborough to the U.S. Senate, where he served for almost 14 years before being unseated by conservative Democrat Lloyd Bentsen, and the defeat of an effort to lock the right-to-work law into the state constitution. The latter cause was a bitter fight that scuttled the Constitutional Convention of 1974. There were more than a majority of legislator-delegates who favored submitting the right-to-work question to the voters, but the convention operated under restrictive rules that required proposals to receive a two-thirds vote. Labor won the fight by a three-vote margin on the last night of the convention.

Before the recession of the 1980s, the Texas AFL-CIO's membership peaked at 300,000 in 1982 under longtime president Harry Hubbard, who retired in 1988 and was succeeded by Joe Gunn. In recent years, labor has generally sided with the trial lawyers on such issues as workers compensation, worker safety, and business liability for faulty products but has been frustrated by strong business support in the legislature, particularly in the House.

Although the Texas AFL-CIO has traditionally endorsed Democratic candidates, its executive committee voted unanimously in 1991 to halt the practice of blanket endorsements and threatened to run labor union members as independent candidates against Democrats who refuse to support labor on key issues. "Too many Democrats are trying to out-Republican Republicans. There's a long list of people who have been disappointing us," AFL-CIO spokesman Christopher Cook said.[54]

## Governmental Lobbyists

Since local governments are significantly affected by state laws and budgetary decisions, counties, cities, prosecutors, metropolitan transit authorities, and various special districts are represented by lobbyists in Austin. The stakes are particularly high now. Most governments are finding revenue harder to raise, particularly with the federal government passing the cost of numerous programs to the states, and the state issuing similar mandates to local governments.

Many local governments belong to umbrella organizations such as the Texas Municipal League, the Texas Association of Counties, and the Texas County and District Attorneys Association, which have full-time lobbyists. Several of the larger cities and counties also retain their own lobbyists, and mayors, city council members and county judges frequently come to Austin to visit with legislators and testify for or against bills. Some legislators complain that Houston and Harris County, the state's largest city and county, take up a disproportionate amount of the legislature's time with perennial fights over fire and police civil service regulations, mass transportation, and other local issues. Some have jokingly referred to the House Intergovernmental Affairs Committee as the "Houston Committee." One reason Houston and Harris County dominate so much of the legislature's time is because political unanimity is seldom achieved among Harris County's large, diverse legislative delegation. Another reason is restrictive state laws, such as those governing fire and police civil service, that may better be left to local discretion.

## Agricultural Groups

Although Texas is now predominantly urban, agriculture is still an important part of the state's economy, and a number of agricultural groups are represented in Austin. Their influence obviously is strongest among rural legislators. But the Texas Farm Bureau, the largest such group and probably the most conservative, was instrumental in the 1990 election defeat of liberal Democratic Agriculture Commissioner Jim Hightower, who had angered many agricultural producers and the chemical industry with tough stands on farm worker rights and pesticide regulation.

Other producer groups include the Texas and Southwestern Cattle Raisers Association, the Texas Nurseryman's Association, and the Texas Corn Producers Board. Populist-oriented groups like the Texas Farmers Union and the American Agriculture Movement were active in the state during the recession-plagued 1980s.

The United Farm Workers Union has been a strong advocate of better conditions for workers and has frequently been at odds with agricultural producers. Represented in court by the Texas Civil Liberties Union and Texas Rural Legal Aid attorneys, farm workers won major lawsuits and legislation in the 1980s on such issues as unemployment compensation, picketing rights, the right to be informed about dangerous pesticides in use in fields, and a higher minimum wage.

## Professional Groups

There are a number of professional groups in addition to trial lawyers with lobbyists in Austin. Several communications organizations, such as the Texas Daily Newspaper Association and the Texas Association of Broadcasters, are interested not only in open meetings and open records laws and other freedom of information developments, but also in tax laws affecting their industries. Several communications groups have formed Texas Media, which monitors freedom of information issues specifically.

One of the better known professional organizations is the Texas Medical Association, which in recent years has joined forces with business against the trial lawyers in support of tort reform and other limitations on malpractice suits and other damage claims against physicians. The TMA's political action committee is a major contributor of campaign dollars to candidates for the legislature and other state offices.

## Religious Groups

Political scientists often place religious groups on the fringe of the interest group system, and many people, influenced in part by their theological beliefs and their views of separation of church and state, think religious groups have little or no legitimate role to play in the political process. Nevertheless, religious groups have helped influence policy in Texas, and the abortion issue plus a series of social and economic issues have increased the presence of religious groups in Austin.

A number of religious groups have emerged since the 1940s with an identifiable right wing orientation. Many organizations in the 1940s and 1950s combined Christian rhetoric and symbols with anti-communism, anti-labor, anti-civil rights, anti-liberal or anti-New Deal themes. While these groups were often very small, they were linked to the extreme right-wing of the Texas establishment, and they were the precursors to many of the right-wing ideological groups that have emerged in American politics in the past 20 years.[55] Many of these organizations have gravitated toward the Republican party.[56] And many of the individuals who have been involved in the rancorous theological and policy debates of the Southern Baptist Convention have been linked to national right-wing political movements.

Many religious denominations have boards or commissions that are responsible for monitoring governmental action. While staff members or volunteers serving in this capacity may not register as lobbyists, they function much like lobbyists. There are select issues that impact specific religious groups, and legislators usually are aware of the positions taken by church groups on these issues.

One well-known religious interest group is the Christian Life Commission of the Baptist General Convention of Texas, which is a strong advocate of human services programs but also lobbies against gambling proposals, including the recent creation of the state lottery.

Churches across the state, particularly the Catholic church, whose policies on social action have been shaped by papal encyclicals and Vatican II, have formed community-based organizations to address the social and economic needs of the poor. In many regards, this is a redefinition of the social gospel, a church-based political movement of the late 19th and early 20th centuries.

The Industrial Areas Foundation—with its member community groups—has steadily grown in influence since making its first appearance in Texas in the mid-1970s. IAF is a non-profit, New York-based organization whose local groups draw financial and lobbying support from churches in their communities. Members are unsophisticated, poor people, but they are persistent and difficult to ignore when they arrive by the busload at the Capitol, intent on winning passage of a program important to them. Their best-known groups are Valley Interfaith in South Texas; Communities Organized for Public Service, or COPS, in San Antonio; and The Metropolitan Organization, or TMO, in Houston.

The first IAF chapter in Texas, San Antonio's COPS, quickly developed a reputation for being confrontational and raucous in demanding better drainage facilities and other capital improvements for the city's impoverished neighborhoods. COPS members would gang up on a city council member, surround him and scream their demands, refusing to take "no" or "maybe" for an answer. After being successful at the local level, IAF didn't entirely lose its confrontational spirit when it expanded its efforts to the statewide arena in the 1980s. But it began to mature politically and develop influential friends in high places—including Democratic Governors Mark White and Ann Richards and Lt. Governors Bill Hobby and Bob Bullock—as it joined other groups in lobbying for a health care plan for the poor and more equity in school finance. IAF, particularly Valley Interfaith, also was instrumental in 1989 in winning approval of $100 million in bonds to bring water and sewer service to some of the "colonias," the unincorporated slums where thousands of poor people live along the Texas-Mexico border. Two years later, the legislature and Texas voters authorized the Texas Water Development Board to increase that allotment.

IAF lobbies for tangible improvements in facilities and services for the poor and doesn't do battle for broader liberal issues like civil rights or putting an end to police brutality. "When we meet with ordinary people in their homes, they are more concerned with crime in the neighborhood and the safety and education of their kids, than they are with police brutality," IAF organizer Ernie Cortes told *Texas Monthly* writer Gary Cartwright. To remain successful, organizers also have to produce visible victories. "A new storm sewer or a paved street is an advance that can be measured, as is an air-conditioned school or a health clinic. The result of Cortes' pragmatic approach is that he takes people who feel that they have no stake in politics and makes them a part of the system," Cartwright wrote.[57]

## WHO ARE THE LOBBYISTS?

During the 1991 regular session of the Texas Legislature, more than 850 individuals representing hundreds of businesses, trade associations, and other interests registered as lobbyists with the secretary of state. (Under an ethics reform law enacted that year, they now register with the new Texas Ethics Commission.) They ran the gamut from well-dressed corporate lobbyists with cellular telephones and generous expense accounts to volunteer consumer and environmental advocates in blue jeans and sneakers. Most were male, although the number of women lobbyists has increased in recent years, and many women now hold major lobbying positions. About 170 of the lobbyists registered in 1991 were women. Most lobbyists came to their career by way of other occupations and jobs, but they have, on the whole, an acute understanding of the policymaking process and the points of access and influence in that process. The most successful lobbyists have developed the ability to pursue a wide range of tactics based on a comprehensive strategy.

At least 60 of the lobbyists registered in 1991 were former legislators, including Ben Barnes, a former lieutenant governor and speaker of the House, and former speakers Bill Clayton, Rayford Price, and Byron Tunnell. These individuals bring to the process their legislative skills, personal relationships with former legislative colleagues, and expertise in substantive policy areas. A number of other lobbyists were former legislative staffers.

Many of the trade and professional associations, labor unions, and public interest groups have full-time staffs in Austin who function as their lobbyists. Many corporations also use their own employees to lobby in Austin. Some companies have governmental affairs departments or offices staffed by employees with experience in government or public affairs. In large corporations that do business across the country, the governmental affairs staffs may be rather large because such companies will attempt to follow the actions of numerous state legislatures, city councils, and the U.S. Congress.

A number of lawyers have developed very successful lobby practices. Some of these professional freelancers, or "hired guns," specialize in specific policy areas, while others represent a wide array of clients. Some may be identified as "super lobbyists" because of their ability to exercise considerable influence in the policymaking process. Many work for the state's largest law firms, which have established permanent offices in Austin. Some of the top-notch freelancers aren't attorneys, but they have a strong knowledge of the governmental process.

There also are some public relations firms that offer their services to interest groups. These companies specialize in "image creation" or "image modification."[58] While they may not handle the groups' direct lobbying efforts, they often are retained to assist in indirect lobbying campaigns. They are particularly adroit in developing relationships with the press, developing media campaigns, and assisting in political campaigns.

## INTEREST GROUPS AND THE POLICYMAKING PROCESS

For many people, the term **lobbying** means sleazy characters lurking in the halls of the state Capitol, attempting to bribe legislators with money, sex, or booze (Figure 4-1). And that perception has been reinforced in recent years by numerous published reports of legislators being treated to trips, golf tournaments, and concerts by lobbyists (see chapter 8). While such tactics are questionable at best, they are only part of the complex relationships between interest groups and policymakers. Lobbying is central to a pluralistic society, and the legal foundations of lobbying activity are found in the U.S. Constitution, which provides for the right to "petition the Government for a redress of grievances."[59]

In the broadest sense, lobbying is "one aspect of the efforts of men, characteristically organized into groups, to influence the making of public policy, wherever it is made..."[60] Most scholars take this view. Lobbying is both indirect and

**FIGURE 4-1**   Cartoon depicting the concerns of some legislators over losing special interest favors to the cause of ethics reform. (©*Houston Chronicle,* reprinted with permission)

direct and includes, but is not limited to, electoral activities, public relations campaigns, protests and demonstrations, and direct contact with policymakers (Table 4-1). According to political scientist Carol Greenwald, "Lobbying may thus be defined as any form of communication, made on another's behalf, and intended to influence a governmental decision."[61]

## Indirect Lobbying

Effective lobbying starts with the election of officeholders supportive of a group's viewpoint on key issues and the building of general public support for a group and its objectives.

*Electoral Activities.* While the electoral activities of interest groups are similar to those of political parties, there are some significant differences. Political parties are broad coalitions of voters concerned with a wide range of issues, while most interest groups are focused on only a limited set of issues. Parties function not only to contest elections but to govern once elected. Interest groups primarily are concerned with influencing and shaping policies that directly affect them, while leaving the day-to-day management of government to political parties. Most interest groups also cross party lines in supporting candidates.

**TABLE 4-1**  Techniques of Exercising Influence in the Policy-Making Process

1. Testifying at hearings
2. Contacting government officials directly to present organization's point of view
3. Engaging in informal contacts with legislators and other officials—at conventions, over lunch and so on
4. Presenting research results or technical information
5. Sending letters to members of the organization to inform them about organizational activities
6. Entering into coalitions with other organizations
7. Making media contacts
8. Consulting with government officials to plan legislative strategy
9. Helping to draft legislation
10. Inspiring letter writing or telegram campaigns
11. Mounting grass roots lobbying efforts
12. Having influential constituents contact their representatives' office
13. Helping draft regulations, rules, or guidelines
14. Serving on advisory commissions and boards
15. Alerting legislators to the effects of a bill on their districts
16. Filing suit or otherwise engaging in litigation
17. Making financial contributions to political candidates
18. Doing favors for officials who need assistance
19. Attempting to influence appointments to public office
20. Publicizing candidates' voting records
21. Engaging in direct-mail fund raising for the organization
22. Running advertisements in the media about organization's position on issues
23. Contributing work or personnel to electoral campaigns
24. Making public endorsements of candidates for office
25. Engaging in protests or demonstrations

Source: Table adapted from *Organized Interests and American Democracy* by Kay Lehman Scholzman and John T. Tierney. Copyright @ 1986 by Kay Lehman Schlozman and John T. Tierney. Reprinted by permission of HarperCollins Publishers.

Interest groups must decide which candidates they will back through campaign contributions, organizational support and public endorsements. Most groups are not interested in political ideology or philosophy but primarily are concerned with electing their "friends" and defeating their "enemies."

Most interest groups generally don't give money to a large number of legislative candidates but spend their money selectively, targeting those legislators who serve on the committees that have jurisdiction over their industry or areas of concern. (See the discussion of the "iron triangles" of government earlier in this chapter and in Chapter 13.) The Texas Legislature's highly centralized leadership also encourages groups to concentrate their resources on a small number of key lawmakers. According to an analysis by the *Houston Post*, special interest contributions accounted for an average 66.5 percent of the campaign donations to House committee chairmen in 1990 and 57.6 percent of the contributions to Senate committee chairs. Seven House chairmen received more than 80 percent of their campaign funds from special interest groups.[62]

In some cases, interest groups will use promises of financial campaign support to recruit opponents for incumbent legislators who consistently vote the "wrong" way. In other instances, incumbents and potential challengers will approach an interest group for support. Although the process has become a permanent fixture of contemporary elections, it still often presents an unsavory image of a mutual shakedown. While a candidate cannot legally promise a specific vote for financial or other campaign support, an interest group will make every effort to assure that a potential recipient of campaign contributions is "sympathetic" and will be "accessible" to the group.

Under state and federal laws, interest groups and many corporations are able to form political action committees (or PACs) for raising and distributing campaign funds. Money is contributed to a PAC by individual members of a group or employees of a corporation and then distributed among selected candidates. In most instances, a PAC is managed by the professional staff of the interest group, and the campaign contributions are a key part of the organization's overall lobbying strategy.

Federal campaign finance restrictions and reporting requirements are much more stringent than the state's. Federal law limits individual contributions to $1,000 per candidate for each election and PAC contributions by corporations, labor unions, trade associations, and other organizations to $5,000 per candidate per election. Texas law also prohibits corporations or labor unions from making direct contributions to state and local political candidates, but state law sets no limits on the amount of money a PAC or an individual can give to candidates (see Table 4-2). There have been instances when a PAC has contributed more than $100,000 to a single candidate. Texas' top 50 PACs reported contributing $10 million in 1990 to legislative campaigns alone.[63]

Interest groups also will often provide in-kind support for political candidates. A group may make its phone banks available to a candidate, it may conduct a poll and provide the candidate with the results, or it may provide office space and equipment to a candidate's campaign at reduced cost. Some organizations may even "loan" the services of their staffers to a campaign or provide postage, cars for travel, printing services, and a variety of other in-kind contributions. In many instances, this is done without full public disclosure, a violation of the law.

A group's election strategy often includes candidate endorsements, which can be publicized through newsletters, news releases, press conferences, or conven-

**TABLE 4–2** Major Special Interest Contributions to Ann Richards' Campaign from July through December 1990.*

| | |
|---|---|
| Business and medical | $431,711 |
| Plaintiffs' lawyers | 82,550 |
| Financial groups | 47,500 |
| Organized labor | 46,914 |
| Agricultural | 21,180 |

*These figures include contributions made by identifiable political action committees, law firms, or other businesses (excluding corporations). They do not include donations from Beaumont trial lawyer Walter Umphrey, the single biggest contributor to Richards' campaign. He and his law firm's political action committee contributed or loaned Richards $350,000 (see Chapter 9). But those donations were not made during the period covered here.

Source: Information compiled and published by Reference Guides, Inc., in the *Guide to Statewide Elected Officials.*

tions. Some groups maintain phone banks during election campaigns to systematically inform their members of their endorsements and encourage them to get out and vote for their chosen candidates. Public endorsements often are sought by candidates when a group's size, prestige, and influence are considered valuable, and candidates often will use these endorsements in their advertising campaigns.

*Public Opinion.* Interest groups also may seek to cultivate favorable public opinion about themselves through media campaigns. One objective is to "develop a reservoir of good will in the minds of the citizenry that can be drawn upon when political battles over specific issues occur."[64] While this practice is more pronounced at the national level, state organizations in Texas associated with national interest groups often participate in national campaigns.

Public relations campaigns also are used to mobilize public support for a group's position on a specific issue under consideration by state government.[65] Voters may be encouraged to write, call or "fax" their legislators. The Texas Medical Association, for example, has sought public support for restrictions on medical malpractice awards by distributing cards to physician waiting rooms that attempt to explain how the high cost of malpractice insurance can affect the costs and quality of health care.

In addition to paid advertisements with emotional language and imagery, interest groups will use press conferences and informal media contacts to attempt to plant stories that are favorable to the group's objectives or at least to put their "spin," or viewpoint, on running media coverage of an issue. For years, Texas legislators resisted parimutuel betting and the lottery. But groups supporting those proposals continued to insist that gambling would boost state revenue, and, eventually, they won the fight.

Public interest advocates, who are at the forefront of efforts to reform such governmental activities as utility and insurance regulation, can't match the financial firepower that utilities, insurance companies and other big industries can muster. Their success depends on their ability to stir up public concern—or outrage—over pocketbook issues and the relationships between monied special interests and government. So they avidly work the news media, which is crucial to their ability to spread their message. They seldom can afford paid advertising campaigns, but they hold frequent news conferences, issue a stream of press releases, and readily return reporters' phone calls. They also recognize strength and efficiency in numbers and frequently issue joint statements or hold joint news conferences on issues of mutual concern. During the 1991 regular legislative session, for example, 32 organizations—representing consumer activists, children, the elderly, the disabled and organized labor—banded together against a bill that would have reduced health insurance benefits for many Texans.

*Protests and Marches.* Staged demonstrations against governmental decisions or inaction have long been used by individuals or groups attempting to influence public policy. While many people have mixed feelings about such tactics, protests and marches can be effective in capturing public attention and focusing on a group's issue or problem. Television coverage of such events, in particular, can convey powerful and intense images. The civil rights movement capitalized on this resource, and that movement's success, in large measure, turned on the ability of minority leaders to show the nation that the discriminatory policies practiced by many governments and individuals were incompatible with the values of a democratic society.

In recent years, both antiabortion groups and abortion rights activists in Texas have marched in support of their positions. Animal rights groups have picketed stores that sell fur coats. Gay and lesbian groups have held vigils to protest incidents of "gay bashing," and a variety of groups have used prayer vigils to dramatize their particular issues or concerns. It is not clear what effects these tactics have. But groups that use them often have limited resources and recognize their value in gaining free media attention.

## Direct Lobbying

While interest groups may spend substantial amounts of time and money attempting to elect "friendly" candidates and building public support for their objectives, their work has only begun. The next, crucial step is direct lobbying, or the communication of information and policy preferences directly to policymakers. Lobbying often is associated with legislatures, but it is directed to the other institutions of government as well. Public officials depend on the information provided by interest groups, and many policy initiatives, including proposed legislation, come from lobbyists. The judicial system also is an arena in which interest groups attempt to play a major role, particularly as the courts become more active in formulating policy or forcing policy changes. By initiating test cases, challenging regulations and filing *amicus curiae* briefs in support of litigants, interest groups can use the courts, a pattern evident in Texas, to advance their policy goals.[66]

Lobbyists engage in a wide range of activities. Most groups understand the necessity to pursue their legislative agendas at every conceivable opportunity in the process, and they also realize it usually is easier to block policy initiatives than to enact new policies.[67]

*Drafting Legislation.* Interest groups often will draft specific proposals for formal introduction in the legislature. In any given legislative session, hundreds of bills are drafted by the legal or technical staff of an interest group. The groups usually work closely with legislative sponsors or their staffs in the drafting process, and staffers from the agencies that would be affected by the legislation also may be consulted.

*Planning and Implementing a Legislative Strategy.* At the beginning of this chapter, we summarized the tactics used by legislative leaders in 1991 to break a deadlock over a tax bill. Interest groups, which had a direct stake in the revenue issue, were called upon to ask their constituencies to bring pressure on a large number of legislators in a short period of time.

That lobby blitz may have been more obvious than most, but it was not unusual. Interest groups supporting a bill usually will work closely with the bill's sponsor, committee chairmen, and other legislative leaders at every stage of the process. Strategy will be planned from the introduction of the legislation through committee hearings and then through final action by the House and the Senate. Potential opposition will be assessed and ways of diffusing that opposition and building support for the bill will be mapped out.

*Personal Contacts and Communications.* If one were to ask most interest groups why they contribute to political candidates and what they expected in return, the overwhelming response would be "access." The interest group system revolves around communication and the exchange of ideas and information with policymakers. To have some prospects of success, a group must have access to lawmakers, something that often is no small task to achieve.

With thousands of bills considered during each regular legislative session, interest groups and individuals have to compete with each other for the opportunity to discuss their programs with lawmakers. Interest groups attempt to gain access through various techniques, but they are all fundamentally trying to tell their story in the hope of convincing a majority of legislators to support their policy positions.

Lobbyists are denied direct access to legislators on the floor of the House and the Senate while the bodies are in session, but there are numerous other opportunities for direct or indirect contact. During House and Senate sessions, many lobbyists will wait outside the chambers to catch the ears of legislators who happen to pass by. Or they will have the doormen send messages asking individual lawmakers to step outside the chambers for brief meetings in the lobby. Hence the term, "lobbyists." It is not unusual for several dozen lobbyists to be gathered at one time outside the House or the Senate chamber on the second floor of the Capitol, particularly on days when major bills are being debated. Lobbyists also frequent the House and Senate galleries. In some instances, a lobbyist's presence in the gallery is simply a matter of minor interest or a way to kill some time before a committee meeting, but sometimes special interest groups will pack the gallery in a show of force to threaten recrimination against lawmakers who don't vote their way.

Effective lobbyists, however, do most of their work long before a bill reaches the House or the Senate floor for a vote. They will stop by legislators' offices to present information and solicit support for or against specific legislation. If they can't meet personally with a legislator, they will meet with his or her staff. In many cases, lobbyists will provide lawmakers with written reports, summarizing the highlights of an issue and their position on it. And many interest groups will back up the personal efforts of their lobbyists with letterwriting and telephone campaigns directed at legislators by the groups' members.

Much of the personal lobbying is done away from the Capitol, sometimes far away—over lunch and dinner tables, at cocktail parties, on golf courses, and even on hunting and ski trips. While a great deal of socializing goes on at these lobby-sponsored affairs, they also provide lobbyists with golden opportunities to solidify friendships with lawmakers and make pitches for or against specific legislative proposals. A five- or ten-minute business conversation reinforced with a few hours of social camaraderie can work wonders, as many interest groups and their lobbyists very well know. Such entertainment is expensive—lobbyists have spent well in excess of $1 million during a regular legislative session entertaining lawmakers—and it can easily be used to abuse the policy-setting process. Repeated news accounts of extravagant and often questionable lobby spending finally convinced the legislature in 1991 to ban most lobby-paid trips for lawmakers and to limit lobby expenditures on entertainment to $500 per year per legislator (see Chapter 8).

*Testifying at Hearings.* During any given legislative session, House and Senate committees and subcommittees hold hundreds of hearings on bills which have to win committee approval before they can be considered by the full House and Senate. Interest groups can use committee hearings to formally present information to legislators or to help mobilize public support for or against a particular bill. Testifying at public hearings is often symbolic and secondary to the personal communications with legislators and their staffs (Figure 4-2).

**FIGURE 4-2**  Lobbyists crowd into the Senate chamber for a committee meeting during the 1991 regular legislative session. (Texas Senate Media Services)

*Coalitions of Interest Groups.* In many instances, a group will not have sufficient resources to effectively influence the outcome of a contested issue, or a legislative or regulatory proposal may affect many different groups. So groups sometimes find it advantageous to form coalitions to coordinate their electoral and direct lobbying activities. These coalitions are informal, tenuous, or short-lived, based on current common interests or objectives and a desire to maximize resources and share costs and expenses.[68]

In 1991, some consumer advocates teamed up with the Texas Trial Lawyers Association to defeat products liability legislation—a priority of the business community—that would have made it more difficult for consumers injured by defective products to sue manufacturers and retailers. Because of their large campaign contributions to legislators, the trial lawyers carried most of the clout that killed the bill in the Senate; and their overriding reason for fighting the legislation was a personal financial interest—the potential loss of lucrative fees. But underfunded consumer advocates welcomed the ally.

## SUMMARY AND CONCLUSIONS

**1.** Political power in Texas is essentially structured around organizations, whether they be corporations, professional associations, or interest groups. There is a great disparity in the distribution of resources among these institutions, and this raises a fundamental question as to whether every individual in the political system has equal access to policymakers and the decision-making process.

**2.** Proponents of pluralist theories, while recognizing the inequities in political resources, argue that individual interests are most adequately represented through membership in interest groups. Groups are the essential players in the policymaking process, and politics is basically group interaction, they say. With so many groups involved in this competition for public resources, no one group can dominate the process. Moreover, there is always the potential for individuals to organize a group to advance their particular concerns, and the organizational structures of most groups provide for the individual to move to leadership positions. Leaders of groups are generally committed to democratic values and representing the concerns, needs, and expectations of their membership.

**3.** An alternative view is offered by the proponents of elite theory, who also identify groups, organizations, corporations, and other institutions as the primary players in the policymaking process. But they recognize the marked differences in the resources and subsequent political influence of these groups and contend that a relative few dominate the policy process. Over the course of the state's political history, the most influential institutions have been dominated by white, Anglo-Saxon males from the higher socio/economic levels of the state's population. While there is some competition among these elites, there is a great deal of consensus, and, historically, the Texas establishment has expressed indifference, if not hostility, toward the interests of labor, minorities, and the lower socio/economic groups of the state. Access to the leadership positions in these wealthy institutions has been limited, and these institutions are tied together with complex interlocking relationships.

**4.** The interest group system in Texas was historically dominated by oil and gas, agriculture, and financial institutions. But dramatic changes in the state's economy, the political mobilization of minorities, and the development of public interest groups have produced considerable change. Not only are there more groups and organizations now participating in the policy arenas, but some of the traditionally dominant groups apparently have experienced a dilution of their power. Policies that have been directed to the interests of the lower socioeconomic groups are modest indications of these changes.

**5.** The effectiveness of an interest group in the policymaking process is related to the group's size, the geographical distribution of its membership, its economic resources, its reputation, and its leadership and staff.

**6.** With the proliferation of interest groups over the past three decades and their increased activities, there is concern that the state's interest group system is subject to deadlock. As different groups win favorable legislation and budgetary allocations, it becomes increasingly difficult for policymakers to deny the claims of groups within the political system.

**7.** In the most fundamental terms, interest groups and other organizations attempt to communicate their wants and needs to policymakers through a variety of techniques. While lobbying has a negative connotation for many Texans, this communication process is essential to elected and appointed policymakers.

**8.** Interest groups engage in indirect and direct lobbying. Indirect activities include electoral activity, campaign financing, and efforts to shape public opinion to benefit the groups' specific objectives. The large volume of contributions to political campaigns by political action committees has raised questions about their influence on the decisions of policymakers. Recently, there has been considerable debate over ethics reform.

**9.** Direct lobbying involves a wide variety of strategies and techniques used by lobbyists to influence and shape the decisions of policymakers. Effective lobbyists know how to gain access to legislators and other policymakers, to build and maintain coalitions with other interests, and to follow systematically a policy decision at every step of the process. The successful pursuit of a comprehensive lobbying strategy requires resources, organizational skills, a sense of timing, and tenacity.

## KEY TERMS

Interest group
Mischief of factions
Pluralism
Elitism
Iron rule of oligarchy
The Establishment

Hyperpluralism
Iron triangles of government
Single-issue groups
Public interest groups
Lobbying

## FURTHER READING

Armstrong, David, "Global Entanglements: The Political Economy of a Texas Oil Company," *The Texas Observer*, September 21, 1991, pp. 11-17.

Bachrach, Peter, *The Theory of Democratic Elitism: A Critique*. Boston: Little, Brown, 1967.

Berry, Jeffrey M., *The Interest Group Society*, 2nd ed. Glenview, Ill.: Scott, Foresman and Company, 1989.

Borges, Walter, "TEXPAC Goes Grass Roots," *Texas Lawyer*, 8 (January 1990), pp. 1, 12-13.

Brewton, Pete, "The Great S&L Robbery," *The Texas Observer*, April 5, 1991, pp. 1, 14-18.

Campbell, Brett, "The Greening of the Legislature," *The Texas Observer*, May 17, 1991, pp. 23-27.

Davidson, Chandler, *Race and Class in Texas Politics*. Princeton: Princeton University Press, 1990.

Domhoff, G. William, *Who Really Rules?* Santa Monica, Ca.: Goodyear Publishing Company, Inc., 1978.

Domhoff, G. William, *Who Rules America Now?* Englewood Cliffs, N.J.: Prentice-Hall, Inc., 1983.

Dye, Thomas R., *Who's Running America? The Bush Era*, 5th ed. Englewood Cliffs, N.J.: Prentice Hall, 1990.

Garcia, John A., and Rodolfo de la Garza, "Mobilizing the Mexican Immigrant: The Role of Mexican-American Organizations," *Western Political Quarterly*, 38 (December 1985), pp. 551-564.

Green, George Norris, *The Establishment in Texas Politics: The Primitive Years, 1938-1957*. Westport, Conn.: Greenwood Press, 1979.

Greenwald, Carol S., *Group Power: Lobbying and Public Policy*. New York: Prager Publishers, 1977.

Hrebenar, Robert J., and Clive S. Thomas, eds., *Interest Group Politics in Southern States*. Tuscaloosa: University of Alabama Press, 1992.

Hrebenar, Ronald J., and Ruth K. Scott, *Interest Group Politics in America*, 2nd. ed. Englewood Cliffs, N.J.: Prentice Hall, 1990.

Leon, Mark, "Watchdog or Lapdog," *The Texas Observer*, April 5, 1991, pp. 6-7.

Lowi, Theodore J., *The End of Liberalism*, 2nd ed. New York: W. W. Norton & Company, 1979.

Morehouse, Sarah McCally, *State Politics, Parties and Policy*. New York: Holt, Rinehart and Winston, 1981.

Rogers, Mary Beth, *Cold Anger: A Story of Faith and Power Politics*. Denton, Texas: University of North Texas Press, 1990.

Rogers, Mary Beth, "Gospel Values and Secular Politics," *The Texas Observer*, November 22, 1990, pp. 6-8.

Sabato, Larry J., *PAC Power*. New York: W. W. Norton & Company, 1985.

San Miguel, Guadalupe, Jr., *Let All of Them Take Heed: Mexican Americans and the Campaign for Educational Equality in Texas, 1910-1981*. Austin: University of Texas Press, 1987.

Schlozman, Kay Lehman, and John T. Tierney, *Organized Interests and American Democracy*. New York: Harper and Row, Publishers, 1986.

## ENDNOTES

1. Alexis de Tocqueville, *Democracy in America: A New Translation by George Lawrence*, edited by J. P. Mayer (Garden City: Anchor Books, 1969, copyright in the English translation by Harper & Row Publishers, 1966), p. 191. Used by permission from HarperCollins Publishers.

2. *Austin American-Statesman*, August 18, 1991.

3. Ibid.

4. See Robert S. Erikson, Norman R. Luttbeg, and Kent L. Tedin, *American Public Opinion*, 3rd ed. (New York: Macmillan Publishing Company, 1988), p. 118; and Robert L. Lineberry, George C. Edwards, III, and Martin P. Wattenberg, *Government in America*, 5th edition (New York: HarperCollins Publishers, 1991), p. 341.

5. Dennis S. Ippolito and Thomas G. Walker, *Political Parties, Interest Groups, and Public Policy* (Englewood Cliffs, N.J.: Prentice Hall, 1990), p. 271.

6. Ibid., pp. 270 - 271.

7. Kay Lehman Schlozman and John T. Tierney, *Organized Interests and American Democracy* (New York: Harper & Row Publishers, 1986), p. 75.

8. Ronald J. Hrebenar and Ruth K. Scott, *Interest Group Politics in America*, 2nd ed. (Englewood Cliffs, N.J.: Prentice Hall, 1990), p. 13.

9. See E. E. Schattschneider, *The Semi-Sovereign People* (Hinsdale, Ill.: Dryden Press, 1975) and Hrebenar and Scott, *Interest Group Politics in America*, p. 29.

10. Robert Salisbury, "Overlapping Memberships, Organizational Interactions, and Interest Group Theory," unpublished paper presented at the annual meeting of the American Political Science

Association, Chicago, 1976. See also Carol S. Greenwald, *Group Power* (New York: Praeger Publishers, 1977), pp. 38-40.

11. Schlozman and Tierney, *Organized Interests and American Democracy*, pp. 73-74.
12. Hrebenar and Scott, *Interest Group Politics in America*, p. 29.
13. Ippolito and Walker, *Political Parties, Interest Groups, and Public Policy*, p. 278.
14. For an extended summary of these incentives, see Jeffrey M. Berry, *The Interest Group Society*, 2nd ed. (Glenview, Ill.: Scott, Foresman/Little Brown, 1989), pp. 50-57. See also Robert H. Salisbury, "An Exchange Theory of Interest Groups," *Midwest Journal of Political Science*, 13 (February 1969), pp. 1-32.
15. Greenwald, *Group Power*, pp. 32-35.
16. Ippolito and Walker, *Political Parties, Interest Groups, and Public Policy*, pp. 279-280.
17. Berry, *The Interest Group Society*, p. 53.
18. Lawrence J. R. Herson, *The Politics of Ideas* (Prospect Heights, Ill.: Waveland Press, Inc., 1990), p. 68.
19. David B. Truman, *The Governmental Process*, (New York: Alfred A. Knopf, 1951).
20. For a succinct summary of the elitist-pluralist debate, see Thomas R. Dye and Harmon Zeigler, *The Irony of Democracy*, 7th ed. (Monterey, Cal.: Brooks/Cole Publishing Company, 1987), chap. 1.
21. David Truman, *The Governmental Process*, chap. 4.
22. Ippolito and Walker, *Political Parties, Interest Groups, and Public Policy*, pp. 275-276.
23. Thomas R. Dye, *Who's Running America: The Bush Years*, 5th ed., (Englewood Cliffs, N.J.: Prentice Hall, 1990), p. 4.
24. Robert Michels, *Political Parties: A Sociological Study of the Oligarchical Tendencies of Modern Democracy* (1915) (New York: Free Press, 1962), p. 70.
25. C. Wright Mills, *The Power Elite* (New York: Oxford University Press, 1956).
26. See Dye and Zeigler, *The Irony of Democracy*, chap. 1.
27. George Norris Green, *The Establishment in Texas Politics: The Primitive Years, 1938-1957* (Westport, Conn.: Greenwood Press, 1979), p. 1.
28. Ibid., p. 17.
29. Ibid., p. 1.
30. Ibid, p. 10.
31. Chandler Davidson, *Race and Class in Texas Politics* (Princeton: Princeton University Press, 1990), p. 54.
32. Ibid, chapters 4 and 5.
33. Ibid., p. 83.
34. Ibid., p. 108.
35. Lineberry, et al., *Government in America*, p. 342.
36. See Theodore J. Lowi, *The End of Liberalism*, 2nd ed. (New York: Norton, 1979).
37. Schlozman and Tierney, *Organized Interests and American Democracy*, p. 103.
38. Hrebenar and Scott, *Interest Group Politics in America*, p. 42.
39. See George Norris Green, *The Establishment in Texas*.
40. Belle Zeller, *American State Legislatures* (New York: Thomas Y. Crowell, 1954), and Sarah McCally Morehouse, *State Politics, Parties and Policy* (New York: Holt, Rinehart and Winston, 1981).
41. Harmon L. Zeigler and Hendrik van Dalen, "Interest Groups in the State Politics," in Herbert Jacob, and Kenneth N. Vines, eds., *Politics in the American States*, 3rd ed. (Boston: Little, Brown, 1976).
42. *Houston Chronicle*, March 22, 1987.
43. Christian, George, "Business Agenda Firmly Opposed in 72nd Legislature," *Texas Chamber of Commerce Report*, September 1991, p. 6.
44. Ibid.
45. *Fort Worth Star-Telegram*, September 8, 1991.
46. *Houston Chronicle*, March 3, 1991.
47. Ibid.
48. *Houston Chronicle*, September 15, 1991.
49. Interview with author, Austin, Texas, March 12, 1991.
50. *Dallas Morning News*, July 11, 1988.
51. *Austin American-Statesman*, July 12, 1990.

52. *Austin American Statesman*, April 27, 1991.
53. See George Norris Green, *The Establishment in Texas Politics* for an excellent analysis of the labor-bashing techniques used by Texas business in the 1940s and 1950s.
54. *Houston Chronicle*, August 21, 1991.
55. See Green, *The Establishment in Texas Politics*, chap. 5.
56. See Davidson, *Race and Class in Texas Politics*, chap. 10.
57. Gary Cartwright, "Who Says One Man Can't Change the World?" *Texas Monthly*, September, 1991, p. 161.
58. Hrebenar and Scott, *Interest Group Politics in America*, p. 83.
59. *U.S. Constitution*, 1st Amendment.
60. Lester Milbrath, *The Washington Lobbyists* (Chicago: Rand McNally, 1963), pp. 7-8.
61. Greenwald, *Group Power*, pp. 61-62.
62. *Houston Post*, March 3, 1991.
63. *Fort Worth Star-Telegram*, May 19, 1991.
64. Ippolito and Walker, *Political Parties, Interest Groups, and Public Policy*, p. 323.
65. Hrebenar and Scott, *Interest Group Politics in America*, pp. 114-115.
66. Ippolito and Walker, *Political Parties, Interest Groups, and Public Policy*, pp. 364-365.
67. The following section draws from the research of Scholzman and Tierney, *Organized Interests and American Democracy*, chap. 7.
68. Hrebenar and Scott, *Interest Group Politics in America*, pp. 148-153.

# 5

# THE MASS MEDIA IN TEXAS POLITICS

You can't live with them. You can't live without them.

The news media and any number of state officials have been expressing similar sentiments for years about each other and their adversarial, yet symbiotic, relationship. The Capitol press corps obviously wouldn't exist without a state government to cover. And although some governors, legislators, and bureaucrats believe they could do their jobs very well without the media looking over their shoulders, they know where to turn when they have a message or an image they want to convey to the public.

Officeholders can communicate directly with their constituents, relaying their own subjective accounts of their accomplishments through personal contact, public speeches, newsletters, or paid television commercials. And political parties and special interest groups regularly disseminate governmental information through their membership networks. But virtually all the information that most citizens have about their government—particularly on the state and federal levels—came directly or indirectly through the mass media. An individual either read a newspaper or magazine article, saw a television newscast or heard a radio summary of a particular event or heard about it from a newspaper or magazine reader, TV viewer, or radio listener.

In adopting First Amendment guarantees of press freedom more than 200 years ago, the framers of the U.S. Constitution recognized that a free press was an independent conduit of information essential to making a representative democracy work. It was to provide a public forum for the exchange of ideas and a means of scrutinizing the actions of public officials so as to establish accountability. The mass media has not always been impartial, and in many cases it has not been as independent as the Constitution drafters probably envisioned. But the unofficial fourth branch of government, for all its flaws, has served—and continues to serve—as a check and balance on the legislative, executive, and judicial branches.

Subjective decisions by a newspaper editor or television news producer can affect the final news product and determine whether it is perceived as fair. Should a paper, for example, publish a story about a minor indiscretion by a political candidate? Or a story suggesting a major indiscretion that is based on circumstantial, largely undocumented, evidence? Or a story about a suggestive joke that a political candidate utters in an informal setting? If any of these stories are published or broadcast, should they be on the front page or used to lead the evening newscast? How much time should be given to a particular issue, event or personality? Editors' and producers' answers to these questions are influenced by the highly competitive nature of the news business, and they can, in turn, help determine who is elected to public office and influence government policymaking.

In fulfilling its watchdog role, the media itself has become a major institution linking governments to their constituents. But, ironically, in the current, so-called **information age**—when it has become easier than ever before to be informed—millions of Americans, particularly young adults, are ill-informed and indifferent to the actions and decisions of their leaders and governmental institutions. This disturbing development threatens the foundations of a democratic society, because democracy depends on an informed and involved public.

## THE DEVELOPMENT OF THE PRESS IN TEXAS

### Newspapers

Frontier Texans, isolated in their farmhouses and small settlements, lacked many creature comforts, but most had the opportunity to keep informed of the political sentiment of the day. In 1860, according to historian T.R. Fehrenbach, there were 71 daily and weekly newspapers in Texas with a total circulation of about 100,000. "Ninety-five percent of the white population could read and write and some publication reached virtually every family."[1] Like other early American newspapers, these publications were often highly partisan and primarily devoted to commentary on public issues—the local, state, and national political events of that turbulent period. Social calendars and stories about floods, fires, murders, and other everyday disasters were not yet standard journalistic fare. Editorial writing, however, already had developed into a backwoods art form. "This writing was often irate, biased, and misinformed—but much of it was clear and sound. It kept the freeholders of Texas fully aware of events; many farmers could quote Senator Stephen Douglas or Sam Houston at length. Texans were already keen political animals."[2]

Throughout much of the 20th century, Texas' major newspapers were active members of the conservative, big-business, big-oil establishment that ran the statehouse and the state. During the pre-television years of the 1940s and 1950s, in particular, publishers of some of the state's major newspapers, such as Amon Carter in Fort Worth and Jesse Jones in Houston, were oilmen and financiers who helped control local and state politics for the dominant conservative wing of the Texas Democratic Party. Another strong voice for the establishment was *The Dallas Morning News*, a tireless anticommunist, antilabor, antiliberal crusader. At various times, *The News* editorialized that "the presidency of Franklin Roosevelt was actually destructive of the Republic, the Senate's censure of Joe McCarthy (was) 'a happy day for Communists,' and the Supreme Court (was) 'a threat to state sovereignty second only to Communism itself.'"[3] There was little pretense of detached, neutral reporting as the newspapers actively participated in the political process.

The establishment's close relationship with the Texas press was convincingly demonstrated in numerous election campaigns, including the 1954 Democratic gubernatorial runoff between Governor Allan Shivers, who had led conservative Texas Democrats in supporting Republican Dwight Eisenhower in the 1952 presidential race, and liberal challenger Ralph Yarborough, a party loyalist and strong supporter of organized labor. In the closing weeks of the campaign, 95 of the state's 100 daily newspapers carried editorials endorsing Shivers, who won the runoff.[4] Yarborough would later win election to the U.S. Senate, but the establishment's opposition to him was rabid. In its editorial endorsement of Shivers in 1954, *The Dallas Morning News*, however, was kind enough to concede that some of Yarborough's Texas supporters were not "reds...radicals or goon squad supporters."[5]

In 1945, the *Texas Spectator*, a short-lived independent weekly newspaper in Austin, conducted a study showing that many Texas weeklies were ready outlets of canned propaganda of the National Association of Manufacturers. Over a 30-day period, the *Spectator* discovered, 52 papers with a total circulation of 97,000 used antilabor columns and cartoons prepared by the manufacturers' association without telling their readers the biased source of the material.[6]

News coverage has changed significantly in the past 30 years, and readers now will rarely find the kind of inflammatory, racist, demagogic writing that characterized much of the earlier Texas press. The media today is much more disposed to cover issues affecting the lower income populations, minorities, and others struggling against the power structure. Texas is still largely a conservative state, and a restructured business community is still influential in the setting of state policy. But the media—particularly the large newspapers and television stations—is much more eager to challenge the political and business establishment today.

For one reason, there is a high level of distrust of government now. A turning point in Texas was the Sharpstown stock fraud scandal that broke in 1971. It revealed that the legislature had given quick passage in 1969 to two banking regulation bills sought by Houston financier Frank Sharp and that high-ranking state officials had profited from insurance stock purchases financed with loans from Sharp's bank (see Chapter 8). That was soon to be followed by the Watergate scandal, which would shake public confidence in government throughout the country, much as the bitter experience of the Vietnam War already had begun to do.

News people have retained their symbiotic relationship with government officials, on whom they still depend for much information. But after Sharpstown and Watergate, reporters seemed to more readily question the motives of the governor, legislators, and other public officeholders and political candidates. The ethical behavior of officeholders and their relationship to the special interests that spend millions of dollars trying to influence state government came under closer scrutiny. The media also reexamined its own ethics. Most news organizations, for example, adopted policies prohibiting their reporters from accepting free airplane rides, junkets, and other freebies from state officials or candidates, practices that had been fairly common in Texas in the past.

Another significant factor in the evolution of the Texas press was the passing of the high-profile publishers who had been part of the conservative establishment. Many of their newspapers were subsequently sold to large national conglomerates with newspapers and broadcast holdings in many cities. Such purchases of major, once independently owned newspapers like the *Houston Chronicle*, the *Fort Worth Star-Telegram*, and the *Austin American-Statesman* are part of a consolidation of media ownership across the country, a development regarded as unhealthy by many within and outside the industry. The only major metropolitan newspapers in Texas still owned by Texas-based corporations are *The Dallas Morning News* and the *Houston Post*.

Such consolidations raise concerns that national owners, who have no personal ties to the local communities, may be more concerned about profits and losses than the quality of news coverage—or diversity of editorial viewpoints—in their local outlets. John Shenefield, the head of the Justice Department's Antitrust Division, in 1979 expressed the view that "the increased concentration of economic and political resources in the hands of a few institutions may unnecessarily threaten those fundamental values of dispersed power and a multiplicity of viewpoints upon which our nation is based."[7]

Perhaps paradoxically, though, national ownership offers Texas newspapers a greater degree of independence than was true in the past. Absentee corporate owners don't have sacred cows to protect in the Texas statehouse, the local courthouse, or city hall and don't feel compelled to defend old provincial prejudices. Some newspaper chains also move editors and publishers around among their various cities, thus increasing the likelihood of putting a fresh perspective on some state and local issues. Had the *Austin American-Statesman*, for example, still had Texas owners, it may not have been so bold as to editorialize for a state income tax when that proposal was still highly unpopular in Texas and opposed by most elected officials and businessmen. The *American-Statesman*, owned by Atlanta-based Cox Enterprises, helped provoke a public debate over a critical issue that is becoming more and more difficult for the legislature to avoid. And the newspaper stepped forward months before Lt. Governor Bob Bullock and some elements of the business community unsuccessfully proposed such a tax in 1991.

It also is difficult to imagine the conservative Texas publishers of only a few years ago endorsing a liberal Democrat like Ann Richards for governor, which many of their successors did in 1990. *The Dallas Morning News*, the state's largest and one of its most influential newspapers, is still owned by a Texas-based corporation. It also still presents one of the most conservative editorial viewpoints in the state on its opinion pages—it endorsed Republican Clayton Williams for governor in 1990—but it aggressively covers governmental and political institutions on its news pages.

For the most part, Texas newspapers have maintained considerable **editorial autonomy** under national owners. That was amply illustrated during the 1990 governor's race by the six Texas dailies owned by the Hearst Corporation, which has diverse media properties throughout the country. The *Houston Chronicle*, the *San Antonio Light*, and the *Beaumont Enterprise* endorsed Richards. *The Midland Reporter-Telegram* endorsed its hometown candidate, Williams, and so did Hearst's other West Texas paper, the *Plainview Daily Herald*. The *Laredo Morning Times*, meanwhile, maintained a local policy of no political endorsements.

The 1970s and 1980s were turning points for many Texas newspapers. Many changed owners during this period, and the overall quality of Texas journalism began to noticeably improve. The most dramatic and most influential change occurred in Dallas, and it was brought about by the brief entry of one of the nation's media giants, the Times Mirror Company, into the Dallas newspaper market.

Times Mirror, publisher of the *Los Angeles Times*, one of the country's most respected newspapers, purchased the *Dallas Times Herald* from local owners in 1970. Within a few years, it precipitated a major newspaper war with its dominant competitor, *The Morning News*. Times Mirror brought in new editors, recruited reporters from all over the country, improved the quality and aggressiveness of its news coverage—"The Only Sacred Cow Here Is Hamburger," read a sign on the newsroom wall—and awakened *The Morning News* from what many media watchers had considered a long provincial slumber. At one point, the *Times Herald* briefly passed *The Morning News* in Sunday circulation. But *The Morning News* responded by bringing in new editors of its own, expanding its news staff, and vastly improving its own product. During this period, both newspapers became major national award winners.

Initially, Times Mirror's foray into Dallas was extremely profitable, but with the precipitous decline in the Texas economy during the 1980s, the *Times Herald* began to lose money and was still second in advertising and circulation. The paper was sold in 1986 to a Texas owner, who was unable to reverse its financial position. It changed hands one more time before *The Morning News* purchased the struggling property and closed it in 1991. *The Morning News* remains one of the state's and nation's premier newspapers, thanks in large part to the swift kick administered by Times Mirror. Moreover, the higher journalistic standards that emerged in Dallas had positive effects on some of the state's other newspapers, which soon began undergoing transformations of their own.

Several hundred newspapers in the United States have ceased publication since 1900, a reflection of changing reader habits, corporate consolidations, the emergence of television, the proliferation of radio stations with targeted audiences, the development of specialized magazines, and other factors. The folding of the

*Dallas Times Herald* left that city with only one major newspaper and Texas with 97 daily and 430 weekly newspapers.[8]

Local newspaper competition can help improve the quality of news coverage, provide alternative views and interpretations of events, and reduce the potential for cozy relationships between the media and the community's establishment. But it is increasingly difficult for a city to support two daily newspapers. Houston and San Antonio are among the few Texas cities that still do, and the papers there are engaged in fierce battles for readership and advertising dollars.

Most weekly newspapers are oriented primarily to their local communities and carry little news of state government or politics. But most of the small towns served by weeklies also are in the circulation areas of daily newspapers. There are 15 African-American-oriented newspapers in Texas, including five in Houston and three in Dallas and San Antonio. There are six Spanish language papers, none of which has a circulation of more than 25,000.

Newspapers can more readily explain a pending issue, its history, and possible options for its resolution than can the electronic media. But newspapers also have their limits, primarily in the amount of space they can or will devote to governmental news. Responding to the popularity of television and TV's drain on available advertising revenue, newspapers in recent years generally have reduced the proportion of space allocated to so-called "hard news." "Newspaper editors, like TV producers, have discovered the American public's insatiable hunger for 'fluff,'" one critic wrote.[9] Many editors also have been influenced by *USA Today*, which specializes in short stories and numerous color photos and charts that make it something of a foldable TV set that can easily be tucked under the arm and carried on an airplane. The larger Texas papers, nevertheless, still set aside a respectable amount of space for national, state, and local government news, alongside the travel and lifestyle stories and the gourmet recipes. A modern daily newspaper is much like a cafeteria. It has a variety of offerings for a variety of tastes and expects its readers to scan the headlines, choosing what they want to try to digest.

## The Electronic Media

Dramatic changes in mass communications, primarily the emergence of television, over the past 40 years have had a major impact on the role of the media in government and politics. Television has replaced the newspaper as the public's primary source of news. An estimated 98 percent of American homes have at least one TV set, approximately 75 percent have VCRs, and close to 60 percent are linked to cable television systems. While there are wide differences in viewing patterns, people in the average home watch television for approximately seven hours a day. According to a recent survey by The Roper Organization, 65 percent of the American public turn to television as the primary source of news and 49 percent rank television as their most believable news source.[10] Television also is now the primary source of news for most Texans. Fifty-three percent of respondents to a

1986 edition of *The Texas Poll* (Table 5-1) said television was their primary source of local news, and 73 percent said TV was their primary source of national news.[11]

With these changes, there has been increased concern about the role of television in shaping our view of politics and setting the agenda for public policies. Even more fundamental are declining levels of news literacy among Americans, particularly the young. While there has been a proliferation of news sources, a recent survey by the Times Mirror Center for The People & The Press (Table 5-2, page 130) concluded that "those under 30 know less than younger people once did, and they are less interested in what's happening in the larger world around them."[12] This decline, which will be discussed in more detail later in this chapter, has implications for the broadcast media, but it has had its greatest impact on newspapers. In 1965, more than 70 percent of Americans indicated they read a newspaper each day, but only 44 percent reported daily readership in 1990.

There are about 20 television markets in Texas, ranging in size from Dallas-Fort Worth and Houston, which rank seventh and tenth nationally, to such small markets as Laredo, 198th, and Victoria, 205th. Coverage of state government and politics varies significantly between the larger and smaller cities. The most consistent coverage comes from Houston and Dallas stations, some of which have fulltime news bureaus in Austin, and the Austin stations themselves. Television stations in many of the smaller cities sometimes will send news crews to Austin for special events, such as a gubernatorial inauguration or the opening day of a legislative session, but their overall coverage is spotty and inconsistent. Some get videotapes of news events through independent news services in Austin.

Even at its best, television is an inadequate substitute for newspaper coverage of government and politics. In a recent study of national evening newscasts on ABC, NBC, and CBS, it was determined that eight minutes of each 30-minute show was consumed by advertising. That left only 22 minutes for national news, international news, special reports (in-depth reports on social issues), soft news (entertainment and human-interest stories), and non-news (greetings, sign offs, and transitions to commercials). The networks varied somewhat in their emphasis, but

**TABLE 5–1**   Texas Survey of Primary Sources of News 1986

|  | Primary Source of Local News | Primary Source of National News |
| --- | --- | --- |
| Newspapers | 34% | 18% |
| Radio | 9 | 5 |
| Television | 53 | 73 |
| Magazines | 1 | 3 |
| Talking to People | 3 | 1 |
| Don't Know/Refused | 1 | 1 |

Totals do not equal 100% because of rounding.

Source: *The Texas Poll,* Summer 1986, Copyright, Harte-Hanks Communications.

**TABLE 5–2**  News Consumption

|                                          | 1965 | 1990 |
|------------------------------------------|------|------|
| Read a Newspaper Yesterday:              |      |      |
| All Respondents 21 and Older*            | 71   | 44   |
| Under 35                                 | 67   | 30   |
| 35-49                                    | 73   | 44   |
| 50+                                      | 74   | 55   |
| Watched TV News Yesterday:               |      |      |
| All Respondents 21 and Older*            | 55   | 53   |
| Under 35                                 | 52   | 41   |
| 35-49                                    | 52   | 49   |
| 50+                                      | 62   | 67   |
| Listened to News on the Radio Yesterday: |      |      |
| All Respondents 21 and Older*            | 58   | 53   |
| Under 35                                 | 58   | 57   |
| 35-49                                    | 61   | 57   |
| 50+                                      | 55   | 48   |

*The 21 and Older categorization is used here to be consistent with Gallup's report of 1965

Source: Times Mirror Center for The People & The Press, *The Age of Indifference*, June 28, 1990.

many stories, including presentations of complex issues, received less than two minutes of air time.[13] And the Cable News Network, or CNN, although it has frequent news programs throughout the day, doesn't offer the depth that is found in most newspapers.

Local television coverage is subject to the same criticism. Political news must compete with weather, sports, crime, and human interest stories. Most TV news programs provide only cursory reports on governmental issues and activities, and people who rely solely on TV for news have little substantive information upon which to make critical and informed judgments. Television is good at taping a protest demonstration on the Capitol steps, getting a sound bite from the governor, or gathering interviews with citizens outraged over the latest tax increase. But the limited air time given to even the most important stories makes it difficult to explain why the protesters marched on the Capitol or explore the economic and political factors that produced the tax bill. Television is visually oriented, and explanations are difficult to depict on videotape within these time constraints.

Most radio news also is of the headline variety, a quick summary of the day's news highlights. Many radio stations make no pretense of offering serious news coverage. And few among those that do have sufficient news staffs to cover major events or issues in Austin. They rely on wire stories or feeds from a news service such as the Texas State Network, which has a full-time Austin correspondent. A handful of news-talk stations, however, offer more in-depth coverage and commentary on political events and public issues. Some of the better radio news stations in Texas are WOAI in San Antonio, which periodically sends a reporter to Austin; KTRH in Houston, which has intermittently had an Austin bureau; and KRLD in Dallas, which owns the Texas State Network. While a large part of the population tunes in to radio regularly, the medium runs a poor third as a primary source of state political news.

Television and radio often take their cues about what to cover from the print media. Most stations don't have large enough reporting staffs to do the extensive background work required to develop many complex stories. But once a story broken by a newspaper has grabbed attention, the electronic media usually will join in pursuit.

Just as there is national concern about growing chain ownership of newspapers, there also is concern about ownership patterns in the TV industry. As an unsettling precedent, some media watchers cite the 1985 purchase of the National Broadcasting Co., or NBC, by General Electric, a non-journalistic conglomerate whose primary business had been "neither news nor entertainment but household appliances, airplane engines, nuclear reactors, and arms."[14]

In Texas, there are several multicity broadcast chains and cross-ownerships of major newspapers, television stations and networks (Table 5-3). The *Fort Worth Star-Telegram*, for example, is now owned by Capital Cities/ABC, Inc., which also owns the ABC television network and KTRK-TV in Houston. When Times Mirror entered the Dallas market in 1970, it purchased KDFW-TV, which it still owns today, and the company also owns KTBC-TV in Austin, both CBS affiliates. A.H. Belo Corp., owner of *The Dallas Morning News*, also owns major television stations in

**TABLE 5–3**  Major Media Owners in Texas

| | |
|---|---|
| The Hearst Corporation<br>*Houston Chronicle*<br>*San Antonio Light*<br>*The Midland Reporter-Telegram*<br>*Plainview Daily Herald*<br>*Laredo Morning Times*<br>*Beaumont Enterprise* | Harte-Hanks Communications, Inc.<br>*Corpus Christi Caller-Times*<br>*Abilene Reporter-News*<br>*San Angelo Standard-Times*<br>*Wichita Falls Times Record News*<br>*Harte-Hanks Community Papers*<br>KENS-TV (San Antonio) |
| A.H. Belo Corporation<br>*The Dallas Morning News*<br>*Arlington Daily News*<br>*Garland Daily News*<br>*Grand Prairie Dailiy News*<br>*Irving Daily News*<br>*Mid-Cities Daily News*<br>*Richardson Daily News*<br>*Metrocrest News*<br>WFAA-TV (Dallas)<br>KHOU-TV (Houston) | Capital Cities/ABC, Inc.<br>*Fort Worth Star-Telegram*<br>KTRK-TV (Houston)<br><br>Times Mirror Company<br>KDFW-TV (Houston)<br>KTBC-TV (Austin) |
| Cox Enterprises, Inc.<br>*Austin American-Statesman*<br>*The Longview News-Journal*<br>*The Lufkin Daily News*<br>*The Daily Sentinel (Nacogdoches)*<br>*Waco Tribune-Herald* | Lin Broadcasting<br>KXAS-TV (Fort Worth)<br>KXAN-TV (Austin) |

Sources: Texas Daily Newspaper Association, *1991 Directory of Texas Daily Newspapers* (Austin: TDNA, 1991); Texas Association of Broadcasters, *Texas Broadcasters Directory, 1990* (Austin: TAB, 1990); *Dallas Morning News Texas Almanac, 1992–1993* (Dallas: A.H. Belo, 1992)

Dallas and Houston. Under current federal regulations, no single corporation may own more than 12 stations in each segment of the electronic media (television or AM or FM radio). The owner of a newspaper may not purchase broadcast properties in the same media market, and a radio station cannot buy a television station in the same market or vice-versa.[15] The conflicting cross-ownerships in Texas, however, pre-dated the regulations and were allowed to remain in place.

During most of his 18 years as lieutenant governor, Bill Hobby's family-owned corporation, H & C Communications, owned three major media outlets in Houston—the *Houston Post*, KPRC-TV, and KPRC radio. The Hobbys sold the *Post* while he was still in office but retained ownership of the two broadcast stations and purchased a third, KSAT-TV in San Antonio. People familiar with the relationships say Hobby "bent over backwards" to avoid influencing his properties' political or governmental coverage while he was in office.

There have been remarkable technological changes over the past decade suggesting that we can anticipate a much greater range of electronic news sources in the future. The emerging media include cable television, satellites, low-power television, videotext, teletext, and computer networking to news sources around the state, nation and world.[16] As these new forms of communication develop, broad-casting as it is traditionally understood may be replaced by narrowcasting, or the communication of a specific news story to a small part of the population. While it is difficult to foresee all of the implications of these developments, one can speculate there will be major changes in the way the electorate receives information about politics and government—and the way the media will be exploited by officeholders and candidates.

## THE CAPITOL PRESS CORPS

The state's major newspapers, wire services, several television stations, and a radio network are represented at the Capitol by reporters who cover state government and politics full-time. The press corps has about 60 permanent members and is larger during legislative sessions when additional media organizations send representatives to Austin and some of the permanent bureaus beef up their staffs. Several insider-type, subscriber newsletters that focus on state government also have been launched in Austin. The muckraking *Texas Observer*, long a favorite of Texas liberals, is still published fortnightly and still has a faithful following, but its influence has been reduced by an increased commitment to investigative governmental reporting by the state's major dailies. And the slick magazine, *Texas Monthly*, offers limited coverage of state government, most notably its ranking of what it considers the 10 best and 10 worst legislators after each regular session.

Individual news bureaus range in size from as many as five or six staffers for the largest newspapers to one-person operations for smaller organizations. Television bureaus usually include a reporter and a camera person. Each multi-person bureau has a bureau chief who not only is a reporter but also makes assignments and handles administrative duties. Some newspaper bureaus also have columnists, and the larger bureaus have clerks and sometimes hire university journalism students as interns. The Associated Press is the only news organization with a full-time still photographer on its Capitol staff, although several freelance photographers are available to newspapers in Austin, and staff photographers are sent to the Capitol from home offices for special assignments.

The small newspaper bureaus usually give priority to covering members of their local legislative delegations and events of particular interest to their communities, while the large papers and the wire services provide more general coverage. But even the large papers find it impossible to cover the entire range of state government activities. So priorities are set, with the legislature, the governor, the attorney general, the courts, and the larger administrative agencies usually receiving the most attention.

The large dailies offer more investigative and interpretive reporting than do the wire services, television, and radio. The large newspapers also are increasingly turning to specialty reporters based in their home offices, rather than at the Capitol, to cover all governmental aspects—state, local, and federal—of such multifaceted issues as environmental protection, health care, and transportation.

The heavyweights in the Capitol press are *The Dallas Morning News* and the *Houston Chronicle*, the two largest newspapers in Texas. *The News*—with six full-time reporters—has the largest statehouse bureau. The *Chronicle* has only four full-time reporters assigned to the Capitol but, like *The News*, frequently supplements its

**FIGURE 5-1**  Lt. Governor Bob Bullock holds a news conference in the Senate chamber with members of the Capitol press corps in 1991.  (Texas Senate Media Services)

Austin staff with reporters from the home office to cover selected issues or subjects of local interest to Houston readers.

The *Austin American-Statesman, Fort Worth Star-Telegram,* and *Houston Post* also have some statewide influence. The *American-Statesman,* which has a high percentage of state employees among its readers and more reporters in Austin than the out-of-town papers, provides the most coverage of the state bureaucracy. One of the *American-Statesman's* strongest areas of state government reporting in recent years has been reporter Denise Gamino's unmatched coverage of the Department of Mental Health and Mental Retardation, an important agency undergoing major changes in the wake of two federal court orders.

The statehouse bureaus are generally considered prestigious assignments and attract capable and aggressive reporters. Nevertheless, there has been considerable turnover on Capitol news staffs in recent years. Only a dozen or so of the reporters and columnists covering the legislature in 1991 had more than 10 years of experience on the Capitol beat. This means many reporters have little historical perspective for comparing the administrations of different governors or the performance of the legislature over a sustained period. When Governor Bill Clements made a successful comeback for a second term in 1986, there were few reporters at the Capitol who had covered the start of his first administration in 1979. And only a handful of reporters who covered Ann Richards' election as governor in 1990 had been around long enough to witness her first statewide election as state treasurer only eight years earlier. But most reporters successfully compensate for their limited institutional memories through research and interviews with longtime Capitol players. Moreover, new reporters can bring a fresh perspective to the Capitol beat and—like new officeholders—challenge the traditional assumptions under which state government operates.

There is no typical pattern to the careers of Capitol reporters. Some were promoted from their organizations' local staffs, while others were hired from competing bureaus or even from out-of-state newspapers. In recent years, relatively few Capitol reporters have chosen to retire in those jobs, but only a handful have gone on to become editors or news directors in their home offices. Some have moved to news bureaus in Washington and jobs in other media markets, while others have become press secretaries or information specialists for elected officeholders or state agencies. Some have even left the news business for unrelated occupations.

Until the mid-1970s, the state provided office space free to the press in the Capitol. But the growth of news staffs prompted the legislature to renovate the longtime Capitol press room to provide more space, and the state started charging news organizations rent. In recent years, most bureaus leased private office space outside the Capitol for their main offices while retaining extra work space in the Capitol. As part of a Capitol restoration project, the press room, which was located just outside the House chamber, was closed at the end of 1991 to be converted to other uses, and the last news organizations moved their offices out of the building. Limited press work space was to be created in an underground addition to the Capitol scheduled to be completed in 1992.

information to constituents that, in effect, amounts to a continuous po.
campaign.

Recent governors have used political funds to purchase statewide
satellite time to communicate directly with the public on major policy issues c
proposals. So far, such efforts have had mixed results. But technology will allow
governors to use the technique more in the future to try to circumvent the
intermediary role of the press and directly mobilize public support for a governor's
programs during critical steps in the legislative process.

Most of the Austin-based trade associations and other special interest
groups have public relations specialists to promote their causes and keep their
members informed of developments at the Capitol. Interest groups are at the center
of the policymaking process, and their proposals and efforts to get them enacted
are inherently newsworthy. Lobbyists also provide a wealth of insider information
to reporters, but newspeople must carefully evaluate it because of the large stakes
that special interests have in the workings of state government.

## MEDIA COMPETITION AND PACK JOURNALISM

To visitors in the House or the Senate gallery, the Capitol press corps must often
resemble a pack of predators intent on devouring the governor or legislative leaders.
Sometimes, a state official also may feel he won't escape with his life when two dozen
newspeople chase him down a Capitol hallway to thrust cameras and microphones
into his face. Capitol reporters and the organizations they represent are very
competitive, and reporters prefer to operate independently of each other. But the
size of the press corps, the logistics of covering major, breaking news events, and
the fear of missing a big story to a competitor often force journalists into a pack,
both physically and mentally.

Any reporter can break a major story on any given day, sending competitors
scrambling to produce followup stories. But more often than not, the large daily
newspapers determine which stories will get the most attention from the wire
services, the broadcast media and other members of the pack. The large papers
generally have the most experienced reporters in the statehouse, and their large
circulations make them attractive outlets for a bureaucrat, a lobbyist, a legislator, or
a concerned citizen who wants to offer a proposal, try to kill a piece of legislation,
or expose wrongdoing.

There are pluses and minuses to **pack journalism**. The pack often is at its
best when devouring a story of major proportions, such as the scandal over the
abusive marketing practices of some private psychiatric hospital chains. The *Houston
Chronicle* and the *San Antonio Express* broke the first stories in 1991 of patients
literally being hauled off to hospitals in Texas against their will by private security
agents employed by the hospitals. The story quickly ballooned into one of national
proportions, and other media outlets began their own investigations. Media competition on such a story helps uncover details that one newspaper or one television
station alone may not have enough resources to do. And it serves to call the attention

With proper credentials, media representatives are granted access floors of the House and the Senate when the legislature is in session. Specia tables at the front of each chamber are provided for reporters, and the Hous the Senate set standards for credentials under their respective rules.

Technology has enhanced the transmission and, in some cases, the prep tion of news reports. Newspaper bureaus transmit their stories to their home off via computer, and TV bureaus in Austin, like TV correspondents throughout world, use satellite transmissions. Among the newspapers, *The Dallas Morning Ne* has taken the further technological step of developing a computerized data base political contributions to certain candidates and officeholders. The paper reporters use that information to more readily develop stories of political influence buying that detail, for example, how many of a governor's appointees to state boards and commissions were political donors and how much money each gave.

But sound news judgment and perseverance are still the basic tools of the successful Capitol reporter, just as they are for thousands of newspeople elsewhere. Statehouse reporters usually have to dig out the best stories, frequently using confidential sources to develop tips or hunches. Legislators, other elected officials, members of their staffs, bureaucrats, and lobbyists love to tell secrets about each other. Such sources, of course, often have their own political or personal axes to grind, and the smart reporter is wary. Campaigns for state office are notorious for whispered accusations or innuendoes directed against opposing camps. Sometimes a legislator, without allowing his name to be used, will leak a controversial proposal to an influential reporter as a trial balloon to see how other lawmakers and the general public react to the idea before deciding whether to actively promote it. Similar anonymous leaks, cast in a negative light, can be used to kill someone else's proposal before he has had a chance to gather support for it. Although reporters run the risk of being used in such situations, they also can be put on the trail of a jewel of a story. A newsperson has to evaluate each tip on its own merits, a task made more difficult by the fact that competitors also are getting similar tips.

## GOVERNMENTAL PUBLIC RELATIONS

Most of the state's top elected officials and administrators of major agencies spend thousands of tax dollars each year on press secretaries and public relations operations to help disseminate public information and also to promote themselves and their agencies. News releases, press conferences, background briefings, slick reports, and videotapes are designed to maintain the visibility of state agencies, cultivate general goodwill, announce new programs, and anticipate budgetary attacks or program changes. In a dispute with the legislature or, perhaps, another state agency, a public official's media specialists often try to put a **spin** on a story that presents information in the best possible light for their boss.

The House and the Senate also provide media services for their members. Taxpayers pay for written news releases, newsletters, and radio and television feeds to local stations. These resources can be used by a legislator to maintain a flow of of more readers and viewers to a problem and increase pressure on public officials to correct it. A potential drawback is the possibility that reporters, under pressure to beat competitors to a new lead on the story, may not take enough time to double check their facts and may report mistakes. Another significant problem is that the pack mentality often causes journalists to focus their attention on a limited number of spectacular stories while ignoring other important issues. In this respect, pack journalism limits the agenda for public debate and discussion.

The fear of being beaten on new developments in major, running stories can also discourage reporters from sitting back and taking a more contemplative look at the implications behind the headlines. During the two summer special sessions in 1991, Capitol reporters gave extensive coverage to the lottery and tax issues and proposals for government reorganization, including Governor Ann Richards' proposal for increased appointment powers over the state bureaucracy (see Chapter 9). But there were virtually no stories attempting to examine whether or how such restructuring of state agencies would improve the administration of public programs and the delivery of services. In their haste to be first with breaking news, media outlets often neglect a thorough examination of the complexities of governance.

## MEDIA BIAS

Most public officials are sensitive about what is written and broadcast about them, particularly if a controversial issue has thrust them into the spotlight. So, consequently, they will often consider news stories slanted against them or their viewpoints. Complaints about alleged **media bias** also are made by readers and viewers, and the issue has sparked considerable debate and research. National studies have indicated that most reporters are more liberal than the general population in personal ideology and on many public policy issues, and conservatives have exploited these findings to support their contention of a liberal media bias.[17] But other people, including many liberals, have pointed to corporate media ownership and concluded that those who make the final decisions as to what news is covered and how it is covered reflect more conservative biases.

Capitol reporters normally attempt to present all sides of an issue. Most believe they are objective, dedicated to principles of fairness and balance, and report events as they happen. A summary of this view of the press as a mirror was presented by Frank Stanton, former president of CBS, when he testified before a congressional committee that "what the media do is to hold a mirror up to society and try to report it as faithfully as possible."[18] Accusations of bias, however, will not go away.

As we have already discussed, the Texas media earlier in this century was characterized by intense political activism with a clear establishment bias in news stories as well as editorial columns. Although this style has largely disappeared, newspeople and the organizations they represent sometimes have strong personal or corporate opinions about the issues or individuals they cover, and bias and the perception of bias are problems the media constantly has to fight.

Subjective decisions—such as a reporter's own strong interest in an issue—may determine which news events are covered on a particular day, or which angle is emphasized in a particular story. Unless they are personal friends, reporters seldom discuss their political preferences with each other, but their personal politics doubtlessly cover the spectrum—Democrats, Republicans, and Independents; conservatives, moderates, and liberals.

More often then not, however, reporters eagerly provide a forum for the viewpoints of consumer and welfare advocates, environmentalists, and other progressive-minded individuals. One reason is that spokespeople for these groups are readily accessible, hold frequent news conferences, and actively cultivate media contacts. They depend on free media exposure to compensate for limited budgets in their battles against the business lobby for the tougher regulations and higher taxes that progressive programs usually require. Another reason is that stories about the age-old struggle between the powerful and the powerless, the rich and the poor, attract considerable reader and viewer interest and center on controversy and conflict.

The prominence with which editors or news directors play stories—front page versus inside the paper, the lead item on the 10 o'clock news versus minor air treatment—is usually determined by the newsperson's perception of the public's interest in a given story. But an editor's or publisher's own opinion of an issue also may be a factor. Newspapers and broadcast stations often disagree with each other—and with their own reporters—on how stories should be played. Ultimately, a relatively few individuals decide what stories will be reported, how prominently they will be presented, and how much space or time will be allotted to them. And people alleging media bias will point out that fact.[19] Michael Parenti, a critic of institutional elites in the United States, concludes that "the very process of selection allows the cultural and political biases and class interests of the selector to operate as censor."[20] Other media watchers argue, however, that the media "gatekeepers"—those who decide what news to publish or broadcast—are constrained, at least in part, by their readers' or viewers' preferences, as determined through market research.

There are five basic criteria used by the media to select what will be reported. First, a story must have a significant impact on its audience. Second, it needs to be something that generates considerable interest, such as violence, conflict, disaster, or scandal. Another component is familiarity—the public identifies with well-known individuals or familiar situations. A reported event also should occur in some proximity to readers and viewers, and finally, a news story should be timely. Conflict, proximity, and timeliness often appear to be the more critical elements of a story's newsworthiness.[21] Yet, public policymaking is complex and often highly technical and doesn't always produce the kinds of stories necessary to sustain general public interest.

Stories about governmental scandals and political corruption often are displayed on page one of newspapers and at the top of evening TV newscasts.

Attempting to follow in the footsteps of the earlier muckrakers of American journalism, some Texas newspeople view themselves as crusaders and are determined to "clean up" government. In their eagerness, however, they can become susceptible to charges of unfair, personal bias against the public officials they are targeting. This is particularly true when haste to be the first with the latest development or newest angle in an ongoing scandal produces reporting or editing mistakes.

Although they usually are adversaries, legislators and the reporters who cover them share one dubious distinction—the public doesn't think very highly of either group. Texans responding to the spring 1991 edition of *The Texas Poll* said they trusted reporters and legislators only slightly more than they did TV evangelists, lobbyists, and insurance salesmen, who were at the bottom of the list.[22] In the case of the media, it may be a desire to "shoot the messenger," or at least partially blame the bearers of bad news for the serious social and governmental problems that no one seems able to resolve.

Some people also may be convinced that the media isn't telling the full story of what's going on in state government—that some Capitol reporters have become insiders and are too close to the institutions and officeholders they cover. Most state officials, however, would find it difficult to subscribe to that theory. Individual reporters have their favorite and least favorite officeholders, and relationships that affect a newsperson's objectivity may occasionally occur. But most reporters are too independent to fall into that trap.

Newspapers and radio and television stations in Texas are big businesses and, as such, sometimes have their own special interests to protect. Media opposition, for example, played a major role in killing an attempt in the 1980s to put advertising under the sales tax. That tax would have raised millions of new dollars for education, human services, and other programs that media outlets generally support, but media owners feared it would have reduced advertising volume and deprived them of critical revenue.

## THE MASS MEDIA AND THE POLICY AGENDA

The media inevitably has some impact on public policy since, as we noted at the beginning of this chapter, the vast majority of the people who elect policymakers receive virtually all of the information on which to evaluate the performances of those policymakers either directly or indirectly through the media.

Some scholars and media experts believe one of the major contributions of the media to politics is **agenda-setting**. By choosing which events and issues to cover and how extensively to cover them, they say, the media helps define what is important for the public and, by omission, what is not important. Maxwell McCombs and Donald Shaw, recognized authorities on the mass media, argue that "the idea of agenda-setting asserts that the priorities of the press to some degree become the priorities of the public. What the press emphasizes is in turn emphasized privately and publicly by the audiences of the press...."[23]

Some extend the agenda-setting role of the media to agenda-building. The media's coverage of specific issues creates a climate for political action by shaping the atmosphere in which these issues will be debated and solutions developed.[24] By helping to make an issue relevant, the media gives people reasons for taking sides and converting the problem into a serious political issue. From this perspective, "the public agenda is not so much set by the media as built up through a cycle of media activity that transforms an elite issue into a public controversy."[25] Issues and concerns of a few individuals now become the concerns of many, and the dynamics of the policymaking process are changed.[26]

The most consistent readers and viewers of governmental and political news are the business, community, and political leaders who actively influence and work on policy formation. Most key public officials and their staffs spend a lot of time keeping up with media coverage of public issues. Clipping and filing news stories is an important part of the routine in many state offices. A number of independent clipping services also compile news articles daily for influential clients from papers across the state, and some firms provide video clips of news stories carried on television.

But some people familiar with the workings of Texas government believe that the policy-building role of the press is overstated. Bo Byers, who spent almost 40 years covering state government and politics for the *Houston Chronicle* and the Associated Press before retiring in 1983, said he found the media's role in the policy setting process primarily reactive. "In most cases, the media is kind of like the politicians. They see public sentiment developing for something, and they get behind it. Then you see the editorials start appearing," he said.[27] This view suggests a less intrusive role of the mass media in the policy process and is similar to the notion that the press merely mirrors what others think about public issues.

This passive view receives some support from the argument that the Texas press has been largely reactive in reporting some of the most crucial issues facing Texans on the threshold of the 21st century—educational equality, criminal justice, and care of the mentally ill and the mentally retarded. Although newspapers were influential in prompting the legislature to make improvements in all three of these areas in the years following World War II, deterioration set in, and the media and the legislature of the next generation took back seats to the judiciary. The media had largely ignored a recurrence of substandard conditions in state prisons and MHMR facilities—and, consequently, so had the legislature—until after the federal courts had stepped in with landmark reform orders. And disparities in property wealth and educational opportunities between rich and poor school districts had been growing wider for years, exacerbating a dropout problem that, in turn, helped keep the prisons overcrowded. But educational disparities received only occasional attention from news reporters until after the Mexican American Legal Defense and Educational Fund had won a state court judgment declaring the school finance system unconstitutional. Once the courts had forced the issues, however, the media devoted extensive coverage to them, keeping the problems, their causes, and potential solutions in the public eye.

The media's attention to public problems and officialdom's response form something of a never-ending cycle. In the early 1980s, to cite but one example, the deaths of several elderly patients at the Autumn Hills Nursing Home in Galveston prompted changes in state law designed to tighten oversight of such facilities. By the early 1990s, however, the *Houston Chronicle* and other newspapers again were reporting widespread deficiencies in state regulation of the nursing home industry. Those reports and a hard-hitting, national network television expose of abuse and neglect at Texas nursing homes—complete with nauseating glimpses shot by a hidden camera—put pressure on Governor Richards, the legislature, and the Texas Department of Health to address the problem again. The media reports suggested that the lax attitudes of some state regulators may have been partly to blame, but inadequate funding of nursing home regulation also may have been a factor. If so, it was an all-too-typical conflict of two governmental policies: a policy to protect vulnerable members of society, but to do so within the confines of a broader policy to limit costs and taxes.

Anthony Downs describes these phases of news coverage and public interest in terms of an **issue-attention cycle**.[28] There is a pre-public phase where a problem, such as poor nursing home conditions, quietly affects numerous individuals. Someone, perhaps a relative of a nursing home resident, then attempts to transform the issue into a public concern through the media. Press coverage starts slowly but rapidly intensifies, prompting more and more outraged citizens to discuss the problem. But initial enthusiasm for solutions gives way to the "realization that significant progress will be costly not only in terms of money but social stability," and many people begin to lose interest. After the enactment of policies to address some of the problems, governmental responses tend to become institutionalized, and many of the initial changes are ignored or become ineffective. While press coverage may continue intermittently, it has limited effect in renewing public opinion or prompting further governmental action—until someone, usually several years later, restarts the cycle.[29]

The media's degree of influence over specific governmental actions, however, can vary considerably, depending on the media's own interest in an issue and the public's reaction to what they read and hear. All too often, an apathetic public and indifferent public officials minimize the media's role in agenda-setting or agenda-building.

Perhaps the greatest potential for media influence in Austin is over the ethical conduct of legislators and other public officials, because of the potential embarrassment and political damage that can befall an elected official caught in an impropriety. But even that influence is sporadic because memories are short and, sooner or later, there will be another scandal (see Chapter 8). Never is the relationship between reporters and governmental officials more adversarial than when the media is questioning the ethical behavior of officeholders.

Governor Preston Smith vividly illustrated that point in a Headliners Club address to reporters, media executives, and lobbyists in Austin shortly after the Sharpstown stock fraud scandal had first hit the headlines in early 1971. Smith never was implicated in any wrongdoing, but reporters had been asking a lot of questions about why the governor had added two banking regulation bills sought by Houston financier Frank Sharp to the agenda of a special legislative session in 1969. Smith later vetoed the bills, but he and other state officials had profited from insurance stock purchases financed with loans from Sharp's bank. Smith surprised his luncheon audience, especially those in the first row of tables, by suddenly holding up a stone in the middle of his speech and proclaiming, "Let he who is without stock cast the first rock." The governor didn't throw the stone, of course, but some heads ducked.

The same kind of tension was evident 20 years later when House Speaker Gib Lewis was fighting two misdemeanor ethics charges stemming from a grand jury investigation of his relationship with a tax collection law firm. After Lewis was indicted on Dec. 28, 1990—12 days before the 1991 legislative session was to convene—the speaker mailed letters to newspapers across the state, urging editors to avoid a "rush to judgment" about his case. Maintaining his innocence, Lewis said, "All I ask is basic fairness—that I be given the time and opportunity to gather the facts and present my case before you judge me." The *Houston Chronicle* ran the letter at the top of its "Viewpoints," or letters-to-the-editor, column, accompanied by the mug shots, front and side views, taken of Lewis when he surrendered to law enforcement officers at the Travis County jail.[30]

Lewis was easily reelected speaker when the legislature convened and maintained a reasonable working relationship with the news media throughout the 1991 session. He had always been personable. But there were some rough spots. He accused the media of manufacturing the ethics issue and suggested news people should monitor their own behavior first. The day before the session convened, he told a group of Capitol reporters, in a seemingly jocular vein: "You guys ought to be lucky I am close-mouthed. I know who every one of you is sleeping with. I now understand where you get some of your leads. My phone has been ringing off the wall the last couple of weeks....So you better be nice to me."[31]

## THE MASS MEDIA AND THE ELECTORAL PROCESS

Candidates for public office in Texas still attend rallies in the park and salute the flag at Fourth of July parades. Some legislative and local candidates, particularly those with more shoe leather than money, still rely heavily on door-to-door campaigning. But in races for statewide offices and many local and district offices as well, the campaign stump has long since been replaced by the **sound bite**, the press conference and the contrived pseudo-event developed by the campaign consultant. Campaigning is now constructed around the mass media, particularly television, and the media, in effect, has displaced the political party as the major information link between the voters and those in government (see Chapter 6).

Journalists and academics repeatedly debate the effects of news coverage on elections. Most journalists believe their job is to be as objective as possible in outlining the issues and reporting and evaluating the backgrounds, philosophies, activities, and policy proposals of candidates. The media tries to determine what issues should be important in a campaign, but journalists are being increasingly challenged by television advertising with which the candidates themselves seek to dictate what the electorate should consider important.

News media reports and paid political advertising obviously play major roles in shaping voters' decisions. Studies have indicated that party identification helps determine voters' choices in general elections, but long ballots in primaries and general elections force voters to also seek other sources of information about the candidates. Consequently, voters may increasingly rely on the "simplification and interpretation inherent in news presentations to clarify candidates' characteristics, issues, positions and prospects."[32] Newspaper editorial endorsements of candidates also provide additional cues to many voters.[33]

The media, however, has been criticized for covering campaigns much as it would a horse race. Some critics argue that reporters often neglect substantive policy issues and the candidates' positions on them in favor of stories about campaign strategies, tactics, and personalities, which usually are easier to develop. Numerous national studies indicate that policy issues receive only a small part of campaign coverage, and a cursory review of campaign reporting in Texas leads to a similar conclusion. There are variations in the way newspapers, television, and news magazines cover political campaigns, but approximately one-half of the news stories focus on who is winning and the strategy and tactics that candidates are using.[34]

The "horse race" approach includes the publication of poll stories indicating candidate voter strength in trial heats at different stages of a campaign. Some polls are leaked to the press by the candidates who commission them—if the polls make a candidate look strong or his opponent appear weak. Other polls are conducted periodically by media organizations. While some of these surveys also attempt to measure public opinion on selected issues, their primary focus is on who is winning and who is losing.

Most candidates for major offices plan their daily campaign appearances with television newscasts in mind. They participate in activities that look good in a 30-second news segment. Unfortunately for the viewers, however, such superficial coverage doesn't even begin to shed light on the complex issues in a race and a candidate's position on them. Neither does a candidate's paid television advertising.

In what has become a ritual for the Capitol press corps in Austin each political season, reporters are regularly summoned to a candidate's campaign headquarters where a staffer or a consultant loads a videotape into a VCR and proudly previews the candidate's latest TV ad. It may be a positive, "feel good" spot, portraying the candidate in the best possible light—playing with his grandchildren, speaking to senior citizens, or shaking hands with the president of the United States. Or it may be an attack ad, charging his opponent with a weakness or an indiscretion unworthy of the public trust, or deliberately misrepresenting the opponent's record or position on an issue. Sometimes, the candidate will attend the press preview but usually doesn't. Reporters—print and electronic—then dutifully troop back to their offices and, more often than not, write reviews of the previews, usually getting reaction from the candidate's opponent or the opponent's campaign consultant.

Several media organizations have started closely analyzing paid TV spots for accuracy and reporting their findings. But most reporters, particularly in the print media, dislike the process of even partially covering a campaign off the well-crafted images on a TV screen. Major Texas newspapers—while still preoccupied with the horse race—devote considerable resources to political coverage, attempting to provide the in-depth perspective missing in the electronic media. But the vast majority of Texas voters become acquainted with a candidate through televised images, and television has come to dominate and, for the most part, trivialize the political process.

Television has allowed a candidate with enough money to legally buy an election. Bill Clements, who had never previously held elective office and was a stranger to most Texans, spent millions of dollars of his own fortune on TV ads in 1978 to become the first Republican to capture the governor's office this century. In 1990, Clayton Williams, another multimillionaire businessman and political neophyte, spent more than $21 million, including $8.4 million from his own pocket, to create an attractive, 30-second TV image that came within a whisker of also being elected governor.

Political scientists, reporters, many voters, and even some candidates loudly criticize what television has done to campaigns for public office, putting style over substance and orchestrated events over thoughtful debate of the issues. But the creators of superficial TV ads know they have a large audience. And since candidates are in the race to win office and not to reform the system, they spend millions of dollars perpetuating the political problem, which actually is part of a larger social problem.

Particularly susceptible to the image creators and media manipulators are the young adults who, according to a 1990 study by the Times Mirror Center for The People & The Press, are less likely to read newspapers, watch TV news programs, and otherwise keep up with current events than their parents or grandparents. "The 30-second commercial spot is a particularly appropriate medium for the MTV generation," noted the study. "Sound bites and symbolism, the principal fuel of modern political campaigns, are well-suited to young voters who know less and have limited interest in politics and public policy. Their limited appetites and aptitudes are shaping the practice of politics and the nature of our democracy."[35]

The more disturbing issue, therefore, is the long-term implications of the superficial, image-oriented campaign and an increasingly indifferent electorate.


## MEDIA COVERAGE OF THE 1990 GUBERNATORIAL CAMPAIGN

The 1990 gubernatorial election is a case study of some of the worst aspects of contemporary political campaigning. The highly acrimonious campaign was characterized by **negative TV ads**, personal attacks on the character and integrity of the candidates, and distortions of their public records. While receiving national attention for new lows in campaign combat, it also demonstrated the effectiveness of well-financed campaigns and political advertising. The news media's performance in covering it was mixed. But the few voters who followed the campaign through the state's major daily newspapers—while periodically wiping off the mud—were given more than enough information to compare the candidates' qualifications and personalities and evaluate their proposed solutions—or lack thereof—to the state's major problems. In the end, Democrat Ann Richards defeated Republican Clayton Williams because Williams couldn't survive his own spontaneity, his lack of governmental and political experience, and the in-depth media scrutiny to which he was finally subjected.

The rancher-oilman from Midland took full advantage of Texas' television markets to swamp three opponents and win the Republican nomination without a runoff. Bankrolling his own campaign to the tune of $6 million for the March primary, Williams literally galloped to the nomination across the small screen. With an ad campaign that included TV spots of him riding horseback in cowboy duds across his ranch, he cultivated an image as an independent, successful businessman and governmental outsider with strong traditional roots who would mount a no-nonsense attack on the problems in Austin. In a televised debate, one Republican opponent insisted that the next governor of Texas couldn't "ride horseback into the 21st century," but Williams and his media consultants had already created a folk hero who was readily embraced by conservative Republican voters.

One of Williams' more memorable TV spots in the primary featured him standing in front of a chain gang and promising to introduce young drug offenders to the "joys of busting rocks." The ad clearly was aimed at widespread concern about crime, drugs, and juvenile delinquency, issues that had been identified in public opinion polls. But it was several weeks after the ad first aired before any reporter questioned in print the legality of imposing such convict labor under a federal judge's reform order that had governed the prison system for several years. Reporters also were slow to take a critical look at Williams' televised claims of having created thousands of jobs with his various businesses.

The Democratic primary, meanwhile, was characterized by rancorous charges and countercharges and—in the minds of many—petty, cheap shots among the candidates. Ann Richards was dogged by allegations that she had once used illegal drugs. Attorney General Jim Mattox, one of her opponents, had planted the allegations with reporters early in the campaign, but they initially remained unreported. The drug question erupted as an issue after a statewide televised debate in February, when Richards refused to fully answer a reporter-panelist's question about whether she had ever used illegal drugs. A recovering alcoholic, Richards said only that she had not used a "mood altering chemical" in the previous 10 years. She said she didn't want to say any more because she didn't want to discourage drug addicts from seeking treatment. The debate question was legitimate because gubernatorial candidates had been promising to fight illegal drugs, and her refusal to answer it with a definitive yes or no was enough to raise doubts about her personal conduct that plagued her throughout the rest of the primary campaign. But some media outlets' subsequent handling of the question was irresponsible.

In the Democratic runoff, Mattox ran a television commercial questioning whether Richards had ever used illegal drugs and even charged on a national TV news show, without offering any proof, that Richards had once been addicted to cocaine. No one ever produced any proof of the drug allegations but, in a particularly poor performance, some media outlets ran uncorroborated allegations about both Richards and Mattox using illegal drugs. Fear of being beaten by a competitor in what had become a virtual feeding frenzy, some news people had thrown basic journalistic standards of substantiation and fairness out the window.

Richards, who eventually defeated Mattox in the runoff, wasn't above launching negative campaign attacks of her own. During the primary campaign, she ran TV ads suggesting that both Mattox and former Governor Mark White, who finished third in the primary, had profited in an unethical fashion from their years in public office.

While the media had four major Republican gubernatorial candidates and three major Democratic contenders to try to cover before the primaries, reporters could concentrate on only two nominees—Williams and Richards—after the primaries and the Democratic runoff. And Williams, in particular, began to be subjected to closer and more critical scrutiny.

Williams' first encounter with this increased media attention occurred in spectacular fashion only a few days after his primary victory, when he invited reporters to visit his West Texas ranch for spring roundup. Sharing a cup of coffee with cowhands, campaign staffers, and three male reporters—R.G. Ratcliffe of the *Houston Chronicle*, Sam Attlesey of *The Dallas Morning News*, and John Gravois of the *Houston Post*—around an early morning campfire and still basking in his electoral success, Williams saw no reason for caution. When he told an old joke comparing the morning's foggy weather to rape—"if it's inevitable, just relax and enjoy it"—he certainly had no idea it would become page one headlines in the next day's newspapers and an issue in the remainder of the campaign. But it did.

In the not too distant past, such remarks in an informal setting, where the candidate was hosting reporters, would have been treated as off-the-record and not been reported. But that time is gone. Now, every aspect of a public official's or candidate's life is subject to public scrutiny, as demonstrated on the national scene by the reporting a few years earlier of one-time Democratic presidential candidate Gary Hart's relationship with model Donna Rice. Reporters are making greater efforts to present voters with a candid view of a candidate, warts and all, something that viewers aren't going to see in the candidate's TV commercials. The media also perceives a significant public concern about the moral behavior of elected officials.

In reporting Williams' rape joke, the media also took into consideration society's increasing sensitivity to sexual abuse and harassment, the fact that a violent crime is no laughing matter, and the question of whether Williams, as governor, would be sensitive to issues of particular concern to half of Texas' population—women. The joke loomed even larger after a woman won the Democratic nomination. At the time of the campfire chat, Richards was still in a runoff with Mattox.

Williams' problems were compounded a few weeks later when, in an interview with the *Houston Post*, he admitted that he had been "serviced" by prostitutes as a young man.[36]

Williams' campaign operatives then resorted to a typical campaign technique. They tried to restrict the media's access to him and to more carefully manage his public appearances. But despite the attempts at damage control, Williams saw a gradual erosion of his early lead with costly losses among Texas women. And he committed other major gaffes late in the campaign.

Just a few days before the general election, in a televised appearance before a panel of reporters, Williams admitted that he did not know what the only constitutional amendment on that year's ballot was about but had already voted for it during the early, or absentee, voting period. His wife had told him to, he said. The admission was particularly devastating because the amendment had been offered to settle a well-publicized controversy over the timing of Senate confirmation of gubernatorial appointments, an issue of crucial importance to the next governor. The faux pas reinforced Richards' claims that Williams lacked the qualifications and the experience to be governor. That impression also was being painted by newspaper stories questioning how Williams could keep promises to build more prisons and attack the illegal drug problem and still keep another promise to veto higher taxes in the face of a severe revenue shortfall being projected by state budget experts.

Also a few days before the November election, Williams admitted that he had paid no federal income tax in 1986 because of business losses, an admission that angered tax-weary voters of more modest means. In the fall, the *Houston Chronicle* also reported allegations that a bank of which Williams was a director had illegally required high risk auto loan customers to purchase credit life insurance.[37] A grand jury investigation was initiated by Travis County Attorney Ken Oden, a Democrat, and months after the election, the bank would enter a guilty plea to criminal charges and pay a $1.2 million fine.

Some newspapers and at least one television station, KVUE-TV in Austin, began regularly analyzing political TV ads during the campaign, pointing out inaccuracies and inflated claims to readers and viewers. *The Dallas Morning News* even used a standing format that made its truth-in-advertising features easily recognizable. The major daily newspapers in Houston, Dallas, Fort Worth, and Austin also published numerous in-depth articles examining the legitimate issues— education, crime, taxes, insurance reform, abortion, and the environment—and how the candidates were addressing, or failing to address, each one. Efforts were made to analyze the political viability of each candidate's stand on an issue, not just to recite what each candidate was proposing. And lengthy investigative profiles of both Richards and Williams were published.

But television—the paid commercials and the sound bites on evening newscasts—was how most Texans formed their impressions of the governor's race and of which candidate was the most qualified, or the least objectionable. And television was made to order for the mudslinging that both Richards and Williams publicly castigated but also perpetuated. Personal attacks or campaign blunders, not substantive issues, also were often featured in the daily front page headlines in the newspapers.

In October, for example, the media turned Williams' calculated snub of a Richards handshake at a joint public appearance before the Greater Dallas Crime Commission into a major event. While a luncheon audience was mingling and TV cameras were rolling, the Republican nominee—who had tipped off some reporters to his plans—walked up to Richards, accused her of lying about him, and refused to shake her offered hand. The two candidates then separately addressed the luncheon about the state's crime problem, but those speeches weren't what was reported on TV that evening and in most newspapers the next morning.

Reporter Cinny Kennard of Dallas' WFAA-TV believed the incident, which looked particularly dramatic on TV, was newsworthy because it showed Richards' performance under fire. "The issue of character enters in there. What kind of character does a candidate have in a situation like that?"[38]

But there were others who felt that the coverage was superficial and poorly served the media's audience. In an article in *The Texas Observer*, Dave Denison asked:

> Was the confrontation, in the final analysis, really that much more important than the real and substantial differences in the two candidates' approach to the crime problem? Even if the snub were inevitably to dominate the next day's news coverage, footage from the two speeches on crime could have been edited down later to show quite a lot about the different ways Williams and Richards were thinking about the issue.
>
> In fact, it was a great day for reporters on the scene. They were rescued from the task of doing speech coverage or issues coverage. They had a dramatic incident with front-page and top-of-the-news appeal. All the reporters who were there, including myself, felt they had gotten a good show.[39]

Denison also argued that commercial television stations should devote more of their evening newscasts to coverage of substantive political issues. He suggested running excerpts from candidates' stump speeches at the end of a newscast or producing documentaries on major political races. But while Denison interviewed voters who indicated they would watch such coverage, TV executives also cited cold statistics indicating that most viewers prefer game shows and sitcoms to public affairs programming. And where the mass of viewers go, so do the advertisers.[40]

Newspapers were split in their endorsements in the governor's race. The only major metropolitan dailies to endorse Williams in the general election were *The Dallas Morning News* and the *Houston Post*. Candidates welcome such endorsements and often feature them in political advertising. But favorable exposure on the front pages, rather than on the editorial pages, and on TV screens normally is more crucial to a candidate's electoral success.

For all its highs and lows, the 1990 campaign coverage was dominated by the governor's race, a fact that highlighted a perennial, major shortcoming of most

Texas news organizations. Down-ballot statewide races aren't completely ignored, but they are traditionally undercovered by the media. The main reasons are logistical and financial. Newspapers and television stations don't have sufficient staff, news columns or air time to provide the in-depth coverage that many of these "other" races deserve. In 1990, there were contested races for lieutenant governor, attorney general, agriculture commissioner, comptroller, state treasurer, land commissioner, the Railroad Commission, and some court seats. The news media's limited attention to such races increases the likelihood that well-financed candidates can win election almost solely on the basis of effective television advertising campaigns. TV certainly was a key factor in Republican Rick Perry's narrow victory over liberal Democratic Agriculture Commissioner Jim Hightower in 1990.

Reporters believed that Hightower, who had used no paid TV, had under-estimated his opponent and may have been too preoccupied with national liberal Democratic causes. But Hightower sharply criticized the media for ignoring foreign trade and other issues that he had discussed in numerous personal appearances throughout Texas. "Frankly there's just a lot of stupidity in the press," he said in a post-election interview in *The Texas Observer.* "I mean there are people who just aren't very bright. They don't get it. I mean, you can talk issues all day long, and they just don't follow you."[41]

To receive any appreciable press coverage, a candidate for statewide office has to establish himself or herself as a serious, viable contender. And one of the standards by which such viability is measured is a candidate's ability to adequately finance a campaign—either through personal wealth or a broad base of financial contributors. The media in 1990, for example, never took Republican nominee Warren G. Harding, Jr.'s candidacy for comptroller seriously because he was over-whelmed at the outset, both in endorsements and financial support, by Democratic nominee John Sharp. A member of the Texas Railroad Commission at the time, Sharp had developed such a broad base of both Democratic and Republican supporters during several years in public office that potentially stronger Republican candidates chose not to run against him.

Perhaps the media's most glaring omission in 1990 was its under coverage of the U.S. Senate race at the top of the ballot. From the very beginning, there was virtually no doubt that well-financed, incumbent Republican Phil Gramm would win re-election over Democratic challenger Hugh Parmer, a state senator from Fort Worth. But the two men represented significant political and philosophical differen-ces that should have been more fully aired before the electorate. Instead, reporters who did write stories about the Senate race liked to speculate on how wide Gramm's victory margin would be, whether a large win by him would produce more votes for down-ballot Republicans and whether it would give him a boost as a potential presidential candidate. While political insiders may have appreciated such specula-tion, most voters would have found stories about Gramm's Senate voting record, his performance on bread-and-butter issues, much more relevant when they entered the voting booth. But Gramm's voting record—for better or worse, one of the most conservative in the U.S. Senate—was ignored by most media organizations.

## GUARDIANS OF OPEN GOVERNMENT

Since the soundness of any governmental policy or program is affected by the motives and capabilities of those officials who design and administer it, most members of the Capitol press corps take very seriously their role as watchdogs over the behavior and performance of elected officials and bureaucrats. In a survey for a master's thesis from the University of Texas at Austin in 1983, Steve Levine, who was then the Capitol bureau chief for the *Beaumont Enterprise*, found that many Capitol reporters rated their government watchdog role as second in importance only to the "neutral transmission of information."[42]

Consequently, the media is a persistent guardian of the public's access to governmental business through the state's **Open Meetings and Open Records acts**. These laws, which apply to state and local governments, basically provide that the public's business is to be conducted in public and that most records produced in the conduct of the public's business are to be made available to the public on demand. Each law provides for certain exceptions. Governmental bodies, for example, are allowed to hold closed-door meetings to consider personnel matters, to discuss lawsuits in which they are involved, and to consider real estate purchases, although all formal actions are to be taken in public. The open meetings law requires a governmental body to post advance notices of all its meetings, even closed-door, executive sessions, and the Open Records Act establishes a procedure whereby the state attorney general's office decides disputes over whether specific governmental records can be kept confidential. But media representatives are engaged in a constant struggle against abuses and outright violations of the laws and attempts by school boards, city councils, and other governments to expand the list of exceptions that allow them to conduct business in private.

A ploy of some governmental officials, for example, is to seek an attorney general's opinion on virtually every request for records submitted by a reporter or other member of the public, even though the attorney general may have previously ruled that similar records are public. Such a practice not only abuses the Open Records Act by slowing down the public's access to the requested information, it often also forces unnecessary legal expenses on the requesting party. In one glaring, recent case of abuse, the Houston Independent School District used a variety of legal maneuvers to circumvent a request by the *Houston Chronicle* for access to records on the educational backgrounds of some HISD administrators. The newspaper was trying to determine how many administrators held degrees from a non-accredited college, something of likely concern to many parents and taxpayers. But the school district continued to resist even after rulings from the attorney general and the Texas Supreme Court that the information the newspaper sought was public.

Some state officials also are not above breaking or bending open government laws. The 1991 ethics law, ironically, was written by House and Senate negotiators behind closed doors in apparent violation of the Open Meetings Act (see Chapter 8). And, that same year, Governor Ann Richards and several key legislators and staffers flew to remote Matagorda Island to discuss budgetary and government reorganization issues in a private meeting whose legality was widely challenged by the news media. What made the meeting questionable was the fact that it was attended by a quorum of the Legislative Budget Board. Attorney General Dan Morales said the Open Meetings Law applied to the board but said the actual legality or illegality of the island meeting was a fact question that had to be evaluated by local law enforcement officials. A Calhoun County grand jury, which looked into the matter, concluded that board members hadn't broken any state laws. Calhoun County District Attorney Jack Whitlow said the meeting was not a formal meeting and noted the law, although vague, allowed governmental bodies to meet privately with staffers so long as there was no discussion of public business.[43] But the incident made some people question the sincerity of Governor Richards and Lt. Governor Bob Bullock, the budget board chairman, who on taking office only a few months earlier had promised to promote openness in their "New Texas."

Several media organizations monitor and actively promote open government issues. The Freedom of Information Foundation of Texas, a non-profit corporation that includes journalists, educators, and attorneys among its directors, maintains a telephone hotline to advise news people on open meetings and open records rights and procedures and generally promotes openness in government. Texas Media, an umbrella organization that includes the Texas Daily Newspaper Association, the Texas Press Association, the Texas Association of Broadcasters, the Society of Professional Journalists, and other media groups, lobbies the legislature on open government issues. It's a difficult struggle because many public officials throughout Texas prefer to conduct the public's business in private. Numerous attempts usually are made each legislative session to weaken the Open Meetings and Open Records laws. In 1991 alone, Texas Media opposed or worked to change about 100 such bills.

Media organizations obviously are in the business of disseminating information. But it is important to remember that they are not the only ones with a stake in strong open government laws. Every taxpaying Texan also has a strong right to know what his or her government is doing, to find open doors in city council chambers and school board meeting rooms, and to have ready access to public documents.

## HOW WELL INFORMED ARE TEXAS CITIZENS?

Despite the media's fight for open government, however, only a small percentage of Texans attempt to keep up with what their elected officials in Austin are doing. High-profile issues, like taxes, the lottery, or horse-race betting, attract a lot of attention. But many taxpayers, particularly those who live in metropolitan areas that have numerous legislators, don't even know who their state representatives or state senators are, much less how they have voted on significant issues.

This may partly be the media's fault. Many small newspapers carry only brief wire service stories about news events in Austin, while others give an incomplete picture by concentrating primarily on issues of local interest. The major newspapers provide more complete coverage, but they seldom publish record votes of legislators within their readership areas. Most radio stations carry only cursory headline versions of statehouse news, at best, and most television stations, through which most Texans apparently get their news, don't do much better than that. Although specialists in communications, reporters don't always tell their readers and viewers how the actions of the legislature, the governor, the bureaucracy, and the courts are relevant to their lives and their futures.

But it is only partly the media's fault. There are ample information sources for anyone to stay informed of major developments in state government. The distractions and demands on a person's time are great in today's fast-paced world, and a person who wants to know what's going on in the governmental and political arena often has to juggle priorities. But the opportunities are there. It is up to the individual to make the time and the effort.

Ignorance among the general electorate plays right into the hands of the special interests, who not only stay abreast of developments in Austin but also spend millions of dollars on political donations and legislative entertainment to influence those developments to their advantage, not to the benefit of the general public. Most governmental actions, whether taken by the legislature or a state regulatory board, eventually will affect the pocketbooks or quality of life of thousands, perhaps millions, of Texans, most of whom will be caught by surprise.

And if recent indications are correct, the influence of special interests over the public's business will become even greater in the future. In one of the greatest ironies of the so-called "information age," young people apparently are paying less attention than their parents to what's going on in their world. At least, that is the conclusion of a national study published in 1990 by the Times Mirror Center for The People & The Press.

The study, *The Age of Indifference*, indicated that newspapers, which have suffered an overall decline in regular readership since the 1960s, have been affected more adversely than the electronic media. But young people today also are less inclined than their parents even to watch news on television. When surveyed, only 30 percent of a national sample of people younger than 35 said they had read a newspaper the previous day. That compared to 67 percent of those younger than 35 in a Gallup Poll in 1965. Only 41 percent of those younger than 35 in the 1990 sample said they had watched television news the previous day, compared to 52 percent in 1965. The Times Mirror study also determined that young Americans are less able than their parents to identify major newsmakers—except, perhaps, for sports figures—are much less critical of political leaders, and are less likely to vote. Only in coverage of sports and the abortion issue—which could directly affect the lives of many young persons—do young people match their parents' interest in news. "Abortion notwithstanding, an overall examination of the surveys conducted by Times Mirror reveals a younger generation with less curiosity about news of all sorts, and one with an especially small appetite for the most serious and complicated of issues," the survey concluded.[44]

Noting that during the previous five decades younger Americans had been at least as well informed as older people, the Times Mirror researchers suggested that the Vietnam conflict and the Watergate scandal, both of which damaged Americans' confidence in their government, may be partly to blame for such a large amount of indifference now. They also cited serious problems in public education, longtime classroom deficiencies which restrict young people's views of the world and which Texas and other states are still trying to resolve.[45] And the increased number of entertainment alternatives now competing for young people's time also is a likely factor.

Whatever the reason, the prospects for a quality state government sensitive to the public interest in the next generation are discouraging. If the survey accurately reflects the attitudes of the young, state government will be controlled well into the 21st century by special interests, perhaps to a greater extent than ever before.

## SUMMARY AND CONCLUSIONS

**1.** Throughout much of this century, Texas' major newspapers were owned by publishers who were members of the conservative, big-business, big-oil establishment that ran the state government.

**2.** The media today is much more independent of officialdom, much more eager to challenge those in power. One reason for that change is the high level of distrust of government produced by the Sharpstown and Watergate scandals and the divisiveness of the Vietnam War. Another factor is the growth in out-of-state corporate ownership of major Texas newspapers and television stations. Absentee corporate owners don't have sacred cows to protect in state and local governments.

**3.** Television is now the primary source of news for most Texans, although most TV news programs provide only cursory reports on government and politics. Major Texas newspapers, meanwhile, have made significant improvements in recent years.

**4.** About 60 journalists now regularly cover the state Capitol, and the number increases when the legislature is in session. The size of the press corps and the logistics of covering major, breaking stories often force journalists into a pack, both physically and mentally. Such intense competition can increase public pressure on officials to correct problems and deficiencies. But the pack mentality also can prompt reporters to focus attention on a few spectacular stories while ignoring other important issues. In this respect, pack journalism limits the agenda for public debate and discussion.

**5.** Although allegations of media bias are exaggerated, subtle, subjective decisions help determine which stories are covered by reporters, what angles are emphasized, and the prominence with which they are displayed. The personal political preferences of the journalists cover the spectrum, and most news people take pains to avoid biased reporting. But more often than not, they eagerly provide a forum for the viewpoints of consumer and welfare advocates and environmentalists challenging big business and big government. Stories about the age-old struggle between the powerful and the powerless center on the controversial and attract considerable viewer and reader interest. Corporate media owners also have their own business interests to protect, sometimes to the point of influencing public policy.

**6.** The media inevitably has some impact on public policy by focusing attention on specific issues and making the causes of few individuals the concerns of many. But in recent years, the Texas press was largely reactive in reporting major deficiencies in criminal justice, education, and the state's care of the mentally retarded—issues that produced landmark court orders for reform. Perhaps the greatest potential for media influence is over the ethical conduct of public officials.

**7.** Political campaigning, especially for major offices, is now primarily constructed around television, particularly paid TV advertising in which candidates give voters 30-second, positive glimpses of themselves or make 30-second, often misleading attacks on their opponents. Major newspapers attempt to penetrate the candidates' carefully crafted TV images and focus attention on the complex policy issues. But even newspapers often divert attention from substantive issues to "horse race" stories about campaign strategies and tactics.

**8.** The 1990 gubernatorial race was one of the most negative and acrimonious in the nation's history, and the media's performance in covering it was mixed. Some reporters let themselves be taken in by the unsubstantiated allegations of illegal drug use that were raised against candidates in the Democratic primary. And the news media only belatedly challenged the accuracy of advertising claims with which multimillionaire Clayton Williams captured the Republican nomination. In the end, though, Ann Richards defeated Williams because Williams couldn't survive his own spontaneity, his lack of political experience, and the in-depth media scrutiny to which he was finally subjected.

**9.** Media organizations are persistent guardians of the public's access to governmental business through the state's Open Meetings and Open Records acts, but the fight against government secrecy is a never-ending battle.

**10.** One of the greatest ironies of the so-called "information age" is that young people apparently are paying less attention than their parents to governmental news and other substantive events occurring in the world around them. This dims the prospects for a quality state government in the next generation because ignorance among the general electorate plays right into the hands of the special interests who make it their business to influence public policy.

## KEY TERMS

Information age
Editorial autonomy
Capitol press corps
Spin
Pack journalism
Media bias
Agenda-setting

Issue attention cycle
Sound bite
Negative TV ads
Open Meetings and Open
    Records acts
*Age of Indifference*

## FURTHER READING

Abramson, Jeffrey B., F. Christopher Arterton, and Gary R. Orren, *The Electronic Commonwealth*. New York: Basic Books, Inc.,Publishers, 1988.

Arterton, F. Christopher, *Media Politics*. (Lexington, Mass.: Lexington Books, 1984.

Bennett, W. Lance, *News: The Politics of Illusion*, 2nd ed. New York: Longman, 1988.

Berkman, Ronald, and Laura W. Kitch, *Politics in the Media Age*.New York: McGraw-Hill Book Company, 1986.

Denison, Dave, "Prime-Time Politics: Why TV News Doesn't Get the Picture," *The Texas Observer*, December 21, 1990, pp. 4-8.

Dugger, Ronnie, "On the Governor's Race," *The Texas Observer*, September 28, 1990, pp. 7-9.

Glendening, Parris N., "The Public's Perception of State Government and Governors," *State Government* (Summer, 1980), pp. 115-120.

Graber, Doris A., *Mass Media and American Politics*, 3rd ed. Washington, D.C.: Congressional Quarterly Press, 1989.

Jamieson, Kathleen Hall, *Packaging the Presidency*. New York: Oxford University Press, 1984.

Jamieson, Kathleen Hall, *Eloquence in an Electronic Age*. New York: Oxford University Press, 1988.

Joslyn, Richard, *Mass Media and Elections*. Reading, Mass.: Addison-Wesley Publishing Company, 1984.

Krasnow, Erwin G., Lawrence D. Longley, and Herbert A. Terry, *The Politics of Broadcast Regulation*. New York: St. Martin's Press, 1982.

Nimmo, Dan, and James E. Combs, *Mediated Political Realities*. New York: Longman, 1983.

Parenti, Michael, *Inventing Reality: The Politics of the Mass Media*. New York: St. Martin's Press, 1986.

Ranney, Austin, *Channels of Power: The Impact of Television on American Politics*. New York: Basic Books, Inc., 1983.

Wolbrueck, David J., "Curtains for the Editor: Freedom of the Press Under Fire in Round Rock," *The Texas Observer*, April 19, 1991, pp. 22-23.

## ENDNOTES

1. T. R. Fehrenbach, *Lone Star: A History of Texas and the Texans* (New York: The MacMillan Company, 1968), p. 302.
2. Ibid., p. 303.
3. George Norris Green, *The Establishment in Texas Politics, 1938-1957* (Westport, Conn.: Green-wood Press, 1979), p. 10.
4. Ibid., p. 162.
5. Ibid., p. 162.
6. Ibid., p. 104.
7. John H. Shenefield, "Ownership Concentration in Newspapers," *American Bar Association Journal*, 65 (September, 1979), p. 1335.
8. *Editor and Publisher Yearbook 1991* (New York: Editor and Publisher, 1991). There are some discrepancies among the various yearbooks regarding these totals. Gale Research, Inc., which publishes the *Gale Directory of Publications and Broadcast Media 1992* (Detroit: Gale Research, Inc., 1991), reports 105 dailies and 442 weeklies.
9. Vittorio Zucconi, "America's Media Empires," *World Press Review* (May, 1986), p. 21. Excerpted from "La Republica" of Rome.
10. "A Short Course in Broadcasting, 1991," *The Broadcasting Yearbook, 1991*, p. A-3.
11. Harte-Hanks Communications, *The Texas Report*, 3 (Summer, 1986). The questions were phrased "Now I would like to ask you where you get most of your news. Where do you get most of your local news? How about news of what's going on in the country—where do you get most of your national news?"
12. Times Mirror Center for the People and the Press, *The Age of Indifference*, June 28, 1990, p. 1.
13. *The New York Times*, July 7, 1991, p. H23.
14. Zucconi, "America's Media Empires," p. 19.
15. "A Short Course in Broadcasting, 1991," *The Broadcasting Yearbook 1991*, p. A-3.
16. Jeffrey B. Abramson, F. Christopher Arterton and Gary R. Orren, *The Electronic Commonwealth* (New York: Basic Books, Inc., 1988), pp. 5-6.
17. *Public Opinion* (August/September 1985), p. 7.

18. Edward Jay Epstein, *News from Nowhere* (New York: Random House Vintage Books), pp. 13-14.
19. Doris A. Graber, *Mass Media and American Politics*, 2nd ed. (Washington, D.C.: Congressional Quarterly Press, 1984), pp. 71-74.
20. Michael Parenti, *Democracy for the Few*, 5th ed. (New York: St. Martin's Press, 1988), p. 170.
21. Graber, *Mass Media and American Politics*, pp. 78-79.
22. *The Texas Poll*, conducted by the Public Policy Resources Laboratory at Texas A & M University for Harte-Hanks Communications, Inc., Spring, 1991.
23. Maxwell E. McCombs and Donald L. Shaw, "The Agenda-Setting Function of the Press," in Doris A. Graber, *Media Power in Politics*, 2nd ed. (Washington, D.C.: CQ Press, 1990), p. 75.
24. Doris Graber, *Mass Media in American Politics*, pp. 268-269.
25. Gladys Engel Lang and Kurt Lang, *The Battle for Public Opinion: The President, the Press, and the Polls during Watergate* (New York: Columbia University Press, 1983), p. 58.
26. Larry N. Gerston, *Making Public Policy: From Conflict to Resolution* (Glenview Ill.: Scott, Foresman and Company, 1983), pp. 55-56.
27. Personal interview with Bo Byers, Austin, Texas, July 12, 1990.
28. Anthony Downs, "Up and Down with Ecology—'The Issue Attention Cycle,'" *Public Interest*, 32 (Summer 1972), pp. 38-50.
29. See Barbara J. Nelson, *Making an Issue of Child Abuse: Political Agenda Setting for Social Problems* (Chicago: University of Chicago Press, 1984), pp. 51-75.
30. *Houston Chronicle*, January 6, 1991.
31. *Houston Chronicle*, January 8, 1991.
32. Ibid., p. 3.
33. Ibid., pp. 3-4.
34. See S. Robert Lichter, "How the Press Covered the Primaries," *Public Opinion*, (July-August, 1988), p. 45; Thomas E. Patterson, "The Press and its Missed Assignment," in *The Elections of 1988*, edited by Michael Nelson (Washington, D.C.: Congressional Quarterly Press, 1989), p. 98; Doris Graber, *Processing the News*, 2nd ed. (New York: Longman, 1988), p. 78; and Marjories Randon Hershey, "The Campaign and the Media," in *The Election of 1988*, edited by Gerald Pomper (Chatham, N.J.: Chatham House, 1988), pp. 96-100.
35. Times Mirror Center for the People and the Press, *The Age of Indifference: A Study of Young Americans and How They View the News* (Washington, D.C.: Times Mirror Center for the People and the Press, 1990), p. 28.
36. *Houston Post*, April 22, 1990.
37. *Houston Chronicle*, September 12, 1990.
38. Dave Denison, "Primetime Politics," *The Texas Observer*, December 21, 1990, p. 5.
39. Ibid.
40. Ibid., p. 6.
41. "Jim Hightower: The Media and the Message," *The Texas Observer*, December 21, 1990, p. 8.
42. Steven Tod Levine, "Application of the Transactional Model to the Interaction between Capitol Reporters and High-Level State Government Bureaucrats," Master of Arts Thesis, University of Texas at Austin, December, 1983, p. 64.
43. *Houston Chronicle*, July 25, 1991.
44. *The Age of Indifference*, p. 9.
45. Ibid., p. 21.

# 6

# THE PARTY SYSTEM
# IN TEXAS

...the common and continual mischiefs of the spirit of party are sufficient to make
it the interest and duty of a wise people to discourage and restrain it.

*George Washington, Farewell Address to the*
*People of the United States–September 17, 1796*

Political parties still do not get much respect or esteem. Many contemporary Texans
go so far as to consider them a joke. Parties have little relevance for the layperson,
and media coverage of party-related activities often is focused on political patronage,
questionable campaign contributions, negative campaigning, petty conflicts that
lead to governmental deadlock, and instances of graft or corruption. Many people
don't view political parties as institutions of virtue or responsiveness, and they hold
clearly defined antiparty attitudes that are often expressed in the simple statement,
"I vote for the person and not the party."

Other people are ambivalent. They don't really know what political parties
do and may not even be able to distinguish between the two major parties. All they
know about parties is that they produce competition and, if nothing else, the ability
to "throw the rascals out" and replace them with another set of rascals.

But part of the electorate is really interested in political parties and is
convinced that parties are essential to developing and maintaining a democratic
society. A political party, these individuals believe, is one of the few mechanisms
available to the general public for reviewing and possibly repudiating the actions of
governmental leaders.

For much of the period since the Civil War, Texas was a one-party Democratic state. There was no organized opposition party available to mobilize the interests of those who felt neglected or excluded from the Democratic party. Electoral politics were based on factions and personalities, and the interests of the lower socioeconomic classes, especially minorities, were blatantly neglected. Over the past 30 years, however, Texas has witnessed the emergence of a viable Republican party, and the state has entered a phase of competitive two-party politics. Minorities have also won admittance to the political system and exercise considerable influence, particularly in the Democratic party.

## POLITICAL PARTIES AND A DEMOCRATIC SOCIETY

As long as a society is ruled by a few individuals and the interests or concerns of the general population have no political significance or influence, leaders have little reason to be concerned with what the masses think or want. But democratic societies are based on an assumption that those who rule have a fundamental obligation to consider the preferences, interests, and opinions of those who are governed. Since it is impossible for every individual to participate in every public policy decision, we have chosen to construct a representative government in the United States. We choose individuals to act in our behalf, which makes it necessary for us to find mechanisms to assure that these individuals are responsive and responsible. We try to accomplish this objective through several means, including elections, interest groups—and political parties.[1]

While political parties share their representative roles with other institutions, scholars tend to agree that parties perform critical functions that other institutions cannot. There is considerable debate about formal definitions of parties, their characteristics, organizational and membership criteria, and the relationship of the parties to the governing institutions and the social system.[2] Our purpose is to focus on that part of the debate that would help us understand the political parties in Texas.

## POLITICAL PARTIES IN PERSPECTIVE

Political parties are complex structures that relate to most other facets of government and politics. V.O. Key suggested that parties are social structures that are best understood from three perspectives: the party in the electorate, the party as an organization and the party in government (Figure 6-1). The party in the electorate involves the party's relationship to voters and election activities. The party organization includes a wide range of activities from the precinct to the state level that are necessary to support the party's structure. The party in government covers the activities of those elected individuals who take office and carry out the functions of government.

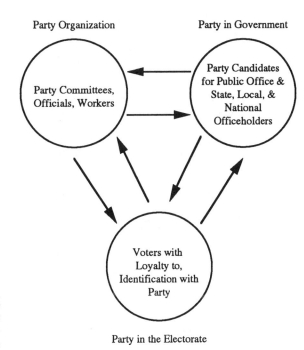

Party Organization                       Party in Government

Party Committees, Officials, Workers

Party Candidates for Public Office & State, Local, & National Officeholders

Voters with Loyalty to, Identification with Party

**FIGURE 6-1**
The Three-Part Political Party.
(*Party Politics in America,* 5th ed. by
Frank Sorauf. Copyright © 1984 by
Frank Sorauf. Reprinted by permis-
sion of HarperCollins Publishers.

Party in the Electorate

## Definition of Political Parties

We find the party definition given by political scientist Leon D. Epstein to be best
suited to Texas. A political party is "any group, however loosely organized, seeking
to elect governmental officeholders under a given label."[3] While we tend to think
only in terms of Democrat and Republican, other political parties have emerged at
both the state and local level in Texas history that met the criteria of this definition.
While political parties share some attributes and characteristics of other groups and
organizations that function in the political arena, they are distinguished from these
organizations by their primary preoccupation with contesting elections and the fact
that "it is only parties that run candidates on their own labels."[4]

## Parties and Interest Groups

At first glance, political parties and interest groups often appear indistinguishable,
but there are differences, which were partially addressed in the earlier chapter on
interest groups. While political parties are coalitions of men and women whose
political behavior is structured under a "common label to recruit, nominate, and
elect candidates for public office," interest groups are concerned with shaping public
policy by influencing the actions and decisions of public officials.[5] An interest group
usually focuses on a narrow range of policy issues. It can attempt to influence the

outcome of elections, but it doesn't nominate candidates or take responsibility for the day-to-day management of government.[6] These are functions of the political parties and officials elected under their banners.

Studies completed during the years of one-party domination in Texas concluded that the interest groups were especially powerful.[7] Some expect the relative power between interest groups and parties to change in the emerging two-party Texas, but that remains to be seen.

## THE FUNCTIONS OF POLITICAL PARTIES

### Intermediaries between the Electorate and Government

The 17 million people who live in Texas have a wide range of interests, needs, and expectations that they expect their government to fulfill. Samuel Huntington, a modernization theorist, noted that political parties, while sharing some characteristics with other social and political institutions, have a unique function in modern societies "to organize participation, to aggregate interests, and to serve as the link between social forces and the government."[8] Simply stated, the political parties link diverse segments of the population to government and thus contribute to the stability and legitimacy of the government.

### Recruit and Nominate Candidates

There are thousands of officeholders in Texas, ranging from justice of the peace to governor. And, except for most city and school district elections, which are nonpartisan, the parties have a virtual monopoly on nominating candidates. It is possible to get an independent on the ballot with no party affiliation, but an independent is not likely to get elected. Under Texas law, an individual who runs for an office in the primary election of one of the parties wins that party's nomination if he or she receives the majority vote in either the primary or a runoff.

Many elected positions do not pay well and are not politically attractive and, in some areas of the state, it is difficult to get people to run for them. In some counties, the parties aggressively recruit candidates. In other counties, they don't.

Parties have not always used the primary to nominate candidates. Prior to reforms enacted in the Terrell Election Laws of 1903 and 1905, candidates were nominated by party conventions, which were attended by the party faithful.

### Contest Elections and Mobilize Voters

While candidate-centered campaigns built on modern media-oriented technology have reduced the role of the political parties in elections (see Chapter 7), parties are still the most important institutions for mobilizing the electorate and channeling votes toward specific candidates. Although most Texans aren't active in party affairs, more than two-thirds of the Texas electorate identifies with one or the other major party, and the two parties have a near monopoly on the votes cast. Given the size of the state, the number of people who participate in elections, the diversity of interests, and the variety of political subcultures within the state, the political parties have had considerable success in mobilizing voters in Texas.[9]

## Organize and Manage the Government

Once elected, officeholders use their party affiliations in carrying out their public responsibilities, and with the development of a two-party system in Texas, the parties have taken on a more significant role in government. Governor Ann Richards, a Democrat, has made hundreds of appointments to policy-setting state boards and commissions, and her appointments have been primarily Democrats. Her first appointment to fill a vacancy on a statewide appellate court was a Democrat, and future, similar appointments can also be expected to be Democrats.

After taking office in 1979 as Texas' first Republican governor in more than 100 years, Bill Clements appointed many Republicans to state boards, but he also named some Democrats, in part to encourage conservative Democrats to switch parties. His successful strategy was instrumental in adding to the strength and influence of the GOP in Texas. One of Clements' most significant Democratic appointments was that of Raul A. Gonzalez to a vacancy on the 13th Court of Civil Appeals in Corpus Christi. Democratic Governor Mark White later appointed Gonzalez as the first Hispanic on the Texas Supreme Court, where Gonzalez still serves. Gonzalez remains a Democrat, but he is one of the Supreme Court's more conservative members.

Despite the growth of the Republican party and increased GOP representation in the legislature—Republicans held 57 of the House's 150 seats in 1991—the legislature's organizational structure is still nonpartisan. But party caucuses are becoming more influential, particularly in staking out positions on issues. In 1991, Lt. Governor Bob Bullock, a Democrat, bumped Republicans from committee chairs in the Senate, where Democrats held a 22-9 majority. But Democratic Speaker Gib Lewis continued to appoint Republicans to committee chairs in the House. If and when Republicans gain a majority or near-majority of House seats and succeed in electing one of their own speaker, they may attempt to organize the House along the partisan lines of the U.S. Congress, where the majority party gets all the leadership positions (see Chapter 8).

The political parties also help to bridge the inherent conflicts between the executive and legislative branches of government. The governor needs legislative support for key programs and, in turn, legislators often need the governor's support and assistance to get their bills enacted. The chances of such cooperation are enhanced if the governor and a majority of the legislature are of the same party. Democrat Ann Richards didn't get everything she wanted from the Democrat-dominated legislature during her first year in office—no governor does—but her relationship with the legislature was smooth sailing compared to Republican Bill Clements' stormy last term.

## Provide Accountability

One of the fundamental problems of a democratic government is how to keep public officeholders responsive and accountable to the people. Elected officials can abuse power. They can engage in graft and corruption. They can pursue policies that conflict with the interests of most of their constituents or pursue foolish or shortsighted policies that produce adverse results. The political parties, in their criticisms of each other as well as their electoral competitiveness, serve to inform the voters of the shortcomings and failures of elected officials. This process provides alternatives for the voters and gives them an opportunity to "turn the rascals out."

## Manage Conflict and Aggregate Interests

The United States generally has had a stable political system that managed conflict among competing groups and interests, and the political parties have played a major role in that process. A party expends a great deal of energy trying to find common ground among competing interests so that successful coalitions of voters can be put together in support of that party's candidates on election day. The Texas Democratic Party, for example, is built on a diverse coalition of African-Americans, Hispanics, lower socioeconomic groups, labor, some professionals, and rural interests, to name a few. To build durable support for its candidates, the party must find compromises and develop accommodations among these groups. As interests within the party agree to support a variety of programs, the party succeeds in resolving conflict.[10]

## Agenda-Setting

Public policy doesn't just happen. It is the result of groups organizing around issues and keeping pressure on elected officials for a response. Some issues are longstanding problems that have produced sharp differences of opinion and will take years to resolve. Others emerge rapidly, perhaps as a result of a catastrophic event, such as the deadly school bus accident in the Rio Grande Valley that produced an immediate outcry for safety barriers between public roadways and open gravel pits like the one in which many young bus passengers drowned. Interest groups often try to build support for their programs through the political parties.

The parties also play a role in establishing policy priorities. Candidates running for public office under a party's banner announce their support or opposition to specific policies and, once elected, they are expected to use the resources of their offices to try to achieve those objectives. In anticipation of future elections, officeholders will spend much time and energy trying to implement policies that will solidify their support among the voters.

# THE CHANGING PARTY SYSTEM IN TEXAS

The significant demographic and economic changes that Texas has experienced over the past three decades have reshaped the politics and, subsequently, the party system of the state.

## One-Party Politics

Immediately after the Civil War, the Republican party was able to capture control of Texas government for a short period. But Republican influence eroded rapidly, and by the time the Constitution of 1876 was implemented, the Republican party's influence in state politics was negligible. The Republican party was perceived by most Texans of that era to be the party of conquest and occupation, and a "people ruled by a military government will retain an antipathy toward the occupying power."[11] Strong anti-Republican feelings were generated by the Reconstruction administration of Radical Republican Governor E. J. Davis, one of the most oppressive officeholders in American history. From 1874 to 1961, no Republican won a statewide office in Texas, and there were only a few scattered areas where Republicans were elected to local offices. In 1928, the state voted for Herbert Hoover, the Republican presidential candidate. For many Texans, however, the salient issue in that campaign was the fact that Al Smith, the Democratic nominee, was a Catholic and favored the repeal of Prohibition. Anti-Catholicism and Prohibition had deep roots among many fundamentalist religious groups in Texas.

The anti-Republicanism that evolved from the Civil War and Reconstruction, however, is only a partial explanation for the Democratic party's longtime domination of Texas politics. V.O. Key in his classic study of *Southern Politics* presents the provocative thesis that Texas politics might be better understood in terms of "modified class politics."[12]

As the conservative agricultural leaders, or Bourbon class of Texans, attempted to regain control over the state's political system after Reconstruction, the postwar economic devastation was dividing Texas along class lines. The small farmers, African-Americans, and an emerging urban labor class suffered disproportionately from the depression of this period. They turned their discontent into support for agrarian third parties, and particularly the Populist Party, which began to threaten the monopoly of the traditional Texas power structure. C. Vann Woodward, an American historian, suggests that Texas Populists approached the African-Americans with "a limited type of equalitarianism quite different from that preached by the Radical Republicans and wholly absent from the conservative approach."[13]

To protect their political power, the established agricultural leaders moved to divide the lower social groups by directing the discontent of the lower income whites against the African-Americans. The rural Bourbon elites, who manifested traditionalistic political values and wanted to consolidate power in the hands of the privileged few, also created alliances with the mercantile, banking and emerging industrial leaders, who reflected the individualistic view of a limited government that served to protect their interests. These two dominant forces consolidated political power and control and merged the politics of race with the politics of economics. Then for more than 80 years, the conservative Texas establishment pursued policies that best served their interests rather than those of the general population.

This analysis is not to suggest that a group of men sat down in a room on a single occasion and developed a strategic plan for a one-party system. The process of domination and control evolved over time. The elites were able to institutionalize their control through the adoption of constitutional restrictions and the enactment of legislation designed to reduce the size of the electorate and thus reduce the potential of a popular challenge to the establishment's political monopoly.[14]

The Jim Crow segregation laws stripped the African-Americans of many economic, social, and political rights and eliminated them from the political process. Restrictive voter registration laws, including a poll tax, which also were designed to exclude African-Americans, served to reduce the participation of low-income whites in the political process as well. Furthermore, the costs of statewide political campaigns maximized the electoral potential of candidates financed by the establishment.[15] The result of all this was a one-party Democratic system, dominated by influential conservatives.

The Texas Democratic party, however, was not homogeneous. There were factions, regional differences, and personal political rivalries. Initially, there were no sustained, identifiable factions as voting coalitions changed from election to election through much of the first third of the 20th century. But the arrival of the Depression in 1929, the election of President Franklin Roosevelt in 1932, and the policies of the New Deal reshaped Texas politics in the 1930s.

State party systems are linked to the national party system, and developments in the Texas party system must be understood as part of this relationship. During the period from the Civil War to Roosevelt's election, the national party system was dominated by the Republican party. The election cycles from 1928 to 1936, however, produced a major national party realignment, and the Democratic party, capitalizing on the devastation of the Depression, replaced the Republicans as the dominant national party.

Roosevelt's administrations articulated and developed a radically different policy agenda than that of the Republican party. Government was to become a buffer against economic downturns as well as a positive force for change. Under Roosevelt, the regulatory function of the federal government was expanded to exercise control and authority over much of the nation's economy. The federal government also enacted programs such as Social Security, public housing, and labor legislation to benefit lower socioeconomic groups.

These national policies had a direct impact on many Texans and produced an active philosophical split within the Texas Democratic party that was to characterize Texas politics for the next two generations. A majority of Texas voters supported Roosevelt in his four elections, and the Democratic party maintained its monopoly over Texas politics. But competing economic interests clearly—and often bitterly—divided Texas Democrats along liberal and conservative lines.

A strong Republican party didn't emerge at this time in Texas or any other southern state because "southern conservative Democratic politicians, who would have been expected to lead such a realignment, or any politicians for that matter, did not relish jumping from a majority-status party to one in the minority."[16] Furthermore, the restrictive voter registration laws designed to reduce participation by minorities and poor whites continued to limit the electoral prospects of liberal Democrats and allowed conservatives to remain largely in control of the state party. "As long as the conservative Democrats remained dominant, they served as a check on the potential growth of the Republican party."[17] There also were residual feelings from the Civil War and an earlier antipathy toward the Republican party that required generations to die off before new voters were willing to change party allegiances.

The emerging liberal wing of the Texas Democratic Party was able to elect Governor James Allred in 1934 and 1936, and considerable progressive legislation was enacted during his administration. But from 1940 to the late 1970s, the conservative wing of the party prevailed in state elections. Democratic presidential candidates carried Texas in 1944, 1948, 1960, 1964, 1968, and 1976, even though some of them were too liberal to suit the tastes of the state's conservative Democratic establishment.

By 1941, the conservative Democrats began to lay the groundwork for an all-out attack on the "New Deal," or liberal, Democrats in the 1944 presidential election. Roosevelt won the nomination for a fourth term, but in Texas there was a bitter intra-party battle between liberal Democrats loyal to Roosevelt and conservative Democrats for control of the party organization and delegates to the Democratic National Convention. This election was followed by three successive presidential elections in which conservative Democrats bolted the party to support either third party candidates or the Republican nominee.[18]

The harbinger of this conservative-liberal split in a statewide political race was the 1946 Democratic gubernatorial race between Homer Rainey and Beauford Jester. Rainey, a former University of Texas president who had been fired after a bitter fight over the UT governing board's censorship of books and efforts to force him to dismiss liberal faculty members, ran as a liberal, or progressive, candidate supporting academic freedom, labor legislation, and civil rights.

He was challenged by four conservatives who attacked him on the university issue, suggested there was rampant atheism at the university, and unleashed anti-labor, anticommunist and anti-African-American attacks. Jester, in a well-financed campaign, eventually defeated Rainey 2-to-1 in a runoff. Many of the allegations raised against Rainey were designed to inject emotionalism into the race and divert attention from the substantive social and economic issues of importance to the lower economic classes. The tactics served the economic and political objectives of the state's corporate establishment.

Similar volatile allegations emerged during many subsequent state elections, and the conservative Democrats were able to capitalize on them. In 1944, the

U.S. Supreme Court declared the white primary—party elections in which only whites could vote—unconstitutional in *Smith* v. *Allwright*. Subsequently, there were a number of candidates who appealed to the sentiments of white supremacy. Texas also had its own brand of "McCarthyism," initiated by right-wing patriotic groups who alleged communist conspiracies throughout the state.[19]

## Modified One-Party Democratic Politics

At first glance, it might appear that the **bi-factionalism** in the Democratic party partially compensated for a competitive two-party system but, in his study of southern politics, Key argued against that perception. Factionalism results in discontinuity in leadership and group support, and the voter has no permanent reference point from which to judge the performance of the party or selected candidates. Key concluded that factionalism resulted in no-party politics. Since there are no clear distinctions as to who holds power and who does not, the influence of pressure groups increases.[20] In one-party Democratic Texas, state government and public policy were conducive to control by wealthy and corporate interests.

In 1948, the Democratic National Convention approved one of the strongest civil rights planks ever adopted up to that point by any political party, but very few Texans (6.5 percent) voted for Strom Thurmond, a southern white supremacist who bolted the Democratic party in protest and became the presidential nominee of the Dixiecrats. In subsequent years, however, the national Democratic party pushed for stronger civil rights legislation, which alienated segments of the white population, prompting many voters to eventually leave the Democratic party and align with the Republicans.

During this period of one-party politics, oil dominated the Texas economy, and Texas oil interests actively lobbied the national government for the reestablishment of state control over the oil-rich tidelands, which extended 10 miles into the Gulf of Mexico off the Texas coast. President Truman, concerned about national security and federal access to these resources, refused to accede to state demands and vetoed legislation favorable to Texas oil interests in 1952. Truman did not plan to run for reelection in 1952, but in the pre-election maneuvering, Texas oil producers, in league with Democratic Governor Allan Shivers, orchestrated a strategy to take the support of conservative Democrats to the Republican party.

While promising to support the Democratic party, Shivers and his allies captured control of the Texas delegation to the 1952 Democratic National Convention. The Democrats nominated Adlai Stevenson, and the Republicans, Dwight Eisenhower. When the Texas Democratic party convened its fall convention, which was called the governor's convention, Shivers succeeded in winning the party's endorsement of Eisenhower. The "Shivercrats," as they were called, were successful in carrying Texas for Eisenhower, and this election helped establish a pattern whereby Texas would retain its Democratic leanings in state and local elections but would vote Republican in many presidential elections.[21]

For years, the Republican party's limited presence in Texas had been basically a patronage base for leaders who were more interested in an occasional appointment than in winning elections.[22] But the 1952 election marked a change in the party's leadership and led to efforts to create a party capable of winning local and statewide elections.[23] The process of developing the necessary organization took years, but it would accelerate after the 1964 election.

In 1960, Lyndon Johnson ran for vice president and re-election to the U.S. Senate from Texas, which was permitted under state law, and won both offices. His Republican opponent in the Senate race was John Tower, a relatively obscure college professor from Wichita Falls, who received 41 percent of the vote. After Johnson won the vice presidency and resigned from the Senate, a special election to fill the Senate seat was called in 1961. It attracted 71 candidates, including Tower, who defeated conservative Democrat William Blakely with 50.6 percent of the vote in a runoff.[24] There is information to suggest that liberal Democrats, in retaliation for having been locked out of the power centers of their party and in anticipation of an ideological realignment of the party system, supported Tower in this election.[25] *The Texas Observer*, an influential liberal publication, endorsed Tower with an argument for a two-party system. "How many liberals voted for Tower will never be known, nor will it be known how many 'went fishing,'" wrote Republican campaign consultant and author John R. Knaggs, who was a volunteer worker for Tower during the 1961 race. "But in reviewing Tower's razor-thin 10,343-vote margin out of 886,091 cast, it must be concluded that the liberal element was pivotal in electing the first Republican United States senator to represent Texas during the 20th century."[26] Texas Republicans, incidentally, hadn't even held a primary in 1960.

Tower was re-elected in 1966, 1972, and 1978, and his successes pointed to the electability of a Republican candidate statewide. No other Texas Republican won a statewide office until 1978, when Bill Clements was elected governor, but many students of Texas politics regard Tower's election in 1961 as the beginning of the state's two-party system.[27] While Republicans made some gains in suburban congressional districts and local elections in the 1960s—including the election to Congress of a Houston Republican named George Herbert Walker Bush—the numbers were inconsequential, and most significant election battles continued to take place for a while longer within the Democratic party.

The only liberal Democratic candidate who was successful on a statewide basis during this period was Ralph Yarborough. After several losing campaigns, he had been elected to the U.S. Senate in a special election in 1957 and held that office until his defeat in 1970 by conservative Democrat Lloyd Bentsen. Yarborough, who had a distinguished legislative career, was "the mainstay of the liberal wing until his primary defeat in 1970 and comeback failure in 1972."[28]

Despite some indications of a revitalized and expanded Republican party and the increased mobilization of minorities in support of the liberal wing of the Democratic party, conservative Democrats controlled state politics until 1978. Conservatives were able to dominate the nominating process in the Democratic primaries through well-financed and well-executed campaigns. In the general elections, liberal Democrats had little choice other than to vote for a conservative Democrat against what was usually perceived to be an even more conservative Republican.[29]

During this period of Democratic factionalism, Texas Democrats played a major role in the U.S. Congress and national politics. Sam Rayburn, the longtime speaker of the U.S. House of Representatives and regarded as one of a handful of great speakers in U.S. history, came from a rural congressional district in northeast Texas. Before moving on to the vice presidency and then the White House, Lyndon Johnson was majority floor leader in the U.S. Senate. In addition, Texas congressmen, as a result of the seniority system, had influential committee posts.

## Two-Party Politics in Texas

On the national level, **realignment** of political parties is often associated with a critical election where there are economic or social issues that cut across existing party allegiances and produce a permanent shift in party support and identification.[30] What apparently has happened in Texas is that the state party system has been integrated into the national party system and more closely approximates the political divisions that exist in states outside the South. Rather than occurring in one single election, this process has occurred over many years.

A major contributor to change was the civil rights movement. African-Americans, and later Hispanics, went to federal court to attack state laws promoting segregation and restricting minority voting rights. Successful lawsuits were brought against the white primary, the pre-primary endorsement, the poll tax, and racial gerrymandering of political districts (see Chapter 7). Then minorities turned to the U.S. Congress for civil rights legislation, a process that produced the 1965 Voting Rights Act, which was expanded to Texas after 1975.

Economic factors also have shaped minority political support and, in turn, contributed to two-party development. African-Americans and Hispanics are disproportionately low-income populations, which means they support and demand such governmental services as public housing, public health care, day care, and income support. These are policies associated with the liberal wing of the Democratic party. Minority organizations across the state have made concerted efforts to register, educate, and mobilize the people in their communities. By 1990, approximately 90 percent of the African-American vote in Texas was Democratic, and while there is less cohesion among Hispanic voters, approximately 75 percent of the Hispanic vote usually is Democratic. As the numerical strength of minorities increased, conservative Anglo Democrats found their position within the party threatened and began to look to the Republican party as an alternative.

The large numbers of people who have migrated to Texas from other states, particularly when the Sun Belt economy of the 1970s and early 1980s was booming and many northern industrial states were struggling, also have contributed to the development of the two-party system. Many of these new arrivals were Republicans from states with strong Republican parties. Using statewide poll data from the mid-1980s, Dyer, Vedlitz, and Hill, scholars who have written extensively on elections and voting trends in Texas, concluded that one-quarter of Texas Republicans were newcomers to the state.[31] Much of the new Republican strength was in the high-income, urban, and suburban Anglo areas where many of these people settled. Other significant factors were President Reagan's popularity in the 1980s, and the 1978 election of Republican Governor Bill Clements, who encouraged many conservative Democratic officeholders to switch parties.

The realignment process also has produced divisions within the growing Republican party. Few Republicans identify themselves as liberals. Most are conservatives who share much of the political philosophy of Texas' traditional conservative Democrats. They are advocates of marketplace economics and oppose many of the social and economic policies originating with the New Deal. The emergence of the **radical right**, however, has produced sharp philosophical differences among Texas Republicans.

The radical right element has long been part of the Texas political landscape.[32] While its influence was occasionally manifested in conservative Democratic politics, the movement found far greater potential in the Republican party for shaping electoral politics. There are secular components of radical right politics, but the movement has a particularly religious overtone and draws considerable support from evangelical groups across the state. Some scholars who study the relationship of religion and politics have suggested that fundamentalist groups described as the Christian Right have been successful in mobilizing segments of the electorate that have been traditionally inactive and brought these voters into the Republican party. In a recent study, Chandler Davidson concludes that this movement has not taken over the Republican party, "but its influence is significant and gives the Texas Republicans their particular stridency and, at times, their appearance of a Know-Nothing movement."[33] The Republicans' difficulty in attracting minority groups and balancing the power and influence of the radical right results in greater influence for this wing of the party. The conflict within the Republican party over the abortion issue is a manifestation of this internal tension, and a pro-choice Republican movement has begun to organize to counter the influence of the radical right.

During the 1970s, the Texas Republican party had an organizational edge on the Democrats. As the minority party, the only way it could successfully challenge the numerical strength of the Democrats was to develop local party organizations capable of mobilizing membership, providing continuity between elections, and providing candidates with campaign resources. After the defeat of Republican presidential nominee Barry Goldwater in 1964, the national Republican party commenced a strategy of rebuilding using modern campaign technology. The national party assisted state parties, and Texas Republicans applied the technology to state and local elections. Organizational strengths between Republicans and Democrats have since pretty well evened out, however. One of the most successful recent statewide organizational efforts, for example, was put together by the Democrats in 1982 through a coordinated fund-raising and get-out-the-vote effort orchestrated by U.S. Senator Lloyd Bentsen and Lt. Governor Bill Hobby, both of whom were on the ballot that year.

Voters develop party perceptions and allegiances on the basis of common political experiences, and each successive generation can perceive and respond to events differently. At present, the Texas Republican party draws disproportionately from young voters, whether born in the state or newcomers. In a recent set of state-wide surveys (1986), 37 percent of the voters in the age group 18-29 identified with the Republican party. By contrast, only 21 percent of the voters over 62 identified with Republicans.[34] Politics is demography in action, and the data provide additional insight into the changes in the state's party system.

If we put all of these changes together, the following generalizations emerge:

> The Republican party is composed disproportionately of those who are college educated, newcomers, Anglos, large metropolitan area residents, higher income and under thirty. Democrats are strongest among minorities, older residents, natives, those with lower levels of income, and those with less education.[35]

Events of the 1970s and the 1980s demonstrated that the transformation of the Texas party system was well on its way. After the Sharpstown scandal (see Chapter 8), the Texas House elected a liberal Democrat, Price Daniel Jr., to the speakership in 1973. Three other moderate to liberal Democrats were elected to statewide office—Bob Armstrong as land commissioner in 1970, John Hill as attorney general in 1972, and Bob Bullock as comptroller in 1974—and these men were successful in implementing policies that were more equitable in the treatment of lower socioeconomic Texans.[36]

In 1978, John Hill defeated Governor Dolph Briscoe, a conservative, in the Democratic primary, and Bill Clements, then a political unknown, defeated Ray Hutchison, a former state legislator who had the endorsement of most Republican state leaders, in the Republican primary. Hill neglected to mend fences with conservative Democrats, and Clements, a multimillionaire, used much of his own money on an effective media campaign to upset Hill by 17,000 votes in the general election. Four years later, Clements lost to Democratic Attorney General Mark White but in 1986 returned to defeat White in an expensive, bitter fight that seemed to center primarily on Clements' desire for revenge (see Chapter 9).

In the 1982 election, Democratic liberals won control of additional statewide offices. Ann Richards was elected state treasurer, Jim Hightower was elected agriculture commissioner, and Garry Mauro was elected land commissioner to succeed Bob Armstrong who had lost a Democratic primary race for governor.

Party realignment also was reflected in the Texas Legislature. In 1971, Republicans held only 12, or seven percent, of the 181 legislative seats. An often-repeated joke was that Republicans were so few they could caucus in a phone booth. But by 1981, there were 45 Republican legislators holding 25 percent of the seats; 10 years later, Republicans held 57 of the 150 House seats and nine of the 31 Senate seats to constitute 36 percent of the legislature.

The 1990 election further demonstrated how far the realignment process has gone. Three major Democratic candidates—Mark White, a conservative-moderate, and Jim Mattox and Ann Richards, both liberals—fought it out in a bitter primary campaign. Mattox and Richards went into a runoff, which Richards won. Conservative businessman Clayton Williams, meanwhile, spent $6 million of his own money to win the Republican primary with a strong majority over three other major candidates. The general election, which received national attention for reaching new depths of manipulated innuendo, mudslinging, and negative attacks, saw Richards prevail.

While the Republican party lost the governor's office, two Republicans were elected to other statewide offices. Kay Bailey Hutchison was elected state treasurer, the job Richards previously had held, and Rick Perry unseated liberal Democrat Jim Hightower to become agriculture commissioner. Republicans gained one seat on the Texas Supreme Court to bring their total to four but lost the two seats they had held on the Court of Criminal Appeals. They also lost three seats in the Texas House from their 1989 all-time high of 60. Republicans retained one of the U.S. Senate seats from Texas when Phil Gramm easily won re-election to the seat once held by John Tower, and the GOP claimed eight of the 27 congressional seats from Texas. (The 1990 census has since increased the number of congressional seats from Texas to thirty.)

Many political observers believe the Texas electorate now generally breaks down as one-third Democratic, one-third Republican, and one-third independent, the classification that Bill Clements used to call **ticket splitters** who played such crucial roles in his two winning elections. The independents, who can cast the deciding votes in any statewide race, tend to be more conservative than liberal, as they clearly demonstrated in the 1988 election. Under the old law that Lyndon Johnson had put to such personal advantage, conservative Democrat Lloyd Bentsen ran simultaneously for re-election to the U.S. Senate and as the Democratic vice presidential nominee. Texas voters overwhelmingly rejected Bentsen and his liberal running mate, Michael Dukakis, at the top of the ticket, but also overwhelmingly re-elected Bentsen over a Republican opponent to the Senate. Many independents obviously split their votes for Bentsen.

## A Caveat to Realignment

Although the party system has been transformed in Texas, there is considerable disagreement as to what these changes will mean in the long run.

Race and class, according to one view, will remain major features of partisan politics. V.O. Key, writing in the 1940s, concluded that race was becoming less important and the electorate was dividing along liberal and conservative lines. He concluded that a "modified class politics seems to be evolving."[37] The parties appear, in part, to be aligning around economic issues that are manifested in liberal and conservative philosophies, but the issues of race continue to shape attitudes. Chandler Davidson argues that "the Republican party's hard-line racial policy" attracted large numbers of conservative Democrats as well as supporters of George Wallace, the conservative American Party's 1968 presidential nominee, and "strengthened the commitment of African-Americans and Mexican Americans to the Democratic Party."[38] Some Texas African-Americans and Hispanics, primarily well-educated, well-to-do individuals, have become Republicans. But the vast majority remain Democrats, and Sunday morning visits to African-American churches in Houston and Dallas and appearances at South Texas pachangas (fiesta-style cookouts) are practically mandatory for Democratic candidates serious about winning statewide office.

A second view of recent changes in the party system is that the party system is undergoing a disintegration or **dealignment**.[39] Underneath all of these changes are factors that point to the decline of the parties' electoral functions and their general organizational weaknesses. Voter participation has declined, and a large number of people hold both major parties in low esteem, can see little difference between them, and no longer identify with either of them. Additionally, the parties have lost control over the nomination processes, and a well-financed candidate such as Bill Clements or Clayton Williams can capture a party's nomination by using sophisticated campaign and media technology. Interest groups may provide more access to policymakers than do the parties and offer sophisticated organizations to shape public policy. Finally, the media plays a much greater role in screening candidates and shaping public opinion than do the parties. In short, according to this argument, political parties no longer perform their traditional functions because other institutions control the political process.

A contradictory view in Texas is that the parties are undergoing a process of revitalization, that there are indications that the parties are attempting to reclaim basic party functions, especially in the areas of elections and campaigns.[40] Rather than resist modern campaign technology, there are party activists who are attempting to adapt technology to the party organization. If the parties were able to provide sophisticated support in fund raising, campaign advertising, phone banks, and a variety of other campaign functions, the candidates are likely to become more dependent on the party organization.

## THE PARTY ORGANIZATION

To carry out their functions, the parties have developed permanent and temporary organizations. The Texas Election Code spells out many of the responsibilities and legal restrictions imposed on the parties, and state and national party rules define many of their operating procedures. Court cases, both federal and state, have further defined their operations.

"Party organization is built around geographic election districts, starting with the basic unit of election administration, the **precinct**."[41] Looking at an organizational chart of the parties, one would get the impression that there is a hierarchical arrangement to party organization, but this is not an accurate conclusion. V.O. Key described the party organization as a "system of layers of organization," with each level—county, state and federal—concentrating on the elections within its jurisdiction.[42] There is a great deal of autonomy at each party level based on the limited sanctions that one level can impose on another and the fact that each level of the party needs the other to carry out electoral functions.[43]

There are no membership requirements for either the Democratic or the Republican party. You do not have to pay dues, attend meetings, campaign for candidates, or make contributions. When you register to vote, you are not required to state your party preference. The right to participate in a party's electoral and nominating activities is based simply on voting in that party's primary election. When you vote in one of the major party primaries, your voter registration card is stamped "Democrat" or "Republican."

## The Permanent Organization

The Texas Election Code makes the county commissioners of each of the 254 counties responsible for creating election precincts, of which there are an estimated 6,500 in Texas. Population, to a large extent, determines the number of precincts within a county. In 1992 Bexar County, with approximately 1.2 million persons, had 514 precincts, while Harris County, with a population of more than 2 million, had 1,225 precincts.

Voters in each precinct elect a **precinct chair** in the party primary (Figure 6-2, page 174). Any eligible voter within the precinct can file for this position, or the names of write-in candidates can be added to the ballot. (One of this book's authors was elected a precinct chair with two write-in votes.) While there are many contested elections for this position, there are numerous other instances when no one runs for the office. Precinct vacancies abound throughout the state, and **county executive committees** often find it impossible to fill them because they have few incentives to offer, a fact that has contributed to the parties' organizational decline. The office has limited legal powers or resources. In some counties, the chair is responsible for staffing the polling places on election day, but increasingly this is a function of the county election administrator. This person calls the precinct convention (which will be discussed below) to order and serves as a member of the county executive committee. Precinct chairs also serve to mobilize party supporters to vote. Many people do absolutely nothing with the position, while others contribute a great deal of time and energy and have successfully delivered the precinct for their party's candidates in the general election.

The second level of the party organization is the county executive committee, which includes each precinct chair and the **county chair**, who is elected to a two-year term by primary voters countywide. Under state law, one of the major functions of the county chair and the executive committee is the organization and management of the primary election. The county executive committee accepts filings by candidates for local offices and is also responsible for planning the county or district conventions. Funds for the management of primary elections are provided to the county party by the state through the secretary of state's office.

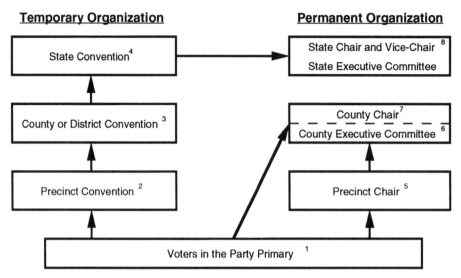

**Temporary Organization**        **Permanent Organization**

| Temporary | Permanent |
|---|---|
| State Convention[4] | State Chair and Vice-Chair[8] / State Executive Committee |
| County or District Convention[3] | County Chair[7] / County Executive Committee[6] |
| Precinct Convention[2] | Precinct Chair[5] |
| Voters in the Party Primary[1] | |

1. Any registered voter may participate in the primaries which are held in even-numbered years on the second Tuesday in March.
2. Any person who has participated in a party primary may attend the precinct convention which is held the same day as the primary.
3. Delegates from the precinct conventions are selected to attend the county convention or the senatorial convention which is held the second Saturday after the second Tuesday in March.
4. Delegates are selected from the district or senatorial conventions to attend the state convention which is held in June.
5. A precinct chair is selected by voters participating in the party primary, and if required, the runoff primary.
6. The precinct chairs and the county chair comprise the party's county executive committee.
7. The county chair is elected by voters countywide in the primary, and if required, the runoff primary.
8. The State Executive Committee and the Chair and Vice Chair are selected by the State Convention held in June of even-numbered years.

**FIGURE 6-2**  Organization of Texas Political Parties.

The county committees may be well-organized and actively work to carry out a wide range of organizational and electoral activities, or they may meet irregularly and have difficulty getting a quorum of members to attend. While the county chair is an unpaid position, the party organizations in some counties have successful ongoing fundraising operations. They support a permanent party head-quarters, retain permanent professional staff, and are engaged in various party activities between elections.

The Texas Election Code provides for other district committees that correspond to a state senatorial, state representative, judicial district, or congressional district. District committees that are solely within a county are comprised of precinct chairs while multicounty districts committees include representatives of all affected counties. These committees fill vacancies between the primary and general election if they occur.

At the state level, a party's permanent organization is the **state executive committee**, which is composed of 64 members, including the party's state chair and vice chair. When the parties meet in their biennial state conventions, two committee members, a man and a woman, are selected by delegation caucuses from each of the 31 state senatorial districts. The **state chair** and the **vice chair**, one of whom must be a woman, also are selected by the convention. The two top state party leaders and other executive committee members serve two-year terms and are unpaid. As might be expected, the incumbent governor often exercises considerable influence, if not control, over the composition of his or her party's state executive committee.

Statewide candidates file for office with the executive committee, which also is responsible for planning and organizing the party's state convention and helps raise funds for the ongoing operations of the party. While the committee serves to establish party policy, the day-to-day party operations are entrusted to the party's executive director and professional staff. The Texas Democratic Party and the Texas Republican Party have permanent staffs and headquarters in Austin.

There are periods when the state committees are highly effective with strong, energetic leadership that carries over into the development and retention of a competent professional staff. At times, however, the state committees can become divided along ideological, factional, or personal lines, producing conflict that sometimes has become open warfare. In those instances, a party finds it difficult to raise funds, maintain a highly qualified staff, and carry out its electoral functions.

## Temporary Organization

The temporary organizations of the political parties are the series of conventions that are held every two years, beginning on the day of the party primaries. They are particularly significant in presidential election years because they—together with the presidential preference primary—help select the state's delegates to the parties' national nominating conventions. The convention system also helps organize the permanent party structure and brings party activists together to share common political concerns and shape party policies. Most Texans, however, have little knowledge of the convention system, and few participate in it.

## The Precinct Convention

Anyone who votes in a party primary, which is conducted on the second Tuesday in March of even-numbered years, is eligible to participate in that party's **precinct convention**, which is normally held in the same place as the primary and begins shortly after voting stops at 7 p.m. After the convention is organized and selects its permanent officers—chair, vice chair, and secretary—it begins its real business, the selection of delegates and alternate delegates to the county or senatorial district convention. Each precinct is assigned a specific number of delegates, based on the party's voting strength. The Democrats since 1972 have used particularly complex procedures designed to assure broad-based delegate representation by ethnicity, gender, and age. A precinct convention also can adopt resolutions to be submitted at the county or district conventions for possible inclusion in the party's **platform**.

In presidential election years, the primary and the precinct conventions are the first steps in the selection of delegates to the national conventions. Before 1988, when Texas' participation in the first regional "Super Tuesday" presidential preference primary changed the delegate selection process, the precinct conventions were extremely crucial to presidential candidates because a candidate had to have strong support among delegates at the precinct level to ultimately capture a significant number of Texas delegates to the national convention. Now, much of that luster has been stolen by the primary, although the conventions still play a role in the Democratic party's presidential nominating process.

The precinct conventions held in non-presidential election years are often poorly attended and, in many precincts, no one shows up. The precinct meeting may last 15 minutes, and those attending may not be able to get enough people to volunteer to be delegates to the upcoming county or senatorial convention. Such low participation rates are cited by those who conclude that the political parties are in decline.

In the past, highly motivated political and ideological movements have been able to capture precinct conventions and advance candidates who had little in common with mainstream party voters. Supporters of Barry Goldwater used this strategy in 1964 to help capture the Republican nomination for their candidate, as did supporters of Democrat George McGovern in 1972. But both men were soundly defeated in the general election. In recent years, the "religious right" has attempted a similar strategy to extend its influence in the Republican party.

## The County or Senatorial District Conventions

County or senatorial district conventions are held two weeks after the precinct conventions. District conventions are held in the larger urban counties, such as Harris, Dallas, Tarrant, and Bexar, which include more than one state senatorial district. Those delegates elected at the precinct conventions comprise the membership of this second level of the convention process which, in turn, elects delegates to the state convention.

Conventions are about politics, selection of candidates, and control of the party apparatus. There have been intermittent periods of lackluster conventions. But during Texas' one-party era, there were frequent, bitter convention fights between conservatives and liberals for control of the Democratic party. And while those fights were most evident at the state convention, they also permeated the precinct, county, and district conventions. As Texas Republicans have increased in number and developed more diversified interests, similar intraparty struggles have surfaced.

## State Conventions

The two major parties hold their **state convention**s in June of even-numbered years. Convention delegates certify to the secretary of state the names of those individuals who were nominated to statewide offices in the March primaries, adopt a party platform, and elect the state party chair, the vice chair, and the state executive committee.

In presidential election years, the state conventions also select delegates to their respective parties' national nominating conventions, elect members to their parties' national committees, and choose presidential electors. Electors from the party that carries Texas in the presidential race will formally cast the state's electoral votes for that party's candidate in December after the general election.

The allocation of all the Texas delegates to the Republican National Convention are determined by the presidential primary. Delegate selection committees named by the candidates nominate lists of delegates, who are selected at the state convention. Texas delegates to the Democratic National Convention are determined through a more complicated process based both on the primary vote and candidate support from attendees at the series of party conventions beginning at the precinct level.

## THE PARTY IN GOVERNMENT

As part of V.O. Key's concept of the tripartite perspective on political parties, we have discussed, in part, the political party in the electorate. In the next chapter, we will expand on this analysis by looking more closely at voting behavior, partisan attitudes, and the party activists. We also have presented a brief summary of the party organization. We will defer a discussion of the party in government until we get to later chapters on the legislature, the executive branch, the bureaucracy, and the judiciary.

However we describe the political parties in Texas, they do not produce cohesive, policy-oriented coalitions in government. Texas politics and political parties have long troubled serious students of government who have concluded that political parties have not been able to hold their elected officials accountable or responsive to those supporting the party. Under ideal circumstances, these governmental experts believe, the two major parties would articulate clearly defined political philosophies and policies they would pursue if their candidates were elected. Once elected, persons supported by the party would be committed to these programs, giving the voters a clear reference with which to evaluate their performances in office. This perspective is often referred to as the "responsible party model."

There are several reasons why Texas parties are incapable of functioning in this manner, none of which serve to lessen the disenchantment and disgust that many voters have toward political parties and those holding public office under their banners.

The political parties in Texas are highly decentralized and unable to impose sanctions or discipline on members who pursue goals at variance with a party's stated objectives. The large number of elected officials at both the state and the local level serves to diffuse the party leadership. Symbolically, we may consider the governor to be the leader of his or her party, but in subsequent chapters, we will demonstrate how little control the governor has in policy formation and implementation.[44]

Secondly, the coalitions that the parties form with groups harboring different objectives, interests, and agendas make it next to impossible to develop clearly stated philosophical or ideological positions that would always differentiate one party from another. There are philosophical, ideological, and programmatic differences among members and supporters of the same party. In the legislature, for example, there are both liberal and conservative Democrats, and there often are ideological voting patterns that cross party lines.

Another explanation for the lack of partisan accountability is the longstanding antiparty tradition of American politics. Many voters are ambivalent, even outright hostile, toward political parties, and the parties make only limited efforts to include a large number of individuals in their organizational activities. And many voters spend little, if any, effort to become informed on issues of politics and public policy.

## THIRD PARTIES IN TEXAS

There has been a long tradition of third parties in Texas, including Grangers, Populists, Progressives, Socialists, Dixiecrats, the American Independent Party, La Raza Unida, and Libertarians. None has had statewide electoral success, and it is rather easy to discount the importance of such political movements. But both the Populists in the 1890s and La Raza Unida in the early 1970s were perceived to be a significant threat to the established state party structure and those who controlled political and economic power.

Major **third party** movements surfaced when Texas was still a one-party Democratic state and, in some respects, they suggested an alternative to the then-weak Republican party. But, both from a state and a national perspective, they were movements of crisis or discontent.[45] The Democratic party, particularly its conservative wing, either co-opted these movements by making minor public policy concessions to them or by getting restrictive legislation, such as the poll tax, enacted to reduce their electoral base. In some instances, economic recriminations were the price individuals paid for participating in these third party movements.[46]

The most recent significant third party movement, La Raza Unida, raised a particularly interesting prospect of a political party built upon an ethnic group. In the 1960s, young Hispanic leaders began to develop student organizations across the state that became the organizational framework on which this party was developed.[47] The low-income Hispanic population had been excluded from any major role in the Democratic party by restrictive voter registration laws, at-large elections, and racial gerrymandering designed to minimize Hispanic voting strength. An even more fundamental problem, though, was the fact that state public policy was not responsive to the educational and economic needs of Hispanics, and conservative Democrats refused to enact legislation that would benefit that major part of the population.

La Raza Unida, led by Jose Angel Gutierrez and Mario Compean, began in 1969 to organize in Crystal City in Zavala County and then extended its efforts to Dimmit, La Salle, and Hildago counties.[48] Overwhelmingly Hispanic and poor, these counties were characteristic of many South Texas counties where the Anglo minority controlled both the political and economic institutions, and there was little sensitivity to the needs of low-income residents.

The struggle for access to the ballot box and fair elections in Zavala County parallels the experience of African-Americans throughout the South. Manipulation of the election laws, economic reprisals, and intimidation by the police and Texas Rangers were used by the Anglo minority to try to retain control. La Raza Unida, however, won control of local and county offices in Crystal City and Zavala County in 1972, the same year that Ramsey Muniz ran as the party's gubernatorial candidate. During the general election campaign, there was considerable speculation in the press and apprehension among conservative Democrats that La Raza would drain a sufficient number of votes away from Dolph Briscoe, the Democratic nominee, to give Henry (Hank) Grover, a right-wing Republican, the governorship. Briscoe won the election, but without a majority of the votes. The subsequent growth of liberal and minority influence within the Democratic party, internal dissension within La Raza Unida and legal problems encountered by Muniz contributed to the demise of this third party after 1978.

In addition to statewide third parties, local political organizations connected to neither the Democratic nor the Republican party have been influential in some cities. Elections for city offices are nonpartisan, and most are held during odd-numbered years when there are no state offices on the ballot. Cities such as San Antonio and Dallas developed citizens associations, which had all of the characteristics of political parties. Many of these local organizations controlled city governments for decades and maintained a virtual monopoly over city elections. In recent years, there has been a decline of these local political parties.

## WHY A TWO-PARTY SYSTEM?

Why are there only two major political parties in Texas and the United States? Many other democratic countries have multiparty systems that function quite well. And given the economic, regional, and social diversification of this nation and this state, one might conclude that multiple parties would be more capable of translating the interests of their members and supporters into public policy. Yet, the United States has a 200-year history of two-party politics.

By historical accident and certainly not by design, the first national party system in this country was configured around two identifiable coalitions of interests who articulated two alternative views of American government. Some have suggested that there was a natural dualism in American politics and parties aligned along these fundamental differences. By itself, that is not a very convincing argument, but subsequent generations have been politically socialized or educated to think that two parties are inevitable and preferred over any alternatives. The Democrats and Republicans can do battle over a wide variety of issues, but one will hear spokespersons of both parties extolling the virtues of two-party politics. Democrats and Republicans just don't talk about multiparty politics.

State election laws also contribute to the persistence of a two-party system. Unlike in the party primaries, where runoffs are held—if necessary—to select a nominee by majority vote, general elections are won by a simple plurality. The candidate who gets more votes than any other candidate, regardless of how many are in the race, is elected. There are no runoffs. That was how Dolph Briscoe won election with less than a majority of the vote in 1972, when La Raza Unida candidate Ramsey Muniz siphoned off traditional Democratic votes. Without a runoff, third party candidates have little chance of winning office over major party nominees. Also, legislative and congressional seats in Texas are filled by the top vote getters in geographic, single-member districts. Elections in multiparty systems are usually structured around the principle of proportional representation, where legislative seats are allocated on the basis of the parties' electoral strength. Election laws in this country also impose specific requirements that make it difficult for third parties to get their candidates listed on the ballot.

Most Texans do not have the intense ideological positions that may prompt the formation of a third party. Winning elections takes precedence over ideological purity, and only a few individuals are "true believers" with a highly cohesive, systematic set of beliefs shaping their political behavior.[49] A conservative Republican may support marketplace economics and deregulation but oppose a ban on abortion. A liberal Democrat who is a Catholic may favor greater economic regulation and expanded social services but oppose government programs subsidizing family planning or sex education.

While class and race shape politics and public policy debates, other issues and concerns cut across these groupings. While we can talk about the tendency of one party to attract more of one group of citizens than the other party, no party has a monopoly on key segments of the electorate. There are Hispanics, Anglos, and African-Americans in both parties. Labor divides its support between the two parties as do religious, economic, and educational groups. The multiclass and heterogeneous base of support for the two parties minimizes the potential for third parties.[50]

## SUMMARY AND CONCLUSIONS

**1.** Historically, Texans, along with most other Americans, have expressed a great deal of ambivalence or indifference toward political parties. In part, this ambivalence is translated into neglect of the political parties with little consideration for the basic roles that parties play in a democratic society.

**2.** While there are other institutions that perform some of the same functions, the political parties are uniquely structured to build electoral coalitions and serve as intermediaries between the electorate and the government. In their primary pursuit to capture the offices of government, the political parties recruit and nominate candidates, mobilize the electorate, provide accountability, resolve conflicts among diverse groups, and set the political agenda.

**3.** Weak party systems are often associated with systems where interest groups play a more prominent role in the policy-making process. For much of its political history, Texas functioned with a one-party system, characterized by two dominant factions. This weak party system, which was based in part on the systematic exclusion of large segments of the state's population through discriminatory election laws, has contributed to a powerful interest group system. In Austin, as well as at the local level, the raw power of interest groups is seen in most aspects of the decision-making process, and with weak political parties, the concerns and needs of the general public are subordinated to those of the special interest groups. It remains to be seen whether the emerging two-party system will change the relative power between the political parties and interest groups.

**4.** Over the past 30 years, there have been significant changes in the state's party structure. One-party Democratic control has been transformed by complex economic, social, and political changes, and the state is rapidly moving toward two-party competition. While some of these changes are appropriately discussed in terms of realignment, another view is that the state has finally become more integrated into the national party system, thus closely approximating the political alignments that exist outside the South.

**5.** Historically, politics in Texas were configured around class and race, and despite all of the partisan changes, these two factors are primary dimensions of partisan alliances.

**6.** While much can be said about partisan realignment, there are those who would argue that the changes are offset by the organizational weaknesses of the political parties and the decline in party identification. Among the more pessimistic scholars, there is the view that the parties are dealigning or disintegrating with some of the primary functions being assumed by other institutions, including the press and the interest groups.

**7.** Much of the realignment-dealignment debate speaks to the party in the electorate, but the parties have rarely functioned as highly cohesive, disciplined organizations in the government. With candidate-centered campaigns, the parties have lost much of their control over those elected under the party label. Legislators, as well as other elected officials, are somewhat like free agents, aligning with other groups or organizations with little concern of recrimination from the political party.

**8.** State statutes spell out much of the details of the formal party organization, but there are wide variations from one area of the state to another in the vitality and strength of the local party organizations.

**9.** A competitive, viable two-party system is directly related to the responsiveness of public officials and governing institutions. Most importantly, public policy is shaped, in part, through responsible and competitive political parties, but the continued neglect of the needs and interests of large segments of the state's population challenges the very premises upon which a democratic society is based.

## KEY TERMS

| | |
|---|---|
| Political party | Precinct chair |
| One-party system | County executive committee |
| Bi-factionalism | County chair |
| Two-party system | State executive committee |
| Realignment | State chair and vice chair |
| Radical right | Precinct convention |
| Ticket splitters | State convention |
| Dealignment | Third party |
| Precincts | Platform |

## FURTHER READING

Anders, Evan, *Boss Rule in South Texas: The Progressive Era.* Austin: University of Texas Press, 1982.

Anderson, James E., Richard W. Murray, and Edward L. Farley, *Texas Politics*, 6th ed. New York: HarperCollins Publishers, Inc., 1992.

Bauer, John R., "Partisan Realignment and the Changing Political Geography of Texas," *Texas Journal of Political Studies*, 12 (Spring/Summer 1990), pp. 41-66.

Beck, Paul Allen, and Frank J. Sorauf, *Party Politics in America*, 7th ed. New York: HarperCollins Publishers, 1992.

Champagne, Anthony, and Rick Collis, "Texas," in Alan Rosenthal and Maureen Moakley, eds., *The Political Life of the American States*. New York: Praeger, 1984.

Davidson, Chandler, *Race and Class in Texas Politics*. Princeton: Princeton University Press, 1990.

Dyer, James and Don Haynes, "Social, Economic and Political Change According to the *Texas Poll*." Paper presented at the Allan Shivers Conference on the New Texas, Austin, Texas, November 7-8, 1986.

Dyer, James A., Arnold Vedlitz, and David B. Hill, "New Voters, Switchers, and Political Party Realignment in Texas," *Western Political Quarterly*, 41 (March 1988), pp. 155-167.

Frantzaich, Stephen E., *Political Parties in the Technological Age*. New York: Longman, 1989.

Garcia, Ignacio M., *United We Win: The Rise and Fall of La Raza Unida Party*. Tucson: Mexican American Studies and Research Center at the University of Arizona, 1989.

Grantham, Dewey W., *The Life and Death of the Solid South: A Political History*. Lexington: University Press of Kentucky, 1988.

Green, George Norris, *The Establishment in Texas Politics: The Primitive Years, 1938-1957*. Westport, Conn.: Greenwood Press, 1979.

Ivins, Molly, *Molly Ivins Can't Say That, Can She?* New York: Random House, 1991.

Jewell, Malcolm E., and David M. Olson, *American State Political Parties and Elections*, rev. ed. Homewood, Ill.: The Dorsey Press, 1982.

Key, V. O., *Southern Politics*. New York: Vintage Books, 1949.

Knaggs, John R., *Two Party Texas: The John Tower Era, 1961-1984*. Austin: Eakin Press, 1986.

Ladd, Everett Carl, Jr. *American Political Parties: Social Change and Political Response.* New York: W. W. Norton & Company, 1970.

Morehead, Richard. *50 Years in Texas Politics: From Roosevelt to Reagan, From the Fergusons to Clements.* Burnet, TX: Eakin Press, 1982.

Quinones, Juan Gomez, *Chicano Politics.* Albuquerque: University of New Mexico Press, 1990.

Sabato, Larry J., *The Party's Just Begun: Shaping Political Parties for America's Future.* Glenview, Ill.: Scott Foresman/Little Brown College Division, 1988.

Stanley, Jeanie R., "Party Realignment and the 1986 Texas Election," *Texas Journal of Political Studies*, 9 (Spring/Summer 1987), pp. 3-13.

Sundquist, James, *Dynamics of the Party System*, rev. ed. Washington, D.C.: Brookings Institution, 1983.

Tower, John G., *Consequences: A Personal and Political Memoir.* New York: Little, Brown, 1991.

## *ENDNOTES*

1. Dennis S. Ippolito and Thomas G. Walker, *Political Parties, Interest Groups, and Public Policy: Group Influence in American Politics* (Englewood Cliffs: Prentice Hall, 1980), p. 2.

2. John F. Bibby, *Politics, Parties, and Elections in America* (Chicago: Nelson-Hall, 1987), pp. 3-4.

3. Leon Epstein, *Political Parties in Western Democracies* (New York: Praeger, 1967), p. 9.

4. Bibby, *Politics, Parties and Elections in America*, p. 15.

5. Sara McCally Morehouse, *State Politics, Parties and Policy* (New York: Holt, Rinehart and Winston, 1981), p. 118.

6. Ibid., pp. 118-119.

7. Ibid., p. 117.

8. Samuel Huntington, *Political Order in Changing Societies* (New Haven: Yale University Press, 1980), p. 91.

9. Robert J. Huckshorn, *Political Parties in America*, 2nd ed. (Monterey, Cal: Brooks/Cole Publishing Company, 1981), p. 23.

10. Bibby, *Politics, Parties and Elections in America*, p. 12.

11. V.O. Key, *Southern Politics* (New York: Vintage Books, 1949), p. 7.

12. Ibid., p. 255.

13. C. Vann Woodward, *The Strange Career of Jim Crow*, 2nd rev. ed. (New York: Oxford University Press, 1966), p. 21.

14. Chandler Davidson, *Race and Class in Texas Politics*, (Princeton: Princeton University Press, 1990), p. 21.

15. Ibid., p. 6.

16. Alexander P. Lamis, *The Two-Party South*, expanded edition (New York: Oxford University Press, 1988), p. 23.

17. Ibid., p. 194.

18. George Norris Green, *The Establishment in Texas Politics: The Primitive Years, 1938-1957* (Westport, Conn.: Greenwood Press, 1979), p. 57.

19. Ibid., pp. 121-134.

20. Key, *Southern Politics*, pp. 302-310.

21. Green, *The Establishment in Texas Politics*, pp. 142-148.

22. V. O. Key, *Southern Politics*, pp. 294-297.

23. Green, *The Establishment in Texas Politics*, p. 148.

24. Lamis, *The Two-Party South*, p. 195.

25. Ibid., p. 195; Davidson, *Race and Class in Texas Politics*, p. 201.

26. John R. Knaggs, *Two-Party Texas: The John Tower Era 1961-1984* (Austin: Eakin Press, 1986), p. 15.

27. Davidson, *Race and Class in Texas Politics*, p. 199.

28. Lamis, *The Two-Party South*, p. 194.

29. Ibid., pp. 196-197.

30. For an excellent summary of realignment theory and conditions under which realignment is likely to take place, see James L. Sundquist, *Dynamics of the Party System* (Washington, D.C.: The Brookings Institution, 1973).

31. James A. Dyer, Arnold Vedlitz, and David B. Hill, "New Voters, Switchers, and Political Party Realignment in Texas," *Western Political Quarterly*, 41 (March 1988), p. 164.

32. Green, *The Establishment in Texas Politics*, chap. 5; Davidson, *Race and Class in Texas Politics*, chap. 10.
33. Davidson, *Race and Class in Texas Politics*, p. 206.
34. Dyer, Vedlitz, and Hill, "New Voters, Switchers and Political Party Realignment in Texas," p. 159.
35. Ibid., pp. 165-166.
36. Green, *The Establishment in Texas Politics*, p. 208.
37. Key, *Southern Politics*, p. 255.
38. Davidson, *Race and Class in Texas Politics*, p. 238.
39. Walter Dean Burnham, *Critical Elections and the Mainsprings of American Politics* (New York: Norton, 1970), chap. 5; Walter Dean Burnham, *The Current Crisis in American Politics* (Oxford: Oxford University Press, 1982).
40. See Robert Huckshorn, *Political Parties in America*, pp. 358-360.
41. Bibby, *Politics, Parties, and Elections in America*, p. 81.
42. V. O. Key, Jr., *Parties, Politics and Pressure Groups*, 4th ed. (New York: Thomas Y. Crowell Company, 1958), p. 347.
43. Bibby, *Politics, Parties, and Elections in America*, p. 82.
44. See Huckshorn, *Political Parties in America*, pp. 16-21.
45. Daniel Mazmanian, *Third Parties in Presidential Elections* (Washington, D.C.: The Brookings Institute, 1974), p. 5.
46. George Rivera, "Building a Chicano Party in South Texas," *New South* (Spring 1971), pp. 75-78.
47. Ibid., pp. 75-78.
48. Juan Gomez Quinones, *Chicano Politics* (Albuquerque: University of New Mexico Press, 1990), pp. 128-131.
49. John Crittenden, *Parties and Elections in the United States* (Englewood Cliffs: Prentice Hall, 1982), p. 11.
50. Huckshorn, *Political Parties in America*, p. 11.

# 7

# ELECTIONS, CAMPAIGNS AND POLITICAL BEHAVIOR

> Politics is show business for ugly people.
> *Bill Miller,* Political Consultant
>
> We just elect them, we don't explain them.
> Texas GOP Consultant
>
> In this crazy business of politics, a lie
> unanswered becomes truth within 24 hours.
> *Willie Brown,* California Assembly Speaker[1]

At a time when millions of people around the world are eliminating authoritarian political systems, clamoring for the right to organize political parties, and demanding free and open elections, Texans congratulate themselves if one-third of the eligible population votes. Such a poor turnout doesn't stem from a lack of opportunity. After decades of denying voting rights to large parts of the population, Texas now has one of the United States' more progressive voter registration laws, and public interest groups such as Common Cause and the League of Women Voters continue to push for the elimination of any remaining barriers. Contemporary political campaigns, especially those for national and statewide offices, have high media visibility. People are bombarded by sophisticated TV ad campaigns, direct mail, phone bank solicitations for candidates, and daily news coverage. Yet low rates of participation in elections indicate that something fundamental is disturbing Texas voters as well as voters across the nation. Statewide turnout rates in Texas are consistently lower than those in other western democracies, and turnout rates in many local elections are downright appalling.

Some suggest that Texans just don't care about what happens in government as long as their own selfish interests are being met. Other people argue that there is a sense of disenchantment, disillusion, or alienation among Texas voters. Texans care about politics, government, and public policy but believe that a single vote will make no difference.

Elected officials, moreover, are perceived to be increasingly insulated from the popular will. While they articulate a commitment to elections and political participation, many are not really interested in cultivating an electorate that is actively involved in the decisions of government. The real brokers of politics and public policy are the interest groups, lobbyists, and political action committees, and with the decline of the political parties, many candidates become free agents who sell their services to the highest bidders.

There is a great deal of literature indicting contemporary elections in Texas and the United States. Elections were designed to give the people the opportunity to direct public policy through chosen officials who would then be held accountable at the next election, but the system won't work properly if people won't vote. Elections are clearly imperfect instruments, but we have found no other vehicle for translating the needs, interests and expectations of the public into public policy.

## THE FUNCTIONS OF ELECTIONS

For more than 200 years, we in the United States have been debating electoral issues. Who should participate? When should elections be held? What percentage of the popular vote is required to win an election? What are the policy consequences of elections? Does it really make any difference who gets elected? While these questions are important and merit our attention, the most important issue is the relationship of elections to our definitions of a democratic society. In the most fundamental terms, "elections are used to assure popular support and legitimacy for those who make governmental decisions."[2] A stable political system depends on popular support, and people freely participating in the process of choosing those who make public policy are more likely to accept and support policy without coercion or force.

While elections provide broad statements of the electorate's expectations for future public policy, they seldom articulate or direct precise programs. Successful political parties and candidates build broad-based campaign coalitions, and the competing demands of the diverse groups courted by candidates make it difficult for candidates to specify in detail the policies they plan to pursue once elected. Most people seeking public office, therefore, prefer to speak in general concepts and try to avoid answering hypothetical "what if" questions posed by reporters. Questions like: "What if the economy doesn't recover as fast as you are predicting and there isn't enough revenue to raise teachers' pay or improve health care? Will you support a tax increase or cut back on your priorities?"

Nevertheless, after an election, a successful candidate is likely to indicate that the people have spoken and claim a mandate to pursue specific public policies of his or her choosing. If there is a mandate, it is for the person elected, not for a specific program.[3]

Elections enable voters to replace public officials or force officeholders to change their policies.[4] They are, in effect, the one institution that a society can use to control its leaders. But this role is based on the assumptions that there is universal suffrage, voters are offered clear alternatives, large segments of the population are informed about those aspiring to public office, and there is significant voter participation. Throughout Texas history, elections often have been manipulated for the advantage and interests of the few.

Texas' political culture has unwritten rules as to how elections should be conducted and what candidates should and should not do. For example, we expect a candidate to shake the hand of his or her opponent even after a bitter defeat or attack. That's why Republican Clayton Williams' snub of the handshake offered by Democrat Ann Richards during one joint appearance in the 1990 gubernatorial campaign received so much media attention. Candidates can attack, counterattack, make charges and countercharges against each other, and still be considered politically acceptable and civilized. Such election rituals are manifestations of the way in which we have institutionalized conflict.

Some would argue that elections and election rituals have only a symbolic function that serves to "quiet resentments and doubts about particular political acts, reaffirm belief in the fundamental rationality and democratic character of the system, and thus fix conforming habits of future behavior...."[5] While this position may be extreme, there is an implicit warning in the author's conclusions. The trivialization of elections may ultimately result in even more disenchantment, disdain, and disgust with politics and government. If the electorate is "fed a steady diet of buncombe, the people may come to expect and to respond with the highest predictability to buncombe."[6]

## CHARACTERISTICS OF TEXAS ELECTIONS

Texans have numerous opportunities to vote, often as many as three or four times a year. Voters in Texas and other states, in fact, get to vote on more candidates and issues than citizens of other democracies.[7]

Except for constitutional amendment elections, which are set by the legislature, and emergency elections set by the governor to fill vacancies in specific offices, elections are held at regular, predictable intervals mandated by state law.[8] There has been a systematic effort to separate elections and thereby minimize the convergence of issues in state and local elections.[9] Most city and school board elections are held in May which has the effect of separating them from party primaries held in March of even-numbered years and general elections held in November. Many constitutional amendment elections are scheduled on the same day as the general election, but they can be held separately. There are all kinds of explanations and justifications for this election scheduling, but there is evidence to suggest that it contributes to "voter fatigue," reduced voter turnout, and the disproportionate influence of a few individuals in many of the local and special elections where voter turnout usually is the lowest.

These election cycles also shape the policymaking process. A tax increase, for example, is likely to take place soon after an election, not immediately prior to one. Voter dissatisfaction, officeholders hope, would be dissipated by the time an election takes place two to three years after their tax vote. This is a double-edged sword. It insulates public officials from immediate public discontent when hard and unpopular decisions must be made, but it also makes it difficult to punish elected officials for pursuing questionable or highly unpopular programs.

## Political Suffrage in Texas

Despite the rhetoric of democratic theory included in the state's constitution and the somewhat venerable view people have of elections and voting, Texas has a dark history of voter disenfranchisement. The systematic exclusion of African-Americans, Hispanics and low-income whites was justified on a variety of grounds, but it was clearly undemocratic. And it created a political system where the interests of a few could prevail over the interests of the majority. A large number of Texans have paid a high price for this early legacy of discrimination.

After the Civil War, the state initiated efforts to organize a civilian government to reestablish its full statehood in the Union. The Constitutional Convention of 1866 accepted the supremacy of the national government and eliminated slavery, but it refused to adopt the 13th Amendment, which would have given African-Americans the right to vote and hold public office.[10] This constitution was rejected by the Radical Reconstructionists in Congress in 1867, and another Texas constitution was adopted that extended full voting rights to African-Americans. African-Americans were elected to subsequent constitutional conventions, and 41 African-Americans served in the Texas Legislature from 1868 to 1894.[11] But while Texas extended political rights to them, African-Americans were threatened with physical violence and economic recriminations that reduced their political participation well into the 20th century.

## The Poll Tax

The conservative Texas establishment's reaction to the Populist movement and its potential for building a coalition between African-Americans and low-income whites resulted in the legislature's adoption of a poll tax that went into effect in 1904,[12] a tax of $1.50 to $1.75 that had to be paid each year before a person could vote. In the early 1900s, that was a large sum of money for low-income people. And it was to be paid between October 1 and January 31, three months before the primaries and nine months before the general elections, long before most people even began to think about voting. Consequently, the tax eliminated large numbers of voters who were likely to support the Populist Party and undermine the political establishment.[13]

The poll tax was in effect for more than 60 years in Texas. It was outlawed for federal elections by the 24th Amendment to the U.S. Constitution, which was adopted in 1964, but Texas retained the poll tax for state and local elections, thus requiring two sets of registered voters and separate ballots. In November of 1966, Texas voters approved an amendment to the state constitution eliminating the poll tax for state elections and implementing annual voter registration. By that time, the U.S. Supreme Court also had ruled that the state poll tax was unconstitutional.[14]

## The White Primary

Texas, along with several other southern states, also implemented the white primary, which was designed to eliminate African-American participation in the elections that really counted.[15] Initially, the Texas legislature in 1923 enacted a law that denied African-Americans the right to vote in the Democratic primary. That law was declared unconstitutional by the Supreme Court in 1927 on the basis of the 14th Amendment.[16] But almost immediately, the legislature authorized the state party executive committee to establish the qualifications for voting in the primaries, and the Democratic party adopted a resolution that only whites could vote. This was challenged in the federal courts, and again the Supreme Court declared the white primary unconstitutional in 1932.[17]

Acting through its state convention and without legislative authorization, the Democratic party then proceeded in May of 1932 to again exclude African-Americans from the primary. The issue was taken a third time to the Supreme Court, which ruled in 1935 that the party, as a voluntary organization, had the authority to determine membership and the right of participation.[18] So for the next nine years, the Texas Democratic party excluded African-Americans from its primary. But African-Americans continued to use the courts to attack the white primary, and finally, in the case of *Smith* v. *Allwright* in 1944,[19] the Supreme Court reversed its earlier decision and declared the white primary unconstitutional.

But those who insisted on excluding African-Americans from participation were extremely imaginative in their efforts to circumvent the court's decisions. If the white primary were unconstitutional, why not use a restrictive, pre-primary selection process to pick candidates, who then would be formally nominated in the Democratic primary and subsequently elected in the general election. Finally, in 1953, the Supreme Court also declared this arrangement unconstitutional.[20]

## Restrictive Registration Laws

Until 1971, Texas had one of the most restrictive voter registration systems in the nation. Voters had to register annually between October 1 and January 31. For voters who didn't register in person at the county courthouse, deputy registrars could deliver or mail in only one registration form at a time, thus minimizing the possibilities of a coordinated voter registration drive. These restrictions discouraged voter registration across the state, and especially among the African-American, Hispanic and low-income populations.[21]

More court intervention forced major changes in the voter registration law in 1971.[22] The highly restrictive system was transformed in a relatively short time into one of the most progressive systems in the country. Common Cause, the League of Women Voters, and minority groups played major roles in forcing the legislature to comply with the court's decision. Annual registration was replaced with permanent registration, and an individual now can register by mail or in person up to 30 days prior to an election. Persons working individually or with a political campaign can be deputized to register voters, and large voter registration drives are encouraged. The elimination of restrictive voter registration requirements has been particularly beneficial to minority and low-income groups. But there continues to be pressure to further liberalize the law even to the point of permitting a person to register to vote on the day of the election.

## Property Ownership and the Right to Vote

From colonial times, one requirement for the right to vote was property ownership, a practice that continued in modified form through the 1970s in many states, including Texas. Property ownership was not a prerequisite to vote in primaries and most other elections, but it was required in bond elections that were used by local governments to win financing of new buildings, roads, sewer systems, and other infrastructure needs. The exclusion of non-property owners from these elections was based on the argument that revenue from property taxes was used to repay these bonds, and if a person did not own property on which to pay a tax, he or she should not have the right to vote for the bonds.

Landlords, however, passed through their property taxes to renters, and many renters, therefore, had a direct interest in the outcome of bond elections. Many urban areas, moreover, had large amounts of rental property and many residents who were barred from participating in those elections. Eventually, the federal courts declared property ownership as a requirement for voting in bond elections unconstitutional.

## Women and the Right to Vote

The national movement for women's suffrage was a long struggle fought in the state capitals as well as Washington. In 1915, the Texas Legislature considered a constitutional amendment extending the right to vote to women but rejected it. In 1918, women were given the right to vote in primary elections and party conventions. And then in 1919, Texas became the first southern state to approve the 19th Amendment to the U.S. Constitution, which, by late 1920, was approved by the required number of states to grant women's suffrage in all elections.[23]

## Extension of the Vote to Those under 21

A long-standing debate over the age at which a person should be permitted to vote became more intense during the Vietnam War. Many people believed that individuals who were required to comply with the draft and risk death in battle should no longer be denied the right to vote. So the 26th Amendment, which lowered the voting age from 21 to 18, was adopted in 1971, and the first election in which 18-year-olds could vote was in 1972. Perhaps because of the political activism of many college students during the Vietnam era, there were expectations that young people would vote at higher rates than older adults, but this has never materialized. The lowest voter turnout rates, in fact, are among voters 18 to 29.

## ELECTION SYSTEMS AND THEIR IMPACT
## ON POLITICAL PARTICIPATION

In contemporary Texas, it often is difficult to understand the widespread systematic discrimination once directed toward minority groups. But even after the most obvious abuses were eliminated, there were more subtle, but just as pervasive, techniques for reducing the political power and influence of these same groups.

One of these techniques is racial **gerrymandering** of political boundaries. State legislators and many city council members are elected from **single-member districts,** each of which represents a specified number of people. After the 1990 census, for example, each member of the Texas House ideally represented 113,243 people, and each member of the state Senate, 547,371 people. To minimize the possibilities of minority candidates being elected, the legislature could divide minority communities and attach them to predominantly non-minority communities. This tactic is called cracking. Conversely, the minority communities could be consolidated into one district, a tactic called packing, with an 80 to 90 percent minority population, thus reducing the number of legislative districts in which minorities might have a chance of winning office. The Voting Rights Act forbids such practices, but minority groups that challenged the 1991 legislative redistricting plans contended lawmakers used such tactics to protect incumbent Anglo senators and House members (see Chapter 8).

**At-large elections** represent another technique that has been used to reduce minority representation. At one time members of the Texas House from urban counties were elected in multimember districts, which required candidates to win election in countywide races, a very difficult prospect for minority candidates. The practice was eliminated in legislative races in the 1970s as a result of federal lawsuits. But many cities, school districts and special districts across Texas continue to use at-large elections requiring candidates to run for office citywide or districtwide. This system has the effect of diluting minority representation in most communities where it is used. In addition to the increased costs of running in citywide or districtwide elections, which discourage minority candidates, a minority group that may account for 60 percent of a city's total population and 52 percent of the voting age population may account for only 45 percent of the registered voters. And with the possibility of polarized voting, where minorities vote for the minority candidates and the non-minorities vote for the white candidates, there is a high likelihood that no minority could get elected in many at-large systems. Under the **Voting Rights Act**, at-large elections are coming under increasing attack, and many local governments have now adopted some form of single-member districting.

## Federal Intervention in the Electoral Process

In order to vote under current Texas law, a person must be 18 years old, a citizen of the United States, a resident of the state and county for at least 30 days before the election, a resident of the voting precinct on election day, and must have registered to vote at least 30 days before the election. The Election Code denies the right to vote to aliens; convicted felons in prison, on probation, or on parole; and individuals deemed mentally incompetent, but the state has eliminated all the other early restrictions.

As outlined above, the state was forced by the federal government to expand suffrage and eliminate discriminatory election practices. Minorities were forced to use the federal courts to overcome the reluctance of state leaders to extend basic voting and political rights. For the first 70 years of the current century, if any obstacles could be found to exclude minorities from the electoral process, they were implemented with dispatch and little concern for the interests of significant segments of the state's population.

In 1965, Congress passed the Voting Rights Act, which in its initial form did not apply to Texas. The sustained pattern of civil rights violations in Texas, as well as other areas of the country, resulted in amendments to the act in 1975 and its extension to Texas. Since then, the law has been central to strategies by minorities in challenging discriminatory election systems and practices.

Under the Voting Rights Act, minority groups can challenge state and local election systems in the federal courts, and the burden of proof in such challenges is on the government. An election system that dilutes minority voting strength is illegal, even if there is no clear intent to discriminate against minorities. Furthermore, any changes in the election systems of the state or local governments, including redistricting plans, must be reviewed and pre-cleared by the U.S. Justice Department or must be approved by the U.S. District Court in Washington, D.C. This legislation has produced changes in election systems across the state, and it has contributed directly to the increase in minority representation in the Texas legislature and on local governing bodies.

## Types of Elections

As indicated earlier in this chapter, a Texan is likely to have the opportunity to vote in three or four elections a year, ranging from general statewide elections to elections for the governing bodies of local, special districts. Turnout and interest is highest in the general election in presidential election years and can be abysmally low in elections for school boards and the governing bodies of single-purpose districts, such as hospital and water districts.

*Primary Elections.* Texas and most other states use the direct primary election to nominate major party candidates for public office. Prior to the adoption of the primary in 1903, the political parties used the party conventions to nominate their candidates, but changes were implemented for two basic reasons. Throughout the country, there was a progressive reform movement that faulted the conventions as undemocratic, corrupt, and dominated by a few of the party elites and advocated the party primary as an alternative.

Second, the personal rivalries and factional disputes that erupted at nominating conventions threatened the monopoly that the Democratic party had over Texas politics during that era, and the primary elections were a solution to excessive intraparty conflict. Any party that received 20 percent of the vote in the last gubernatorial election is required to nominate candidates by the primary. Other parties can continue to use the nominating convention.

Primaries are now held on the second Tuesday in March in even-numbered years, a change that was implemented in 1988 as part of the strategy of southern states to increase the region's influence in the presidential nominating process. For practical purposes, the primaries in Texas are open because no party membership is designated on an individual's voter registration card. Only after a person has voted in a party's primary is the party's name stamped on the card, and that restricts a person to voting only in that party's runoff, if there is one.

Some students of Texas politics suggest that the structure of the state's primary stymied the development of the two-party system and contributed to the conservative establishment's long domination of state politics. Comparisons between earlier primary elections and general elections suggest that Republicans voted in the Democratic primaries and then voted for Republicans in the general election. Conservative candidates were usually nominated by both parties, so it was assured that conservatives would be elected in the general election.[24]

Voter turnout in the primary elections is traditionally lower than in the general election, but the emergence of a two-party system is producing appreciable changes in participation patterns in the Democratic and Republican primaries. During the period of one-party politics, the person who won the Democratic primary was the individual who was finally elected. From the 1920s through 1970, the rate of turnout for the Democratic primary never exceeded 35 percent of the voting age population, and after the 1978 primary, the turnout rate dropped below 20 percent.[25] In 1988, a presidential election year, some 1.8 million Texans, or approximately 15 percent of the voting age population, voted in the Democratic primary. In 1990, during a heated gubernatorial campaign, the Democratic primary turnout was 1.5 million, or 13 percent of the voting age population. This low rate of participation was again repeated in the 1992 presidential primary when only 9.6 percent of the voting age population voted in the Democratic primary.[26]

Through 1982, participation in the Republican primaries never exceeded 2.4 percent of the voting age population.[27] In 1986, the turnout in the Republican primary was 4.6 percent. That increased to 1 million voters, or 8 percent of the voting age population, in the 1988 Republican presidential primary. In 1990, some 855,000, or 7 percent of the voting age population, voted in the Republican gubernatorial primary. Again in the 1992 presidential primaries, only 5.1 percent of the voting age population voted in the Republican presidential primary.[28] Despite these low turnouts, Republicans now are staging serious statewide contests in their primaries, which will attract more voters as the party becomes more competitive in the general elections.[29]

A candidate must receive an absolute majority of votes cast for a specific office to receive the party's nomination. If no candidate receives a majority, the two top vote-getters must face each other in a **runoff election**. And voter turnout rates for runoffs are lower than those for the first primary.

Minority groups have argued that the absolute majority requirement discriminates against African-American and Hispanic candidates. While there has been no successful challenge to the requirement under the Voting Rights Act, it has been successfully challenged in many school district elections where candidates usually are elected on a nonpartisan ballot. Where the challenges have been successful, pluralities rather than majorities are required for election.

Texas, along with a handful of other states, gives the political parties the responsibility of administering the primary elections. A party's county chairman and the county executive committee are responsible for printing the ballots, locating polling places, providing for voting machines, hiring the election judges and clerks and canvassing the election returns.

Prior to 1972, the costs of the primaries was borne by the political parties, and the major source of funding was the filing fees paid by candidates running for office. Those fees could be extremely high. Statewide and legislative candidates paid $1,000, and the filing fees for some local offices were as high as $8,900. This system was perceived by many as a way of eliminating potential candidates from running for public office, and the system was successfully challenged in the federal courts in the early 1970s.[30]

Under current law, modest filing fees are still permitted and the parties still conduct the primaries, but the state picks up most of the cost. Administration costs for the 1990 primaries totaled $13.4 million. Almost $2.9 million of that was raised through filing fees, but the state paid the balance. It cost about $2 million to administer the primaries in Harris County (Houston), $1.1 million in Dallas County and $691,000 in Bexar County (San Antonio).

A person can win a place on the primary ballot without paying a filing fee by submitting a designated number of registered voters' signatures on petitions to party officials.

While the primary has helped make the political process more democratic, some party advocates argue that the primary has contributed to the decline of the political parties. The parties no longer control the nomination process because any eligible individual can get on a primary ballot by paying the required filing fee or submitting the required petitions. And potential officeholders, organizing and funding their own campaigns, have little allegiance to the parties. A person who is even hostile toward the party's leadership, the party's platform, or its traditional public policy positions can win the party's nomination. A supporter of political extremist Lyndon LaRouche, for example, was elected chair of the Harris County Democratic Party in 1988. Not only was this person an embarrassment to the party, but the party regulars had to pass rules to bypass his authority in order to minimize potential political damage.

Parties function primarily to win elections, but the primaries may result in an unbalanced ticket and minimize the party's electoral strength. A primary also can potentially produce a weak candidate who receives a small portion of the votes in the general election.[31]

*General Elections.* General elections for state and federal offices are held on the first Tuesday after the first Monday in November in even-numbered years. Unlike the primaries, the administration and costs of the general election are the responsibility of the county.

The names of the candidates nominated in the primaries by the two major parties are placed on a ballot along with the names of third party and independent candidates who have submitted petitions bearing the names of registered voters equal to 1 percent of the vote in the last gubernatorial election. While some areas still use paper ballots and mechanical voting machines, many counties use punch cards that permit the election returns to be counted by computer. The ballot is styled in such a way to permit straight party voting by pulling one lever, marking one block or punching one hole.[32] In campaigns, candidates and political leaders often urge voters to "pull one lever" in support of one party's entire slate of candidates, but there is an increased pattern of ticket-splitting by voters.

In the election of 1896, the turnout rate was more than 80 percent of the eligible voting age population, but only 12 years later in 1908, four years after the effective date of the poll tax, turnout had fallen to approximately 35 percent. During much of the period from 1910 to 1958, turnout rates in non-presidential elections were less than 20 percent. Presidential elections generated a somewhat higher turnout, but in very few instances did the turnout rate exceed 35 percent of eligible voters. The 1968 presidential election produced a turnout of approximately 48 percent of the eligible voters, the highest turnout rate since 1900.[33]

Forty-seven percent of Texas' voting age population cast general election ballots in the 1984 presidential race and 44 percent in the 1988 presidential race. Only 29 percent of the voting age population cast general election ballots in the 1986 gubernatorial race and 31 percent in the 1990 gubernatorial race. Democratic and Republican primaries combined often attract only about half of the votes cast in the general election.

State officials quoted in the media often will refer to the voter turnout in terms of a percentage of registered voters. It sounds better, but it is misleading. The

1988 general election turnout, for example, was 66 percent, or about two-thirds, of the registered voters. But one-third of Texans of voting age had not even bothered to register.

*City, School Board, Single-Purpose Districts.* Elections for most city councils, school boards, and single-purpose districts are conducted in May. These are non-partisan elections in which no candidate is identified by party label. Across the state, there are wide variations in the competitiveness of these elections, campaign costs, and turnout.

While turnout rates in **local elections** rarely match those in the general elections, competition for control of local governments became more intense in the 1970s and 1980s. Much of this can be attributed to the increased political mobilization of minority voters. And contested campaigns in urban areas can be as expensive as state legislative and congressional races.

School board and single-purpose district elections usually have abysmally low rates of voter participation. It is not uncommon for many seats to go uncontested, and turnout rates can be as low as 2 percent to 5 percent. Candidates often spend little, if any, money on these elections, and their campaigns are usually informal.

*Special Elections.* The legislature can submit constitutional amendments to the voters in a general election or schedule them in a special statewide election, where voter turnout is much lower. If low turnout is perceived to be beneficial to passage of the amendment, legislators and interest groups supporting the proposal will attempt to schedule a special election. If a higher voter turnout is viewed as advantageous, sponsors will attempt to put the proposal on a general election ballot. Two amendments, one pertaining to public school finance reforms and the other to college student loan bonds, were submitted in a special election in August 1991, which attracted a statewide turnout of 11.4 percent of eligible voters. Thirteen constitutional amendments, including a proposal legalizing a state lottery, were submitted in a November 1991 election, which had a turnout rate of 26.4 percent. The student loan bonds were the only issue on both ballots. They were rejected in August but were approved only three months later by the larger number of voters.

Although there were no state or federal offices on the November 1991 ballot, there was greater voter participation than in most constitutional amendments elections because of high interest in the lottery, which won easy approval, and mayoral and city council races in Houston and Dallas, the state's two largest cities. Houston is an exception to most cities in that its city elections are held in November, rather than May. And the Dallas elections had been postponed from the previous spring by a federal court order in a dispute over city council districts.

Local governments also conduct special elections for bond issues, local initiatives and referenda, and the recall of public officials, and while there are occasional high-interest, emotionally-charged elections, turnout rates in these elections tend to be extremely low. People who do vote in these elections tend to be those with higher incomes and educational levels.

The governor also can call special elections to fill vacancies in legislative and certain other offices.

*Extended Absentee Balloting.* Beginning in 1988, Texas made a major change in the requirements for absentee voting. Prior to that time, if a voter was not going to be in the county on election day or was incapacitated so it would be impossible to get to the polls, he or she could vote absentee in person at a designated polling place or by mail before election day. The new law permitted anyone to vote early without having to state an excuse and created an extended period for absentee, or early, balloting. Urban counties, in particular, now maintain multiple voting places, including stations conveniently located in shopping malls, during the extended voting period, which runs from the 20th day to the 4th day before the scheduled election day. Consequently, there has been a notable increase in the number of votes cast early—20 percent to 30 percent of all votes in some areas.

The extended early voting has radically changed campaign strategies and tactics. One part of the new strategy is for a candidate to communicate earlier to that part of the population that has a high likelihood of voting absentee. With a large portion of the vote cast early, a candidate might well carry the election day totals but lose the absentee vote and lose the election. Another part of the strategy is to mobilize those voters who cast their votes on election day. Thus, a campaign must "peak" twice.

## THE NEW CAMPAIGN TECHNOLOGY

In the earlier chapter on political parties, we discussed the long history of one-party politics in Texas. The only elections that counted then were the Democratic primaries, and they would often include five or six candidates for a single office. In statewide or local campaigns, candidates seldom ran as a ticket or coalition. Each candidate developed his or her own campaign organization, thus precluding the development of a statewide party organization that could be mobilized in an election campaign. Individuals who became involved in a campaign were primarily motivated by their personal loyalties to a candidate and not to the political party.

With extremely low rates of voter participation in the primaries and the absence of any real threat of a Republican challenge in the general election, Democratic candidates were able to stumble through the election process building loose coalitions that tended to disintegrate within a short period. While there was competition, conservative candidates, tied to the establishment, generally prevailed. Moreover, although there might have been differences in personality and style among these conservatives candidates, they were fundamentally committed to the policy agendas of the economic elites of the state.

By today's standards, political campaigns through the 1950s seemed amateurish and unsophisticated. Modern political campaigns have been reshaped by a number of factors, including an expanded electorate that is highly mobile, the increased competitiveness of the Republican party, the organizational weaknesses of both political parties, the continuation of the candidate-centered campaign, and the increased reliance on the electronic media for news and political information.[34] Today's successful campaigns rely on sophisticated public opinion polling, slick campaign ads contrived by media experts, analysis of demographics, and targeting of selected populations through direct mail and phone banks—all orchestrated by a stable of campaign consultants.

Contemporary campaigns—state, local, and national—increasingly rely on the professional **campaign consultant**. Such consultants have been around in some form or another in Texas for a long time. W. Lee "Pappy" O'Daniel, the owner of a flour mill that produced "Hillbilly Flour" and master of ceremonies of a daily radio talk show, ran for governor in 1938 exploiting a rustic image couched in religious, evangelical language that had a wide reception in the rural areas of the state. His speeches were designed to create an identification with the "common folks," but he was a wealthy businessman who had ties to Texas' corporate leaders. His "homespun style" was contrived, and O'Daniel relied heavily throughout his campaign on public relations expert Phil Fox of Dallas.[35] What is different about contemporary campaign consulting is that it is an identifiable industry with diversified expertise. More significantly, few candidates for statewide office or major local offices now run without utilizing the services of campaign consultants.

## Public Opinion Polling

In a society based on mass consumption, it is no wonder that techniques were developed to measure public attitudes and opinions. The origins of the industry are usually linked to George Gallup, who conducted a statewide poll in 1932 for his mother-in-law who ran for secretary of state in Iowa. Survey research or public opinion polling has a variety of applications, most of which are non-political, and market research is now a multibillion-dollar industry.

Public opinion polling is used in political campaigns for a number of purposes. As would-be candidates consider running for office, they will often hire pollsters to conduct benchmark surveys of voters and those who are likely to vote in the upcoming election. Using well-tested sampling techniques, the pollster will conduct either a telephone survey or a face-to-face survey of a representative sample of the voters. The length and type of the survey usually is determined by available funds and the information desired by the candidate and those developing the campaign. Surveys are expensive. If the required number of completed interviews is 1,200 for a statewide race at a cost of $25 each, it is clear that polling can consume a hefty chunk of the campaign budget.

Surveys are used to develop campaign strategy, monitor the progress of the campaign, and modify the campaign as changes take place in the attitudes, perceptions, or mood of the electorate. The benchmark survey, often taken some time before the official campaign gets underway, is rather lengthy and attempts to assess current public opinion as it relates to the office a candidate is seeking. Issues are identified, perceptions of candidates are probed, and trial heats with potential opponents are tested. A wide range of demographic questions are included to permit the segmentation of the electorate into small groups whose specific interests or concerns can be identified and targeted.

As the campaign proceeds, tracking surveys are used to determine shifts in attitudes, perceptions, and support for the candidate. Does the candidate now have greater name identification? Do more people perceive the candidate positively and express their support? Is there a particular event or emerging campaign issue that might spell defeat? This information is used to adjust the campaign to changing conditions. Toward the end of the campaign, surveys are often taken nightly to permit further fine-tuning of the campaign in the final days.

A variation on the survey is the use of a focus group. As television ads are developed, the campaign staff may choose to test them before they are aired. A series of focus groups, each including 8 to 12 persons recruited for specific demographic characteristics, will be asked to review these ads and provide their impressions and reactions. An experienced staff will watch these proceedings to identify subtle responses to the ads, the theme or the message. On the basis of these qualitative assessments, the media consultants will decide which ads should be used and which should be discarded.

## Segmentation and Targeting of the Electorate

A political campaign is fundamentally an organized effort to communicate with the electorate with the goal of convincing a majority of those who participate to vote for a specific candidate. There are several million registered voters statewide, and hundreds of thousands in each of the largest counties. It is impossible for a candidate to communicate with every voter, and it wouldn't make sense to even attempt to do so considering the low voter turnout in elections. The problem is made even more difficult by the fact that voter turnout rates vary among different ethnic, income, and educational groups, and some of these voters will not support a particular candidate no matter what he or she says or does. In a partisan election, many people will vote for or against a candidate strictly on the basis of party identification. Finally, not every voter shares a candidate's concerns and priorities.

Census data, surveys, and past election returns with turnout and party voting patterns are used to segment the population. There are research specialists who are able to integrate and organize this information to permit the campaign to target its messages to small, well-defined populations. Whether direct mail, television, radio, newspapers, phone banks, or block walking is used to reach its audience, the modern campaign will direct a specific message with high issue or interest saliency to these segmented populations.

For example, the survey data may suggest that a disproportionate number of women between the ages of 45 and 54 have not heard of the candidate but are concerned about health care and medical insurance. Based on demographic data and television program ratings, the media specialist knows that a large number of these women watch daytime television programs. To get a specific message to these voters, television spots with a health care message oriented to the specific concerns of women from 45 to 54 will be developed and aired during these times of the day. Most populations can be segmented and targeted in this manner, increasing the likelihood that a desired message gets to the specific voters whose perceptions and attitudes the consultant wants to influence.

The segmentation of the electorate may well lead to a fracturing of the political debate. Various segments of the electorate are exposed to narrow slices of the candidate's image, personality, and concerns. The campaign hopes that each group of voters will respond favorably to their own limited knowledge of the candidate, but some critics would argue that this segmentation "further diminishes the importance of language, logic, and reason in the articulation of campaign issues."[36]

## Media and Advertising

It is easy to assume that a campaign can market a candidate much like a pack of cigarettes or a box of soap, and our increasing cynicism often leads to this facile conclusion. But voter response to candidates, the progress of the campaign, and the various ads and messages the voters receive form an extremely complex process. Scholars in various disciplines have attempted to unravel the effects of news reports and campaign advertising on voter behavior, but the conclusions are only tentative.

## Controlled Media

There are numerous media through which candidates can communicate their messages to the voters, and for those that can be purchased commercially, the only limitations are availability and finances. The media that is purchased by the candidate is often referred to as the controlled media. That is to say, the decisions on which media to use, when to purchase advertisements, and what message to convey is under the control of the candidate. There are some technical and legal questions pertaining to campaign advertising, but the candidate has a wide range of options.

Billboards, bench signs, advertisements on buses and cabs, and electronic signs can be purchased for the purpose of establishing voter awareness and name identification. While such ads are not likely to convert or mobilize voters, they establish the candidate's visibility.

Although candidates continually talk about "pressing the flesh" and making direct contacts with the voters, it is simply impossible to talk personally to the number of people necessary to win an election, particularly in a statewide or urban race. Candidates stage block walks and rallies in which they personally participate and meet with supporters, but many of these are **media events** they hope will be covered by the press. Campaigns still rely on block walking and phone banks, but in a sophisticated campaign, these tactics are coordinated with the media blitz and direct mail.

In many local elections across Texas, it is too costly or inefficient to use radio and television advertising. But it is impossible to run a viable statewide campaign without the use of the electronic media. Texas is large and diverse and has about 20 separate media markets.[37] Candidates often spend 50 percent of the campaign budget for television and radio advertising, and the media specialists—ranging from the creative staff to the time buyers—have taken on increased importance in modern campaigns.

The 30-second spot is now the standard for television advertising, and the candidate's consultants attempt to carefully craft advertisements that address concerns, perceptions, and expectations of varied segments of the electorate.[38] The media blitz usually picks up steam as the campaign moves closer to election day, because it is assumed that it takes several exposures to a given ad for a voter to respond and, in many cases, allegations raised in an opponent's ads must be addressed.

Campaign advertising became an issue in the 1990 gubernatorial race with what seemed to be an endless series of negative campaign ads and related tactics (see Chapter 5). Democrat Ann Richards' previous problems with alcoholism were raised, and inferences were made, but never substantiated, that she had used illegal drugs. Gay-bashing ads were used against Richards when the Democrat received the endorsement of groups alleged to be linked to lesbian rights, and a Democratic fund-raising letter from Ron Brown, the party's national chairman, attempted to link Republican nominee Clayton Williams with the neo-Nazism and racism of David Duke of Louisiana.[39]

The negative ad is not new to Texas politics, but most observers agreed that ads in the 1990 gubernatorial race were more vitriolic, aired with more frequency, and were seemingly more irrelevant to the issues facing the state (Figure 7-1, page 202). As the ads continued, newspapers began to analyze their themes and veracity, and voters indicated that they were displeased with them. But consultants continued to convince their clients that negative attacks worked and that people, while they objected to them, had higher recall of negative ads than many other TV spots.

## Uncontrolled Media

Positive news stories about the candidate and campaign are potentially more valuable than paid advertising and don't cost the campaign money. Candidates and their handlers thus attempt to exploit the press by getting positive coverage and reducing as much as possible any negative slants in campaign stories. But the relationship between political candidates and the press is adversarial. And the news media, ever alert for weaknesses in a candidate and tips spread by political opponents, can make or break a candidate by the coverage and slant given to the candidate's personality, reputation, view of the issues, and campaign activities.

**FIGURE 7-1**   Cartoon depicting Mark White and Ann Richards exchanging charges about negative campaign ads. (© *Houston Chronicle*.  Reprinted with permission)

Many campaigns hire press secretaries who specialize in media relations, and one author has suggested that a successful media strategy entails the following: "Keeping the candidate away from the press; feeding the press a simple, telegenic political line of the day; and making sure the daily news line echoes ('magnify' may be the better word) the images from the campaign ads, thus blurring the distinction between commercials and 'reality.'"[40]

Members of the press are keenly aware of these efforts to manipulate them, and the best reporters are usually able to resist. But the hectic, irrational nature of statewide campaigns, the pressure of news deadlines, the propensity for pack journalism, and the fear of being beaten to a major story by a competitor often work against a reporter's sincere efforts to avoid being used and to get the "straight skinny" on the candidate's abilities and potential and his or her stand on the issues.

Clayton Williams used his millions to win the 1990 Republican gubernatorial nomination with an effective paid TV campaign that portrayed an attractive image of an independent, can-do, cost-conscious businessman. But he lost the general election to Democrat Ann Richards after the uncontrolled news media painted a less-attractive picture: that of a coarse, chauvinistic individual who had only the vaguest notion of what he would do as governor (see Chapter 5).

## Direct Mail and Fund-Raising

People like to receive mail. Some people even like to receive junk mail, experts say, and direct mail has become a highly sophisticated component of modern campaigns. Direct mail specialists provide campaigns with a technique for "persuasion and fundraising."[41] As a further refinement of the segmentation and targeting of voters, this technique permits the campaign to craft a specific message for a narrowly defined population and assure, with high probability, that households with the specified demographic or psychographic characteristics will receive the campaign message. In a sense, it is "narrowcasting" a specific message to an identifiable audience.

Direct mail is big business in the United States, and it has been easily adapted to political campaigns. In many instances, the campaign messages and appeals are very emotional, designed to push the voters' hot buttons on specific issues. They are crafted by specialists who have studied the emotional appeals of such communications, and the attention to detail often astonishes the uninitiated. The length of a letter, the color of the paper on which it is printed, the underlining and highlighting of specific words or phrases, and teasers on the envelope to get the recipient to open the letter receive critical attention by the specialist.

Evidence indicates that people respond to direct mail appeals, and if the technique is integrated with phone banks, block walks, and the media campaign, it becomes an extremely valuable campaign tool.

Direct mail also has become a major tool in campaign fund-raising. Massive mailing lists segmenting virtually every population group in the state have been developed, and names of persons with probable political attitudes and beliefs are easily extracted from these files by computer. Successive mailings to probable supporters have a high likelihood of producing campaign dollars. The continued use and refinement of these lists increase the rate of return, and while campaigns still rely on large contributions, the more modest contributions received from direct mail solicitation have taken on increased importance.

## TEXAS CAMPAIGN CONSULTANTS

When Larry Sabato published *The Rise of the Political Consultants* in 1981, the only major national political campaign firm he identified from Texas was V. Lance Tarrance and Associates, Inc., of Houston, which specialized in polling. But throughout the state, there are other consultants with national or regional reputations.

Some of the better known Democratic campaign specialists in Texas today include George Shipley of Austin, whose clients have included Governor Ann Richards and Attorney General Dan Morales; Jack Martin of Austin, a strategist and former treasurer of the Texas Democratic party who has done work for Richards, Lt. Governor Bob Bullock and U.S. Senator Lloyd Bentsen; Dan McClung of Houston, whose clients have included Bentsen; and Bill Emory and Peck Young of Austin, who handle numerous congressional and local races.

On the Republican side, Tarrance is still a major pollster. So is David Hill of Houston, a former Tarrance associate. Strategist and direct mail specialist Karl Rove of Austin has worked for former Governor Bill Clements, U.S. Senator Phil Gramm, Texas Supreme Court Chief Justice Tom Phillips, state Treasurer Kay Bailey Hutchison, and Agriculture Commissioner Rick Perry. He also has handled fundraising campaigns for the Texas Republican party. Carol Reed and Jeanne Johnson of Dallas are major Republican fundraisers, Bryan Eppstein of Fort Worth has handled a number of legislative races for Republican candidates, and John Weaver of Austin, a former executive director of the Texas Republican party, has been involved in presidential and statewide campaigns. And there are others—media advisers, direct mail specialists, pollsters, and strategy wizards—in both parties, operating in what seems to be a growth industry.

## MONEY AND CAMPAIGNS

### Campaign Costs

We really don't know precisely how much is spent every year on political campaigns in Texas. There is no single place where all this information is collected. Candidates for state office file their campaign finance reports with the state Ethics Commission, where they are scrutinized by the news media and public interest groups. Candidates for city councils, county offices, and school districts file their campaign spending reports with the jurisdictions in which they are running. With more than 2,000 governmental units and no requirement that local campaign data be reported to the state, we can provide only some examples of contemporary campaign costs and finances.

Modern campaign technology and paid media are extremely expensive, even on the local level. City council races in major cities such as San Antonio, Houston, Fort Worth, and Dallas can easily cost $50,000 to $100,000. All of the candidates in the 1991 mayor's race in San Antonio spent more than $1 million combined, and winner Nelson Wolff spent more than $500,000 alone. Mayoral candidates in Houston and Dallas spent $5 million and $1.8 million respectively the same year. There have been reports of candidates running for county commissioner spending $40,000, and district judges in metropolitan counties spending more than $100,000. Historically, school board elections have been low-budget, but it is not uncommon for slates of candidates in large urban school districts to spend $10,000 to $15,000 in low-turnout elections.

Frank Sorauf, a specialist on political parties and campaigns, reported that the costs of U.S. congressional campaigns had risen from $77 million in 1972 to $450 million in 1986. Even after accounting for inflation, the increase was 122 percent over 14 years.[42] While there is no comprehensive hard data for political races in Texas, there is every indication that campaign costs in Texas have risen at a comparable rate.[43]

Many people believe that campaign expenditures in statewide races in Texas, particularly gubernatorial races, now skirt on the obscene. But fueled by the rising costs of television advertising and other modern campaign techniques—and two-party competition—expenditures continue to increase.

In the 1968 Democratic primary and runoff, the total spent by seven candidates was $3.75 million, with the winner, Preston Smith, spending approximately $850,000.[44] This was at a time when winning the Democratic nomination effectively meant winning the election because statewide Republican opposition was still weak.

Three Democratic gubernatorial candidates spent more than $13 million in the 1990 primary and runoff, and four Republican candidates spent more than $18 million in their primary. Total expenditures in the 1990 governor's race exceeded $50 million, making it the most expensive governor's race ever waged in the United States up to that point. The winner, Democrat Ann Richards, spent more than $12 million, while the losing Republican nominee, Clayton Williams, spent more than $21 million.

More than $10 million was spent on six races for the Texas Supreme Court in 1988, making them the most expensive judicial races in Texas history. Philosophical control of the court (see Chapter 11) was at stake, and the business and medical community battled the trial lawyers in a feeding frenzy.[45]

## Campaign Finances

The soaring campaign costs have raised considerable concern about campaign fund-raising and contributions. There is concern that elections are being bought and that major campaign contributors are purchasing influence in the policymaking process. Some critics of contemporary campaigns have argued that current practices are a form of legalized bribery which infers that public officials are available to the highest bidder. The debate is often ill-defined, and sometimes only single case studies of legislative votes are used to demonstrate the alleged relationship between political contributions and a recipient's performance in office. But the issue is ultimately a question of the "impact of campaign finance on American politics and American democracy."[46]

There is no question that money is critical to most successful campaigns for public office because it permits the candidate to purchase the resources for communicating to an expanded electorate.

But money is not the only factor that bears on an election. Incumbency, existing party loyalties, the availability of party or campaign activists, the public's perceptions of a candidate, and a candidate's campaign skills or expertise also help determine electoral success. There have been numerous elections in which well-financed candidates were defeated by opponents with far fewer dollars. And they may suggest that "there are genuine limits" on what money can accomplish in a campaign.[47]

Contributions are made to influence the outcome of an election and, subsequently, to shape public policy by electing persons who share similar political views with or who will be sympathetic or accessible to those making contributions. As the stories of large campaign contributions are circulated, it is not uncommon to hear the phrase that Texas has the "best Supreme Court money can buy" or the "best legislature money can buy." When key policy votes seem to be influenced by an officeholder's relationship to his political contributors, credence is given to these claims.

Undoubtedly, some individuals make contributions to candidates out of a sense of civic duty, general concern for good public policy, partisan loyalty, or personal friendship. But large contributions of thousands of dollars, either from individuals or political action committees, raise different questions about intent and purpose.

Rarely will anyone admit publicly that he is attempting to buy a candidate. Individuals and PACs—particularly the PACs—making large political contributions usually say they are doing so for the purpose of "gaining access" to elected officials.[48] Since officeholders have limited time to consider and assess competing interests, lobbyists representing interest groups and their PACs contend that campaign contributions are necessary to facilitate access and give them an opportunity to present their cases on specific legislation.

Political scientists and others have attempted to prove that there is a relationship between campaign contributions and public policy, but so far the research is inconclusive. Multiple factors shape the decisions of public policymakers, including an officeholder's personal views, the views of his constituents, legal and technical issues, and the merit of the requests made by specific individuals or groups.[49] Yet, the strong appearance of a relationship between money and public policy is there, and advocates of campaign finance reform can make strong arguments for change.

## The Fat Cats

Unlike the federal government, Texas places no limits on the amount of money a single individual or political action committee can contribute to a political candidate. And there are no limits on how much a candidate can contribute to his or her own campaign. Large contributions have always played a role in Texas politics and, over the years, most large contributions have gone to the conservative candidates, both Democrat and Republican. In the 1972 Democratic gubernatorial primary, for example, approximately 89% of the 824 campaign contributions larger than $500 went to the conservative candidates.[50] Potentially, the use of direct mail to solicit small campaign donations may begin to partially offset some of the large campaign contributions, but large donors are still prominent in Texas political campaigns.

Some of the better known stories of large campaign contributions center on Clinton Manges, a South Texas rancher-oilman who, ironically, was not Texas' typical political **fat cat**. Manges, in fact, was a maverick who battled Texas' corporate establishment for years. In 1982, he outdid the fat cats at their own game by contributing $1.8 million to several Democratic candidates, either personally or through a political action committee administered by his attorney, Pat Maloney of San Antonio. His contributions included more than $300,000 to gubernatorial candidate Bob Armstrong; $65,000 to Garry Mauro, a candidate for land commissioner; $50,000 to Jim Mattox, a candidate for attorney general; more than $100,000 to Texas Supreme Court Justice Ted Z. Robertson; and more than $200,000 to Supreme Court candidate Woodrow Wilson Bean of El Paso. All of those individuals except Armstrong and Bean won election that year, and while in office they were periodically plagued by questions about their relationship—either real or imagined—to Manges, who was frequently involved in litigation and for several years had millions of dollars at stake in a dispute over mineral leases that involved the state.

A number of recent candidates for state office have been wealthy in their own right and willing to spend a considerable amount of their own money to get elected. In his first election in 1978, Bill Clements used his personal wealth to guarantee $4.5 million in bank loans to his campaign, which were later repaid. In his campaign in 1986, Clements racked up another $4.5 million in debt, which he later raised money to repay. He loaned his losing 1982 campaign $3 million.

Republican Clayton Williams spent about $8.5 million of his own money on his 1990 gubernatorial campaign, but his defeat left him holding an empty bag. Had he won, he also would have been able to raise enough contributions to repay himself, but most donors aren't interested in giving money to a defeated candidate. Governor Ann Richards, who beat Williams, asked the legislature in 1991 to limit the size of campaign contributions. She also said that for the sake of fairness, limits needed to be placed on the amount of money that a wealthy candidate could be repaid by donors for his own personal investment in a race. But the legislature refused to put any limits on campaign contributions.

## The Political Action Committees

In Chapter 4, we discussed the development of political action committees as an extension of interest groups. These committees have increased their importance at the state and local level by bringing sophisticated fund-raising skills to political campaigns. Year in and year out, they collect money from their members and are a ready source of campaign dollars. PACs are in the business of influencing elections, and the well-organized PACs anticipate elections well in advance of the candidate filing date, when campaigns begin in earnest.

Another kind of political action committee is the super-PAC, which represents a wide range of interests extending beyond a single industry. These are ad hoc coalitions formed prior to an election to attempt to get a "bigger bang for their buck" by coordinating their political contributions. A coalition of lobby groups organized in 1982 under the designation of the Associated Research Group. Its membership included the Texas Medical Association, the Texas Association of

Realtors, the Texas Automobile Dealers Association, and others. Its members gave more than $1 million to 150 campaigns in 1982.[51]

## Attempts at Reforms

On the heels of the Sharpstown scandal (see Chapter 8), the legislature enacted a major campaign finance reporting and disclosure law in 1973 that, with some changes, is now administered by the state Ethics Commission. Although it didn't limit the size of political contributions, for the first time it required candidates to list the addresses as well as the names of donors and the amounts and dates of contributions. It also required political action committees contributing to candidates or officeholders to report the sources of their donations, which usually had been hidden in the past. Also for the first time, officeholders were required to file annual reports of their political contributions and receipts—even during years when they were not seeking re-election—and candidates were required to report contributions and other financial activity that occurred after an election. And a candidate had to formally designate a campaign treasurer before he or she could legally accept political contributions.

## POLITICAL PARTICIPATION

In 1991, a small group of protesters pitched tents and erected a series of crude displays outside the offices of the Texas Water Commission in Austin. They came from a small town south of Dallas, where, they claimed, a plant was polluting the environment with cancer-producing agents. People living in the community had experienced disproportionately high cancer rates and immunity and respiratory problems. These were middle-aged Texans who had never before participated in, much less organized, a demonstration. They appeared to be uncomfortable, but there was a sense of desperation as they talked about their families and friends.

A month or so later in San Antonio, several thousand antiabortionists organized a three-mile-long demonstration along a major highway. The demonstration took place after church on a Sunday, and many of the well-groomed protesters carried Bibles and had their young children in tow. Waving placards, singing songs and praying, they used tactics that have been used across the nation by antiabortion groups.

On any given day in newspapers across Texas, there are hundreds of "letters to the editor" that address a wide range of state and local political issues. People contact public officials every day about stop signs, public facilities, garbage collection, and a multitude of governmental functions and responsibilities. Thousands of people are involved in politics as they attempt to shape the actions and decisions of public officials.

When we think about political participation, we have a tendency to think primarily in terms of voting or running for office. But these two activities are just a small part of the ongoing process necessary to sustain a democratic political system, translate the interests and demands of the general public into specific policies and assure governmental responsiveness.

Most people who participate in politics engage in what scholars call conventional political behavior. This includes voting, running for office, contributing to and campaigning for candidates, writing letters, gathering petitions, participating in other **grass roots** activities, and lobbying.

Fewer individuals participate in what is considered unconventional political behavior. These are acts that are likely to offend or enrage large segments of the population. In the view of some people, they can include boycotts, protest marches, and other non-violent demonstrations, although many individuals consider any lawful, peaceful demonstration a very conventional means of exercising their constitutional rights. To virtually everyone, however, destruction of property, personal injury, assassination, and other forms of violence are totally unacceptable forms of political behavior.[52]

Not everyone, of course, participates in politics at the same level. Why some people get actively involved in politics and public life while others seem totally uninterested in government, current events, or public policy is a question that has challenged scholars, candidates, journalists, and reform groups for years. And it has generated a great deal of research.

From the day a person is born, he or she is subject to a socialization or learning process. As the individual approaches adulthood, the process includes the shaping of political attitudes, beliefs, and behaviors. The process is complex, lifelong, and structured by the interaction of the individual with the environment in which he or she lives.

**Political socialization,** the process by which people learn to behave politically, "transmits a broad array of values and opinions, from general feelings about trust in government to specific opinions" about the economy, political leaders and institutions.[53] The agents of political socialization include the family, where the young child first learns of the views and attitudes of parents and relatives toward government, the political process, and leaders. The process is expanded through the schools, where children are exposed to national and state history, government, heroes, and values. Civics lessons and courses are taught to further shape commitment to the dominant values of the society. Other institutions such as the church and the mass media also contribute to this molding process. So do a person's peers and life experiences. Individuals tend to validate their perceptions and attitudes through the opinions of friends and acquaintances, and a major life experience, such as a tour of duty in the military or extended unemployment, has a potential effect on one's political behavior.

Political behavior is complex and changes over time. The limited space dedicated to this topic here is insufficient to "flesh out" its nuances and complexities, and we warn you to avoid drawing hard and fast conclusions. But a few of the broadest generalizations about political behavior are in order.

A number of scholars have developed classifications of political behavior that run from high levels of involvement in a wide range of activities to virtual passivity. Such classifications permit us to produce generalizations on the different levels of political participation. Utilizing a national study by Sidney Verba and Norman H. Nie, well-known American political scientists specializing in political socialization, we can identify six categories of political participation.

At one end of the spectrum of political participation are the complete **activists** (approximately 11 percent of the population) who are engaged in all types of political activity. Not only are these individuals involved in political campaigns, but they participate in almost every other arena of community life. By contrast, there are the inactives (22 percent) who participate rarely if at all in the political life of the community. In some of the literature, this first group has been referred to as political gladiators, and the second group, apathetics.

Another group which is relatively inactive and shares many of the characteristics of the inactives are the voting specialists (21 percent). These individuals report that they vote regularly in presidential and local elections and rely primarily on elections to shape the decisions of government. These individuals seldom engage in other organizational activities or attempt to personally contact policymakers.

There are a small number of parochial participants (four percent) who vote but do not engage in collective activity or campaigns. Nevertheless, they do contact policymakers over specific issues that affect their personal lives.

A group which demonstrates a high rate of participation in community life but low levels of campaign activity are the communalists (20 percent). These individuals engage in community activities such as PTA and neighborhood associations, but rarely engage in the high conflict game of political campaigns.

A group which engages at a high rate in political campaigns but a low rate in community activities are the campaigners (15 percent). This groups appears to be attracted to the conflict of campaigns but shows little interest in other community organizational activities.[54]

While we have limited survey data for Texas, some generalizations emerge from national studies to provide insights into the patterns of participation in the state:

1. **Income**. Individuals with higher income levels are more likely to be active participants in a wider range of political activities than those with low incomes.
2. **Education**. Rates of participation increase as the level of education increases. People with college degrees are more likely to participate in politics than those less well educated.
3. **Sex**. Historically, men have participated in politics at higher rates than women, but in recent years women and men have been participating at comparable levels.
4. **Age**. The highest rates of participation are among middle-aged people.
5. **Race and ethnicity**. Rates of participation among Anglos are highest. But African-Americans, despite the historical patterns of discrimination, are now moving toward the Anglo level. Hispanics participate at rates considerably lower than those of Anglos and African-Americans.

Historically, if you were a middle-aged Anglo male, well-educated and wealthy, you were more likely to participate in politics than most other people.

Changes in the social and economic composition of the state's population are producing changes in political participation.

## CHANGING PATTERNS OF PARTY SUPPORT AND IDENTIFICATION

Statewide data collected over the past 40 years from various public opinion polls confirm the argument made in the previous chapter that Texas is becoming a two-party state. In 1952, according to a survey conducted by Belden Associates of Dallas, 66 percent of Texans called themselves Democrats, and only six percent claimed to be Republicans.[55] There was little change in party identification from 1952 to 1964, but during the next decade, Republican party identification increased to 16 percent, and Democratic party identification declined to 59 percent (Figure 7-2).

Between 1975 and 1984, there was a dramatic decline in voter identification with the Democratic party and a significant increase in Republican party identification. By 1989, approximately 31 percent of Texas voters called themselves Republicans, and 32 percent identified as Democrats. This shift in party identification is reflected in the increased competitiveness of local and state Republican candidates and Republican electoral victories across the state. Moreover, both parties must focus a great deal of their attention on the independent voter, who now is the key to electoral success. The data from *The Texas Poll* (Table 7-1) conducted in the fall of 1991 provide a detailed demographic profile of voters now identifying themselves as Democrats, Republicans, or independents.

**FIGURE 7-2**   Changing Party Affiliation in Texas, 1964-1989. (*The Texas Poll,* © Harte-Hanks Communications, Inc., Fall 1989.)

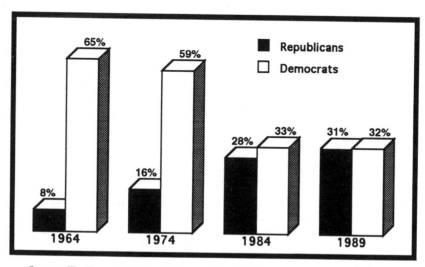

Source: *The Texas Poll,* Fall, 1989, copyrighted by Harte-Hanks Communications, Inc.

**TABLE 7-1**   Party Affiliation of Texas Voters, Texas Poll–Fall 1991

| | Party Identification | | | |
|---|---|---|---|---|
| | **Republican** | **Democrat** | **Independent** | **Not Ascertained** |
| ALL RESPONDING | 31.8% | 31.4% | 30.7% | 6.2% |
| **EDUCATION** | | | | |
| Less Than High School | 16.4% | 47.0% | 28.4% | 8.2% |
| High School Grad | 31.3 | 30.5 | 32.2 | 6.0 |
| College Grad | 41.6 | 24.7 | 29.2 | 4.5 |
| Not Ascertained | 12.5 | 43.7 | 18.7 | 25.0 |
| **INCOME** | | | | |
| Less Than $20,000 | 24.6% | 40.4% | 28.4% | 6.6% |
| $20,000–$40,000 | 29.0 | 35.2 | 30.6 | 5.2 |
| $40,000–$60,000 | 36.9 | 25.5 | 33.6 | 4.0 |
| $60,000 and over | 45.4 | 18.9 | 31.1 | 4.5 |
| Not Ascertained | 33.3 | 14.0 | 29.8 | 22.8 |
| **AGE** | | | | |
| 18 to 29 | 36.4% | 24.4% | 34.2% | 4.9% |
| 30 to 44 | 31.2 | 28.5 | 33.1 | 7.1 |
| 45 to 61 | 33.2 | 33.6 | 27.6 | 5.6 |
| 62 to 95 | 26.1 | 42.6 | 25.6 | 5.6 |
| Not Ascertained | 20.0 | 20.0 | 20.0 | 40.0 |
| **GENDER** | | | | |
| Male | 30.8% | 29.3% | 34.1% | 5.8% |
| Female | 32.8 | 33.6 | 27.0 | 6.6 |
| **ETHNIC BACKGROUND** | | | | |
| Anglo | 39.8% | 24.1% | 30.9% | 5.2% |
| African-American | 5.8 | 67.4 | 24.4 | 2.3 |
| Hispanic | 14.3 | 44.6 | 30.9 | 10.1 |
| Other | 23.1 | 28.2 | 41.0 | 7.7 |
| Not Ascertained | | 20.0 | 20.0 | 60.0 |
| **NUMBER OF YEARS IN TEXAS** | | | | |
| 10 Years or Less | 44.1% | 21.3% | 29.4% | 5.1% |
| Over 10 not life | 32.8 | 31.0 | 29.7 | 6.4 |
| Entire life | 27.5 | 34.7 | 31.9 | 5.8 |
| Not Ascertained | 50.0 | 8.3 | 16.7 | 25.0 |
| **RELIGION** | | | | |
| Catholic | 30.0% | 33.3% | 30.4% | 6.2% |
| Baptist | 31.2 | 36.8 | 26.0 | 6.0 |
| Methodist | 30.8 | 31.9 | 29.8 | 7.4 |
| Other Protestant | 40.8 | 24.8 | 30.7 | 3.7 |
| Other | 26.2 | 31.5 | 35.3 | 6.9 |
| Not Ascertained | 13.3 | | 60.0 | 26.7 |
| **SELF REPORT IDEOLOGY** | | | | |
| Liberal | 21.9% | 43.8% | 29.8% | 4.5% |
| Moderate | 31.6 | 34.8 | 30.9 | 2.7 |
| Conservative | 42.1 | 20.6 | 31.5 | 5.9 |
| Not Ascertained | 6.9 | 27.6 | 27.6 | 37.9 |

Source: *The Texas Poll,* copyright Harte-Hanks Communications, Inc. Fall, 1991

A careful review of this table will demonstrate that there are marked differences in the social and economic characteristics among party identifiers (see Chapter 6).

Ticket-splitting, a practice associated with the realignment process, is now characteristic of contemporary Texas elections. In 1990, there was clear evidence that Texans cast their votes selectively as they went down the general election ballot. There were a number of Democratic votes cast for Republican U.S. Senator Phil Gramm and a sizable number of Republican defectors to Bob Bullock, the successful Democratic candidate for lieutenant governor.[56]

The 1990 gubernatorial contest between Ann Richards and Clayton Williams generated a great deal of speculation about gender gap differences between men and women over policy issues and potential party support. Williams' rape joke gaffe (see Chapter 5) certainly prompted a negative reaction among women across the state. But there was no unanimity among pundits, pollsters, and professors as to whether the difference in support the two candidates received was based on gender or age differences.[57] There is evidence suggesting that older and younger voters view the world in markedly different ways, and these differences are manifested in their support or opposition to specific public policy issues, parties, and candidates. Based on survey data, younger voters, for example, are more tolerant of candidates who have experienced problems with alcohol or drug abuse.

## POLITICAL PHILOSOPHY

There is a wide spectrum of political beliefs among Texans. While the state's dominant individualistic and traditionalistic subcultures (see Chapter 1) tend to be characterized by conservative attitudes, a sizable part of the state's population has moderate to liberal viewpoints (Table 7-2). These philosophical differences were prominent in the liberal-conservative battles in the Democratic party from 1940 through the 1970s. Generally, persons describing themselves as liberal now vote Democratic, moderates split between the two parties, and conservatives tend to vote for Republican candidates.

**TABLE 7–2**   Political Philosophy of Texas Adults 1968–1988

|  | 1968 | 1988 |
| --- | --- | --- |
| Liberal | 15% | 19% |
| Middle of the road/Moderate* | 40 | 40 |
| Conservative | 34 | 35 |
| Don't know, not sure, etc. | 11 | 6 |

*In the 1968 study, the phrase middle of the road was used. The Texas Poll uses the term moderate.

Sources: Chandler Davidson, *Race and Class in Texas Politics;* Harte-Hanks Communications Inc., *The Texas Poll,* Spring, 1988.

In his book, _Race and Class in Texas Politics_, Chandler Davidson argues that opinion data, voting patterns, and the recurring liberal-conservative contests in the Democratic primaries challenge the "myth of overwhelming conservatism" of Texas adults. Very few liberals were elected to public office in one-party Texas because the political playing field was biased toward the conservative Democratic establishment. Previous election laws served to reduce participation among lower-income groups and minorities, many of whom had more moderate-to-liberal views of government's role in setting public policy.[58]

But by the 1980s, moderate-to-liberal Democrats had gained control of their party's organization, and while the party retained some conservative members, a large number of conservatives switched to the Republican party.

Texas Republicans also have philosophical and ideological differences, and in recent years, these divisions often have been rancorous and bitter. Overwhelmingly conservative, Republicans are split along the lines of economic conservatism and "life style" conservatism, such as that preached by the "Religious Right." During the period of one-party politics, religious fundamentalists exercised what political influence they had in the Democratic party. Now, after 30 years of utilizing direct mail linked to televised religious programs, or the "electronic church," many of the evangelical fundamentalists have been politically mobilized and have settled primarily within the Republican party. There are some fundamental differences between the Religious Right and mainstream Republicans, and party activists speak of the intensity of these intraparty divisions.

## MINORITIES AND POLITICAL PARTICIPATION

Over the past 20 years, African-Americans and Hispanics have realized substantial gains in the electoral process. Elimination of restrictive voting laws and adoption of a liberal voter registration system have contributed to an increase in minority voters across the state. The federal Voting Rights Act, meanwhile, has been used with considerable success to attack racial gerrymandering of political districts and eliminate at-large elections, thus enhancing election opportunities for minority candidates. Concerted voter registration and mobilization drives coordinated by groups such as the National Association for the Advancement of Colored People (NAACP) and the Southwest Voter Registration Education Project (SVREP) also have contributed to an increased electoral role for minorities.

### Hispanics

After the 1990 census, Hispanics comprised 25 percent of Texas' population. But the Hispanic population is younger than the Anglo and African-American populations and, consequently, Hispanics accounted for only 22 percent of Texans of voting age (Table 7-3). Hispanics also include a significant number of immigrants (an estimated one out of seven) who are not eligible to vote, thus reducing the Hispanic population to 19 percent of adult citizens. Approximately 14 percent or

**TABLE 7–3**  1990 Population and Voting Age Population

| | Total Population | Percent of Total | Population of Voting Age | Percent of Total |
|---|---|---|---|---|
| Anglo/White | 10,291,680 | 60.6% | 7,828,352 | 64.4% |
| Hispanic | 4,339,905 | 25.6 | 2,719,586 | 22.4 |
| African-American | 1,976,360 | 11.6 | 1,336,688 | 11.0 |
| American Indian | 52,803 | 0.3 | 39,316 | 0.3 |
| Asian | 303,825 | 1.8 | 213,294 | 1.8 |
| Other | 21,937 | 0.1 | 13,435 | 0.1 |
| Total | 16,986,510 | | 12,150,671 | |

Source: U.S. Bureau of Census, *PL94–171 Census Tape for 1990 for Texas.*

1,097,851 of the 7,701,499 Texas voters registered in November 1990 had Hispanic surnames. According to a study by Robert Brischetto of the Southwest Voter Research Institute, Inc., Hispanics comprised an estimated 9.1 percent of the registered voters in 1976.[59]

Voter turnout rates among Hispanics are lower, in part, because of the lower educational and income levels of large segments of the Hispanic population. It is estimated that only 10 percent of voters participating in the 1990 general election in Texas were Hispanic.[60]

While the Republican party has attempted to penetrate the Hispanic vote with a message of shared conservative values on family and social issues, most Hispanic voters in Texas continue to identify with the Democratic party.

Approximately 45 percent of all Hispanic adults interviewed in *The Texas Poll* said they identified with the Democratic party (Table 7-1), but given the large number of Hispanics who are not registered to vote, this figure tells only part of the story. Based on statewide exit interviews conducted on election day by the Southwest Voter Research Project, Democratic candidates consistently receive more than 70 percent of the Hispanic vote. Walter Mondale, the Democratic nominee for president in 1984, received 75 percent of the Hispanic vote; Governor Mark White received 79 percent in his 1986 loss to Bill Clements; Michael Dukakis, the 1988 Democratic presidential nominee, received 83 percent; and Ann Richards, the 1990 Democratic gubernatorial nominee, received 78 percent.[61]

With a decline in Anglo identification and participation in the Democratic party, Hispanic and African-American votes now constitute a larger part of the total Democratic vote. Moreover, as the realignment process has accelerated, there has been an increase in polarized voting along ethnic and racial lines.

The increased electoral strength of the Hispanic population is borne out in Table 7-4, which compares the number of Hispanic elected officials in 1974 to those elected in 1991. The marked increase can be attributed to a more equitable apportionment of city, county, and school district political boundaries as well as the growth of the Hispanic population during this period.

**TABLE 7–4**   Latino Elected Officials in Texas 1974–1991

|  | 1974 | 1984 | 1991 |
|---|---|---|---|
| Federal | 2 | 3 | 4 |
| State | 13 | 25 | 27 |
| County | 102 | 152 | 205 |
| Municipal | 251 | 401 | 593 |
| Judicial/<br>   Law Enforcement | 172 | 291 | 358 |
| School Board | – | 555 | 706 |
| Special District | – | – | 76 |
| Total | 540 | 1,427 | 1,969 |

Sources: Juan A. Sepulveda, Jr. *The Question of Representative Responsiveness for Hispanics*, Cambridge, Mass.: Harvard College, Honors Thesis March 1985; 1984 and 1991 *National Roster of Hispanic Elected Officials*, National Association of Latino Elected and Appointed Officials.

## African-Americans

African-Americans comprise approximately 12 percent of the state's population, 11 percent of the voting age population, and nine percent to 10 percent of those who vote. Approximately 67 percent of Texas African-Americans call themselves Democrats, and 80 percent to 90 percent of the African-American vote normally is cast for Democratic candidates. Voting cohesively as a group, African-Americans, like Hispanics, have considerable potential to influence the outcome of both primaries and general elections.

The increased political clout of the African-American population also is manifested in the number of African-American elected officials (Table 7-5). In 1970, there were only 29 African-Americans elected to public office in Texas. The number increased to 196 in 1980 and 305 in 1990.

**TABLE 7–5**   African-American Elected Officials in Texas 1970–1990

|  | 1970 | 1980 | 1990 |
|---|---|---|---|
| Federal | – | 1 | 1 |
| State | 3 | 14 | 14 |
| County | – | 5 | 17 |
| Municipal | 16 | 75 | 138 |
| Judicial/Law Enforcement | – | 21 | 40 |
| School Board | 10 | 78 | 95 |
| Special District | – | 2 | – |
| Total | 29 | 196 | 305 |

Sources: Metropolitan Applied Research Center, Inc. and Voter Regional Council, Inc., *National Roster of Black Elected Officials*. Joint Center for Political Studies, *National Roster of Black Elected Officials*, 1980, 1990.

## SUMMARY AND CONCLUSIONS

**1.** Elections, although imperfect mechanisms, provide the general population with an opportunity to indirectly shape public policy through the selection of leaders. One of the more disturbing aspects of the contemporary Texas political system is the low rates of participation in elections, and among some parts of the electorate that participation is meaningless or inconsequential.

**2.** During much of the period since Reconstruction, the state has systematically excluded significant segments of the population from participating in state and local elections through the poll tax, restrictive voter registration laws, and intimidation. The exclusion of African-Americans, Hispanics, and many individuals from lower socio/economic groups often served the purposes of the historically dominant economic interests of the state.

**3.** The most discriminatory aspects of the state's election laws have been eliminated, but minority groups continue to challenge racial gerrymandering and at-large election systems. Through litigation and reliance on the Voting Rights Act, minority groups have been increasingly successful in challenging discriminatory election systems which dilute minority voting strength.

**4.** With the multiple levels of government and the varied election cycles for these governmental units, Texans are subjected to a continuous election process. Within the course of a year, voters may have the chance to vote in three or four different elections. Voter participation in many of these elections, but especially in special district races, is extremely low. Individuals who will have control over hundreds of millions of dollars are elected to public office with a small fraction of the total voting-age population participating in low visibility elections with limited competition and news coverage.

**5.** Historically, political parties played a central role in elections, but with the weakened parties, the increased role of the mass media, and the candidate-centered campaign, candidates increasingly rely on paid campaign consultants. These consultants, trained in the use of mass communications, have taken over many of the traditional party functions. The consultants' primary objective is to win campaigns, and in this process limited consideration appears to be given to the subsequent effects of campaigns on governance and policymaking.

**6.** The costs of statewide campaigns, as well as many regional and local campaigns, have escalated over the past three decades. While there have been some efforts to solicit small campaign contributions from thousands of voters through direct mail, the large campaign contributions from political action committees or wealthy individuals comprise a major share of funds raised by candidates. While money may not buy public officials, it certainly buys access to them, and, more importantly, it creates the impression that well-organized interests, corporations, or wealthy individuals have a disproportionate influence on policymakers.

**7.** There has been a dramatic shift in party identification over the past two decades as the state has moved from one-party Democratic dominance to a two-party state. Approximately one-third of the electorate identify themselves as Democrats, one-third as Republicans, and one-third, independents.

**8.** Texans have not expressed a significant shift in their philosophical orientations over the past 20 years, and given the characteristics of the dominant political culture, it is not surprising that the majority of Texans classify themselves as moderate to conservative.

**9.** While elections are important, political participation takes a variety of other forms, many of which have a greater impact on the policymaking process than voting. There are some individuals who do little more than vote or hold general opinions about politics, government, and public policy. By contrast, there are segments of the state's population who can be characterized as political activists. Simply stated, higher socio/economic individuals participate in a wider range of political activities and at greater rates than do people in the lower SES groups.

**10.** Over the past 20 years, African-Americans and Hispanics have realized substantial gains in the electoral process and successes in electing minorities to public office. Organizations and leaders within their communities have played a major role in politicizing the minority population, and with the projected demographic changes, the political clout of the minority populations, especially the Hispanics, will accelerate in the future.

## KEY TERMS

| | |
|---|---|
| Suffrage | Special election |
| Poll tax | Absentee (or early) voting |
| White primary | Campaign consultant |
| Gerrymandering | Public opinion polling |
| Single-member districts | Media event |
| At-large election | Fat cat |
| Voting Rights Act | Political Action Committee |
| Primary election | Grass roots |
| Run off election | Political socialization |
| General election | Activist |
| Local election | |

## FURTHER READING

Bennett, W. Lance, *The Governing Crisis: Media, Money, and Marketing in American Elections*. New York: St. Martin's Press, 1992.

Diamond, Edwin, and Stephen Bates, *The Spot: The Rise of Political Advertising on Television*, rev. ed. Cambridge, Mass.: The MIT Press, 1988.

Dunham, Patricia, *Electoral Behavior in the United States*. Englewood Cliffs, N.J.: Prentice Hall, 1991.

Erikson, Robert S., Norman R. Luttbeg, and Kent L. Tedin, *American Public Opinion*, 4th ed. New York: Macmillan Publishing Company, 1990.

Garcia, John A., "The Voting Rights Act and Hispanic Political Representation in the Southwest," *Publius*, 16 (Fall, 1986), pp. 49-66.

Godwin, R. Kenneth, *One Billion Dollars of Influence*. Chatham, N.J.: Chatham House Publishers, Inc., 1988.

Harte-Hanks Communications, Inc., *The Texas Poll*. This is quarterly survey is conducted by the Public Policy Resources Laboratory of Texas A&M University.

Hershey, Marjorie Randon, *Running for Office*. Chatham, N.J.: Chatham House Publishers, Inc., 1984.

Holcombe, John, "The 1982 Legislative Elections in Texas," *Texas Journal of Political Studies*, 5 (Spring/Summer 1983), pp. 10-18.

Lozano, Vince, "Endorsements and the Paper Chase," *The Texas Observer*, November 22, 1990, pp. 21-22.

Martel, Myles, *Political Campaign Debates*. New York: Longman, 1983.

Olien, Roger M., *From Token to Triumph: The Texas Republicans Since 1920*. Dallas: SMU Press, 1982.

Sabato, Larry J., *PAC Power: Inside the World of Political Action Committees*. New York: W. W. Norton & Company, 1985.

Sorauf, Frank J., *Money in American Elections*. Glenview, Ill.: Scott, Foresman and Company, 1988.

Yeric, Jerry L., and John R. Todd, *Public Opinion: The Visible Politics*. Itasca, Ill.: F. E. Peacock Publishers, Inc., 1989.

## ENDNOTES

1. These quotes were reported in Sam Attlesey, "Politicians Sometimes say the Funniest Things," *The Dallas Morning News*, October 13, 1991, p. 44A. Used by permission of the publisher.
2. L. Sandy Maisel, *Parties and Elections in America* (New York: Random House, 1987), p. 1.
3. Gerald Pomper, *Elections in America* (New York: Dodd, Mead and Company, 1968), p. 12.
4. Herman Finer, *The Theory and Practice of Modern Government* (New York: Holt, 1949), p. 219.
5. Murray Edelman, *The Symbolic Uses of Politics* (Urbana: University of Illinois Press, 1964 ), p. 17.
6. V. O. Key, Jr., with the assistance of Milton C. Cummings, Jr., *The Responsible Electorate* (Cambridge: Harvard University Press, 1966), p. 7.
7. Maisel, *Parties and Elections in America*, p. 1.
8. Ibid., p. 3.
9. Ibid., p. 3.
10. Rupert Richardson, Ernest Wallace and Adrian Anderson, *Texas: The Lone Star State*, 5th edition (Englewood Cliffs: Prentice Hall, 1988), p. 231.
11. See Merline Pitre, *Through Many Dangers, Toils and Snares: Black Leadership in Texas 1868-1890* (Austin, Texas: Eakin Press, 1985).
12. Richardson, et al., *Texas: The Lone Star State*, p. 312.
13. Wilbourn E. Benton, *Texas Politics: Constraints and Opportunities*, 5th edition (Chicago: Nelson-Hall Publishers, 1984) pp. 72-73.
14. *Harper* v. *Virginia State Board of Elections*, 86 S. Ct. 1079 (1966).
15. Benton, *Texas Politics*, pp. 67-72.
16. *Nixon* v. *Herndon, et al*, 273 U.S. 536 (1927).
17. *Nixon* v. *Condon*, 286 U.S. 73 (1932).
18. *Grovey* v. *Townsend*, 295 U.S. 45 (1935).
19. *Smith* v. *Allwright*, 321 U.S. 649 (1944).
20. *John Terry, et al., Petitioners* v. *A.J. Adams, et al.*, 345 U.S. 461.
21. Beryl E. Pettus and Randall W. Bland, *Texas Government Today: Structures, Functions, Political Process*, 3rd edition (Homewood, Illinois: The Dorsey Press, 1984), pp. 85-86.
22. *Beare, et al* v. *Preston Smith, Governor of Texas*, 321 F. Supp. 1100 (1971).
23. Benton, *Texas Politics*, p. 65.
24. Frank J. Sorauf, *Party Politics in American*, 5th edition (Boston: Little, Brown and Company, 1984), p. 213; George Norris Green, *The Establishment in Texas Politics: The Primative Years, 1938-1957*, (Westport, Conn.: Greenwood Press, 1979), p. 164.
25. Davidson, *Race and Class in Texas Politics*, p. 24.
26. *San Antonio Express News*, story based on Cox News Service, March 15, 1992, 19A.
27. Ibid., p. 24.
28. *San Antonio Express News*, March 15, 1992, 19A.
29. *Dallas Morning News, Texas Almanac 1992-1993* (Dallas: A.H. Belo, 1992) and estimates based on the 1990 census.
30. *Carter* v. *Dies*, 321 F. Supp. 1358, (1970); *Bullock* v. *Dies* 405 U.S. 134 (1972).
31. Sorauf, *Party Politics in America*, p. 220.
32. Robert S. Loarch, *State and Local Politics*, 3rd. ed. (Englewood Cliffs, N.J.: Prentice Hall, 1989) p. 63.

33. Davidson, *Race and Class in Texas Politics*, p. 24.
34. For an excellent analysis of the development of campaign professionals, see Larry J. Sabato, *The Rise of Political Consultants* (New York: Basic Books, Inc., 1981).
35. Norris, *The Establishment in Texas Politics*, pp. 24-25.
36. W. Lance Bennett, *The Governing Crisis: Media, Money and Marketing in American Elections* (New York: St. Martin's Press, 1992), p. 32.
37. David Saffell, *State Politics* (Reading, Mass.: Addison-Wesley Publishing Co., 1983), p. 113.
38. See Edwin Diamond and Stephen Bates, *The Spot: The Rise of Political Advertising on Television*, rev. ed. (Cambridge, Mass.: The MIT Press, 1988).
39. *The Texas Observer*, September 28, 1990, p. 8.
40. Bennett, *The Governing Crisis*, pp. 33-34.
41. Sabato, *The Rise of Political Consultants*, p. 220.
42. Frank Sorauf, *Money in American Elections*, (Glenview, Ill.: Scott, Foresman and Company, 1988), p. 1.
43. See Herbert Alexander, *Financing the 1976 Election* (Washington, D.C.: Congressional Quarterly Press, 1979) and Herbert E. Alexander and Brian A. Haggerty, *Financing the 1984 Election* (Lexington, Mass.: Lexington, 1987).
44. Davidson, *Race and Class in Texas Politics*, p. 138.
45. Anthony Champagne, "Campaign Contributions in Texas Supreme Court Races," forthcoming in *Crime, Law and Social Change.*
46. Sorauf, *Money in American Elections*, p. 297.
47. Ibid., pp. 298-307.
48. Larry Sabato, *PAC Power* (New York: W. W. Norton, Inc., 1985), pp. 126-128.
49. Sorauf, *Money in American Elections*, pp. 306-317.
50. Davidson, *Race and Class in Texas Politics*, p. 141.
51. Ibid., pp. 146-147.
52. Samuel H. Barnes and Max Kaase, *Political Action* (Beverly Hills, Cal.: Sage, 1979), chap. 2.
53. Lance T. LeLoup, *Politics in America*, 2nd edition (St. Paul, Minn.: West Publishing Co., 1989), p. 156.
54. Sidney Verba and Norman H. Nie, *Participation in America* (New York: Harber and Row, 1972), pp. 79-80, pp. 118-119. Seven percent of the sample was not classified.
55. James A. Dyer and Arnold Vedlitz, "New Voters, Switchers, and Political Party Realignment in Texas," *Western Political Quarterly*, 41 (March 1988), p. 156.
56. *The Texas Poll*, 7 (Spring 1990) p. 4.
57. *The Texas Poll*, 7 (November 1990) pp. 4-5.
58. Davidson, *Race and Class in Texas Politics*, chap. 2.
59. Robert R. Brischetto, *The Political Empowerment of Texas Mexicans 1974-1988*, (San Antonio: Southwest Voter Research Institute, Inc., *Latino Electorates Series*, 1988), p. 5.
60. Robert R. Brischetto, Southwest Voter Research Institute, Inc., telephone conversation November 1, 1991, San Antonio, Texas.
61. Brischetto, "The Political Empowerment of Texas Mexicans, 1974-1988" and phone conversation with Robert R. Brischetto, November 1, 1991.

# 8

# THE TEXAS LEGISLATURE

> During one recent, hectic session of the Texas legislature, a few weary lawmakers began wearing buttons that read, "Maybe They Meant Two Days Every 140 Years."

For the many Texans who have the notion that their state government does little more than raise their taxes, make them wear seat belts, and otherwise meddle with their lives, even that would probably be too often for legislators to convene. In reality, however, the 140 days that lawmakers are in regular session every two years have proved insufficient for finding realistic, political solutions to the complex problems facing the nation's third most populous state. Additional, or special, legislative sessions have become commonplace, as state leaders struggle to operate under 19th century constitutional restrictions written for a rural, frontier state.

Enormous social, political, and economic changes have occurred in Texas during the past generation alone. Thirty years ago, a rural dominated legislature was still controlled by groups and interests that showed little concern for the problems of the urban areas and minority groups. Operating within the context of one-party Democratic control and an interest group system dominated by oil, finance, and agriculture, legislative leaders tied to conservative factions in the Democratic party pursued selected policies that benefited those sectors of the Texas economy.

Now, more than 80 percent of the state is urban. The ethnic and racial characteristics of the population have changed, and still more changes are projected in the state's social composition. Texas is now a two-party state, the economy is diversifying, and there is evidence of a transformation of the key sectors of the economy to high technology, information, and services. Consequently, there are more demands today on lawmakers than in the past. The issues and policy questions that confront the legislature are much more complex, and the special interests demanding attention are more numerous and diverse.

The Constitution of 1876 still shapes the formal legislative organization and structure, but there have been significant changes in the dynamics of the legislative process.

## THE ORGANIZATION AND COMPOSITION
## OF THE TEXAS LEGISLATURE

Following the oppressive efforts of Governor Edmund J. Davis and the Reconstruction Republicans to centralize power and authority in the state, the rural delegates who dominated the constitutional convention in 1875 were distrustful, even fearful, of the excesses and abuses of big government. They created a part-time, bicameral legislature comprised of a 31-member Senate and a 150-member House of Representatives. To curb the power of lawmakers, they limited the **regular legislative session** to a maximum of 140 days every two years and gave the governor the authority to call special sessions whenever necessary. Lawmakers convene in regular session on the second Tuesday of January in odd-numbered years. Special sessions are limited to a maximum of 30 days each and are limited to consideration of subjects submitted by the governor, but there is no limit on the number of **special sessions** that a governor can call.

Recent years have seen frequent special sessions. From midsummer of 1986 through midsummer of 1987, during a lingering budgetary crisis spawned by a depressed oil industry, the legislature convened for its regular 140-day session and four special sessions. Two of those special sessions lasted the maximum 30 days. The 71st legislature in 1989-1990 held six special sessions to deal with workers' compensation and equalization of school funding. The 72nd legislature had two special sessions to write a new budget, pass a tax bill, make major changes in the criminal justice system, and redraw congressional district lines in the summer of 1991, only a few weeks after the regular session had ended.

Some state officials and government experts believe the frequency of special sessions is more than enough evidence that Texas legislators should have annual regular sessions, at least for budgetary purposes. Texas is one of only seven states without regularly scheduled annual legislative sessions, and such a change would require a constitutional amendment.

All other states also have **bicameral legislatures**, except Nebraska, which has a unicameral system with only one lawmaking body of 49 members. The sizes of other state Senates range from 20 in Alaska to 67 in Minnesota, while Houses vary in size from 40 in Alaska to 400 in New Hampshire.[1]

### Terms of Office and Qualifications

Representatives serve two-year terms, while senators are elected to four-year, staggered terms. A senator has to be a qualified voter, at least 26 years old, a resident of Texas for five years preceding his or her election, and a resident of the district from which elected for at least one year. A representative must be a qualified voter, at least 21 years old, a Texas resident for two years, and a resident of the district represented for one year. There is no limit on the number of terms an individual can serve in the legislature.[2]

In 1991, a bipartisan group of influential Texans began lobbying for term limits for legislators and most other state officials to rid state government of "professional politicians" and, they argued, make it easier to elect officeholders who would be more responsive to the public. Texans for Term Limitations was co-chaired by Houston oil executive Rob Mosbacher, a Republican, and James Calaway, a major Democratic fund-raiser, also from Houston. It was interesting that those two individuals would be leading such an attack. Calaway had helped raise large sums of money for numerous career politicians over the years, and Mosbacher already had run unsuccessfully for statewide office twice—most recently as the 1990 Republican nominee for lieutenant governor. Some suspected Mosbacher was at least partly using the campaign for term limitations to increase his statewide exposure and name identification for still another political race of his own.

Several constitutional amendments that would have imposed varying limits on terms for legislators and all statewide elected officials except judges were proposed during the 1991 regular legislative session, but all died in committee. The campaign for term limitations faced a major obstacle in Texas—the lack of an initiative process, which many other states have, to allow private citizens to force action on an issue. Amendments to the Texas Constitution, which the term limitations would require, have to first be approved by the legislature, and lawmakers seemed to be in no hurry to place limits on their own tenure. Opponents of term limitations argued that the forced retirement of the most experienced legislators would serve to increase the power of the bureaucracy, the non-elected agency heads and staffs who have no direct accountability to the voters. As will be discussed in more detail later, turnover in the Texas Legislature already is high anyway, much higher than in the U.S. Congress, which has also been targeted by term limitation campaigns.

## Pay and Compensation

Members of both the House and the Senate and their presiding officers have a base pay of $7,200 per year, which also is set by the state Constitution and can be raised only with voter approval. It is one of the lowest legislative pay levels in the country and was last increased in 1975 by a constitutional amendment that also set lawmakers' per diem allowance at $30 a day while they were in session. The House and the Senate authorize additional expense allowances for members to cover staff salaries and other costs of operating legislative offices.

A constitutional amendment was proposed in 1989 to increase legislators' salaries to more than $20,000 per year, but the voters turned the proposal down by a 2-to-1 margin. The amendment also would have removed voter control over legislative pay and given lawmakers the power to give themselves raises by setting their pay at one-fourth the governor's salary, which the legislature sets and regularly increases. The proposition was endorsed, as most proposals for higher legislative pay are, by many special and public interest groups that lobby the legislature and must retain good relationships with lawmakers. But the timing was bad. The amendment was offered as the legislature was tightening spending on most public programs during a prolonged budget crunch, and it followed by only a few months a national furor over a major pay increase proposed for members of Congress.

Some newspaper columnists and editorial writers also accused the legislature of trying to sneak something past the voters by putting a misleading caption on the pay raise amendment. The language on the ballot said the proposition was to limit legislative pay to one-fourth that of the governor. The problem was that many voters didn't realize the governor's salary—then about $90,000 a year—was so much greater than legislative pay. And the caption didn't clearly point out that approval of the amendment would remove voters' longtime right to review and reject legislative pay raises.

In 1991, however, Attorney General Dan Morales, a former legislator, provided lawmakers with a long-sought way to bypass the voters. Responding to an inquiry initiated by the House, Morales issued a formal legal opinion that said legislators could claim additional expenses—at a level to be set by the legislature— while they were in session. The House and the Senate then took steps to allow all members except those from the Austin area to claim an additional $85 a day while in session, or an extra $11,900 for each regular session. This was on top of the $30 per diem set in the constitution.

Also in 1991, Texas voters approved a constitutional amendment creating a state Ethics Commission that could recommend legislative pay raises to the voters and change legislative per diem on its own. One of the commission's first actions was to raise the per diem for lawmakers from $30 to $85 per day while the legislature was in session. In return, legislative leaders agreed to give up the additional $85 in daily expenses that had been authorized by the attorney general.

In the mid-1960s, Texas was one of 26 states that set legislative salaries in their constitutions, and those states paid their legislators less than other states. By 1990, however, only Texas and five other states still retained constitutional limits. Compensation commissions now recommend legislative pay levels in some states, while legislatures in 28 states set their own salaries. In 1990, legislative pay ranged from a high of $57,500 a year in New York, where lawmakers set their own salaries and are considered a full-time legislature, to a low of $100 a year in New Hampshire, which has annual sessions but a constitutional limit on salaries.[3]

Supporters of higher legislative pay in Texas say it is only fair because legislative service has become much more than a part-time job for many lawmakers, particularly with the large number of recent special sessions. They argue that the present low compensation level pretty well restricts legislative service to wealthy individuals or those who have law practices or own businesses in which partners or employees can help take up the slack while they are in Austin. Supporters admit that higher pay wouldn't necessarily improve the overall quality of people elected to the legislature, but they believe it would broaden the potential pool from which legislators are drawn—and perhaps improve the prospects for quality—by encouraging more salaried, working people to run for legislative office.

The outside, personal income of many legislators obviously does suffer while they are in office, but legislative service can also enhance business and professional connections. Critics of higher legislative pay also note that candidates, many of whom spend thousands of dollars to get elected to the legislature, know the pay level before they run for the office. And Texas lawmakers have provided themselves one of the best legislative retirement plans in the country.

Retirement is computed on the basis of state district judges' salaries, which legislators raise during virtually every regular session, thereby increasing their own retirement benefits as well. Many former legislators receive pensions that are much larger than their paychecks were while they were in office. In 1991, legislators sweetened their retirement plan even more by quietly amending a state employee retirement bill to allow former legislators to receive full retirement benefits at age 50 instead of 55, as set in earlier law, and reduce the required time for service in office. The sponsor of the amendment, Representative Nolan "Buzz" Robnett, a Republican from Lubbock who, incidentally, was 50 at the time, helped make himself eligible for $1,780 a month in retirement pay, almost triple his legislative salary.[4] Despite some belated, negative publicity over that provision, Governor Ann Richards didn't veto the bill because it also boosted retirement benefits for thousands of state workers. She let it become law without her signature. But such self-serving legislative actions reinforce the negative opinion that many Texans have of the legislature.

## Physical Facilities

The House chamber and representatives' offices have been traditionally located in the west wing of the state Capitol, and the Senate chamber and senators' offices in the east wing. The pink-granite building was completed in 1888, but the legislative chambers, offices, and public galleries have been renovated and refurbished several times since. A major Capitol restoration and expansion project (Figure 8-1), including a four-story underground addition to the building, was begun in 1990 and forced the temporary relocation of many legislators' and support staff offices to nearby buildings.

Senate committee rooms also were located in the Capitol, but most House committee rooms, as well as offices for House and Senate committee staffs, were in nearby state office buildings before the renovation got underway. Some support services, such as the Legislative Reference Library, the Legislative Budget Board, and the Legislative Council, had offices and facilities in the Capitol. But they also were moved temporarily to other buildings during the renovation project. The new underground addition will house some legislative offices and committee hearing rooms.

When the legislature is in session, access to the floor of each chamber is restricted to lawmakers, certain state officials, some staff members, and accredited

**FIGURE 8-1**  Legislators pose in construction pit in 1991 after work on an underground Capitol extension was underway. The addition to the historic building was to house some legislators' offices and committee hearing rooms. (Texas Senate Media Services)

media representatives. The galleries, to which the public is admitted, overlook the chambers from the third floor of the Capitol.

In both the House and Senate chambers, members have desks facing the presiding officer's podium which, in turn, is flanked by desks of the clerical staff (Figure 8-2). Unlike the U.S. Congress, where seating is arranged by party affiliation, seats are assigned to state legislators by seniority. Occasionally by chance or choice, members of similar party affiliations or interests will be assigned seats together. During the early 1980s, a number of moderate-to-liberal House Democrats chose seats on the same side near the rear of the chamber, an area that some jokingly came to refer to as "Red Square." Yet, many of their immediate neighbors were some of the House's most conservative Republicans.

## Membership

In 1971, the Texas legislature was overwhelmingly white, male, and Democratic. There were two African-Americans in the 150-member House and one in the 31-member Senate. The one African-American senator was also the only woman in

**FIGURE 8-2** The Texas House of Representatives chamber with the computerized voting boards and the speaker's podium in the background. (Texas House of Representatives)

the Senate. She was Barbara Jordan of Houston who, two years later, would begin a distinguished career in Congress. Frances Farenthold of Corpus Christi was the only woman in the House. She was a reform-minded lawmaker who was often referred to as the "Den Mother of the Dirty Thirty," a coalition of liberal Democrats and Republicans who challenged the power of House Speaker Gus Mutscher while the Sharpstown stock fraud scandal was unfolding. In 1972, Farenthold ran a strong race for governor in the Democratic primary but lost a runoff election to Uvalde rancher Dolph Briscoe. There was only one Hispanic senator and 11 Hispanic members of the House, and there were 10 Republicans in the House and two in the Senate.

Changing political patterns and attitudes, redrawn political boundaries and court-ordered single-member districts for urban House members had significantly altered the composition of the legislature by 1991 (Table 8-1). During the regular session that year, the House included 13 African-Americans, 20 Hispanics, 19 women, and 57 Republicans. The Senate had two African-American members, five Hispanics, four women, and nine Republicans. Representation from the urban and suburban areas of the state had grown, reflecting the population shifts accommodated by redistricting. In a special election to fill a House vacancy early in the

**TABLE 8–1**  Comparative Profile of Texas Legislators 1971, 1981, and 1991

|                    | House |      |      | Senate |      |      |
|--------------------|-------|------|------|--------|------|------|
|                    | 1971  | 1981 | 1991 | 1971   | 1981 | 1991 |
| Democrats          | 140   | 112  | 93   | 29     | 24   | 22   |
| Republicans        | 10    | 38   | 57   | 2      | 7    | 9    |
| Males              | 149   | 139  | 131  | 30     | 30   | 27   |
| Females            | 1     | 11   | 19   | 1      | 1    | 4    |
| Hispanics          | 11    | 17   | 20   | 1      | 4    | 5    |
| African-Americans  | 2     | 13   | 13   | 1      | 0    | 2    |
| Anglos             | 137   | 120  | 117  | 29     | 27   | 24   |

Source: Texas House and Senate Rosters 1971, 1981, 1991.

1991 session, Austin voters elected Texas' first openly gay legislator, Representative Glen Maxey.

The legal profession was the dominant occupation of those legislators serving in 1991. Sixteen of the 31 senators and 50 of the 150 House members were attorneys, although not all of them made their living practicing law. Business was the second most frequently reported occupation, and there were several farmers and ranchers. The House included one retired airline pilot, one orthodontist, one dentist, one chiropractor, one registered nurse, and one firefighter. Two representatives and one senator identified themselves as housewives or homemakers. Senators' ages ranged from 37 to 69, with an average age of 48. The age range for members of the House was 22 to 82, with an average age of 46.

There are various career patterns leading to election to the legislature.[5] Lawmakers include former members of city councils and school boards, former prosecutors, former legislative aides, and longtime Democratic and Republican party activists. Many, however, arrive in Austin as freshmen legislators with relatively little political experience. Nineteen of the 31 senators in 1991 had previously served in the House. For many, service in the Texas House or Senate is a stepping stone to other elected or appointed offices. Many other legislators become lobbyists after leaving office.

Turnover in the legislature is high, and relatively few individuals who serve can be considered career legislators. Only four senators and six House members entered the 1991 regular session with 20 or more years of legislative service. The average legislative experience in the Senate was 10.5 years, while House members had served an average of 6.2 years. In addition to the effects of redistricting of legislative seats every 10 years, the high turnover is due to the low pay and the personal costs involved in running for public office. While in session, many legislators lose income from their regular sources of employment. Political ambition also is a factor. Many lawmakers who want to move up the political ladder will serve only a few terms in the House before making a move for the Texas Senate, the U.S. Congress, or other state or local offices.

## REPRESENTATION AND REDISTRICTING

Representative government is one of the essential components of American society, and there are continued debates as to how a person elected to public office should identify the interests and preferences of those people he or she represents.[6] Political theorists as well as legislators struggle with the problem of translating the will of the people into public policy.

Most legislators represent diverse groups and interests in their districts. During a normal legislative session, there will be thousands of proposed laws to consider, and legislators must constantly make decisions that will benefit or harm specific constituents. There will be hundreds of bills that do not have a direct bearing on the interests of a particular legislator's district, but nonetheless, the legislator develops a representative style that helps him or her to accommodate these competing demands.

Many European legislatures use a system called proportional representation where legislative seats are allocated on the basis of each party's vote. By contrast, the Texas legislature and most other American legislatures allocate seats geographically on the basis of single-member districts. The long legal and political battles over apportionment and redistricting address some of the fundamental questions of who should be represented and how they should be represented.

The Texas Constitution of 1876 provided that the legislature redraw state representative and senatorial districts every 10 years, "at its first session after the publication of each United States decennial census," to reflect changing population patterns. Despite this requirement, members of earlier rural-dominated legislatures were reluctant to apportion the legislative seats equitably to reflect the increased urbanization of the state, and inequities grew. In 1948, Texas voters approved a constitutional amendment creating the Legislative Redistricting Board to carry out redistricting responsibilities if the legislature failed to do so during the required session. The board includes the lieutenant governor, the speaker of the House, the attorney general, the comptroller, and the commissioner of the General Land Office. The board is directed to meet within 90 days after a session in which the legislature fails to redistrict itself and must complete the redistricting job within another 60 days.

But for many more years, the urban areas of the state still were denied equality in representation. After the 1960 census, it was possible for approximately 33 percent of the state's population to elect a majority of the members of both the House and the Senate. Rural legislators tended to neglect urban issues and urban problems, and Texas, like most other states, soon was to enter the political thicket of the reapportionment revolution.

Equality in redistricting finally came to Texas as a result of federal court intervention. Prior to 1962, the U.S. Supreme Court refused to intervene in issues involving malapportionment of Congress or the state legislatures. In 1962, the court reversed its earlier position and ruled in the case of *Baker* v. *Carr* that it had jurisdiction in issues of congressional redistricting. The principle of equality was initially applied to congressional districts, and in the case of *Reynolds* v. *Sims* (1964), the court held that state legislative districts had to be apportioned on the "one man, one vote" principle. Litigation in 1965 (*Kilgarlin* v. *Martin*) extended this ruling to Texas, and the reapportionment revolution was to produce dramatic changes in the composition and structure of the Texas legislature. To a large degree, the increased representation of minorities and Republicans in Texas' lawmaking body is a result of the legal and political redistricting battles.

The state Senate has always been elected by single-member districts, and after the 1970 census, the application of the "equality principle" to the Senate resulted in districts that were comparable in size. The issues of racial and partisan gerrymandering—the practice of drawing lines to favor a particular individual or group—were still to be resolved through subsequent litigation and federal legislation.

Rural members of the Texas House also were elected from single-member districts, but in the urban counties that had been allocated more than one representative, the elections were held in multi-member districts. Each candidate for a House seat in an urban area had to run for election countywide, a practice that put ethnic and political minorities at a disadvantage because their votes were diluted by the dominant Anglo and Democratic populations.

In 1972, a three-judge federal court ruled that multimember districts in Dallas and Bexar counties were unconstitutional because they diluted the voting strength of African-Americans in Dallas and Hispanics in Bexar. Coincidentally, the at-large districts diluted the voting strength of the Republicans in both counties.

Despite the fact that 50 percent of Bexar County's population was Hispanic, under the at-large election system only one Hispanic from Bexar had served in the Texas House in 1971. Dallas County, which had a large African-American population, had only one African-American House member. Single member districts in Harris County had been drawn by the Legislative Redistricting Board in 1971, and after the U.S. Supreme Court upheld the lower court's decision regarding Dallas and Bexar counties, multimember districts were soon eliminated in all other urban counties.

After 1975, Texas was covered by the provisions of the federal Voting Rights Act, which prohibits the dilution of minority voting strength, requires pre-clearance of redistricting plans by the Department of Justice, and gives African-Americans and Hispanics a strong weapon to use in challenging a redistricting plan in court. By 1991, however, minorities believed their fight for equal representation was still far from over.

The Mexican American Legal Defense and Educational Fund, Texas Rural Legal Aid, and the Texas Civil Rights Project sued the state over the 1991 redistricting plans drawn by the legislature, alleging that Texas House and state Senate districts had been gerrymandered to protect incumbents at the expense of minorities. After a state district judge in Edinburg ruled that the plans were unconstitutional, state Democratic leaders attempted to work out a compromise with the minority plaintiffs. But in a separate lawsuit brought by Republicans, a three-judge federal court in Austin took over the redistricting process.

The Republicans challenged the new districts as discriminatory against the GOP. The court upheld the redistricting plan for congressional districts, which had been pre-cleared by the Department of Justice and, thanks to population gains, increased the number of congressional districts in Texas from 27 to 30. But the court, all of whose members were Republican appointees, voted 2 to 1 to order its own plans for Texas House and state Senate districts. The court-ordered plan wasn't expected to significantly change the proportion of Democratic and Republican seats in the House after the 1992 elections, but political experts believed the court order could increase Republican strength in the Senate by several seats at the expense of incumbent Democrats. And minority groups complained that it could reduce the number of minority senators.

With so much at stake, the court's Senate order sparked a bitter political fight. Texas Attorney General Dan Morales, a Democrat, accused one of the federal judges, Jim Nowlin, of having possible improper contact with one or more Republican legislators in the drawing of the plan. State Representative George Pierce, a Republican Senate candidate from San Antonio, acknowledged he had made some changes in San Antonio Senate districts at Nowlin's request the day before the order was issued, but Pierce denied any wrongdoing. The 5th U.S. Circuit Court of Appeals in New Orleans appointed a special committee of federal judges to investigate the allegations against Nowlin, but the U.S. Supreme Court refused to block the March 1992 primary elections for Senate seats under the court's redistricting plan.

Further complicating the 1991 redistricting effort was U.S. Commerce Secretary Robert Mosbacher's refusal to use 1990 census figures that Texas officials believed more accurately reflected the state's population. The initial census results indicated Texas had about 17 million residents, of whom 25 percent were Hispanic and 12 percent African-American. An updated, revised count would have boosted the state's total population to about 17.5 million. But Mosbacher (the father of the Mosbacher who was heading the campaign to limit legislators' terms in office) ruled that the earlier figures would become law. The state sued the federal government over the issue, contending the lower figures represented a census undercount that would cost Texas $1 billion in lost federal aid for education, health care, transportation, welfare, and other critical needs over the next decade. Democrats also contended that Mosbacher's decision to use the lower figures was politically motivated because the undercount was greater among minority groups, which were more likely to vote Democratic than Republican.

Based on the initial 1990 census results, the ideal population for a state senatorial district was 547,952 and for a House district, 113,243.

## LEGISLATIVE LEADERSHIP

The highly institutionalized leadership structure that is found in Congress is only now beginning to emerge in the Texas legislature—and to only a limited extent.[7] The legislature is a part-time institution that has been historically dominated by a small group of Democratic lawmakers. With no significant party opposition or minority representation until recent years, legislative leadership was highly per-sonalistic and dependent on the political relationships between the presiding officers and key legislators.

The presiding officer of the House of Representatives is the **speaker**, who is elected by the House from among its own membership. Thanks to the long tenures of Speaker Gib Lewis and his immediate predecessor, Bill Clayton, there wasn't a contested speaker's race between 1975 and 1991. But Lewis' decision not to seek re-election in 1992 created the possibility of a spirited speaker's race in preparation for the 1993 legislative session. Thousands of dollars were expected to be spent by several candidates seeking the votes of 76 House members, the majority necessary to be elected presiding officer. It is illegal for a speaker candidate to make outright promises in return for members' support, but legislators know that the earlier they hop onto a winning bandwagon, the better chance they probably will have at getting their preferred committee assignments or getting a chance to run with their legislative programs.

Until the 1950s, it was unusual for a speaker to serve more than one two-year term. The position was circulated among a small group of legislators who dominated the House. Clayton, a lawmaker from Springlake in West Texas, set a record by serving four consecutive terms before retiring in 1982. His successor, Lewis of Fort Worth, broke Clayton's record when he was elected to his fifth term in January 1991. That was only 12 days after Lewis had been indicted on mis-demeanor ethics charges for allegedly accepting an illegal gift from a San Antonio-based law firm—a partial payment of about $5,000 on a delinquent tax bill for a business Lewis partly owned.

Despite the charges—which Lewis denied and were later dismissed in a plea bargain with prosecutors—and a well-publicized Travis County grand jury investiga-tion into legislative ethics that continued for several more weeks, Lewis wasn't opposed for re-election, and only one House member voted against him. That was largely because Lewis had locked up his fifth term months earlier, well before the November election, by securing promises of support on signed pledge cards from House members and legislative candidates. And as popular as Lewis was among most of his colleagues, it would have been virtually impossible for any challenger to wage a late campaign against him.

Unlike most of their predecessors, Clayton and Lewis devoted long hours to the job and kept large full-time staffs. With the complexities of a growing state putting more demands on the legislative leadership, recent lieutenant governors also have made their jobs virtually full-time and, like the speaker, have hired large staffs of specialists to research issues and help develop legislation. The presiding officers also depend on key committee chairmen to take the lead in pushing the speaker's and the lieutenant governor's priorities.

The **lieutenant governor** is chosen by the voters in a statewide election to serve a four-year term as presiding officer of the Senate. Unlike the vice president of the United States—his counterpart in the federal government, who has only limited legislative functions—the lieutenant governor is the Senate's legislative leader. He is often called the most powerful officeholder in state government because he is capable of merging his statewide electoral base into a dominant legislative role.[8] There are conditions attached, however. The lieutenant governor gets most of his power from the Senate, not from the Constitution, and to be successful he must learn to accommodate the individual senators—31 of the strongest egos in Texas—who set the rules. Even a strong-willed individual such as Bob Bullock, who became lieutenant governor in January 1991 after 16 years of running the comptroller's office with an iron hand, found that he couldn't strong-arm the Senate.

The lieutenant governor's power is based in part on the same coalitional strategies that are used by the speaker through committee assignments and relationships with interest groups. But the lieutenant governor has more direct control over the Senate's agenda than the speaker has over the House's. Under longstanding Senate rules, the lieutenant governor determines when—and if—a committee-approved bill will be brought up for a vote by the full Senate. In the House, the order of floor debate is determined by the Calendars Committee. Although that key panel is appointed by the speaker and is sensitive to the speaker's wishes, it represents an intermediate step that the lieutenant governor doesn't have to encounter.

Bill Hobby, a quiet-spoken media executive who served a record 18 years as lieutenant governor before voluntarily leaving the office in January 1991, patiently sought consensus among senators on most major issues and rarely took the lead in promoting specific legislative proposals. One notable exception occurred in 1979 when Hobby tried to force Senate approval of a presidential primary bill opposed by most Democratic senators. After Hobby served notice that he would alter the Senate's traditional operating procedure to give the bill special consideration, 12 senators, dubbed the "Killer Bees," hid out for several days to break a quorum and keep the Senate from conducting business. They also succeeded in killing the primary bill and reminding Hobby that the senators set the rules. Another exception occurred in 1989 when Hobby, in an effort to break an impasse over workers' compensation reform, proposed a plan generally supported by business but vigorously opposed by trial lawyers and some of Hobby's own key Senate leaders. This time, much of Hobby's proposal eventually was adopted.

Hobby's successor, Bob Bullock (Figure 8-3), had demonstrated strong leadership and a mercurial personality during his long tenure as state comptroller. Upon taking office as lieutenant governor, he had major policy and structural changes in mind for state government and was impatient to see them carried out by the legislature. Unlike Hobby, Bullock took the lead in making proposals and then actively lobbying for them. He reportedly had shouting matches with some lawmakers behind closed doors and one day abruptly and angrily adjourned the Senate when not enough members were present for a quorum at the scheduled starting time. But his experience and knowledge of state government and his tireless work habits won the respect of most senators and their support for most of his proposals.

**FIGURE 8-3** Lt. Governor Bob Bullock, at the podium, presides over a session of the Texas Senate. (Texas Senate Media Services)

Bullock's most controversial proposal during his first session was a state income tax to improve state government's revenue base and reduce the high property taxes that Texans had to pay for the support of public schools (see Chapter 13). Texas was one of only a handful of states that didn't have an income tax, and opposition to one had traditionally been very high. Governor Ann Richards and Speaker Gib Lewis remained opposed to an income tax, as did a majority of the House which, under the state constitution, has to initiate action on tax bills. So only a hybrid corporate income tax was passed, not a personal income tax.

Another major Bullock priority, the creation of a new, consolidated state environmental protection agency, was approved by the Senate but died in the House during the 1991 regular session. The proposal was revived, modified, and approved that summer during a special session that restructured a handful of state agencies in an effort to cure a potential $4.8 billion state deficit without a major tax increase. A governmental overhaul also was supported by the governor and the speaker but was initiated by Bullock, who advocated intensive performance audits of all state agencies and programs. At the legislature's direction, those audits were supervised by the new comptroller, John Sharp, who recommended a $4 billion deficit reduction package. Thanks to pressure from special interests, many of Sharp's recommendations were rejected, but the legislature adopted enough of the proposals to limit the increase in taxes and fees for the next biennium to $2.7 billion.

The lieutenant governor has more control over the membership of Senate committees than the speaker has over House panels. The Senate allows the lieutenant governor to appoint members of all standing committees without restrictions, while the membership of most House committees is determined partly by seniority. The speaker has total discretion, however, in naming committee chairs and vice chairs and in appointing all the members of some of the House's most powerful panels. These include the Appropriations Committee, which decides how to spend the state's money, the Calendars Committee, and the Redistricting Committee, which redrew the lines of legislative and congressional districts in 1991.

The power of each presiding officer to determine which committee will have jurisdiction over a specific bill gives the speaker and the lieutenant governor tremendous influence over the lawmaking process. House and Senate rules provide that an extraordinary majority of members can force the re-referral of a bill that is languishing in one committee and allow it to be considered by a more favorable panel, but such challenges to the leadership are rare.

Ironically, a presiding officer occasionally can be trapped by the very powers that generally result in his control of the legislative process. In January 1985, Speaker Lewis stacked the House Ways and Means Committee with Republicans and conservative Democrats who joined him in opposing higher taxes. The next year, after the bottom fell out of the oil prices that traditionally had produced considerable state tax money, Lewis was convinced by Governor Mark White and Lt. Governor Bill Hobby that additional revenues were necessary. But the Ways and Means Committee refused to approve the tax legislation, forcing Lewis to arrange the introduction of a new tax bill that he referred to the State Affairs Committee, which was more receptive to the speaker's wishes.

The speaker and the lieutenant governor control the legislative process through the application of the rules, and they each rely on a parliamentarian who provides advice and counsel on procedures. They do not participate in House or Senate debate on bills and usually attempt to present an image of neutral presiding officers. In fact, however, through their relationships with their committee leaders and interest groups, they rarely lose control of the process.

In the Senate, the lieutenant governor can vote to break a tie. The Speaker can vote on any issue in the House, but he normally abstains from voting except to break a tie or to send a signal to encourage reluctant or wavering House members to vote a particular way on an issue of importance to him.

The Senate has a president pro tempore, or assistant presiding officer, who is chosen by senators from among their membership. This position is rotated among the senators on a seniority basis. It is held for a limited period of time, and the holder of the position is third in line of succession to the governorship. There is a tradition that the governor and the lieutenant governor both allegedly "leave" the state on the same day so that the president pro tempore can serve as "governor for a day" at one point during his term.

The speaker appoints a speaker pro tempore, usually a close ally. In 1981, Speaker Clayton named the first African-American, Representative Craig Washington of Houston, to the post. Although Clayton was a rural conservative and Washington was an urban liberal, Washington was a critical member of the speaker's team. He also exercised considerable influence in the House on a wide range of issues of importance to minorities. Ten years later, Gib Lewis named another African-American legislator, Representative Wilhelmina Delco of Austin, as the first woman speaker pro tem.

There is no formal division along party lines or a formal system of floor leaders in either the Texas House or the Senate. The longtime one-party legislative system with the speaker's and lieutenant governor's control of committee appointments did not produce a leadership structure comparable to that of the U.S. Congress. The committee chairs comprise the speaker's and lieutenant governor's teams and usually act as their unofficial floor leaders in developing and building support for the leadership's legislative priorities. With few exceptions, the chairs are philosophically, if not always politically, aligned with the presiding officers.

But committee chairs sometimes exercise independence and political differences with the speaker or the lieutenant governor. Representative Mike Toomey, a Republican from Houston, for example, was named chairman of the House Judiciary Committee by Democrat Lewis in January 1987. A few months later, Toomey was one of the outspoken Republicans who fought against a tax increase backed by Lewis and most other Democrats.

Although Texas is now largely an urban state, many legislators who represent primarily rural areas still hold key leadership positions. Former Lt. Governor Bill Hobby of Houston, who took office in 1973 and served for 18 years, broke a long string of Senate presiding officers who had rural or small city backgrounds (Table 8-2). His successor, Bob Bullock, had small town roots but had lived in Austin for many years before becoming lieutenant governor. Gib Lewis of Fort Worth in 1983 became the first House speaker from a large city in many years—and the first in the age of long-term speakers. Lewis appointed a number of rural legislators to important committee chairs, and, like Hobby before him, so did Bullock.

In 1991, four of the most important legislative committees—House Appropriations, House State Affairs, Senate Finance, and Senate State Affairs—were chaired by lawmakers with large rural constituencies. Representative Jim Rudd's rural roots were often reflected in the West Texas Democrat's conservative approach to budget writing as chairman of the appropriations panel. His counterpart in the Senate, John Montford, was from the same part of the state and represented some of the same constituents but had a more progressive approach to budget setting. The difference was that Montford, chairman of the Senate Finance Committee, also represented and lived in Lubbock, a medium-sized city, and had to balance the concerns of both urban and rural constituents. The growth in urban representation in the legislature as a whole has produced a more urban-oriented lawmaking body

**TABLE 8–2**   Recent Presiding Officers

|                          | When Served | Home          |
| ------------------------ | ----------- | ------------- |
| **Lieutenant Governors** |             |               |
| Ben Ramsey               | 1951–1963   | San Augustine |
| Preston Smith            | 1963–1969   | Lubbock       |
| Ben Barnes               | 1969–1973   | DeLeon        |
| Bill Hobby               | 1973–1991   | Houston       |
| Bob Bullock              | 1991–       | Hillsboro     |
| **Speakers**             |             |               |
| Reuben Senterfitt        | 1951–1955   | San Saba      |
| Jim T. Lindsey           | 1955–1957   | Texarkana     |
| Waggoner Carr            | 1957–1961   | Lubbock       |
| James A. Turman          | 1961–1963   | Gober         |
| Byron M. Tunnell         | 1963–1965   | Tyler         |
| Ben Barnes               | 1965–1969   | DeLeon        |
| Gus Mutscher             | 1969–1972   | Brenham       |
| Rayford Price            | 1972–1973   | Palestine     |
| Price Daniel Jr.         | 1973–1975   | Liberty       |
| Bill Clayton             | 1975–1983   | Springlake    |
| Gib Lewis                | 1983–1993   | Fort Worth    |

Source: Texas Legislative Council, *Presiding Officers of the Texas Legislature, 1846–1982* (Austin: Texas Legislative Council, 1982).

than sat in Austin in the not-too-distant past. But rural legislators generally present a unified conservative bloc, while urban lawmakers, who include suburban Republicans and inner city liberal Democrats, are more diverse.

## THE COMMITTEE SYSTEM

The committee system is the backbone of the legislative process, and it is molded by the lieutenant governor and the speaker.[9] The fate of most of the several thousand pieces of legislation that are introduced during a regular session will be determined by a **committee**.

The number and names of committees are periodically revised under House and Senate rules, but there have been few changes in recent years. During the 1991 regular session, the Senate had 11 standing committees, varying in membership from seven to 13. One panel, the Nominations Committee, reviews and holds confirmation hearings on appointments made by the governor to state boards and commissions. Additionally, Lieutenant Governor Bullock designated the entire Senate as a Committee of the Whole on redistricting and named Senator Chet Brooks, a Democrat from Pasadena who was the Senate dean, or longest tenured member, as the chair. The Committee of the Whole was divided into two subcommittees on legislative and congressional redistricting. There were 36 standing committees in the House with memberships ranging from five to 23 (Table 8-3). Most of these committees are substantive. That is, they hold public hearings and evaluate bills related to their particular subject areas, such as higher education, natural resources, or public health. A few committees are procedural, such as the Rules and Resolutions Committee, which handles many routine congratulatory

**TABLE 8–3**  Senate and House Standing Committees: 72nd
Legislature, 1991

|  | Number of Members |
|---|---|
| **Senate Committee** | |
| Administration | 11 |
| Criminal Justice | 7 |
| Economic Development | 11 |
| Education | 11 |
| Finance | 13 |
| Health and Human Services | 9 |
| Intergovernmental Relations | 11 |
| Jurisprudence | 7 |
| Natural Resources | 11 |
| Nominations | 7 |
| State Affairs | 13 |
| Committee of the Whole on Redistricting | 31 |
| **House Committee** | |
| Agriculture and Livestock | 9 |
| Appropriations | 23 |
| Business and Commerce | 9 |
| Calendars | 9 |
| Corrections | 9 |
| County Affairs | 11 |
| Criminal Jurisprudence | 11 |
| Cultural and Historical Resources | 9 |
| Elections | 9 |
| Energy | 9 |
| Environmental Affairs | 9 |
| Financial Institutions | 9 |
| General Investigating | 5 |
| Government Organization | 9 |
| Higher Education | 9 |
| House Administration | 9 |
| Human Services | 9 |
| Insurance | 9 |
| Judicial Affairs | 9 |
| Judiciary | 9 |
| Labor and Employment Relations | 9 |
| Liquor Regulation | 9 |
| Local and Consent Calendars | 9 |
| Natural Resources | 9 |
| Public Education | 9 |
| Public Health | 9 |
| Public Safety | 9 |
| Redistricting | 15 |
| Retirement and Aging | 9 |
| Rules and Resolutions | 9 |
| Science and Technology | 9 |
| State Affairs | 13 |
| State, Federal and International Relations | 9 |
| Transportation | 9 |
| Urban Affairs | 11 |
| Ways and Means | 13 |

Source: Texas House and Senate

resolutions, and the Calendars Committee, which for several years has scheduled bills for debate by the full House and created considerable controversy over its power.

Some committees play more dominant roles in the lawmaking process than others, particularly in the House. The House State Affairs Committee, for example, will handle many more major statewide bills than the committees on Cultural and Historical Resources or Agriculture and Livestock. The House Urban Affairs and County Affairs committees will handle several hundred bills of importance to local governments each session. The importance or the status of a committee is determined by the area of public policy over which it has jurisdiction, and most legislators will seek appointment to these important committees.

The House **Calendars Committee** has had more life and death power over legislation than any other committee because it has set the order of debate on the House floor. During each regular session, it has killed hundreds of bills that had been approved by various substantive committees by refusing to set them for debate by the full House or scheduling them so late in the session they didn't have time to win Senate approval. This committee has traditionally worked in a close relationship with the speaker, and the adroit use of the power of this committee has been one means by which the speaker and his team controlled the House. Although many legislators have bitterly complained about the committee keeping their priority bills bottled up, some lawmakers have defended the panel as a means of keeping controversial legislation—on which many members would rather not have to cast votes—from reaching the House floor. "You have to realize that all bills do not get to the floor," Speaker Lewis said in 1991. "You have to realize also that a lot of committee chairmen who have taken a great deal of heat over a long period of time—from authors or special interest groups—they'll finally pass a bill out and say, 'I hope we can kill it in Calendars.'"[10]  Almost 400 bills died in the Calendars Committee at the end of the regular session that year, including controversial, Senate-approved measures to allow Texans to legally carry concealed handguns and to shorten the period for which failing students would be disqualified from extracurricular activities under the no-pass, no-play law. Several candidates running to succeed Lewis as speaker in 1993 said they would consider changes in the Calendars Committee's powers.

The state budget is the single most important piece of legislation enacted by the legislature because through it, lawmakers determine how much money is spent on the state's public programs and services. In the House, the Appropriations Committee, which includes representatives of other standing committees, takes the lead in drafting state budgets, while the House Ways and Means Committee is responsible for producing any tax or revenue measures necessary to balance the budget.

The two most important committees in the Senate are the Finance Committee, which handles both the budget and tax bills, and the State Affairs Committee, which handles a variety of legislation of major, statewide importance. During special budget sessions in 1986, Lt. Governor Bill Hobby designated the entire Senate as a

Committee of the Whole to consider tax legislation. Hobby also used the same approach to develop workers' compensation legislation in 1989.

Although committees have general subject areas of responsibility, legislative rules allow the lieutenant governor and the speaker latitude in assigning bills. If he wishes, the presiding officer can assure the death of a bill by sending it to a committee he knows will oppose it or guarantee quick action on a measure by referring it to a receptive, or friendly, panel.

During a special budget session in 1991, when the legislature also was considering the reorganization and consolidation of many agencies, Lt. Governor Bullock and Speaker Lewis made some unusual committee referrals in an effort to keep bureaucrats and lobbyists off balance. Education bills, for example, went to the House and Senate State Affairs committees instead of the education panels. Legislation to create a new Department of Transportation went to the House Government Organization Committee, not to the Transportation Committee. And the Senate Administration Committee, which normally handles housekeeping functions, such as determining the size of Senate staff payrolls, had to vote on a huge prison construction package.

The committee system is a legislative screening process. Only 970 of the 4,684 bills and constitutional amendments introduced in the 1991 regular legislative session won final legislative approval. And most of those that didn't make it died in a Senate or a House committee, many without ever being heard. The committee is where technical drafting errors and oversights in bills can be corrected and where compromise, if possible, can begin to work. Rarely does a committee kill a bill on an outright vote, because there are much easier, less obvious ways to scuttle legislation. A bill can be gutted, or so drastically amended or weakened, that even its sponsor can hardly recognize it. Or it can simply be ignored.

The committee chairman has considerable power over the disposition of any legislation that comes to his or her committee. He may kill a bill by simply refusing to schedule it for a hearing. Or, after a hearing, the chairman may send a bill to a subcommittee that he either stacks with members opposed to the legislation or that he never appoints, thus allowing the bill to slowly—and quietly—die in the legislative deep freeze. Even if a majority of committee members want to approve a bill, the chairman can simply refuse to recognize such a motion. Most chairmen, however, are sensitive to the wishes of the presiding officers. If the speaker or the lieutenant governor wants a bill to win committee approval or another measure to die in committee, a chairman usually will comply.

The U.S Congress has developed a highly diversified subcommittee system.[11] Standing committees are divided into standing subcommittees which operate from one session to the next. These standing subcommittees are defined by the rules and have jurisdiction over specific legislative matters. Such a formal subcommittee structure is absent in the Texas House and has only recently begun to develop in the Senate. In the House, a committee chairman will name **subcommittees** for bills as needed, while the Senate has several standing subcommittees. In 1991, the Senate Economic Development Committee had a standing subcommittee on insurance; the

Health and Human Services Committee had a subcommittee on health services; the Intergovernmental Relations Committee, a subcommittee on urban affairs; the Natural Resources Committee, subcommittees on agriculture and water; and the State Affairs Committee, a subcommittee on elections and ethics.

Referral to a subcommittee doesn't always mean the death of a bill. Subcommittees also help committees spread out the workload. Some bills are sent to subcommittees so that a small number of lawmakers—usually three on an ad hoc subcommittee but slightly more on a Senate standing subcommittee—can work out differences or draft substitute legislation that accommodates competing interest groups or corrects technical problems.

Legislation must be passed in exactly the same form by the House and the Senate. If one chamber refuses to accept the other's version of a bill, a **conference committee** can be requested to try to resolve the differences. Conference committees of five senators and five representatives are appointed by the presiding officers. A compromise bill has to be approved by at least three senators and three House members who serve on the conference committee before it is sent back to the full House and the full Senate for subsequent approval or rejection. Over the years, conference committees have been used to draft legislation in dramatically different forms than was approved by either the House or the Senate in the earlier versions of the bills. But since conference panels are supposed to only adjust the differences between the House and the Senate in a bill, both chambers have to pass a concurrent resolution to allow a conference committee to add new language.

Select committees are occasionally appointed by the governor, the lieutenant governor, and the speaker to study major policy issues, such as tax equity or school finance. Select panels usually include private citizens as well as legislators, and they usually recommend legislation. Standing legislative committees also study issues in their assigned areas during the interims between sessions, and the presiding officers can ask them to conduct special investigations or inquiries pertaining to governmental matters. In a few circumstances, the presiding officer has appointed a special committee to carry out such a task, but normally, special investigations in the House are the primary responsibility of the House General Investigating Committee.

## RULES AND PROCEDURES

Laws are made in Texas according to the same basic process followed by Congress and other state legislatures.[12] But, as the discussion of the committee system already has indicated, the rules that determine how and when legislation is considered are complex and loaded with traps where legislation can be killed (Figure 8-4). One often hears the remark around the Capitol that "there are a lot more ways to kill a bill than to pass one," and it is true. So the legislators and lobbyists who learn to master the rules can wield a tremendous amount of influence over the lawmaking process. The House and the Senate each has a detailed set of rules governing the disposition

This diagram displays the sequential flow of a Bill from the time it is introduced in the House of Representatives to final passage and transmittal to the Governor. A Bill introduced in the Senate would follow the same procedure in reverse.

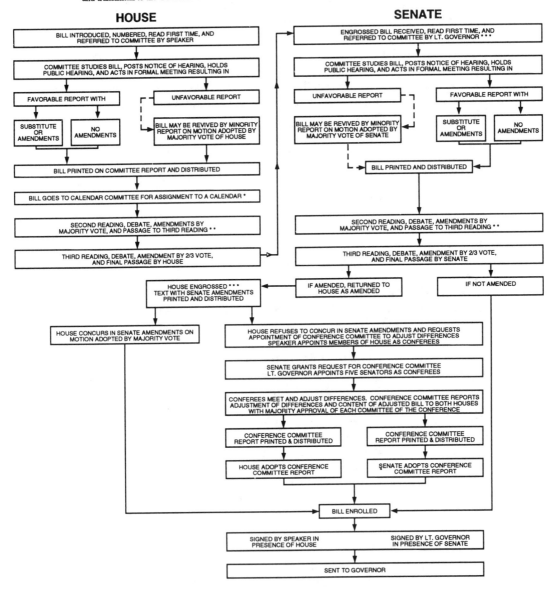

FIGURE 8-4  Basic Steps in The Texas Legislative Process. Reprinted with permission from *Texas Business Today* (September 1990), a monthly publication from the office of Commissioner Mary Scott Nabers of the Texas Employment Commission.

of legislation, and each has a parliamentarian to help interpret them. Previous rules interpretations also are of critical importance.

The basic, simplified outline of the process by which a bill becomes a law starts with the introduction of a bill in the House or the Senate and its referral to a committee by the presiding officer, which constitutes **first reading**. That is the only reading that most bills will ever get. But a bill that wins committee approval can be considered on **second reading** by the full House or Senate where it is debated and often amended. Some amendments are designed to improve a bill, while others are designed to kill it by loading it down with controversial or objectionable provisions that will prompt legislators to vote against it. Still other amendments that may be punitive toward particular individuals or groups are sometimes offered. Such an amendment, which may be temporarily added to a bill only to be removed before the measure becomes law, is designed to give a group or perhaps a local official a message, or warning, that the sponsoring legislator expects the group or individual concerned to heed his wishes on a particular issue. Lawmakers also may offer amendments that they know have little chance of being approved merely to make favorable political points with constituents.

If a bill is approved on second reading, it has to win one more vote on **third reading** before it goes to the other chamber for the same process. If the second chamber approves the bill without any changes, or amendments, it then goes to the governor for signature into law or veto. The governor also can allow a bill to become law without his or her signature. This procedure is just the opposite of the pocket veto power afforded the president of the United States. If the president doesn't sign a bill approved by Congress by a certain deadline, it is automatically vetoed. If the governor of Texas doesn't sign or **veto** a bill by a certain deadline, it becomes law.

The governor has to accept or reject a bill in its entirety, except for the general **appropriations bill**, or state budget, from which the governor can delete specific spending proposals while approving others. This power is called a **line item veto**. The budget and any other bill approved by the legislature that appropriates money has to be certified by the comptroller before it is sent to the governor. Texas has a pay-as-you-go state government, and the comptroller has to certify that there will be enough available revenue to fund the bill.

If the second chamber amends the bill, the originating house has to approve, or concur in, the change or request a conference committee. Any compromise worked out by a conference committee has to be approved by both houses, without further changes, before it is sent to the governor. A gubernatorial veto can be overridden and the bill allowed to become law by a two-thirds vote of both houses, although this process is rarely attempted.

All bills except revenue-raising measures can originate in either the House or the Senate. Tax bills must originate in the House, although the legislative leadership severely bent that rule to win approval in a special session in 1991 of a tax bill necessary to balance a new state budget. After the House had dismantled a $3.3 billion revenue bill recommended by its Ways and Means Committee and sent the Senate nothing but a $30 million shell, Lt. Governor Bullock and the Senate, in consultation with lobbyists, took over the writing of a new tax bill. At the same time, House and Senate negotiators worked out compromises on a $59 billion budget without a formal conference committee being appointed. The Senate then approved the budget and a $2.7 billion tax and fee bill that had been written in Bullock's office, and the House followed suit.

Pieces of legislation also encounter other significant procedural obstacles. In the House, there is the Calendars Committee, which we discussed earlier in this chapter. And in the Senate, there is the two-thirds rule.

The **two-thirds rule** for debating bills on the Senate floor is a strong obstacle to controversial bills because it means only 11 senators, if they are determined enough and one isn't absent at the wrong time, can keep any proposal from becoming law. This rule also is a source of the lieutenant governor's power. After a bill is approved by a committee, its sponsor can have it placed on the daily intent calendar. If the sponsor is recognized by the lieutenant governor, he or she will seek Senate permission to consider the bill. A sponsor can have majority Senate support for a measure but will watch it die if he can't convince two-thirds of the senators to let the body formally debate it.

The two-thirds rule also gives a senator the opportunity to vote on both sides of an issue. Sometimes a senator will vote to bring up a bill and then vote against the measure when it is actually passed and only a majority vote is required for approval. This enables the senator to please the bill's supporters, give the sponsor a favor that can be repaid later, and, at the same time, tell the bill's opponents that he voted against the measure.

There was speculation that Democratic senators would move to repeal or change the two-thirds rule during the 1993 session if a court-ordered redistricting plan significantly increased Republican strength in the Senate. Only nine of the 31 senators were Republicans in 1991, but the addition of two more Republicans would give the GOP enough senators to form a one-third bloc.

The Senate rules also provide for **tags** and **filibusters**, both of which can be effective in killing bills near the end of a legislative session. A tag allows an individual senator to postpone a committee hearing on any bill for at least 48 hours, a delay that is often fatal in the crush of unfinished business during a session's closing days. The filibuster, a procedure that allows a senator to speak against a bill for as long as he or she can stand and talk, is usually little more than a nuisance to a bill's supporters early in a session, but it also can become a potent and ever-present threat against controversial legislation near the end of a session (Figure 8-5). Sometimes several senators will engage in a tag-team filibuster, taking turns speaking against a bill. Often, the mere likelihood of a senator speaking against a bill is sufficient to kill a measure. In the last few days of a session, the lieutenant governor may refuse to recognize the sponsor of a controversial bill for fear a filibuster will fatally delay other major legislative proposals. Former state Senator Bill Meier of Euless, who spoke for 43 hours in 1977 against a bill dealing with the public reporting of on-the-job accidents, still held in 1991 the world's record for the longest filibuster.

**FIGURE 8-5** Senator Carlos Truan, a Democrat from Corpus Christi, filibusters against a coastal development bill in 1991. The bill was approved by the Senate but died in the House. (Texas Senate Media Services)

Sponsors of legislation languishing in an unfriendly committee or subcommittee often try to resurrect their proposals by attaching them as amendments to related bills when they are debated on the House or Senate floor. Such maneuvers often are successful, particularly if opponents are absent or if the sponsor succeeds in "mumbling" his amendment through without challenge. But the speaker or the lieutenant governor must find that such amendments are germane to the pending bill if an alert opponent raises a point of order against them.

To facilitate the passage of non-controversial and local pieces of legislation, the House and the Senate have periodic local and consent or local and uncontested **calendars**, which are conducted under special rules that enable scores of bills to be routinely and quickly approved by the full House or Senate without debate. Bills of major statewide significance, even controversial measures, sometimes get placed on these calendars, but it takes only one senator or three representatives to have any bill struck. Legislators will sometimes knowingly let a controversial bill slip by on a local calendar without moving to strike it so as not to offend the sponsor or the presiding officer. But to protect themselves politically, should the bill become an issue later, they will quietly register a vote against the measure in the House or Senate journal.

Speaker Lewis attempted to reduce floor fights in the House by insisting that compromises on controversial legislation be worked out as much as possible in committee (Figure 8-6). It can be argued that this approach to consensus building is an efficient, businesslike way to enact legislation. But, since most of the compromises that emerge from committee have been worked out by legislators and lobbyists behind closed doors or over a lunch table, it also serves to discourage the free and open debate that is so important to the democratic process.

Lewis also discouraged the taking of **record votes** during House floor debate on most bills. During one week of the 1989 regular session, for example, the House acted on dozens of amendments to an important bill determining manufacturers' potential liability for faulty products, a $46.5 billion appropriations bill and far-reaching health care legislation but took only a handful of record votes. There was sharp debate over many of the amendments, but the leadership was in control. Few members demanded record votes because they would have antagonized the speaker and exposed themselves to the scrutiny of interest groups. These issues were settled with "division" votes taken on the computerized voting machine, but

**FIGURE 8-6** Then-Speaker Gib Lewis explains his ruling on a parliamentary point of order to House members gathered around the podium in 1991. (Texas House of Representatives)

there was no formal record left once the voting boards were cleared. Lewis insisted this approach saves the taxpayers money because each record vote costs about $100, including the printing costs in the House Journal. It also can afford lawmakers some respite from lobby pressure. But more significantly it serves to keep the taxpaying public back home in the dark about significant decisions made by their elected representatives. The fewer the record votes a legislator has to make, the more he is able to dodge accountability to his constituents, who have a right to know how he is voting in Austin.

Many legislators either have their minds made up on an issue before the matter is debated on the floor or, in many cases, aren't familiar with a bill and will simply vote the way the sponsor votes or the way the House or Senate leadership wants them to vote. Despite what tourists in the gallery may think, legislators who raise their fingers above their heads when a vote is taken are not asking the presiding officer for a rest break. They are signaling the way they are voting and encouraging other lawmakers to vote the same way. One finger means yes. Two fingers mean no.

When record votes are taken, House rules technically prohibit members from punching the voting buttons on other members' desks, but the practice occurs regularly. Sometimes a member will instruct his deskmate or some other legislator to cast a specific vote for him if he expects to be absent when the vote is called for. Other legislators make a habit of punching the voting buttons at all the empty desks within easy reach. This practice is normally challenged only in cases of extremely close votes, when members of the losing side request a roll-call verification of the computerized vote, and the votes of members who don't answer the roll call are struck. The House was embarrassed in 1991 when a dead lawmaker was recorded as answering the daily roll call and voting on several record votes. The legislator had died in his Austin apartment, but his body wasn't discovered for several hours. Meanwhile, colleagues had been pushing his voting button. This practice is not a problem in the Senate, where the secretary of the Senate orally calls the roll on record votes.

Partly because of the rules under which the legislature operates, partly because of the heavy volume of legislation and partly because of political maneuvering, the closing days of a regular session are extremely hectic. Legislators are asked to vote on dozens of conference committee reports they don't have time to read. House members similarly have to decide whether to accept Senate changes in bills without a conference committee, and vice versa. With hundreds of bills being rushed to the governor's desk, mistakes occur. And deliberate attempts are made—often successfully—to slip major changes in law through the confusion.

Three days before the 1991 regular session ended, the House without debate unanimously approved Senate amendments to a routine liquor regulation bill that the House had approved earlier in the session. Only after the bill was already on its way to Governor Ann Richards did most House members learn that the Senate changes provided numerous favors for the alcoholic beverage industry and included a particularly controversial provision to allow the sale of alcohol at Texas Stadium in Irving, home of the Dallas Cowboys football team. The latter provision would have superseded an Irving city ordinance. The House bill had been expanded from its original two pages to 17 pages by liquor and beer lobbyists, and the Texas Stadium provision had been prepared by an attorney for the Cowboys and sponsored in the Senate by Senator Bob Glasgow of Stephenville. Glasgow said he had been unaware of the dispute over sale of alcohol at Texas Stadium, and he criticized Irving officials and their legislators and lobbyists for sleeping on the job.[13] But Senator John Leedom of Dallas complained that the maneuver reflected poorly on the Senate, and he criticized beer and liquor lobbyists for their role in it. "It made us appear that we might not know what we're doing and that we were doing things in a sly way," Leedom said in a speech on the Senate floor. "I think it's time we realize that the integrity of this organization can be questioned by the last-minute introduction of bills we are receiving and passing."[14] Lt. Governor Bob Bullock added, "The last 48 or 72 hours (of a session) are very dangerous periods."[15] Governor Richards later vetoed the bill. But for every surprise bill or special interest amendment that is caught, dozens of others usually slip through and become law.

## THE EMERGING PARTY SYSTEM

A newcomer to Texas or a casual observer of state government may have thought it strange when the media in 1987 made much ado of the partisan conflicts in the legislature over a record tax increase. After all, don't Democrats and Republicans usually wage political war? For the most part, however, such partisan divisiveness in Texas had been limited to the ballot box and the campaign trail. Except for some fights over legislative and congressional redistricting, the state's lawmaking process had seldom experienced such overt partisan conflict. Now, that was changing because of the realignment of the state's party system and the increased number of Republicans elected to the legislature, particularly the House.

Unlike Congress, the legislature is not organized along party lines. This is due primarily to the absence of Republican legislators for many years and the more recent practice of rural Democrats aligning themselves with the Republican minority to produce a conservative coalition. As recently as 1971, the year before a federal court declared urban, countywide House districts unconstitutional, there were only 10 Republicans in the House and two in the Senate. As Republicans increased their numbers, they aligned themselves with conservative Democrats to control the policy-setting process. This ideological coalition became increasingly important as single-member districts boosted not only the number of Republican lawmakers but also the number of moderate and liberal Democratic legislators elected from urban areas. It became a means of maintaining some legislative control for conservative Democrats as the base of power shifted in their own party.

Many Republicans and conservative Democrats formally organized the Texas Conservative Coalition in the House in the 1980s. One of the early major fights between this group and the Democratic caucus occurred over health care legislation for the poor in 1985. The conflict was so divisive that a final resolution was achieved only when Speaker Gib Lewis sided with the Democratic majority to break a tie on one key vote. The Democratic caucus prevailed and won approval of a new health care law, but the Conservative Coalition reflected an intense level of conflict among House Democrats and the ability of ideology to undermine partisan loyalty.

There have been occasions when liberal Democrats and conservative Republicans formed unholy alliances, but these coalitions were usually short-lived. During the controversy over the Sharpstown stock fraud scandal in 1971, liberal Democrats and Republicans formed a loose coalition called the "Dirty Thirty" that continually harassed House Speaker Gus Mutscher, who was not only a key figure in the scandal but also epitomized the rural conservative Democratic tradition of the statehouse.

With the growth of the Republican Party in Texas, it was inevitable that partisan differences would have greater impact on the legislature. Bill Clayton, a conservative, rural Democrat who was speaker during the 1981 redistricting debates, was accused by many Democrats of having been excessively helpful to the Republicans in the creation of House districts where Republicans could be elected. As speaker, Clayton's base of power included Republicans, and after he retired from the legislature, he became a Republican.

Gib Lewis continued the tradition of appointing Republicans to major committee chairs. Lewis, however, was challenged by a Republican opponent in 1986 in his legislative district in Tarrant County, an area of growing Republican strength. His challenger, K. Wayne Lee, was believed to have been encouraged by prominent Fort Worth Republicans who were more interested in the growth of the Republican party than the maintenance of legislative harmony. The state GOP leadership disavowed any involvement in the recruitment of Lee, but state Republican Chairman George Strake criticized a number of Republican House members who openly supported Lewis. While the Republican leadership outside the legislature appeared to be clearly committed to electing additional Republicans, GOP legislators were more concerned with maintaining friendly relationships with the speaker. After easily defeating his challenger, Lewis was again elected speaker in 1987. He replaced some Republicans on the House Ways and Means Committee who had refused to approve an emergency tax bill during a special session in 1986, but he appointed or reappointed Republicans to nine committee chairs.

Partisan divisions increased in 1987 as Lewis, Democratic Lt. Governor Bill Hobby and Republican Governor Bill Clements fought over a new state budget in the face of a huge revenue shortfall. On one side of the debate were moderate and liberal Democratic legislators, including inner city and South Texas minorities whose constituents had the most to gain from a tax increase and the most to lose from deep cuts in spending on human services and educational programs. On the other side were a handful of conservative, primarily rural Democrats and a number of Republicans with middle-to-upper-middle class suburban constituents who insisted on fiscal restraint. In spite of Clements' eventual support of a tax bill, all but a few of the House Republicans repeatedly refused to vote for it. Lewis had enough votes to win majority approval of the legislation in a summer special session. But he needed a two-thirds vote, or 100 votes, to put the bill into immediate effect and begin producing enough revenue to balance the budget in time for the September 1 start of the new fiscal year. Lewis and the Democrats finally gave in and let Republicans vote against the tax bill. Despite their public claims of fiscal restraint, most of these Republicans then voted for a parliamentary maneuver to put the tax increase into immediate effect and keep state government operating and the universities and other state facilities—many in Republicans' districts—open. Lewis, Hobby, and Clements expressed dismay over the partisan nature of the tax fight.

Now that Texas is a two-party state, partisanship will remain part of the legislative process. Before too many more years, the legislature may even organize itself along the same partisan lines as Congress—with distinct party positions, such as floor leaders, caucus leaders, and whips. That development will depend on how fast Republican strength in the statehouse continues to grow and on the future leadership personalities that emerge in both parties.

In 1989, Republicans formed their first **caucus** in the House, prompting speculation that they were preparing for an eventual partisan organization if and when they gained a majority of seats. Representative Tom Craddick of Midland, the Republican Caucus chairman, dismissed suggestions that the formal organization of the House was the objective. But Democratic caucuses in the House and the Senate are also taking on more importance and play key roles in marshalling legislative support on selected issues. Representative Sam Russell of Mt. Pleasant was chair of the House Democratic Caucus in 1991, and Senator Carl Parker of Port Arthur chaired the Senate Democratic Caucus.

Responding to stepped-up, well-financed Republican challenges of Democratic incumbents in the 1980s, both House and Senate Democratic caucuses formed political action committees to raise campaign funds for Democratic legislators and legislative candidates. The Associated Republicans of Texas, which operates independently of the Texas Republican party, has raised large sums of money for Republican legislative candidates, as have a number of national Republican organizations. And in 1991, wealthy Midland businessman Clayton Williams, whose loss to Democrat Ann Richards in the 1990 gubernatorial race was blamed for costing Republicans major gains in legislative races, organized a political action committee to raise funds for future GOP legislative candidates, particularly for those seeking House seats held by Democrats. The goal was to gain a majority of the House's 150 seats, a target that had eluded the strong GOP push in the previous decade. The House Republican Caucus planned to work closely with Williams' new Republicans in Majority, or RIM-PAC.[16]

Upon taking office in January 1991, Lt. Governor Bob Bullock appointed only Democrats to committee chairs in the Senate, although his longtime Democratic predecessor, Bill Hobby, had named two Republican chairmen. Even though Lewis in 1990 had to beat a second Republican challenger for his Tarrant County legislative seat, he continued his practice of naming Republicans to House committee chairs. He appointed Republicans to head eight of the House's 36 standing committees in 1991, although the GOP's share of House seats had dropped slightly in the 1990 elections, from 60 to 57 members. Republicans, meanwhile, had picked up a ninth seat in the 31-member Senate.

Republicans actively fought the Democratic leadership over the 1991 state budget and tax increase, much as they had done in 1987. If and when they gain a majority of House seats, Republicans are expected to attempt to elect one of their own speaker. How that speaker chooses his committee chairs would be the next key test in the development of a two-party system in the Texas legislature.

## OTHER LEGISLATIVE CAUCUSES

Hispanic and African-American House members formed their own caucuses as their numbers began to increase in the 1970s in the wake of redistricting and creation of urban single-member districts. Their cohesive blocks of votes have proved influential in speaker elections and the resolution of major statewide issues, such as health care for the poor, public school finance, and taxation. Their ability to broker votes has won committee chairs and other concessions they may not otherwise have received. The Mexican American Legislative Caucus, which included almost one-fifth of the House membership, was chaired by Representative Eddie Cavazos, a Democrat from Corpus Christi, in 1991. Representative Fred Blair, a Democrat from Dallas, chaired the Black Legislative Caucus.

Some urban delegations, such as the group of legislators representing Harris County, the state's most populous county, have formed their own caucuses to discuss and seek consensus on issues of local importance. In Harris County's case, however, consensus is rarely found on major local controversies because of the political, ethnic, and urban-suburban diversity found within the delegation itself. Twenty-six House members—almost one-fifth of the body's membership—represented various parts of Houston and Harris County in 1991, and six senators had districts that were wholly within or dominated by the county. On many occasions, debate in committees and on the House or Senate floor has bogged down into Houston fights over mass transportation or fire and police civil service, and many non-Harris County legislators have complained about being drafted into service on the Houston City Council.

## LEGISLATIVE NORMS

In addition to the formal rules of each legislative body, there are unwritten rules, or **norms**, that shape the behavior of legislators and other actors in the lawmaking process. The legislature is much like most other social institutions in that its members have perceptions of the institution and the process as well as the way they are expected to behave or carry out their responsibilities. Other participants also impose their views and expectations on lawmakers. Beginning with studies of the folkways of the United States Senate, there is a considerable body of literature pertaining to these informal norms within the legislative process.[17]

With about 4,600 pieces of legislation introduced during a regular session, the level reached in 1991, no legislator could possibly read and understand each bill, much less the hundreds of amendments offered during floor debate. And while there are moments of high drama when issues of major, statewide importance are being debated, the majority of the legislative workload is tedious, dull, and produces little direct political benefit for most senators and representatives. So it becomes clear why these norms have evolved and function to expedite decision-making.

To make the process work, legislators must accommodate the competing interests that they represent and achieve a great deal of reciprocity among each other. A legislator lays out chits, or obligations, as he or she supports another lawmaker's bill with the full expectation that the action will be returned in kind. One individual legislator usually will have no direct political or personal interest in most of the bills that are introduced each session. So for practical purposes, he often will defer to the wishes of colleagues.

The legislative process is designed to institutionalize conflict, and the rules as well as the norms of the legislature are designed to give this conflict an element of civility. Debate is often intense and vigorous, and it may be difficult for some lawmakers to separate attacks on their positions from attacks on their personalities. But most legislators have learned the necessity of decorum and courtesy. Even if lawmakers believe some of their opponents on the House or Senate floor are deceitful, personal attacks on other legislators are considered unacceptable. Legislative leaders and other members have a tacit understanding that personalized conflict is disruptive to the lawmaking process. Personal attacks, even to the point of fisticuffs, occasionally occur, but they are rare.

Some legislators become known for their commitment to producing good legislation. These workhorses spend endless hours developing programs, and they seem to overload themselves with legislation and are repeatedly turned to by presiding officers to handle tough policy issues. Other lawmakers tend to defer to their leadership, direction and cues. Knowledge, expertise, and commitment to moving legislation through the various stages of the process result in these legislators exercising considerable influence and power. And they are essential to a productive legislative session.

Senator Ray Farabee, a Democrat from Wichita Falls and one of the more influential members of the Senate during his tenure, sponsored more than 100 bills during the 1987 regular session, including major legislation dealing with prisons and utilities. He also chaired the important State Affairs Committee, which considered hundreds of bills, many of major significance, and served on the budget conference committee. His workdays, Farabee estimated, averaged 10 to 12 hours while the legislature was in session and included four to five hours on legislative business between sessions when the senator also practiced law. For a while, Farabee was considered a potential candidate for statewide office, but he quit the legislature to accept a high-ranking position with the University of Texas System.

Other legislators earn reputations as grandstanders. Almost every legislator has shown off for the media or the spectators in the gallery at one time or another, but there are a number who have developed a distinct reputation for this style of behavior. These individuals appear to be more interested in scoring political points with their constituents or interest groups—with the objective of being re-elected or seeking higher office—than with mastering the substance of legislation. Many of these lawmakers are lightweights who contribute little to the legislature's product. And while they may introduce many bills during a session, they are not interested in the details of the lawmaking process and are unable to influence other legislators to support their legislation.

The legislature also has a number of opportunists, including members who pursue issues in an effort to produce personal or political benefits for themselves. They may sponsor legislation or take a position on an issue to curry favor with a special interest group or exploit an issue that they hope will benefit their personal businesses or professions. Legislative rules prohibit legislators from voting on issues in which they have a personal monetary interest, but individual lawmakers can interpret that prohibition as they see fit. Many lawmakers will try to cash in on their legislative experience by becoming lobbyists after they leave office at considerably higher pay than they were making while they were in the legislature.

By disposition or personality, some legislators appear to be little more than spectators. They discover they enjoy the receptions, the free lunches with lobbyists, and the other perks of the office much more than the drudgery of the committee hearings, research, and floor debates. Some quickly become weary of the legislative process and, after a few sessions, decide against seeking re-election.[18]

## LEGISLATORS AND THEIR CONSTITUENTS

Except for an occasional emotional issue, such as mandatory seat belt use or drinking while driving, most Texans pay little attention to what the legislature is doing. That's why they often are surprised to discover they have to pay a few extra dollars to get license plate stickers for their cars or learn that the fee for camping in a state park has suddenly—or so it seems—been increased. Very few Texans—particularly in the large cities divided up among numerous lawmakers—can identify their state representatives or senators by name, and far fewer can tell you what their legislators have voted for or against. In a very significant sense, this gives a legislator great latitude when voting on public policies. It also is a major reason that most incumbent lawmakers who seek re-election are successful. Most legislative turnover is the result of voluntary retirements, not voter retribution.

News media coverage of the legislature is uneven. Large daily newspapers in Houston, Dallas, Fort Worth, and Austin make commendable efforts to cover the major legislative issues and players and provide both spot news accounts and in-depth interpretation of the legislature's actions. All too frequently, however, they are limited by insufficient space and rarely publish individual voting records or attempt to evaluate the performances of legislators from their readership areas. Newspapers in San Antonio and smaller cities, which have smaller Austin staffs, give greater coverage to their local legislators and local issues but often neglect issues of statewide significance. Many rural Texans have access to even less media coverage. And most television and radio news shows, the primary source of legislative information for thousands of Texans, provide only cursory coverage.

While legislators are always aware of latent public opinion, they tend to be more responsive to the interest groups, or attentive publics, that operate in their individual districts or statewide.[19] There are some people who are well-informed and attentive to public policy issues. As a proportion of the total population, this group of voters is relatively small, but they can be mobilized in opposition to or support of an individual legislator. In some instances, these are community opinion leaders who, directly or indirectly, are able to communicate to other individuals information about a legislator's performance. Or they may belong to any number of public interest and special interest groups that compile legislative voting records on selected issues of importance to their memberships. While these records are only sporadically disseminated by the news media to the general public, they are mailed to the sponsoring groups' members.

Those constituents associated with interest groups are usually the most attentive publics. Many groups can contribute thousands of dollars to a legislator's re-election campaign, or to the campaign of an opponent, and they hire lobbyists who are well-versed in the legislative process. But the politically astute legislator will duly take note of all the letters, phone calls, telegrams, petitions, and visits by all his constituents—plus local media coverage—lest he lose touch with a significant number of other voters with a different view of an issue and become politically vulnerable.

Another favorite voter-contact tool of many legislators is an occasional newsletter that they can mail to households in their districts at state expense. These mailouts usually include photos of the lawmaker plus articles summarizing his or her accomplishments in Austin. Sometimes, legislators will also include a public opinion survey seeking constituent responses on a number of issues.

Even with all their tools of communication, legislators sometimes don't get the message, or simply refuse to hear what the public is telling them. An obvious example of such non-responsiveness occurred in 1991, when the legislature was asked to approve a so-called "potty parity" bill that would have required extra toilets in women's restrooms in newly constructed or heavily renovated stadiums or other large entertainment facilities. The idea was to reduce the long restroom lines that women, unlike men, had to endure at some public events. A Houston woman who had been ticketed for using the men's room during a concert had attracted considerable public sympathy. Texas' new woman governor wanted the bill, the lieutenant governor and the speaker of the House were willing to support it, and it won easy Senate approval. No one stepped forward to publicly oppose it, but it never became law. It was quietly ambushed with a crippling amendment in the House, where it had become the victim of a number of factors. Some conservative legislators apparently feared that the bill would have led to unisex restrooms, while others may have refused to take the issue seriously. Some lawmakers, perhaps influenced by the quiet opposition of stadium owners who didn't want the extra expenses, said the state shouldn't be writing local building codes.[20]

## LEGISLATIVE DECISION-MAKING

Even the most conscientious lawmaker doesn't have time to study most of the hundreds of bills and amendments on which he or she will have to make decisions during a legislative session. And many of those bills contain hidden traps and potential controversies that can haunt a legislator later, often during a re-election campaign. So obviously, legislators use numerous information sources to assist them in decision making.

Much legislation is of a local nature and affects only a limited number of lawmakers and their constituents. In those cases, most legislators defer to the wishes of colleagues who are directly affected by the proposed legislation, with the expectation that their wishes on their own local bills will be similarly respected.

A number of factors will help shape lawmakers' decisions on major legislation.[21] The wishes of constituents will be considered, particularly if there is a groundswell of dominant opinion coming from a legislator's district. Legislators also exchange information among themselves, particularly with members of the same caucus, members who share the same political philosophy, or colleagues from the same counties or regions of the state. Lawmakers often will take their cues from bill sponsors or the speaker's and lieutenant governor's leadership teams. As the political parties develop more formal legislative structures, there are likely to emerge more identifiable patterns of cue-giving and cue-taking along party lines. That already has begun to some extent, particularly on budgetary, taxation, and redistricting issues.

A legislator's staff also assists in the decision-making process, not only by evaluating the substantive merits of proposed legislation but also by assessing the political implications of a lawmaker's decisions. The Legislative Budget Board and the Legislative Council provide technical information and expertise that also can be weighed by legislators.

Interest groups are major sources of information and influence. Although an individual legislator will occasionally rail against a specific group, most lawmakers consider them absolutely essential to the legislative process. Through their lobbyists, interest groups provide a vast amount of technical information and can signal the level of constituency interest, support, or opposition to proposed laws. A senator or representative can use interest groups to establish coalitions of support for a bill, and some legislators become closely identified with powerful interest groups because they almost always support a particular lobby's position.

There also are several ways the governor can significantly influence the legislature. One is by raising the public's consciousness of an issue or need—and the governor's position on how it should be addressed—through speeches to civic and lobby groups and communications through the media. The governor also can establish indirect communications to individual lawmakers through the governor's legislative liaisons, party leaders, and influential persons in a lawmaker's district who are willing to bend the legislator's ear on the governor's behalf. Governors also can personally appeal to lawmakers in direct one-on-one meetings or in periodic meetings with groups of legislators. At the beginning of each regular session, the governor outlines his or her legislative priorities in a "state of the state" address to a joint session of the House and the Senate, and the governor usually has frequent meetings with the lieutenant governor and the speaker throughout a session. The governor also will visit the House or the Senate chamber in a personal show of support when legislation that he or she strongly advocates is being debated. Unlike her immediate predecessors, Governor Ann Richards even personally testified before legislative committees on several of her priorities, including ethics reform and government reorganization. The severity of a governor's arm twisting is often in the eye of the beholder, but it can include appeals to a lawmaker's reason or conscience, threats of retaliation, appeals for party support, and promises of a *quid pro quo*. The greatest threat that a governor can hang over a legislator is the possible veto of legislation or a budget item of importance to him. In special sessions, the governor also has the power to negotiate with a lawmaker over whether to add a bill that is important to the legislator to the special session's agenda, which is controlled by the governor.

Legislators also rely on information and support from other elected statewide officeholders, such as the attorney general, the comptroller, or the land commissioner. These officials and lawmakers, particularly if they belong to the same party, also can assist each other in achieving political agendas.

Legislators also rely on the news media, which provides information about substantive policy issues and perspective on those issues in broader political terms. In part, the policy agenda is established by those issues that the media perceives to be of importance and, ever sensitive to public opinion, legislators receive some of their cues from the press.

The relative importance of one or more of the above groups or actors on decision making is difficult to measure and varies from lawmaker to lawmaker and from issue to issue. The outside influences also can be tempered by a legislator's own attitude and opinion. On many issues, of course, legislators will get competing advice and pressure. As much as a lawmaker may like to be all things to all people, he can't be. He can't please a chemical lobbyist, who is seeking a tax break for a new plant on the Gulf coast and also happens to be a large campaign contributor, and environmentalists, who fear the facility would spoil a nearby wildlife habitat. He can't please the governor, who is promoting a lottery as a new state revenue source, and most of the voters in his district, who have consistently voted against gambling. The ultimate decision and its eventual political consequences are the legislator's.

Should a lawmaker cast a particular vote on the basis of the specific concerns of his district, personal convictions, the position of his political party, or the wishes of the special interest groups that helped fund his campaign? Each of these criteria reflect complex relationships between the legislator and the people represented. And since the overriding consideration for most lawmakers is to get re-elected, the legislator must carefully balance them.

## THE DEVELOPMENT OF LEGISLATIVE STAFF

The quality of a legislator's staff often can help determine his or her success, and both the quantity and quality of legislative staffs were significantly enhanced during the 1970s and 1980s.[22] This reflected an emerging professional approach to lawmaking and meeting the needs of an increasingly complex, urban state. During the 1991 regular session, the House had about 940 employees, including part-time workers, and the Senate about 800. These figures included Capitol and district office staff for individual senators and representatives, the committee staffs, assistants to the lieutenant governor and the speaker, and other support staff hired directly by the House and the Senate.

Additionally, there are permanent staff members assigned to the Legislative Budget Board, which functions as the research arm of the appropriations and tax-writing committees; the Legislative Council, which researches issues and drafts bills and resolutions for introduction by legislators; and the Legislative Reference Library, which provides resource materials for lawmakers, their staffs, and the general public. Other support staff are assigned to the Sunset Advisory Commission, which assists the legislature in periodic reviews of state agencies, and the state auditor, who is chosen by and reports to the legislative leadership.

In the 1979 regular session, 3,596 bills were filed in the House and the Senate, and 890 were enacted into law. In 1989, the number of bills filed had grown to 5,069, and 1,318 were enacted. Although the number of bills filed and enacted dropped off by a few hundred during the 1991 regular session—thanks, in part, to a large projected revenue shortfall—the general increase in bills considered over the years may be partly attributable to the larger and better-prepared legislative staffs. "Staffs certainly are a lot more active than when I first came here in the late 1960s," noted Robert Kelly, the Legislative Council's executive director. "They tend to spawn ideas. The more laws you have on the books, the more tinkering they require. It's exponential."

Legislative staffers range from part-time secretaries and clerks who also attend college to lawyers and professionals who draft bills and direct research that results in major state laws. There are limits on the number of staff members and the funds allocated for legislators' personal staff and, as a general rule, senators have more personal staff than House members. Staffing levels are usually reduced between sessions, and some members shut down their Capitol offices entirely. Most lawmakers, however, maintain offices both in Austin and in their districts, even if staffs function only to answer the phone.

A key support group in the House is the House Research Organization, which was organized as the House Study Group in the 1970s by a handful of primarily liberal lawmakers. The name was later changed, and its structure was reorganized to represent the entire House, but it still fills a strong research role. It is supported by funds from the general House budget and is governed by a steering committee that represents a cross section of Democratic and Republican House members. During legislative sessions, its staff researches major pieces of legislation for House members and media subscribers and provides detailed analyses, including pro and con arguments, of bills on the daily House calendar. During interims between sessions, it provides periodic analyses of proposed constitutional amendments and other issues. The Senate took steps to form a similar organization in 1991.

The quality of other resources available to lawmakers also has improved in recent years. Legislators and staff can routinely check the status of bills on computer terminals in their offices, and interest groups as well as the public can get access to this data system through the Legislative Reference Library. In years past, before the installation of a computer system, legislators often had trouble determining where a bill was in the process, and this lack of information could be exploited by the leadership when it wanted to kill or expedite consideration of legislation.

## LEGISLATIVE ETHICS AND REFORMS

The vast majority of legislators are honest, hard-working individuals. But the weaknesses of a few and the millions of dollars spent by special interests to influence the lawmaking process serve to undermine Texans' confidence in their legislature and their entire state government. While legislators can't pass laws guaranteeing ethical behavior, they can set strong standards for themselves, other public officials, and lobbyists and provide stiff penalties for those who fail to comply. Such reform efforts are periodically attempted. But, unfortunately, they usually are the result of scandals and fall short of creating an ideal ethical climate.

The **Sharpstown stock fraud scandal** rocked the Capitol in 1971 and 1972 and helped produce some far-reaching legislative and political changes.[23] It involved banking legislation sought by Houston banker-developer Frank Sharp and approved by the legislature in special session in 1969, only to be vetoed by then-Governor Preston Smith. After the federal Securities and Exchange Commission filed a lawsuit in 1971, the scandal broke with news that Smith, then-House Speaker Gus Mutscher, Representative Tommy Shannon of Fort Worth, who had sponsored the bills, and other individuals had profited from stock deals involving Sharp's National Bankers Life Insurance Company. Much of their stock was purchased with unsecured loans from Sharp's Sharpstown State Bank. Mutscher, Shannon, and an aide to the speaker were later convicted of conspiracy to accept bribes. Mutscher, who had consolidated power in the House and was often regarded as iron-handed and arbitrary, was forced to resign. Later, the House moved to formally limit the speaker's power through a modified seniority system for committee appointments. While subsequent speakers still exercised a great deal of power, it was constrained by expectations that the speaker would be more responsive to the membership. The media also started giving greater scrutiny and coverage to the activities of the speaker.

Fallout from the Sharpstown scandal helped an outsider, Uvalde rancher Dolph Briscoe, win the 1972 gubernatorial race and helped produce a large turnover in legislative elections. In 1973, the legislature responded with a series of ethics reform laws, including requirements that lobbyists register with the secretary of state and report their total expenditures in trying to influence legislation. State officials also were required to file public reports identifying their sources—although not specific amounts—of income.

Weaknesses in those laws, however, were vividly demonstrated in 1989, when a wealthy East Texas poultry producer named Lonnie "Bo" Pilgrim distributed $10,000 checks to several senators in the Capitol while lobbying them on workers' compensation reform and the Travis County district attorney could find no law under which to prosecute him. There also were published reports that lobbyists had spent nearly $2 million entertaining lawmakers during the 1989 regular session without having to specify which legislators received the "freebies," thanks to a large loophole in the lobby registration law. The revelations—including frequent news stories about lobbyists treating lawmakers to golf tournaments, ski trips, a junket to Las Vegas for a boxing match, and limousine service to a Cher concert—created an uproar. The legislature was in special session six times in 1989 and 1990 on workers' compensation and school finance reform, but then-Governor Bill Clements, who controlled the special sessions' agendas, refused to include ethics.

Some senators had angrily rejected Pilgrim's checks on the spot, while others returned them after the media had pounced on the story. But the very next year, the businessman—a longtime political contributor and a former member of the Texas Water Development Board—again contributed thousands of dollars to several statewide officeholders and candidates. Those checks weren't offered under the Capitol dome but were more traditionally sent through the mail, and they were gratefully accepted. Only one officeholder, who was passed over by Pilgrim in favor of his opponent, tried to make a campaign issue of the new contributions.

Despite all the headlines over ethical problems, legislative turnover was minimal in 1990. Democrats Ann Richards and Bob Bullock made ethics reform major issues in their successful campaigns for governor and lieutenant governor. And Speaker Lewis won re-election from his Fort Worth district over a Republican challenger who had tried to use the ethics issue against him. Lewis' problems, however, had only begun.

In early December 1990, about a month after the general election, a Travis County grand jury began investigating Lewis' ties to a San Antonio-based law firm, Heard Goggan Blair and Williams. The firm had made a fortune collecting delinquent taxes for local governments throughout Texas under a law that allowed it to collect an extra 15 percent from the taxpayers as its fee. For several years, it had successfully defeated legislation that would have hurt its business. The *Fort Worth Star-Telegram* had reported that Heard Goggan had paid about half of a $10,000 tax bill owed to Tarrant County by a business that Lewis partly owned.[24] And the *Houston Chronicle* reported that the grand jury also was looking into a trip that Lewis had taken to a Mexican resort during the 1987 legislative session with four Heard Goggan partners and a lobbyist (all males) and six women (including a waitress from a topless night club in Houston).[25] The trip had been taken while a bill opposed by Heard Goggan was dying in a House committee.

On Dec. 28, only 12 days before the 1991 regular legislative session was to convene and Lewis be re-elected to his record fifth term as the House's presiding officer, grand jurors indicted Lewis on two misdemeanor ethics charges. He was accused of soliciting, accepting, and failing to report an illegal gift from Heard Goggan—the partial payment of the tax bill. Lewis, who had pleaded guilty to an earlier misdemeanor and paid an $800 fine during his first term as speaker in 1983 for failing to report all of his business interests on an annual financial disclosure statement, insisted he was innocent this time and vowed to fight the charges. He said the tax payment was the settlement of a legal dispute. And he angrily accused Travis County District Attorney Ronnie Earle, who headed the prosecution and had been publicly advocating stronger ethics laws, of using the grand jury to "influence the speaker's election." Lewis said Earle was guilty of "unethical and reprehensible behavior."[26]

Lewis won a postponement of his trial under a law that automatically grants continuances to legislators when they are in session. The grand jury investigation—which prosecutors said would include other legislators or former legislators—continued for several more weeks, but no more indictments were issued. Representative Hugo Berlanga, a Corpus Christi Democrat who was a key Lewis lieutenant, chairman of the House Calendars Committee, and a former speaker pro tem, was investigated for alleged business ties to Heard Goggan and, one day during the 1991 session, spent six hours in the Travis County jail for refusing a judge's order to give prosecutors his business records.

Meanwhile, considerable attention was focused on an ethics reform bill, with Richards personally testifying before House and Senate committees for tougher ethical requirements for state officials and lobbyists. The Senate approved an ethics bill fairly early in the session, but the House didn't act on its version of the bill until late. The final bill was produced by a conference committee on the last night of the regular session in a private meeting that apparently violated the Texas Open Meetings Act. The measure was approved by the House and the Senate only a few minutes before the legislature adjourned at midnight, even though there wasn't time to print and distribute copies and very few legislators knew for sure what was in the legislation.

This performance and the bill itself left a bad taste all around (Figure 8-7). Despite complaints that the measure wasn't strong enough and the controversy over the secretive way in which the final compromise had been written, Richards signed the bill. But she did so in the privacy of her office, not in the public ceremony that governors usually hold for their priority pieces of legislation. Ronnie Earle, the Travis County district attorney, was among those displeased with the legislation, and the best that former Congresswoman Barbara Jordan, the governor's ethics adviser, could say about the measure was that it was a "worthy effort." But Richards called the new law a "very strong step in the direction of openness and ethics reform in this state."

The new law required more reporting of lobby expenditures and conflicts of interest between lobbyists and state officials, prohibited special interests from treating legislators to pleasure trips, prohibited lawmakers from accepting honoraria—or fees—for speaking before special interest groups and created a new state Ethics Commission to review complaints about public officials.

**FIGURE 8-7**  This cartoon is representative of the Texas press' opinion of the ethics reform bill approved by the legislature in 1991. (© *Houston Chronicle*. Reprinted with permission.)

But the measure didn't put any limits on financial contributions to political campaigns, nor did it prohibit legislator-attorneys from representing clients before state agencies for pay. Moreover, it authorized the Ethics Commission to slap a bigger fine, $10,000, on someone who files a frivolous complaint against a public official than the maximum fine, $5,000, that could be levied on an officeholder for violating the ethics law. That latter provision was viewed by many critics as an unreasonable effort to discourage citizen complaints. The new law also provided that complaints filed with the Ethics Commission would remain confidential unless the commission took action, a provision that would allow the commission to dismiss or sit on legitimate complaints without any public accounting. And the haste in which the final compromise was drafted produced several mistakes.

The legislature's failure on another significant bill during the 1991 regular session also left doubts about the commitment of lawmakers to true ethics reform. Another effort was made to pass legislation that Heard Goggan Blair and Williams, the law firm that figured in the Gib Lewis indictment, had been killing for several years. It would have allowed local governments to collect the same fees as private law firms on delinquent tax collections. This time, the Senate delayed action on the bill for several weeks early in the session before approving it. The House Ways and Means Committee delayed action for several more weeks. Finally, the House Calendars Committee, chaired by Representative Hugo Berlanga, another subject of the grand jury investigation, set the bill for floor debate three days before the end of the session, the last possible day that a bill could win initial House approval under the House rules. But the House calendar, or agenda, was long that day, and legislators never got to the bill before the restrictive "72-hour rule" went into effect. The tax collection bill automatically died at midnight as House members were stalling action on a gambling bill that was just before it on the calendar. Lewis insisted he wasn't responsible for the bill's death. Lengthy debate on bills higher on the calendar had done it in, he said. All the media attention over the grand jury investigation and Lewis' indictment hadn't been enough to at least embarrass the legislature into passing the bill. There obviously was still a lot of opposition, at least in key places, to the measure, but no one had wanted to be blamed for killing it. As reporter Edward M. Sills wrote in the *San Antonio Light,* the measure died "without much in the way of fingerprints."[27]

In January 1992, Lewis announced that he wouldn't seek re-election to another term in the House. In a plea bargain later the same month, prosecutors dropped the two ethics indictments against Lewis in return for the speaker's "no contest" plea to two minor, unrelated charges. Lewis paid a $2,000 fine for failing to publicly disclose a business holding in 1988 and 1989, for which he had already paid a minor civil penalty to the secretary of state.

Lewis' decision to retire set off the first speaker's race in the House since 1975, and many House members, including most of the freshmen, hoped to use the campaign to bargain for reforms in the way the House conducted its business. The freshmen, in particular, had complained in 1991 that the House rules had been used to create an un-democratic process that catered to special interests and favored an inner circle of legislators close to the speaker. Much of their unhappiness centered on the Calendars Committee, which operated in a manner that allowed it to kill bills without any individual member having to take public responsibility. Reform-minded members also sought changes in the rules to limit the number of terms an individual could serve as speaker, and some wanted to have the speaker elected by secret ballot. Proponents argued that a secret ballot would make members more independent and less fearful of being punished with poor committee assignments or having their legislative programs scuttled by a speaker who they voted against. Opponents of the secret ballot, however, argued that taxpayers had the right to know who their individual legislators supported for the critical leadership post.

Nationwide, there have been coordinated efforts to address the weaknesses and deficiencies of state legislatures. In the 1960s and the early 1970s, these efforts, working through the National Conference of State Legislatures, conducted extensive research and recommended a host of reforms. Texas legislators were influenced by these efforts at modernization, and many changes in staff, support services, and procedures were implemented during the 1970s.

Reforms also have been the result of the efforts of public interest groups. Common Cause, the self-styled "people's lobby," has had a specific interest in elections and campaign costs. In the early 1970s, Common Cause was influential in obtaining changes in laws pertaining to voter registration and campaign finance disclosure. With the increased influence of fund-raising through political action committees, Common Cause also has lobbied, so far unsuccessfully in Texas, for limitations on the amount of campaign funds that a legislator can receive from PACs.

Much of the debate over revising the Texas Constitution in the 1970s focused on modernizing the legislature. Recommendations included annual sessions and a compensation commission to set legislative pay. But the concerted effort to rewrite the constitution was defeated by voters in 1975.

## SUMMARY AND CONCLUSIONS

**1.** The nation's third most populous state has only a part-time legislature that operates under strict, antigovernment restrictions drafted by 19th century Texans in the wake of the repressive Reconstruction era. It is a lawmaking body that is not structured to readily respond to pressing, late 20th century needs and crises. A series of emergencies has required frequent special legislative sessions in recent years and increased financial and personal pressures on lawmakers, who are among the lowest paid state legislators in the country. Legislative turnover in Texas is high.

**2.** As recently as 1971, there were only a handful of African-Americans, Hispanics, Republicans, and women in the 150-member House of Representatives and the 31-member Senate. But federal court intervention in redistricting, particularly the ordering of single-member House districts for urban counties in 1972, has significantly increased the number of women, ethnic minorities, and Republicans in the legislature.

**3.** Unlike the U.S. Congress, the Texas legislature is not organized along party lines and has only the tentative beginnings of an institutionalized leadership structure. The presiding officer of the House is the speaker, who is elected by the other House members. The presiding officer of the Senate is the lieutenant governor, who is elected by the voters statewide. The speaker appoints a speaker pro tempore, or assistant presiding officer, who usually is a close ally. Senators choose a president pro tempore from among their membership and periodically rotate the office, which is third in line of succession to the governorship, on a seniority basis.

**4.** The most significant powers of the speaker and the lieutenant governor are the appointment of House and Senate committees that screen and draft legislation and the assignment of bills to committees. The fate of most pieces of legislation is decided at the committee level. While most House committees are partially appointed on the basis of seniority, the lieutenant governor has absolute control over the composition of Senate committees. The presiding officers also play key roles in the development of major legislative proposals and, to a great extent, depend on their handpicked committee chairs to sell their legislative programs to House and Senate colleagues.

**5.** Traditionally, the powers of the presiding officers have been enhanced by the Calendars Committee in the House and the two-thirds rule in the Senate. The Calendars Committee, composed entirely of speaker appointees, sets the schedule for floor debate in the House and, each session, has killed hundreds of bills approved by substantive committees by simply refusing to schedule them. The two-thirds rule provides that two-thirds of the Senate's membership must approve before any bill can be debated on the floor of that body. That means that 11 senators can block, or kill, any piece of legislation that has majority support. The lieutenant governor decides which Senate sponsors get recognized for consideration of specific bills.

**6.** To be sent to the governor for signature into law, a bill must be approved after three readings in both the House and the Senate. Referral to committee is first reading, and that's as far as most bills get. Many are never scheduled for a hearing by the chairmen of the committees to which they are assigned. Many others die in subcommittees to which they are sent after being heard by the full committee. And others don't survive the Calendars Committee in the House or the two-thirds rule in the Senate. Those that do win committee approval are often amended, or changed.

**7.** For those bills that survive the committee process, second reading is a crucial step. That is where most floor debate on legislation occurs and where many bills are further amended. If a bill is approved on second reading, it advances to third reading and then to the other legislative chamber, where it is referred to a committee and has to repeat the process.

**8.** Bills that originate in the House are called House bills, while bills that originate in the Senate are called Senate bills, and a bill has to be approved in exactly the same form by each chamber. If the Senate, for example, approves a House bill after making some changes in it, the House will have to concur in—or accept—the Senate version, or a conference committee of House and Senate members will have to be appointed to try to work out a compromise.

**9.** The governor can sign a bill, veto it, or let it become law without his or her signature. The governor can use the line-item veto to delete specific spending provisions from the general appropriations bill, or state budget. But all other bills have to be accepted or rejected in their entirety.

**10.** Tax bills have to originate in the House. All other bills can originate in either chamber.

**11.** Proposed constitutional amendments require the approval of two-thirds of the House and the Senate before they can be submitted to the voters.

**12.** The legislative rules and heavy volume of bills considered enable lawmakers to frequently sneak major, controversial proposals into law by adding little-noticed amendments to other bills.

**13.** The growth of Republican strength, particularly in the House, has increased partisan activity in the legislature leading to speculation that if and when Republicans gain a majority, attempts may be made to organize the legislature along the partisan lines of Congress. Both parties already have active legislative caucuses.

**14.** There is considerable diversity among legislators in their styles and work habits. Many lawmakers take their cues from a handful of legislators who are recognized as experts on selected issues and are assigned leadership roles by the presiding officers.

**15.** Legislators' decisions are influenced by a number of factors, including constituents, interest groups, colleagues, staff, the governor, and the media.

**16.** Although most legislators are honest, hard-working individuals, the weaknesses of a few and the millions of dollars spent by special interests to influence the lawmaking process serve to undermine Texans' confidence in state government. Lawmakers make periodic efforts to strengthen their ethical standards but usually only after well-publicized scandals.

## KEY TERMS

Legislature
Regular session
Special session
Bicameral legislature
Speaker
Committee
Calendars Committee
Subcommittee
Conference committee
First reading
Second reading
Third reading

Veto
Appropriations bill
Line item veto
Two-thirds rule
Tag
Filibuster
Calendar
Record vote
Caucus
Legislative norms
Sharpstown stock fraud scandal
Lieutenant governor

## FURTHER READING

Anderson, Arthur J., "Texas Legislative Redistricting: Proposed Constitutional and Statutory Amendments for an Improved Process," *Southwestern Law Journal*, 43 (October 1989), pp. 719-757.

Armstrong, David, Bret Campbell, Suzanne Donovan, Scott Henson, and Jennifer Wong, "The 72nd Legislature," *The Texas Observer*, June 28, 1991, pp. 4-14.

Barber, James David, *The Lawmakers*. New Haven: Yale University Press, 1965.

Bickerstaff, Steve, "State Legislative and Congressional Reapportionment in Texas: A Historical Perspective," *Public Affairs Comment*, 37 (Winter, 1991), pp. 1-13.

Blondel, J., *Comparative Legislatures*. Englewood Cliffs, N.J.: Prentice Hall, 1973.

Campbell, Brett, "The Greening of the Legislature," *The Texas Observer*, May 17, 1991, pp. 15, 23-27.

Deaton, Charles, *The Year They Threw the Rascals Out*. Austin: Shoal Creek Press, 1973.

Dubose, Louis, "The Best Ethics Money Can Buy," *The Texas Observer*, January 11, 1991, pp. 3-4.

Dubose, Bert, and Glen Utter, "Formal and Informal Rules Regulating Public Officials' Behavior," *Texas Journal of Political Studies*, 10 (Fall/Winter 1988), pp. 3-16.

Edwards, Julie, "The Right to Vote and Reapportionment in the Texas Legislature," *Baylor Law Review*, 41 (December 1989), pp. 689-730.

Fenno, Richard F., *Home Style: House Members in Their Districts*. Boston: Little, Brown and Company, 1978.

Jewell, Malcolm E., and Samuel C. Patterson, *The Legislative Process in the United States*, 4th ed. New York: Random House, 1986.

Keefe, William J., and Morris S. Ogul, *The American Legislative Process: Congress and the States*, 7th ed. Englewood Cliffs, N.J.: Prentice Hall, 1989.

Kingdon, John W., *Congressmen's Voting Decisions*, 2nd ed. New York: Harper & Row, Publishers, 1981.

Mayhew, David, *Congress: The Electoral Connection*. New Haven: Yale University Press, 1974.

Pettus, Beryl E., "Escape from Modernization: Legislative Institutions Out of Synchronization with Environmental Changes," *Texas Journal of Political Studies*, 2 (Spring, 1980), pp. 27-41.

Rosenthal, Alan, *Legislative Life: People, Process and Performance in the States*. New York: Harper & Row, Publishers, 1981.

Rosenthal, Alan, *Governors and Legislatures: Contending Powers*. Washington, D.C.: Congressional Quarterly Books, 1990.

Texas Legislative Council, *Presiding Officers of the Texas Legislature, 1946-1982*. Austin: Texas Legislative Council, 1982.

Thorburn, Wayne, "The Growth of Republican Representation in the Texas Legislature: Coattails, Incumbency, Special Elections, and Urbanization," *Texas Journal of Political Studies*, 11 (Spring/Summer 1989), pp. 16-28.

Wong, Jennifer, "The Highwayman," *The Texas Observer*, March 8,1991, pp. 10-11, 23.

## ENDNOTES

1. *Book of the States, 1990-1991 Edition* (Lexington, Ky.: The Council of State Governments, 1990), p. 123.
2. See Article 3 of the *Texas Constitution* for the constitutional provisions pertaining to the structure, membership and selection of the Texas Legislature.
3. *Book of the States, 1990-91 Edition*, pp. 110-112, 120, 131.
4. *Austin American-Statesman*, June 11, 1991.
5. For a comprehensive analysis of the literature on legislative recruitment and careers, see Donald R. Matthews, "Legislative Recruitment and Legislative Careers," *Legislative Studies Quarterly*, IX (November 1984), pp. 547-85.
6. For a brief overview of the "representative problem," see Neal Riemer, ed., *The Representative: Trustee? Delegate? Partisan? Politico?* (Boston: D. C. Heath and Company, 1967). For a more comprehensive treatment of the subject, see Hanna F. Pitkin, *The Concept of Representation* (Berkeley: University of California Press, 1967).
7. On the general concept of legislative institutionalization, see Nelson W. Polsby, "Institutionalization in the U.S. House of Representatives," *American Political Science Review*, 62 (1968), pp. 144-168.
8. Fredd Gantt, Jr., *The Chief Executive in Texas: A Study of Gubernatorial Leadership* (Austin: University of Texas Press, 1964), p. 238.
9. For a good summary of the scholarly work on legislative committees, see Heinz Eulau and Vera McCluggage, "Standing Committees in Legislatures: Three Decades of Research," *Legislative Studies Quarterly*, IX (May 1984), pp. 195-270.
10. *Austin American-Statesman*, May 13, 1991.
11. See Steven H. Haeberle, "The Institutionalization of the Subcommittee in the United States House of Representatives," *Journal of Politics*, XL (November, 1978), pp. 1054-65.
12. See Malcolm E. Jewell and Samuel C. Patterson, *The Legislative Process in the United States* (New York: Random House, 1966), chap. 11, for a good summary of the function of legislative rules and procedures.
13. *Dallas Morning News*, May 26, 1991.
14. *Dallas Morning News*, May 27, 1991.
15. *Dallas Morning News*, May 27, 1991.
16. *Houston Chronicle*, July 7, 1991.
17. Donald R. Matthews, *U.S. Senators and Their World* (New York: Vintage Books, 1960). For the adaptation of this concept to state legislatures, see Alan Rosenthal, *Legislative Life: People, Process, and Performance in the States* (New York: Harper & Row, Publishers, 1981), pp. 123-127.
18. These legislative styles are similar to those developed by James David Barber, *The Lawmakers* (New Haven: Yale University Press, 1965), chaps. 2-5.
19. For an excellent treatment of the relationship of U.S. legislators to their districts and constituencies, see Richard F. Fenno, Jr., *Home Style: House Members in Their Districts* (Boston: Little, Brown and Company, 1978).
20. *Houston Chronicle*, June 2, 1991.

21. The general concepts for this discussion are based on John W. Kingdon, *Congressmen's Voting Decisions*, 2nd ed. (New York: Harper & Row, Publishers, 1981).

22. For a general discussion of staff in state legislatures, see Alan Rosenthal, *Legislative Life: People, Process, and Performance in the States* (New York: Harper & Row, Publishers, 1981), chap. 10.

23. Richard Morehead, *50 Years in Texas Politics* (Burnet, Texas: Eakin Press, 1982), pp. 236-237.

24. *Fort Worth Star-Telegram*, Dec. 4, 1990.

25. *Houston Chronicle*, Dec. 12, 1990.

26. *Houston Chronicle*, Jan. 1, 1991.

27. *San Antonio Light*, May 26, 1991.

# 9

# THE TEXAS EXECUTIVE

I just love this job.

*Governor Ann Richards,* on more than one occasion soon after taking office.

The Governor's office is not the primrose path of pleasure. Every time you throw yourself in opposition to what somebody wants, you immediately become the target for many a poisoned arrow.

*Governor Pat M. Neff* [1]

The salary isn't bad, the fringe benefits are pretty good, and there is a lot of prestige and status associated with the job. One might definitely get a sense of power and influence from holding the position, and if your personality thrives on publicity, it may be satisfying to have a pack of journalists following your moves and hanging on to your every word. But sooner or later, the reporters will become a pain in the neck. It will be hard to get time to yourself and, if you are not careful, your efforts to relax may be subject to criticism. You will be authorized a large staff, but it will attempt to structure most of your waking hours. You can easily spend $10 to $12 million and a year's worth of 16-hour days winning the job and, in the process, be subjected to all kinds of ridicule and personal attacks. And once elected, you may catch all kinds of flak for developments over which you have little, if any, control. Finally, eight or ten other people will want your job and will be eager to make you look bad so they can challenge you when your term of office is up.

If there is any one office that comes to mind when people think of state government, it is the office of governor. It clearly is the most visible office in the state, and the person holding the position is the focus of considerable media attention. But while the popular image of the office is one of power, those elected to it discover that the office, by design, is institutionally weak. The term, "chief executive," is almost a misnomer, thanks to constitutional restrictions ensuring that no other governor would ever be able to repeat the oppressive abuses of the Reconstruction administration of Governor Edmund J. Davis.

Unlike the president of the United States, the governor of Texas has no formal appointive cabinet through which to impose his or her own policy over the entire governmental bureaucracy. Several other major state agencies are headed by executive officers independently elected of the governor, including such key players as the attorney general and the comptroller. The governor appoints hundreds of members of boards and commissions that set policy for numerous other state agencies. But, despite limited governmental reorganization during Governor Richards' first year in office (Figure 9-1), most of those boards are structured in such a way that a new governor has to wait until halfway through his or her first term to appoint a majority of panel members.

All of this is not to suggest that the governor is merely a figurehead. The governor can veto legislation and has the exclusive authority to schedule special

FIGURE 9-1  Governor Ann Richards greets the crowd at her inauguration ceremony in January, 1991.  (Texas Senate Media Services)

sessions of the legislature and set their agendas. And despite its limitations, the appointments power offers the opportunity to make a strong mark on state government. The high visibility of the office also offers a governor a ready-made public forum. So while the state constitution limits the formal powers of the office, a governor's influence is shaped by his or her personality, political adroitness, staff appointments, and ability to define and sell an agenda that addresses broad needs and interests within the state.

## A HISTORICAL PERSPECTIVE
## ON THE EXECUTIVE FUNCTION IN TEXAS

Texas, like many other states, functions with a **plural executive**, but this has not always been the case. In the 1836 constitution of the Republic, the powers of the president of Texas "closely resembled the powers of the American president, except he was forbidden to lead armies without the consent of Congress."[2] When Texas was annexed to the United States in 1845, a new constitution, regarded by most scholars as the best that the state has had, was written. It continued the office of a strong single executive and gave the governor significant powers and resources, including the appointment of other executive officials.[3] When Texas adopted a revised constitution upon joining the Confederacy in 1861, there were some minor reductions in the powers of the governor. The new charter called for the election of two other executive officeholders, the state treasurer and the comptroller of public accounts.[4]

Under the Constitution of 1866, written at the end of the Civil War, the governor retained extensive appointment powers, except the treasurer and the comptroller remained elected. The Constitution of 1866 also expanded the legislative power of the governor through the line-item veto, a power still retained today. But the Constitution of 1866 was short-lived and replaced by the Constitution of 1869 to bring the state into compliance with the Reconstruction policies of the Radical Republicans who had taken over Congress. The Constitution of 1869 was influenced by Jacksonian democracy, which led to the diffusion of the executive function among eight officeholders, six of whom were to be elected statewide.[5]

Radical Reconstruction policies and the excesses and abuses of the Davis administration produced a political reaction that culminated in the Constitution of 1876, which still forms the basic framework of state government. Public hostility toward Davis resulted in strict constitutional limits on the governor. The new constitution retained the plural executive structure of independently elected officeholders. The only executive officer the governor was given the power to appoint was the secretary of state. Terms of elected officials were limited to two years, their salaries were defined by the constitution, and the duties of each office were specified in great detail, thus limiting their discretionary powers. Restrictions also were placed on outside employment and holding any other office or commission.[6]

Over the years, a few of the constitutional restrictions on the executive branch have been loosened, but the changes have not significantly enhanced the governor's authority. By constitutional amendment, voters have empowered the legislature to raise the governor's salary.[7] To correct an oversight, a provision was added in 1948 to provide for the succession of the governor if the incumbent died or was disabled. In 1972, the term of office for the governor and most other statewide executive officeholders was extended to four years and in 1980, the governor was given the power, with the approval of the Texas Senate, to remove persons from boards and commissions whom the governor had personally appointed.[8] But when Richards in 1991 tried to revive interest in giving the governor cabinet-style appointment powers over major state agencies, she met with only limited success.

## The Structure of the Plural Executive

Article 4, Section 1 of the 1876 constitution created the executive branch, which "shall consist of a Governor, who shall be the Chief Executive Officer of the State, a Lieutenant Governor, Secretary of State, Comptroller of Public Accounts, Treasurer, Commissioner of the General Land Office, and Attorney General." Added to the executive branch later were the Agriculture Commissioner, the three-member Railroad Commission and the 15-member State Board of Education. Only the Secretary of State is appointed by the governor. Members of the education board are elected from districts, while the other officeholders are elected statewide. The constitution requires most of these officials to be at least 30 years old and a resident of Texas for at least five years.[9]

The agencies headed by these elected officials are autonomous and—except for limited budgetary review—independent of the governor's control. In a confrontation with the governor over policy matters, the agency heads can claim an electoral mandate just as the governor can. Writing in 1964, Fred Gantt concluded that there had been only "scattered incidents of hostility within the executive branch" and said that generally "elected officials have cooperated remarkably well with their chief executives."[10] Gantt's observations were based on a period in which Texas was a one-party Democratic state. While there was a liberal wing of the Democratic party, party politics were dominated by conservatives, and their interests were generally reflected by statewide elected officials. Most potential institutional conflicts were subordinated to political interests, and it was usually in the self-interest of the various elected officials to cooperate.

But the potential for conflict between the governor and other executive officials increased as Texas became a two-party state, and conflict is likely to become commonplace in the future, even between officials within the same party. During Republican Governor Bill Clements' first term, the other elected officers in the executive branch were Democrats, including Attorney General Mark White, who frequently feuded with the governor and jockeyed for the political advantage that allowed him to unseat Clements in 1982.

Democrat Jim Mattox also used the attorney general's office, which he held from 1983 to 1991, to prepare for a gubernatorial race. There was frequent speculation that some of his official actions were designed to increase his name identification and position himself on popular issues at the expense of Governor White, a fellow Democrat, and then Governor Clements, who returned to office in 1987.

There also can be conflict between any members of the executive branch. In 1991, for example, Lt. Governor Bob Bullock and Attorney General Dan Morales went head to head over the issue of who would serve as legal counsel to the state in the redistricting process.

One may argue that the effect of the plural executive on state politics and the governor's control of the executive branch is minimal because, for the most part, conflict among these elected officials still appears to be minimal. But one may also argue that the governor, in an effort to avoid conflict with officials over whom he or she has no control, pursues policies that are not likely to be disruptive, innovative, or responsive to pressing contemporary issues.

In contemporary state and national government, there is a tendency to look to the chief executive for policy initiatives. If those holding office in a plural executive system have sharply different or competing agendas, it is difficult to develop coordinated policies. But proponents of the plural executive contend that it does what it was intended to do: control and constrain the governor. While collegial or collective decision-making is often inefficient and potentially leads to deadlock, the advocates of the plural executive contend that democracy, in most instances, is to be preferred over efficiency.

## The Governor of Texas in a Comparative Perspective

For more than 30 years, scholars have ranked the various state governors on the basis of formal constitutional and legal powers, such as budgetary authority, appointment and veto powers and term limitations. And from the earliest to the latest studies, the governor of Texas has ranked consistently with the weakest state governors.[11] Even when the measure is expanded to include additional institutional and political variables, the Texas governor ranks with the weakest of them (Table 9-1).[12]

## OFFICES OF THE EXECUTIVE BRANCH

### The Lieutenant Governor

The lieutenant governor is the second highest ranking official in the state, but the executive powers of this office are limited. Were the governor to die, be in-

**TABLE 9–1**  The Institutional Powers of the Governorship 1990

| Very Weak | | | Weak | | | Moderate | | | Strong | | | Very Strong | | | |
|---|---|---|---|---|---|---|---|---|---|---|---|---|---|---|---|
| 14 | 15 | 16 | 17 | 18 | 19 | 20 | 21 | 22 | 23 | 24 | 25 | 26 | 27 | 28 | 29 |
|  | RI | TX | NC | NH | AL | IN | AZ | CA | AK | AR | MN | NY | MA |  | MD |
|  |  |  |  | SC | ME |  | FL | CO | DE | CT |  |  | WV |  |  |
|  |  |  |  | VT | NV |  | ID | GA | IL | HI |  |  |  |  |  |
|  |  |  |  |  | NM |  | KY | MS | IA | KS |  |  |  |  |  |
|  |  |  |  |  | OK |  | MO | MT | LA | NE |  |  |  |  |  |
|  |  |  |  |  |  |  |  | WA | MI | NJ |  |  |  |  |  |
|  |  |  |  |  |  |  |  | WI | ND | OR |  |  |  |  |  |
|  |  |  |  |  |  |  |  | WY | OH | TN |  |  |  |  |  |
|  |  |  |  |  |  |  |  |  | PA | UT |  |  |  |  |  |
|  |  |  |  |  |  |  |  |  | SD |  |  |  |  |  |  |
|  |  |  |  |  |  |  |  |  | VA |  |  |  |  |  |  |

Source:  From "Governors" by Thad L. Beyle in *Politics in the American States: A Comparative Analysis* edited by Virginia Gray, et al. Copyright © 1990 by Virginia Gray, Herbert Jacob, and Robert B. Albritton. Reprinted by permission of HarperCollins Publishers.

capacitated, or removed from office, the lieutenant governor would become governor, but that eventuality has occurred only three times since 1900. In 1917, William P. Hobby replaced James E. Ferguson, who was impeached. Governor W. Lee O'Daniel resigned in 1941 to enter the United States Senate and was succeeded by Coke Stevenson. And Governor Beauford Jester died in office in 1949 and was replaced by Allan Shivers. The fact that the lieutenant governor is only a heartbeat away from the governor's office has little of the significance of the relationship of the vice president to the president of the United States.

From a political perspective, a governor could run with a lieutenant governor on an unofficial "ticket" and incorporate the lieutenant governor into the administration. But historically, the governor and the lieutenant governor, while usually members of the same party, often came from different factions and were potential political adversaries.

In Texas, the office of lieutenant governor primarily is a legislative office. The lieutenant governor is the presiding officer of the Senate and, as such, is given enormous power over the legislative process by the Senate rules (See Chapter 8). His legislative powers and prerogatives far exceed those of the vice president on the federal level. Many experts consider the lieutenant governor, because of his key legislative role and statewide constituency, one of the most powerful officeholders in state government. In addition to presiding over the Senate, he also chairs the Legislative Budget Board, which plays a key role in the state budgetary process. Bill Hobby, son of the former governor, served a record 18 years as lieutenant governor and was an influential state leader before retiring in 1991. He was succeeded by Bob Bullock, a former state comptroller. From early indications, Bullock's perceptions of the office and his role were markedly different from

Hobby's but, like Hobby, he apparently viewed himself as primarily a legislative, rather than an executive, leader.

## The Attorney General

The attorney general is the state's chief legal officer and represents the state in litigation. This office is called upon to defend state laws enacted by the legislature and orders adopted by regulatory and environmental protection agencies. It also is responsible for enforcing the state's antitrust and consumer protection laws. Recent attorneys general also have been kept busy defending the state or negotiating settlements in federal and state court actions challenging the constitutionality of state prisons, the public school finance system, the method of selecting state judges, and other major policies. Unlike his counterparts in the federal government and some other states, the Texas attorney general is primarily a civil lawyer. Except for representing the state in the appeals of death penalty cases and assisting local prosecutors in certain other cases, he has virtually no responsibility for criminal law enforcement. Many candidates for the office like to campaign on tough law and order platforms, but responsibilities for criminal prosecution are vested in locally elected county and district attorneys (see Chapter 12).

The attorney general, who also gives advisory opinions on the legality of actions of other state and local institutions, is at the center of the policymaking process.[13]

In 1990, Attorney General Jim Mattox used an advisory opinion to drop a bombshell on Governor Bill Clements, the legislature, and numerous state agencies. Reversing opinions by his predecessors, Mattox ruled that 163 board and commission members who had been appointed since the 1989 regular legislative session were holding their positions illegally because they had not been confirmed by the Senate during the first special session after their appointments. The opinion cast a legal cloud over the validity of thousands of governmental decisions and temporarily threw state government into a turmoil.[14] A compromise was negotiated to protect the appointments and amend the constitution to clarify the timing of confirmations, but the event demonstrated the political power of the attorney general's office.

Three recent attorneys general—John Hill, Mark White, and Mattox—have attempted to use the influence and visibility of the office to advance to the governorship. Hill won the Democratic gubernatorial nomination in 1978 but lost to Bill Clements in the general election. White was elected governor in 1982, but Mattox lost in a Democratic runoff to Ann Richards in 1990.

Dan Morales, a Democratic state representative from San Antonio, was elected attorney general in 1990 and, in the process, became the second Hispanic elected to statewide office in Texas (Figure 9-2).

## The Comptroller of Public Accounts

The comptroller is the state's primary tax administrator and accounting officer. During his tenure (1975-1991), Bob Bullock modernized this office with the intro-

**FIGURE 9-2** Attorney General Dan Morales announces the filing of an antitrust lawsuit against manufacturers of infant formula. At left is Assistant Attorney General James Mullenix. (Office of the Attorney General of Texas)

duction of state-of-the-art computer and accounting technology and reduced tax delinquency, expedited the processing of checks and aggressively pursued the collection of out of state taxes.[15]

Texas functions under a **pay as you go** principle, which means that the state cannot borrow money for its current operating budget. Unlike the federal government, the Texas legislature cannot adopt a budget that exceeds anticipated revenue. The comptroller is responsible for providing the revenue estimates on which biennial state budgets are drafted, and a budget can't become law without the comptroller's certification that it falls within his official revenue projection. The comptroller's office produces a revenue estimate of all projected state income for the two-year budget period by using sophisticated models of the state's economy.[16] If the revenue estimate is below the legislature's budget proposals, appropriations must be reduced or taxes must be raised. In a volatile, changing economy, it is often difficult to accurately project revenues two years in the future, and in the mid-1980s Bullock had to adjust his revenue estimate downward several times to account for plunging oil prices.

The comptroller's powerful role in budgetary affairs was supplemented by the legislature in 1990 with the additional authority to conduct management audits of local school districts and again in 1991 with similar oversight authority over other state agencies. Reacting to a large revenue shortfall, the legislature in 1991 authorized Bullock's successor, John Sharp, to conduct intensive performance audits of state programs, which resulted in a limited financial and structural reorganization of the executive branch (Figure 9-3).

## The State Treasurer

The state treasurer is the custodian of state funds. Revenues received by the state are administered by this office and placed in financial institutions until they are needed to pay the state's bills. The treasurer and the State Depository Board can increase state revenues through the careful choice of financial institutions with higher interest rates. For years, the state had surpluses in its various accounts, but after the economy turned sour in the 1980s, cash flow shortages have been a periodic problem. The legislature has to pass a balanced budget, but sometimes there may not be enough money on hand on a particular day to cover all the state's bills. The treasurer plays a key role in taking steps to resolve that problem, including the issuance of cash management notes to raise short-term cash from investors. Republican Kay Bailey Hutchison was elected to the office in 1990 (Figure 9-4).

**FIGURE 9-3**   Comptroller John Sharp, at the podium, announces the results of his performance audits of state agencies in 1991. Listening are Governor Ann Richards, other state officials, and his team of auditors. (State Comptroller of Public Accounts)

**FIGURE 9-4**   State Treasurer Kay Bailey Hutchison inspects a cache of unclaimed coins discovered in a safe deposit box.  Her office helped locate the owner.  (Office of the Texas Treasury)

## Commissioner of the General Land Office

When Texas became a state, it retained ownership of its public lands. Much of that land has since been sold to individuals or corporations, but the state still retains ownership, including the mineral rights, to approximately 22 million acres, which are managed by the state land commissioner. Revenues generated by mineral leases and other uses of the public lands are earmarked for education through the Permanent University Fund and the Permanent School Fund. This agency also is responsible for the Veterans Land Program, which provides low interest loans to veterans for the purchase of land and houses.

In recent years, Democratic Land Commissioner Garry Mauro has developed environmental programs, including concentrated beach cleanup efforts. And the legislature in 1991 gave the land office the responsibility of administering a new comprehensive program for cleaning up oil spills off the Texas coast.

## Commissioner of Agriculture

This office, created by statute rather than by the constitution, is responsible for the implementation of laws regulating and benefiting the agricultural sector of the state's economy. In addition to providing support for agricultural research and education, the agency also is responsible for the administration of select consumer protection laws in the areas of weights and measures, packaging and labeling, and marketing. Former Agriculture Commissioner Jim Hightower, a Democrat who held the office for eight years before being unseated by Republican Rick Perry in 1990 (Figure 9-5), aggressively pursued strong regulation of herbicide and pesticide use and attempted to establish safety and health programs to protect farm laborers.

**FIGURE 9-5**
Agriculture Commissioner Rick Perry (right) inspects a crop of peanuts with Lee County extension agents. (Texas Department of Agriculture)

## Secretary of State

The secretary of state, the only constitutional official appointed by the governor, has a variety of duties, including granting charters to corporations and processing the extradition of prisoners to other states. The primary function of this office, however, is to administer state election laws. That responsibility includes reviewing county and local election procedures, developing statewide policy for voter registration, and receiving and tabulating election returns. For many years, this office also registered lobbyists, maintained lobby expenditure reports, and was the custodian of campaign finance reports and personal financial disclosure statements of officeholders. But these duties were transferred to the new state Ethics Commission in 1992.

## Elected Boards and Commissions

*The Texas Railroad Commission.* This body was originally designed to regulate intrastate (within Texas) operations of railroads, but as the federal commerce clause was expanded by court interpretation and legislation, many of its original functions were taken over by the federal government. It does, however, regulate intrastate trucking and bus service and oil and natural gas production in Texas.

The commission includes three members who serve for staggered six-year terms and rotate the chairmanship among themselves. As might be expected, the oil and gas industry has historically focused much attention and political support on this agency, given its powers in controlling and regulating energy production in the state. The commission is charged with balancing energy supply, market demand, and conservation. After the discovery of the East Texas oil fields in the 1930s, the uncontrolled exploration for oil resulted in prices dropping to 10 cents a barrel. Major producers convinced the commission to stabilize prices and supply by limiting production. Many of the agency's critics have claimed it is a prime example of a regulatory body that has been co-opted by those interests it was created to regulate.

In 1991, Governor Richards appointed state Representative Lena Guerrero of Austin to the commission to replace John Sharp, who had resigned after being elected comptroller. Guerrero, who had to run for election in 1992 to retain the seat, was the first woman and non-Anglo to serve on the regulatory body.[17]

*The State Board of Education.* Since the early settlers declared their independence from Mexico, public education has been a major policy issue in Texas, and in recent years it probably has attracted more attention than ever before. The debate has focused not only on educational quality and financing, but also on how best to implement and manage public education programs. The state has bounced back and forth between an elected state education board and an appointed one.

Prior to the educational reforms implemented in 1984 under House Bill 72, the State Board of Education included 27 members elected from congressional districts across the state. At the urging of reformers dissatisfied with student performance, the legislature provided in House Bill 72 for a new education board of 15 members to be appointed by the governor and confirmed by the Senate. The idea was to reduce the board's independence while new education reforms ordered by the legislature were being carried out. But the law also provided that the board would again become an elected body within a few years. Some state leaders later proposed that the board remain appointive and put the question to the voters, who opted for an elected board in 1986. The present education board includes 15 members elected from districts established by the legislature and oversees an area of public policy that accounts for a large percentage of the state's budget.

The day-to-day administration of the Texas Education Agency, the agency responsible for public education, is under the direction of the commissioner of education, a person nominated by the State Board of Education and appointed by the governor. The governor was given the appointment power under a 1990 law. Previously, education commissioners were hired and fired by the education board.[18]

## THE QUALIFICATIONS OF THE GOVERNOR

The constitution has few requirements for a person who desires to run for governor. A governor must be at least 30 years old, a United States citizen, and a resident of Texas for at least five years. There also is a vague requirement that no individual can be excluded from office for his religious beliefs "provided he acknowledges the existence of a Supreme Being."[19] The constitution, however, doesn't spell out all the roadblocks to winning the office.

Until the election of Bill Clements in 1978, for example, every governor since 1874 had been a Democrat. Clements served two terms (1979-1983 and 1987-1991) and, with the development of a two-party system in Texas, additional Republicans can be expected to be elected to the office in the future.

The majority of governors have been white males who were Protestants, well-educated, middle-aged, and affluent. In many cases, their families also were active in public life and helped shape their careers. No minorities and only two women have been elected to the office. Miriam A. (Ma) Ferguson, whose husband, James E. (Pa) Ferguson, had earlier been governor, served two terms (1925-1927 and 1933-1935), and Ann Richards was elected to the state's top office in 1990. (By 1990, only three women have ever been elected to any other statewide executive offices in Texas. Richards served two terms as state treasurer and was succeeded by Kay Bailey Hutchison. From 1919 to 1923, Annie Webb Blanton was state superintendent of schools.)

Statewide political campaigns are costing more and more money each election year (see Chapter 7). Access to financial resources or the ability to raise large sums of money to run an effective campaign have taken on increased importance. Otherwise qualified prospects are dissuaded from running for governor and other offices because of the difficult and grueling burden of fund-raising. Former Governor Bill Clements and fellow Republican Clayton Williams, a Midland businessman who lost the 1990 gubernatorial race to Richards, spent millions of dollars out of their own pockets in their first election bids, although neither had previously held elective office. This raises the possibility that personal wealth and the willingness to spend it on one's election campaign will take on more importance in future races.

Modern campaigns are increasingly shaped by the mass media, particularly television, and media-driven campaigns usually are concerned more with image than substance. Several candidates have had difficulty utilizing or exploiting the mass media to their advantage, and candidates—no matter how qualified—who do not understand the electronic media are likely to be rebuffed in their efforts to win major statewide office.

Just as there are career patterns in business and industry, there have been general career patterns that have led to the governor's office. As might be expected, previous public service has provided a gubernatorial aspirant with public visibility and linkages to party leaders, interest groups, and public officials around the state. Such relationships help a candidate develop broader electoral support. Texas governors have previously served in local and statewide offices, the legislature, and Congress. Preston Smith (1969-1973) was a legislator and lieutenant governor prior to being elected governor. Dolph Briscoe (1973-1979) also served in the legislature. Mark White (1983-1987) served as secretary of state and then attorney general, and Ann Richards was a county commissioner and then state treasurer. Although he had never previously held elective office, Clements was a deputy United States secretary of defense prior to winning his first gubernatorial race.

## IMPEACHMENT AND INCAPACITATION

A governor can be removed from office through impeachment proceedings initiated in the House of Representatives and conviction by the Senate in a trial of the impeachment charges. Texas is one of only a few states that have removed a governor with this procedure. The administration of James E. "Pa" Ferguson was marked by a controversy that erupted in 1917 over the governor's efforts to remove five University of Texas faculty members. The governor vetoed the UT appropriations, and when he called a special legislative session to consider other appropriations, he was immediately faced with articles of impeachment based primarily on the misuse of public funds. He ultimately was convicted and removed from office. For two more decades, the husband and wife team of Ma and Pa Ferguson and the controversy that continued to surround them dominated a great deal of Texas politics.[20]

If the governor dies or is incapacitated, the lieutenant governor replaces the governor until the next general election. In instances when the governor leaves the state, the lieutenant governor serves as acting governor. After World War II, when there was general concern that a nuclear attack on the United States might simultaneously eliminate a large number of public officials, a law was enacted which included 17 officeholders in the line of gubernatorial succession.

## THE SALARY AND "PERKS" OF THE OFFICE

As noted earlier, the salary of the governor is now established by the legislature. In 1990, the latest year for which comparative data were available, the governor of Texas was the eighth highest paid chief executive among the states with a salary of $93,432. The state also provides the governor with a mansion and staff to maintain it, travel expenses, and access to state-owned planes and cars.

## THE POWERS OF THE GOVERNOR

There are competing views of the function of the chief executive, and these views have changed over time. Early state constitutions limited gubernatorial powers, and governors in many states found themselves in a subordinate position to their legislatures. Throughout the 19th century, those relationships were often redefined. At times, the governors' powers were increased and those of the legislatures reduced. During other periods, such as the era of Jacksonian democracy, the powers of both institutions were subjected to strong restrictions and control to assure greater representation and responsiveness to the public. Reform movements of the early 20th century, responding to political corruption and non-responsiveness, focused on management and efficiency in the governors' offices; in some states, the office of governor was restructured around the organizational principles of an executive cabinet. Events such as the Great Depression contributed to a further redefinition of executive leadership with an emphasis in some states on policy initiatives, administrative control and coordination, and expanded political leadership.[21] The Texas Constitution of 1845, adopted when the state was admitted to the Union, modeled the governor's authority on the strong executive principle found in the United States Constitution, but every successive Texas constitution reduced the powers of the office, reflecting apprehension of strong executive and political authority.

Yet Texans appear to have high expectations of their governors. Ultimately, governors are evaluated in terms of their policy agendas and the leadership they exercise in achieving those goals. But how does a governor meet such expectations when the formal powers of the office are limited? The following discussion analyzes the formal powers and reviews the informal resources that are available to the governor to complement them. The adroit exploitation of political resources explains gubernatorial successes despite the institutional weakness of the office.

### Legislative Powers

The governor has the opportunity to clearly outline his or her legislative priorities at the beginning of each biennial regular session through the traditional "state of the state" address to the legislature. The governor also can communicate with lawmakers—collectively or individually, in person, through written messages, or through intermediaries—throughout the session. In this fashion, the governor can establish a policy agenda, recommend specific legislation, and set the stage for negotiations with legislative leaders, other state officials, and interest groups. The governor's addresses and other formal messages to the legislature are well covered by the media, which affords the governor the opportunity to also mobilize the public support that may be essential to the success of his or her initiatives.

The governor's effectiveness as a negotiator and salesperson can be enhanced by the office's two major constitutional powers over the legislature—the veto and the authority to call and set the agenda for special legislative sessions.

The complex needs of a major, industrialized state and heightened partisan differences over such critical issues as budget and tax policies have made it more and more difficult for the legislature to complete its work during regular sessions, which are held for 140 days every other year. The 71st legislature held six special sessions in 1989 and 1990, and the 72nd legislature held two special sessions after its regular session in 1991. The governor can call the legislature into any number of special sessions that can last as long as 30 days each and designate the subjects to be considered during each one.

Sometimes, the mere threat of a special session can be enough to convince reluctant lawmakers to approve a priority program of the governor or reach an acceptable compromise during a regular session. Most legislators, who are paid only part-time salaries by the state, dread special sessions because they interfere with their regular occupations and professions and become a financial burden. They also further disrupt a lawmaker's family life. Governor Bill Clements, who called two special sessions on workers' compensation reform in 1989, used the threat of a third to finally convince a handful of senators to break a year-long impasse and approve legislation backed by the governor, a majority of the House, and the business community.

There also are risks in calling special sessions. The governor's influence and reputation are on the line, and further inaction by the legislature can become a political liability or embarrassment. There also have been instances when the legislative leadership has liberally interpreted the subject matter of a governor's special session proclamation and considered bills not sought by the governor. Since the speaker and the lieutenant governor make the parliamentary rulings that determine whether a specific piece of legislation falls within the governor's call, the governor has to carefully draft a proclamation setting a special session's agenda. Once a special session is called, the governor can increase his or her bargaining power by adding legislators' pet bills to the agenda in exchange for the lawmakers' support of the governor's program.

The governor of Texas has one of the strongest veto powers of any governor. While the legislature is in session, the governor has 10 days to veto a bill or let it become law without his or her signature. A veto can be overridden by a two-thirds vote of both the House and the Senate. During the past 50 years, Governor Clements was the only governor to have a veto overridden. It was a local bill related to game management that the Democrat-dominated legislature voted to override during the Republican governor's first term. The governor has 20 days after the legislature adjourns to veto bills passed in the closing days of a session. Such vetoes are absolute because the only way the legislature can respond is to have the bill reintroduced in the next session.

The governor also has line item veto authority over the state budget. That is, the governor can strike specific spending items that he or she considers objectionable without vetoing the entire bill. This power applies only to the budget, which also is known as the general appropriations bill. All other bills have to be accepted or rejected in their entirety by the governor.

Historic records on gubernatorial vetoes are not complete, but Dan Moody apparently was one of the more frequent veto users. He vetoed 117 bills and resolutions during four years in office from 1927-1931. Governor Richards vetoed 36 bills and resolutions, the lowest number in 10 years, in one regular and two special sessions in 1991. She allowed 228 bills out of 959 to become law without her signature, and gave few explanations for her actions. A governor may veto a bill for a number of reasons, including doubts about a bill's constitutionality, its wording, the possibility that it duplicates existing law, or because of substantive policy differences. A governor's threat of a veto often is as effective as an actual veto because such threats usually prompt legislative sponsors to make changes in their bills to meet a governor's objections.

## Budgetary Powers

The state budget is the primary instrument for policy coordination, but the governor of Texas has weaker budgetary authority than the governors of most states and the president of the United States. Since successful policy initiatives depend on funding, the budget constraints facing the governor limit the governor's ability to develop a comprehensive legislative program. The budgetary process will be discussed in more detail in Chapter 13, but the legislature has the lead in budget-setting with a major role played by the Legislative Budget Board, or LBB, a 10-member panel that includes the lieutenant governor, the speaker, and eight key lawmakers. The LBB and the governor's office both make budgetary recommendations to the legislature, but lawmakers will give greater attention to the LBB's product. There have been instances when the legislature rejected the governor's budget out of hand and virtually excluded the governor from the budgetary process. But when the governor and the legislature share similar policy goals, there can be considerable cooperation on budgetary matters.

As discussed above, the governor does have line-item veto authority over the budget, a power that the president doesn't have on the federal level. But in recent years, the legislature has restricted the use of the line-item veto by making more lump sum appropriations to agencies and giving agency heads more discretion in how to allocate the money among specific programs.

Under a constitutional amendment adopted in 1985, the governor shares limited budget execution authority with the Legislative Budget Board. To meet emergencies between legislative sessions, the governor can propose the transfer of funds between programs or agencies, and the LBB can modify or reject the governor's proposal.

## Appointive and Removal Powers

One indication of a strong governor is the power to hire and fire the persons responsible for implementing public policy. But as we discussed earlier in this chapter, the Texas governor's administrative authority is severely limited by the plural executive structure under which independently elected officeholders head several major state agencies.

Most of the remainder of the state bureaucracy falls under more than 200 boards and commissions that oversee various agencies created by statute. Most of these are part-time, unpaid positions whose occupants are heavily dependent on agency staffs and constituents for guidance. This hydra-headed structure reflects the convergence of several theories of administrative organization, but the ultimate consequence is to further fragment policy management and implementation. Although members of those boards are appointed by the governor and confirmed by the Senate, the structure creates the potential for boards and commissions to become captives of the narrow constituencies they are serving and reduces their accountability to both the governor and the legislature.

Most board members serve six-year **staggered terms**. That means it takes a new governor two or three years to get majorities favoring the governor's policies on most boards. Resignations or deaths of board members may speed up the process, but a governor can't remove a predecessor's appointees. A governor, with the approval of two-thirds of the Senate, can fire only his or her own appointees.

At the beginning of her administration in 1991, Governor Ann Richards used public pressure to prompt the early resignation of a Clements' holdover appointee and gain a majority on the three-member State Board of Insurance. (The term of a second board member had expired soon after Richards took office.) Richards, who had made insurance reform a key issue in her 1990 campaign, went so far as to threaten to have legislative leaders put the insurance agency in conservatorship if holdover appointees didn't step down.[22] Richards also attacked the Department of Commerce over questionable spending and forced the resignation of that agency's executive director.

Richards continued her campaign for more "accountability" over the bureaucracy by also asking the legislature in a 1991 special session to give her the power to directly appoint the executive directors of state agencies. Those officials historically had been hired by the various boards and commissions. In reorganizing a handful of agencies, the legislature gave the governor a small taste of the cabinet-style authority she had sought. The governor was given the authority to appoint a new commissioner, or "czar," to oversee several health and human service agencies, the new executive director of the Department of Commerce, and the executive director of a new Department of Housing and Community Affairs. The governor also retained her previous authority to appoint the secretary of state, the adjutant general, and the director of the Office of State-Federal Relations.

The governor appoints individuals to boards and commissions with approval of two-thirds of the Senate. **Senatorial courtesy**, an unwritten norm of the Senate, permits a senator to block the governor's nomination of a person who lives in that senator's district. The governor and staff members involved in appointments spend considerable time clearing potential nominees with senators because political considerations are as important in the confirmation process as a nominee's qualifications.

All across the state, there are individuals who, for a variety of reasons, seek gubernatorial appointments. The appointments process coordinated by the governor's appointments secretary, or assistant, is particularly hectic at the beginning of a governor's administration. As the campaign of a successful candidate is dismantled and the transition team takes over, there are immediate requirements to identify upcoming appointments available to the governor and, just as crucial, to identify individuals who are available, competent, politically acceptable, and supported by key interest groups. And while most governors would deny it, campaign contributions are a significant factor in board appointments. A number of Governor Clements' appointees had made substantial contributions to his campaign.[23] Richards likewise appointed several major contributors to important posts. One of Richard's most controversial appointments was that of Beaumont attorney Walter Umphrey to the Texas Parks and Wildlife Commission. Umphrey had ties to a company with a poor environmental record, but he had been the single biggest contributor to Richards' gubernatorial campaign and actively sought the parks and wildlife post. He and his law firm's political action committee had either donated or loaned Richards $350,000.

In recent years, there also has been a great deal of political symbolism associated with governmental appointments, and Richards has been particularly sensitive to constituencies that historically have been excluded from full participation in the governmental process. Thus many of her appointees have been women and minorities.

In addition to making administrative appointments, the governor appoints individuals to fill vacancies on all courts at the district level or above. If a United States senator dies or resigns, the governor appoints a replacement. When a vacancy occurs in another statewide office except for the lieutenant governor, the governor also appoints a replacement. All of these appointees must latter win election to keep their seats.

## Judicial Powers

The State of Texas has an 18-member Board of Pardons and Paroles which is appointed by the governor. This board decides when prisoners can be released early, and their decisions do not require action by the governor.[24]

The governor, however, does have the authority to grant executive clemency, acts of leniency or mercy, toward convicted criminals. One is a 30-day stay of execution for a condemned murderer which a governor can grant without a recommendation of the parole board. The governor, on recommendation of the board, can grant a full pardon to a criminal, a conditional pardon, or the commutation of a death sentence to life imprisonment.[25]

Over the years, some governors have been accused by their opponents of abusing these powers. These charges were particularly prevalent during the administrations of Ma and Pa Ferguson. The Board of Pardons and Paroles was created, in part, to reduce the powers of the governor in granting clemency.[26] In the future, particularly since the Republicans used executive clemency as an effective campaign issue against Democratic nominee Michael Dukakis in the 1988 presidential race, Texas governors are likely to take pains to avoid any suggestion that they are soft on criminals.

If a person flees a state to avoid prosecution or a prison term, the United States Constitution, under the rendition clause, requires that person, upon arrest in another state, to be returned to the state from which he or she fled. The governor is legally responsible for ordering state officials to carry out such extradition requests.[27]

### Military Powers

The Texas Constitution authorizes the governor to function as the "commander-in-chief of the military force of the state, except when they are called into actual service of the United States."[28]   The governor appoints the adjutant general, who is responsible for the administration and implementation of this duty. Texas can't declare war on another country, and the president has the primary responsibility for national defense and protecting the country against foreign invasion. But when riots or natural disasters occur within the state, the governor can mobilize the Texas National Guard to protect lives and property and keep the peace. Should the United States go to war, the National Guard can be mobilized by the president as part of the national military forces. Although the "Desert Shield" and "Desert Storm" military operations against Iraq in the Persian Gulf in 1990-91 weren't part of an official declared war, a number of Texas National Guard units were called into active duty by the president and sent overseas.

### INFORMAL RESOURCES OF THE GOVERNOR

Governors can compensate for some of the constitutional limitations on their office through such resources as their perceptions of problems and issues, their leadership capabilities, their personalities, their work habits, and their administrative styles. Some governors want to get involved in the minutiae of building policy coalitions, and they are willing to give a great deal of their personal time to effecting compromises and agreements. Other governors find such hands-on involvement distasteful, inefficient, and time-consuming and leave such detail work to subordinates.

The governor's position as the single most visible state official can be both a blessing and a curse to the occupant of the office. The governor sometimes gets credit that may belong to others but can just as readily be blamed for problems beyond his or her jurisdiction or control. A major factor, for example, in Mark White's loss of his 1986 re-election bid was falling oil prices that had devastated the state's economy earlier the same year. White had no choice but to call a special legislative session only a few months before the November election and, under the circumstances, probably exercised the best leadership that he could in convincing lawmakers to cut the budget and raise taxes. But it was the type of leadership that wasn't appreciated by most voters.

## The Governor's Staff

Nineteenth-century governors had only three or four individuals to assist them in carrying out their responsibilities, but with the increased complexity of state government and increased demands on the governor's time, successive governors obtained budget authorization to expand their staffs. By 1963, under John Connally, the governor's staff had grown to 68 full-time and 12 part-time employees.[29] Under the administration of Dolph Briscoe in the 1970s, the staff had further expanded to more than 300, but in subsequent administrations, staff sizes leveled off to about 200 people.

The staff's organization reflects the governor's leadership style. Some governors create a highly centralized office with a chief of staff who functions to screen contacts and information going to the governor. Other governors want greater personal contacts with numerous staff members. However the governor structures the staff, the critical question is whether the governor is getting sufficient information upon which to make decisions that produce good public policy and minimize the potential for unforeseen controversy, conflict, or embarrassment. Under ideal circumstances, the staff enhances the governor's political, administrative, and policy-making capabilities. There have been instances, though, when a governor has permitted his staff to insulate him by denying access to persons with significant information or recommendations.

Governors generally choose staffers who are loyal and share the governor's basic political attitudes. A great deal of staff functions are political, and it stands to reason that governors select persons whom they believe to understand the complexities of the political process and the governor's view of it and are not likely to embarrass the governor by committing obvious political errors. Since communications with the governor's various constituencies are fundamental to success, some staffers also are chosen for their skills in mass communications and public relations. Other staffers are hired for their knowledge and skills in specific public policy areas.[30] In many respects, staff members function as the governor's surrogates. That means if one makes a mistake, particularly a serious mistake, the public will perceive it as the governor's error.

A governor needs information to make decisions, and the staff functions to collect, organize, and screen relevant information. People—legislators, agency administrators, lobbyists, reporters, and members of the general public—want to talk to the governor, and the staff schedules the governor's time. Contemporary politics are media oriented, and the governor's office spends considerable time orchestrating events that are deemed newsworthy.

Finally, staffers work on strategies to garner support for the governor's proposals from legislators, agencies, and interest groups. Since the governor often lacks the time to conduct discussions and negotiations, key staff members represent the governor in such meetings and in personal lobbying of lawmakers. Sometimes, the governor gets involved personally, particularly if his or her participation is needed to break an impasse and effect a solution.[31]

## The Governor and the Mass Media

The mass media helps shape the political and policy options of the governor. And governors, as well as gubernatorial candidates such as Clayton Williams, the unsuccessful 1990 Republican nominee, who have failed to understand the impact of the mass media often have courted disaster. A governor who is readily accessible to the media and understands the working constraints under which the media operates is likely to develop a good working relationship with the press. But success with the media is more than being accessible and friendly.

Governors call press conferences to announce new policies or explain their positions on pending issues. They stage pseudo-news events, such as visiting a classroom to emphasize concern for educational quality or an industrial plant to demonstrate a commitment to economic development. They or their staffers sometimes leak information to selected reporters to embarrass the opposition, to put an action of the administration in the best possible light, or to float a trial balloon to gauge legislative or public reaction to a proposal. Some governors have purchased radio or television time to try to mobilize public opinion in support of pet proposals that are failing in the legislature. Overall, the timely use of the media can contribute significantly to the power and influence of a governor.

Periodic statewide public opinion polls, which have taken on increased importance in state politics, often include questions about the governor's performance. Those ratings are considered an indirect measure of the governor's support among the electorate and are widely monitored by a variety of players in the political arena.

## The Governor and the Political Party

One of the functions of a political party is to build sustainable coalitions for the support of public policy. The historic political factions within one-party Democratic Texas were somewhat ill-defined. Factionalism was often described in terms of liberal or conservative, but within these general categories were complex urban-rural, regional, and economic interests. Democratic governors built policy coalitions around these factions, but there was little stability or continuity. While some governors could claim wider support than others, most governors derived only limited power from their position as party leader.

With the emerging two-party system, however, political parties are taking on more importance, and there are indications that the party will provide a greater resource to the governor. During his second term, Bill Clements, for example, had a sufficient number of Republican votes in the House to thwart the will of the Democratic majority, particularly during the 1990 special sessions over school finance reform. Assuming that the Republican party gains additional seats in future legislatures, there is likely to be a pattern of greater party cohesion and less bipartisan voting. As this takes place, a governor of either party will attempt to use the party to garner support for his or her legislative program.

### The Governor and Interest Groups

Successful governors seem to be consummate political animals who continually nurture relationships throughout the political system. A gubernatorial candidate aggressively solicits the endorsements and contributions of groups and organizations throughout the state. These groups, in turn, develop a stake in the governor's election and usually assume that the candidates they support will be responsive to their interests. A governor's policy initiatives can be expected to include legislation of benefit to key support groups, and these groups will maintain an active role throughout the policy process.

## LEADERSHIP STYLES OF RECENT TEXAS GOVERNORS

Gubernatorial leadership styles have been as varied as the personalities that molded the chief executives' approaches to their jobs. While the formal constitutional powers of the governor have changed little over the years, there have been significant policy and political differences among holders of the office.

Some governors have come to the office with a well-defined policy agenda, which they were prepared to pursue aggressively. While they were often hampered by the reactions of other elected officials and interest groups, these activist governors attempted to exploit every resource available to them. Other governors have appeared to take a more limited view of the office and/or their responsibilities to initiate new programs. They preferred to take an administrative or managerial view of the office while leaving policy initiatives to other institutions or elected officials. New programs, especially those with far-reaching tax or social implications, were pursued with considerable caution.

Some governors have thrived on the constant attention and political and social interactions that center on the office. They have worked long hours, continually engaged in public relations and coalition building. Strange as it may seem, however, there have been other governors who were introverted, even shy, and apparently found many aspects of the office distasteful. They often insulated themselves from the public and other political officials through their staffs and seemed detached from the activities necessary to influence public policy.[32]

## Dolph Briscoe (1973-1979)

Dolph Briscoe (1973-1979), a wealthy rancher-banker from the small southwest Texas town of Uvalde, served eight years in the Texas House in the late 1940s and early 1950s and was best known then for his sponsorship of legislation to build farm-to-market roads, a crucial transportation network for agriculture. After dropping out of politics for several years to concentrate on his ranching and banking interests, Briscoe ran for governor in 1968, finishing fourth in a field of 10 candidates in the Democratic primary. In the wake of the Sharpstown stock fraud scandal that had rocked voter confidence in state leaders, Briscoe ran successfully in 1972 as an "outsider" challenging the stewardship of incumbent politicians. He defeated Governor Preston Smith and Lt. Governor Ben Barnes in the Democratic primary and in the general election defeated Republican state Senator Henry "Hank" Grover of Houston and Ramsey Muñiz, the candidate of the Hispanic La Raza Unida party. Briscoe won re-election in 1974 to become the first Texas governor elected to a four-year term under a constitutional amendment adopted in 1972.

Briscoe favored limited government and made a pledge of "no new taxes" a popular campaign theme for years to come. Unlike his immediate successors, he was able to keep the promise because high oil prices during the 1970s enabled the legislature to balance state budgets without major tax changes. The prison system, however, was deteriorating, disparities in educational opportunities were growing greater between property-poor and wealthy school districts, and Texas was lagging behind virtually every other state in the amount of money it spent on vital health and human services programs. Eventually, the inaction of the 1970s caught up with the state in the 1980s. Federal and state court intervention forced the state to address some of these problems at great cost to taxpayers. Briscoe was not singularly responsible for these subsequent developments—including an oil industry recession that exacerbated the problems—but he and the legislators of his time contributed to the costly dilemmas now confronting the state.

During his two terms, Briscoe's interest in state policy and his involvement in policy planning and implementation were topics of frequent public discussion. Despite expectations of a gubernatorial presence in Austin, Briscoe spent most weekends—and many working days as well—at his ranch near Uvalde. An Associated Press survey of flight logs of the governor's state airplane indicated that Briscoe spent 90 days, including 39 working days, in Uvalde during the first 10 months of 1975, at the beginning of his second term.[33] Briscoe's response to these criticisms indicated that, even as governor, he still considered himself an outsider to state government. "I'm responsible for the office wherever I am, and I think it's important to get out and see people, to get away from the artificial atmosphere which exists in the capital city, and particularly around the Capitol," he said.[34] Briscoe was uncomfortable in the public eye and despite the potential value of the news media to the governor, he held very few news conferences in Austin during his tenure.

Legislators also complained that they had difficulty getting audiences with the governor, even to discuss legislation of importance to him. Representative John Hoestenbach, a conservative Democrat from Odessa, complained that "dealing with Briscoe's office was like trying to deal with Howard Hughes. You were never sure there was a Dolph Briscoe, he was so inaccessible."[35]   While this was a common perception of Briscoe, there were legislators who disagreed. Representative D. R. "Tom" Uher, a conservative Democrat from Bay City who chaired the important House State Affairs Committee during Briscoe's administration, observed years later that he had no trouble getting access to Briscoe. He concluded that the criticisms of Briscoe were due to the perception that the governor was not as dynamic or progressive as some of his detractors would have liked him to be.[36]

Briscoe's leadership was woefully lacking during the single most important event of his administration, the Constitutional Convention of 1974. Except for expressing opposition to some proposals that he believed would further weaken the governor's office, he did nothing to promote modernization of the state's 19th century constitution. Deadlocked over the volatile "right to work" issue, the convention ended in failure, three votes short of the two-thirds vote necessary to submit a new constitution to the electorate. Many observers believed that personal lobbying by the governor could have made a difference with some legislator-delegates to the convention, but Briscoe didn't intervene. The legislature attempted to salvage the convention's work by submitting extensive constitutional amendments to the voters in 1975, but Briscoe actively opposed the entire package, and the voters rejected it.

Associates said Briscoe usually insisted on personally reviewing items of business before taking action— "a characteristic alternately described by supporters as meticulous decision-making and by opponents as inefficient foot-dragging."[37] But when he reappointed a dead man to a minor state board, his reputation as an "absentee governor" was further enhanced, and it raised questions as to how much Briscoe was in control of his office.

Interestingly enough, Briscoe indirectly contributed to the occupancy of the governor's mansion for the 12 years after he left office, a period during which two bitter enemies would take turns as chief executive. The failure of Democratic factions to resolve their personal and ideological conflicts after Briscoe's loss to Attorney General John Hill in a heated party primary in 1978 helped set the stage for Bill Clements to upset Hill in November and become Texas' first Republican governor since Reconstruction. Clements eventually would serve two terms, but they would be interrupted by Democrat Mark White, who had been given his political start by Briscoe.

## Bill Clements (1979-1983, 1987-1991)

Clements, a self-made multimillionaire who had founded an international oil drilling firm, personally funded much of his first campaign in 1978, effectively using a sophisticated media strategy. The man who shocked the Democratic establishment by defeating John Hill by 17,000 votes had held no previous elected office. His only governmental experience had been as deputy secretary of defense under Presidents Nixon and Ford. He was an outsider, a Republican, highly opinionated and blunt, and had a reputation for solid management skills. All the other elected statewide officials were Democrats, as were the vast majority of legislators, although many lawmakers shared his conservative views.

Upon arriving in Austin, Clements did not understand the limitations of the powers of the governor.[38] In his election campaign, he had tapped a rather widely-held view that state government was wasteful and had proposed that 25,000 state jobs be eliminated. He also appealed to popular notions of limited government and proposed that the Texas Constitution be amended to allow private citizens to propose laws through the initiative and referendum process. Although he pushed for these changes in speech after speech, he gradually learned that he couldn't singlehandedly run the statehouse and the bureaucracy the way he had the corporate boardroom. He learned there were enormous constraints on the governor's office, and he didn't accomplish either of those major goals.

In an interview years later, Clements admitted that he didn't fully understand how state government worked when he first took office. "Until I came to Austin and until I actually was in office and everything, I really didn't understand the detailed nuance of how the state government really functioned. I'd say it took me at least through that first legislative session. And by the time that was over, well, I began to understand exactly how the state government works."[39]

In a system of divided government where the governor was a Republican and the legislature was predominantly Democratic, Clements eagerly exercised his veto power. During his first legislative session in 1979, he vetoed a near-record 51 bills.[40] He also freely exercised his line-item veto power over the appropriations bill by striking $252 million from the $20.7 billion state budget for 1980-1981.[41] His veto of a $16 million appropriation for construction of a new prison unit was to haunt him, however, after a federal court declared the overcrowded prison system unconstitutional. That veto was widely criticized by Clements' Democratic opponents as having contributed to the overcrowding problem.

Clements generally received high marks for the quality of his staff and board appointments during his first term. Republicans, who for years had been shut out of appointments to boards and commissions, were appointed by the Republican governor, but Clements also appointed many Democrats, especially conservatives. In part, his appointment strategies were designed to convert conservative Democrats to the Republican party, thus extending and consolidating Republican gains across the state. Clements made many judicial appointments during his two terms, including the first two women to the Texas Supreme Court and the first African-American to the Court of Criminal Appeals.

But Clements never developed effective public relations with the legislature, the news media, and the general public, and he often found himself at odds with other elected officials and interest groups, primarily because of his outspokenness.

He often was portrayed as mean-spirited and insensitive, as someone inclined to "shoot from the lip" and worry about the consequences later. After learning at a meeting at Texas A&M University that scuba diving by a pregnant woman could damage a fetus, he angered many women by saying, in jest, that diving could serve as a form of birth control. After an offshore Mexican oil well blew out and threatened Texas beaches in 1979, Clements advised coastal residents against "crying over spilt milk." The insensitive remark was compounded by revelations that SEDCO, the drilling firm he had founded, had leased the drilling equipment used on the blown-out well.

At the end of his first term in 1982, Clements' job performance rating had dropped, his image had suffered, and the Texas economy had begun to show signs of weakness. A revitalized Democratic statewide political effort organized by United States Senator Lloyd Bentsen and Lt. Governor Bill Hobby helped White unseat Clements in a bitterly fought campaign that Clements wasn't soon to forget.

In 1986, Clements became only the second person in Texas history to regain the governor's office after losing it. And while his motivations for staging a comeback effort weren't totally clear, it was widely believed that his main interest was revenge. His hostility toward White remained so intense that he snubbed White's offer of a handshake on Inauguration Day, a clear violation of the unwritten rules of American politics.

Clements' second administration thus got off to a controversial start, and it went downhill from there. By the time Clements left the governor's office the second time in 1991, he was widely viewed more as an obstructionist who would rather fight the Democratic majority in the legislature than as a leader who was ready to seek solutions to major state problems.

A major distraction at the beginning of Clements' second term was the governor's admission of his involvement in a "pay-for-play" football scandal at Southern Methodist University that prompted the National Collegiate Athletic Association to suspend SMU's intercollegiate football program for two years. Clements didn't initiate the illicit payments to athletes but admitted that, as chairman of SMU's governing board during the period between his two terms as governor, he participated in a decision to let previously approved payments continue.

Clements also spent his first six months back in Austin battling Lt. Governor Bill Hobby and Democratic legislators over the state budget. Clements insisted on deep service cuts that would have enabled him to keep a 1986 campaign promise against higher taxes, but he finally gave in during a summer special session in 1987 and signed a record $5.6 billion tax increase. The public's opinion of Clements, meanwhile, was plummeting. Two-thirds of the respondents to *The Texas Poll* that summer said they disapproved of the governor's job performance.[42] And Clements' negative ratings remained high throughout the remainder of his term.

Clements suffered a stroke in the summer of 1988 at the age of 71. Staffers said he fully recovered, but there later was periodic speculation—much of it coming from Clements' political enemies—that the stroke had further reduced his effective-

ness. During a three-month standoff between the governor and Democratic legislators over school finance reform in 1990, some Democrats even contended that
Clements' then-chief-of-staff Mike Toomey was actually running the governor's
office. Toomey, a tight-fisted, former Republican House member, had a highly
visible and hard-nosed role in negotiations with legislative leaders. But Toomey
insisted that Clements remained in charge, and the governor personally participated
in the final, successful negotiations with legislative leaders.[43]

By then, Clements already had called a fourth, consecutive special session
on school finance. Although Democrats controlled the legislature, a solid bloc of
Republicans in the House—slightly more than one-third of that body's membership—
had strengthened the governor's hand by keeping the House from mustering the
two-thirds vote necessary to override a Clements' veto. In the end, though, faced
with a Texas Supreme Court deadline to provide more equity in public education
funding, Clements again gave in on the tax issue and signed a $512 million tax
increase. The increased revenue helped pay for the school finance bill—which
ironically was struck down as unconstitutional by the Supreme Court the next
year—and meet revenue shortfalls in the Texas Department of Human Services and
the Texas Department of Health.

The $6.1 billion in tax increases that Clements, an avowed fiscal conserva-
tive, signed during his second term was more than any other governor in Texas
history. The Texas economy was undergoing a painful transition in the wake of the
oil bust, and state government's existing tax base was strained at a time of increasing
budgetary demands. Those factors weren't the governor's fault, but Clements, like
White before him, had further eroded the credibility of public officials by making
anti-tax campaign promises he couldn't keep.

Clements counted the enactment of a major overhaul of the workers'
compensation system a major victory during his second term. At his insistence, the
legislature in 1989 created a new state agency and established new legal standards
under which workers injured on the job could seek compensation from their
employers or insurance companies. But it took two special sessions after lawmakers
failed to resolve an impasse over the issue in the 1989 regular session. Although
Clements strongly promoted workers' compensation reform, he never presented
the legislature with a specific proposal of his own. House Speaker Gib Lewis, Lt.
Governor Bill Hobby and key legislators exercised the leadership. Clements' role
was to hold a gun to the legislature's head by threatening to keep lawmakers in
Austin as long as it took to get a bill that he would accept. It was an effective exercise
of the governor's power to call and set the agenda for special sessions.

Clements' two terms converged with the emergence of a two-party system
in Texas, and his candidacy and elections contributed significantly to this historic
development. John Tower was the first Republican elected to the United States
Senate from Texas since the end of Reconstruction, but no other Republican had
been able to win any other statewide office until Clements tried. After proving that
a Republican could win the governorship, Clements made the Republican party
attractive to many conservative Democrats across the state who were becoming

increasingly disenchanted with the direction of the Democratic party, and many switched to the GOP.

There were only a handful of Republicans in the legislature and none in any other elected state offices when Clements was elected to his first term. After Clements had completed his second term in January 1991, Republicans held four of the nine seats on the Texas Supreme Court, two other statewide offices (in addition to a United States Senate seat), and more than one-third of the seats in the Texas House. They also had made major inroads in county and other local offices throughout the state.

In an interview in late 1990, Clements assessed his contribution to the development of a two-party system: "The electorate out there breaks down into about one-third Democrats, one-third Republicans and one-third independents. Well, that is a significant change in the political profile of Texas. That's a historic change, and I guess I'd like to say that I put a brick in place to bring that about."[44]

### Mark White (1983-1987)

White was a young, unknown Houston attorney when he was appointed secretary of state by Briscoe in 1973. But he soon learned the role of the electronic media in contemporary state politics and used his appointment as a stepping stone to higher office. White was considered the underdog by most political experts when in 1978, he ran against former House Speaker Price Daniel, Jr. for attorney general in the Democratic primary. After winning the nomination, White defeated James Baker— who later would serve in the cabinets of both Presidents Reagan and Bush—in the general election.

White's obvious ambition over the next four years created a great deal of animosity between him and Governor Clements, whom he unseated in 1982 with populist-style campaign attacks on high utility rates, promises to improve education (especially teachers' salaries), and a strong Democratic campaign effort. Assuming that the Texas economy would continue to expand and provide additional tax revenues, White also claimed he could keep his campaign promises without higher taxes. But he didn't count on his administration being plagued by a recession that arrived about the time he moved into the governor's office and worsened throughout his tenure.

Clements had been the first governor to competently exploit television in a political campaign, but White was the first governor to make television a major tool of his administration. He was photogenic, understood the format of the medium, and used it to promote public support of his legislative programs. He quickly earned the nickname, "Media Mark," with such stunts as leading reporters on a walking tour of a shantytown that homeless people had established near the Capitol.

But the effective use of the mass media in the policy-making process is much more than getting on the evening news. Governors must understand that legislators and other elected officials have their own programs and priorities and also interpret their own elections as mandates to pursue specific courses of action, which may conflict with the governor's. They also are trying to balance the demands of their constituents and various interest groups. A governor cannot continually use the media to try to run roughshod over these other policymakers. Effective leadership requires the governor to combine confrontation, accommodation, and compromise; in his first year as governor, White often seemed to lose sight of the latter two ingredients. Instead of establishing rapport with lawmakers through effective, personal lobbying, White chose to be confrontational by using the media to publicly attack those who opposed his positions on education and utility regulation, and his tactics backfired.

White fulfilled a campaign promise to appoint a housewife to the embattled Public Utility Commission, but lawmakers overwhelmingly defeated his proposal to make the PUC an elective, rather than appointive, body. The House defeated the proposal 104-39, even after the governor had spent $175,000 in political funds to promote it in a television ad campaign.[45] The legislature also shut the door on White's proposed two-year, 24 percent pay raise for teachers after the governor had spent another $100,000 in political funds on another TV blitz to promote that cause.

White, however, had some successes during the 1983 legislative session. He played a high-profile role in breaking a stalemate over interest rates on credit cards when he paid a surprise visit to the Texas Bankers Association headquarters across the street from the governor's mansion.[46] He and his staff also played a key role in convincing Microelectronics and Computer Technology Corp. (MCC), a highly sought computer research consortium, to choose Austin over cities outside Texas as its headquarters. And at the end of the regular session, the governor and legislative leaders agreed on an education compromise—an intensive study of the public schools that would lead to far-reaching education reforms a year later.

White's administration is probably best remembered for its role in the education reform effort. At a time of increasing concern throughout the country about deteriorating academic performances by public school students, White joined Lt. Governor Bill Hobby and Speaker Gib Lewis in appointing the Select Committee on Public Education, which was charged with conducting a comprehensive study of the state's public educational system and recommending changes.

The committee was chaired by billionaire computer magnate Ross Perot of Dallas. A strong-willed individual who was determined to turn the educational establishment on its head and overhaul the public school system, Perot, in many instances, appeared to eclipse the governor as the chief proponent of education reform in Texas. But White also delivered the same message.

The committee was successful in carrying out its charge and crafted legislation that would become known as House Bill 72, a landmark measure passed during a special session in the summer of 1984 (see Chapter 13). The bill, however, included two particularly controversial provisions that, like the recession, would prove politically damaging to White. It provided a teacher pay raise but also outraged many teachers by requiring them to pass a one-time-only literacy test to keep their jobs. It also imposed a so-called "no-pass, no-play" rule that disqualified failing students from athletics and other extracurricular activities for six weeks, despite the fact that football and other high school activities were the main sources of entertainment in hundreds of small Texas towns.

In this special session, White also broke his campaign pledge against higher taxes by signing a $4.8 billion tax bill. The tax increase not only helped pay for the education improvements, but it also financed another need—more highway construction. By selling the two issues together, White was able to muster more support from the business community for education reform and higher taxes.

That tax increase and the approaching 1986 election prompted White to approach the 1985 legislative session with considerably more caution than the previous sessions. Walter Mondale, the 1984 Democratic presidential nominee, and Lloyd Doggett, the Democratic nominee for the United States Senate, had been thrashed in Texas, and White had supported both. President Ronald Reagan's re-election coattails had helped Republican candidates capture additional seats in the Texas House, and White's negative job performance rating was rising, apparently in response to the tax bill, the no-pass, no-play rule, and the teacher literacy test. White vowed not to retreat on any of the major education reforms, and they remained in place.

He also was instrumental in the development of a new health care plan for the poor, an area of continued neglect in the state's political history. An active statewide coalition of groups representing lower socioeconomic Texans had focused on the issue, and White embraced their cause. But his determination to avoid another tax increase almost torpedoed this initiative. Eleventh-hour uncertainty over funding played into the hands of Republicans, who helped kill the plan on the House floor as the regular session was ending. White, nevertheless, turned the potential disaster into a public relations victory for himself by promptly calling—to the cheers of human services advocates—a special session on indigent health care. The session convened the next day and quickly approved a funding plan belatedly proposed by the governor.

Throughout most of the 1985 session, however, legislators complained that the governor offered virtually no leadership on anything else.

By 1986, Texas was in a recession. The oil industry—which had been the cornerstone of the Texas economy and a major source of revenue for the state treasury for more than half a century—was devastated by plunging oil prices, and tax revenues, in turn, declined precipitously. White was forced to call the legislature into an election-year special session that summer to rewrite the state budget. But even in the face of disaster, the prospect of cutting spending and raising taxes was so painful and politically divisive that the task wasn't completed in the first 30-day session. After calling a second session, White addressed the legislature on September 8—two months before election day—and asked for a tax increase. Lawmakers, he said, could blame him. The legislature made deep budget cuts and enacted a $763 million tax bill, which White signed.

Despite the political risks he took on the revised budget and tax increase, White abandoned his leadership role on the controversial issue of parimutuel betting. Proponents of horse and greyhound race betting took advantage of the same budgetary crisis to convince lawmakers to legalize wagering on a local option basis—subject, first, to voter approval in a statewide referendum. The parimutuel backers argued that racetrack betting would give state government an important new source of tax revenue and would help boost the economy. To avoid antagonizing parimutuel supporters, White let the bill become law without his signature but issued a preachy statement against the evils of gambling, which he personally opposed. Texas voters approved the parimutuel referendum the next year.

Most political observers believed that White, who was only 46 when he left the governor's mansion, aspired to national office and, as governor of a crucial, major state, considered himself a possible choice for the 1988 Democratic vice presidential nomination. He attracted national attention by frequently criticizing the policies of President Reagan's Republican administration and cultivated the national media on visits to Washington and appearances at national governors' conferences. One day during the 1986 gubernatorial campaign, White's staff even bumped a reporter for a major Texas newspaper from the governor's plane and gave the seat to a reporter for *The New York Times*. But White was saddled with the political liabilities of the state's economic plight, program cuts, and tax increases. And many schoolteachers and rural Texans hadn't forgiven him for the teacher literacy test and the no-pass, no-play rule. So Clements staged a successful comeback at the polls in 1986.

## Ann Richards (1991-   )

As discussed in previous chapters, gubernatorial politics reached a low level in the 1990 campaign. While that election may be an exception, it certainly did not add to the stature of the office of governor. And although it is difficult to measure the impact of such campaigns on the public, some would argue that the contemporary negative campaign at all levels of government has contributed to widespread disenchantment and cynicism.

Upon taking office in January 1991, Richards attempted to redirect the public's attention to the idea that her election symbolized a "New Texas." A governor uses the inauguration to set the tone and outline an agenda for the new administration, and Richards invited supporters to join her in a march up Congress Avenue to symbolically retake the Capitol for "the people." Then, hitting on the progressive Democratic themes of her campaign, Richards promised in her inaugural address a user-friendly, compassionate state government that would expand opportunities for everyone, particularly minorities and women. She promised to clean up the environment, improve education, attack crime, cut red tape, and boost ethical standards for public officeholders.

But the euphoria of the day was tempered by the reality of a $4 billion-plus potential deficit, a court order for school finance reform that could make the shortfall even greater, and a grand jury investigation into legislative behavior that had further eroded public confidence in state government. Richards also was

sharing inauguration day with a new, strong-willed lieutenant governor, Bob Bullock, who shared most of her political views but was impatient enough to try to take
over the leadership role and embarrass the new governor if she faltered or showed
any sign of timidity.

Richards moved quickly to establish herself as an activist governor (Figure
9-6). The day after her inauguration, she continued a campaign assault against high
insurance rates by marching over to a meeting of the State Board of Insurance to
publicly speak against a proposed increase in auto insurance premiums. Unlike her
recent predecessors, she also testified before House and Senate committees, ensuring that her legislative priorities would receive maximum media coverage. As
discussed earlier, she also used the media to attack the state bureaucracy, picking
two agencies—the insurance board and the Department of Commerce—for repeated
verbal assaults, finally prompting the resignations of a holdover appointee on the
insurance panel and the executive director of the commerce agency.

Meanwhile, Richards also was quickly fulfilling a campaign promise to
appoint more women and minorities to key positions in state government. She
appointed the first African-American to the University of Texas System Board of
Regents, the first African-American woman to the Texas A&M University governing

**FIGURE 9-6**  This cartoon illustrates Governor Ann Richards' attempt to convince the legislature to
grant the governor more control over the executive branch through cabinet-style appointment powers.
(© *Houston Chronicle*.  Reprinted with permission.)

board, and the first Hispanic to the Court of Criminal Appeals. Twenty-five percent of her appointees during her first three months in office were Hispanic, 21 percent were African-American, and 49 percent were women. Richards also named a disabled person to the Board of Human Services and a crime victim to the Board of Criminal Justice.[47]

With the state facing a revenue crunch, Richards took the lead in lobbying legislators for a constitutional amendment to create a state lottery. She failed to muster the necessary two-thirds vote in the House during the 1991 regular session but finally prevailed in winning legislative approval in a special session that summer. The lottery was a relatively safe issue on which to stake a leadership claim because polls indicated it had the strong support of most Texans as a new source of revenue for state government.

Most other major issues before the legislature during Richards' first year in office, however, weren't so simple, and the new governor was less willing to strike specific policy positions. She preferred to support the initiatives of Democratic legislative leaders, or take the best bill they were willing to give her, rather than demand that legislators enact a specific plan. Richards, for example, didn't submit any plan of her own for school finance reform. She outlined strong provisions for a new ethics law for legislators and other public officials but ended up signing a much weaker bill rather than trying to force a showdown. She also accepted a watered-down version of a bill creating a new, consolidated environmental protection agency. And she had little input in the budget- and tax-writing process, which Lt. Governor Bullock dominated. Detractors would say Richards' leadership wilted in the heat of legislative battle. Supporters would say she was a pragmatist who knew the limits of her office and recognized the necessity of political compromise.

Although some of the issues were different, Richards' early leadership experiences in office were not unlike those encountered by other newly elected governors. While issues are often articulated during a campaign, the substantive details of a complete legislative package are generally not considered then. After the election, the most pressing issue is recruiting staff and getting organized to take office. The transition from election day to inauguration day is only about two months, which still leaves precious little time to develop a comprehensive legislative package. A new governor thus is often forced to take the best bill available.

The progressive goals that Richards had outlined in her campaign also were tempered by the reality that Texas was still a predominantly conservative state. Despite promoting a vision of a "New Texas" that offered more compassion for the poor, improved health care for the sick, and greater educational opportunity for all, Richards also took pains to establish credentials of fiscal restraint. She opposed Lt. Governor Bullock's proposal for a personal income tax, even though it could have provided a big boost in health and human services programs and education spending. And she eagerly embraced a thorough review of state spending practices that helped reduce the size of the revenue and tax bill that she eventually signed during her first year in office.

Richards' proposal for the direct gubernatorial appointment of state agency heads was prompted by her frustration from the outset at a new governor's limited ability to influence the decisions of policymaking boards loaded with holdover appointees from a previous administration. Richards' position was that a new governor whose proposals presumably were endorsed by the voters shouldn't have to wait through most of her first term to begin implementing new policies. "The public views the governor as head of the executive branch and holds her responsible," said Paul Williams, Richards' executive assistant. "This (proposal) actually gives governors the power the public perceives them to have."[48]

The cabinet concept was not new, and neither was the legislature's reluctance to fully embrace it for fear of tipping the balance of governmental power away from the legislature. Lawmakers gave Richards some additional appointment powers over selected agencies, most notably in the health and human services area. But the governor's power over the bureaucracy remained limited.

### SUMMARY AND CONCLUSIONS

**1.** The governor is the most visible public office in state government, and the general public ascribes considerable power and influence to the office, but in terms of formal powers the office is weak. The governor shares administrative and policy functions with many other elected officials and, while there is a great deal of collaboration and cooperation among these officials, there is always the potential for conflict that can produce inertia or deadlock.

**2.** Unlike the president of the United States who functions with a cabinet that serves at his pleasure, the governor of Texas is part of a plural executive structure which also includes, among others, the lieutenant governor, the attorney general, the comptroller, the treasurer, the land commissioner, and the commissioner of agriculture. This structural arrangement is a direct consequence of Radical Reconstruction and the excesses of the Davis administration. It was the intention of the constitutional framers to constrain administrative power by distributing it among several statewide elected officials. Advocates of reform have argued that this structure diminishes the capacity of the executive branch to respond to the problems confronting the state.

**3.** There have been instances when one of the other elected, executive officeholders has been more influential than the governor. Such circumstances can arise when there are partisan differences, scandals that have crippled the governor's influence, or a governor who is passive in the policy and administrative processes.

**4.** Administrative responsibilities are further fragmented through 200-plus boards and commissions authorized by statutory law. While the governor appoints individuals to these agencies, the governor's control is diluted by board members' staggered terms, senatorial approval of the governor's appointments, and legal requirements relating to the composition of these boards. A governor's cabinet, most recently advanced by Governor Richards, has long been advocated by many critics of state government as a solution to this fragmentation of the administrative branch. In addition to giving the governor more control over the administrative branch, it would integrate executive agencies along functional lines and subordinate state agencies to the policy objectives of the governor. But the legislature has been reluctant to expand the governor's power in this fashion.

**5.** State laws assign major policy and some administrative responsibilities to the governor. A governor's success in policy formation is based on the adroit use of his or her resources, and there are some historic examples of Texas governors exercising considerable leadership and influence in the policy-making process despite the institutional limitations on the office. The governor's veto power, including line-item veto authority over the budget, has been used effectively by Texas governors to put their imprint on state policy.

**6.** Potentially, the governor has a number of informal resources that can be used to shape public policy and the administrative process. Governors have used their access to the mass media, their party roles, and their relationships to key interest groups within the state to bring pressure to bear on the legislature and other elected officials.

**7.** There have been marked differences in the leadership styles of Texas governors. A number of factors contribute to these variations, including a governor's personality, perceptions of the office, attitudes toward the role and function of government, prior career patterns, and a variety of intangible personal attributes, such as a sense of political timing and a sustained involvement in the development and execution of strategies to achieve policy objectives.

## KEY TERMS

Plural executive
Governor
Lieutenant Governor
Attorney General
Comptroller of Public Accounts
Pay as you go
State Treasurer
Land Commissioner

Agriculture Commissioner
Secretary of State
Railroad Commission
State Board of Education
Impeachment
Staggered terms
Senatorial courtesy

## FURTHER READING

Beyle, Thad L., and Lynn Muchmore, eds., *Being Governor: The View from the Office*. Durham, N.C.: Duke University Press, 1983.

Beyle, Thad L., and J. Oliver Williams, *The American Governor in Behavioral Perspective*. New York: Harper Row & Publishers, 1972.

Davis, J. William, *There Shall Also Be a Lieutenant Governor*. Austin: Institute of Public Affairs, University of Texas at Austin, 1967.

Dickson, James D., *Law and Politics: The Office of Attorney General in Texas*. Austin: Sterling Swift, 1976.

Fairbanks, James David, "The Textbook Governor," *Texas Journal of Political Studies*, 6 (Fall/Winter 1983), pp. 54-63.

Gantt, Fred, Jr., *The Chief Executive in Texas: A Study of Gubernatorial Leadership*. Austin: University of Texas Press, 1964.

Lipson, Leslie, with an introduction by Marshall E. Dimock, *The American Governor from Figurehead to Leader*. Chicago: The University of Chicago Press, 1939.

Morehouse, Sarah McCally, "The Governor as Political Leader," in Herbert Jacob and Kenneth N. Vines, *Politics in the American States*, 3rd ed. Boston: Little, Brown and Company, 1976.

Prindle, David, *Petroleum Politics and the Texas Railroad Commission*. Austin: University of Texas Press, 1981.

Reston, James, Jr., *The Lone Star State: The Life of John Connally*. New York: HarperCollins, 1989.

Richards, Ann, *Building from the Blueprint: A Plan for Texas State Government*. Austin, TX: Office of the Governor, 1991.

Sabato, Larry, *Goodbye to Good-Time Charlie: The American Governorship Transformed*, 2nd ed. Washington, D.C.: Congressional Quarterly Press, Inc., 1983.

Texas General Land Office, *The Land Commissioners of Texas*. Austin: Texas General Land Office, 1986.

Weaver, Jacqueline Lang. *Unitization of Oil and Gas Fields in Texas: A Study of Legislative, Administrative and Judicial Politics*. Washington, D.C.: Resources for the Future, Inc., 1986.

Welch, June R., *The Texas Governor*. Dallas: Yellow Rose Press, 1988.

Wiggins, Charles, Keith E. Hamm, and Howard Balanoff, "The Gubernatorial Transition in Texas: Bolt Cutters, Late Trains, Lame Ducks, and Bullock's Bullets," in Thad L. Beyle, ed., *Gubernatorial Transitions: The 1982 Elections*. Durnham, N.C.: Duke University Press, 1985.

## *ENDNOTES*

1. Pat M. Neff, *Messages of Pat M. Neff* (Austin: A.C. Baldwin, 1921), pp. 34-35.
2. Fred Gantt, Jr., *The Chief Executive in Texas* (Austin: The University of Texas Press, 1964), p. 24.
3. Ibid., p. 24-25.
4. Ibid., p. 27.
5. Ibid., pp.27-32.
6. Ibid., pp. 32-36.
7. Ibid., p. 37.
8. Charles F. Cnudde and Robert E. Crew, *Constitutional Democracy in Texas* (St. Paul: West Publishing Co., 1989) p. 90.
9. *The Texas Constitution*, Article 4, Section 4.
10. Gantt, *The Chief Executive in Texas*, p. 116.
11. Joseph A. Schlesinger, "The Politics of the Executive" in Herbert Jacob and Kenneth N. Vines, editors, *Politics in the American States*, 2nd ed. (Boston: Little, Brown and Company, 1971), chap. 6; Thad L. Beyle "The Governors, 1988-89," in *The Book of the States*, 1990-91 Edition (Lexington, Ky.: The Council of State Governments, 1990), p. 54.
12. Thad L. Beyle, "The Governors, 1988-89," p. 58.
13. Daniel Elazar, "The Principles and Traditions Underlying State Constitutions," *Publius* 12 (Winter 1982), p. 17.
14. *Austin American-Statesman*, May 4, 1990.
15. Texas Comptroller of Public Accounts, *Fiscal Notes*, (December 1990), p. 8.
16. Ibid., p. 9.
17. *Texas Government Newsletter*, 18 (December 10, 1990).
18. *Texas Government Newsletter*, 19 (July 15, 1991).
19. *The Texas Constitution*, Article 1, Section 4.
20. Gantt, *The Chief Executive in Texas*, pp. 229-230.
21. For an excellent treatment of the American governor through the depression years see Leslie Lipson, *The American Governor from Figurehead to Leader*. (Chicago: University of Chicago Press, 1939.)
22. *Texas Government Newsletter*, February 11, 1991.
23. *Dallas Morning News*, April, 1987, p. H-2.
24. *The Texas Constitution*, Article 4, Section 11.
25. Wilbourne E. Benton, *Texas Politics: Constraints and Opportunities*, 5th ed., (Chicago: Nelson-Hall Publishers, 1984), pp. 164-166.
26. Gantt, *The Chief Executive in Texas*, pp. 150-155.
27. Benton, *Texas Politics*, pp. 166-167.
28. *The Texas Constitution*, Article 4, Section 7.

29. Gantt, *The Chief Executive in Texas*, pp. 90-107.
30. Robert S. Lorch, *State and Local Politics* 3rd ed., (Englewood Cliffs, NJ: Prentice Hall, 1989) pp. 115-116.
31. Ibid., pp. 116-119.
32. See James E. Anderson, Richard W. Murray, and Edward L. Farley, *Texas Politics*, 6th ed. (New York: HarperCollins Publishers 1992), pp. 166-191, for an excellent analysis of the leadership styles of Governors Shivers, Daniel, Connally and Smith.
33. The Associated Press, as reported in the *Dallas Morning News*, November 23, 1975.
34. *Austin American-Statesman*, May 9, 1978.
35. *Dallas Times-Herald*, April 23, 1978.
36. Interview with Tom Uher, Feb. 26, 1991.
37. *Dallas Times-Herald*, April 23, 1978.
38. *Fort Worth Star-Telegram*, January 1, 1980.
39. *Houston Chronicle*, December 2, 1990.
40. *Houston Post*, June 17, 1979.
41. *Austin American-Statesman*, June 16, 1979.
42. *The Texas Poll*, Summer, 1987, conducted for Harte-Hanks Communications, Inc., by the Public Policy Resources Laboratory at Texas A & M University.
43. *Houston Chronicle*, December 2, 1990.
44. Ibid.
45. *Dallas Morning News*, June 5, 1983.
46. *Houston Chronicle*, June 5, 1983.
47. *Texas Government Newsletter*, 19 (February 25, 1991).
48. *Austin American-Statesman*, July 4, 1991.

# 10

## THE BUREAUCRACY AND POLICY IMPLEMENTATION

> One thing Texans have today is a state government that doesn't work very well....It is time to rethink Texas government and how it provides basic services to the state's citizens.
>
> *State Comptroller's Office*[1]

The **bureaucracy**, which includes more than 800,000 state and local employees in Texas, often is on the receiving end when someone complains about government. It is the favorite whipping boy of taxpayers who are dissatisfied with the quality of public services and of elected officeholders who ultimately are responsible for government's failures. But without the bureaucracy, government would come to a grinding halt. The bureaucracy issues driver's licenses, builds highways, distributes welfare checks, and, for better or for worse, performs a myriad of other public services. On an individual basis, the bureaucracy is the clerk, the inspector, the highway patrolman, the computer programmer, the engineer, or one of hundreds of other occupational specialists. On a larger scale, it is an assortment of agencies, some employing thousands of individuals, with designated responsibilities for specific public programs and services.

Statewide, there is a loosely connected, highly fragmented—and often confusing—network of approximately 250 agencies and universities with more than 200,000 employees responsible for carrying out programs and policies approved and funded by the Texas legislature and the governor. There are an additional 600,000 individuals employed by the school districts, cities, counties, and special districts.

Although it is an exaggeration to say, as some people do, that the bureaucracy dominates state government, its role is enhanced because the legislature meets in regular session only five months every other year and the governor has only limited powers over the executive branch. As discussed in Chapter 9, most agencies are administered by part-time boards or commissions appointed by the governor, while several others are run by statewide officeholders elected independently of the governor. In many cases, agency governing boards and administrators exercise considerable independence in interpreting policies and thus in determining the character and the quality of the services their agencies deliver. And many of the part-time, citizen boards are heavily dependent on the guidance of veteran administrators and career bureaucrats in governing their agencies.

## DEFINING BUREAUCRACY

Each one of us comes into regular contact with organizations that can be defined as bureaucracies. A large college or university has its bureaucracy as do many large corporations. If you have spent any time in a hospital, you were provided services that were administered through a bureaucracy. The legal system which many of us will come into contact with at one time or another is a bureaucracy. To speak of contemporary institutions—either public or private—in Texas and the United States is, in part, to speak of bureaucracies.

Max Weber, a German sociologist writing in the early part of the 20th century, regarded bureaucracies as efficient means of organizing large numbers of individuals to carry out the required tasks for accomplishing specific goals.[2] Bureaucratic structures are inevitable in large, complex societies where there is a great deal of individual and group interdependence. And to a large extent, these complex organizations are "superior to other methods of organizing people to perform tasks."[3]

Scholars have identified a number of attributes of bureaucracies, the first of which is size. Whether defined in terms of the number of employees, size of budgets, or number of programs administered, size suggests complex relationships among the people working for an organization. Employees of some large state agencies are scattered among many cities, and both the size and geographic dispersion of these agencies contribute to their organizational hierarchy.[4]

Within governmental organizations, specific positions are assigned specific responsibilities or given specific authority in a hierarchical arrangement. Most agency staffs have one individual at the top with the organization divided into bureaus, divisions, field offices or other units. The organization develops complex rules for supervision, management, and reporting of activities.

Bureaucracies require a division of labor among employees and contribute to the subsequent development of expertise based on experience and education. Thousands of state and local employees are engaged in routine tasks that require them to specialize and concentrate their attention on a limited number of activities. The organization, or agency, breaks down the responsibilities given to it by the legislature into narrowly defined tasks for its employees.

The specialization and division of labor in large organizations require rules and procedures to coordinate the activities of many individuals. Rules reduce the requirements for continued supervision of employees, and they lay the foundation for standardized behavior.[5] Rules define how tasks are to be carried out, who is responsible for carrying out a specific task or function, and who qualifies for the organization's services.

Contemporary bureaucracies also are characterized by impersonal relationships. People often complain about having to deal with faceless bureaucrats. But responsibilities within an agency are assigned to positions, which can be held by any number of individual workers who are supposed to be able to provide the requested service. When you go to get a voter registration card or your driver's license renewed, it should make no difference who the specific individual is who is assisting you. People come and go in large organizations, and the ongoing functions of an organization are not dependent on any specific individuals.[6]

## THE GROWTH OF GOVERNMENT IN TEXAS

Governments in Texas have grown significantly over the past three decades. In 1967, there were 388,000 full-time, state and local government employees in Texas. Twenty years later, the number had more than doubled (Table 10-1).

In 1967, the state's population was 10.6 million, which meant there was one public employee at the state or local level for every 27 Texas residents. By 1987, the state's population had increased to approximately 16.8 million persons, and there was one public employee for every 20 individuals (Table 10-2). During this period there was a substantial expansion of programs at all levels of government. State spending during the 1982-1983 biennium was $26.3 billion and, only 10 years later, the legislature appropriated $60 billion for the 1992-1993 biennium. State spending grew at an annual rate of 8.4 per cent which, in relation to the state's population growth, was close to the national average. More significantly, though, even with the increase in state employees, Texas' per capita spending is only 70 per cent of the national average. It is only in the area of education that the state's spending approaches the national average, but that level has declined since 1985.[7]

The citizens of Texas have come to expect a wide range of public services and, as the population grows, these expectations increase. The federal government

TABLE 10–1   Employment by Type of Government 1967–1987

| Unit of Government | Full-Time Employees | | |
|---|---|---|---|
|  | 1967 | 1977 | 1987 |
| State | 88,734 | 163,870 | 198,769 |
| Total Local | 299,578 | 477,177 | 646,913 |
| Counties | 32,978 | 60,287 | 77,851 |
| Municipalities | 75,168 | 115,481 | 139,340 |
| School Districts | 177,734 | 282,492 | 400,035 |
| Special Districts | 13,698 | 18,917 | 29,687 |
| Total for the State | 388,312 | 641,047 | 845,682 |

Sources:   U.S. Department of Commerce, Bureau of the Census, *Census of Governments,* 1967, Vol 3, No. 2, Table 15; *Census of Governments,* 1977, Vol 3, No. 2, Table 13; *Census of Governments,* 1987, Vol 3, No. 2, Table 14.

**TABLE 10–2** Texas Public Employment in Comparison to the State's Population

| Unit of Government | Number of State and Local Employees Per Capita | | |
|---|---|---|---|
| | 1967 | 1977 | 1987 |
| State | 1:119 | 1:80 | 1:84 |
| Local | 1:35 | 1:27 | 1:26 |
| All Levels | 1:27 | 1:21 | 1:20 |

Sources: U.S. Department of Commerce, Bureau of the Census, *Census of Governments*, 1967, Vol 3, No. 2, Table 15; *Census of Governments*, 1977, Vol 3, No. 2, Table 13; *Census of Governments*, 1987, Vol 3, No. 2, Table 14; U.S. Department of Commerce, Bureau of the Census, *Statistical Abstract of the U.S.*, 1971, Table 12; *Statistical Abstract of the U.S.*, 1981, Table 8; *Statistical Abstract of the U.S.*, 1991, Table 26.

also has imposed mandates on state and local governments that require additional expenditures and personnel. And the success of interest groups in winning approval of new programs adds to the growth of public employment. There have been efforts to curtail government growth and spending, but they have met with only marginal success in slowing down the expansion of state and local bureaucracies. The state's ongoing financial problems may yet result in a tighter squeeze on public employment, but affected groups and interests will attempt to minimize reductions.

Eighty percent of state government employees work in three areas: higher education; public safety and corrections; and social services that include public welfare and health care. While counties have a major responsibility for providing social services, a much larger percentage of county employees work in public safety and corrections and general governmental administration. Approximately one-third of city employees are engaged in fire and police protection, while another 30 percent work for city utilities and in housing, sewerage, sanitation, parks and recreation and natural resources departments (Table 10-3).

**TABLE 10–3** State and Local Employment by General Functions, 1987

| | State | Counties | Cities/ Towns | School Districts | Special Districts |
|---|---|---|---|---|---|
| Education | 39.6% | .9% | 2.5% | 100% | – |
| Social Services* | 30.4 | 28.9 | 6.8 | – | 43.4% |
| Public Safety & Corrections | 10.4 | 24.1 | 31.7 | – | – |
| Transportation | 7.6 | 10.1 | 8.4 | – | 7.1 |
| Government Administration | 5.0 | 24.2 | 8.6 | – | – |
| Environment/Housing | 4.2 | 3.8 | 17.0 | – | 18.7 |
| Utilities | – | – | 13.9 | – | 29.5 |
| All Other | 2.8 | 7.8 | 11.0 | – | 1.3 |
| Total Employees | 198,769 | 77,851 | 139,340 | 400,035 | 29,687 |

*Includes income maintenance.

Sources: U.S. Department of Commerce, Bureau of the Census, *1987 Census of Government, Public Employment*, Vol. 3, No. 2, Table 14.

## THE BUREAUCRATS AND PUBLIC POLICY

There is a tendency to think of bureaucrats as simply responsible for executing policies and decisions made by the legislative branch of government, but the bureaucracy is involved in virtually every stage of the policy-making process. In addition to the elected administrative officials who are invested with policy-making authority by the state constitution and statutes (see Chapter 9), there are many appointed officials with political ties to interest groups that are affected by the work of their agencies. These officials help develop policy alternatives, and during any given session of the legislature, it is possible to identify many pieces of legislation that originated with state agencies. Legislators are dependent on the information sources and expertise of bureaucrats, and as administrators develop reputations for technical knowledge and political skills, they have the potential to expand the policy roles of their respective agencies.

The legislature usually broadly defines a program and gives the affected agency the responsibility of filling in the details.[8] In the process of interpreting the intent and clarifying the objectives of the legislature, the agency transforms statutory law into administrative law. These actions speak to the broad role of bureaucracies in the policy-making process. Agency interpretations can even change a vague law from its original legislative purpose. Legislative oversight and the budgetary process can be used to control the bureaucracy, but administrative agencies often have resources and political influence that protect their prerogatives.

### Policy Implementation

"Implementation represents the conscious conversion of policy plans into reality."[9] While one state agency is attempting to translate legislative intent into a specific program, other governmental bodies also will maintain a presence. The courts, for example, shape the actions of the bureaucrats through their interpretation of statutes, administrative rules, and regulations. And there may be any number of jurisdictional and political battles over program goals and objectives with other agencies or elected officeholders. Such conflicts often result from Texas' plural executive system of government, in which the governor and several other statewide officials are elected independently of each other and numerous other agencies are headed by appointed boards and commissions (see Chapter 9).

Implementation "encompasses those actions by public and private individuals (and groups) that are directed at the achievement of goals and objectives set forth in prior policy decisions."[10] It involves the organization and staffing of a new agency to carry out the defined goals of new legislation or the assignment of responsibilities to an existing agency or agencies. Agencies develop the necessary new rules, procedures, or guidelines for operating the new program. Additional employees are hired if the legislature provided the necessary funding. If not, responsibilities are reassigned among existing personnel. Sometimes, tasks are coordinated with other agencies. Ultimately, all this activity translates into the hundreds of thousands of daily transactions between governmental employees and the public.

All of us have heard horror stories of persons who have suffered from abuse, neglect, incompetence, or capriciousness at the hands of public employees and agencies. Whether it is an indigent family that fell through the cracks of the welfare system or a county jail prisoner who was lost in the administrative process of the judicial system, these stories tend to reinforce the suspicion and hostility that many people have toward bureaucracies and public employees. There is no question that these abuses deserve attention and demand correction. In that respect, the mass media plays a significant role in the administrative process by bringing these issues to the attention of the general public as well as policymakers.

On the other hand, thousands of governmental programs are successfully carried out with little or no fanfare and are consistent with the intent and purpose of the authorizing legislation (Figure 10-1). Most public employees take pride in what they are doing and attempt to be conscientious in translating policy objectives into workable public services. They are citizens and taxpayers who also have to receive services from other state and local agencies. A complex, interdependent state with 17 million people depends on the effectiveness and efficiency of governmental agencies in program implementation. And that activity appears, on the whole, to be mutually satisfactory or beneficial to most parties involved.

**FIGURE 10-1** Transportation is a major function of the state bureaucracy. This is one of many freeway interchanges in Houston. (© *Houston Chronicle*. Reprinted with permission)

## Obstacles to Policy Implementation

As noted above, when things go wrong in state government and problems go unresolved, there is a tendency to point the finger at the bureaucrats and blame them for excessive red tape, inefficiency, mismanagement, or incompetence. But while some of these charges are occasionally valid, other factors usually are responsible for the failure of public policies. "Bureaucrat bashing" plays well politically, and many candidates for public office run on such campaigns. But in many cases they are unfairly blaming government employees for complex problems that policymakers have been unable—or unwilling—to resolve and that will continue to be difficult. One high profile issue is the perennial struggle to improve the quality of the public education system. Much of the criticism directed at educational bureaucrats has been justified, but the legislature and the governor are ultimately responsible for the enactment of sound educational policies—and the development of a sufficient and equitable system of paying for them.

Some legislative policies may be misdirected with little potential for producing the intended results. Or economic and social conditions upon which laws were based may change, making programs inappropriate. Administrators also may find that alternative approaches would have worked much better than those outlined by the legislature, and the legislature frequently fails to appropriate enough money to adequately fund programs. Moreover, it also is possible that those who are charged with implementing a new policy do not have the know-how or the resources to make it work.[11] Finally, programs often produce unintended results that were overlooked or unanticipated when the original policy was designed.[12]

## POLITICAL CONTROL AND THE RESPONSIVENESS OF THE BUREAUCRACY

Taking a cue from political scientist Robert Lineberry, policymakers can use several strategies to control bureaucracies and assure that policies are implemented as intended:[13]

- Change the law to reduce or eliminate the discretionary authority of an agency.
- Overrule the bureaucracy and reverse or rescind an action or decision of an agency. With the independence of many agencies, boards, and commissions at the state level, the governor can reverse few agency decisions. So this step often requires legislative action.
- Transfer the administration of a program to another agency through administrative reorganization, a strategy attempted by the legislature in 1991.
- Replace an agency head who refuses or is incapable of carrying out program objectives. But there are only a few agencies over which the governor can directly exercise such authority in Texas.
- Cut or threaten to reduce the budget of an agency to force compliance with policy objectives.
- Abolish an agency or program through sunset legislation.

- Make legislation more detailed and eliminate agency discretion in interpreting policy.
- Pressure the bureaucracy to change with legislative hearings and public disclosures of agency neglect or inadequacies.
- Protect public employees who reveal incompetence, mismanagement, and corruption through whistle-blower legislation.
- Enact revolving-door restrictions to reduce or eliminate the movement of former state employees to industries over which they had regulatory authority.

Although these tools are available to policy makers, the accountability and responsiveness of state and local agencies also are affected by a number of other factors, not the least of which is the influence of special interests.

The special interests that have great influence over the legislature also carry a lot of clout throughout the bureaucracy. Thanks to laws influenced by special interest lobbyists, many regulatory agencies, in fact, are headed by boards that have to have a majority of members from the professions or industries they are supposed to regulate. Many taxpayers may feel this system is merely a legalized way of letting the foxes guard the henhouse, but it is an extension of the "iron triangles" concept (see Chapters 4 and 13), whereby special interests seek to influence not only the legislators responsible for enacting proposed laws but also the agencies responsible for enforcing them.

## Appointments to State Agencies

Business and professional groups argue that their professions can be effectively regulated only by individuals knowledgeable of the industries or vocations. While that argument has some validity, it also increases the potential for incestuous relationships that make a mockery of the regulatory process. There is always the possibility—and often the likelihood—that industry representatives serving on boards or commissions—or the chief executive of an agency—will be inclined to protect their industries against the best interests of consumers. This pattern of influence and control is often referred to as **cooptation**. Licensing agencies also may seek to adopt unfair regulations designed to restrict new competitors from entering an industry.

Historically, many nine-member state regulatory boards included only industry representatives. But under the sunset review process, which will be discussed in more detail later in this chapter, laws have gradually been changed to turn over three of the positions on most of those boards to public members. The Sunset Advisory Commission has concluded: "Boards consisting only of members from a regulated profession or group affected by the activities of an agency may not respond adequately to broad public interests. This potential problem can be addressed by giving the general public a direct voice in the activities of the agency through representation on the board."[14]

The legislature provided in 1991 that the Texas Funeral Service Commission, which underwent sunset review that year, would have a majority of public members, because most of the complaints against funeral homes were consumer-oriented and not technical in nature. But most industries were still able to flex their muscles with lawmakers. That same year, Comptroller John Sharp recommended that most regulatory agencies be consolidated into an umbrella Department of Licensing and Regulation that not only could have saved the state millions of dollars but also could have reduced the influence of some special interests over the bureaucracy. Lawmakers rejected the proposal and retained a hodgepodge of separate, small, industry-dominated agencies.

The "fox and the henhouse" approach to state regulation was highlighted again when Governor Ann Richards demanded that the Texas Department of Health crack down on poor nursing home care and deplorable conditions in some facilities. It was revealed that state inspectors had repeatedly found unsanitary conditions in three nursing homes partly owned by a member of the Texas Board of Health. The board member, an appointee of former Governor Bill Clements, denied any allegations of improper care but resigned after moving to another state.[15] Texas law required that one member of the 18-member health board be involved in the nursing home industry, while other members included other health care professionals.

The danger that regulators can become too friendly with the special interests they regulate and become protective of the status quo is not exclusive to boards dominated by industry representatives.

One recent target of public outrage was the Texas Alcoholic Beverage Commission, or TABC, which developed a reputation of being too friendly to the liquor industry, despite the fact that the law in this case forbids any of its three board members from being directly involved in the industry. This agency was thrust into the spotlight in the 1980s by the problem of drunken driving and the carnage that it was leaving on Texas streets and highways.

Led by groups such as Mothers Against Drunk Driving, or MADD, and the Texas Parent-Teacher Association, Texans started demanding that both the legislature and the commission crack down on the problem. The legislature enacted tougher laws and penalties against driving while intoxicated but, influenced by pressure from beer and liquor lobbyists, refused to pass another key demand of MADD, a law that would prohibit anyone—drivers or passengers—from having an open container of alcohol in an automobile or truck. Lawmakers eventually produced a compromise—a difficult-to-enforce ban against drinking-while-driving that didn't apply to passengers. While that law angered thousands of Texans who had become accustomed to drinking a beer on their way home from work in evening rush-hour traffic, it didn't satisfy MADD and other groups which believed Texas still had a long way to go in making its roadways safe.

So, in February 1990, these citizen groups urged the Alcoholic Beverage Commission to adopt administrative rules to prohibit "happy hours" in bars and restaurants, which they believed encouraged excessive drinking, and take other steps to discourage drinking by minors and drivers. The approach, as proposed by Mothers Against Drunk Driving and other members of a citizen coalition called

Texans for Responsible Alcohol Consumption, would have given the hospitality industry a greater financial incentive to exercise more care in serving patrons because the TABC had the authority to suspend the lucrative liquor licenses of rules violators. Restaurant and bar owners opposed the proposed restrictions, and the TABC rejected them, contending that many of the proposals were beyond the agency's administrative authority and would require changes in state law by the legislature.

Two months later, however, the commission's own staff proposed a more limited set of rules changes to clamp down on happy hours and other reduced-price drink promotions, which the commission unanimously adopted in June 1990. "We've reached a point now where we feel it's time to take some action," said the agency's general counsel, Joe Darnall.[16] The liquor industry still opposed some of the proposals, but the commission apparently realized that most Texans favored some restrictions. A *Texas Poll* published about three weeks before the commission's decision indicated that 52 percent of Texas adults believed two-for-one drink prices and similar happy hour offerings should be banned. Sixty-four percent of the survey's respondents said such promotions caused people to drink more than they normally would.[17] Among practices banned by the commission were sales of multiple drinks for the price of one; one price, all-you-can-drink promotions; and ladies' nights, where women drank free or for reduced prices. Half-price drinks and nickel beer promotions weren't prohibited because, according to the commission's then-chairman, Louis M. Pearce Jr. of Houston, "We can't fix prices."[18] MADD and other anti-drunk-driving crusaders called the commission's new rules a step in the right direction but felt the agency still didn't go far enough.

As a result of a legislative-ordered review of state agencies in 1991, Comptroller John Sharp recommended that the Alcoholic Beverage Commission be abolished and its functions transferred to other state agencies at an estimated annual savings of $8 million. The legislature didn't adopt that proposal, but it did order the commission, which had previously been granted two postponements of sunset review, to undergo sunset review in 1993.

## The Revolving Door

Over the years, many regulatory agencies had become training grounds for young attorneys and other professionals taking their first jobs out of college or law school. They would work for state agencies for a few years for relatively low pay while gaining valuable experience in a particular regulatory area and making influential contacts in the state bureaucracy. Then they would leave state employment for higher paying jobs in the industries they used to regulate and represent their new employers before the state boards and commissions for whom they had worked. Or they would become consultants or join law firms representing regulatory clients. Former gubernatorial appointees to boards and commissions—not just hired staffers—also participated in this so-called **revolving-door** phenomenon, which raised ethical questions about possible insider advantages. One former member of the Texas

Water Commission, Lee Biggart, a 1981 appointee of Governor Bill Clements, developed a successful Austin law practice representing clients before the Water Commission after he left the agency. He was by no means the only former policymaker to profit in such fashion from his state experience, but he attracted more attention than many others because the Water Commission had major environmental protection responsibilities. (A few years later, the legislature would combine the commission with other environmental offices into a larger environmental protection agency.) "The bulk of lawyers who practice here were once associated with water agencies in one way or another," then-Commissioner John Houchins told the *Austin American-Statesman* in 1986.[19]

Revolving-door restrictions in the 1975 law that created the Public Utility Commission prohibited PUC members and key staffers from going to work for regulated utilities immediately after leaving the agency. But that was the only agency that had such restrictions until the ethics reform law of 1991 expanded them to other agencies. Legislators, however, refused to place similar restrictions on themselves. State senators and state representatives who also were lawyers could continue to represent clients for pay before the state boards and commissions that operated under the laws and the budgets that the legislators enacted. For the first time, though, the 1991 ethics law did require legislators to publicly report who they represented for pay before state agencies.

## Citizen Complaints

In her inaugural address, Governor Ann Richards said she expected state government to provide "legendary customer service" to the taxpayers and announced the appointment of an **ombudsman**, a special assistant in her office, to handle citizen complaints. Three months later, the governor—who spent much of her first year in office trying to shake up the bureaucracy and make it more responsive—reported that the ombudsman was receiving thousands of phone calls and letters each week. "The sad fact is that the people don't trust state government. They don't believe we have their interests at heart, and I think they may be right," Richards told a meeting of state agency heads, whom she had called on the carpet to complain about a "crisis of competence" in state government.[20]

## Legislative Budgetary Control

Every two years, the legislature has traditionally set the budgets for state agencies and then provided little scrutiny over how effectively the money actually was spent, unless there was a financial crisis that required a special legislative session or an emergency transfer of funds by the governor and the Legislative Budget Board. Perhaps the most control that lawmakers exercised over agency spending, besides setting the bottom line, was by approving a number of line items in agency budgets that restricted portions of an agency's budget to specific programs. That pattern also made those budgetary items vulnerable to the governor's line-item veto power, but it didn't necessarily guarantee that money eventually was spent for designated purposes.

Prompted by a major revenue shortfall and the fearful prospect of a state income tax, the legislature in 1991 made some significant changes in the budgetary approach. The biennial appropriations bill included fewer individual spending items and a greater lumping of funds in agency budgets. Some 160 of the approximately 250 state agencies and universities were given lump sum appropriations. Although that saved those agencies from any program vetoes by the governor, Lt. Governor Bob Bullock and other proponents predicted the change in the budget pattern would lead to a more cost efficient bureaucracy. They said it would give agency administrators greater flexibility in managing funds and meeting critical public needs.

The legislature also gave the Legislative Budget Board, or LBB, a 10-member body that is chaired by the lieutenant governor and also includes the speaker of the House and other key legislators, the power to join the governor in initiating emergency transfers of money between agencies when the legislature was not in session. This was an expansion of the budget execution laws under which the governor could propose emergency transfers subject to the LBB's approval. And, finally, lawmakers ordered agencies to cut a total of $300 million from their appropriations during the 1992-93 budget period and empowered the comptroller to make a list of proposed reductions for LBB action if the agencies failed to reach that goal.

At Bullock's urging, the LBB later took other steps to increase its scrutiny of agency spending by ordering performance audits of agencies every three months and establishing a computer link that would enable the LBB, the governor, and other key elected officials to more closely monitor spending by major agencies and universities. "No state agency can pass muster under this new system without doing good advance planning, both as to its purpose in government and its resources," Bullock said in a guest column in the *Amarillo Daily News*.[21]

The legislature in 1991 also initiated steps to establish a long-term, strategic planning process for state government, an idea that had always been short-lived before. The goal was to establish two-year, four-year, and six-year plans to assist the legislature in the budget-writing process. "Agencies will be required to re-justify their most basic missions, explain what is needed to meet goals to carry out those missions and then be subjected to cross-examination in an evaluation of their performance in those areas."[22]

## Sunset Legislation

Although Texas has been slow to modernize its budgetary process and other key functions of state government, it became one of the first states to require formal, exhaustive reviews of how effectively agencies are doing their jobs. The **sunset** law enacted in 1977 was so named because most agencies have to be periodically re-created by the legislature or automatically go out of business.[23] Relatively few agencies—except for a number of obscure, inactive ones like the Pink Bollworm Commission and the Stonewall Jackson Memorial Board—have actually been abolished. But the obligatory review has produced some significant structural and policy changes in the state bureaucracy that the legislature may not have otherwise ordered. It also has expanded employment opportunities for lobbyists, because numerous special interest groups have much to win or lose in the sunset process. And in many cases special interests have succeeded in protecting the status quo.

Each agency is up for sunset review every 12 years under a rotating order set out in the sunset law. The review begins with the Sunset Advisory Commission, which includes four state representatives appointed by the speaker of the House, four senators appointed by the lieutenant governor, and two public members, one named by the speaker and the other by the lieutenant governor. Each legislative member serves a four-year term and each public member a two-year term. The chairman is designated every two years alternately by the speaker and the lieutenant governor. The commission employs a staff that studies each agency up for review during the next regular, biennial legislative session and reports its findings to the panel, which makes recommendations to the legislature. In a few cases, the commission will propose that an agency—usually a minor one—be terminated or consolidated with another agency. In most cases, though, the commission will recommend the continuation of an agency but outline suggested changes in its organizational structure and/or operations. The future of the agency is then debated by the full legislature. If lawmakers fail to approve a sunset bill for any agency by September 1 of the year the agency is scheduled for review, the agency will be phased out of existence over the next year or be terminated abruptly on September 1 if the legislature also refuses to approve a new budget for the agency. The Texas Higher Education Coordinating Board is subject to sunset review but individual universities are not. Also exempted from sunset review are the courts and state agencies created by the constitution, such as the governor's office, the attorney general, the comptroller, the treasurer, and the General Land Office.

The sunset process hasn't reduced the size of the state bureaucracy. By fiscal 1991, there were almost 224,000 state employees, calculated on a full-time equivalent basis and including higher education, compared to about 163,000 in 1977, the year the sunset law was approved. The number of state employees per 10,000 population also increased from 127 in 1977 to 131 in 1991, although Texas still trailed most other states in that category.[24] While 45 agencies had been terminated or merged, Bill Wells, the Sunset Advisory Commission's executive director, estimated that a like number of new agencies were created by the legislature for a variety of reasons during that same period (Table 10-4). But Wells believes the statistics don't tell the full story. He believes the sunset process has served to slow down the creation of new agencies. "You can't say how many (new agencies) would have been created if sunset hadn't heightened the awareness of the fact that we've got maybe too many agencies now," he said. "There is a heightened awareness of the fact that you need to go a little slower and you need to really have a problem before you create an agency."[25]

**TABLE 10–4** Overview of Sunset Action from 1979 to 1991

|  | 1979 | 1981 | 1983 | 1985 | 1987 | 1989 | 1991 | Totals |
|---|---|---|---|---|---|---|---|---|
| Legislative Session | 66th | 67th | 68th | 69th | 70th | 71st | 72nd | |
| Agencies Reviewed | 26 | 28 | 32 | 31 | 20 | 30 | 30 | 197 |
| Agencies Continued | 12 | 22 | 29 | 24 | 18 | 25 | 22 | 152 |
| Agencies Abolished Outrright | 8 | 2 | 3 | 6 | 1 | 3 | 3 | 26 |
| Agencies Abolished & Functions Transferred | 1 | 3 | 0 | 0 | 1 | 2 | 5 | 12 |
| Agencies Combined | 4 | 1 | 0 | 0 | 0 | 0 | 0 | 5 |
| Agencies Separated | 1 | 0 | 0 | 1 | 0 | 0 | 0 | 2 |

Source: Texas Sunset Advisory Commission, *Sunset Review in Texas: Summary of Process and Procedure*, September,1991.

The sunset review process has helped rid state government of some dead-wood, modernized some state laws and bureaucratic procedures, and made some agencies more responsive and accountable to the public. As a sunset policy, which was discussed earlier in this chapter, public members also have been added to the boards of numerous small regulatory agencies that previously had included only representatives of the professions or industries that they regulated.

The largest agencies and those with influential constituencies usually are the most difficult to change because special interests are working overtime and making large political contributions to protect their turf. According to an analysis by the *Dallas Times Herald*, for example, industries regulated by agencies that were up for sunset review in 1983—including the Public Utility Commission, the Railroad Commission, the State Board of Insurance, and the State Banking Board—gave $1.3 million to legislators and legislative candidates during the 1982 election campaigns. Contributions from the five largest political action committees concerned with the 1983 sunset bills increased 66 percent over 1980, the previous election year. Utility companies, whose rates and services are regulated by the Public Utility Commission, contributed more than $349,000 to legislative campaigns. Insurance companies, agents and underwriters gave more than $320,000. "The utilities want us to leave the Public Utility Commission alone, the truckers want us to leave the Railroad Commission alone, the oil companies want us to leave the Railroad Commission alone, the bankers want us to leave the banking board alone," said Representative Ernestine Glossbrenner, D-Alice, then a member of the Sunset Advisory Commission. "That just tells me that they would rather live with the chains they have. The industries know how to work with these agencies, and they don't want to learn a new way of operating."[26]

Whatever else the sunset process may have accomplished in 1983, the legislative review of the State Board of Insurance, which attracted little attention at the time, failed to head off a major controversy over that agency's operations five years later. The collapse in October 1988 of the Dallas-based National County Mutual Fire Insurance Co., one of the largest insurance failures in Texas history, raised questions about how well the board was protecting consumers from financially troubled insurers. A Senate committee launched a well-publicized investigation of the board, and the legislature approved some minor insurance regulatory reforms in 1989. More changes were made in 1991, after Ann Richards had made insurance reform a priority in her successful 1990 gubernatorial race.

Since it is obvious that major state agencies have to be re-created in some form, they can be held hostage by legislators for any number of purposes during their review year. In 1983, lawmakers seeking the creation of a state human rights commission to investigate complaints about job discrimination won Senate approval of an amendment that tacked that agency onto the Texas Employment Commission sunset bill. The House refused to accept the amendment but the human relations advocates had a strong upper hand. There was no question that the governor and the legislature weren't going to let the TEC, which administers unemployment compensation benefits and provides job placement services, go out of business. So rather than give in to the House's opposition, senators let the bill die at the end of the regular session. Governor Mark White then promptly called a special session to pass the TEC sunset bill and a separate measure creating a human relations commission.

In 1989, then-Governor Bill Clements and other foes of Agriculture Commissioner Jim Hightower used the sunset process to trim Hightower's influence. Unlike most other statewide, elected offices, the agriculture commissioner's post wasn't created by the state constitution. It is statutory, which made it vulnerable when the Department of Agriculture had to pass sunset review. Hightower, a liberal Democrat, had cultivated the enmity of conservative agricultural producers and the chemical industry by, among other things, proposing tighter restrictions on the use of pesticides and more protection for agricultural workers. Clements, a Republican who opposed most of Hightower's politics, backed efforts to change the law to replace Hightower's job with a commissioner or multi-member commission appointed by the governor. Hightower had strong support in the Democrat-dominated Senate for keeping his post elective. But he had trouble in the House, where one-third of the members were Republicans and many rural, conservative Democrats shared a dim view of his policies and politics. Hightower had survived attacks in previous legislative sessions, but this time, with the future of the agricultural agency at stake, he was forced to accept a distasteful compromise. His job remained elective, but he had to share his authority to regulate pesticides with a new board created in the sunset law. The agriculture commissioner would chair a new, nine-member Agricultural Resources Protection Authority. But the board also would include two members appointed by the governor and six members who would be administrators from the Texas Department of Health, the Texas Water Commission, and other agencies. Environmentalists and consumer advocates warned that the new setup would weaken the public's protection against pesticide use. "Because of the actions of the governor and the chemical industry, the sunset review was misused and manipulated far beyond its original intent," said John Hildreth of Consumers Union. Hightower's political troubles were so deep that he was unseated the next year by Rick Perry, one of the legislative sponsors of the pesticide regulation compromise. Perry, a farmer from Haskell in the Texas Panhandle, had been a conservative Democrat. He became a Republican to run against Hightower and win the agriculture commissioner's post in his first campaign for statewide office.

## Whistle Blowing

Governmental agencies make mistakes. Agencies can be very inefficient, and like any other organization, public or private, they can be mismanaged and make gross errors in judgment. These actions may, in fact, be very costly to the general public. In addition to the financial costs, regulatory neglect also may jeopardize the health of individuals or contribute to the loss of lives. Governments spend huge amounts of money for supplies, construction, and basic services, and there is always the potential for public employees to be offered kickbacks or bribes to influence decisions that would benefit particular corporations or individuals. Elected and appointed officials are not above **influence-peddling**, and there are numerous instances cited throughout this book of breaches of ethical conduct as well as out-and-out corruption.

At the same time, there are many ethical public employees who are concerned with the performance of the agencies for which they work. They too are citizens and taxpayers, and they bring to their positions their own personal and professional values. Having discovered irregularities, mismanagement, or corruption, what options are available to them? How do they handle the ethical dilemmas with which they come into contact?

On the one hand, employees can succumb to institutional loyalty, peer pressure, and the real potential for retaliation by their bosses or administrators and choose to do nothing. Some agencies have formal procedures for bringing such issues to the attention of policymakers, but there are risks to careers and reputations. Employees could confidentially leak information about abuse or mismanagement to the press, which could be instrumental in exposing the activities of an agency and producing legal, administrative, or legislative action. Over the years, leaked information by public employees has precipitated investigations and sufficient pressure to effect changes.

But some public employees choose to go public with information about problems within their agencies. These individuals are known as **whistleblowers**, and they subject themselves to the possible loss of their jobs, reassignment to less desirable positions, and other forms of retaliation from their supervisors and fellow employees.

Texas has a "whistleblower protection law," which is designed to protect public employees from such retaliation. If an employee is subjected to such tactics after having come forward, the law permits the worker to file a lawsuit against the offending agency. A major test of the effectiveness of the law was brought by George Green, an architect for the Texas Department of Human Services.[27]

Assigned to supervising the construction of DHS facilities, Green publicly complained of shoddy construction, kickbacks and non-compliance with contracts and said his supervisors had refused to take action against the offending contractors. After he went public with his charges, Green eventually was fired by the agency for abusing sick-leave time and making unauthorized telephone calls. Criminal charges were brought against him and, although they were eventually dropped, he spent $130,000 in legal fees, could not find a job, and depleted many of his personal assets. He sued the state and won a $13.6 million judgment from a Travis County jury in 1991, but the state appealed, which meant the case could remain unresolved for months or years to come.

Green's story speaks to a major problem in state government. Few public employees can afford to be subjected to this type of retaliation, and few have the resources to fight the legal and administrative tools available to agencies. Although the legislature intended to protect whistleblowers and to encourage their inside information, most state and local employees may have learned a broader lesson: keep your mouth shut.

## REGULATION

In the process of implementing state policy, the legislature delegates a great deal of authority to regulatory agencies. And cities, operating under similar authority, regulate select areas of the local economy.

One aspect of state economic regulation affects the prices that certain businesses can charge for their services. Major state regulators in this area include the State Board of Insurance, which determines maximum rates that can be charged for automobile and homeowners insurance, and the Public Utility Commission, which has authority over rates charged for intrastate telephone services as well as electric rates charged by some utility companies.

A second regulatory function is the **licensing** of professions and franchising of corporations. Under state law, some occupations require formal training, testing, and subsequent licensing from a state agency. These include doctors, nurses, accountants, lawyers, and a host of other professions. To open a barber shop, a funeral home, or a nursing home—among other facilities—an individual or a corporation also must obtain a state license. Licensing implies regulation, and the acceptance of a license implies a willingness to comply with state controls. On the local level, contractors are required to meet building codes established by city councils.

State agencies also can regulate the allocation of resources. Over the years, the state has developed a body of legislation and rules directly related to water resources that are enforced by the Texas Water Commission, which soon will be merged with other agencies into a new environmental protection department. In the San Antonio area, recent disputes over the use of water from the underground Edwards Aquifer prompted state intervention. The days of virtually unrestricted water use are gone, and the state claims a right to make the hard decisions as to which areas and interests will get what amount of water. Likewise, the Texas Railroad

Commission is authorized to establish the rate at which a well can pump oil from the ground.

State and local governments also can regulate by providing operating subsidies to businesses in the form of tax abatements and other tax breaks. These often are offered for specified periods to entice businesses to locate or expand in a specific community. In return, the businesses may agree to stipulations or conditions imposed on them by the participating government. Cities also grant franchises to cable TV systems, which agree to provide a specific level of service in return for the operating rights.

State agencies also regulate companies for fairness and competition. While there are many federal laws dealing with price-fixing, monopolies, and unfair competition, there also are state statutes relating to the competitiveness of the state's economy.

The state also is involved in what some writers term social regulation.[28] In effect, social regulation is much broader than the economic regulation described above. Social regulations affect "the conditions under which goods and services are produced and the physical characteristics of products that are manufactured."[29] While the federal government has preempted many state policies in these areas, there are state agencies involved in regulating work- place safety, air quality, water quality, and consumer protection.

## MERIT SYSTEMS AND PROFESSIONAL MANAGEMENT

At the turn of the century, public employees in Texas were hired on the basis of **political patronage** or the personal relationships and friendships they had with elected or appointed public officials. Under a patronage system, there was limited consideration for the skills, competence, or expertise of those hired to carry out state policies. There were few rules concerning terms of employment, advancement, or the rights or conduct of public employees, and there were wide variations in wages and salaries from agency to agency. There also were high rates of employee turnover with subsequent declines in responsiveness to the needs and interests of the public.

Some reform advocates pushed for a **merit system** based, in part, on the example established by the federal government when it passed the Pendleton Act in 1883 and created a Civil Service Commission. But while some other states have developed comprehensive, statewide employment or personnel systems administered by a single agency, the reform movement in Texas has not been as successful, and state government here continues to function under a decentralized personnel system.[30]

Merit-based public employment was inconsistent with the individualistic views of government, politics, and public administration evolving from the dominant political subcultures of Texas (see Chapter 1). And the plural executive worked against efforts to centralize and coordinate personnel policies because the various elected, executive officeholders jealously guarded their prerogatives to hire and fire the people who worked for them.

Governmental functions have expanded since the turn of the century, and policy implementation has become more complex and technical.[31] Many programs require highly specialized skills, and it is impossible to administer most programs with political hacks who have no formal training or expertise for technical jobs. Furthermore, the public has gradually developed higher expectations of their government and reacts unfavorably to incompetent public employees. There also has been pressure on state government to establish some system of merit employment in order to attract employees who demand job protection and predictability in advancement. Additional pressure for merit employment has come from the federal government. Since the 1930s, numerous federal grants have been tied to a requirement that the state enact a merit system for those state employees administering the grants. In more recent years, federal laws prohibiting hiring discrimination on the basis of sex, age, disability, race, or ethnicity have been extended to state and local governments. These requirements, in turn, have forced Texas government to pay more attention to employment practices.[32]

While politics have not been totally eliminated in the hiring and promotion of public employees, the state has developed some elements of a personnel system. It is not a merit system but a highly fragmented system with different agencies assigned various responsibilities for developing and implementing personnel policies. Ultimately, the legislature has the legal authority to define personnel practices for state government, and the biennial budget is the major tool used by legislators to establish some 1,300 job classifications and corresponding salary schedules. The legislature also establishes policies on vacations, holidays, and retirement. During interims between legislative sessions, the Legislative Audit Committee can exercise some authority in reclassifying job positions.

The legislature's control over personnel policies is enhanced by a classification officer appointed by the state auditor to collect personnel information and advise state agencies on compliance with state law. Other agencies involved in the personnel system include the attorney general's office, which has the final authority to interpret how the personnel procedures and policies are to be applied, and the comptroller, who is charged with maintaining the state's payroll system and issuing state paychecks.

As part of the budgetary process, the governor can make recommendations regarding salaries of state employees and changes in job classifications. He or she also has the responsibility of enforcing state classification and salary policies and can order the comptroller to withhold paychecks from employees whose positions violate those policies.

But the primary responsibility for carrying out personnel policies is delegated to the various state agencies. An administrator can develop specific policies for an agency as long as the agency works within the general framework defined by the legislature. As might be expected, some agencies have developed sophisticated personnel plans for their employees while others have only the most rudimentary procedures. Some have begun to implement merit system principles, including competitive examinations for initial placement and advancement, probationary periods for first-time employees, job evaluation and counseling, and programs for career development.

All state agencies are required to comply with affirmative action and nondiscrimination policies, and several have personnel programs that include employee assistance with personal and family problems. Many agencies also have developed procedures for filing grievances about work conditions, performance evaluations, terminations, demotions, and employee-supervisor conflict. In the face of efforts to organize state employees through labor unions and demands for more comprehensive personnel procedures, agencies are beginning to develop formal procedures for addressing the broad concerns of their employees.

But how do people get jobs in state government? Many positions still are filled as a result of friendships, other personal contacts, and the influence of individuals who play in the policy arenas of state government and politics. Historically, many agencies recruited their employees informally through employee referrals and political contacts but, increasingly, state agencies advertise job openings through the Texas Employment Commission, private employment agencies, the mass media, and college placement centers. In highly technical fields, agencies are forced to compete with employers in the private sector and, consequently, there is greater emphasis on systematic recruitment and hiring practices. Beginning in 1991, all state job openings were required to be listed with the Texas Employment Commission.[33]

Higher and public education employees are subject to different employment procedures and policies which are determined by individual university governing boards and local school districts. Unlike state government, many cities across Texas have adopted centrally administered merit systems organized around the accepted principles of modern personnel management. Their personnel departments include independent civil service commissions that have some rule-making authority and hear appeals of personnel matters.

## ADMINISTRATION IN TEXAS

Two of the biggest budget items in state government are public and higher education, and each is administered differently.

### Public Education

Public education is administered through local school districts, but regulations and coordination are provided on a statewide level through the State Board of Education and the Texas Education Agency, the latter headed by a state education commissioner. The State Board of Education includes 15 members elected on a partisan basis from single-member districts for four-year terms. Board members are not paid for their services but are reimbursed for official expenses, such as travel. The chairman of the board is designated by the governor.

This board was at the center of considerable controversy during the 1980s. Prior to reforms adopted in 1984, it included 27 members elected from each of the state's congressional districts. But reformers, including Dallas computer billionaire Ross Perot who chaired the Select Committee on Public Education, which produced many of the reform proposals, believed the old board stood in the way of meaningful change. It was replaced by a 15-member board that initially was appointed by the governor with a provision that it would automatically revert to an elected board within a few years. In 1986, when the legislature gave voters the option of an appointed or elected State Board of Education, voters overwhelmingly chose an elected board.

The Texas Education Agency, or TEA, is responsible for the day-to-day administration of educational policies set by the legislature and the state board. The agency accredits school districts, provides curriculum and technical assistance to districts, operates research and information programs, monitors school districts for compliance with federal and state guidelines, and distributes state and federal funds to the local districts.[34]

For many years, the education commissioner was hired directly by the State Board of Education, but the legislature changed the selection process in 1990 to give the governor the authority to approve or veto the board's choices. The commissioner also has to be confirmed by the Texas Senate. In 1991, Lionel "Skip" Meno became the first education commissioner selected by the new process and, with the board's approval, he moved quickly to impose a major reorganization on the TEA and improve assistance to school districts. Among other steps, Meno, who had been deputy superintendent of schools in New York, eliminated several top-level jobs in Austin in favor of beefing up regional offices. State board chair Carolyn Crawford said it was the first significant reorganization of the TEA since it was created in 1949. Before the overhaul, the agency frequently had been criticized by local school officials and some state leaders for being a bureaucratic obstacle to education reforms.[35]

Texas has approximately 1,050 individual school districts (see Chapter 12), which are administered by locally elected school boards but are subject to state laws and regulations and are heavily dependent on state funding.

## Higher Education

Texas has 12 separate university governing boards responsible for the administration of specific universities and professional schools plus the Texas Higher Education Coordinating Board, which administers the state's major student loan program and—unless bypassed by the legislature—has the authority to approve or reject all university construction projects and proposed degree programs.

The Coordinating Board has 18 members appointed by the governor to six-year staggered terms. Other university boards have nine members, also appointed by the governor. Like most other appointed policymakers in state government, all higher education board members are unsalaried but are compensated for expenses. The two most prestigious university boards are the University of Texas System and the Texas A&M University System boards of regents (Figure 10-2). They govern the state's two largest university systems.

## Other State Agencies

As noted earlier in this chapter, higher education, public safety and corrections, and social service agencies account for 80 percent of state government's work force.

The Department of Criminal Justice and the Department of Public Safety are the two major agencies responsible for public safety and corrections. The criminal justice agency is governed by a nine-member board appointed by the

**FIGURE 10-2** Alison Leland (second from right in the foreground) testifies before the Senate Nominations Committee in 1991 on her appointment to the Texas A&M University Board of Regents. She was the first African-American woman to be named to the board. (Texas Senate Media Services)

governor. One of its major functions is oversight of the state prison system, one of the largest in the world, which is administered through the department's institutional division. The agency also includes a community justice assistance division, which assists local governments with probation programs and other alternatives to incarceration, and a pardons and paroles division. Actual parole decisions, however, are the responsibility of a separate, 18-member, full-time parole board appointed by the governor.

The most visible employees of the Department of Public Safety are the highway patrol officers, who monitor highway traffic, issue speeding tickets and assist in emergencies. The DPS also includes a section responsible for issuing driver's licenses and operates a crime investigation laboratory and criminal law enforcement division that assist local police agencies. The Texas Rangers, a law enforcement organization that handles a variety of difficult assignments, is part of this agency.

State government's major social service agencies are the Texas Department of Human Services, the Texas Department of Health, and the Texas Department of Mental Health and Mental Retardation. DHS is the state's primary welfare agency. It administers the Aid to Families with Dependent Children welfare program and Medicaid assistance programs. MHMR supervises state hospitals for the mentally ill and state schools for the mentally retarded and supports community-based programs. In 1991, the legislature created an umbrella-type board in an attempt to provide more coordination between these agencies' programs and gave the governor the authority to appoint a "supercommissioner" of health and human services to give the governor more oversight over this critical and traditionally underfunded area of state government.

## *SUMMARY AND CONCLUSIONS*

**1.** Despite a historical ambivalence, if not animosity, toward government, Texans have come to expect good roads, public university systems affording inexpensive education, safe drinking water, and a host of other public programs to meet their needs and interests. With a population approximating 17 million people living in densely populated areas, it is almost axiomatic that government must grow and expand to meet the needs of this expanding population.

**2.** The biennial state budget now exceeds $60 billion, with more than 200,000 state employees. When the employees of local governments are added to this figure, there are more than 800,000 Texans employed by 4,000 governments spread across the state. Collectively, we refer to state and local administrative agencies as the bureaucracy.

**3.** State and local administrative agencies have the primary responsibility for implementing public policies that have been adopted by the legislature and local governing bodies. At the same time, it is quite evident that the administrative agencies also are involved in virtually every stage of the policy-making process. Legislative bodies depend on administrative agencies for counsel and advice when they formulate public policy, and they also rely on these same institutions for information in the assessment and evaluation of the success or failure of public policies.

**4.** When things go wrong and problems go unresolved, there is a tendency to blame bureaucrats. Big, bad government (the bureaucracy and bureaucrats) is a convenient whipping boy for those seeking public office, the mass media, and the general public. Often, government employees are unfairly blamed for complex problems that policymakers have been unwilling or unable to resolve.

**5.** The fragmented structure of the executive branch of state government is, by itself, a major obstacle to the efficient, responsive delivery of public services. Problems of public administration are further compounded by the fact that there are dozens of appointed, part-time, policy-setting boards that determine much of the activity of these agencies. Consequently, there is always the potential for these agencies to become unaccountable to the electorate and, in too many cases, susceptible to the influence of special interest groups.

**6.** The size of agencies, inefficient organizational structures, the agencies' self-interest, poor performance by some public employees, and the agency autonomy from public control are all legitimate criticisms of bureaucratic structures or behavior. There are a number of strategies available to policymakers to control bureaucracies and assure that policies are implemented as intended.

**7.** Through sunset legislation, Texas became one of the first states to require formal exhaustive review of how effectively agencies are doing their jobs. Within a specified period of time, most state agencies are subject to periodic reviews and must be reauthorized by the legislature. The procedure has not reduced the size of the state bureaucracy, but it has helped rid state government of obsolete agencies and produced greater accountability. Administrative agencies are closely linked to businesses, industries, and interest groups, and public employees can develop close relationships with these organizations. To minimize collusion and collaboration that benefit private industry, Texas has adopted revolving-door restrictions. That is, board members and key employees of regulatory agencies are prohibited from going to work for a regulated company within a certain period after leaving state employment.

**8.** While many local governments have adopted the merit system for employees, state government in Texas functions under a decentralized personnel system. It is highly fragmented with each agency largely free to set its own personnel policies. While some agencies have adopted high standards for the recruitment and advancement of their employees, other agencies continue to use political favoritism as the basis for their employment practices. Consequently, there are major differences in the quality of public employees among the state agencies.

## KEY TERMS

| | |
|---|---|
| Bureaucracy | Influence-peddling |
| Cooptation | Whistleblower |
| Revolving door | Licensing |

Ombudsman                                                    Political patronage
Sunset                                                          Merit system


## FURTHER READING

Campbell, Brett, "Killing the Messenger: Did DHS Retaliate Against a Whistleblower," *The Texas Observer*, July 12, 1991, pp. 8-11.
Curry, Landon, "Politics of Sunset Review in Texas," *Public Administration Review*, 50 (January-February, 1990), pp. 58-63.
Davis, Edwin S., "Rule Making Activity of Selected Texas Regulatory Agencies," *Texas Journal of Political Studies*, 8 (Fall/Winter 1986), pp. 26-36.
Dubnick, Melvin J., and Barbara S. Romzek, *American Public Administration*. New York: Macmillan Publishing Company, 1991.
Knabe, Eileen, et al., *Guide to Texas State Agencies*. Austin: Lyndon B. Johnson School of Public Affairs, The University of Texas at Austin, 1990.
Leon, Mark, "Watchdog or Lapdog?" *The Texas Observer*, April 5, 1991, pp. 6-7.
Meier, Kenneth J., *Regulation: Politics, Bureaucracy and Economics*. New York: St. Martin's Press, 1985.
Office of Governor, Division of Planning Coordination, *Quality Texas Government: People Make the Difference*. Study conducted by the Texas Research League, Austin, Texas, 1972.
Palumbo, Dennis, and Steven Maynard-Moody, *Contemporary Public Administration*. New York: Longman, 1991.
Schuman, David and Dick W. Olufs, III, *Public Administration in the United States*. Lexington, Mass: D.C. Heath and Company, 1988.
Slack, James D., "Bureaucracy and Bureaucrats in Texas," in Gerry Riposa, ed., *Texas Public Policy*. Dubuque, Iowa: Kendall/Hunt Publishing Company, 1987.
Slack, James D., "Representative Bureaucracy and Affirmative Action Policy in Texas Government: Implementing Federal Policy in the Lone Star State," in Gerry Riposa, ed., *Texas Public Policy*. Dubuque, Iowa: Kendall/Hunt Publishing Company, 1987.
Straussman, Jeffrey D., *Public Administration*, 2nd ed. New York: Longman, 1990.
Sunset Advisory Commission, *Recommendations to the Governor of Texas and Members of the Seventy-Second Legislature*, Final Report, March, 1991.
Ripley, Randall B., and Grace A. Franklin, *Policy Implementation and Bureaucracy*, 2nd ed. Chicago: The Dorsey Press, 1986.
Ripley, Randall B., and Grace A. Franklin, *Congress, the Bureaucracy, and Public Policy*, 3rd ed. Chicago: The Dorsey Press, 1984.


## ENDNOTES

1. State Comptroller's Office, "Breaking the Mold: A Report of the Texas Performance Review," Volume 1, July, 1991, p. 1.
2. See Max Weber, "Bureaucracy," in *Max Weber Essays in Sociology*, ed. H. H. Gerth and C. Wright Mills (New York: Oxford University Press, 1971), pp. 196-244.
3. Jeffrey D. Straussman, *Public Administration* (New York: Longman, 1990), p. 65.
4. The following discussion is based on Dennis Palumbo and Steven Maynard-Moody, *Contemporary Public Administration* (New York: Longman, 1991), pp. 26-31; and Jeffrey D. Straussman, *Public Administration* (New York: Longman, 1990), pp. 63-64.
5. Melvin J. Dubnick and Barbara S. Romzek, *American Public Administration* (New York: MacMillan Publishing Company, 1991), p. 248.
6. Dubnick and Romzek, *American Public Administration*, pp. 248-249.
7. Governor's Task Force on Revenue, *Charting a Course for Texas' Future: Toward a More Equitable System of Taxation*, July 19, 1991, pp. 8-9.
8. Theodore J. Lowi, *The End of Liberalism*, 2nd ed. (New York: W. W. Norton, 1979), p. 274.
9. Larry N. Gerston, *Making Public Policy* (Glenview, Ill.: Scott, Foresman and Company, 1983), p. 95.
10. Donald S. Van Meter and Carl E. Van Horn, "The Policy Implementation Process: A Conceptual Framework," *Administration and Society*, 6 (February 1975), p. 447.

11. Dennis Palumbo and Steven Maynard-Moody, *Contemporary Public Administration* (New York: Longman, 1991), p. 304.
12. Jeffrey D. Straussman, *Public Administration*, 2nd ed. (New York: Longman, 1990), p. 246.
13. Robert Lineberry, *American Public Policy* (New York: Harper & Row, 1977), pp. 84-85.
14. Sunset Advisory Commission Report, October 1991.
15. *Dallas Morning News*, October 24, 1991.
16. *Houston Chronicle*, April 18, 1990.
17. *The Texas Poll*, Harte-Hanks Communications, Inc., June 1990.
18. *Houston Chronicle*, June 26, 1990.
19. *Austin American-Statesman*, May 12, 1986.
20. *Houston Chronicle*, April 25, 1991.
21. *Amarillo Daily News*, September 18, 1991.
22. *Texas Weekly*, November 11, 1991, p. 5.
23. Colorado was the first state to adopt sunset legislation in 1976. See Straussman, *Public Administration*, p. 39.
24. Data provided by State Comptroller's office.
25. The Associated Press, as published in the *Dallas Times Herald*, August 14, 1983.
26. *Dallas Times Herald*, December 2, 1982.
27. Brett Campbell, "Killing the Messenger: Did DHS Retaliate Against a Whistleblower," *The Texas Observer*, July 12, 1991, pp. 8-11.
28. Straussman, *Public Administration*, p. 286.
29. William Lilley III and James C. Miller III, "The New Social Regulation," *The Public Interest*, 47 (Spring 1977), p. 53.
30. Council of State Governments, *The Book of the States, 1990-1991 Edition*, vol. 28 (Lexington, Ky.: Council of State Governments, 1990), p. 346.
31. For an excellent summary of the merit system movement, see Dennis Palumbo and Steven Maynard-Moody, *Contemporary Public Administration* (New York: Longman, 1991), pp. 165-174.
32. Office of the Governor, Division of Planning Coordination, *Quality Texas Government*, 1972. Much of the following discussion is based on this report.
33. Eugene W. Jones, Joe E. Ericson, Lyle C. Brown, and Robert S. Trotter, Jr., *Practicing Texas Politics*, 8th ed. (Boston: Houghton Mifflin Company, 1992), p. 319. For an extended discussion of the state's personnel policies, see James E. Anderson, Richard W. Murray, and Edward L. Farley, *Texas Politics: An Introduction*, 6th ed. (New York: HarperCollins Publishers, 1992), pp. 213-216.
34. Texas Education Agency, *Snapshot '90: 1989-1990 School District Profiles* (Austin: Texas Education Agency, 1991), p. 2.
35. *Austin American-Statesman*, October 12, 1991.

# 11

# THE JUDICIAL SYSTEM IN TEXAS

> It is fair to suggest that Texas does not have a "court system" or "judicial system."
>
> *Texas Research League*[1]

Texas, of course, does have courts—about 2,600 of them. It's the system that is missing in an assortment of courts of various, often overlapping jurisdictions that grows and becomes more unwieldy almost every time the legislature meets. Courts resolve civil disputes over property rights and personal injuries. They determine guilt or innocence and set punishment in criminal cases involving offenses against people, their property, and public institutions. And they help set public policy by reviewing the actions of the executive and legislative branches of government. A civil dispute may stem from something as simple as a tenant breaking an apartment lease to something as complex and potentially expensive as an auto manufacturer's liability for a defective brake system that contributes to the deaths or injuries of dozens of motorists. Criminal cases range from traffic offenses, punishable by fines, to capital murder, for which the death penalty can be imposed. Court-imposed changes in public policy have included such national milestones as desegregation and orders specifically directing Texas to make extensive improvements in public education financing, the care of the mentally ill and the mentally retarded, and the state prison system.

Some streamlining of Texas judicial processes, especially at the appellate level, was accomplished in 1981. But the Texas judiciary, particularly in urban areas, has become overloaded by a high crime rate and an increasingly litigious approach to civil disputes. It can take months to get a civil or a criminal case—one that isn't settled out of court or in a plea bargain with prosecutors—to trial. By the 1980s, the judiciary also had become a philosophical and political battleground, the subject of embarrassing national media attention and the target of numerous calls for reform.

## THE STATE COURTS IN THE FEDERAL SYSTEM

Like people in every state, Texans are subject to the jurisdiction of both state and federal courts. The federal judiciary, created by Article III of the United States Constitution, has jurisdiction over violations of federal laws—including criminal offenses that occur across state lines, such as illegal drug trafficking—and banking, securities, and other activities regulated by the federal government. Federal courts also have had major effects on state government policies and Texas' criminal justice system through interpretations and applications of the U.S. Constitution and federal laws, including the Bill of Rights. Texas has a bill of rights in its constitution, but the federal courts have taken the lead in forcing policies protecting civil and political rights. The U.S. Supreme Court declared the white primary election unconstitutional in *Smith* v. *Allwright* in 1944. And federal court intervention continues in the redistricting of legislative and congressional district lines to avoid the dilution of minority votes under the Voting Rights Act. The federal judiciary also has ordered far-reaching improvements in the state prison system and in facilities for treating the mentally ill and the mentally retarded. And when a policeman reads a criminal suspect his rights, he is complying with constitutional requirements determined by the U.S. Supreme Court in the so-called Miranda case.

It is estimated, however, that 95 percent of all litigation is based on state laws or local ordinances. So if any of us is involved in litigation, it is likely to take place in state rather than federal court.

## THE LEGAL FRAMEWORK FOR THE JUDICIAL SYSTEM

The United States and Texas constitutions form the basic legal framework of the Texas court system. Building on that framework, the Texas legislature has enacted codes of criminal and civil procedure to govern conduct in the courtroom and statutory laws for the courts to apply. Most criminal activities are defined and their punishments established in the **Penal Code**. The most serious crimes, which can be punished by imprisonment, are classified as felonies, while more minor offenses, punishable by fines or county jail terms only, are called misdemeanors. In criminal cases the state, often based on charges made by another individual, initiates action against a person accused of a crime.

**Civil lawsuits** can be brought under numerous statutes and involve conflicts between two or more parties, be they individuals, corporations, governments, or other entities. There are laws governing contracts and property rights between private citizens, consumer protection laws that afford individuals an avenue for relief against corporate abuses, liability laws governing personal injuries, and administrative laws that give state regulators enforcement powers against environmental polluters.

An individual with a grievance to be addressed has to take the initiative of going to court. A person can experience problems with a landlord who refuses to return a deposit, a dry cleaner who lost a suit, or a friend who borrowed and wrecked a car. But in a civil dispute, there is no legal issue to be resolved unless a lawsuit is filed. An injured person filing a lawsuit is a plaintiff. Since even the most minor disputes in the lowest courts can require professional assistance from a lawyer, a person will soon discover that the pursuit of justice can be very costly and time-consuming.

Statutes and constitutional laws also are subject to change through legislative action and popular consent of the electorate, and over the years there have been significant changes in what is legal or illegal, permissible or impermissible. At one time, for example, state law provided for a potential life prison sentence for the possession of a few ounces of marijuana; small amounts are now considered a misdemeanor punishable by a fine. The legal drinking age was lowered to 18 for a few years but reestablished at 21 after parents and school officials convinced the legislature that the younger age had helped increase alcohol abuse among teenagers.

## THE STRUCTURE OF THE TEXAS COURT SYSTEM

There are five levels of Texas courts, but because of constitutional and statutory provisions, courts at different levels have overlapping authority and jurisdiction (Figure 11-1). Two different levels of courts may have jurisdiction over the same type of criminal or civil cases. Some courts have only **original jurisdiction**. That is, they can only try or resolve cases being heard for the first time. They weigh the facts presented as evidence in a case and apply the law in reaching a decision or verdict. Other courts have only **appellate jurisdiction**. They review the decisions of lower courts to determine if constitutional and statutory principles and procedures were correctly interpreted and followed, and they are empowered to reverse the judgments of the lower courts and order cases retried if constitutional or procedural mistakes were made. Still other courts have both original and appellate jurisdiction.

At the highest appellate level, Texas has a **bifurcated court system** with the nine-member Texas Supreme Court serving as the court of last resort in civil cases and the nine-member Texas Court of Criminal Appeals functioning as the court of last resort in criminal cases. Only one other state, Oklahoma, has a similar structure.[2]

Unlike federal judges, who are appointed by the president to lifetime terms, state judges, except for those on municipal courts, are elected to limited terms in partisan elections.

### Courts of Limited Jurisdiction

The lowest ranking courts in Texas are municipal courts and justice of the peace courts. There is a high probability that you or someone you know has appeared before a judge in one of these courts because both handle a large volume of traffic

# COURT STRUCTURE OF TEXAS
## SEPTEMBER 1, 1991

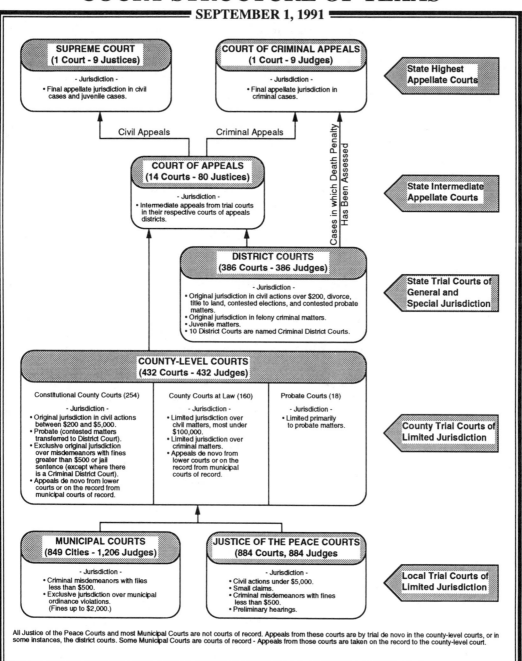

FIGURE 11-1   Court Structure of Texas.  (Office of Court Administration.)

tickets. Some of these courts are big revenue raisers for local governments, and they often are accused of subordinating justice and fairness to financial considerations.

There are about 800 **municipal courts** established under state law. In many of the larger cities, multiple courts have been authorized to handle the heavy workload. The qualifications, terms of office, and method of selecting municipal judges are determined by the individual cities, but they are generally appointed by the city council. Municipal courts have original and exclusive jurisdiction over city ordinances, but most of these courts are not courts of record, where a word-for-word transcript is made of trial proceedings. Only very rudimentary information is officially recorded in most of these courts, and any appeal from them is heard *de novo* by the higher court. That means the second court has to conduct a complete new trial and hear the same witnesses and evidence all over again because no official record of the original proceedings was kept. The informality of these proceedings and the absence of a record reduce the probability of appeals and add to the confusion and cost of using the system.[3] In response to these problems, the legislature in recent years has created municipal courts of record for some cities.

Each county in Texas is required to provide for one **justice of the peace court**, and county governments in the larger metropolitan areas may each create 16 of them. Justices of the peace are elected to four-year terms from precincts, or subdivisions of the county drawn by commissioners court, which also sets their salaries. Justices of the peace are not required to be licensed attorneys, which has been one of the major criticisms of these courts. Each justice of the peace precinct has an elected constable who serves warrants and performs other duties for the court.

Although their duties vary from county to county, justice of the peace courts, with certain restrictions, have original jurisdiction in civil cases when the amount in dispute is $5,000 or less and have original jurisdiction over criminal offenses that are punishable by fines only. In some areas of criminal law, they have overlapping jurisdiction with municipal courts. Justices of the peace also sit as judges of small claims courts, and in many rural counties they serve as coroners. They also function as state magistrates with the authority to hold preliminary hearings to determine if there is probable cause to hold a criminal defendant. These are not courts of record, and cases appealed from these courts generally start de novo in county courts.

## County Courts

If there is confusion about the authority and jurisdiction of the two courts mentioned above, the problem is compounded by the county courts. They were created by the constitution to serve the needs of the sparsely populated, rural society that existed when the charter was written in 1876. But population growth and urbanization have placed enormous demands on the judicial system and, rather than modernize the system, the state has added additional courts while making only modest changes in the structure and jurisdiction of the older courts.

Each county has a **constitutional county court**. The holder of this office, the county judge, is elected countywide to a four-year term. This individual is the chief executive officer of the county and presides over the county commissioners court, the policy-making body of county government. Most urban county judges don't perform judicial duties. But county judges in many rural counties perform both executive and judicial functions, which some experts believe is inconsistent with the constitution's separation of powers doctrine. While a large number of the county judges are lawyers, they are not required to be. They are required only to be "well informed in the law" and must take appropriate courses in evidence and legal procedures.

The county court shares some original civil jurisdiction with both the justice of the peace and the district court and has civil appellate jurisdiction over justice courts when the amount in dispute is $20 or more. The county court has no criminal jurisdiction in counties that have a criminal district court. Otherwise, it has exclusive original criminal jurisdiction over misdemeanors, except those involving official misconduct or those where the maximum fine is $200 or less. The county court has criminal appellate jurisdiction over the justice of the peace and municipal courts. One of the primary functions of these courts is probating the wills of deceased individuals.

Over the years, the legislature has also created 178 **statutory county courts** in 69 counties that initially were designed to deal with specific local problems and, consequently, have inconsistent jurisdictions. All judges on these courts have to be lawyers, but the authority of a particular court is defined by the legislation creating it. Some of these courts can't hear civil disputes of more than $2,500, while others can hear disputes of as much as $100,000. Some have exclusive probate jurisdiction in their respective counties. Drunken driving cases are the primary criminal cases tried before these courts.

## Courts of General Jurisdiction

The primary trial court in Texas is the **district court**. While there is some overlapping jurisdiction with county courts, the district courts have original jurisdiction over civil cases involving $500 or more in damages and criminal felony cases. The legislature has created a number of district courts with specialized jurisdictions over criminal or civil law or over such specialties as family law—divorces and child custody cases. In a number of the large metropolitan counties that have several district courts, the jurisdictions of the respective courts are determined by informal agreements among the judges. District court judges are elected to four-year terms, must be at least 25 years old, and must have practiced law or served as a judge of another court for four years prior to taking office.

The constitution gives the legislature the responsibility to define judicial districts, and as the expanding population produced greater caseloads, new districts were created. In 1981, there were 328 district courts. By 1991, there were 386 judicial districts, with one judge per district. A single county may be allocated more than one district court with overlapping geographical jurisdiction. Harris County, the state's most populous county, had 59 district courts in 1991, each covering the entire county. By contrast, one rural district court may include several counties. As these courts evolved, there was little systematic consideration of the respective workloads of individual courts, and now there are great disparities in the number of people that district courts serve.

Although new courts have been added in the counties of greatest growth, many urban counties suffer from a heavy backlog of cases that can delay a trial date in a civil lawsuit for months or years and has prompted a widespread use of plea bargains in criminal cases. In a **plea bargain**, a criminal defendant, through his lawyer, will negotiate a guilty plea with prosecutors that will get him a lesser sentence than he could expect to receive if convicted in a trial. The process saves the state the time-consuming expense of a full-blown trial and has become an essential tool in clearing urban court dockets.

District Attorney John B. Holmes Jr. has estimated that 90 percent of the 25,000-plus felony cases filed in Harris County (Houston) each year are disposed of through plea bargains. Without plea bargains, the caseload would simply overwhelm the 22 Harris County district courts that handle criminal cases. In 1991, Holmes said, it took an average 45 to 60 days to get the remaining criminal cases to trial in the county. Some judges worked faster than others, but much of the remaining delays, he said, were "self-imposed" by prosecutors or defense lawyers through various motions.

Harris County's remaining 37 district courts, meanwhile, disposed of more than 86,000 civil lawsuits—divorces, workers compensation claims, personal injuries, tax disputes, and others—in fiscal 1990 but left almost 98,000 other cases pending. With more than 26,000 of the dispositions involving cases that were more than 18 months old—many were much older than that—individuals seeking justice through the courts can legitimately ask how long does justice have to be delayed before it is denied. Many civil lawsuits are resolved through negotiations between the opposing parties, but those that are tried and appealed can take several years to be resolved.

The wide disparities in populations and caseloads served by the various district courts prompted the adoption of a constitutional amendment in 1985 that created the Judicial Districts Board, chaired by the chief justice of the Texas Supreme Court. That panel will be responsible for redistricting judicial districts with an eye toward a more equitable distribution of the workload if the legislature fails to act by 1993.

Although the district court is the state's primary trial court, and the state pays the district judges' base salaries, the counties pick up virtually all the other district court expenses. The counties provide courtrooms, pay the courts' operating expenses, and supplement the judges' state pay.

## Intermediate Courts of Appeal

There are 14 intermediate **Courts of Appeals** covering 13 multicounty regions that hear appeals of both civil and criminal cases from the district courts. Two courts, the 1st and 14th, are based in Houston and cover the same area. The constitution provides that each court has a chief justice and at least two other justices, but the legislature can add to that number and has done so for most courts. Each Houston court has nine judges, and the 5th Court of Appeals in Dallas has 13 judges. Five of these intermediate courts, however, have only three members. Appellate judges are elected to six-year terms. They must be at least 35 years old and have at least 10 years of experience as an attorney or a judge on a court of record.

These courts had a combined total of more than 14,000 cases on their dockets in 1990, with criminal cases accounting for more than 50 percent of their load. But there are wide disparities in the caseloads between individual courts, with those in Houston and Dallas handling the lion's share. The Texas Supreme Court partially balances the load by transferring cases between courts. The courts of appeals normally decide cases in panels of three judges, but an entire court can hear some appeals *en banc*. It takes the courts an average of eight months to dispose of a civil appeal and nine months for a criminal appeal.[4]

## The Appellate Courts

The creation of separate courts of last resort for civil and criminal cases resulted from a commitment by the constitutional framers of 1876 to fragmenting political power and decentralizing the structure of state and local government. It also was based on the rationale that criminal cases should be tried more expeditiously, and the way to accomplish this was through a separate appellate court.[5]

Although it decides only civil appeals, the **Supreme Court** is probably viewed by most as the titular head of the state judiciary, and it has been given some authority to effect coordination of the state judicial system.[6] The Supreme Court is charged with developing administrative procedures for the state courts and rules of civil procedure. It appoints the Board of Law Examiners, which is responsible for licensing attorneys, and the court has oversight of the State Bar, the professional organization to which all lawyers in Texas must belong. The Supreme Court also has disciplinary authority over state judges, through recommendations of the State Commission on Judicial Conduct. All of these responsibilities, however, do not compensate for the lack of a unified judicial system.

The Supreme Court is comprised of a chief justice and eight justices who serve staggered, six-year terms. Three members are up for election every two years on a statewide ballot. Members must be at least 35 and have been a practicing attorney, a judge of a court of record, or a combination of both for at least 10 years.

The **Court of Criminal Appeals**, which hears only criminal cases on appeal, includes a presiding judge and eight other judges elected statewide to staggered, six-year terms. The qualifications for members of this court are the same as those for the Supreme Court.

Under the federal system, some decisions of the Texas Supreme Court and the Court of Criminal Appeals can be appealed to the U.S. Supreme Court. Those cases have to involve a federal question or a constitutional right assured under the U.S. Constitution.

## IN SEARCH OF A JUDICIAL SYSTEM

Judicial reform has been a recurring issue in Texas politics. Small, incremental changes have been made since the 1970s, but there are many jurists and scholars who continue to push for an overhaul of the state courts. In September 1989, Texas Supreme Court Chief Justice Thomas R. Phillips requested an in-depth study of the Texas judiciary by the Texas Research League, a privately financed, nonprofit organization specializing in studies of state government.

The Research League concluded that the court system was fundamentally flawed and sorely in need of an overhaul. It made 27 recommendations, including one that the legislature rewrite the judiciary article of the state constitution to provide a fundamental framework for a unified court system. It also recommended that:

- the statutory and constitutional county courts be  abolished with the county judge being given only administrative and executive duties over county  government.
- the state be divided into new geographic judicial  districts, each with only one district court. The  legislature could provide for more than one judge per  court, where necessary.
- there be only one intermediate court of appeals with multiple divisions composed of at least three judges each.
- the Court of Criminal Appeals be retained as the court of last resort in criminal cases but the Supreme Court be recognized as the head of the state court system and be responsible for its management. "Ideally, a court system should have only one court at its head. However, current workloads and backlogs mitigate against the merger of the state's two top courts."[7]

Despite a series of similar studies and reports, however, reform of Texas courts has been difficult. The public may have a lot to gain from judicial restructuring, but the primary stakeholders—the judges, the attorneys, the court administrative personnel, and litigants who benefit from delays, confusion, and inefficiency—have resisted such change. Unless there is a spontaneous popular demand for reform, there will be few structural changes in the judiciary until some or all of these participants perceive some advantages from reform.[8]

## THE COURT PERSONNEL

### Texas Judges

In November 1990, the last month for which extensive data were available, most members of the intermediate and highest appellate courts had served on lower courts prior to their election or appointment to the appellate benches. Most district judges had come to the bench directly from private law practice or from a prosecutor's office, rather than from county or justice of the peace courts. There was a much greater diversity in career patterns for judges on the county courts, justice of the peace courts, and municipal courts, given the limited constitutional requirements for many of those positions.

The ages of Supreme Court justices ranged from 41 to 64, while the ages of the judges on the Court of Criminal Appeals ranged from 41 to 68. The age range on the Courts of Appeals was 39 to 73 with an average of 57, and on the district courts, 32 to 75, with an average of 52. The average length of service on the Supreme Court was four years, nine months; on the Court of Criminal Appeals, six years, nine months; on the Courts of Appeals, seven years, two months; and on the district courts, eight years. At that time, the most experienced district judge had been in office for 33 years.[9]

By 1990, about one-third of the judges at the district court level and higher were Republicans. The development of a two-party system in Texas has impacted the partisan affiliation of state judges. Republicans have seen election gains and, thanks to the recent tenure of Republican Governor Bill Clements, more appointments to fill judicial vacancies. A number of judges also have switched from the Democratic party. Dallas County, in particular, has experienced considerable party switching by incumbent judges.[10]

The majority of Texas judges are white males. With greater frequency, however, women as well as Hispanics and African-Americans are now entering the legal profession and running for judicial offices. Their success may be further enhanced if the federal courts order changes in the judicial selection process.

## Other Participants in the State Judiciary

There are a number of other elected and appointed offices that are part of the judicial system. County and district clerks, both elected offices, are custodians of court records. Bailiffs are peace officers assigned to the courts to help maintain order and protect judges and other parties from physical attacks. Other law enforcement officers play critical roles in the arrest, detention and investigation of persons accused of crimes.

The officeholders responsible for prosecuting criminal cases are the county attorneys and the district attorneys, both of whom are elected (see Chapter 12). Some counties don't have a county attorney. In those that do, he or she is the chief legal advisor to county commissioners, represents the county in civil lawsuits, and prosecutes misdemeanors, the more minor criminal offenses. The district attorney prosecutes felonies and, in counties that don't have a county attorney, also handles misdemeanors. The district attorney exercises considerable power in the criminal justice process by deciding which cases to take to a grand jury for an indictment, whether to seek the maximum penalty for an offense or whether to plea bargain with a defendant for a reduced sentence. The office represents one county in metropolitan areas and several counties in less populated areas of the state.

## The Jury Systems

Other important players in the judicial process are the private citizens who serve on juries, of which there are two kinds—grand juries and trial or petit juries. While there is some debate about the competency of a jury of ordinary citizens to make reasonable decisions on complex and technical civil and criminal matters, we have not been able to develop any acceptable or viable alternatives.

The **grand jury**, which has its origins in early English law, functions, in theory, to assure that the government has sufficient reason to proceed with a criminal **prosecution** against an individual. It includes 12 persons selected by a district judge from a list proposed by a jury commission, which was appointed by the local district judge or judges. Although the grand jury evolved to protect the individual against arbitrary and capricious behavior by governmental officials, there have been allegations over the years that grand juries represented the interests and concerns of upper social and economic groups and underrepresented minorities. A district attorney also can exercise great control over a grand jury because he or she decides what evidence and which witnesses jurors will hear. Grand jury meetings and deliberations are conducted in private, and the accused is not allowed to have an attorney present during grand jury questioning.

A grand jury usually meets on specified days of the week and serves for the duration of the district court's term, usually from three to six months. If at least nine grand jurors believe there is enough evidence to warrant a trial in a case under investigation, they will issue an **indictment**, or a "true bill," a written statement charging a person or persons with a crime. A grand jury investigation also may result in no indictment, or a "no bill."

In some cases, grand juries will issue indictments alleging misdemeanors. That often happens after an investigation fails to produce a strong enough case for a felony indictment. Most misdemeanors, however, aren't handled by grand juries. A district or county attorney can prepare an information, a document formally charging an individual with a misdemeanor, on the basis of a complaint filed against the accused by a private citizen.

The jury on which most people are likely to be called to serve is the trial or **petit jury** (Figure 11-2). Texas and United States citizens who are at least 18 and meet other minimal requirements are eligible, and anyone refusing to comply with a jury summons can be fined for contempt of court. The legislature in 1991 increased the likelihood of an individual being called to jury duty by providing that county and district clerks prepare jury summonses from lists of those Texans who have drivers' licenses or hold Department of Public Safety identification cards. Previously, prospective jurors were chosen from voter registration lists, and it was believed that many Texans had not been registering to vote so as to avoid jury duty. Persons older than 65, individuals with legal custody of young children and fulltime students remain exempted from jury duty.

Six persons make up a jury in a justice of the peace or county court, and 12 in a district court. Attorneys for both sides in a criminal or civil case screen the

**FIGURE 11-2**  A pool of prospective jurors is assembled in Harris County.  The state's most populous county, Harris has 59 state district courts.  (© *Houston Chronicle*.  Reprinted with permission.)

prospective jurors, known as veniremen, before a jury is seated. In major felony cases, such as capital murder, prosecutors and defense attorneys may take several days to select a jury from among hundreds of prospects. Attorneys for each side are allowed a certain number of peremptory challenges, which allow them to dismiss a prospective juror without having to explain the reason, and an unlimited number of challenges for cause. In the latter case, the lawyer has to state why he or she believes a particular venireman wouldn't be able to impartially hear and evaluate the evidence in the case. The judge decides whether to grant each challenge for cause but can rule against a peremptory challenge only if he believes the prosecutor is trying to exclude prospective jurors because of their race, such as keeping African-Americans off a jury that is to try an African-American defendant. If that happens, the defendant is entitled to a new group, or panel, of prospective jurors. The prosecution and defense are each allowed as many as 15 peremptory challenges in capital cases, those in which the death penalty can be imposed. Fewer are allowed in other criminal trials.

In civil cases, attorneys for both sides determine whether any persons on the jury panel should be disqualified because they are related to one of the parties, have some other personal or business connection, or could otherwise be prejudiced. For example, a lawyer defending a doctor in a malpractice suit probably would not want to seat a prospective juror who had been dissatisfied with his own medical treatment. Such potential conflicts are discovered by attorneys' careful screening and questioning of veniremen. In addition to those challenges for cause, which aren't limited, attorneys for each side are allowed a limited number of peremptory challenges.

Unanimous jury verdicts are required to convict a defendant in a criminal case. Agreement of only 10 of the 12 members of a district court jury and five of the six on a county court jury, however, are necessary to reach a verdict in a civil suit. In a criminal case, jurors have to be convinced "beyond a reasonable doubt" that a defendant is guilty before returning a guilty verdict.

## JUDICIAL PROCEDURES AND DECISION MAKING

At the trial court level, civil litigants and criminal defendants (except those charged with capital murder) can waive their right to a jury trial if they believe it would be to their advantage to have their cases decided by a judge rather than a group of their peers. Following established procedures, which differ between civil and criminal cases and which are enforced by the judge, the trial moves through the presentation of opening arguments by the opposing attorneys, examination and cross examination of witnesses, presentation of evidence, rebuttal, and summation. Some trials can be completed in a few hours, while the trial of a complex civil lawsuit or a sensational criminal case can take weeks, or months. Convicted criminal defendants or parties dissatisfied with a judge or jury's verdict in a civil lawsuit can then appeal their case to higher courts.

The procedure in the appellate courts is markedly different from that in the trial courts. There is no jury at the appellate level to rehear evidence. Instead, judges review the decisions and the procedures of the lower court for conformance to constitutional and statutory requirements. The record of the trial court proceedings plus legal briefs filed by attorneys are available for appellate judges to review.

Most civil and criminal appeals are initially made to one of the 14 intermediate Courts of Appeals. (Death penalty cases are appealed directly to the Court of Criminal Appeals.) Parties dissatisfied with decisions of the Courts of Appeals can appeal to the Texas Supreme Court or the Court of Criminal Appeals.

Cases reach the Supreme Court primarily on **writs of error** alleging a lower court has ruled erroneously on points of law. Applications for writ of error seeking reversals of lower court decisions are rotated among the nine Supreme Court justices (Figure 11-3). The justices and their briefing attorneys then prepare memos on their assigned cases for circulation among the other court members. Meeting in private conference the court decides which applications to reject outright—thus upholding the lower court decisions—and which to schedule for oral, attorneys' arguments. A case won't be heard without the approval of at least four of the nine justices.

Differences over legal points can be debated at length behind the closed doors of the conference room. But Franklin Spears, a Democrat who served in the

**FIGURE 11-3** Texas Supreme Court, 1992. Front row, left to right: Eugene A. Cook, Raul A. Gonzalez, Chief Justice Thomas R. Phillips, Oscar H. Mauzy, Jack Hightower. Back row, left to right: John Cornyn, Nathan L. Hecht, Lloyd Doggett, Bob Gammage. (© 1991, Thomas P. Murray)

legislature from 1959 to 1967 and then served 12 years on the Supreme Court before retiring at the end of 1990, said the debate among court members never got acrimonious. "It's a different kind of debate than the robust debate in the legislature," he said. "In the legislature it's every member for himself. Everybody competes with everybody else." Since legislators debate in public, they are keenly aware of the political impressions they make on special interest groups and other constituents. Members of the court who debate in private have to make convincing legal, rather than political, arguments to their peers.

Attorneys' oral arguments, however, are presented in open court. The lawyers argue their perspectives on the legal points that are at issue and answer questions from the justices. Three cases usually are scheduled for oral arguments each week, and three justices on a rotating basis are responsible for writing the opinions on cases heard in a particular week. The three justices draw slips of paper to determine who writes which opinion. It usually takes several weeks—and sometimes several months—after oral arguments before a decision is issued. Supreme Court orders and opinions are issued once a week, except for the several weeks each year that the court is in summer recess.

Most cases taken to the Supreme Court on appeal are from one of the Courts of Appeals, but occasionally the Supreme Court will receive a direct appeal from a district court. In 1980, the high court agreed to hear about one in every eight applications for writ of error that it received. That percentage had been reduced to about one in 14 by 1990, after the court had changed its rules to increase from three to four the number of justices required to approve a hearing.

The Supreme Court also acts on hundreds of petitions for **writs of mandamus,** or orders directing a lower court or another public official to take a certain action. Many of those involve disputes over procedure or evidence in cases still pending in trial courts. In fiscal 1990, there were 866 applications for writ of error and 780 other writs and motions filed with the Supreme Court.

The Court of Criminal Appeals has appellate jurisdiction in criminal cases that originate in the district and county courts (Figure 11-4). It must sit as a full, nine-member court when considering appeals of capital murder cases, and decisions must be rendered by a five-person majority. For other criminal cases, the court is divided into three-member panels with two judges constituting a majority. Although capital murder cases are appealed directly to the Court of Criminal Appeals, other cases are appealed first to the intermediate Courts of Appeals and are reviewed by the criminal court at its discretion.

**FIGURE 11-4** Texas Court of Criminal Appeals, 1992. Front row, left to right: Charles F. Campbell, Sam Houston Clinton, Presiding Judge Michael J. McCormick, Chuck Miller, Bill White. Back row, left to right: Frank Maloney, Charles Baird, Morris Overstreet, Fortunato Benavides. (© 1991, Thomas P. Murray)

Before the adoption of a constitutional amendment in 1981, all criminal appeals went directly from the trial court to the Court of Criminal Appeals because the intermediate courts handled only civil cases—they were, in fact, then known as the Courts of Civil Appeals. The change greatly reduced a backlog of cases before the Court of Criminal Appeals from more than 4,000 in 1983 to 550 only three years later. Over the next several years, the criminal court granted approximately 13 percent of the petitions for discretionary review that it received.[11]

## JUDICIAL SELECTION IN TEXAS

As previously noted, all judges, except for those on municipal court benches, are elected in partisan elections. Midterm vacancies, however, are filled by appointment. Vacancies on the justice of the peace and county courts are filled by county commissioners courts, while vacancies on the district and appellate benches are filled by the governor.

Most Texans apparently believe that the popular election of judges is the best way to keep the judiciary responsive to the public. In a non-binding primary referendum in 1988, Texas Democrats approved the continued election of judges by a 4-1 margin. But the election process has been significantly diluted by a large number of appointments to judicial vacancies. Many retiring judges will leave office in mid-term to give the governor the opportunity to appoint a successor—if the governor belongs to the same political party. And in some cases, the legislature will create new district courts with effective dates between elections so that the governor gets to appoint their first judges. In reality, therefore, Texas has a mixed judicial selection system.

As of November 1990, three of the nine members of the Texas Supreme Court and three of the nine judges on the Texas Court of Criminal Appeals had initially been appointed to the bench. Slightly more than half of the Courts of Appeals judges and about 60 percent of the state district judges had initially been appointed.[12] Appointees are required to run for office in the next general election to keep their seats, but their incumbency enhances their election chances.

In recent years, the legislature has been under increasing political and legal pressure to change the way state judges are selected. Among the most frequently mentioned alternatives are nonpartisan elections, elections from geographic districts, or a so-called **merit selection**, or Missouri, plan for appointing judges. Under the latter proposal, the governor would initially appoint judges from lists of potential nominees recommended by committees of experts. The appointed judges would have to run later in retention elections to keep their seats, but they wouldn't have opponents on the ballot. Voters would simply decide whether a judge should remain in office or be removed—to be replaced by another gubernatorial appointee.

## CONTEMPORARY ISSUES IN JUDICIAL SELECTION

Throughout much of the 1980s and into the 1990s, the state courts were at the center of conflict and controversy. Reports of large campaign contributions from lawyers to judges and judicial candidates raised allegations that Texas had the best justice money could buy. The philosophical makeup of the Supreme Court underwent a major change in favor of plaintiffs, and suddenly billions of dollars were at stake in crucial legal decisions that the corporate establishment was beginning to lose. Meanwhile, minorities, who held a disproportionately small number of judicial offices, pressed for greater influence in electing judges, and lengthy ballots, particularly in urban areas, made it increasingly difficult for most voters to choose intelligently among judicial candidates.

## Judicial Activism

In earlier chapters, we noted the historical domination of state politics and policies by the conservative business-oriented establishment. For decades, that domination also applied to the judiciary, as insurance companies, banks, utilities, and other large corporate entities became accustomed to favorable rulings from a Democratic, but conservative, Texas Supreme Court.

Establishment-oriented justices, usually elected with the support of the state's largest law firms, tended to view their role as strict constructionists. The legislature had the authority to enact public policy, and the responsibility of the courts, they believed, was to narrowly interpret and apply the law. Within this strict framework, judges were not to engage in setting policy but were to honor legal precedent and prior case law, which had generally favored the interests of corporations over those of consumers, laborers, and the lower social classes.

The establishment began to feel the first tremors of a philosophical earthquake in the 1970s. The Texas Trial Lawyers Association, whose members represent consumers in lawsuits against businesses, doctors, and insurance companies, increased its political activity. And in 1973, the legislature, with increased minority and female membership from single-member House districts ordered by the federal courts, enacted the Deceptive Trade Practices-Consumer Protection Act, which encouraged plaintiffs, or injured parties, to take their grievances to court. Among other things, the new law allowed consumers to sue for attorneys' fees as well as compensatory and punitive damages.

Trial, or plaintiffs', attorneys, who usually receive a healthy percentage of monetary damages awarded their clients, began contributing millions of dollars to successful Supreme Court candidates, and judicial precedents started falling. A revamped court issued significant decisions that made it easier for consumers to win large judgments for medical malpractice, faulty products, and other complaints against businesses and their insurers. The new activist, liberal interpretation of the law contrasted sharply with the traditional record of the court. "All of a sudden, we have a magnificent Supreme Court, which is not controlled by a sinister, rich, opulent elite," trial attorney Pat Maloney of San Antonio, a major contributor to Supreme Court candidates, said in a 1983 interview with the *Fort Worth Star-Telegram*.[13]

The business community and defense lawyers accused the new court majority of exceeding its constitutional authority by trying to write its own laws. Some business leaders contended the court's activism endangered the state's economy by discouraging new businesses from moving to Texas, a fear that was soon to be put to partisan advantage by Republican leaders.

At various times in the early and mid-1980s, the lineup on the Supreme Court was viewed as 5-4 or 6-3 in favor of positions advocated by plaintiffs' attorneys. But the court also issued unanimous major opinions, sometimes coming down on the side of the plaintiffs, sometimes on the side of the defense.

## Campaign Contributions and Judicial Politics

The controversy over the Supreme Court escalated into a full-blown storm in 1986 when the Judicial Affairs Committee of the Texas House investigated two justices, Democrats C.L. Ray and William Kilgarlin, for alleged improper contact with attorneys practicing before the court. The two justices denied the allegations, largely made by former briefing attorneys, but never testified before the legislative panel. Both justices had consistently sided with trial lawyers and had received considerable campaign support from the plaintiffs' bar, but they contended the investigation was politically motivated and orchestrated by defense lawyers and corporate interests opposed to their judicial activism.

Questions also were raised about the motivation of the committee chairman, state Representative Frank Tejeda, a Democrat from San Antonio who received much publicity from the investigation while successfully campaigning for a state Senate seat. Even some legislators on the committee believed the investigation should have been left to the State Commission on Judicial Conduct, a state agency charged with investigating complaints of ethical violations by state judges.

Chief Justice John L. Hill voluntarily testified before the committee and said he suspected but couldn't prove that information about the Supreme Court's deliberations on some cases had been improperly leaked to outsiders. But Hill also urged the committee to let the judicial conduct commission investigate the allegations and "let the chips fall where they may."[14] The committee eventually concluded its investigation without recommending any action against the justices.

Hill, a former attorney general who had narrowly lost a gubernatorial race to Republican Bill Clements in 1978, had been a strong supporter of electing state judges and had spent more than $1 million winning the chief justice's seat in 1984. As did his colleagues on the court, he accepted many campaign contributions from lawyers. Reversing his position in 1986, Hill announced that the "recent trend toward excessive political contributions in judicial races" had prompted him to change his mind.[15] He now advocated the so-called merit selection, or Missouri, plan of gubernatorial appointments and periodic retention elections. But Hill was the only Supreme Court member to endorse such a change. The other eight justices—like Hill, all Democrats—still favored the elective system, and the legislature ignored pleas for change.

According to reports filed with the secretary of state, campaign contributions to Supreme Court candidates between 1982 and 1984 averaged nearly $340,000.[16] Some candidates received more than $100,000 from a single individual. In 1984, the average total contributions to a campaign for district judge was $53,000. Again, there were some candidates who depended on large contributions from a handful of people, while others built their campaign war chests on small contributions from numerous supporters.[17] Reformers argued that such large contributions were creating an appearance of impropriety and eroding public confidence in the judiciary's independence.

## Legislative Reaction to Judicial Activism

Initially unable to defeat activist justices, the business community moved its battle to the legislature, which in 1987 enacted a so-called **tort reform** package that attempted to put some limits on personal injury lawsuits and damage judgments entered by courts. A tort is a wrongful act over which a lawsuit can be brought. Insurance companies, which had been lobbying nationwide for states to set limits on jury awards in personal injury cases, were major proponents of the legislation. They were joined by the Texas Civil Justice League, an organization of trade and professional associations, cities, and businesses formed in 1986 to seek similar changes in Texas tort law. The high-stakes campaign for change was enthusiastically supported by Governor Bill Clements but was opposed by consumer groups and plaintiffs' lawyers, who had been making millions of dollars from the judiciary's new liberalism.

Cities, businesses, doctors, and even charitable organizations had been hit with tremendous increases in insurance premiums, which they blamed on greedy trial lawyers and large court awards in malpractice and personal injury lawsuits. Trial lawyers blamed the insurance industry which, they said, had started raising premiums to recoup losses the companies had suffered in investment income in the late 1970s and early 1980s, after interest rates had fallen.

In an article in the March 1, 1987, editions of the *Houston Chronicle*, reporter R.G. Ratcliffe explained what the tort reform battle was all about:

> It is a debate in one of those gray areas of society about how we, as a people, will define justice—and its limits. It is a fight over the price of pain and suffering; the limits of punishment; the question of how much one person can be held responsible for the wrongs of another; and whether law can evolve through court rulings or whether the expansion of law is the exclusive province of the legislature.[18]

Ratcliffe pointed out that it also was a fight over money, lots of money. Members of the Senate Economic Development Committee alone, he reported, had received $158,850 in political contributions from tort reform advocates in 1986 and $101,100 from those opposed to change. This Senate committee played a key role in developing the reform legislation.

Among other things, the new tort reform laws set limits on punitive damages in lawsuits, limited governmental liability, attempted to discourage frivolous lawsuits, and limited the ability of claimants to collect damages for injuries that were largely their own fault. Governor Clements said the new laws would assure the business community that Texas was "serious about holding down the cost of doing business," assure consumers that "we are devoted to holding down the cost of products and liability insurance," and send a message to the judiciary that "we are tired of frivolous lawsuits clogging up our courts and making it harder for the real victims of injustice to plead their cases."

George Christian, a consultant to the Texas Civil Justice League, said it probably would take several years to evaluate the full effect of the tort changes. But he believed the public attention focused on the issue contributed to the major philosophical and political changes that were soon to occur on the Texas Supreme Court. "Just the furor over it, the publicity, the interest it sparked had to have some impact on the judicial elections in 1988," he said.

## Judicial Impropriety

For the Supreme Court, meanwhile, 1987 was even stormier than 1986 had been. In June, the State Commission on Judicial Conduct, which also had investigated Justices Ray and Kilgarlin, issued public sanctions against each. Ray was reprimanded for seven violations of the Code of Judicial Conduct, including the acceptance of free airplane rides from attorneys practicing before the court and improper communication with lawyers about pending cases. Kilgarlin received a milder admonishment because two of his law clerks had accepted a weekend trip to Las Vegas, Nevada, from a law firm with cases pending before the court. Both justices also were cited for soliciting funds from attorneys to help pay for litigation the justices had brought against the House Judicial Affairs Committee and a former briefing attorney who testified against them. There was some talk among legislators of initiating removal proceedings against the two Democratic justices, but nothing came of it. Governor Clements, a Republican, demanded their resignations, but he was ignored. Kilgarlin lost a close re-election race to Republican Nathan Hecht in 1988, and Ray didn't seek re-election when his term was up in 1990.

Later in 1987, the Texas judiciary, particularly the Supreme Court, received even more negative publicity—this time on a national scale—when the high court upheld a record $11 billion judgment awarded Pennzoil Company in a dispute with Texaco Inc. Several members of the Supreme Court also were featured on a network television program that questioned whether justice was "for sale" in Texas.

The record judgment was awarded to Pennzoil after a state district court jury in Houston had determined that Texaco had wrongfully interfered in Pennzoil's attempt to acquire Getty Oil Company in 1984. The 1st Court of Appeals in Houston upheld the judgment and the Supreme Court, ruling there was no reversible error in the lower courts, refused to hear Texaco's appeal. Texaco, which already had sought protection under federal bankruptcy laws, later reached a settlement with

Pennzoil, but it also waged a massive public relations campaign against the Texas judiciary.

In a segment on CBS-TV's "60 Minutes" program, correspondent Mike Wallace pointed out that plaintiff's attorney Joe Jamail of Houston, who represented Pennzoil, had contributed $10,000 to the original trial judge in the case and thousands of dollars more to Supreme Court justices. The program also generally criticized the elective system that allowed Texas judges to legally accept large campaign contributions from lawyers who practiced before them. Democrat Oscar Mauzy, one of several justices elected with the financial backing of Jamail and other trial lawyers, defended the system in an interview with Wallace. Chief Justice John Hill, the only Supreme Court member who wanted to scrap the elective system, told Wallace it had become "outrageous." The program presented what already had been reported in the Texas media, but after the national exposure, Governor Clements and other Republicans renewed their attacks on the activist, Democratic justices. And some newspapers published editorials calling for a merit selection system of appointing judges.

In August 1987, a few months before the CBS program aired, Chief Justice Hill unexpectedly announced that he would leave the court in the middle of his six-year term on January 1, 1988, to return to private law practice and lobby as a private citizen for changing the judicial selection method. The legislature had refused to change the elective system earlier that year, and Hill's relationship with the other eight justices was strained. Part of the problem stemmed from the fact that all the other justices favored the continued election of judges. But personality differences were another source of friction. Many court observers believed that Hill had difficulty in adjusting to the fact that he couldn't "run" the court the way he had the attorney general's office or a private law firm. He was chief justice, but the other eight justices had been elected independently and they jealously guarded that independence.

## Increased Partisanship and Republican Gains

Hill's resignation and the subsequent resignations in 1988 of two other Democratic justices—Robert M. Campbell and James Wallace—gave the Republicans a golden opportunity to make historic inroads on the high court. Party realignment, including midterm judicial appointments by Clements, already had increased the number of Republican judges across the state, particularly on district court benches in urban areas. But only one Republican had ever served on the Supreme Court in modern times. Will Garwood was appointed by Clements in 1979 to fill a vacancy on the court but was defeated by Democrat C.L. Ray in the 1980 election.

Prior to Hill's decision to step down, GOP leaders had been planning to recruit a Republican slate of candidates for the three Supreme Court seats that normally would have been on the ballot in 1988. Now, six seats were contested, including those held by three new Republican justices appointed by Clements to fill the unexpected vacancies. Even though a full Supreme Court term is six years, the governor's judicial appointees have to run in the next election to keep their seats.

Clements appointed Thomas R. Phillips, a state district judge from Houston, to succeed Hill and become the first Republican chief justice since Reconstruction. Clements named Barbara Culver of Midland, a state district judge, to succeed Campbell and become the second woman to serve on the Supreme Court. Attorney Eugene Cook of Houston was appointed to replace Wallace.

Republicans won three of the six races in 1988. Phillips defeated Democratic Justice Ted Z. Robertson, who challenged the chief justice rather than run for re-election to his own seat. Phillips joined Hill in advocating a change in the judicial selection process. He also voluntarily imposed limits on his own fund raising but still spent $2 million, while Robertson, with heavy support from trial lawyers, spent $1.8 million.

Culver was unseated by conservative Democrat Jack Hightower, a former congressman and state senator. Cook retained his seat, and Republican Nathan Hecht of Dallas, a member of the 5th Court of Appeals, unseated activist Democratic Justice William Kilgarlin in a close race. Liberal Democrat Lloyd Doggett of Austin, a trial lawyer and former state senator, defeated Republican Paul Murphy, a Houston appellate judge, for the seat vacated by Robertson. In the sixth race, Democratic Justice Raul A. Gonzalez, the first Hispanic to serve on the Supreme Court and one of its most conservative members, defeated Republican challenger Charles Ben Howell.

The Democratic resignations and the subsequent 1988 elections enabled the GOP to make strong partisan gains from the controversy over judicial activism. But the Republican gains probably hindered, more than helped, the cause of reforming the judicial selection process. The business and medical communities, which had considerable success fighting the trial lawyers under the existing rules—with large campaign contributions of their own—viewed the new Supreme Court as more conservative. "I'm a happy camper today," said Kim Ross, lobbyist for the Texas Medical Association, whose political action committee had supported conservative Democrats Gonzalez and Hightower as well as the three Republican winners.[19]

The Supreme Court's philosophical orientation didn't change overnight, and two of the justices—Hightower and Gonzalez—weren't as predictable as many observers expected them to be. But change was on the way. The first major departure from a previous plaintiff-oriented ruling occurred in September 1990 when the court, in a 5-4 decision, upheld the constitutionality of limits on medical malpractice awards in wrongful death cases. Three years earlier a more liberal court, in a 7-2 ruling, had struck down malpractice caps in personal injury cases. The new ruling was a major victory for the Texas Medical Association, which had contributed about $180,000 through its political arm to Supreme Court candidates in 1988 and helped unseat the author of the previous opinion, former Democratic Justice William Kilgarlin. The new majority opinion was written by Republican Justice Eugene Cook, one of the five successful candidates supported by the TMA.[20]

Conservatives made additional gains on the Supreme Court in 1990. Chief Justice Phillips handily turned back a challenge from liberal Democratic Justice Oscar Mauzy, who nevertheless remained on the court because he still had two years remaining on his own term. C.L. Ray, one of the most liberal justices, retired and was succeeded by the more-moderate Bob Gammage, a Democratic Court of Appeals judge and former congressman and state legislator. Republican John Cornyn, a state district judge from San Antonio, won the seat vacated by the retirement of Democratic Justice Franklin Spears to give the GOP four of the court's nine seats.

The Texas Medical Association supported all three of the 1990 winners. Joined by business groups, the TMA distributed about 2 million slate cards publicizing its endorsements. The single biggest factor in the 1990 races, however, may have been television advertising.[21]

As he had in 1988, Phillips put a $5,000 limit on individual contributions to his campaign but still spent more than $2.5 million and ran a TV campaign attacking Mauzy over the 1987 "60 Minutes" show that had identified Mauzy as a recipient of large campaign contributions from trial lawyers. More than half of Phillips' financial support came from doctors, bankers, and businessmen.[22]

Gammage defeated controversial appellate judge Charles Ben Howell of Dallas, a perennial Republican candidate who received only lukewarm support from his own party's leaders. In television ads, Gammage noted that Howell had previously been sanctioned by the Commission on Judicial Conduct and had once worn a "Judge Kook" sign to a televised debate. Cornyn took no chances against an opponent with few credentials but a famous name, Gene Kelly, who had spent practically no money and didn't campaign but had upset an experienced, well-financed Court of Appeals judge in the Democratic primary. Cornyn ran TV spots and received editorial endorsements from newspapers that focused attention on Kelly's lack of credentials. Kelly was a retired Air Force judge from San Antonio who had virtually no civilian courtroom experience.

## Long Ballots and Familiar Names

Kelly's candidacy raised the haunting memory of Donald B. Yarbrough, an example repeatedly cited by proponents of judicial appointment. Yarbrough was an unknown attorney from Houston who claimed that God had told him to run for the Supreme Court and, thanks to his familiar name, upset a much more qualified candidate, appellate judge Charles Barrow, for a seat on the high court in 1976. Yarbrough's name was similar to that of Don Yarborough, who had run unsuccessfully for governor two times in the 1960s, and to that of former U.S. Senator Ralph Yarborough and sounded familiar enough to fool voters who didn't pay much attention to down-ballot races. Yarbrough spent approximately $350 campaigning, while Barrow had the endorsement of the legal establishment.

Yarbrough served about six months on the Supreme Court but became the target of a criminal investigation and resigned as the legislature was preparing to remove him. After he left the court, he was convicted of lying to a grand jury investigating allegations he plotted to have a banker killed and was sentenced to five years in prison. While free on bond during an appeal, he left the country to attend medical school in Grenada and refused to return when his appeal was denied. He finally was apprehended in the Caribbean, sentenced to two additional years for bond jumping, and imprisoned. After he was paroled from state prison, he was convicted in 1986 on federal conspiracy and bribery charges in connection with a money-laundering scheme and sentenced to six years in federal prison.

Texas voters are confronted with long ballots that in some counties may include 40 or 50 names for judicial offices alone, making it virtually impossible for most voters to recognize the names of all the judges, much less weigh their qualifications against those of competing candidates. In such instances, people often vote for names with which they are vaguely familiar, whether it be Gene Kelly or Jesse James, the name of a former longtime state treasurer. A vote cast on this basis is not rational, but it is difficult to criticize the overwhelmed voter. Studies in other states have indicated that many voters cast ballots for unknown judicial candidates on the basis of party label or ethnic surname.[23]

## Minorities Fight for Representation

As the high-stakes battles were being waged over the Supreme Court's philosophical and political makeup, minorities also were actively seeking more representation in the Texas judiciary. But instead of pouring millions of dollars into judicial races to change the composition of the state courts, Hispanics and African-Americans filed lawsuits to force change through the federal courts.

The first Hispanic was seated on the Texas Supreme Court in 1984, but by 1991 there had been no African-Americans on that court. The first African-American was seated on the Court of Criminal Appeals in 1990 and the first Hispanic in 1991. Throughout Texas history, Hispanics and African-Americans have had a great deal of difficulty winning election to state courts. Even though they comprise a large percentage of the population of various counties and judicial districts, the high cost of judicial campaigns plus polarized voting and low rates of minority participation in elections have minimized their electoral successes.

As of February 1989, a few months before a major lawsuit went to trial over the issue, only 35 of 375 state district judges were Hispanic, and seven were African-American. There were only three Hispanics and no African-Americans among the 80 judges on the 14 intermediate Courts of Appeals. Although they comprised at least one-third of the Texas population, African-Americans and Hispanics held only 11.2 percent of the district judgeships and less than 4 percent of the intermediate appellate seats.[24] African-Americans sat on only three of the 59 district court benches in Harris County (Houston), although they accounted for 20 percent of that county's population. African-Americans held only two of 36 district judgeships in Dallas County, where they made up 18 percent of the population. Hispanics held three district court seats in Houston and one in Dallas. Three

African-American judges in Dallas, who had been appointed by Governor Mark White to fill judicial vacancies, had been unseated in countywide elections. One was Jesse Oliver, a former legislator who had won election to the Texas House from a sub-district within Dallas County but couldn't win a 1988 judicial race countywide. Oliver, a Democrat, had overwhelming African-American support but lost about 90 percent of Dallas' white precincts, which is an example of polarized racial voting.[25]

In a landmark lawsuit tried in September 1989 in federal district court in Midland, attorneys for the League of United Latin American Citizens, or LULAC, and other minority plaintiffs argued that the countywide system of electing state district judges violated the Voting Rights Act by diluting the voting strength of minorities. Section 2 of the Voting Rights Act allows a federal court to strike down an electoral system that prohibits a protected class of voters an equal opportunity to elect officeholders of their choice.

Two months later, U.S. District Judge Lucius Bunton ruled in *League of United Latin American Citizens et al.* v. *Mattox et al.* that the countywide system was illegal in nine of the state's largest counties—Harris, Dallas, Tarrant, Bexar, Travis, Jefferson, Lubbock, Ector, and Midland. Those counties elected 172 district judges, almost half of the state's total, but had only a handful of minorities serving on the district courts. Bunton did not order an immediate remedy but strongly urged the legislature to address the issue in an upcoming special session that Governor Clements had scheduled on workers' compensation.

Clements, Lt. Governor Bill Hobby and House Speaker Gib Lewis said they favored replacing the present system with one under which judges would be appointed by the governor and periodically reviewed by the voters. This so-called "Missouri plan" was basically what former Supreme Court Chief Justice John L. Hill had been actively promoting. But most legislators opposed making any changes in the judicial selection process. And Clements, who opposed electing judges from subdistricts within a county, refused to add the issue to the special session's agenda.

Some Democratic leaders, including state party chairman Bob Slagle and Attorney General Jim Mattox, agreed with the plaintiffs and favored the partisan election of trial judges from districts. Mattox, who was campaigning for the 1990 Democratic gubernatorial nomination and eager to win the support of minority leaders, enraged Governor Clements and many Republican judges by agreeing to a district plan with the LULAC plaintiffs. Under that proposal, which would have required judges in the largest counties to run from state representative districts in the 1990 elections, many minority candidates would have been elected at the expense of incumbent judges. Bunton, however, rejected the Mattox-LULAC proposal. On January 2, the deadline for candidates to file for places on the 1990 party primary ballots, Bunton ordered judges in the nine counties to run for election from districts but in nonpartisan elections. Mattox then belatedly joined Secretary of State George Bayoud, the state's chief elections officer, and two district judges in asking the 5th U.S. Circuit Court of Appeals to block Bunton's order and give the state time to appeal. The federal appellate court granted the stay, and partisan, countywide judicial elections were held as scheduled in 1990.

Mattox also had another reason for favoring single-member judicial districts over at-large elections. Without districts, he may never have been elected to public office. As a liberal Democrat, he probably could not have won his first race for the Texas House from Dallas in 1972 if the federal courts had not intervened and ordered single-member districts for legislators that year. Mattox's victory in a district election for the statehouse launched a political career that later included service in Congress as well as the attorney general's office and made Mattox a strong, although unsuccessful, contender in the 1990 governor's race.

Ironically, one minority judge was outspoken in his opposition to district elections for trial judges. State District Judge Felix Salazar of Houston didn't seek re-election in 1990, at least in part because he disliked the prospect of having to run from a district rather than countywide. A Democrat, Salazar lived in a predominantly non-Hispanic white Houston neighborhood and in previous elections had been endorsed by a diversity of groups. He claimed that small districts could work against the interests of minorities because a judge from a conservative Anglo district could feel political pressure to sentence minority criminal defendants more harshly than whites. "The judge will have to espouse the feeling of the community. His district may think that's all right, and it will be hell unseating him," he told the *Houston Chronicle*.[26]

Other opponents of district elections argued that districts also could put undue pressure from minority communities on judges. But Jesse Oliver, the former African-American legislator and judge who had been unseated in a countywide race in Dallas and was a plaintiff-intervenor in the LULAC lawsuit, didn't agree that judicial districts would distort the administration of justice any more than countywide elections. "For one thing, if the community does exert pressure, then the white community is exerting all the pressure now because they are electing the judges in Dallas County," he said.[27]

In September 1990, the 5th U.S. Circuit Court of Appeals in New Orleans reversed Bunton and upheld countywide judicial elections. The appellate court held that Section 2 of the Voting Rights Act applied only to elections for legislative and executive officers, not judges. "Judicial offices are not representative ones, and their occupants are not representatives," Judge Thomas Gee wrote for the majority. "Indeed, the state processes for filling them need not even be elective, as those for all representative offices presumably must be."

The LULAC plaintiffs appealed to the U.S. Supreme Court and, ruling in their case and one from Louisiana in June 1991, the Supreme Court held that the Voting Rights Act does apply to elections for the judiciary. "If a state decides to elect its trial judges, as Texas did in 1861, those elections must be conducted in compliance with the Voting Rights Act," Justice John Paul Stevens wrote for the majority.

Minority groups hailed the landmark decision as a major victory. But the ruling didn't produce an immediate change in the way Texas judges were elected because it didn't specifically strike down the at-large election system. "We believe that the state's interest in maintaining an electoral system—in this case, Texas' interest in maintaining the link between a district judge's (countywide) jurisdiction and the area of residency of his or her voters—is a legitimate factor to be considered" in determining whether the Voting Rights Act has been violated, the high court wrote. But it also emphasized that the state's interest was only one factor to be considered and didn't automatically outweigh proof of diluting minority votes.

The Supreme Court returned the Texas lawsuit to the 5th Circuit for further action, and attorneys for the plaintiffs promised to continue to press their case for district elections. Noting that only 14 of the 172 district judges in the nine counties directly affected by the ruling were minorities, LULAC attorney Rolando Rios of San Antonio noted: "If we elect them by state legislative seats, we could have as many as 60 minorities elected. So, the implications are tremendous for the minority community."[28]

The Supreme Court's decision had potential far-reaching effects on the way the entire Texas judiciary was selected, including the statewide elections of members of the highest appellate courts. When the ruling in the LULAC case was handed down, minority plaintiffs had already filed a suit attacking the at-large election of judges on the state's 13th Court of Appeals. In *Rangel* v. *Mattox*, U.S. District Judge Filemon Vela of Brownsville ruled in July 1989 that the at-large election scheme for the Corpus Christi-based court violated the Voting Rights Act. Only one member of the court at that time was Hispanic despite heavy concentrations of Hispanic voters in many of the 20 counties served by the court. A minority lawsuit challenging the statewide elections of the nine members of the Texas Court of Criminal Appeals also was pending.

The suit to force judges on the Court of Criminal Appeals to seek election from specific geographic regions—an Hispanic, for example, would be heavily favored in a South Texas district—was filed by the Mexican American Legal Defense and Educational Fund in federal district court in 1989 when there were no minority judges on the criminal court. The death of Democratic Judge M.P. "Rusty" Duncan in an automobile crash created an unexpected vacancy, which Governor Bill Clements filled on March 16, 1990, with the historic appointment of the first African-American to the court, Louis Sturns, a Republican state district judge from Fort Worth. Since the vacancy had occurred after the filing deadline for the 1990 party primaries, the State Republican Executive Committee put Sturns on the general election ballot as the GOP nominee for the seat. The State Democratic Executive Committee nominated another African-American, Morris Overstreet, a county court-at-law judge from Amarillo, who had lost a primary race for another seat on the criminal appellate court to a white candidate (Figure 11-5). Overstreet narrowly defeated Sturns in the November general election to become the first African-American elected to a statewide office in Texas.

Democratic Governor Mark White appointed the first Hispanic, Raul A. Gonzalez, the son of migrant workers, to the Texas Supreme Court in 1984 to fill a vacancy created by a resignation. Gonzalez made history a second time in 1986 by winning election to the seat and becoming the first Hispanic to win a statewide election in Texas (Figure 11-6). A native of Weslaco in the Rio Grande Valley, Gonzalez had been a state district judge in Brownsville and had been appointed to

**FIGURE 11-5** Morris Overstreet of Amarillo became the first African-American to win a statewide election in Texas when he won a seat on the Court of Criminal Appeals in 1990. (Courtesy of Morris Overstreet)

the 13th Court of Appeals in Corpus Christi by Republican Governor Bill Clements in 1981. Governor Ann Richards appointed the first Hispanic, Fortunato P. Benavides, to the Court of Criminal Appeals in 1991 to fill a vacancy created by the death of Justice Marvin O. Teague. Benavides had been a justice on the 13th Court of Appeals and a district judge and a county court-at-law judge in Hidalgo County.

Despite his background, Gonzalez, a Democrat, is generally considered one of the more conservative members of the Supreme Court. He calls himself "independent." An analysis by the *Texas Lawyer* showed that Gonzalez wrote 12 dissents to majority court opinions during a 15-month period in 1989-90. "The record speaks for itself," he said. "It shows my independence. I am a person of strongly held views. I've agreed with every judge and disagreed with every judge. I'm not concerned with who is voting with me or against me."[29]

**FIGURE 11-6** Raul A. Gonzalez was the first Hispanic to serve on the Texas Supreme Court and the first Hispanic to win election to a statewide office in Texas. (Courtesy of Raul Gonzalez)

Only two women have ever served on the Texas Supreme Court and none on the Court of Criminal Appeals. But by 1989, according to the Office of Court Administration, 58 other women were serving or had served on district or appellate court benches. Most of those had taken office after 1980. The first woman to become a state district judge in Texas was Sarah T. Hughes of Dallas, who was appointed to the bench in 1935 by Governor James V. Allred and served until 1961, when she resigned to accept an appointment by President John F. Kennedy to the federal district bench. Ironically, Hughes is best known for swearing a grim-faced President Lyndon B. Johnson into office aboard Air Force One on November 22, 1963, following Kennedy's assassination in Dallas.

Ruby Sondock of Houston was the first woman to serve on the Texas Supreme Court. She had been a state district judge before Governor Bill Clements named her to the high court on June 25, 1982, to temporarily fill a vacancy. Sondock chose not to seek election to the seat and served only a few months. She later returned to the district bench. Barbara Culver, a state district judge from Midland, became the second female Supreme Court justice when Clements appointed her in

February 1988 to fill another vacancy. Culver also served less than a year. She was unseated by Democrat Jack Hightower in the 1988 general election.

The debates and lawsuits centering on judicial elections and representation in Texas speak to the significant role of the courts in policymaking as well as day-to-day litigation. The composition of the courts makes a difference. While some may argue that the role of a judge is simply to apply the law to the facts and issues of a specific case, judges bring to the courts their own values, philosophical views, and life experiences, and these factors serve to filter their interpretations of the law.

## CRIME AND PUNISHMENT

Under the United States and Texas constitutions, a person charged with a crime is presumed innocent until the state can prove to a judge or a jury that he or she is guilty beyond a reasonable doubt. The state also has the burden to prosecute fairly, to follow principles of procedural due process outlined in constitutional and statutory law and interpreted by the courts. Even persons charged with the most heinous crimes retain these fundamental rights, and while there is often a public outcry about coddling criminals, the process is designed to protect an individual from governmental abuses, to lessen the chance that an innocent person will be wrongly convicted of a crime.

In Texas, as well as in other states, these rights have sometimes been violated. Historically, there have been instances of lynchings, suspects murdered by police, confessions extorted by physical violence, persons incarcerated without cause, and individuals denied a variety of rights. But over the years the federal courts, in particular, have strengthened the enforcement of these rights. Through a case-by-case process, the U.S. Supreme Court has applied the U.S. Bill of Rights to the states by way of the "due process of law" and the "equal protection of law" clauses of the 14th Amendment to the U.S. Constitution. The failure of police or prosecutors to comply with specific procedures for handling a person accused of a crime may result in charges against an individual being dropped or a conviction reversed on appeal.

An arrested suspect must be taken before a magistrate—usually a justice of the peace or a municipal court judge—to be formally informed of the offense or offenses with which he is charged and told his legal rights. Depending on the charges, a bond may be set to allow the defendant to get out of jail and remain free pending a trial of the case. A person has the right to remain silent, to consult with an attorney and have an attorney present during questioning by law enforcement officers or prosecutors, and to be warned that any statement he makes can be used against him in a trial. A defendant who can't afford to hire a lawyer must be provided with a court-appointed attorney at taxpayer expense. Many of these protections were extended to the states by the U.S. Supreme Court in the landmark **Miranda ruling** in 1966. In 1991, however, the high court ruled that a person jailed for an armed robbery could be questioned about an unrelated murder without his lawyer in the robbery case being present.[30]

Every criminal defendant has the right to a trial by jury but, except in capital murder cases, may waive a jury trial and have his case decided by a judge. A defendant may plead guilty, not guilty or **nolo contendere** (no contest). Prosecutors and defense attorneys settle many cases through plea bargaining, in which the defendant pleads guilty—often to a lesser offense than which he was originally charged—in return for the prosecution's promise to recommend a lighter sentence or probation. The trial judge doesn't have to accept the plea bargain but usually does. If the defendant chooses to have his guilt or innocence determined by the judge, the judge also determines the punishment if there is a conviction. A judge also may disregard a jury verdict and order a new trial if he or she believes the jury verdict is unjust. The jury can return a guilty verdict only if all jurors agree that the defendant is guilty beyond a reasonable doubt. If the jury can't reach a unanimous verdict—even after lengthy negotiations and prodding from the judge—the judge must declare a mistrial. In that case, the prosecution has to seek a new trial with another jury or drop the charges. In a jury trial, a defendant may choose to have his punishment also set by the jury. If not, it is determined by the judge.

In 1991, the Court of Criminal Appeals took the major step of ordering, for the first time, an official definition of "reasonable doubt" that was to be submitted to every jury deciding a criminal case. According to the definition, evidence against a criminal defendant must be so convincing that jurors would be willing to rely upon it "without hesitation" in the most important events in their own lives.[31]

Jury trials are required in **capital murder** cases, which are punishable by death or life in prison. Use of the death penalty is much more restricted in Texas and other states now than it was little more than a generation ago. Executions in Texas used to be carried out by electrocution at the state prison unit in downtown Huntsville. Some 361 individuals were executed in Texas from 1924 to 1964, when executions were suspended because of legal challenges. In 1972, the U.S. Supreme Court halted executions in all the states by striking down all the death penalty laws then on the books as unconstitutional. The high court held that capital punishment, as then practiced, violated the constitutional prohibition against cruel and unusual punishment because it could be applied in a discriminatory fashion. Not only could virtually any act of murder be punished by death under the old Texas law, so could rape and certain other crimes.

In 1973, the legislature rewrote the death penalty statute to try to meet the Supreme Court's standards by defining capital crimes as murder committed under specific circumstances. The list was expanded later and presently includes the murder of a law enforcement officer or firefighter who is on duty, murder committed during the course of committing certain other major crimes, murder for hire, murdering more than one person, murder of a prison guard or employee, or murder committed while escaping or attempting to escape from a penal institution.

A jury that has found a person guilty of capital murder must also answer certain questions about the defendant before choosing between death or life imprisonment, the only punishments available. Jurors are required to consider whether a convicted murderer will be a continuing danger to society and to consider other mitigating circumstances, including evidence of mental retardation, before deciding punishment.[32] Capital murderers sentenced to life in prison become eligible for parole after serving 35 years.

The first execution under the 1973 Texas law was carried out in 1982. By then the legislature, acting in 1977, also had changed the method of execution from the electric chair to the intravenous injection of a lethal substance. By mid-1992, there had been 50 executions in Texas by lethal injection.

Despite a longstanding federal court order limiting the population of the prison system, each legislative session has added new criminal offenses or increased the penalties for existing crimes. That adds to the pressure on prisons and county jails, many of which have been overcrowded with convicted felons for whom there was no room in state prisons.

Although punishments for most criminal offenses are set in the Penal Code, the law grants considerable leeway to judges and juries, and penalties assessed can vary widely in an inequitable pattern from county to county—and even from courtroom to courtroom in the same courthouse. After capital murder, the most serious criminal offense is a first degree **felony** punishable by a prison sentence of five to 99 years or life and a $10,000 fine. This classification includes such widely disparate offenses as non-capital murder, aggravated robbery in which a deadly weapon is used, and burglary of someone's house. So it's quite possible for a jury in one county to sentence a burglar to 50 years in prison and a jury in the next county to sentence a murderer to five years. The result becomes seemingly more unfair if the convicted murderer's sentence is probated. That means he isn't sent to prison if he promises to behave himself and meet certain conditions, such as restrictions on where he travels and with whom he associates. **Probation**, however, usually is given first time offenders convicted of non-violent crimes.

Lesser felonies are second degree felonies, punishable by 2 to 20 years in prison and a $10,000 maximum fine, and third degree felonies, punishable by 2 to 10 years in prison or one year in a community corrections facility. The most minor crimes are classified as Class A, B, or C **misdemeanors**. Class A misdemeanors are punishable by a maximum $3,000 fine and/or one year in county jail. Class B misdemeanors carry a maximum sentence of 180 days in jail and a $1,500 fine, while Class C misdemeanors are punishable by a maximum $500 fine.

Except for those under the death penalty, a convicted felon sentenced to prison is eligible for **parole** after serving one-third of his or her sentence—or 20 years of a life sentence. But the actual time in prison is often shortened considerably by so-called good time credits, which were originally designed to reward inmates for good behavior or for participating in educational programs but have been liberally given in recent years merely to speed up parole dates and make room in the prison system for new convicts. Many of those released early have gone on to commit more crimes—including murder and other violent offenses—soon after parole. In recent years, the legislature has spent hundreds of millions of dollars to build new prisons but still hasn't been able to keep up with the demands on the criminal justice system.

Defenders of the present Penal Code say it enables judges and juries to follow the standards of the local community in sentencing convicted criminals. But public outrage over the early prisoner releases prompted the legislature in 1991 to create a special commission to study criminal punishment with an eye toward reducing the long sentences assessed many non-violent offenders and leaving more prison space for murderers and rapists. The commission was part of a comprehensive criminal justice law that also provided for construction of more prisons, created an alcoholism and drug abuse treatment program for inmates, and encouraged judges to sentence more non-violent offenders to alternative rehabilitation programs rather than prison. (See Chapter 13.)

## THE POLITICS OF CRIMINAL JUSTICE

While the legislature continues to try to address the criminal justice crisis, the Texas Court of Criminal Appeals must try to balance the constitutional rights of convicts against the public welfare. That role puts the court at the center of major philosophical and political battles. Reversals of convictions, lengthy delays in the executions of those convicted of capital murder, concerns with procedural technicalities, and the release of individuals who are perceived by the public to be guilty have prompted accusations that the judiciary in general and the Court of Criminal Appeals in particular are soft on crime. Whether these perceptions are correct or not, they must be confronted in the political arena.

The combatants include the prosecutors, the district and county attorneys who don't like to see the convictions they have won reversed. The future careers of these elected officeholders can be tied to their conviction rates. Judges of the trial courts, who also must periodically face the voters, also are sensitive to reversals, as are the police and sheriffs departments that arrest the defendants and provide the evidence on which criminal convictions are based.

From a different perspective, defense attorneys have an obligation to protect the rights and interests of their clients and in their appeals often attack procedures used by police, prosecutors, and trial judges. Also participating in the debate are civil libertarians, who insist that a criminal defendant's every right—even the most technical—be protected, and minority groups, who have challenged the conduct of trials when minorities have been excluded from juries weighing the fate of minority defendants.

Randall Dale Adams and Clarence Lee Brandley owe their lives to the appellate process. Both men came perilously close to being executed for murders they apparently didn't commit. Adams spent more than a decade behind bars before he was released in 1989, after a documentary film indicated he had been wrongfully convicted of the murder of a Dallas police officer. The Court of Criminal Appeals ordered a new trial, but the Dallas County district attorney chose not to retry him. Brandley, an African-American janitor at Conroe High School, was convicted by an all-white jury of the rape and murder of a 16-year-old girl, but the Court of Criminal Appeals reversed the conviction after being presented with evidence that Brandley had not received a fair trial and had been a victim of racial prejudice. Neither man would have lived long enough to win freedom had not the appellate process, which most prosecutors attack as too time-consuming and too "technical," worked to delay their scheduled executions.

Some people may argue that the Court of Criminal Appeals, in some cases, has been somewhat indifferent to constitutional guarantees of due process. Throughout much of the court's history, though, it has been charged with excessive concern with legal technicalities that benefit convicted criminals.[33] During the first quarter of the century, the court reversed 42 percent of all the cases appealed to it, although there is evidence that trial courts in Texas during that period did not demonstrate a great deal of concern for due process of law. In that era, Texas, as did many other states, had a harsh system of criminal justice that often reflected class and racial bias. In the 1940s and early 1950s, the criminal appellate court was criticized for a number of reversals, and a restructured court in the late 1950s appeared to be more favorably inclined toward the state. By 1966, the reversal rate had dropped to 3 percent. But electoral defeat of incumbent judges, retirements, and the expansion of the court from three to five members in 1967 and to nine members in 1977 again changed its composition.

In the late 1980s, the Court of Criminal Appeals began to give mixed signals to the lower courts and other participants in the judicial system. Exercising a philosophy that was tagged "new federalism" by some critics, the court, using the Texas Constitution, appeared to be moving in the direction of placing greater limitations on permissible evidence than what had been required by the U.S. Constitution and federal law. A 1987 ruling prohibited the use of videotaped testimony by a child who was sexually abused, and a 1988 ruling expanded a defendant's right to legal counsel. But the court subsequently issued contradictory decisions in 1989 and 1990 that suggested it was backing down from its new federalism approach.[34] Prosecutors, incidentally, had unsuccessfully lobbied the legislature in 1989 for a constitutional amendment to prohibit the Court of Criminal Appeals from granting defendants any right not spelled out in the U.S. Constitution and deny the court the authority to liberally interpret the Texas Constitution.

After the 1990 elections produced significant changes in the court's membership, the new federalism issue resurfaced in the case of *William Randolph Heitman v. State.* In this 1991 decision, the court ruled 7-2 that the Texas Constitution granted criminal defendants more protection against illegal searches and seizures by police than the U.S. Constitution. The court majority included three judges elected in 1990 and Governor Ann Richards' recent appointee, Fortunato Benavides. Neil McCabe, a professor at South Texas College of Law and an expert on new federalism, called the decision a "declaration of independence for the Texas judiciary in criminal cases" and said it followed a national trend. But prosecutors continued to express concern, fearing the decision could have a broader effect on criminal appeals.[35]

In 1990, a former Harris County assistant district attorney, Rusty Hardin, had formed a group called Texas People Against Crime, or TPAC, to try to unseat Judge Sam Houston Clinton, one of the criminal court's more liberal members.

Hardin asserted that Clinton, a Democrat, had voted to reverse convictions in 64 percent of all published cases over the previous nine years, while the court as a whole had ordered reversals in only 47.4 percent of the cases. Hardin attempted to buttress his statistics with the emotional presentation of two crime victims at a state Capitol news conference. The Court of Criminal Appeals had reversed the convictions and ordered new trials for the assailants of both victims. The victims said their lives had been further traumatized by those decisions, one of which was written by Justice Clinton. And Hardin attacked what he called a "philosophical bias" that "does not consider the victim or the rights of society."

Clinton and his supporters, however, criticized Hardin's report as misleading because it didn't take into account thousands of unpublished opinions in which the court upheld convictions. Clinton argued that the published opinions dealt with critical points of law and constitutional questions or with issues on which some of the lower appellate courts disagreed and were more likely to include reversals.

Hardin's group raised only about $50,000 for its campaign, far short of its $200,000 goal, and Clinton narrowly defeated state District Judge Oliver Kitzman of Brookshire, the Republican challenger backed by TPAC.

Five Court of Criminal Appeals seats were on the 1990 ballot, including those of the first two Republicans ever to serve on the court. David Berchelmann Jr., a former state district judge from San Antonio, became the first Republican on the court when he was appointed by Governor Bill Clements to fill a vacancy in 1988. Louis Sturns, a former state district judge from Fort Worth, became the second Republican and first African-American on the court when he was picked by Clements to fill a vacancy in 1990. Both Republicans lost to Democratic opponents in the 1990 general election, with Sturns falling before the challenge of another African-American, Morris Overstreet of Amarillo.

## INCREASED POLICY ROLE OF THE COURTS

At the federal level of government, there has been an ongoing debate about the policy role of the courts. This debate is often framed in terms of judicial activism versus judicial restraint or strict construction of the U.S. Constitution versus loose construction. As indicated in previous sections of this chapter, this action also has become an issue in the Texas judiciary. The state courts are playing a more aggressive role in the policy-making process.

The U.S. Supreme Court, through the writ of certiorari, has near-total discretion over the cases it decides to hear. Texas laws establish the right of appeal to the Texas Supreme Court, which decides most appeals on writs of error. While the U.S. Supreme Court emphasizes cases that involve constitutional issues, the Texas Supreme Court largely rules on procedural matters. "As a consequence, very little of the court's resources remain for the occasional 'landmark' cases," then-Justice Ted Z. Robertson and attorney James W. Paulsen wrote in the March 1986 *Texas Bar Journal*.[36]

But the Texas Supreme Court ordered major, basic changes in one of the most critical issues affecting the future of Texas—the equitable financing of public education. After years of legislative inaction, a state district court in Austin accepted jurisdiction over a lawsuit in which poor school districts attacked the school finance system and, after a trial, declared the system unconstitutional. In a landmark decision in 1989, the Supreme Court unanimously agreed and ordered the legislature to enact a new education finance law. After a 1990 law failed to meet the court's standards, the court issued another order in 1991.

In its two unanimous decisions in *Edgewood* v. *Kirby*, as the school finance lawsuit was called, the Supreme Court mandated new public policy that will affect every school child and taxpayer in Texas. (See Chapter 13.) The unanimity of the first opinion, written by Democratic Justice Oscar Mauzy, surprised many legislators and school officials because two of the three Republican justices had initially been appointed to the court by Governor Bill Clements, who had insisted that the courts had no business trying to tell the legislature what to do about school finance. The decision, which held that the school finance law violated a constitutional requirement for an efficient education system, obviously was the product of considerable compromise among the nine justices. Their deliberations were secret, but Democratic Justice Franklin Spears told the *Fort Worth Star-Telegram*: "We wanted to speak with one voice. The opinion is a composite of many ideas, much brainstorming, much compromising."[37] University of Texas Law School Dean Mark Yudof said the court may have been determined to offer a united front because it attached as much importance to the school finance case as a united U.S. Supreme Court had to the landmark *Brown* v. *Board of Education* desegregation case in the 1950s.[38]

The Texas high court, however, lost its unanimity on the issue in 1992 when a 7-2 majority struck down a 1991 law that had established special County Education Districts with a minimum property tax. In a challenge brought this time by wealthy school districts, the court majority ruled that the tax was a statewide property tax prohibited by the Texas Constitution, but Mauzy and fellow Democratic Justice Lloyd Doggett sharply dissented.

That left the school finance issue still unresolved, but the Edgewood case demonstrated that Texas courts have the potential to increase their role in the policy-making process. Moreover, in 1992, a state district judge in Brownsville ruled that the state's system of funding higher education was unconstitutional because it shortchanged Hispanics in South Texas. That decision also could have major policy ramifications for state government.

## SUMMARY AND CONCLUSIONS

**1.** Texas has a confusing array of courts, many with overlapping jurisdictions. It is one of only two states with a bifurcated court system at the highest appellate level. The Texas Supreme Court is the court of last resort in civil cases and the Court of Criminal Appeals in criminal cases.

**2.** The judicial system is particularly inadequate in urban counties, where thousands of criminal cases each year are disposed of through negotiated sentences between prosecutors and defendants and where it can take years to resolve civil disputes that aren't settled out of court.

**3.** All state judges, except those on municipal court benches, are elected in partisan elections. But there has been increasing political and legal pressure in recent years to change the judicial selection process. Possible alternatives are nonpartisan elections, elections from geographic districts or a merit selection plan under which the governor would appoint judges from lists of nominees recommended by experts. The latter plan would require the appointed judges to run later in retention elections to keep their seats, but they wouldn't have opponents on the ballot.

**4.** Part of the pressure for change is the result of a continuing war for philosophical and political control of the Texas Supreme Court. That court became a battleground in the 1980s between trial attorneys who represent injured parties—or plaintiffs—in damage lawsuits, and the businesses, doctors, and insurance companies they sue. After trial lawyers began contributing millions of dollars to successful Supreme Court candidates, longtime judicial precedents that had favored the corporate establishment began to fall, and it became easier for plaintiffs to win huge damage awards.

**5.** The business and medical communities retaliated by winning some legislative changes in the procedures under which lawsuits are tried and by increasing their own contributions in judicial races.

**6.** Party realignment, including appointments by Governor Bill Clements to fill midterm vacancies, had increased the number of Republican judges on trial courts in the 1980s. And the philosophical confrontation gave Republicans, with support from the business and medical communities, a significant bloc on the Supreme Court.

**7.** Another argument advanced by proponents of change in the judicial selection system are long ballots, particularly in urban areas, where voters don't know the comparative qualifications of judicial candidates and often respond by voting for an unqualified individual with a familiar sounding name.

**8.** Only a handful of women and minorities have ever served on the state's highest appellate courts, and minorities historically have been underrepresented on the lower court benches as well. In a lawsuit by minority plaintiffs, U.S. District Judge Lucius Bunton of Midland ruled in 1989 that the countywide system of electing district, or trial judges in nine of the state's largest counties violated the Voting Rights Act by diluting the voting strength of minorities. In an appeal of that case, the U.S. Supreme Court held for the first time in June 1991 that the Voting Rights Act does apply to judicial elections. While it didn't overturn Texas' judicial election system, the high court's decision had potential far-reaching effects on the way all Texas judges are selected.

**9.** The Texas Court of Criminal Appeals is at the center of philosophical and political disputes as it weighs the constitutional rights of convicted criminals against a growing public concern about crime. In a few key cases, the court has ruled that the Texas Constitution provides criminal defendants more protection than the U.S. Constitution does.

**10.** So far, the federal judiciary has exercised a much greater role than the state judiciary in molding public policy. But in declaring the state's system of funding public education unconstitutional, the Texas Supreme Court demonstrated that state courts have the potential to increase their role in the policy-making process.

## KEY TERMS

Penal Code

Civil lawsuits

Original jurisdiction

Appellate jurisdiction

Bifurcated court system

Municipal courts

Justice of the peace courts

Statutory county courts

District courts

Plea bargain

Court of Appeals

Supreme Court

Court of Criminal Appeals

Grand jury

Prosecution

Indictment

Petit jury

Writ of error

Writ of mandamus

Merit selection

Tort reform

Miranda ruling

Nolo contendere

Capital murder

Felony

Probation

Misdemeanor

Parole

## FURTHER READING

Burka, Paul, "Trial by Technicality," *Texas Monthly*, April 1982, pp. 126-131, 210-218, 241.

Champagne, Anthony and Greg Thielemann, "Awareness of Trial Court Judges," *Judicature*, 74 (February-March 1991), pp. 271-276.

Champagne, Anthony, "Campaign Contributions in Texas Supreme Court Races," forthcoming in *Crime, Law and Social Change*.

Champagne, Anthony, "The Role of Personality in Judicial Reform," *State Constitutional Commentaries and Notes*, 2 (Winter 1991), pp. 5-8.

Champagne, Anthony, "The Selection and Retention of Judges in Texas," *Southwestern Law Journal*, 40 (May 1986), pp. 53, 95-99.

Dubose, Louis, "Impatient Justices," *The Texas Observer*, December 7, 1990, pp. 3-5.

Hill, John, "Taking Texas Judges Out of Politics: An Argument for Merit Election," *Baylor Law Review*, 40 (1988).

House Research Organization, *1988 Primary Referendum Proposals: Official English and Judicial Selection*, 141 (February 23, 1988).

Jacob, Herbert, *Justice in America: Courts, Lawyers, and the Judicial Process*, 3rd ed. Boston: Little, Brown, 1978.

Murray, Richard, "The Selection of Judges in Texas," in Donald S. Lutz and Kent L. Tedin, eds., *Perspective on American and Texas Politics*. Dubuque, Iowa: Kendall/Hunt, 1987.

Parrish, James R., *A Two-Headed Monster: Crimes and Texas Prisons*. Austin: Eakin Publications, 1989.

Reamy, Gerald S., *Criminal Offenses and Defenses in Texas*. Norcross, Georgia: Harrison Company, Publisher, 1987.

Riddlesperger, James W., "Judicial Attitudes Toward Judicial Selection in Texas," *Texas Journal of Political Studies*, 10 (Spring/Summer 1988), pp. 3-18.

Schaefer, Roger C., "Implementing Criminal Justice Policy-Texas Style," in Gerry Riposa, ed., *Texas Public Policy*. Dubuque, Iowa: Kendall/Hunt, 1987.

Schaefer, Roger C., "Texas Criminal Justice: The Policy Arena and Actors," in Gerry Riposa, ed., *Texas Public Policy*. Dubuque, Iowa: Kendall/Hunt, 1987.

Teske, H.C., Jr., ed., *Crime and Justice in Texas*. Huntsville, Criminal Justice Center, Sam Houston State University, 1988.

Texas Judicial Council, Office of Court Administrator, *Texas Judicial System, 62nd Annual Report*. Austin: Texas Judicial Council, 1990.

Texas Research League, *Texas Courts: A Proposal for Structural- Functional Reform*, Report 2. Austin: Texas Research League, 1991.

Texas Research League, *The Texas Judiciary: A Structural-Functional Overview*, Report 1. Austin: Texas Research League, 1990.

## ENDNOTES

1. Texas Research League, *Texas Courts: A Proposal for Structural-Functional Reform*, Report 2, May, 1991. Used by permission from the Texas Research League.
2. Texas Research League, *The Texas Judiciary: A Structural-Functional Overview*, Report 1, August, 1990.
3. Allen E. Smith, *The Impact of the Texas Constitution on the Judiciary* (Houston: University of Houston, Institute for Urban Studies, 1973), p. 45.
4. Texas Research League, *The Texas Judiciary: A Structural-Functional Overview*.
5. Smith, *The Texas Constitution: Its Impact on the Judiciary*, p. 28.
6. Ibid., p. 31.
7. Texas Research League, *Texas Courts: A Proposal for Structural-Functional Reform*, Report 2, May, 1991.
8. Ibid., pp. 1-15.
9. Texas Judicial System, Office of Court Administration, *Texas Judicial System: 62nd Annual Report* (Austin: Office of Court Administration, 1990).
10. Anthony Champagne, "The Selection and Retention of Judges in Texas," *Southwestern Law Journal*, 40, (May, 1986), pp. 79-80.
11. Texas Research League, *The Texas Judiciary: A Structural-Functional Overview*.
12. Texas Judicial Council, *62nd Annual Report*.
13. *Fort Worth Star-Telegram*, September 4, 1983.
14. *Houston Chronicle*, April 12, 1986.
15. *Houston Post*, May 18, 1986.
16. Champagne, "The Selection of Judges in Texas," p. 84.
17. Ibid., p. 41.
18. *Houston Chronicle*, March 1, 1987.
19. *Houston Post*, November 10, 1988.
20. *Texas Lawyer*, September 17, 1990.
21. *Texas Lawyer*, November 12, 1990.
22. Ibid.
23. Champagne, "The Selection of Judges in Texas," pp. 95-103.
24. Samuel Issacharoff, *The Texas Judiciary and the Voting Rights Act: Background and Options* (Austin: Texas Policy Research Forum), pp. 2, 13.
25. *Texas Lawyer*, September 18, 1989.
26. *Houston Chronicle*, December 24, 1989.
27. *Texas Lawyer*, September 18, 1989.
28. *Austin American-Statesman*, June 21, 1991.
29. *Texas Lawyer*, June 18, 1990.
30. *Houston Chronicle*, June 14, 1991, p. A-2.
31. *Texas Lawyer*, November 11, 1991.
32. *Texas Lawyer*, June 3, 1991.
33. Paul Burka, "Trial by Technicality," *Texas Monthly*, April 1982, pp. 126-131, 210-218, 241.
34. *Texas Lawyer*, July 16, 1990.
35. *Texas Lawyer*, July 8, 1991.
36. "Discretionary Review for the Texas Supreme Court?" *Texas Bar Journal* (March 1986).
37. *Fort Worth Star-Telegram*, October 4, 1989.
38. Ibid.

# 12

# LOCAL GOVERNMENTS IN TEXAS

## CITIES, TOWNS, COUNTIES, AND SPECIAL DISTRICTS

> ...the best school of democracy and the best guarantee of its success is the practice of local self-government.
>
> *James Bryce*[1]

Local governments, which were created by the state and operate under limits set by the Texas Constitution and the legislature, have increasingly found their capabilities and resources strapped by the pressing needs of a growing, urban state. State and federal governments have ordered significant improvements in environmental, educational, health, and a host of other programs that affect local governments but have let cities, counties, and school districts pick up much of the tab. For several years, a financially strapped state government, for example, forced counties to spend millions of local taxpayer dollars to house state prisoners in county jails because the state had failed to build enough prisons and adequately address a criminal justice crisis. Local school districts and their property taxpayers also are at the mercy of the legislature, which has repeatedly ordered expensive, new educational programs and raised classroom standards without fully paying for them. Cities likewise find their budgetary problems exacerbated by state mandates.

Local governments have always been important to Texans. Mayoral and city council races are among the most heated political campaigns in the state. But most people don't realize that the mayor, the county judge, or the school board member had his or her hands partly tied long before taking office. Local governments are the governments closest to the people. But they have to shoulder much of the responsibility—and often take much of the public outrage—for policy decisions made in Austin and Washington.

Most of the major city governments can operate with more flexibility than counties or school districts, but no local government is sovereign. The powers that local governments exercise have been delegated to them by the state. Now, obviously, if the state attempted to radically change local government in Houston or any other city there would be a widespread political outcry and, most likely, an electoral revolt against state officials. So few, if any, politicians are likely to pursue such a drastic course of action. But they will continue to pass the buck to local governments for a host of programs and services.

## THEORIES OF LOCAL GOVERNMENT

Prior to the adoption of the U.S. Constitution in 1787, Americans already believed in the "right to local self-government."[2] In many areas of the young country, local governments existed before there was a viable state or federal government, and many communities didn't expect a state or federal government to provide them with basic services. Fearful of the potential abuses of a strong national government, Thomas Jefferson developed a theory of local government, designed in part to strengthen the powers of the states, which is still part of the American political culture. For Jefferson, there was a sense of local sovereignty rooted in the sovereignty of the individual. Local governments, which he termed wards, would have a wide range of responsibilities, including education, police, roads, caring for the poor, conducting elections, some minor judicial functions, and a semblance of a militia to maintain local defenses.[3]

In light of the expanded role of state and federal governments, we might find Jefferson's view rather romantic, outdated, and naïve. Nonetheless, the concept has permeated American attitudes toward government and continues to shape citizen responses to government initiatives. Writing in the 1950s, political scientist Roscoe Martin argued that this Jeffersonian view was manifested in the notions of grass roots politics and political control. Other authors have argued that the flight to suburbia and the creation of small towns and cities near large metropolitan centers are an indication of this enduring value.[4] More recently, the emphasis on neighborhood organizations as a means of empowering people living in urban communities is a restatement of this tradition.

There is a markedly different view of local government that is best expressed in what is commonly referred to as the Dillon Rule, named after an eminent 19th century jurist, John Forrest Dillon. Under this interpretation, there is no sovereignty of local governments in the federal system. Local governments are creations of state governments, and their powers, functions, and responsibilities are defined by the state. There have been numerous state court cases enunciating this principle, but the best known summary of the **Dillon rule** is an Iowa case in which a court held:

> The true view is this: Municipal corporations owe their origin to, and derive their powers and rights wholly from, the legislature. It breathes into them the breath of

life, without which they cannot exist. As it creates, so it may destroy. If it may destroy, it may abridge and control. Unless there is some constitutional limitation on the right, the legislature might by a single act, if we can suppose it capable of so great a folly and so great a wrong, sweep from its existence all of the municipal corporations in the State, and the corporations could not prevent it. We know of no limitation on this right so far as the corporations are concerned....They are, so to phrase it, the mere tenants at will of the legislature.[5]

The Dillon rule is now the dominant theory defining the relationships of states and local governments. From this perspective, local governments are fundamentally the administrative subdivisions of the state and have no rights except those granted to them by the state. As discussed in Chapter Three, these relationships are based on the unitary principle.

## LOCAL GOVERNMENTS IN THE TEXAS POLITICAL SYSTEM

While the legal position expressed by the Dillon rule subordinates local governments to the state, there are practical and political limitations on what the state can do with local governments.[6] One is the system of local self-rule, which Texas recognized when it granted cities home rule authority in 1912. Home rule cities have considerable authority and discretion over their own local policies, but within limits set by state law.

Texas voters approved a constitutional amendment in 1933 that also gave counties home rule authority, but no county established home rule government before the amendment was repealed in 1969. In principle, the amendment was quite progressive, but it was subject to contradictory interpretations, and procedures for a county to adopt home rule were excessively restrictive and difficult to comply with. Many experts continue to advocate home rule as a solution for local problems.[7] As will be discussed later in this chapter, the lack of home rule authority greatly limits the ability of county governments to efficiently meet public needs.

In a 1980 study, the Advisory Commission on Intergovernmental Relations ranked the states according to the discretionary authority they granted to their local governments. Texas ranked 11th in a composite that included all local subdivisions—cities, counties, school districts, and other special districts. But Texas ranked 43rd in the discretionary authority given to its counties alone and first in the discretionary authority given to its cities.[8]

There also is considerable variation among the states in the major responsibilities assigned to different levels of government. Texas, like most other states, assigns the primary responsibility for public education to local school districts, while retaining the primary responsibility for highways, public welfare, and public health at the state level. Police protection, sanitation services, parks, recreation, and libraries are the primary responsibility of municipal governments. Public hospitals are a shared function of the state, county, and special districts.[9] Texas counties share with the state a primary responsibility for the court and criminal justice system.

Local governments can influence state policy. A coalition of counties, cities, or school districts with shared problems, common political objectives, and a large number of determined voters and local leaders can be a formidable political force.

## MUNICIPAL GOVERNMENT IN TEXAS

Despite popular images of wide open spaces dotted with cattle herds and oil wells, Texas is an urban state. Some areas, particularly in West Texas, still have a lot of elbow room, but most Texans live in cities. First-time visitors to the state often express surprise at the size and diversity of Houston and Dallas and the more relaxed charm of San Antonio whose riverwalk reminds many tourists of some European cities. Austin, the seat of state government and location of a world class university, is highly attractive to young professionals and high technology businesses.

When the Texas Constitution was adopted in 1876, the state was rural and agrarian with less than 10 percent of the population living in cities. According to the 1880 census, Galveston was the largest city with a population of 22,248, followed by San Antonio with 20,550. Dallas, a relatively new settlement, had 10,358 residents and Houston, 16,513. For most of the period from 1880 to 1920, San Antonio was Texas' largest city, but it yielded that position to Houston after the 1930 census, and Houston has maintained it ever since.[10]

The United States became an urban society between 1910 and 1920, but Texas did not become an urban state until the period between 1940 and 1950. Only 45 percent of Texas' population lived in cities in 1940, but during World War II there was a 58 percent increase in the urban population. By 1950, approximately 60 percent of Texans were reported to be living in urban areas. Since the 1970 census, eight of every ten Texans have been living in cities.

The 1,000-plus incorporated municipalities in Texas are diverse, and urban life, politics, and government have developed different styles across the state. The basic forms of city government are defined by statutory and constitutional law, but cities vary in their demographic makeup, their economies, the historical experiences that shaped their development, and their quality of life. There are dramatic local differences in economic stability, public safety, public education, health and environmental quality, housing, transportation, culture, recreation, and politics.[11]

Houston, Dallas, and San Antonio are among the 10 largest cities in the United States. According to the 1990 census, Houston had a population of 1.6 million; Dallas, 1 million; and San Antonio, 935,000 (Table 12-1). Five additional Texas cities—El Paso, Fort Worth, Austin, Corpus Christi, and Arlington—each had more than 250,000. But growth rates have varied widely from city to city, thanks to such factors as local differences in economic expansion, annexation policies, in-migration from other areas, and fertility and mortality rates. Statewide, the population increased by 19.4 per cent from 1980 to 1990 but, among the 10 largest cities, growth rates ranged from 2.2 per cent for Houston to 63.5 per cent for Arlington. In some instances, the growth rate for the central city was relatively modest, while growth in surrounding suburban areas was quite high, reflecting continued urban sprawl.

Compared with many other parts of the country, Texas cities have a relatively low ratio of population to incorporated area. Texas cities are relatively young and had a lot of inexpensive land available to them during their early development. So, unlike older cities in other states, they tended to expand outward rather than upward. Texas cities also have used some rather liberal **annexation powers** granted by the legislature to block the development of nearby, small municipalities that would block their expansion. Houston covers approximately 540 square miles, the largest land mass of any city in the state, and has a **population density** of approximately 3,000 persons per square mile. Fort Worth covers 281 square miles with 1,592 persons per square mile. Population density affects policy and budgetary issues relating to virtually every public service provided by the city. Land use, zoning laws, police and fire protection, the location of libraries and parks, and the development of water and sanitation systems are all related to the density of a city's population.

The racial and ethnic composition of Texas cities also is a major factor in urban diversity. Arlington, located between Dallas and Fort Worth, reported in the 1990 census a combined African-American and Hispanic population of 17 percent. By contrast, El Paso had a combined minority population of 72 percent with 69 percent of the population identified as Hispanic. Five of Texas' 10 largest cities— Houston, Dallas, San Antonio, El Paso, and Corpus Christi—have minority populations exceeding 50 percent. Along the Texas-Mexico border, Laredo is 94 percent Hispanic; Brownsville, 90 percent; McAllen, 77 percent, and Harlingen, 71 percent.

**TABLE 12-1  Select Characteristics of the Ten Largest Cities in Texas, 1990**

| City | Total | % 65+ | % Under 18 | Median Age | % African- American | % Hispanic | Persons Per Square Mile |
|------|-------|-------|------------|------------|---------------------|------------|-------------------------|
| Houston | 1,630,553 | 8.3 | 26.7 | 30.4 | 28.1 | 27.6 | 3020 |
| Dallas | 1,006,877 | 9.7 | 25.0 | 30.6 | 29.5 | 20.9 | 2941 |
| San Antonio | 935,933 | 10.5 | 29.0 | 29.8 | 7.0 | 55.6 | 2810 |
| El Paso | 515,342 | 8.7 | 31.9 | 28.7 | 3.4 | 69.0 | 2100 |
| Austin | 465,622 | 7.4 | 23.1 | 28.9 | 12.4 | 23.0 | 2138 |
| Fort Worth | 447,619 | 11.2 | 26.6 | 30.3 | 22.0 | 19.5 | 1592 |
| Arlington | 261,721 | 5.0 | 27.1 | 29.1 | 8.4 | 8.9 | 2814 |
| Corpus Christi | 257,453 | 10.1 | 30.2 | 30.6 | 4.8 | 50.4 | 1907 |
| Lubbock | 186,206 | 9.8 | 25.6 | 28.4 | 8.6 | 22.5 | 1789 |
| Garland | 180,650 | 5.5 | 30.0 | 30.1 | 8.9 | 11.6 | 3150 |
| State | 16,986,510 | 10.1 | 28.5 | 30.8 | 11.9 | 25.5 | 64 |

Source:  U.S. Department of Commerce, Bureau of the Census, *Selected Population and Housing Characteristics, 1990*, from the 1990 Census, Summary Tape File 1A (STF1A), Texas and Texas Counties; U.S. Department of Commerce, Bureau of Census, *Statistical Abstract of the U.S. 1991*, Table 40.

In 1990, the African-American population in Dallas was 29.5 percent. Houston's African-American population was 28 percent, and Fort Worth's, 22 percent. But the African-American population in El Paso was only 3 percent; in Corpus Christi, 5 percent, and San Antonio, 7 percent.

Home values, an indication of the income and personal wealth of a city and a major factor in determining the level of tax support for public services, vary widely across the state. The 1990 statewide median home value, which means half of the homes were above the figure and half were below, was approximately $60,000. The median values were $50,000 in San Antonio, $56,000 in Lubbock but $79,000 in Dallas and $83,000 in Arlington.

Ten percent of the Texas population is 65 years of age or older, but there are variations from city to city. Austin and Garland, for example, have a smaller percentage of residents older than 65, while San Antonio and Fort Worth have a slightly larger-than-average proportion of senior citizens.

All these demographic characteristics represent people who have desires, needs and aspirations. And while we have broad categories with which we can describe and classify cities, we must remind ourselves that individuals and groups ultimately make the decisions that shape city governments and politics.

## The Cities and the State

Although Texas became an urban state in the late 1940s, a rural-dominated legislature was slower in redrawing House and Senate districts to reflect the population changes. Urban areas did not receive a fair share of legislative seats until the 1970s, when the federal courts finally forced the state to redistrict using the principle of "one man, one vote." So, historically, state public policy and expenditures were tilted toward rural areas and interests, while urban areas were often neglected. The early neglect contributed to many of the problems now confronting cities, although recent policies enacted by a more urban-oriented legislature have been more responsive to cities' concerns.

Unlike counties and special districts, the state has granted Texas cities a wide range of discretionary power over organizational structure and local public policy. Texas, in fact, is first among the states in that regard, but cities still are strongly affected by state laws and policies.

Cities, therefore, actively lobby the legislature and other state officials on numerous issues. The Texas Municipal League is supported by member cities and maintains a full-time staff in Austin to monitor the activities of the legislature and state agencies. Many of the larger cities also designate staff members to serve as legislative liaisons, or they retain professional lobbyists. Dallas coordinates its legislative activities through its city attorney's office. San Antonio retains the services of an outside consultant. In the larger cities, there usually is a legislative committee of the city council that works with the city staff to establish a legislative agenda. And, increasingly, representatives of numerous cities are collaborating on issues that affect them all.[12]

More than 840 pieces of legislation that could have affected Texas cities were introduced during the 1991 regular legislative sessions and more than 180 of them were enacted. According to an assessment by the Texas Municipal League, cities fared rather well that session. While they didn't win every battle, the cities' collaborative efforts to enact favorable, and block hostile, legislation was testimony to their increased political clout.[13]

## General Law and Home Rule Cities

The Texas Constitution provides for two general categories of cities: **general law** and **home rule**. General law cities have fewer than 5,000 residents and have more restrictions in organizing their governments, setting taxes, and annexing territory than do home rule cities. They are allowed only those powers specifically granted to them by the legislature. Most Texas cities—more than 800—are general law cities.

Cities with more than 5,000 population can adopt any form of government its residents choose, provided it doesn't conflict with the state constitution or statutes.[14] This option is called home rule and is formalized through the voters' adoption of a charter, which is the fundamental document—something like a constitution—under which a city operates. A charter establishes a city's governing body, the organization of its administrative agencies and municipal courts, its taxing authority, and procedures for conducting elections and annexing additional territory. It also includes a procedure for later charter amendments. There are about 270 home rule cities in Texas.

## FORMS OF CITY GOVERNMENT IN TEXAS

Texas cities have experimented with three forms of government—the mayor-council, the council-manager, and the commission. According to the *1987 Census of Governments*, there were 1,156 municipal governments in Texas, 716 of which were some variation of the mayor-council form and 273 of which had council-manager governments.[15]

## Mayor-Council

The mayor-council form was derived from the English model of city government, and throughout the United States, as well as Texas, it has been the most common form of municipal government. The legislative function of the city is invested in the city council, and the executive function is assigned to the mayor. This type of government is based on the separation of powers principle that also characterizes the state and federal governments.

In principle, the mayor is the chief executive officer and is elected citywide to a term usually corresponding to those of council members. In terms of power, however, there are two distinguishable forms of mayor—the **weak mayor** and the **strong mayor**—and in most Texas cities, the mayor is weak.

The city charter determines a mayor's strength. The weak mayor has little control over policy initiation or implementation. His powers may be constrained by one or more of the following: limited or no appointment or removal power over city offices, limited budgetary authority, and the election of other city administrators independently of the mayor (Figure 12-1). Under these circumstances, the mayor shares power with the city council over city administration and policy implementation, and "is the chief executive in name only."[16]

These restrictions constrain both the political and administrative leadership of the mayor, much like the state constitution restricts the powers of the governor. While it is possible for a person to use non-institutional resources to extend his or her influence over the city council and other administrators and to provide energetic leadership, there are formidable obstacles to overcome.[17]

Under the strong mayor form of government, the mayor has real power and authority, including appointive and removal powers over city agency heads (Figure 12-2). Such appointments often will require city council approval, but the appointees are responsible to the mayor and serve at his or her discretion. The mayor has control over budget preparation and also exercises some veto authority over city council actions. This form of city government clearly distinguishes between executive and legislative functions.

The strong mayor form of government is found in many of the larger American cities, but it has been adopted by only two major cities in Texas—Houston and El Paso. There are a few possible explanations for its unpopularity here. For one, the strong mayor often was associated with urban political machines, and reformers in Texas feared this form of government would contribute to political corruption and ward politics. Secondly, the fragmentation of authority and responsibility in local government parallels that found in state government and is another reminder of the deep distrust of government that Reconstruction produced in Texas. Finally, the state's individualistic and traditionalistic subcultures (see Chapter 1) reinforce

**FIGURE 12-1**   Example of the Weak Mayor Form of Government.

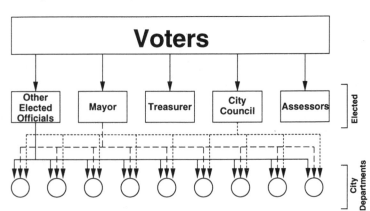

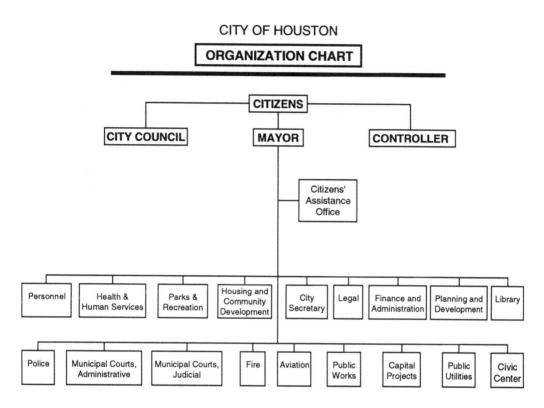

CITY OF HOUSTON

**ORGANIZATION CHART**

**FIGURE 12-2** Example of a Strong Mayor Form of Government, Houston, Texas. (Office of the Mayor, Houston)

hostile attitudes toward governmental institutions that could produce wholesale policy changes.

Houston has a variation of the strong-mayor government. The mayor nominates the fire and police chiefs and other city department heads, who then must be confirmed, or approved, by city council. The mayor can fire agency heads without council's assent. The only executive elected independently of the mayor is the city comptroller, who pays the city's bills. The mayor, however, is responsible for preparing the city budget for council action. The mayor also is a voting member of the council and presides over council meetings.

## City Commissions

The commission and council-manager forms of governments are products of the 20th century and reflect, in part, efforts to reform city governments through administrative efficiency and the reduction of partisan conflict.

The origin of the **city commission** usually is traced to the Texas island city of Galveston. After a hurricane and subsequent flooding devastated most of the city in 1900, the government then in office proved incompetent and incapable of responding to the crisis. That prompted a group of citizens to win the legislature's approval of a new form of government designed to be more responsive by combining the city's legislative and administrative functions in the offices of five city commissioners. City commissions also were soon adopted by other major Texas cities, including Dallas, Houston, and San Antonio. Reform groups across the nation also began to advocate this form of government and, by 1917, which was probably its peak of popularity, more than 500 cities nationwide had adopted some variation of commission government.[18] But with the subsequent development of council-manager government as an alternative, there has been a marked decline in the city commission's popularity. It has been replaced in Houston, Dallas, and San Antonio, and only a few cities in Texas still have this form of government.

Cities with commissions usually will have about five commissioners elected citywide on non-partisan ballots. In some cities, a person will run for a specific commissioner's post, such as commissioner of police or commissioner of public works. In other cities, a person will be assigned to head a specific department after being elected to the commission. Individually, each commissioner serves as an administrator. Collectively, the commission serves as the city's policy-making body. Depending on the city's charter, the mayor can be elected directly by the voters or chosen by the other members of the commission. While there are some variations from city to city, the mayor's formal powers are minimal. He or she presides over commission meetings, but the office is primarily ceremonial.

Initially, the commission was supported as a businesslike approach to running city government. By eliminating partisan elections and combining the executive, administrative, and legislative functions, it was argued, cities could provide services more efficiently. But critics have identified several problems. The commission minimizes the potential for effective political leadership because no single individual can be identified as the person in charge. Moreover, there is minimal policy and budget oversight and review. Commissioners are elected primarily as policymakers, not administrators, and there are downsides to electing amateurs to administer increasingly technical and complex city programs.

## Council-Manager Government

After enthusiasm for the city commission waned, urban reformers, both in Texas and nationally, looked to the **council-manager** form of government (Figure 12-3). Its specific origins are disputed, but it was influenced by the commission. The first cities in Texas to use council-manager government were Amarillo and Terrell in 1913, and it soon became popular. Dallas and San Antonio have been the largest cities in the state to adopt it. Its principal characteristics are a clear distinction between policy making and administration, a professional city management, and non-partisan city elections.

In some council-manager cities, the mayor is chosen by the city council from among its membership to preside over council meetings and fulfill a primarily

# CITY OF SAN ANTONIO
## Organizational Chart

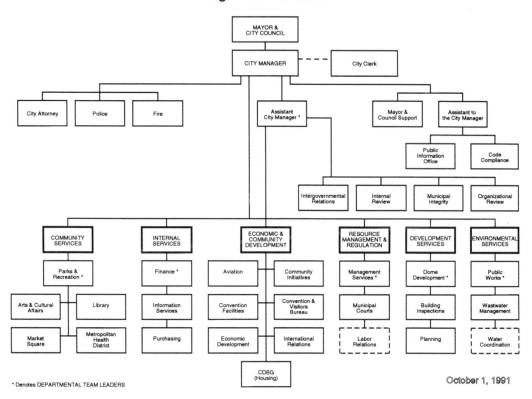

FIGURE 12-3   Example of a Council-Manager Form of Government, San Antonio, Texas. (City of San Antonio, *Adopted Annual Budget, Fiscal Year 1991-1992.*)

symbolic role. Prior to 1975, for example, San Antonio's mayor was elected by the council, but an amendment to the city charter provided for the mayor to be elected directly by the voters. This change enhanced the stature of the office but gave it no additional powers. The mayor remains a voting member of city council but has few other institutional powers in a council-manager government. He or she, however, has the opportunity to become a visible spokesperson for the city and has a forum from which to promote ideas and programs.

The city council, meanwhile, is primarily responsible for developing public policy. It creates, organizes, and restructures city departments, approves the city budget, establishes the tax rate, authorizes the issuance of bonds (subject to voter approval), enacts local laws—or ordinances—and conducts inquiries and investigations into the operations and functions of city agencies.[19]

The council hires a full-time city manager, who is responsible for administering city government on a day-to-day basis. The manager hires and fires assistants and department heads, supervises their activities, and translates the policy directives of the city council into concrete action by city employees. The city manager is also responsible for developing a city budget for council approval and then supervising its implementation. Professionalism is one of the key attributes of the council-manager form of government. Initially, many city managers were engineers, but in recent years there has been a tendency for managers to become generalists with solid skills in public finance. City managers are fairly well paid: the city manager of San Antonio was paid $107,100 in 1992, and the city manager of even a small city such as Seguin was paid $51,300 in 1991.

There is a delicate line between policy making and administration, and a city manager is, in principle, supposed to be politically neutral. The overall effectiveness of city managers depends on their ongoing relationships with their city councils, their ability to develop support for their recommendations within the council and the community at large without appearing to have gone beyond the scope of their authority, and the overall perception of their financial and managerial skills. In the real world of municipal government, city managers play a central role in setting policy as well as carrying it out, and the adroit use of their resources and their sensitivity to political factions and the personal agendas of elected officials are key to determining their success.

## City Council Service, Often a Thankless Job

Regardless of the form of government, most city councils in Texas are small, five to fifteen members elected for two-year terms. More than 90 percent of council seats are elected at-large, or citywide, and council elections are non-partisan. In most cities, a council office is part-time with little or no compensation. In most of the large cities, the pay is nowhere commensurate with the time spent on the job. Council members in San Antonio are paid $20 per meeting, and those in Dallas, $50 per meeting. Low salaries were part of the early urban reform tradition. The idea was that persons would run for office out of a sense of civic duty rather than to advance themselves financially. Houston, whose strong mayor gives it a different form of government than most other Texas cities, pays its council members about $35,000 a year plus an auto allowance and certain other perks, but most council members don't consider that a full-time salary. The mayor of Houston is paid about $133,500 a year.

The frequency of council meetings varies. In many small towns, councils may meet for only a few hours each month, but councils in large cities will meet much more frequently, usually weekly with meetings often lasting for several hours. Cities are dealing with a wider range of complex issues than ever before, and demands on a council member's time are great. In addition to their policy-making roles, council members in large cities are faced with increased demands for constituent services—from assisting in the organization of neighborhood associations to handling complaints about garbage pickup and pornography sold in local stores. Many council members are finding that public service is extremely costly in terms of time lost from their families and the jobs or professions that provide their livelihoods.

Council members in most cities can serve for an unlimited number of terms. There have been recent efforts, however, to place term limitations on many public offices, and referenda on term limitations have been held in several Texas cities. In 1991, San Antonio and Houston imposed a two-term limitation on council members.

## Changing the Forms of City Government

Most major Texas cities have functioned under more than one form of government. Both Houston and San Antonio have functioned under all three primary forms described earlier in this chapter. Changes in city charters often follow periods of intense political conflict, inertia, or inability to respond to long-term problems, but change, nevertheless, doesn't come easily. Proposed changes in governmental structures and elections systems often threaten groups and interests that have a stake in the way business is currently being conducted, and charter revisions have a tendency to polarize a community.

Does the form of government under which a city operates make any significant difference anyway? Political scientists have spent a lot of time trying to answer that question and, while there is some consensus on the general weaknesses of the city commission, opinions are divided on the other forms of local governments. The general public appears to pay little attention to city charters or governmental structures, but elected officials and other city leaders, public employees, special interest groups, minority leaders, and some reform-minded citizens consider the structure of city government a crucial issue.

A **city charter** spells out how a city chooses to run its affairs and helps determine which citizens will have access to policy making and which citizens will find it difficult to influence governmental decisions. In part, a charter is an expression of a city's social, economic, and political structure. In the next section, we will discuss non-partisan city elections, which were intended to reconfigure city politics by eliminating party influences in local elections. Some scholars have concluded that the urban reform movements that advocated non-partisan elections, which often were tied to council-manager government, were advancing middle- and upper-middle class views and interests. While the original intent of these changes may have been to encourage managerial efficiencies, many urban governments became less responsive to the needs and interests of the lower income groups and minority populations.[20]

## MUNICIPAL ELECTION SYSTEMS

### Non-partisan City Elections

Virtually every city in Texas elects its council members in non-partisan elections. Mayoral and council candidates are not identified by party on the ballot and do not run under a partisan label. Claiming that there was "no Democratic or Republican way to pave a street," city reformers who were part of the non-partisan movement (1890s to 1920s) expressed a strong aversion to political parties and particularly to the urban political machines that were identified with parties. To further separate city elections from party politics, most municipal elections also are held at times other than the party primaries or the general election. As noted in the chapter on political parties, Texas politics were dominated for 100 years by the Democratic party, and most city council members elected during that period, which ended only recently, were doubtlessly Democrats. But the party itself plays a minimal role, if any, in most cities in recruiting candidates or building electoral coalitions.

City council campaigns in the smaller cities are generally low budget and heavily reliant on the politics of acquaintances, or a candidate's personal relationships with friends, civic organizations, and a network of community opinion makers. Local newspapers can play a significant role with news stories, candidate profiles, and candidate endorsements. While some candidates volunteer to run for mayor or a council seat, many others are recruited informally by a small number of individuals who may be community leaders or comprise a loose electoral coalition.[21]

The effects of the non-partisan ballot have been particularly evident in large cities with diverse ethnic, racial, and economic groups. The non-partisan ballot and at-large, citywide elections historically have benefited the higher social and economic groups. Parties and party labels normally serve as cues for many voters, and with those eliminated in city elections, voters were forced to find alternative sources of information about candidates. Many local newspapers, which endorsed candidates and decided how much coverage to give them, had ties to the dominant urban elites. Candidates from lower socio-economic groups had few contacts with the influential organizations that recruited, supported, and endorsed candidates. In San Antonio and Dallas, for example, economic and social leaders formed citizens associations, which had all the characteristics of local political parties, to control elections. Although no longer in existence, San Antonio's Good Government League and Dallas' Citizens Charter Association controlled the recruitment and election of candidates in those two cities for several decades. While both groups drew members from both the Democratic and Republican parties, they reflected and pursued the interests of the higher socioeconomic groups, often to the detriment of lower-income and minority populations.

With recent Republican gains in statewide politics, there have been indications that partisanship is beginning to penetrate city elections. While labels are still excluded from the ballot, some city council candidates are beginning to be identified by their party affiliations through news stories, endorsements, and campaign advertisements. When Mayor Nelson Wolff of San Antonio first ran for city council in 1987, his opponent unsuccessfully attempted to exploit Wolff's active role in the Democratic party. The council district in which Wolff was seeking election usually produced sizable Republican majorities in partisan elections, and his opponent assumed that Wolff's Democratic partisanship would become a liability. But although partisan affiliations have come to the surface in some city elections, the non-partisan ballot still tilts the electoral process and city governance toward the interests of the higher social classes. The absence of political parties to mobilize voters in city elections serves to reduce participation among lower socioeconomic groups.

## At-Large Elections

Another notable feature of city politics in Texas is the general use of at-large, or citywide, elections. In 1987, there were 6,183 individuals elected to the governing bodies of 1,156 cities and towns in Texas. Some 5,588, or 90.4 percent, were elected at-large. Only 9.6 percent were elected from single-member districts.[22]

In an at-large election, all of a city's voters participate in the selection of all the members of the city council. In a pure at-large system, every candidate runs against every other candidate. If there are eight candidates running for five positions on the city council, the candidates with the five highest vote totals are the winners. A variation of the at-large system is the place system. Candidates still run citywide but the places, or positions, that are up for election on the council are identified by number, and a candidate files for a specific council seat. Cities that use the place system may require that the winning candidate receive a simple plurality of votes (more votes than any other candidate running for the same position) or an absolute majority of votes (more than half of the votes cast.) If a city requires the latter and there are more than two persons in a race, runoff elections between the two highest vote getters often are required.

During most of the state's history, general law cities were limited to the pure at-large election system. But home rule cities have had more flexibility in conducting elections, and most home rule cities that still have at-large elections use the place system.[23]

## Single-Member Districts

An alternative to at-large elections is the single-member district, or ward. Under this system, a city is divided into separate geographic districts, each represented by a different council member. A candidate must live in and run for election from a specific district, and a voter can cast a ballot only in the race for the council seat that represents his or her district. A person elected from a single-member district can, depending on the city's charter, be elected by a plurality or an absolute majority of votes.

## The Debate over Electoral Systems

There has been much debate over what is the most desired form of city election system. Advocates of at-large elections often warn of ward politics and the potential relationship of single-member districts to political machines and bosses, once readily associated with the older cities of the Northeast and the upper Midwest. These cities were purported to be corrupt and mismanaged with the needs and interests of the general public subordinated to the greed and interests of the few. Even without corruption, they argue, council members elected from districts are concerned primarily with the interests of their own neighborhoods and may be more susceptible to trade-offs, swapping votes for programs and services that would benefit small segments of the community rather than benefiting the entire city. It also has been argued that district elections divide communities along racial, ethnic, or economic lines, thus resulting in high levels of political conflict. Ward elections in other states also have been associated with partisan politics, which early city reformers in Texas deplored. Moreover, proponents of at-large elections argue that their system produces higher caliber candidates, results in more media exposure for political campaigns, and permits a voter to participate in the selection of the entire city council rather than just one individual.[24]

But critics of the at-large system believe that single-member districts make elected officials more responsive to the needs and interests of specific constituencies. They also argue that at-large elections discriminate against African-Americans and Hispanics because of racially polarized voting. Minorities historically have been underrepresented on city councils in Texas and even have had difficulty winning in cities with large minority populations. Furthermore, citywide election campaigns, especially in the larger cities, are much more expensive than district campaigns, thus adversely affecting the electoral chances of candidates from low-income, often minority, areas. It has also been argued that single-member districts produce a more diverse group of elected officials and ensure that a city council considers more diverse views and interests. At-large elections, critics say, permit a small group of individuals, the city's elites, to control the electoral process and the council by recruiting and financially supporting candidates to protect their interests.

## Legal Attacks on At-Large Elections

Election systems are not politically neutral, and the system a city uses makes a difference in local politics. In Houston, for example, whites have historically voted for white candidates for the city council, African-Americans for African-American candidates, and Hispanics for Hispanics.[25] Between 1956 and 1977, only four African-Americans and no Hispanics were elected in citywide council elections in Houston.[26] The number of minority council members increased after 1980, when Houston started electing nine of its 15 council members from districts. Six council members, including the mayor, are still elected citywide. San Antonio had an at-large system prior to the adoption of single-member districts in 1976. And while the Good Government League, a local political organization that dominated the city's politics from 1955 to 1975, slated some minority candidates of its choosing, independent minority candidates, running without the group's endorsement, had little chance of being elected.

Several Texans, including Congresswoman Barbara Jordan of Houston and U.S. Senator Lloyd Bentsen, led the successful effort in 1975 to extend coverage of the Voting Rights Act to Texas, retroactive to 1972. Prior to that development, minority groups challenging city election systems in the federal courts often had been thwarted by conservative judges. Under the Voting Rights Act, any changes in a city's electoral system that altered or modified minority voting strength had to be pre-cleared by the Department of Justice or approved by the federal district court in Washington, D.C.

Many Texas cities, including San Antonio and Houston, had annexed considerable amounts of territory between 1972 and 1975, and they anticipated additional annexations in the future. Annexation was critical to expanding the jurisdiction of a city, expanding its tax base, and thwarting the efforts of suburban communities to create separate cities encircling the central city. Annexation, which also changed local election systems by adding voters, then became the vehicle by which cities were forced under the Voting Rights Act to consider changing from at-large elections to single-member districts in order to give minority voters a more equitable voice in electing city council members.[27] Minority groups also have been able to use the Voting Rights Act to achieve greater representation on city councils after each census and redistricting cycle for city governments.

Hispanics and African-Americans, through various advocacy groups such as the National Association for the Advancement of Colored People, the Mexican American Legal Defense and Educational Fund, Texas Rural Legal Aid, and the Southwest Voter Registration and Education Project, have challenged in federal courts the election systems used by numerous Texas cities. From the small East Texas town of Jefferson to El Paso, Houston, and Dallas, minority groups have, with considerable success, challenged the inequities of at-large elections and forced city governments to adopt electoral plans that give minorities a better chance of electing candidates to city councils. The ethnic and racial composition of city councils have changed dramatically over the past 20 years with a marked increase in the number of Hispanics and African-Americans elected to these governing bodies.

## CITY REVENUES AND EXPENDITURES

Despite a growing number of expensive needs that they are expected to address, Texas cities have limited financial options. City governments are disproportionately dependent on regressive taxes and fees and have state-imposed limits on their taxing powers. The Texas Constitution and statutes limit the tax rate that cities can impose on property, a primary source of local revenue. Cities of 5,000 residents or less can levy a maximum tax rate of $1.50 per $100 assessed valuation, while cities larger than 5,000 can levy as much as $2.50 per $100 assessed valuation. Type B general law municipalities, which are small cities defined under state statutes, can levy a maximum of 25 cents per $100 assessed value.[28] If a city increases its **property tax** rate more than 8 percent in a given year, state law permits citizens to petition the city council for a **rollback election** to nullify the increase. Rollback elections are part of a growing taxpayer revolt that has become a real threat to public officials—and the quality of public services.

The economic problems of the 1980s continued to plague Texas cities into the 1990s as they attempted to maintain acceptable service levels. When the state's economy went sour in 1985 and 1986, cities experienced revenue shortfalls from a decline in sales tax revenues, reductions in the assessed value of property, and the elimination of many federal assistance programs. Cities have responded by increasing taxes and fees, reducing services and staff and postponing capital improvements.[29] By late 1991, property values in most cities were no longer on a precipitous decline, and some additional sales tax revenues were forthcoming from the legislature's expansion of the sales tax base to more goods and services. But still confronted with a near-recessionary economy, cities were practicing austerity.

As discussed in Chapter 3, some of the stated objectives of the New Federalism of the Reagan administration were to eliminate many of the categorical federal grants, consolidate other grants, and reduce federal outlays for them. While Reagan was not successful in many of his programs, the growth rate of federal grant-in-aid spending slowed down dramatically during the 1980s, placing additional financial pressures on local governments. Many cities have increased their already regressive taxes, with the burden falling disproportionately on middle- and low-income households.[30]

Cities, like state government, are prohibited by the Texas Constitution from borrowing money to pay for current operating expenses and have to find other alternatives for bridging revenue shortfalls. Nearly one-third of Texas cities responding to a 1991 survey by the Texas Municipal League reported that they had experienced a shortage of revenue in the previous fiscal year, and close to one-fourth expected their losses to continue. To compensate, approximately half of the cities reported they had increased user fees, particularly fees for solid waste, water, and wastewater, increases directly linked to federally-mandated environmental policy. Fifty-six percent of the cities had raised property taxes, with most reporting a two to three percent increase. Cities also reported hiring freezes, wage freezes, salary reductions, employee layoffs, reduction in services, elimination of some services, and the postponement of capital improvements during the previous two years.[31]

Although cities are required by law to balance their operating budgets, many municipal construction projects are financed by loans through the issuance of general obligation bonds which are subject to voter approval. These bonds are secured by the city's taxing power. The city pledges its full faith and credit to the lender and, over a number of years, repays the bonds with tax revenue. Cities also fund various projects through revenue bonds which are payable solely from the revenues derived from an income-producing facility developed by the city.[32] The poor economy of the late 1980s made it more difficult for cities to borrow money. And with a pent-up demand for improving their infrastructure (streets, waste disposal systems, libraries, and other facilities), cities are entering an era of bond financing that has been radically altered by the performance of Wall Street and changes in state and federal tax laws.[33]

## COUNTY GOVERNMENT IN TEXAS

Prior to Texas independence, local government was organized both under Spanish and Mexican law around the municipality. This unit consisted of large land areas with "presidios for military protection, missions established by the Catholic Church, and settlements established by various colonists and impresarios."[34] There were 23 such municipalities at the time of independence, and they became the first 23 counties organized under the Texas Constitution of 1836. As the population expanded to other parts of the state and demands on local government increased, additional counties were created from the original 23. Texas now has 254 counties, more than any other state. The constitution gives the legislature the power to create, abolish, or alter counties. But it prescribes certain requirements for a new county, including its size and the proximity of its boundaries to the county seat of the county from which it is created. The last county created was Kenedy in 1921.[35]

Counties are administrative subunits of the state that were developed initially to serve a predominantly rural population. Created primarily to administer state law, they possess powers delegated to them by the state and have relatively few implied powers.[36] Unlike home rule cities, counties lack the basic legislative power of enacting ordinances. They can carry out only those administrative functions granted them by the state. Counties administer and collect some state taxes and enforce a variety of state laws and regulations. They also build roads and bridges, administer local welfare programs, aid in fire protection, and perform other functions primarily local in nature.[37]

### The Diversity of Counties

All Texas counties function under the same constitutional restrictions and basic organizational structure despite wide variations in population, local characteristics, and public needs. According to the 1990 census, Loving County, the state's least populous, had only 107 residents, compared to 2,818,199 in Harris County, the most populous (Table 12-2 on page 390). From 1980 to 1990, Denton County grew by 91 percent, while other predominantly rural counties lost many residents. Rockwall County includes only 147 square miles, while Brewster County covers 6,204 square miles. Jeff Davis County reported a 1990 budget of $517,918, paid its county judge $17,687 a year and its county commissioners $5 per meeting. The county judge in Cottle County, the lowest paid in Texas, received $1,020 a year. Harris County's 1990 budget was $576,288,369. Its county judge was paid $92,592, and each of its commissioners, $82,524.[38] Fifty-five percent of Texas' residents live in the 10 most populous counties.

### The Structure of County Government

The organizational structure of county government is highly fragmented, reflecting the principles of Jacksonian democracy and the reaction of late 19th century Texans

**TABLE 12–2**   Ten Largest and Ten Smallest Texas Counties, 1980–1990

|  | 1980 Population | 1990 Population |
|---|---|---|
| Harris County | 2,409,547 | 2,818,199 |
| Dallas County | 1,556,390 | 1,852,810 |
| Bexar County | 988,800 | 1,185,394 |
| Tarrant County | 860,880 | 1,170,103 |
| El Paso County | 479,899 | 591,610 |
| Travis County | 419,573 | 576,407 |
| Hidalgo County | 283,229 | 383,545 |
| Nueces County | 268,215 | 291,145 |
| Denton County | 143,126 | 273.525 |
| Collin County | 144,576 | 264,036 |
|  |  |  |
| Glasscock County | 1,304 | 1,447 |
| Sterling County | 1,206 | 1,438 |
| Terrell County | 1,595 | 1,410 |
| Roberts County | 1,187 | 1,025 |
| Kent County | 1,145 | 1,010 |
| McMullen County | 789 | 817 |
| Borden County | 859 | 799 |
| Kenedy County | 543 | 460 |
| King County | 425 | 354 |
| Loving County | 91 | 107 |

Source: U.S. Censuses, 1980 and 1990.

to Radical Reconstruction. The governing body of a county is the **commissioners court,** but it shares administrative functions with other independently elected officials (Figure 12-4). Moreover, the name, commissioners court, is somewhat misleading because that body has no judicial functions.

*The Commissioners Court and the County Judge.* The **commissioners court** includes a county judge, who is elected countywide, and four county commissioners, who are elected from a county's four commissioners precincts. Until recent years there were gross inequities in the population distributions among commissioners precincts in most counties. This issue of malapportionment came to a head in the 1968 case of *Avery v. Midland County,* where 97 percent of the population, which lived in the city of Midland, elected only one commissioner, and the remaining three percent of the county's residents elected the other three. Similar inequities were prevalent all over the state, but the U.S. Supreme Court applied the "one man, one vote" principle to the counties and required that districts be equally apportioned.[39] Subsequently, Texas was included under the Voting Rights Act in 1975 and counties

# HARRIS COUNTY ORGANIZATION CHART

## MARCH 1991

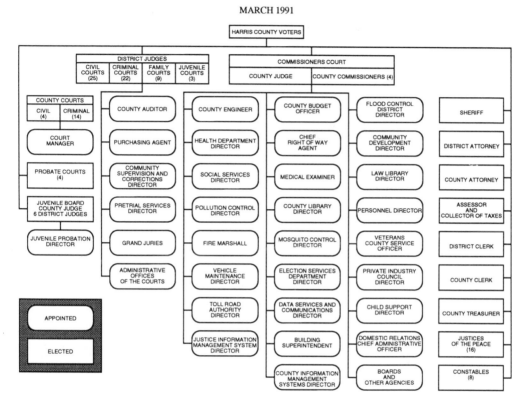

**FIGURE 12-4** Example of county government organization, Harris County, Texas. (Harris County, *Annual Budget, Fiscal Year 1991-1992.*)

were required to consider the interests of minority populations. African-Americans and Hispanics across the state have challenged county electoral systems and increased minority representation on county commissioners courts.

Like other elected county officials, the judge and the commissioners serve four-year terms and are elected in partisan elections. In urban counties, both countywide and precinct campaigns are increasing in cost because of growing numbers of voters and the widespread use of sophisticated campaign technology. The **county judge** presides over commissioners court, participates in the court's deliberations, and votes on issues before it. In many of the smaller counties, the judge serves as the budget officer for the court. If the county judge vacates his or her office, the commissioners choose a replacement.

The constitution also gives the county judge some judicial responsibilities but doesn't require the officeholder to have a law license. Most urban counties have county courts-at-law that relieve the county judge of judicial duties, but county judges in rural counties preside over the county court, which has limited jurisdiction in both civil and criminal cases.

The commissioners court's responsibility is diffused by a number of other elected county offices created by the constitution and state law. But the court fills midterm vacancies in those offices. It also has authority over the county budget, which permits the court to exercise some influence, if not control, over other officeholders.[40] The court sets the annual tax rate, which is limited by the constitution, approves the tax roll and supervises all expenditures of county money (Table 12-3). Other county officials must obtain the court's authorization for personnel positions, salaries, and office expenses. Consequently, the budgetary process often sparks political disputes and other conflicts. On numerous occasions, a Republican sheriff in Bexar County requested additional funds for patrols and jail administration, but the Bexar County Commissioners Court, controlled by Democrats, often denied his requests, sparking political controversies over administrative efficiency versus law and order.

Historically, county road construction and maintenance were primary functions of commissioners court. The Optional Road Law of 1947 gave counties the authority to create a consolidated road system under the supervision of a county engineer, who relieved commissioners of road maintenance and construction headaches. But the importance of roads to the commissioners and their constituents can still generate political disputes.

*The County Clerk.* The constitution provides for an elected **county clerk** to serve as the clerk of the commissioners court, the clerk of the county courts, and in the smaller counties, the clerk of the district court. Over the years, the legislature has enacted hundreds of statutory provisions defining specific responsibilities of the office, prompting one writer to describe the office as the "dumping ground for miscellaneous functions" of the county.[41] All legal documents related to real estate transactions in a county are filed with the county clerk. The office also is the

**TABLE 12-3**  Major Duties of the Commissioners Court

1. Set tax rate and adopt county budget
2. Appoint county officials authorized under statutory law and hire personnel
3. Fill county elective and appointive vacancies
4. Administer elections, including the establishment of voting precincts, the appointment of an election administrator, the appointment of precinct judges, the calling of county bond elections and the certification of election returns
5. Let contracts and authorize payment of all county bills
6. Build and maintain county roads and bridges
7. Build, maintain and improve county facilities, including jails
8. Provide for libraries, hospitals and medical care for the indigent
9. Provide for emergency relief and civil disaster assistance
10. Provide for fire protection and sanitation

Source: Texas Commission on Intergovernmental Relations, *An Introduction to County Government* (Austin: TCIR, 1985), p. 9.

depository of vital statistics, such as birth and death records, and issues marriage licenses and various other licenses required by state law.[42] The county clerk also serves as a county's chief election administrator if commissioners court hasn't created a separate election administrator's office.[43] In 1990, Cottle County paid its county clerk $1,070, while Harris County paid its county clerk $72,948. [44]

*The District Clerk.* This position, also elected countywide, assists a county's district court or courts by maintaining custody of court documents and records.[45] In small counties, the county clerk is authorized to double as the district clerk, and 70 counties combined these two offices in 1990.[46]

*The County and District Attorneys.* The state's interests in both civil and criminal matters is represented at the local level by one of three officers—the county attorney, the **district attorney**, or the criminal district attorney. The legislature has enacted numerous provisions for legal departments that vary from county to county. A county can elect a county attorney unless the legislature provides for another option. Some counties have no county attorney but have a criminal district attorney. Others have two district attorneys, and still others are authorized both a county attorney and a district attorney. And there are inconsistencies in the specific functions and responsibilities of the offices. A district attorney serving in a county with two or more district courts, for example, may be authorized to appear before one court but not another, while a county attorney would handle cases before the second district court.[47]

The county and district attorneys represent the state in bringing charges against criminal suspects and trying them in the appropriate courts. District attorneys prosecute the more serious cases, usually felonies, in the district courts, while the county attorneys prosecute lesser offenses, primarily misdemeanors, in the county courts.[48]

These officers also have other responsibilities. They can provide legal advice and opinions to other county officials and provide legal counsel to any public official or employee who has been sued for acts committed in carrying out his official duties. Upon request of the commissioners court, the district attorney or county attorney may initiate lawsuits on behalf of the county. Various other laws charge these attorneys with protecting the public health, assisting the attorney general in cases involving deceptive trade practices, enforcing the state's election laws, collecting delinquent taxes, and even enforcing the Texas Communist Control Act of 1951.[49]

*The Tax Assessor-Collector.* The property tax is the primary source of revenue for counties. And although commissioners court sets property tax rates, the **county tax assessor-collector**, another elected county officer, has the task of determining who owns what property, how much tax is owed on that property, and then collecting the tax. In counties with fewer than 10,000 people, these responsibilities are assigned to the sheriff, unless voters decide to create a separate tax assessor-collector office. A number of counties, especially those below 5,000 in population, continue to let the sheriff handle the job.

Prior to the 1980s, the tax assessor-collector also was responsible for appraising property, or determining its value. This process often was steeped in politics because the higher the value of a piece of property, the more taxes its owner has to pay. Lowering property values for select friends or supporters gave those holding this office considerable power, which often was abused. In an effort to move toward greater consistency across the state and to enhance the professionalism of tax appraisals, the legislature required each county to create an appraisal district that was separate from the tax office.[50] Property tax appraisals are now conducted countywide by an appraisal district whose members represent other governmental units in the county. The district also certifies the tax rolls, and other governmental units are required by law to use its appraisals.[51]

*County Law Enforcement.* Sheriffs and constables, a county's law enforcement officers, are part of an old tradition under the Anglo-Saxon legal system. Each county has one **sheriff** with countywide jurisdiction, but the number of **constables** can vary. In counties with fewer than 18,000 residents, commissioners court can designate the entire county as a single justice of the peace precinct or can create as many as four precincts, with each precinct assigned one constable. In the large counties, as many as eight justice of the peace precincts can be created with a constable assigned to each. Most counties have four constables.[52]

In a small rural county, the sheriff is the primary law enforcement officer for the entire county. But in the urban counties, city police departments generally assume exclusive jurisdiction in the incorporated municipal areas, leaving the sheriff jurisdiction over the unincorporated areas. Sheriffs have considerable discretion in the hiring, promotion, and firing of deputies and other employees, although some counties have adopted a merit employment system for the sheriff's office. The sheriff also serves as the administrative officer for the district and county courts.

Constables are authorized to patrol their precincts, make arrests, and conduct criminal investigations, but their primary function is to serve as administrative officers of the justice of the peace courts. They are responsible for serving subpoenas, executing judgments of the court, and delivering other legal documents.[53]

County governments are responsible for constructing and staffing county jails, which are managed in most counties by the sheriff and in some counties by a jail administrator. With the state's recent problems in controlling the size of its prison population under a federal court order (see Chapter 13), jail construction has been something of a growth industry in Texas and jail management has taken on increased significance.

All counties are authorized to create an office of medical examiner. This individual is appointed by commissioners court and determines the cause of death of murder victims or others who die under suspicious or unusual circumstances. In counties that don't have a medical examiner, the justice of the peace is charged with conducting an inquest to determine if there are conditions to merit an autopsy.

Counties, either individually or as part of multicounty judicial districts, are required to provide facilities for a criminal probation office. There are statewide standards for probation developed by the Texas Adult Probation Commission and the Texas Juvenile Probation Commission. Funded by the state, the chief adult probation officer of a county is chosen by the district judges, who supervise the office.

*County Auditor.* All counties with 10,000 or more population are required to have an auditor, while smaller counties may have one if commissioners court chooses. Two counties with fewer than 25,000 residents may jointly agree to hire an auditor to serve both counties. The auditor is appointed by the district judges of the county for a two-year term. He or she is primarily responsible for reviewing every bill and expenditure of a county to assure its correctness and legality. Such oversight can, in effect, impose budgetary restrictions on commissioners court and produce political conflict with other county officers.

The role of the auditor varies from county to county. In counties with more than 225,000 people, the auditor is the budget officer who prepares the budget submitted to the court,[54] but recent legislation permits the commissioners court in counties with 125,000 or more people to appoint a budget officer.

*The County Treasurer.* This officer is responsible for receiving and disbursing county funds. While this office has existed since 1846, its primary functions are now carried out by the county auditor, and constitutional amendments have eliminated the office in a number of counties.

*Outdated Offices.* The Texas Constitution created the office of county surveyor, and state laws provided for a county inspector of hides and animals and a public weigher. These offices, which served important functions during the rural, formative period of Texas history, have since been abolished in many counties, and few counties where they remain on the books actually elect anyone to fill them.

## CRITICISMS OF COUNTY GOVERNMENT

The structure of county government in Texas was designed for a rural state and has inhibited efforts of urban counties to respond to growing needs for public services. While the state has experimented with county home rule, the provisions, as noted earlier, were so poorly written, confusing, and contradictory that local self-rule at the county level never was given a real chance.

But even though the county functions primarily as an extension, or administrative subdivision, of state government, there is little supervision of the counties by the state and a wide disparity in the way counties interpret and administer their functions. And the state rarely acts to hold county governments responsible for compliance with state mandates.

Some county judges have been able to develop strong political bases and expand their influence over commissioners court and other county offices. But the fragmentation represented by several independently elected officers always poses a danger of jurisdictional conflict, administrative inefficiency, and even government deadlock.

Like other local governments in Texas, counties rely heavily on the property tax for revenue but can't exceed tax rate limits set by the state constitution. While those limits reflected a general apprehension about government when they were initially set in 1876, they now further restrict the counties' ability to provide services.

Historically, county courthouses have been associated with political patronage and the spoils system. Victorious candidates have claimed the right to appoint personal and political friends to work for them, and state courts have held that elected county officials have wide discretion in the selection of their employees. Reformers have advocated a civil service system for county employees based on merit and competitive examinations and offering job security from one election to the next. A 1971 law allows counties with more than 200,000 population to create a civil service system but it excludes several county offices, including the district attorney. An elected public official retains considerable control over the initial hiring of employees through a probationary period of six months.[55]

## MODERNIZING COUNTY GOVERNMENT

City governments provide most basic public services in urban areas, and as cities expand to county boundaries and beyond, the jurisdiction of county government becomes more limited. Counties, nevertheless, continue to play an important role in Texas. Rural Texans, in particular, continue to rely on counties to provide a number of services, and demands on many counties will likely increase. Recommendations to modernize county government include another attempt at county home rule, granting counties some legislative or ordinance-making authority and creating an office of county administrator, who would be appointed by commissioners court to run the departments now assigned to commissioners. Another recommendation is to extend the civil service system to smaller counties and to all county employees, including those of elected officials.[56]

## SPECIAL DISTRICTS IN TEXAS

When is the last time you or your family dealt with a MUD or a WCID? Have you ever contacted a mosquito abatement district to request assistance in insect control? Or has anyone in your family ever used the medical services of a hospital district? There are approximately 2,000 governmental units across Texas classified as **special districts**. These include drainage districts, navigation districts, fresh water supply districts, river authorities, underground water districts, sanitation districts, housing authorities, soil conservation districts, MUDs (municipal utility districts), and

WCIDs (water conservation and improvement districts), among others. School districts also are considered a form of special districts.

Special districts are units of local government created by the state to perform specific functions. Wide variations in their functions, taxing and borrowing authority, governance and performance permit us in a few paragraphs to make only a few generalizations. Most are authorized to perform a single function and are designated single-purpose districts. But some are multi-purpose districts because the laws creating them permit them to provide multiple services to constituents. For example, in addition to providing water to people in their service areas, MUDs may assume responsibility for drainage, solid waste collection, fire fighting, parks, and other recreational facilities.[57] Some districts, such as hospital districts, normally cover an entire county. Others, such as MUDs, cover part of one county, while still others, such as river authorities, cover a number of counties.

A special district is governed by a board either appointed by other governmental units or elected in non-partisan elections. The board members of hospital districts are appointed by county commissioners courts, while city housing authority boards are appointed by mayors or city councils. Many of these districts have taxing and borrowing authority, but others have no taxing powers and are supported by user fees or funds dedicated to them by other governmental agencies. Many special districts are eligible for federal grants-in-aid.

Special districts exist for a variety of reasons. Independent school districts were created, in part, to depoliticize education and remove the responsibility for it from county and city governments. Reformers in the late 19th and early 20th centuries argued that the governance of schools had to be autonomous and insulated from partisan politics. That goal could be accomplished only by the creation of districts that had their own governing bodies and tax bases. Similar arguments also have been made about other specialized governmental functions.[58]

Special districts also are established after general purpose governments refuse to provide basic services to some areas. Numerous municipal utility districts, for example, have been created as a means of providing water and sewer service and helping developers open up new subdivisions in areas that cities haven't annexed.

In some cases, existing governments are unable to provide essential services to new developments because of state restrictions on the tax and debt authority of cities and counties. Counties are particularly limited by the state constitution and statutory law. They simply do not have the authority to provide many of the services now demanded by their citizens, and the legislature has repeatedly refused to expand their powers. So special purpose districts were created to fill the gap. Since many districts can be created by statute, it has been far easier to create an additional layer of government than change the authority or powers of existing governments by constitutional amendment.[59]

The cost of providing a particular governmental service is another reason for the growth of special districts. Medical care and public hospitals can be extremely expensive, and many cities cannot issue sufficient bonds or raise taxes high enough to pay for them. By creating a special district that includes a number of governmental units and a larger population and tax base, the costs are spread over a wider area.

In some instances, the creation of a special district was related to the geographical area to be served. River basins that extend for thousands of square miles and cover 10 or 20 counties presented a particular problem. Since no existing governments had jurisdiction over the use of water resources in these basins, river authorities with multicounty jurisdictions were created.[60]

Special districts also are often promoted by individuals, groups, or corporations for selfish gains. During the high growth periods of the state when there was a lot of residential and commercial construction, builders would develop plans for large tracts of land in the unincorporated areas of a county. Then they would get local governments or the legislature to create municipal utility or water districts to provide water and sewer services. Often the easiest route was the legislature, where developers would get friendly lawmakers to sponsor special bills for their subdivisions. Eighty-four laws creating water districts in Texas were enacted in 1969 alone.[61] Once the authorization had been granted, the builder would proceed to incorporate a new water district. There were numerous instances when only a handful of people who lived in an area or had a financial interest in a proposed development would vote to create a district, elect its governing body and approve the sale of millions of dollars in bonds. The costs of servicing the bonds would then be assessed against future homeowners or business owners in the area.[62] Before reforms were approved in 1973, this process produced considerable temptation for builders and developers to use special districts to "create business opportunities, make a quick profit, or provide jobs for friends and relatives."[63]

## Consequences of Single-Purpose Districts

From one perspective, special districts are used to compensate for the fragmentation of local government that exists throughout Texas. But, ironically, these districts also contribute to further fragmentation and delay the more-difficult development of comprehensive, multipurpose governmental units that could more efficiently provide public services.

A special district has been called a "halfway house between cityhood and noncityhood, between incorporation and nonincorporation."[64] Residents of a developing community or subdivision may not want to create a new city or become part of a nearby existing city, but they need certain fundamental services, such as water, electricity, and fire protection, some of which could be provided through the creation of special districts.

Many special districts are small operations with limited financial resources and few employees. Salaries often are low, and some districts have difficulty retaining the licensed technical people required to perform daily operations. In some cases, record keeping and management operations are shoddy and amateurish, and the costs of providing services by many of these operations may actually be higher than what similar services cost in larger governmental systems.

Special districts also must use outside legal and professional assistance, which can be very costly, and many districts lack the expertise to maximize their investments or borrowing potential.[65]

Some of these special governmental units also expand their functions beyond the original purpose for which they were created. The metropolitan transit authority in San Antonio, for example, which is authorized under state law to impose a 1 percent sales tax, has gotten into the business of building the Alamodome, a multifunction convention and sports facility. This same organization also is beginning to implement comprehensive planning, a function that normally is carried out by the city of San Antonio. As governments expand their functions, there is a greater potential for intergovernmental rivalry, conflict, potential deadlock, and duplication of costs.

Special districts sometimes are referred to as the "invisible governments" of Texas.[66] Except for the 1,000-plus independent school districts and a small number of other highly visible districts, such as river authorities, most special districts operate in anonymity. The public has only limited knowledge of their jurisdiction, management, operations, or performance. Many taxpayers may not even be aware they are paying taxes to some of these entities. There is little media coverage of their work, few individuals attend their board meetings, and turnout for their elections is extremely low. In the case of the governing boards that are appointed by other governmental agencies, the appointment process often is dominated by a small number of individuals or groups who also dominate the activities of the special district. This is probably the most damning indictment of special districts.

## INDEPENDENT SCHOOL DISTRICTS

The current controversies over educational quality and equity in Texas have roots in the early organization and governance of the public schools. Education was an issue in the Texas independence movement, but it was the Reconstruction period that set the stage for many of the long-term issues of school finance and governance. During Reconstruction, the Republicans attempted to centralize the education system at the state level. But with the end of Republican control prior to the Constitutional Convention of 1875, the centralized system was eliminated and the control and finance of public education were transferred to the counties.

In place of an orderly, comprehensive system that assured public education to every child in the state, community schools were created. They could be formed by any group of parents petitioning the county judge, who had considerable influence and control over the schools. County judges could appoint trustees nominated by the organizing parents and distribute money from the state's available school fund to the organized schools within their respective counties. This produced marked differences in the availability, funding, and quality of public education across the state. Community schools also were self-selective. Those who initiated the creation of a school could decide which children could attend. Consequently, there was racial and economic segregation, and the children of Texans with limited political clout were denied access to an adequate public education. These characteristics dominated public education in Texas at the end of the 19th century, and vestiges remained until 1909.

The independent school district, currently the basic organizational structure for public education in Texas, also had its origins in the Constitution of 1876. Cities and towns were allowed to create independent school districts and to impose a tax to support them. Initially, the city government served as the school board, but in 1879, school districts were permitted to organize independently of the city or town, elect their own boards of trustees, and impose their own school tax. But residents of rural areas, where most 19th century Texans lived, were denied these powers and had only the option of forming community schools. So, in effect, Texas operated under a dual school system with the majority of students subject to the discretionary and often arbitrary powers of county governments.

From the very beginning, the inequities in such a school system were clear to many parents, elected officials, and educators, and there were early efforts to reform and modernize public schools. Most were linked to national education reform movements. For example, the Peabody Education Board, a national organization, provided financial aid and technical support to the leaders of the state reform movement during the early part of the 20th century. More recently, national attention has been directed to the problems of public education through widely publicized studies such as "A Nation at Risk—The Imperative for Educational Reform," which was conducted by the National Commission on Excellence in Education. There have been many national, state, and local organizations that have attempted to identify and articulate the most serious problems with public education, develop alternatives for resolving these problems, and initiate litigation or legislative and administrative initiatives.

Reformers have focused much of their attention on compulsory education laws, adequacy, and equity in school funding, quality curricula, and teacher preparation. Some reform efforts also were directed at the structure and governance of local school districts. The diverse and fragmented structure of Texas schools was modified over the years through consolidations, greater uniformity in the organization of school districts and the extension of the independent school district to virtually every community in the state. More recently, the state also has taken a more active role in setting classroom curricula and requirements for teachers and school district management. (For a more complete discussion of the recent struggles over funding equity and educational quality in the classroom, please see Chapter 13.)

## Local School Governance

Although regulation and coordination are provided on a statewide level through the State board of Education and the Texas Education Agency (see Chapter 10), public education is now administered through the local school districts. In 1990, there were 1,058 school districts in Texas. The smallest, the Allamoore Consolidated

Independent School District in sparsely populated Hudspeth County, had three students, and the largest, the Houston Independent School District, had 174,340 students. Four hundred districts had fewer than 500 students each. More than 3.3 million students attended grades pre-kindergarten through 12 in Texas public schools during the 1989-90 school year.[67] By 1991, minority students (Hispanics, African-Americans, and other minority groups) comprised a majority of the public school population in Texas, and their numbers were expected to increase. As discussed in Chapter 1, the Hispanic population is increasing at the greatest rate for all ethnic and racial groups in Texas, and this growth is reflected in the changing composition of public school enrollment.

School districts are governed by boards of trustees ranging in size from three to nine members. Most have seven. Trustees' terms vary from two to six years, with most serving three-year terms. Board members receive no salaries but are reimbursed for travel related to board business.

School board members are elected in non-partisan elections, although there are some districts, such as the North East Independent School District in San Antonio, where voters will organize political action committees to recruit and fund school board candidates. Most school board elections are held on the first Saturday in May, the same day most cities hold their elections. Some cities and school districts try to share election costs, but many school districts refuse to do that for fear a hotly contested city campaign could affect a school board election. School board election turnouts are low, usually less than 10 percent of registered voters. But turnout will increase when there are highly visible issues, such as the firing of a superintendent or a dramatic increase in taxes.

It often is difficult to recruit qualified candidates for school boards, and many times the offices are uncontested. Persons are asked to run by the superintendent, other members of the board, or key community leaders, and many superintendents indicate that it is difficult to find people who are willing to give the required time and energy. Individuals often have little knowledge of what school board members do, and many trustees will serve for only one term, giving some boards high turnover rates. Moreover, there is no way for a potential trustee to anticipate the amount of time it will take for briefings by the superintendent and his staff, preparing for and participating in board meetings, and taking phone calls from parents and taxpayers. And in addition to his or her policy-making responsibilities, a board member must deal with the political aspect of the job, including attendance at community functions and major school programs and meeting with teachers and taxpayer groups.

The most important decision that a school board makes is the hiring of a school superintendent. In organization and management structure, the school district is similar to the council-manager form of government used by many cities. The board hires a superintendent who is in charge of the district's day-to-day operations. While the board has the primary policy-making responsibility for a district, part-time board members often are dominated by the superintendent and his staff. School trustees and superintendents tend to talk about keeping politics out of education, and superintendents often attempt to convey the impression that they serve simply to carry out the will of their boards. In most instances, though, a school board's agenda is established by the superintendent, and the board members depend on the superintendent and other professional staff members for information and policy recommendations. Very few board members have much time to give to the district, and most have only limited knowledge of the laws affecting education. State law, in fact, restricts the intrusion of board members into the daily management and administration of a district. An excessively politicized school board that becomes involved in day-to-day administration can be called to task by the Texas Education Agency. In an extreme case, the TEA can even take over the management of a school district.

Studies suggest that few school board members expect to pursue further political careers once they have completed their education service. In addition to being concerned about general educational issues and school taxes, many individuals who run for school boards do so out of a sense of civic duty rather than with the intent of launching a political career.

All but 61 of the 1,058 school districts in Texas elect their board members in at-large elections, where every candidate runs district-wide. With only a few exceptions, the 61 districts that elect their board members from single-member districts or a combination of single-member districts and at-large elections are doing so because of lawsuits or a threat of lawsuits by minority plaintiffs. As they have also done against similar city election systems, minority groups have challenged the at-large systems as discriminatory and a dilution of the minority vote in violation of the federal Voting Rights Act. In many districts, Hispanics and African-Americans who comprised a majority or a large part of the population found it virtually impossible to elect anyone to the school board under a district-wide election scheme. They were stymied by lower than average voter registration and turnout rates among minorities and various socioeconomic factors—plus the tendency of Anglo voters to cast ballots for Anglo candidates. Even though only about 6 percent of school districts have adopted single-member districting, it has helped boost the number of African-Americans and Hispanics elected to public office in Texas.[68]

## COUNCILS OF GOVERNMENT

Councils of government, or regional planning commissions, were created under the Texas Regional Planning Act of 1965. That law was enacted, in part, to comply with federal regulations requiring local planning and review procedures.[69] These organizations evolved over the years to take on additional duties, including comprehensive planning and service responsibilities for employment and job training, criminal justice, economic development, health, aging, early childhood development, alcoholism, drug abuse, transportation, land resource management, environmental quality, and rural development programs.[70]

There are 24 regional councils of government, or COGs, in Texas, each one serving a specific geographic area determined by the state (Figure 12-5). In 1991,

# State Planning Regions

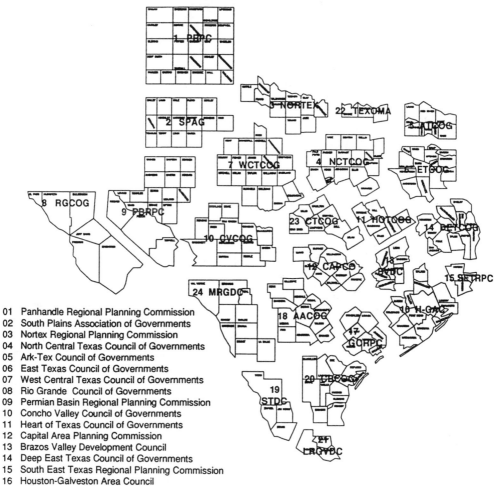

01 Panhandle Regional Planning Commission
02 South Plains Association of Governments
03 Nortex Regional Planning Commission
04 North Central Texas Council of Governments
05 Ark-Tex Council of Governments
06 East Texas Council of Governments
07 West Central Texas Council of Governments
08 Rio Grande  Council of Governments
09 Permian Basin Regional Planning Commission
10 Concho Valley Council of Governments
11 Heart of Texas Council of Governments
12 Capital Area Planning Commission
13 Brazos Valley Development Council
14 Deep East Texas Council of Governments
15 South East Texas Regional Planning Commission
16 Houston-Galveston Area Council
17 Golden Crescent Council of Governments
18 Alamo Area Council of Governments
19 South Texas Development Council
20 Coastal Bend Council of Governments
21 Lower Rio Grande Valley Development Council
22 Texoma Council of Governments
23 Central Texas Council of Governments
24 Middle Rio Grande Valley Development Council

**FIGURE 12-5**  State Planning Regions and Regional Council Membership.  (Office of the Governor, *Regional Councils in Texas*, 1990-1991.)

every county but Val Verde were members of COGs. Membership is voluntary and includes counties, cities, school districts, and other special districts. Each COG decides the composition and structure of its governing body, so long as two-thirds of its members are elected officials from counties or cities. Regional councils have no regulatory authority or powers comparable to those of other local governments, and decisions of the COGs are not binding on their members.[71]

Member governments pay dues, but the primary sources of funding for COGs have been the state and federal governments. The state pays a regional council a flat fee for each county that is a member and provides a per capita payment for each person residing in the COG. At one time, the regional councils relied extensively on federal grants-in-aid, but there was a 70 percent decrease in direct federal funding of the COGs during the 1980s. Seventy-two percent of the $180 million spent by regional councils in 1989 was indirect federal pass-through money administered by state agencies. Several COGs have expanded their technical support and some management services to offset these lost revenues.[72]

## LOCAL PROBLEMS IN TEXAS

During the 1970s and through the early 1980s, Texas cities were key participants in the dramatic economic growth of the state, and many of the older cities of the country—particularly in the East and the Midwest—"looked at their Texas counterparts and envied their capacity to attract population and business."[73] Texas cities had low taxes, a pro-business tradition, few labor unions with significant economic clout, an abundant work force, proximity to natural resources, and governing bodies that favored economic growth and development. By the late 1980s, however, economic conditions had changed dramatically and many problems associated with the older urban areas of the country had arrived in Texas. Furthermore, the benefits of the earlier economic growth had not been distributed equally throughout the state's population. Low-income and minority Texans benefited far less than other groups.[74]

### Graying of Texas Cities

A number of problems are likely to become more pronounced during the 1990s. As is true of the entire nation, the Texas population is aging, or graying. Americans are living longer, and the older age groups are now some of the fastest growing segments of the population. As the population ages, additional demands are placed on city governments for public services, and additional pressures are placed on city budgets. The local property tax, a major source of revenue for city governments, is almost stretched to its limits. Moreover, many Texas cities have granted, in addition to the standard homestead exemption, additional property tax exemptions for individuals older than 65. And as more and more people become old enough to claim these exemptions, younger taxpayers will be called upon to shoulder the burden through higher tax rates. While a consistent trend is not clear, older populations with fixed incomes may increasingly resist bond issues for capital improvements out of fear that these expenditures will increase their property taxes.

## White Flight

Demographically, Texas cities are extremely dynamic. Their population characteristics change over time. The large urban areas are experiencing, in addition to aging populations, some white flight to the suburbs. There has been a dramatic increase in the growth rate of minority populations, especially Hispanics, and a very small growth rate among Anglos in the central cities.[75] Income levels for most minority Texans have always been lower than those of Anglos, and a larger proportion of the minority population falls below the poverty level. These income disparities are clearly identified from income data taken from the 1990 census. For the white or Anglo population, the mean household income in 1989 was above $40,000. By contrast, the mean household income for African-Americans was $23,275 and for Hispanics, $24,354.[76] Moreover, the Hispanic population is much younger than the Anglo population, and many people below the poverty level in the cities are children and young people. The increased concentration of lower income people in the central cities increases pressure for more public services, while a declining proportion of affluent property owners weakens the local tax structures that pay for the services.

## Declining Infrastructures

There has been much concern across Texas and the United States about the declining infrastructures of local governments. Streets, bridges, water and sewer systems, libraries, and other facilities must be constantly maintained or expanded to support a growing population. Moreover, many Texas cities are out of compliance with federal standards for treating water and sewage and disposing of solid waste and must spend millions of dollars on physical improvements to avoid or reduce exposure to fines. But many cities, such as San Antonio, have reached the maximum bonded indebtedness permitted by state law and the constitution. And with the decline of the property values that are necessary to generate the taxes to repay capital improvement bonds, cities are forced to curtail additional construction or find alternatives for dealing with their infrastructure problems.

## Crime and Urban Violence

Crime is a growing problem in Texas cities and counties, just as it is in many other parts of the country. Much of the problem is related to drug abuse and an overloaded criminal justice system and has been compounded by the state's failure—or inability—to take adequate steps to address it. Police departments across the state are being pushed to their limits at the same time that Texas citizens are feeling more insecure and more fearful. Expanded law enforcement forces are proposed by political candidates and elected officials, but most city and county budgets cannot absorb the costs. Much of the increase in crime has been in violent crimes, including a growth in urban warfare between youthful gangs.

## State and Federal Mandated Programs

As we previously discussed in Chapter 3, both federal and state governments have increasingly used mandates in recent years to implement public policy. A mandate is a law or regulation enacted by a higher level of government that compels a lower level of government to carry out a specific action. In simpler terms, it is a form of buck-passing. Despite a decrease in federal funding for many urban problems during the 1980s, there has been an increase in federal mandates on the states, counties and the cities—and an increase in state mandates on local governments, often with no financial support. In some cases, the state will simply pass the responsibility for—and the costs of—carrying out federal mandates to local governments.

While the practice may seem unfair and illogical, it is politically attractive to policymakers because they can "appease a large and vocal interest group which demands an extensive program without incurring the wrath of their constituents." While they get the credit for such programs, they do not get the blame for its costs.[77] Starting with the New Federalism of Ronald Reagan in the 1980s, the debate over financing many programs was transferred to state and local governments.[78] Cities across Texas, for example, claim that these unfunded requirements are pushing them against the wall, and unless there are changes in such practices, the cities will be out of compliance and subject to litigation. They are then likely to reduce other services or seek alternative sources of funding now denied them.

Local governments have been particularly hard hit by mandated environmental policies, which are now estimated to cost $100 billion annually and expected to increase to $148 billion a year by the year 2000. Cities across the nation will pick up one-third of the cost. Responding to the demands of environmentalists and recognizing the basic necessities of clean air and water, both Congress and the Texas legislature have enacted broad changes in laws requiring cities to comply with defined standards. Mandates pertaining to waste water discharge, for example, will require many Texas cities to upgrade their sewage treatment facilities. While some federal funds are available to local governments, Texas, unlike many other states, provides no money to the cities to comply with its environmental mandates.[79]

## SOLUTIONS TO THE PROBLEMS OF LOCAL GOVERNMENTS

### Privatization of Functions

As local governments attempt to juggle their financial problems with increased demands for public services, there has been a recent trend toward contracting some services to private companies. Many governments believe **privatization** can reduce costs through businesslike efficiency, and they consider it an attractive alternative in the face of voter hostility toward higher taxes. Cities, for example, are contracting for garbage pickup, waste disposal, towing, food services, security, and a variety of other services. Privatization also provides a way for cities that have reached their limit on bonded indebtedness to make new capital improvements. For example, a civic center or other facility can be constructed by a private contractor and leased back to a city for an extended period. The city is obligated to pay for the facility over the duration of the lease, but such an arrangement is not subject to the legal limits on the debt that a city may incur.

## Annexation and Extraterritorial Jurisdiction

Population growth in the areas surrounding most large Texas cities has forced municipalities, as well as counties, to wrestle with urban sprawl. In 1950, El Paso included 26 square miles but had expanded to 239 square miles by 1990. Houston grew from 160 square miles in 1950 to 540 square miles in 1990, and similar expansions have been repeated in most of the state's other metropolitan areas. The cities' ability to expand their boundaries beyond suburban development derives from their annexation powers and **extraterritorial jurisdiction** over neighboring areas. Other city policies, though, have contributed to urban sprawl as cities linked economic growth to road and highway construction and the development of new commercial and residential areas to expand municipal tax bases.

With the Municipal Annexation Act of 1963, the legislature granted cities considerable discretionary authority over nearby unincorporated areas. The specific annexation powers and extraterritorial jurisdiction vary with the size of a city and the charter under which it functions. But, generally, cities have extraterritorial jurisdiction over unincorporated areas within one-half mile to five miles of the city limits, making development in those areas subject to the city's building codes, zoning and land use restrictions, utility easement requirements, and road and street specifications. In other words, a developer or anyone else planning to build a home or office there is required to comply with the city code. This authority restricts the use of unincorporated land and, more importantly, requires those building outside of the city to build according to minimal standards. Later, when those areas are annexed by the city, they are less likely to quickly degenerate into suburban slums that will require a high infusion of city dollars for basic services.

Cities can annex area equivalent to 10 percent of their existing territory in a given year, and if this authority is not exercised in one year, it can be carried over to subsequent years. Annexation does not require a vote of those people to be incorporated into the city. However, a city is required to provide annexed areas with services comparable to those provided in its older neighborhoods within three years. Otherwise, individuals living in these newly annexed areas can exercise an option to be de-annexed, a situation that rarely occurs.

Unlike cities in many other parts of the country, Texas cities have used their annexation powers to limit the number of small towns surrounding them. Aggressive use of annexation has permitted cities to expand geographically with population growth. Cities would even annex thin strips of land along major roads and arteries leading into the cities while such additions were still miles from urban development. These actions were taken because a city's extraterritorial jurisdiction extended as far as five miles on either side of the narrow strip that was annexed, thus enabling the city to control future growth and development in a large area. In San Antonio, these annexation policies often were referred to as "spoke annexation," and it has taken more than 30 years for much of the territory brought under the city's jurisdiction to be developed and annexed by the city.[80]

## Economic Development

We have repeatedly suggested that there is a close relationship between economics and politics, and that is as true for local governments as for state government. But the same sluggish economic conditions that have made it necessary for cities to spend more money to support development and growth also have restricted their ability to embark on aggressive economic expansion initiatives.

Historically, cities have attempted to collaborate with the private sector to stimulate local economies. Private sector initiatives have come from chambers of commerce or economic development foundations, and city governments have participated. It also is not unusual for a developer to plan a new residential community with the expectation that the city will assist in constructing some parts of the utility systems to serve it. Cities used to pay for these capital improvements through increased property taxes, fees, or some form of bonds. Now, many cities are being forced to find alternatives. They are using a variety of new financing techniques to assist in economic development, including development impact taxes and fees, user charges, the creation of special district assessments, tax increment financing, and privatization of governmental functions.[81]

A state law was enacted in 1989 to permit cities, with the approval of local voters, to impose a one-half percent sales tax for local industrial development. By late 1991, some 74 cities had held elections to authorize the additional tax, and 47 cities had won voter approval.[82]

The economic development strategies of Texas cities also include the aggressive courting of American and foreign companies to relocate or develop new plants or operations in their communities. Cities and local chambers of commerce sponsor public relations campaigns touting local benefits and attractions, and elected city officials and key city administrators often will be actively involved in recruitment efforts. Since competition between communities often is intense, cities also will offer tax abatements, favored treatment on utility bills, or other financial incentives to companies being courted. Specific city agencies often are given the responsibility of developing economic development plans. Many cities also have established relationships with "sister cities" in foreign countries, and state government has assisted cities by establishing trade and commerce offices in a few key foreign cities.

County governments also have recognized the importance of economic development. The legislature has permitted counties to form industrial development corporations or enterprise zones and relax regulatory policies to encourage the redevelopment of depressed areas. Portions of a county can be designated as reinvestment zones, where tax abatements can be offered to attract new businesses. Like a city, a county also may reduce the property taxes of a business for a specified period to encourage a company to locate or expand in the county. Counties also can create county boards of development, civic centers, foreign trade zones, and research and development authorities.[83]

## Interlocal Contracting

Because many small governments have limited tax bases and staffs, they enter into contracts with larger governments for various public services. In 1971, the legislature, following a constitutional amendment, enacted the Interlocal Cooperation Act, which gave cities, counties, and other political subdivisions rather broad authority for such contracts.[84] The law has been amended several times to expand the scope of these agreements, and local governments are now contracting with each other for services in 25 functional areas ranging from aviation to water and wastewater management.[85]

While these agreements do not resolve many of the jurisdictional problems resulting from the highly fragmented character of local government, they can help officials find less costly and more efficient ways of providing services through economies of scale and the adaptation of technological innovations.[86] Contracting is not an alternative to consolidation of local governments, but it does hold out some promise for improving the quality of local services and reducing their costs.

## Metro Government and Consolidation

In the metropolitan areas of Houston, Dallas, and San Antonio, there are literally hundreds of cities and special districts providing public services. In Harris County (Houston) alone, there are 492 separate governmental units (Table 12-4 on page 410). Legislators, scholars, and reform groups have given a lot of study to the duplication and other problems produced by such proliferation and fragmentation and have made numerous recommendations over the years. One proposed solution is a consolidation of city and county governments. This has been done in a dozen or so metropolitan areas outside Texas, including Baltimore, Denver, New York, St. Louis, San Francisco, and Jacksonville.

Another alternative is the partial union of city and county governments, one variation of which has been tried in Louisiana with the partial consolidation of the city of Baton Rouge and East Baton Rouge Parish (the Louisiana equivalent of a Texas county). The governing bodies of the two levels of government remain but are integrated through representation of one government on the governing body of the other. Both governments share a chief executive officer, and some select

**TABLE 12–4** Local Governments in the Ten Largest and Ten Smallest Counties, 1987

| | Total | County | Municipal | School District | Special District |
|---|---|---|---|---|---|
| State | 4,415 | 254 | 1,156 | 1,113 | 1,892 |
| Harris | 492 | 1 | 28 | 24 | 439 |
| Dallas | 70 | 1 | 26 | 16 | 27 |
| Bexar | 54 | 1 | 22 | 16 | 15 |
| Tarrant | 68 | 1 | 34 | 18 | 15 |
| El Paso | 26 | 1 | 4 | 10 | 11 |
| Travis | 75 | 1 | 14 | 8 | 52 |
| Hidalgo | 75 | 1 | 18 | 15 | 41 |
| Nueces | 38 | 1 | 7 | 14 | 16 |
| Denton | 56 | 1 | 34 | 11 | 10 |
| Collin | 49 | 1 | 24 | 15 | 9 |
| Glasscock | 3 | 1 | | 1 | 1 |
| Sterling | 4 | 1 | 1 | 1 | 1 |
| Terrell | 4 | 1 | | 1 | 2 |
| Roberts | 4 | 1 | 1 | 1 | 1 |
| Kent | 4 | 1 | 1 | 1 | 1 |
| McMullen | 4 | 1 | | 1 | 2 |
| Borden | 2 | 1 | | 1 | |
| Kenedy | 2 | 1 | | 1 | |
| King | 3 | 1 | | 1 | 1 |
| Loving | 2 | 1 | | | 1 |

Source: U.S. Department of Commerce, Bureau of the Census, *1987 Census of Governments, Government Organization*, Vol. 1, Table 26.

governmental functions have been consolidated. Since 1956, Miami and Dade County, Florida, have used another version of county-city consolidation. The county has been granted home rule powers and is authorized to perform most municipal functions in the county as well as in Miami and other local cities.[87]

A third alternative is the creation of a "supergovernment" that spans the cities, counties, and special districts in an area. While alternative forms have been proposed, "this new level of government might be totally independent of other governments in the area, or it might be their agent."[88] While several U.S. cities have proposed such a system, none have adopted it.

There has been little interest in consolidated or metropolitan government in Texas. The response to the proliferation of local governments here is more likely to take the form of increased intergovernmental contracting and the informal cooperation that local governments develop out of necessity and mutual self interests.[89]

## Public Improvement Districts

Under a recent state law, property owners in a specific area of a city or its extraterritorial jurisdiction can petition the city to create a special public improvement district. These districts can undertake a wide range of improvements—landscaping, lighting, signs, sidewalks, streets, pedestrian malls, libraries, parking, and water, wastewater, and drainage facilities. Public improvement districts do not have the same autonomy as other special districts. They are created solely through the discretionary powers of the city and are funded by assessments on property within their boundaries.[90] While their budgets and assessments must be approved by the city, they can be operated and managed by private management companies or by the citizens themselves. Fort Worth created a special improvement district for its downtown area in 1986, and other cities have considered the option.

These special districts certainly are not a solution to the broad range of problems confronting Texas cities. Their widespread use without a coordinated citywide improvements policy could produce a number of problems, including financial and management troubles and the pursuit of programs that conflict with the city's overall objectives.

### *SUMMARY AND CONCLUSIONS*

**1.** Local governments in Texas are the creations of the state and have only those powers granted to them by the state constitution and state statutes. In addition to the traditional functions assigned to local governments, they are charged with carrying out many policy decisions made in Austin and Washington. With limited discretionary authority but with a great deal of responsibility, local governments often find it difficult to respond effectively to the needs of their citizens.

**2.** More than 80 percent of the state's population lives in urban areas. Texas cities have highly diverse social structures, economies, and historical traditions, and, subsequently, there are marked differences in urban politics across the state. Five of the 10 largest cities have more than 50 percent minority populations, a factor which has contributed to a long-standing controversy over urban electoral systems.

**3.** Texas cities smaller than 5,000 people are designated general law cities and are fairly limited as to what form of government they can use. By contrast, cities larger than 5,000 can function as home rule cities, choosing a form of government that satisfies community needs as long as it doesn't conflict with the state constitution or statutes.

**4.** Texas cities have experimented with three forms of government—the mayor-council, the commission, and the council-manager. Over the course of their history, many Texas cities have used variations on these three forms. The institutional structures chosen by cities reflect complex political dynamics, and as the underlying social, economic, and political environment change, cities have a tendency to change their institutions of governance.

**5.** A notable feature of city politics in Texas is the widespread use of at-large, or citywide, election systems. In homogeneous communities, these election systems appear to work quite well. In communities with highly diverse racial, economic, and social groups with polarized voting, however, the at-large election system adversely affects key segments of the population. Since the adoption of the Voting Rights Act there has been an on-going legal attack on the at-large system, and many cities have adopted single-member districts, thus increasing minority representation on local governing bodies.

**6.** Texas cities are now experiencing many of the same problems of the older cities of the North and Midwest. Populations in many cities are aging, and there is some evidence of white flight from the core urban centers. A disproportionately larger share of the population in the central cities is low income and least able to pay taxes to support municipal services. In addition to experiencing high crime rates, cities are faced with significant problems of deteriorating infrastructures. Federal and state governments have imposed additional requirements on the cities that are increasingly difficult to meet.

**7.** County governments, which originated to serve a rural population, function primarily as the administrative subdivisions of the state. Much like state government, county government is highly fragmented with administrative powers shared by a variety of elected administrative officials. County governments have limited discretionary powers, and while there was a limited effort to experiment with county home rule, it was abandoned. Urban counties have many of the same problems that cities face but continue to be limited by statutory and constitutional restrictions.

**8.** One of the major functions of county government is to provide support for the state's judicial system. Counties provide the physical facilities and support personnel for the state's courts. The county is also a key element in the state's criminal justice system, and the explosion in crime and subsequent convictions have pushed many county jail systems to their capacities.

**9.** For a variety of reasons, including the legal restrictions on cities and counties, jurisdictional conflicts, and the private interests of businesses or corporations, there has been a proliferation of special purpose districts. These districts provide a variety of functions, including education, water service, and sanitation. They add to the complex mosaic of local governments, and while they generally provide needed functions, most citizens have limited information about many districts. This often results in extraordinarily low rates of political participation in the district elections.

**10.** Texas has more than 1,000 independent school districts. A wide disparity in the wealth and resources of these districts has contributed to a multitude of problems with the state's educational system. As a result of litigation initiated by poor school districts, the state has attempted to find solutions to these funding inequities.

**11.** Local governments are experimenting with a variety of techniques to deal with their problems. In addition to charter modifications, cities have used their

annexation powers and extraterritorial jurisdiction to expand their tax bases as well
as to exercise limited controls over development in adjacent areas. Cities are also
using public improvement districts to permit targeted areas to impose additional
taxes for needed services. Both counties and cities are privatizing governmental
functions to decrease costs and increase efficiency. Interlocal contracting permits
governments to provide services to each other on a contractual basis, and many
counties and cities are engaged in aggressive economic development programs.

**12.** While Harris County wins the prize for its 400-plus local governments,
many of the urban counties have 40 to 50 local governments with overlapping tax
bases and jurisdiction. There are some advocates of governmental consolidation,
but there is little interest in the state in restructuring local governments, consolidating governmental functions, and providing for greater political accountability.

## KEY TERMS

Dillon rule
Annexation Powers
Population density
General law city
Home rule city
Weak mayor
Strong mayor
City commission
Council-manager government
City charter
Property tax
Rollback election
Commissioners court
County judge

County clerk
County attorney
District attorney
County tax assessor-collector
Sheriff
Constable
County auditor
County treasurer
Special district
Independent school district
Council of government
Privatization
Extraterritorial jurisdiction
Metro government

## FURTHER READING

Bernard, Richard M., and Bradley R. Rice, eds., *Sunbelt Cities: Politics and Growth since World War II.* Austin: University of Texas Press, 1983.
Brooks, David B., *Texas Practice: County and Special District Law,* Vols. 35 and 36. St. Paul, Minn.: West Publishing Company, 1989.
Bullard, Robert D., *Invisible Houston: The Black Experience in Boom and Bust.* College Station: Texas A&M University Press, 1987.
Cole, Richard L., Ann Crowley Smith, and Delbert A. Taebel with a foreword by Marlan Blisett, *Urban Life in Texas: A Statistical Profile and Assessment of the Largest Cities.* Austin: University of Texas Press, 1986.
Davidson, Chandler and Luis Ricardo Fraga, "Slating Groups as Parties in a Nonpartisan Setting," *Western Political Quarterly,* 41 (June, 1988), pp. 373-390.
De Leon, Arnoldo, *Ethnicity in the Sunbelt: A History of Mexican Americans in Houston.* Houston: University of Houston Press, 1989.
Domhoff, G. William, *Who Really Rules? New Haven and Community Power Reexamined.* Santa Monica, Calif.: Goodyear Publishing Company, Inc., 1978.
Feagin, Joe R., *Free Enterprise City: Houston in Political-Economic Perspective.* New Brunswick, N.J.: Rutgers University Press, 1988.
Goodall, Leonard E., ed., *Urban Politics in the Southwest.* Tempe: Arizona State University Institute of Public Administration, 1967.

Harrigan, John J., *Political Change in the Metropolis*, 4th ed. Glenview, Ill.: Scott, Foresman, 1989.

Hawley, Willis D. *Nonpartisan Elections and the Case for Party Politics*. New York: John Wiley & Sons, 1973.

Herzog, Lawrence A., *Where North Meets South: Cities, Space, and Politics on the United States-Mexico Border*. Austin: University of Texas Press, 1990.

Johnson, David R., John A. Booth, and Richard J. Harris, eds., *The Politics of San Antonio: Community, Progress, and Power*. Lincoln: University of Nebraska Press, 1983.

Jones, Laurence, Curtis Hawk, and Delbert A. Taebel, "Political Changes and Partisanship in Texas County Government," *Texas Journal of Political Studies*, 11 (Spring/Summer, 1989) pp. 28-42.

Lineberry, Robert L., *Equality and Urban Policy: The Distribution of Urban Services*. Newburby Park, Calif.: Sage. 1977.

Lorch, Robert S., *State and Local Politics: The Great Entanglement*, 3rd ed. Englewood Cliffs, N.J.: Prentice-Hall, 1989.

Marando, Vincent L., and Robert D. Thomas, *The Forgotten Governments: County Commissioners as Policy Makers*. Gainesville: The University Presses of Florida, 1977.

McComb, David G., *Houston: A History*. Austin: University of Texas Press, 1981.

Miller, Char, and Heywood T. Sanders, eds., *Urban Texas*. College Station: Texas A&M Press, 1990.

Murray, Richard W., "Power in the City: Patterns of Political Influence in Houston, Texas" in Donald S. Lutz and Kent L. Tedin, eds., *Perspectives on American and Texas Politics*. Dubuque, Iowa: Kendall/Hunt, 1987.

Murray, Richard W., and Kent L. Tedin, "The Emergence of Two-Party Competition in the Sunbelt: The Case of Houston," in William Crotty, ed., *Political Parties in Local Areas*. Knoxville: The University of Tennessee Press, 1986.

Norwood, Robert E., and Sabrina Strawn, *Texas County Government: Let the People Choose*, 2nd ed. Austin: Texas Research League, 1984.

Orum, Anthony M., *Power, Money and the People: The Making of Modern Austin*. Austin: Texas Monthly Press, 1987.

Polsby, Nelson, *Community Power and Political Theory*, 2nd ed. New Haven: Yale University Press, 1980.

Perrenod, Virginia Marion, *Special Districts, Special Purposes: Fringe Governments and Urban Problems in the Houston Area*. College Station: Texas A&M University Press, 1984.

Perry, David C., and Alfred J. Watkins, eds., *The Rise of the Sunbelt Cities*. Beverly Hills, Calif.: Sage Publications, 1977.

Reynolds, Morgan O., "General Ordinance-Making Powers for County Governments in Texas," Special Report, Texas Real Estate Research Center, College Station: College of Agriculture, Texas A&M University, August, 1985.

Rice, Bradley R., "The Galveston Plan of City Government by Commission: The Birth of a Progressive Idea," *Southwestern Historical Quarterly*, 78 (April 1975), pp. 36-408.

Syed, Anwar, *The Political Theory of American Local Government*. New York: Random House, 1966.

Tees, David W., Richard L. Cole, and Jay G. Stanford, *Interlocal Contract in Texas*. Arlington, Tex.: Institute of Urban Studies, The University of Texas at Arlington, 1990.

Thomas, Robert, "City Charters and Their Political Implications," in Donald S. Lutz and Kent L. Tedin, eds, *Perspectives on American and Texas Politics*. Dubuque, Iowa: Kendall/Hunt, 1987.

Thometz, Carol Estes, *The Decision-Makers: The Power Structure of Dallas*. Dallas: Southern Methodist University Press, 1963.

Thrombley, Woodworth G., *Special Districts and Authorities in Texas*. Austin: The University of Texas, 1959.

Weaver, Robert R., and Sherman M. Wyman, *Economic Development in Texas: New State and Local Initiatives*. Arlington, Tex.: Institute of Urban Studies, The University of Texas at Arlington, 1988.

Young, Roy E., *The Place System in Texas Elections*. Austin: Institute of Public Affairs, The University of Texas, 1965.

Zax, Jeffrey S., "Election Methods and Black and Hispanic City Council Membership," *Social Science Quarterly*, 71 (June, 1990), pp. 339-355.

## ENDNOTES

1. James Bryce, *Modern Democracies*, Vol. I (New York: Macmillan, 1921), p. 133. Used by permission of the publisher.

2. Anwar Hussain Syed, *The Political Theory of American Local Government* (New York: Random House, 1966), p. 27.

3. Ibid., pp. 38-52. Syed presents an excellent analysis of Jefferson's theory of local government.

4. Roscoe C. Martin, *Grass Roots* (Tuscaloosa: University of Alabama Press, 1957), p. 5.; Robert C. Wood, *Suburbia* (New York: Houghton, Mifflin, 1958), p. 18.

5. *City of Clinton v. The Cedar Rapids and Missouri River Railroad Co.*, 24 Iowa 455 (1868).

6. Roscoe C. Martin, *The Cities in the Federal System* (New York: Atherton Press, 1965), pp. 28-35.

7. David B. Brooks, *Texas Practice: County and Special District Law*, Vol. 35 (St. Paul, Minn.: West Publishing Company, 1989), pp.41-46. A good part of the materials presented on county government rely on this comprehensive work by Brooks.

8. Advisory Commission on Intergovernmental Relations, *Measuring Local Government Discretionary Authority*, Report M-131 (Washington, D.C.: ACIR, 1981).

9. Advisory Commission on Intergovernmental Relations, *State and Local Roles in the Federal System* (Washington, D.C.: ACIR, 1982), pp. 32-33.

10. For an excellent overview of urban development in Texas, see Char Miller and David R. Johnson, "The Rise of Urban Texas," in *Urban Texas: Politics and Development*, ed. Char Miller and Heywood T. Sanders, (College Station: Texas A&M University Press, 1990).

11. See Richard L. Cole, Ann Crowley Smith, Delbert A. Taebel with a foreward by Marlan Blissett, *Urban Life in Texas: A Statistical Profile and Assessment of the Largest Cities* (Austin: University of Texas Press, 1986) for an example of rankings of larger Texas cities on various dimensions measuring aspects of urban "quality of life."

12. Randy Cain, "TML and Large Cities Approach Legislature Together," *Texas Town and City*, LXXIX (January 1991), pp. 18-19.

13. For a summary of the cities' legislative agenda for the 72nd Legislature, see "Legislature Adjourns," *Texas Town and City* LXXIX (June 1991), pp. LA-LP.

14. *Texas Constitution*, Article 11, Sections 4 and 5.

15. U.S. Department of Commerce, Bureau of the Census, *1987 Census of Government, Government Organization*, Vol 1, Table 9. Three additional cities functioned under forms unclassified.

16. Murray S. Stedman, *Urban Politics*, 2nd ed. (Cambridge, Mass: Winthrop Publishers, Inc., 1975) p. 51.

17. Beryl E. Pettus and Randall W. Bland, *Texas Government Today*, 3rd ed. (Homewood, Ill.: The Dorsey Press, 1984), p. 347.

18. Stedman, *Urban Politics*, p. 48.

19. Wilbourn E. Benton, *Texas Politics*, 5th ed. (Chicago: Nelson-Hall Publishers, 1984), p. 260.

20. William Lyons, "Reform and Response in American Cities: Structure and Policy Reconsidered," *Social Science Quarterly*, 59 (June 1978), p. 130. Robert Lineberry and Edmund Fowler, "Reformism and Public Policies in American Cities," *American Political Science Review*, 61 (September 1967), pp. 701-717; Willis D. Hawley, *Nonpartisan Elections and the Case for Party Politics* (New York: John Wiley and Sons, 1973).

21. See Willis D. Hawley, *Nonpartisan Elections and the Case for Party Politics* (New York: John Wiley & Sons, 1973).

22. U.S. Department of Commerce, Bureau of the Census, *1987 Census of Governments, Government Organization*, Vol. 1, Table 10.

23. Roy E. Young, *The Place System in Texas Elections* (Austin: Institute of Public Affairs, The University of Texas, 1965), pp. 1-9. This is an excellent analysis through 1964 of the election systems used by cities and school districts in Texas.

24. Tom Albin, et al., *Local Government Election Systems* (Austin: Local Government Election Systems Policy Research Project, The University of Texas, 1984), p. 2.

25. Richard W. Murray and Arnold Vedlitz, "Racial Voting Patterns in the South: An Analysis of Major Elections from 1960 to 1977 in Five Cities," *Annals of the American Academy of Political and Social Science*. Vol 439 (September 1978), pp. 29-39.

26. Robert Thomas, "City Charters and Their Political Implications," in Donald S. Lutz and Kent L. Tedin, editors, *Perspectives on American and Texas Politics: A Collection of Essays* (Dubuque, Iowa: Kendall/Hunt Publishing Company, 1987), p. 288.

27. Ibid., pp. 288-291.

28. "1991 Annual TML Taxation and Debt Survey," *Texas Town and City*, LXXIX (March, 1991), p. 261a.

29. Frank Sturzl, "Texas Cities Face Troubling Times," *Texas Town and City*, LXXIV (March 1987), pp. 30-31.

30. Cole, et al, *America's Cities and the 1980s: The Legacy of the Reagan Years*, p. 13.

31. "Texas Cities Continue to Face Fiscal Squeeze," *Texas Town and City*, LXXIX (March 1991), pp. 26, 32-34.
32. Ibid.
33. Lawrence E. Jordan, "Municipal Bond Issuance in Texas: The New Realities," *Texas Town and City*, LXXIX (December 1991), pp. 12, 25.
34. Brooks, *Texas Practice: County and Special District Law*, Vol. 35. p. 2.
35. Ibid., p. 14.
36. For a sample of Texas court decisions that affirm the general principle of the Dillon Rule that the county can only perform those functions allocated to it by law, see Robert E. Norwood and Sabrina Strawn, *Texas County Government: Let the People Choose*, 2nd ed. (Austin: The Texas Research League, 1984), p. 11-12.
37. Norwood and Strawn, *Texas County Government*, p. 9.
38. The Texas Association of Counties, *1990 County Officials Salary Survey* (Austin: The Texas Association of Counties, 1990).
39. *Avery v. Midland County*, 88 S. Ct. 1114 (1968).
40. Norwood and Strawn, *Texas County Government*, p. 22.
41. Brooks, *Texas Practice: County and Special District Law*, Vol. 35, p. 331.
42. Texas Commission on Intergovernmental Relations, *An Introduction to Texas County Government* (Austin: TCIR, 1980), p. 10.
43. Brooks, *Texas Practice: County and Special District Law*, Vol. 35, pp. 392-393.
44. Texas Association of Counties, *1990 County Officials Salary Survey*.
45. David R. Brooks, *Texas Practice: County and Special District Law*, Vol 36 (St. Paul, Minn.: West Publishing Company, 1989), pp. 104-105.
46. Texas Association of Counties, *1990 County Officials Salary Survey*.
47. Brooks, *Texas Practice: County and Special District Law*, Vol. 36, pp. 4-8.
48. Ibid., pp. 49-50.
49. Ibid., pp. 18-49.
50. Norwood and Strawn, *Texas County Government*, p. 24.
51. Brooks, *Texas Practice: County and Special District Law*, Vol. 35, p. 495.
52. Brooks, *Texas Practice: County and Special District Law*, Vol. 36, pp. 122-123.
53. TCIR, *An Introduction to County Government*, pp. 75-81.
54. Norwood and Strawn, *Texas County Government*, p. 27.
55. Brooks, *Texas Practice: County and Special District Law*, Vol. 35, p. 273-274.
56. Norwood and Strawn, *Texas County Government*, p. 75-81.
57. Virginia Marion Perrenod, *Special Districts, Special Purposes: Fringe Governments and Urban Problems in the Houston Area* (College Station: Texas A&M University Press, 1984), p. 34.
58. Woodworth G. Thrombley, *Special Districts and Authorities in Texas*, (Austin: Institue of Public Affairs, The University of Texas, 1959), pp. 17-18.
59. Wilbourn E. Benton, *Texas Politics: Constraints and Opportunities*, 5th ed. (Chicago: Nelson-Hall Publishers, 1984), p. 282.
60. Thrombley, *Special Districts and Authorities in Texas*, p. 13.
61. Perrenod, *Special Districts, Special Purposes*, p. 18.
62. Ibid., Chapter 2; Thrombley, *Special Districts and Authorities in Texas*, pp. 15-16.
63. Thrombley, *Special Districts and Authorities in Texas*, p. 15.
64. Robert S. Lorch, *State and Local Politics*, 3rd ed. (Englewood Cliffs, N.J.: Prentice Hall, 1989), p. 246.
65. Ibid., p. 247.
66. Perrenod, *Special Districts, Special Purposes*, p. 4.
67. Texas Education Agency, *Snapshot '90: 1989-1990 School District Profiles* (Austin: Texas Education Agency, 1991), pp. 2-7.
68. L. Tucker Gibson, Jr., "The Effects of Single-Member Districting on Texas School Board Politics," Prepared for delivery at the annual meeting of the Southwest Political Science Association, San Antonio, Texas, March 1991.
69. Governor's Planning and Budget Office, *Regional Councils in Texas: A Status Report and Directory, 1980-1981*, p. 9.
70. Governor's Budget and Planning Office, *Regional Councils in Texas: Annual Report and Directory, 1990-1991*, p. 8.
71. Ibid.

72. Brooks, *Texas Practice: County and Special District Law*, Vol 36, pp. 380-384.

73. Miller and Sanders, eds., *Urban Texas: Politics and Development*, p. xiv

74. Ibid., p. xv.

75. *Texas Almanac, 1992-1993* (Dallas: A.H. Belo Corp., 1991), pp. 137-138.

76. U.S. Department of Commerce, Bureau of the Census, *Money Income of Households, Families, and Persons in the United States: 1988 and 1989*, Series P-60, No. 172, 1991.

77. Frank Sturzl, "The Tyranny of Environmental Mandates," *Texas Town and City*, LXXIX (September 1991), p. 14.

78. Susan A. MacManus, "'Mad' about Mandates: The Issue of Who Should Pay for What Resurfaces in the 1990s," *Publius*, 21 (Summer 1991), pp. 59-75.

79. Frank Sturzl, "A Necessary Heresy," *Texas Town and City*, LXXIX (July 1991), pp. 12, 35-36.

80. For a more detailed discussion of annexation authority, see Wilbourn E. Benton, *Texas Politics*, pp. 264-266.

81. Joel B. Goldsteen and Russell Fricano, *Municipal Finance Practices and Preferences for New Development: Survey of Texas Cities* (Arlington, Texas: Institute of Urban Studies, The University of Texas at Arlington, 1988), pp. 3-11.

82. Bill R. Shelton, Bob Bolen, and Ray Perryman, "Passing a Sales Tax Referendum for Economic Development," *Texas Town and City*, LXXIX (September 1991), p. 10.

83. Brooks, *Texas Practice: County and Special District Law*, Vol. 36, pp. 229-242.

84. Tom Adams, "Introduction and Recent Experience with the Interlocal Contract," in Richard W. Tees, Richard L. Cole, and Jay G. Stanford, *The Interlocal Contract in Texas* (Arlington, Texas: Institute of Urban Studies, University of Texas at Arlington, 1990), p. 1.

85. Tees, et al., *Interlocal Contract in Texas*, pp. B1-B7.

86. Adams, "The Introduction and Recent Experience with the Interlocal Contract," pp. 1-7.

87. Lorch, *State and Local Politics*, pp. 278-280.

88. Ibid., pp. 280-281.

89. Vincent Ostrom, *The Meaning of American Federalism* (San Francisco: Institute for Contemporary Studies, 1991), p. 161. Ostrom suggests that advocates of metropolitan government often overlook the "rich and intricate 'framework' for negotiating, adjudicating, and deciding questions" that are now in place in many urbanized areas with multiple governmental units.

90. Ann Long Diveley and Dwight A. Shupe, "Public Improvement Districts: An Alternative for Financing Public Improvements and Services," *Texas Town and City*, LXXIX (September 1991).

# 13

CONTEMPORARY
PUBLIC POLICY ISSUES
IN TEXAS

It's as big as the House and Senate want to make it, and it's as big as the needs of Texas are. I mean, goodness gracious, how long is a piece of string? How do we rank (in spending)? How do we look, compared to other states throughout the country?

*Lt. Governor Bob Bullock*[1]

With the 21st century rapidly approaching, Texas government was still struggling to keep up with the demands of the 20th. Many of Texas' problems with crime, poverty, pollution, inadequate public schools, and an outdated tax structure were no different from those faced by other states. But they had been compounded when the state's traditional oil-based economy and then its real estate industry collapsed in the 1980s. There were greater demands for public assistance at a time when Texas also was being forced to comply with court orders for major, expensive improvements in prisons and mental health and mental retardation facilities and a more equitable distribution of public education dollars. The court orders indicated a lack of foresight and a neglect of public programs on the part of many state leaders, and reflected strong political differences over how critical needs should be addressed. State government was operating in a continual crisis. But necessity finally began to produce significant changes in policy, changes that were promising but weren't going to occur without controversy, or without more pain.

The issues that we will discuss in this chapter are not new. They are enduring problems, and the policy decisions made in recent years are part of a long sequence of actions and inactions by state officials.

## THE POLICY PROCESS

Except for an occasional federal judge, individuals acting alone haven't forced changes in public policy. The political power necessary to shape policy is exercised through groups and, as we have pointed out throughout this book, some groups or interests have been more influential than others. Before we discuss specific policy changes, we will attempt to outline the concepts involved in the process.

### The Elements of Public Policy

Setting public policy usually involves questions of costs and benefits. The ultimate political problem to resolve is who will benefit from specific policy decisions and who will pay the bill.[2] Certain groups, businesses, or individuals receive direct benefits from governmental decisions—benefits that are paid for by other individuals through a variety of taxes. In this process there is, in effect, a transfer of money from one segment of the population to another, and critical decisions must be made on the allocation of the tax burden, which will inevitably produce intense political conflict.

Public policies also provide indirect benefits. While low-income Texans, for example, receive the direct benefits of welfare assistance, job training programs, and subsidized housing and health care, the entire population eventually stands to benefit if the poverty cycle is interrupted. Similar arguments have been made in the lengthy search for funding equity between property-poor and rich school districts. The state's economic growth and future prosperity will be adversely affected and its crime rate will continue to rise if serious problems of illiteracy and school dropouts aren't successfully addressed now.

Public policy also includes the regulation of the private sector. The indiscriminate use of land, water, and other natural resources is being increasingly curtailed by environmental policies seeking to protect the best interests of the state as a whole. And as policymakers, prompted in part by federal laws and environmental activists, become more sensitive to the extensive problems posed by pollution, state government may impose additional restrictions on corporations and individuals.

Public policy also affects the governmental process itself. Decisions on political redistricting, revisions in election laws, and changes in the structure and organization of state and local governments ultimately address the issue of how power is distributed. They help determine how many people will be able to accomplish personal and collective objectives and improve their lives.

Another dimension of public policy is rooted in the notion of the general good of the community. Related to the concept of indirect benefits, it reflects the values upon which a political culture is based. Whether defined in terms of "it's the right thing to do," or a more systematic theory of the bonds that create the political community, there are elements of public policy that reflect the common needs or interests of those who live in the state.

## The Stages of the Policy Process

Political scientists and policy analysts spend a lot of time defining public policy and all its critical elements. The attention directed to these questions is important, but for our purposes we will use the definition developed by James Anderson, who said policy was "a purposive course of action followed by an actor or set of actors in dealing with a problem or matter of concern."[3]

There are many activities in the private sector that bear on public policy, such as a decision by a large corporation to close its operations in a city, but the following discussion focuses on the governmental institutions that make binding and enforceable decisions affecting all those who live in the state.[4]

A number of scholars have approached policy making as a sequential process. While this approach may suggest an artificial start and stop point, the process is dynamic and continuous (Table 13-1).

Before people try to get government to adopt a new policy or change an old one, they discover they have a problem.[5] People in a particular neighborhood, for example, may experience increased respiratory problems. Right away, they suspect a nearby chemical plant, and their suspicions are reinforced every time winds blow across the neighborhood from the direction of the plant. After complaints to the plant manager bring no satisfaction—or relief—the unhappy neighbors hope government will be more responsive. To make sure they are heard, they identify others affected by the same problem and join forces in a citizens group. Such groups are central to the policy-making process. By banding together, people increase their financial resources, leadership capabilities, and political strength.

Their next step is to find a governmental body or agency that can address the problem and then convince it to do so. They may first approach the city council,

**TABLE 13-1**

| Stages of the Policy Process | Actions Taken |
|---|---|
| IDENTIFICATION AND FORMATION OF AN ISSUE | Defining a common problem and building coalitions to force the issue on the public agenda. |
| ACCESS AND REPRESENTATION | Gaining access to elected or administrative officials and getting them to see the problem. |
| FORMULATION | Getting those in government to initiate action on the problem by sifting through alternative solutions |
| ADOPTION OR LEGITIMATION | The government's specific solution to the problem including the authorization of programs and the allocation of funds |
| IMPLEMENTATION | The application of the government's policy to the problem |
| EVALUATION | Assessing the effects of the policy and determining if its objectives were achieved |

Sources: Charles O. Jones, *An Introduction to the Study of Public Policy*, 2nd ed. (North Scituate, MA: Duxbury Press, 1977) and James E. Anderson, David W. Brady, Charles S. Bullock, III, and Joseph Stewart, Jr., *Public Policy and Politics in America*, 2nd ed. (Monterey, CA: Brooks/Cole Publishing Company, 1984).

only to learn that state laws and regulations govern emissions from the plant. They then will turn to the Texas Air Control Board, which may determine that the plant is violating its state permit and may impose an administrative fine or seek legal action by the attorney general. The Air Control Board, however, may find its hands tied by a loophole in the state's antipollution laws. In that case, the concerned citizens would need help from the legislature, where they would have to convince elected representatives to translate their concerns into a change in policy.

Simply identifying a problem and getting a large number of other people to share your concerns is not a solution. Solutions must be developed and enacted through specific laws, regulations, or other policy changes. Philosophically, there is little disagreement that every child in Texas should have access to a quality education. But what does that mean in practical political terms? Proposed solutions have been extremely diverse. Legislative staffs, blue ribbon committees, independent research organizations, academicians, and consultants from various points on the political spectrum have all contributed studies and opinions. The resolution of their differences is essentially a political process. In the final analysis, "successful policy formulations must deal with the question of selecting courses of action that can actually be adopted."[6]

The legislature is primarily responsible for setting policy at the state level, but the separation of powers doctrine under which our government operates gives the judiciary important scrutiny over legislative action—or inaction. In recent years, there have been several major federal and state court decisions forcing the legislature to make far-reaching changes in education, criminal justice, and mental health and mental retardation programs. Those court orders have prompted some lawmakers and other critics to complain that the judiciary has overstepped its authority and attempted to preempt the legislature. Others believe, however, that the legislature had neglected its responsibilities and needed some shoving.

Virtually every public policy has a cost. It is not enough for the legislature to merely create a program. Programs have to be funded, or they are meaningless. Sometimes, the legislature requires local governments to pick up the tab, but most programs have to compete with hundreds of other programs for a limited number of state tax dollars. Thus the state's complex budgetary process is at the heart of policymaking and is closely monitored by individuals and organizations interested in policy development. Conflicts over the budgetary process can be very intense.

Once legislation has been enacted and funded, its specific provisions must be implemented, or carried out. Much of this activity is the responsibility of state and local agencies that have been created to carry "a program to the problem."[7] Earlier political scientists referred to this stage of the policy process as public administration, and much of it falls within the domain of administrative agencies and departments. But government bureaucrats aren't the only ones involved in carrying out policy. So are legislators, judges, interest groups, and others. The activities in this implementation phase include:

- **Interpretation**—the translation of program language into acceptable and feasible directives;
- **Organization**—the establishment of units and methods for putting a program into effect; and
- **Application**—the routine provision of services, payments, or other agreed-upon program objectives or instruments.[8]

Governments spend a lot of time evaluating the effects of public policy. An enormous amount of information is gathered to determine if programs have met stated goals and, if not, what changes or adjustments are required. Legislative committees, in their oversight function, demand information from agencies to help determine whether to continue to fund programs, expand them, or change them. With an eye on future funding, agencies also spend considerable resources assessing the impact of their own activities and performance. Program evaluation also is part of the broader issue of accountability of public officials and their responsiveness to the needs, demands, and expectations of their constituents. So interest groups, think tanks, scholars, and the news media also actively participate in this phase of the policy process.

Program assessment and evaluation become the basis for future policy and funding decisions. We have found some comprehensive solutions to a limited number of problems, including some diseases, but most governmental policy produces only limited or partial solutions. Problems and issues are on-going, and policymakers often have to adjust or redirect their efforts at problem solving. A solution enacted today can produce additional problems requiring further attention tomorrow. As we will discuss later in this chapter, for example, recent changes in public education policies and funding are part of a long history of efforts to improve the quality of education in Texas.

## Iron Triangles and Issue Networks

There are thousands of players in the policy arenas of state and local government, including bureaucrats, the courts, interest groups, businesses, the mass media, and policy specialists. While some of these have a broad perspective on state policy and a wide range of policy interests, most have narrow and highly specialized interests. One way to think about the relationships among policy participants is to "identify the clusters of individuals that effectively make most of the routine decisions in a given substantive area of policy."[9]

At the state level, these clusters—sometimes referred to as iron triangles of government—include members of the House and the Senate, their staffs, high-level bureaucrats, and representatives of interest groups. Both houses of the legislature are divided into standing committees, which have jurisdiction over specific policy areas, and key committee members usually form one leg of each triangle. There are hundreds of these subsystems in state government, although the use of this concept to explain policy development does not always identify all of the critical players or explain the complexity of the process.

Political scientist Hugh Heclo argues that "the iron triangle concept is not so much wrong as it is disastrously incomplete," and he offers a more complex model—**issue networks**—for mapping out the relationships inherent in the policy process.[10] This concept acknowledges the key roles of the iron triangle players but also takes into account other factors, including the increased interdependence of state and local governments on the federal government. Specialists from all three levels of government are frequently involved in developing specific policies. And groups such as the National Governors' Association, the Conference of State Governments, and the U.S. Conference of Mayors actively seek to influence federal policies that affect state and local governments. State and local policies are increasingly shaped by the federal government through federal funds for domestic programs and federal mandates that require states and local governments to carry out specific programs.

The policy process also is increasingly dominated by specialists who may be identified with interest groups, corporations, legislative committees, or administrative agencies. These experts, or "technopols," understand the technical nature of a problem and, more importantly, the institutional, political, and personal relationships of those involved in trying to solve it.[11]

The number of actual participants in policy development will vary, of course, from issue to issue. Sometimes, only a few individuals are involved in shaping a specific policy. But on other occasions, when changes are being considered in tax law, health care, or public education, for example, there is a "kaleidoscopic interaction of changing issue networks."[12]

In the following discussion of contemporary state policies, you will see some practical applications of these concepts.

## THE BUDGETARY PROCESS

Recent years have not been easy times for legislative budget writers in many states. Twenty-four states raised taxes in 1990, while 30, including Texas, faced potential budget deficits in 1991. Several factors were to blame, including a national recession that increased the number of people seeking public assistance and federal mandates and court orders that required increased state spending on various programs. Some of the most expensive federal mandates have been in Medicaid coverage, which accounted for 9 percent of the average state budget in 1980 but had grown to about 14 percent in 1990. Federal judges, meanwhile, had clamped down on overcrowded prisons and jails in nearly 40 states, while public education funding systems in about 20 states had either been struck down in court or were being challenged.[13]

In 1991, several states failed to pass budgets in time for the start of their fiscal years, forcing the temporary suspension of some services and the temporary layoffs of thousands of state workers. Texas balanced its budget on time, but in the process the legislature put even more stress on an already strained budget and tax system.

Like most other states and unlike the federal government, Texas operates on a pay-as-you-go basis that prohibits **deficit financing**. The comptroller must certify that each budget can be paid for with anticipated revenue from taxes, fees, and other sources. And like other states, Texas greatly increased its spending on state government programs in the 1970s and 1980s. Population growth and inflation were major factors, in addition to the federal mandates and court orders cited above.

The lion's share of state expenditures (including federal funds appropriated by the legislature) is for education, which accounted for 43 percent of state spending in 1991. Welfare and other human services were second at 21 percent, although Texas lags behind virtually every other state in actual dollars spent in that category. Transportation—thanks to a dedicated draw on fuel taxes for highway construction—accounted for almost 10 percent. Those three categories have consistently led state spending from year to year (Figures 13-1 and 13-2).

The Texas legislature's budget-writing problems are compounded by the length of the budget period and the structure of the budget itself. Since the state constitution provides that the legislature meet in regular session only every other year, lawmakers write two-year, or biennial, budgets for state government. That means state agencies, which begin preparing their budget requests several months before a session convenes, have to anticipate some of their spending needs three years in advance. Critics, including many legislators and agency directors, say two-year budgets require too much guesswork and cause inadequate funding of some programs and wasteful spending in other areas. They believe that Texas, which

**FIGURE 13-1**   State Expenditures by Function, 1991. (*State Comptroller of Public Accounts*)

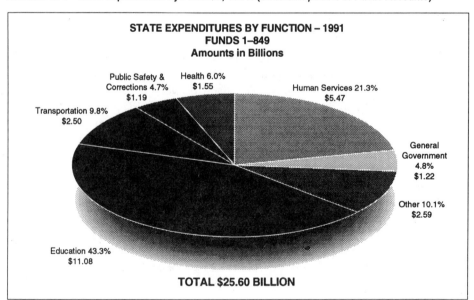

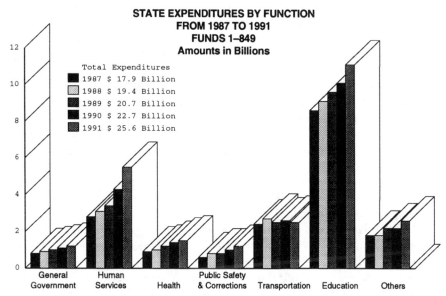

STATE EXPENDITURES BY FUNCTION
FROM 1987 TO 1991
FUNDS 1–849
Amounts in Billions

Total Expenditures
■ 1987 $ 17.9 Billion
□ 1988 $ 19.4 Billion
▨ 1989 $ 20.7 Billion
▦ 1990 $ 22.7 Billion
▨ 1991 $ 25.6 Billion

**FIGURE 13-2**   State Expenditures by Function, from 1987 to 1991. (*State Comptroller of Public Accounts*)

is the nation's third most populous state and has a wide diversity of needs in a changing economy, should have annual budget sessions of the legislature, a change that would require a constitutional amendment.

Since the adoption of a related constitutional amendment in 1985, the governor and legislative leaders have had the authority to order transfers of funds between programs and agencies to meet some emergencies. The governor proposes transfers to the Legislative Budget Board, a 10-member panel that includes the lieutenant governor, the speaker, and eight key legislators, and the LBB can accept, reject, or modify the governor's proposal, or vice versa.

## Dedicated Funds

The legislature's control over the budget-setting process is further restricted by legal requirements that dedicate or earmark a major portion of state spending to specific purposes. The legislature had total discretion over only about $34 billion of the $60 billion budget adopted for 1992-93. The remainder included federal funds earmarked for specific purposes by the federal government or monies dedicated to specific uses by the state constitution or state law. The state treasury included more than 600 separate funds, including 56 that were dedicated to highways, education, parks, schoolteacher retirement, and dozens of other specific purposes. The restrictions hamper the legislature's budget-writing abilities, particularly during lean periods. But the dedicated funds are jealously guarded by the interest groups that benefit from them, and many funds have become "sacred cows" that most legislators dare not try to change.

One of the major **dedicated funds** is the Highway Trust Fund, which automatically gets three-fourths of the revenue from the gasoline, or motor fuels, tax. Under the constitution, that highway user revenue can be spent only to purchase right of way for highways or construct, maintain, and police highways. The remainder of the motor fuels tax revenue goes to public education. Any legislative proposal to tap into the highway fund for other state needs would be fought by a strong lobbying effort from highway contractors as well as chamber of commerce presidents, mayors, and county judges with local road projects they wanted completed.

Other major constitutional funds include the Permanent School Fund and the Permanent University Fund, land and mineral-rich endowments that help support the public schools and boost funding for the University of Texas and Texas A&M University systems. In 1991, the legislature gave the comptroller the authority to consolidate many of the 600-plus funds, a process that was to be completed by 1993, but the comptroller couldn't change the constitutionally dedicated funds.

Agencies submit their biennial appropriations, or spending, requests to the Legislative Budget Board. After its staff reviews the requests, the LBB normally recommends a budget that the full legislature uses as a starting point in its budgetary deliberations. The LBB never formally endorsed a budget before the 1991 legislative session, but the LBB staff drafted a so-called "current services" budget, which projected a $4.8 billion revenue shortfall for the next two years. Despite what its name may have implied, this proposal actually represented an increase in spending. It added money to meet federal regulations to expand certain health and public assistance programs, to staff and operate new prisons already under construction, to fund a new school finance law that had been enacted under court order, and to continue to meet court mandates for improvements in mental health and mental retardation programs.

## STATE TAXES

Texas had entered the 1990s as one of only about a half dozen states without a personal or corporate income tax. Public and political opposition to an income tax remained high, but it was beginning to be openly discussed as an option. Each previous budgetary crisis had seemingly stretched the existing tax structure to the breaking point, only to see the legislature come up with another patch. Critics compared the tax structure to an ugly patchwork quilt that had been stitched together over the years by legislators making accommodations with various special interest groups to cover an assortment of emergencies. Senator Carl Parker, a Port Arthur Democrat, in Senate floor debate in 1991 argued, "They (existing taxes) hit the poor people worse than they do rich folks. They let some people off scot-free, while they tax others heavily. And the direction we seem to be going is worse, not better."[14]

## The Regressive Tax System

In a 1991 study released by Citizens for Tax Justice (CTJ), Texas was ranked as having the second most **regressive tax system** among the fifty states. The state's tax system is based largely on the sales tax, the property tax, and fees which consumes a larger portion of the incomes of the poor and the middle classes (Table 13-2). Based on the calculations of CTJ, Texas taxes its poor families at more than 17 percent of their incomes, and the middle class pays more than 8 percent of their incomes to state and local governments. By contrast, the wealthiest Texans (the richest one percent of the families) pay 3.1 percent of their incomes. Political leaders and chambers of commerce have long touted the state as a low-tax state, but these low taxes are not for the poor or the middle class but for the wealthy, the study concluded.[15]

The last major change in Texas' general tax policy occurred in 1961, when the legislature, over the objections of then-Governor Price Daniel, enacted the state's first **sales tax**. By 1991, the initial 2 percent rate had climbed to 8.25 percent for many Texans, and the tax had become state government's revenue workhorse, producing about 60 percent of the state's tax revenue. A statewide rate of 6.25 percent was tied with Illinois for fifth highest in the nation. The 8.25 percent rate charged in most metropolitan areas, where city and mass transportation authority taxes of 1 percent each were added to the state tax, was tied for third highest with Illinois, New York, and Tennessee.[16]

With each financial crisis (Figure 13-3, page 429),  it was becoming more and more politically difficult for the legislature to consider raising the sales tax rate. And even though groceries and medicine were tax exempt, critics charged that the sales

**TABLE 13–2**  Inequities in State Tax Structures. States with the Highest Taxes on Poor and Middle-Income Families Compared to Taxes on the Richest One Percent.

| "The Terrible Ten" States | Tax Rates on | | | Ratio of Rates | | |
|---|---|---|---|---|---|---|
| | Poor | Middle | Rich | Poor/ Rich | Middle/ Rich | Income Tax? |
| Nevada | 10.0% | 5.7% | 1.8% | 556% | 314% | No |
| Texas | 17.1 | 8.4 | 3.1 | 553 | 273 | No |
| Florida | 13.8 | 7.6 | 2.7 | 518 | 283 | No |
| Washington | 17.4 | 9.5 | 3.4 | 509 | 278 | No |
| South Dakota | 16.2 | 8.7 | 3.5 | 465 | 249 | No |
| Tennessee | 15.2 | 7.7 | 3.6 | 418 | 211 | No* |
| Wyoming | 9.0 | 5.3 | 2.4 | 372 | 218 | No |
| New Hampshire | 12.7 | 7.6 | 3.8 | 329 | 198 | No* |
| Pennsylvania | 15.9 | 9.8 | 5.5 | 287 | 176 | Flat |
| Illinois | 16.5 | 10.8 | 6.0 | 273 | 179 | Flat |

*Only interest and dividends taxed

Source: Citizens for Tax Justice, *A Far Cry From Fair*, CTJ's Guide to State Tax Reform, April, 1991.

tax was regressive because it affected low income Texans disproportionately more than wealthier citizens. Moreover, the sales tax was heavily weighted toward products and left many services—including legal and medical fees and advertising—untaxed. Thus sales tax revenue didn't automatically grow with the state's economy because the Texas economy was becoming more and more service-oriented.

The **franchise tax**, meanwhile, was the state's major business tax, and it also was under widespread attack as inequitable because it applied only to certain corporations. Partnerships, proprietorships, professional associations, and business trusts weren't taxed. Paying most of the franchise tax burden were capital intensive corporations because the tax was based primarily on assets. Service businesses that didn't require much equipment or capital expenditures were much more lightly taxed, and those were the industries that had been accounting for much of Texas' economic growth in the wake of the 1980s oil bust. The administration of the franchise tax also had been successfully challenged in court and had cost the state more than $1 billion in refunds. The oil and gas severance tax revenue that had helped the legislature balance the budget with relative ease when oil prices were high in the 1970s had slowed to a trickle after prices had plummeted and the energy industry had crashed.

State government also had several volume-based taxes—including taxes on cigarettes, alcoholic beverages, and motor fuels—that had set rates per pack or per gallon and didn't produce more revenue when inflation raised the price of the product. Those taxes, particularly the so-called **sin taxes** on cigarettes and alcohol, had been raised frequently over the years. By 1991, Texas' cigarette tax was the second highest in the nation at 41 cents per pack, up from 18.5 cents per pack in 1982.[17]

The biggest source of taxpayer dissatisfaction and anger in Texas, however, was the local property, or ad valorem, tax, the major source of revenue for cities, counties, and school districts. State government no longer levied a **property tax**—a statewide ad valorem tax that used to fund construction of university facilities was repealed by constitutional amendment in 1982—but state government policies had forced local governments to  raise their taxes frequently.

School districts were particularly hard hit, especially by the requirements of House Bill 72, the education reform law passed in 1984, and the school finance equalization law that ordered the transfer of millions of dollars from wealthy to poor school districts in 1991 (see later section in this chapter). In pushing unsuccessfully for an overhaul of the state and local tax structure in 1991, Lt. Governor Bob Bullock said local property tax increases in Texas averaged 28.9 percent, the highest jump in the country, from 1980 to 1988 and moved Texas up to 10th place among the states in total local tax burden. Still more property tax increases were in store in 1991, when many school districts raised taxes to compensate for lost revenue under the new school finance law. Bullock also reported that, despite major state tax increases, state tax revenue compared with personal income had declined 14.9 percent from 1978 to 1987, while local property tax revenue had increased 18.7 percent, when compared with personal income, during the same period.[18]

## The Income Tax: An Alternative to a Regressive Tax System?

Various liberal legislators and groups seeking more funding for state services have long advocated a state **income tax**. But until recently their proposals were ignored, and no major officeholder or serious candidate for major office dared even hint at support for such a politically taboo alternative. Finally, in late 1989, then-Lt. Governor Bill Hobby broke the ice for serious discussion of the issue in a speech to the Texas Association of Taxpayers, whose members included executives of many of the major corporations and other businesses operating in Texas. Hobby, who had waited until he was a lame duck—he had already announced that he wouldn't seek re-election in 1990—proposed that a personal and corporate income tax be enacted, coupled with abolition of the corporate franchise tax and reductions in property and sales taxes. Hobby also told his audience that it would take the business community to convince the legislature to pass an income tax.

There was little public debate on an income tax in 1990 because Republican Governor Bill Clements, who adamantly opposed the proposal, was still in office. But in early 1991, shortly after Clements' departure, the executive committee of the Texas Association of Taxpayers became the first major business group in Texas—at least in modern times—to endorse a state income tax. The group to which Hobby

**FIGURE 13-3**  It was much easier for Sam Houston and his rag-tag Texas army to turn and fight Santa Anna than it is for today's Texas leaders to confront the state's fiscal problems with a realistic long-term solution. (© *Houston Chronicle.* Reprinted with permission)

had made his initial appeal proposed both a corporate and a personal income tax as part of an overhaul of Texas' tax system. The proposal also included repeal of the corporate franchise tax, reductions in property and sales taxes, and restrictions on future tax increases. Bill Allaway, the association's executive vice president, declared, "The current tax system has been demonstrated to be flawed, inequitable, unfair and inconsistent. You name it, it's been called that, and it's all true."[19]

The business group also was motivated by another goal: to transfer much of the state and local tax burden from businesses to consumers. At that time, about 60 percent of taxes levied in Texas had their initial impact on business. The TAT's proposal would have reduced business' share.

Lt. Governor Bob Bullock then shocked much of the political establishment by announcing in March 1991, less than two months after he had been sworn into his new office, that he would actively campaign for a state income tax. The former longtime state comptroller said it was the only way to fairly and adequately take care of the state's present and future needs while also providing relief from two existing unpopular taxes. Bullock proposed making local school property taxes deductible from the income tax, and he recommended the repeal of the franchise tax. "I personally dislike—and I imagine most Texans do—any type of new taxes. But I also know deep down in my heart, deep down in my heart, that it's the right thing to do for Texas," he said.[20]

Although surveys indicated there was still widespread opposition to an income tax among Texans, *The Texas Poll* published that spring signalled that Bullock had struck a favorable chord with many property taxpayers. Half of the poll's 1,003 respondents said they would favor a 5 percent state income tax if it insured that local property taxes would be cut in half, and 54 percent said they would support an income tax to pay for public schools if property taxes were greatly reduced.[21]

Several groups, in addition to the Texas Association of Taxpayers, either endorsed Bullock's proposal or applauded the lieutenant governor for opening up debate on the income tax. They included the Texas Association of School Administrators, the Texas Trial Lawyers Association which feared the possible alternative of a sales tax on legal services, and the Sierra Club. Even Harris County Judge Jon Lindsay, a Republican, said he could support an income tax if revenue from it were dedicated to building more prisons and relieving his overcrowded county jail.[22] The Texas Association of Business, however, opposed it, arguing that an income tax could promote more government spending at a time when the legislature should be trying to tighten its belt. More importantly, the House, which must initiate legislative action on tax bills, also remained strongly opposed to an income tax, and so did the new governor, Democrat Ann Richards.

## Alternatives to Finding New Revenues

The governor and legislative leaders, meanwhile, agreed to postpone the adoption of a new budget and any tax bill until a summer special session. Biennial budgets normally are set in the spring during the regular session. But in this case the legislature would wait for the completion of two new studies: one on state spending, the other on revenue alternatives. Adopting a proposal by Bullock, lawmakers instructed John Sharp, the new comptroller, to supervise unprecedented performance audits of all state agencies and programs with an eye toward eliminating inefficiency and mismanagement and producing savings. Richards, Bullock, and House Speaker Gib Lewis also appointed the Governor's Task Force on Revenue, a panel of private citizens and legislators, to "review and evaluate the current system of revenue and taxation with an aim toward suggesting modifications and improvements."[23] The audit results and the revenue recommendations were to be submitted to the legislature by July 1.

Richards, who wanted to avoid a major tax increase, particularly an income tax, insisted the comptroller's intensive review of state spending was essential before the legislature consider raising any taxes. But privately, legislators, lobbyists, and other Capitol insiders said they didn't expect Sharp to find enough savings to avoid a big tax bill. Maybe he would find several hundred million dollars, perhaps $1 billion, but certainly not enough to bridge the projected $4.8 billion revenue shortfall, they thought. Meanwhile, Richards told the revenue task force at its first meeting that there must be "no sacred cows" in state government. For too long, she said, legislators had been adopting Band-Aid solutions to one financial crisis after another because of an outmoded tax and budget structure. She told the panel, "We want you to work with us to take this current system apart, tell us what should be kept and what should be discarded, and help us build a new system that will work well into the next century."[24]

But Sharp surprised a lot of people by producing a $4 billion deficit reduction plan that included some spending cuts, some agency and funds consolidations, increases in university tuition and various other state fees, and some minor tax increases. Lobby pressure from special interests killed many of Sharp's recommendations, but the legislature approved enough savings and cost-cutting steps to balance a new $60 billion budget without imposing a personal income tax, an increase in the sales tax, or a major expansion of the sales tax base. For the most part, a $2.7 billion revenue package approved by lawmakers was an assortment of more patches, or Band-Aids, to the old tax structure, including increases in college tuition and the gasoline tax. The tax bill, however, included one major change in state tax policy. It replaced the old franchise tax with a hybrid corporate income tax that would apply to an estimated 150,000 to 200,000 of the state's 2 million businesses. It didn't apply to non-corporate businesses, such as partnerships or sole proprietorships, but corporations would have to pay a new tax on income or a reduced tax on assets, whichever was greater.

Meanwhile, the Governor's Task Force on Revenue—over the objections of its chairman, former Governor John Connally, and to the political discomfort of Governor Richards, who had decided some more Band-Aids, after all, were preferable to a personal income tax—recommended that the legislature enact both corporate and personal income taxes in 1993. Key support for the proposal, adopted 7-5, came from two of Lt. Governor Bullock's strongest Senate allies, Democrats

John Montford of Lubbock and Bob Glasgow of Stephenville. "I'm one of those members who want to put the ship of state in drive," said Montford, the Senate Finance Committee chairman whose district included a large chunk of rural, conservative West Texas. "I think it's time to make some tough—what I call 'gutty'—decisions." Montford also warned of a "great taxpayer revolt" because of Texas' continued heavy reliance on the property tax. But Connally argued that an income tax would raise too much money and encourage excessive spending by the legislature. And, he added, "The people don't want it."[25]

The task force also proposed that 75 percent of the revenue from a personal income tax be dedicated to education and used to reduce local school property taxes by 40 percent. The panel also recommended containment of the sales tax rate and a transfer of more of the overall burden of state and local taxes from businesses to individuals. It recommended that the legislature set a goal of splitting the state and local tax load equally between individuals and businesses. Under the existing tax structure, almost 60 percent of the initial impact of state and local taxes fell on business.

If the legislature does enact a personal income tax—and many observers believe it's only a matter of time—support from the business community will be crucial. The sales tax was first adopted after the business lobby got behind it, and business interests remain influential today. State government's ability to provide quality education, highways, and other public support systems is essential to the business community's long term success. A personal income tax also would offer businesses the opportunity to transfer more of their tax load to consumers. That, ironically, could produce a conflict with some of the more liberal, longtime supporters of an income tax. A likely solution would be the enactment of generous tax exemptions for low-income Texans.

A conservative taxpayer group, Taxpayers Against a State Income Tax, accused the 1991 legislature of violating a constitutional provision limiting the growth of the state budget to Texas' economic growth. The 1992-93 budget, the group charged, called for a 17 percent increase in general revenue spending, while the Legislative Budget Board's staff had estimated economic growth at 12 percent to 14 percent during the previous budget period. The critics of the new budget claimed that the legislature could have legally exceeded the growth rate only by formally declaring an emergency, which the legislature had not done. But an attorney on Lt. Governor Bullock's staff said lawmakers had not violated the constitution because the LBB had never officially adopted its staff's economic growth estimates as spending limits for the legislature.[26]

## Gambling on New Revenue

For years, Texas government maintained a strong moralistic opposition to gambling. Charitable bingo games were tolerated and eventually legalized. But the state constitution prohibited lotteries, and horse race betting was outlawed in the 1930s. After the oil bust in the 1980s, however, most legislators began to view gambling as a financial opportunity rather than a moral evil, and in key elections most Texas voters indicated they agreed. In a special session in 1986, when spending was cut and taxes were raised to compensate for lost revenue from plummeting oil prices, the legislature legalized local option, parimutuel betting on horse and dog races, subject to voter approval in a binding referendum, which occurred the next year. And in 1991, under strong pressure from Governor Ann Richards, the legislature approved a constitutional amendment to legalize a state **lottery**, which the voters also endorsed that year. Limited casino gambling on cruise ships operating off the Texas coast also has been legalized by the legislature.

Gambling, however, has not been a panacea for the state's intermittent financial problems. Several years after the parimutuel referendum had been approved, the horse racing industry still had not produced any significant revenue for the state treasury, because there still were no Class 1 tracks in the major metropolitan areas. A number of smaller tracks were operating successfully in smaller communities, but potential investors in the larger tracks complained that the state's 5 percent tax on gambling revenue was too steep for them to make a profit during the first critical years of a track's operation. In 1991, the legislature finally gave in and lowered the horse race tax to a sliding scale starting at 1 percent for the first $100 million wagered at a track. Lawmakers also lowered the state tax on dog racing from the initial 6 percent to a similar sliding scale beginning at 2 percent, to encourage greyhound track owners to drop their opposition to the lottery, which they feared would cut into business at dog tracks.

Opponents accused Richards of overselling the lottery as a revenue source, of leading some voters to think that the lottery would remove the need for a tax increase, which it didn't. Comptroller John Sharp estimated that the lottery would raise about $460 million during the 1992-93 budget period, or less than 1 percent of the $60 billion state budget. It would likely produce more revenue in future years, once it became established, but opponents warned that it was not a stable source of funding for state government. In fact, revenue from established lotteries in some other states has fallen off in recent years. But Texas isn't the only state banking on gambling enterprises to help ease financial problems. Several other states also have recently approved lotteries or begun to experiment with casino-style gambling.

## Bonds: Build Now, Pay Later

Although the Texas Constitution has a general prohibition against state government going into debt, the state has built up $1.7 billion in taxpayer-supported debt since 1980, debt that will have to be paid off with tax dollars over the next generation. There have been a series of constitutional amendments authorizing the state to issue **general obligation**, or tax-backed, bonds to finance new construction, mainly prisons, mental health, and mental retardation facilities. Texas had only $16 million in taxpayer-supported debt in 1980, but it ballooned during tight budgetary periods when state government also was under federal court orders affecting the prison system and the Department of Mental Health and Mental Retardation. Another significant source of debt were bonds issued to support the Superconducting Super Collider research facility.[27]

Some legislators have been uneasy about loading up the additional tax liability on future legislative sessions—and taxpayers. By 1991 debt service was costing state government $160 million a year, and that figure would increase on the heels of a $1.1 billion prison bond authorization that lawmakers and voters approved the same year. The interest on those bonds will about double their cost over the next 20 years, experts say. Bond issues, however, have been widely supported by Democrats and Republicans, liberals and conservatives alike. In promoting a smaller prison bond issue in 1989, then-Governor Bill Clements said, "If there ever was anything that was proper for us to bond, it's our prison system, where those facilities will be on line and in use for a 25- or 30-year period."[28]

Over the years, the state also has issued hundreds of millions of dollars in bonds for such self-supporting programs as water development and veterans assistance. Those programs use the state's credit to borrow money at favorable interest rates. Then they lend that money to a local government to help construct a water treatment plant or to a veteran to help purchase a house, and the debt is repaid by the loan recipients, not by the state's taxpayers.

## EDUCATIONAL POLICIES AND POLITICS

### Public Education: A Struggle for Equity and Quality

More tax dollars are spent on education than any other governmental program in Texas. In 1949, the legislature enacted the Gilmer-Aikin law, which made major improvements in the administration of public education and significantly boosted funding for public schools, but it was soon outdated. By the 1970s, it was obvious that quality and equity were lacking in many classrooms. Hundreds of functional illiterates were being graduated from high school each year, and thousands of children in poor school districts were being shortchanged with substandard facilities and educational aids.

Public elementary and secondary education in Texas is financed by a combination of state and local revenue, a system that produced wide disparities in education spending among the state's approximately 1,050 school districts. The only local source of operating revenue for school districts is the property, or ad valorem, tax. Districts with a wealth of oil production or expensive commercial property had high tax bases that enabled them to raise large amounts of money with relatively low tax rates. Poor districts with low tax bases, on the other hand, had to impose higher tax rates to raise only a fraction of the money that the wealthy districts could spend on education. While poor districts had to struggle to maintain minimal educational programs, rich districts could attract the best teachers with higher pay, build more classrooms, purchase more books and computers, and in some cases, have enough money left over to put astroturf in their football stadiums and construct indoor swimming pools. The glaring inequities didn't exist just between different counties or regions of the state. In many cases, educational resources varied greatly between districts within the same county. But many of the poorest districts were in heavily Hispanic South Texas, and ethnicity became a significant factor in a protracted struggle between the haves and the have-nots. Hispanic leaders played major roles in the fight to improve the futures of their children.

In 1968, a group of parents led by Demetrio P. Rodriguez, a San Antonio sheet metal worker and high school dropout, filed a federal lawsuit (*Rodriguez* v. *San Antonio Independent School District*) challenging the system. The plaintiffs had children in the Edgewood Independent School District, one of the state's poorest. A three-judge federal panel agreed with the parents and ruled in 1971 that the school finance system was unconstitutional. But the state appealed and the U.S. Supreme Court in 1973 reversed the lower court decision. The high court noted that the Texas system of financing public education was unfair, but it held that it didn't violate the U.S. Constitution. Its consciousness raised, the legislature started pumping hundreds of millions of dollars in so-called "equalization" aid into the poorer school districts. But lawmakers didn't change the system, and the inequities persisted and worsened.

By the early 1980s, there was a growing concern among Texas leaders over not just the financing of public education but also the quality of education. Their concerns were shared by leaders in other states in the wake of a national study called "A Nation at Risk" that had sharply criticized the nation's educational systems as inadequate. In 1983, newly elected Governor Mark White tried to raise schoolteachers' salaries to keep a campaign promise to the thousands of teachers who had been instrumental in his election. When the legislature refused to increase taxes for higher teacher pay without first studying the educational system with an eye toward reform, White joined Lt. Governor Bill Hobby and House Speaker Gib Lewis in appointing the Select Committee on Public Education and picked computer magnate Ross Perot of Dallas to chair it. In an exhaustive study, the panel found that high schools were graduating many students who could barely read and write and concluded that major reforms were necessary if the state's young people were to be able to compete for jobs in a changing and highly competitive state and international economy.

With Perot spending some of his own personal wealth on a strong lobbying campaign, the legislature in a special session in 1984 enacted many educational reforms in a landmark piece of legislation known as **House Bill 72** and raised taxes to boost education spending. The bill raised teacher pay, provided for a **career ladder** to reward experienced teachers, limited class sizes, required pre-kindergarten classes for disadvantaged 4-year-olds, required students to pass a basic skills test before graduating from high school, required school districts to provide tutorials for failing students, and prohibited "social promotions" by requiring students to pass all their courses before moving on to the next grade. It also replaced the elected State Board of Education, viewed as antireform by state leaders, with a new panel appointed by the governor. The new board became an elected body four years later, after the appointed panel had time to oversee the initial implementation of the new law.

The two most controversial provisions in the new law, however, were a literacy test for teachers and the so-called **no pass, no play** rule, both of which were to contribute to White's re-election defeat in 1986. Most teachers easily passed the one-time literacy—or competency—test, a requirement for keeping their jobs, but many resented it as an insult to their abilities and professionalism. The no pass, no play rule, which prohibited students who failed any course from participating in athletics and other extracurricular activities for six weeks, infuriated many coaches, students, parents, and school administrators, particularly in the hundreds of small Texas towns where Friday night football was a major social activity and an important source of community pride. Education reformers, however, viewed the restriction as an important statement that the first emphasis of education should be on the classroom, not on the football field or the band hall.

Although the legislature pumped more money into poor school districts in 1984, it still didn't change the basic, inequitable finance system, and the state was soon back in court over that issue. This lawsuit (***Edgewood v. Kirby***) was filed in state district court in Austin, and it contended the inequities violated the Texas Constitution. It was initially filed in 1984, shortly before the enactment of House Bill 72, by the Edgewood Independent School District, 12 other poor districts, and a number of families represented by the Mexican American Legal Defense and Educational Fund, or MALDEF. Dozens of other districts and individuals joined the case as plaintiff-intervenors, and in 1987 state District Judge Harley Clark of Austin ruled the school finance system violated the state constitution. Clark ordered the legislature to come up with a new plan by September 1, 1989, thus giving the state time to appeal his ruling.

The 3rd Court of Appeals reversed Clark in December 1988. But the Texas Supreme Court, in a unanimous, landmark decision in October 1989, struck down the finance system and ordered lawmakers to replace it by May 1, 1990, with a new law that gave public school children an equal opportunity at a quality education. The bipartisan opinion, written by Democratic Justice Oscar Mauzy, a former chairman of the Senate Education Committee, didn't outline a specific solution. In an obvious effort to reach consensus among all nine justices, it was purposefully vague in some areas. But the court said the existing finance system violated a state constitutional requirement for an efficient system of public education. It warned the legislature that merely increasing the amount of state education aid wasn't enough. The decision concluded that "a Band-Aid will not suffice; the system itself must be changed."

The high court cited glaring disparities among school districts' abilities to raise revenue from property taxes because of wide differences in taxable wealth. In 1985-86, the court noted, the 100 poorest districts in Texas had an average tax rate of 74.5 cents per $100 valuation and spent an average of $2,978 per student, while the 100 wealthiest districts had an average tax rate of only 47 cents and spent an average of $7,233 per pupil. "The amount of money spent on a student's education has a real and meaningful impact on the educational opportunity offered that student," the court wrote. "High-wealth districts are able to provide for their students broader educational experiences including more extensive curricula, more up-to-date technological equipment, better libraries and library personnel, teacher aides, counseling services, lower student-teacher ratios, better facilities, parental involvement programs, and drop-out prevention programs. They are also better able to attract and retain experienced teachers and administrators."

But the court, in an obvious attempt to include the more conservative justices in a consensus opinion, said a legislative overhaul of the school finance system didn't have to prohibit wealthier districts from continuing to enrich their programs with local tax dollars. Since local enrichment helped produce the inequities in spending between districts, that part of the opinion would further complicate the legislature's efforts to reach a solution.

To illustrate how extreme inequities could be between districts in the same area, the *Fort Worth Star-Telegram* contrasted the anemic tax base of the mobile homes in the Venus Independent School District, south of Fort Worth, with the tax resources of the Comanche Peak nuclear power plant in the nearby Glen Rose Independent School District. Students in Venus attended most of their classes in portable buildings, while those in Glen Rose had plush throw pillows in their library and a two-story, open-air cafeteria. Venus was able to spend only $4,000 a year per child, while Glen Rose spent $9,500. The tax bill on an $80,000 house in Venus was $935 a year, but only $134 in Glen Rose, where taxes on the power plant made a huge difference.[29]

For several years, the legislature had been making the problem worse by forcing school districts to rely more and more upon local property taxes to meet the costs of education. Most notably with House Bill 72 in 1984, legislators had ordered districts to make a number of expensive improvements, such as smaller class sizes, without fully paying for them at the state level. The legislature persisted in passing the buck because it had serious financial problems of its own after the collapse of the oil industry and the recession of the mid-1980s. On the same day that the Texas Supreme Court issued its school finance order in 1989, the Texas Association of School Boards released the results of a survey that indicated local school property taxes were increasing at a rate about two and one-half times that of state aid. "This decline (in the state's share of funding) does not bode well for school finance equity. As reliance upon disparate local wealth increases, the fiscal equity of the system worsens," the survey concluded.[30]

Governor Bill Clements called the legislature into special session in February 1990 to address the Supreme Court order. But even the threat of a court takeover of the public school system wasn't enough to produce an equitable, constitutional school finance plan, at least not yet. Two alternatives were a massive consolidation of school districts or a Robin Hood-type redistribution of state aid from rich to poor districts. But both of those were extremely unpopular politically, and Clements opposed raising state taxes to increase aid to poor districts while minimizing losses to the more wealthy.

The legislature missed the Supreme Court's May 1 deadline. State District Judge Scott McCown of Austin, who had taken over jurisdiction of the school finance lawsuit from the retired Harley Clark, extended the deadline but hung a heavy hammer over the state's head. He appointed a special master to devise a Robin Hood plan for redistributing available state aid and threatened to put it into effect if the governor and the legislature didn't enact a new law by June 21. Shortly after convening a fourth consecutive special session on the issue, the Republican governor and Democratic legislative leaders agreed on a one-quarter of a cent per dollar increase in the state sales tax to pay for a new school finance plan to boost funding to poor districts. But the plaintiffs in the Edgewood lawsuit called the new law inadequate and promptly took the state back to court.

After a trial on the new law, McCown agreed. Although he allowed the new law to remain in effect for the 1990-91 school year, McCown ruled in September 1990 that the plan that had taken the legislature four special sessions to produce was, like its predecessor, unconstitutional because it didn't narrow the huge gap in wealth between rich and poor school districts.

In January 1991, two weeks after the legislature had convened its 1991 regular session, the Texas Supreme Court upheld McCown's ruling and gave lawmakers another deadline, April 1, to correct the problem. The high court determined that the new law left "essentially intact the same funding system with the same deficiencies" as the law it had struck down 15 months earlier. Like its initial school finance opinion in 1989, the court's ruling was unanimous, but this time it was written by Chief Justice Tom Phillips, a Republican. And, for the first time, the court suggested possible—although highly controversial—solutions. "Consolidation of school districts is one available avenue toward greater efficiency in our school finance system. Another approach to efficiency is tax base consolidation."

There were more than 5,000 school districts in Texas in 1947, and that number was greatly reduced over the next several years. But consolidations have been relatively few in recent years. In many small towns, the school district is not only a major employer, it is also the center of social activities and the heart of the community itself. And be it rich or poor, local residents don't want to give it up. The *Houston Chronicle* vividly illustrated that point at the beginning of the 1990-91 school year with a visit to sparsely populated Cochran County in West Texas. The Whiteface Consolidated School District, which sits atop an oil field, had a tax base of $1.3 million per student and a tax rate of only 46 cents per $100 valuation. It had an indoor swimming pool that the entire community of 450 people shared, and it paid its teachers, on the average, about $3,500 a year more than the neighboring Morton Independent School District did. Morton, the county seat, is a slightly larger town only 12 miles away, but the oil field ends somewhere between the two communities. With a tax base of only $73,400 per student, Morton was one of the state's poorest school districts, and its tax rate was 96.5 cents per $100 valuation. But Morton Superintendent Charles Skeen said consolidation was no more popular with the people of Morton than it was with their neighbors in Whiteface.

"When you have two communities and you take the school out of one of them, the people fear they will lose their town," Skeen said. Whiteface Superintendent David Foote said virtually the same thing: "A lot of people live in this town so their children can go to a small school. They know that if a community loses its school, where the school is the center of the community, the community dies."[31]

The equalization task was further complicated when the Supreme Court in February 1991 took the unusual step of issuing a supplemental school finance ruling, seeking to clarify its January order. This opinion was split 5-4, with a conservative Democratic justice joining the four Republicans on the court to form the majority. Without backing away from its earlier opinions that the school finance system was unconstitutional because of the wide disparities in money available for spending between rich and poor districts, the high court ruled that there didn't have to be total equity among all the districts. The court said the wealthier districts could still enrich their programs with higher tax rates beyond an equalization level set by the state. The new order was issued after the Senate already had approved a school finance bill that would have restricted local education supplements, and Senator Carl Parker, Democrat of Port Arthur, and chairman of the Senate Education Committee, accused the Republicans on the court of trying to protect "big property owners" in the wealthiest districts. "Basically the Supreme Court...did more for political posturing for some members of the court than it did to bring clarity to the issue of education," Parker said.[32]

Despite—or perhaps because of—the clarification order, the legislature missed the court's April 1 deadline when the House and the Senate couldn't agree on a compromise. McCown extended the deadline to April 15. A Supreme Court injunction cutting off state education aid went into effect, but the schools remained open because the state's monthly education payments to local districts weren't due to be distributed until April 25. The new deadline, however, was critical because McCown had again threatened to impose his own "Robin Hood" plan for drastically redistributing state aid if lawmakers again came up empty handed.

The legislature met the new deadline by approving a plan to transfer hundreds of millions of dollars from rich to poor districts and significantly alter the way Texas paid for public schools. The new law, which Governor Richards signed on April 15, just minutes before McCown's next scheduled court hearing, divided the state into 188 county education districts, or CEDs, for taxing purposes. Individual school districts within each CED remained intact, but the new law set a minimum local property tax rate and required funds generated by that rate to be equitably distributed among districts within the same CED. Although the new plan boosted state education aid by about $1.2 billion over the next two years, many wealthy districts lost money to their poorer neighbors and had to consider significant increases in local property taxes or reductions in programs.

Lt. Governor Bob Bullock, who had unsuccessfully proposed a state income tax to pay for public education and provide property tax relief, predicted the new law would raise local school property taxes by an average of 34 percent over the next five years. "Education is a state function, and we should be paying for it with state dollars," he said. "Instead, we've once again strapped property owners with a bill that will push their property taxes through the roof." Bullock's statement was sharply disputed by some House members, who contended Bullock was unnecessarily raising a red flag to promote his own political agenda for an income tax. But the new law was blamed for significant tax increases and budget cutbacks in many school districts later that year.

One of the most widely publicized reactions to the new law occurred in the Dallas Independent School District, which laid off more than 200 teachers at the beginning of the 1991-92 school year to compensate for millions of dollars in lost state aid. The action sparked angry student protests, which convinced the school district to back down and rehire most of the teachers with money transferred from other sections of its budget.

Presented with the new law, Judge McCown lifted the injunction and allowed state aid to continue flowing to school districts on time. The plaintiffs in the Edgewood lawsuit did not challenge the new plan but, a few weeks later, two wealthy Dallas-area school districts filed a countersuit against the new law. They contended it was unconstitutional for the legislature to order the redistribution of local tax money from one district to another and to require each district to levy a minimum tax rate. They were soon joined by a number of other rich districts.

McCown upheld the new law on August 7, but the wealthy districts appealed to the Supreme Court, which struck down the statute in January 1992 in a 7-2 decision. The majority opinion, written by Democratic Justice Raul Gonzalez, held that the new minimum tax amounted to a statewide property tax in violation of the Texas Constitution. The court majority also said local residents should have been allowed to vote on the tax rate. The court, however, allowed the tax to remain in effect until the legislature came up with still another school finance plan, and it gave lawmakers a new deadline of June 1, 1993. Democratic Justices Lloyd Doggett and Oscar Mauzy strongly dissented. "So many words—so little justice," they said in a scathing dissenting opinion. "For the school children, there is delay—perhaps infinite delay—in achieving equal educational opportunity," they wrote. The majority ruling angered Governor Ann Richards and legislative leaders, who complained that they had been led to believe by the 1991 Edgewood ruling that countywide taxing districts with a minimum tax rate would be an acceptable solution to the state's long search for school finance equity.

So the struggle for educational equity and quality continued, as it had for most of the state's history. Since 1925, there have been numerous studies of public education, and issues identified 30 or 40 years ago are only now being addressed in a comprehensive manner (Table 13-3).

Average spending per Texas pupil grew from $2,998 when House Bill 72 went into effect in 1984 to $4,380 in the 1989-90 school year but, according to the National Education Association, remained well below the national average of $5,100 per student. The proportion of Texas students mastering the Texas Educational Assessment of Minimum Skills, or TEAMS, test, which measured basic language and mathematical skills, increased from 75 percent in 1987 to 80 percent in 1989.[33] But

## TABLE 13-3   An Abbreviated History of Interim Studies of Texas Education

Texas has spent a sizable amount of resources over the years examining its public school system and searching for ways to make it work better. Following is a synopsis of major interim studies.

### 1925

The legislature creates the first Texas interim committee on education, the Texas Educational Survey Commission, chaired by Gov. Pat Neff. Among its recommendations: the legislature should structure county and state funds to equalize educational opportunities and to stimulate local tax effort.

### 1938

The State Board of Education publishes its Report of the Results of the Texas Statewide School Adequacy Survey, advocating school district consolidation, among other proposals. It is never implemented.

### 1947

The Gilmer-Aikin Committee is formed at the insistence of Gov. Beauford Jester to study education finance. The committee's report leads to the passage of legislation in 1949 which establishes a Minimum Foundation Program for public education in Texas with the state and local districts sharing the cost of public education. Other changes include a minimum salary for teachers and the creation of a state Department of Education.

### 1958

The 55th Legislature creates the Hale-Aikin Committee of Twenty-Four for the Study of Texas Public Schools. It collects data on the performance of the Gilmer-Aikin reforms in all counties and calls for the continuation and strengthening of those reforms.

### 1965

Gov. John Connally appoints the Governor's Committee on Public School Education to develop a long-range plan to improve education in Texas. This is the first official body in the history of the state to address the issue of inequity in public school finance. The committee issues its report, The Challenge and the Change, in 1968, recommending sweeping changes including massive increases in state aid and widespread consolidation of school districts. The suggestions are ignored.

### 1972

The Joint Interim Senate Committee to Study School Finance recommends a plan to eliminate wealth discrimination in school finance. The model, which was never adopted, called for increased levels of state support and the imposition of maximum and minimum property tax rates statewide.

### 1974

The Governor's Office of Educational Research and Planning issues a report on school finance. This leads to the passage of House Bill 1126, which establishes the Foundation School Program in place of the Minimum Foundation Program; it creates Local Fund Assignments based on actual market value of taxable property and weighted personnel units for funding allocation.

### 1979

House Concurrent Resolution 90 mandates a Curriculum Study Panel to study Texas Public School curriculum. Gov. Bill Clements creates an Advisory Committee on Education to study public education. These studies result in the passage of House Bill 246 which requires the development and implementation of a standardized "essential elements" curriculum in the public schools.

### 1983

Gov. Mark White appoints the Select Committee on Public Education, chaired by Dallas businessman Ross Perot. The Committee's report (1984) results in passage of House Bill 72 during a special session of the legislature. This major reform bill increases state aid to education, along with some equalization measures, changes the funding allocation from a weighted personnel base to a weighted pupil base, increases teachers' salaries, establishes a career ladder, limits class size in grades K-4, and establishes the "no pass, no plan" rule for extracurricular activities.

### 1987

The Joint Interim Committee on High School Dropouts Report results in legislation aimed at lowering the dropout rate, focusing programs on at-risk children, and establishing pilot programs for dropout prevention.

### 1988

Gov. Clements appoints a Select Committee on Education that recommends changes in funding of public education to achieve funding equity among school districts. The 71st Legislature (1989) passes Senate Bill 1019 that implements a guaranteed yield for equalizing aid to schools (declared unconstitutional by the Texas Supreme Court in 1989).

### 1989

The Governor's Task Force on Public Education recommends fundamental changes in assessing the costs of education and in determining how schools are run, how educational success is measured and how the educational system is made accountable to communities and taxpayers.

### 1991

Gov. Ann Richards convenes the Texas School Assembly, a statewide meeting of Texas educators and others involved in Texas public education. Among the issues addressed by the assembly are the under-utilization of school facilities, local autonomy, health insurance for teachers, and testing for student achievement.

Sources: William N. Kirby and Billy D. Walker, *The Basics of Texas Public School Finance*, (Austin, Texas Association of School Boards, 1988) and Gwen Warnock Newman, *The Select Committee on Public Education*, Professional Report, (Austin, University of Texas at Austin, 1983-1984). Cited in Comptroller of Public Accounts, *Fiscal Notes*, March, 1991.

the scores of Texas high school students on the verbal part of the Scholastic Aptitude Test, which is an entrance requirement of many colleges, declined for the third straight year in 1990-91. The average Texas score on the math portion of the SAT increased slightly, but both the average Texas verbal score of 411 and the math average of 463 were well below the national averages of 422 and 474, respectively. The scores of African-American and Hispanic students in Texas lagged behind the scores of Anglo students, while the scores of students from low-income families were lower than those of students in higher-income families. There was a bright spot in the Texas SAT scores, however. Students with 20 or more academic or college preparatory courses recorded scores substantially higher than their peers.[34]

Lionel Meno took office as Texas' new education commissioner in 1991, promising to be innovative in his quest for educational improvements. A few months after arriving in Texas from New York, where he had been deputy superintendent for schools, Meno announced a pilot program to give selected schools more flexibility in teaching students. As many as 80 schools across the state were to be selected for the Partnership Schools Initiative Program and be exempted from regulations that they considered counterproductive to improving learning. One goal was to close the gaps in student performance between ethnic groups.

Not only would an improved level of public education help boost Texas' long-range economic prospects, it also could reduce the state's crime rate, experts predicted.

## Higher Education: The Quest for Excellence and Equity Continues

Texas has 37 state-supported, general academic universities, seven medical schools and health science centers, four law schools, 49 community (or junior) colleges, and four campuses of the Texas State Technical College System. Several universities and health science centers were created by the legislature during the 1960s to accommodate increases in higher education enrollment. But after enrollment growth slowed in the 1980s and the state's economy took a nosedive, the Texas Higher Education Coordinating Board, which must approve new university facilities and degree programs, began to restrict university construction projects.

Meanwhile, the struggle to keep higher education funding competitive with other industrial states has been intense throughout a series of budgetary crises. But compared to most other state agencies, universities have fared pretty well. In the face of a $4 billion-plus revenue shortfall in 1991, for example, higher education received a $250 million increase in its biennial budget and convinced the legislature to reject several controversial budget-cutting proposals made by Comptroller John Sharp. Whatever success higher education has had with the legislature can be attributed to a highly effective lobbying effort (see Chapter 4) and to a recognition by state leaders of the crucial role that education plays in the state's future. Students also are pitching in. The budget increase approved in 1991 was to be partially funded with a tuition increase in 1992. Resident undergraduate tuition was to increase $2 per semester hour to $24, which would still be one of the lowest tuition levels in the country.

The state makes no pretense that all its universities were created equal. The University of Texas at Austin and Texas A&M University at College Station were afforded first class status by the Texas Constitution. They are the state's largest universities, have higher entrance requirements than other schools, fulfill important research functions, and, thanks to a constitutional endowment, have the state's best educational facilities. They receive revenue generated by the land- and mineral-rich **Permanent University Fund,** or PUF. UT receives two-thirds of the money in the Available University Fund, which is dividends, interest, and other income earned by the PUF, and A&M receives one-third. UT and A&M regents also can pledge that revenue to back bonds issued for land acquisition, construction, building repairs, purchase of capital equipment, and purchase of library materials for all the universities within the UT and A&M systems. A statewide property tax used to generate money for a building fund for universities outside the UT and A&M systems, but that tax was repealed in 1982 and replaced by a constitutional provision requiring the legislature to appropriate $100 million a year to a similar fund.

Responding to a federal desegregation lawsuit, the state in the 1980s made a commitment to improve higher educational opportunities for minority students and employment opportunities for minority faculty members. More funding was provided for predominantly African-American Texas Southern University in Houston and Prairie View A&M University in nearby Waller County. Prairie View, which is part of the Texas A&M System, was guaranteed a special share of Available University Fund revenue in a constitutional amendment adopted in 1984. Texas agreed to a five-year desegregation plan with the U.S. Department of Education in 1983 and subsequently created the Texas Educational Opportunity Plan, under which traditionally Anglo schools, including UT-Austin and Texas A&M, increased minority recruitment efforts.

Residents of heavily Hispanic South Texas, however, challenged the state's distribution of higher education dollars and facilities. In a lawsuit filed in state district court in Brownsville in 1987, several Hispanic groups and individuals represented by the Mexican American Legal Defense and Educational Fund, which represented the plaintiffs in the Edgewood school finance case, contended the state's higher education system discriminated against Mexican American students by spending less on universities in the border area. The plaintiffs pointed out that there were no state-supported professional schools south of San Antonio and only one doctoral program—in bilingual education at Texas A&I University in Kingsville.

After the lawsuit was filed, Texas A&I, Laredo State University, and Corpus Christi State University were made part of the Texas A&M System, and Pan American University campuses in Edinburg and Brownsville were added to the University of Texas System. But extensive efforts to negotiate a settlement of the suit failed, and it went to trial in late 1991 as a class action on behalf of all Mexican Americans who allegedly suffered or stood to suffer discrimination in higher education in the Mexican border area of Texas. In January 1992, state District Judge

Benjamin Euresti, Jr. of Brownsville ruled the higher education funding system unconstitutional because it discriminated against South Texas, putting still another major policy area of state government under a court order.

## CRIMINAL JUSTICE

Texas did away with public hangings on the courthouse square years ago but nevertheless retained a frontier attitude toward crime and criminals, an attitude that produced a criminal justice system based more on revenge than rehabilitation. Politicians were elected to the legislature on tough, anticrime promises, vows to "lock 'em up and throw away the key." Once in office, they passed laws providing long sentences for more and more offenses and built more prisons until, eventually, the system was overwhelmed by sheer numbers.

Legislators and most other state policy makers ignored deteriorating prison conditions until U.S. District Judge William Wayne Justice of Tyler declared the prison system unconstitutional in 1980 in a landmark lawsuit brought by inmates (*Ruiz v. Estelle*). He cited numerous problems, including overcrowded conditions, poor staffing levels, inadequate medical and psychiatric care for prisoners, and the use of so-called "building tenders," armed, often abusive inmates given positions of authority over other prisoners. Justice ordered extensive reforms with which the state agreed to comply, and he appointed a monitor to help him supervise what was then known as the Texas Department of Corrections, and is now the institutional division of the Texas Department of Criminal Justice.

One key order by Justice limited the population of prison units to 95 percent of capacity to guard against a recurrence of overcrowding and to allow for the housing of inmates according to their classifications, which were designed to separate youthful, first-time offenders from more-hardened criminals and those with special needs from the general prison population. Between 1980 and 1990, Texas spent hundreds of millions of dollars building more than 38,000 new prison beds and had another 15,000 under construction or authorized when the legislature convened in 1991.[35] Texas had one of the largest prison populations in the United States, and it couldn't build new prisons fast enough to comply with the court order.

Thousands of convicts, many of them dangerous murderers and rapists, were being paroled each year after serving only a small fraction of their sentences in order to make room for new inmates. The prison system came to be known as a "revolving door," and the Board of Pardons and Paroles, which was powerless to slow down the rate of releases, became a political scapegoat for frustrated legislators and outraged, fearful constituents. By 1991, several thousand convicted felons also had become backlogged in overcrowded county jails because the state couldn't accept them without violating Justice's limit on the prison population. The state prisoners were a burden to county taxpayers and were a source of contention between the state and counties, several of whom sued the state over the issue.

Part of the large increase in prisoners resulted from an overall increase in the violent crime rate during the 1980s. But many of the convicts overloading the system were relatively minor, nonviolent, repeat offenders, and many of them were alcoholics and drug addicts who continued to get in trouble because they were unable to function in the free world. Experts believed that alcoholism, drug addiction, or drug-related crimes were responsible for about 85 percent of the prison population.[36]

Meeting in special session in the summer of 1991, the legislature authorized the construction of 25,300 more prison beds, to be funded from $1.1 billion in tax-backed, general obligation bonds that Texas voters approved that November. When completed, they would bring the state's total prison capacity to about 90,000 beds. More significantly, however, lawmakers set aside 12,000 of the new beds for a new alcoholism and drug abuse treatment program which they hoped would reduce the recidivism that was spinning the prison system's door.

The plan was part of a far-reaching criminal justice reform law that also encouraged the development of special probationary programs and other alternatives for minor offenders. It also provided for the repeal of the Penal Code in 1994 and the appointment of a special study commission to encourage the legislature to enact a more equitable punishment structure for criminal offenses. Under the existing Penal Code, a burglar could be sentenced to life in prison, while in the next county or the next courtroom, a murderer could get probation. That's because a long list of offenses were lumped together as first degree felonies, punishable by 10 years to life, with the discretion for sentencing within that wide range left to trial judges and juries.

The new law also offered counties financial incentives to drop their lawsuits against the state over housing state prisoners. But the provision that could have the greatest long-range impact on the criminal justice crisis, legislators hoped, was the drug abuse treatment program. "If you can break the cycle of addiction, you can break the cycle of crime," said Senator Ted Lyon, a Democrat from Rockwall and former police officer who co-sponsored the bill in the Senate with Senator Jim Turner of Crockett.[37] The program also had the strong support of Governor Ann Richards and Lt. Governor Bob Bullock, both recovering alcoholics. The commitment of 12,000 prison beds to such a program was "absolutely unprecedented," Lyon said. The revolutionary effort, he added, would put Texas well ahead of other state prison systems in the treatment of substance abusers. The closest state in terms of commitment, Lyon said, was New York, which had 3,900 drug treatment beds in its prison system in 1991.[38]

The new law gave judges the option of sentencing eligible defendants who were substance abusers to regular prison terms or to the drug abuse treatment program, which was to be segregated from the general prison population in units that the Department of Criminal Justice was to acquire or construct in regional locations. Defendants convicted of violent, aggravated offenses were ineligible for the program. The Texas Commission on Alcohol and Drug Abuse was to help develop a regimen of structured work, education, and treatment requirements. The success or failure of the program will depend, to a large extent, on the criminal trial judges, some of whom have been accused of imposing lengthy sentences to make political points with the voters they must face on election day. Representative Allen Hightower, a Democrat from Huntsville who also co-sponsored the new law, predicted judges would cooperate and "fill it (the program) up."[39] Although this is a major step, the success or failure of other public programs, such as education, health care, and welfare assistance, will also help determine Texas' future criminal justice needs because many prison inmates, including substance abusers, also are indigent and are high school dropouts.

State officials, meanwhile, were hoping that Judge Justice would soon lift his order and let the state regain control of its prison system. One of the first things that Attorney General Dan Morales did after taking office in January 1991 was to file a motion asking Justice to end the lengthy litigation. The legislature in 1991 also enacted another law, which could be implemented once the court dismissed the lawsuit, establishing guidelines for maintaining a constitutional prison system but providing a means of increasing the population of existing prison units while new prisons were being built.

## HEALTH AND HUMAN SERVICES

This is where state government weighs its conscience for compassion against the cold realities of its budget, and Texas historically has been stingy. Texas traditionally has spent less money on health and welfare than most states. It ranked 49th among the states in 1989 at $227 per capita, well below the national average of $403 and the high of $870 in Alaska.[40] Even in the 1970s, when the oil industry was still pumping a healthy amount of tax revenue into the state treasury, Texas was slapped with two federal court orders for providing inadequate care to the mentally ill and the mentally retarded in state institutions. Perhaps the tight-fisted attitude springs from the legacy of frontier colonists standing on their own two feet to fight adversity and win a better life. That view has been perpetuated by countless politicians claiming that Texans could prevail in hard times by pulling up their bootstraps and hanging tough. It, however, ignores the reality that many people in modern Texas can't find their bootstraps because they don't have any boots.

The lobbying efforts of health and human services advocates are made even more difficult by the fact that Texas has no dedicated fund to guarantee a source of revenue for health and welfare programs. They have nothing akin to the Highway Trust Fund which automatically earmarks three-fourths of the revenue from the state gasoline tax and motor vehicle registration fees to build, maintain, and police roads and highways. The difference in outlook reflects the individualistic political view that has long been dominant in Texas (see Chapter 1). It holds that governmental interference in the private lives of its citizens should be limited, unless action is necessary to guarantee a stable marketplace where individuals can freely pursue their own interests. And a good highway or transportation system has always been considered essential to the success of Texas' most influential marketplace, the business and industrial community.

Ron Lindsey, then the commissioner for the Department of Human Services, the state's primary welfare agency, warned legislators in 1991 that widespread poverty threatened to make Texas a "Third World nation within our lifetime." More than 3 million of Texas' 17 million people were living in poverty, he said, including one out of every four children. Lindsey said his agency provided food stamps to more than 750,000 households and monthly welfare grants of $57 each to more than 650,000 recipient households. In 1990, he added, the department confirmed more than 82,000 child abuse cases but was able to assist only 30,199 children. Caseloads for most of the agency's major programs would increase by 150 percent to 190 percent over the next few years, Lindsey predicted.[41] Indigent, at-risk children, other experts warned, were more likely to end up becoming criminals and being an even greater strain on society as adults if they weren't provided assistance and an opportunity for a quality education while they were young. Attempts to break the cycle of poverty weren't new, but they were becoming more critical.

Medicaid and other assistance programs administered by the Department of Human Services, the Department of Health, and other state agencies are largely federally funded, and state officials believe that Texas has not been spending all the federal funds to which it is entitled. It was estimated that the state may have failed to spend millions of dollars a year for the Medicaid program alone, thanks primarily to a lack of coordination among numerous state and local agencies.[42] Medicaid provides health care assistance to pregnant women, infants and young children, the elderly, and the disabled.

Efforts to avoid tax increases or to keep them as small as possible usually limit budgetary increases for health and human services programs during each legislative session. The Department of Human Services, in particular, was plagued by budgetary shortfalls for several years. Part of the problem stemmed from the federal government making more people eligible for Medicaid and other assistance after the legislature had already adopted a budget.

Legislative leaders also blamed mismanagement within the agency. In 1991 the legislature attempted to provide more oversight and coordination for those programs by creating an umbrella-type board over 10 agencies and giving the governor the authority to appoint that board and a "supercommissioner" of health and human services. Most advocates of human services programs apparently were willing to give the reorganization a try, but they warned that better administration—if that's what the reorganization produced—wouldn't make up for a shortage of money. "Good systems—and good people—cannot make up for our failure to allocate adequate resources to respond to human needs in Texas. Whatever our rhetoric, our actions on behalf of those in need are inferior to virtually every other state in the nation," said Phil Strickland, director of the Christian Life Commission of the Baptist General Convention of Texas.[43]

The adequacy of Texas' care for the mentally ill and the mentally retarded was challenged in two lawsuits filed in federal court against the state in 1974. They resulted in court orders requiring the legislature to spend millions of dollars improving facilities and treatment programs in state hospitals and state schools for the mentally retarded. In an agreement tentatively reached in 1991 for settling one suit, the state took steps to close two of its 13 state schools and transfer at least 600 mentally retarded residents to community homes.[44]

## ENVIRONMENTAL PROBLEMS AND POLICIES

After signing a bill consolidating several environmental protection programs into one new state agency in 1991, Governor Ann Richards said the compromise measure was only a beginning because "much remains to be done in environmental enforcement."[45] Appropriately enough, she made her remarks the same week that researchers released a report ranking Texas 46th among the 50 states in healthy environmental conditions and environmental protection policies. The so-called "Green Index" compiled by the Institute for Southern Studies in Durham, N.C., said Texas released the most toxic substances into the environment while spending less than any other state on environmental protection. Most other Southern states also miserably failed the review, which was based on data from the Environmental Protection Agency and other federal agencies, as well as private groups. The report put the blame on "the legacy of policymakers who promote the proposition that everything in the South is cheap—available for the taking, no questions asked."[46] Compounding the problem in Texas is the fact that the state has one-fourth of the United States' oil refining, two-thirds of its chemical manufacturing, and auto-clogged major cities where mass transportation is largely an afterthought.

Over the years, Texas leaders often have displayed a pro-business attitude that seemed indifferent, or worse, to environmental concerns. Former Governor Bill Clements, for example, actively recruited Formosa Plastics Corporation to expand its Calhoun County facilities on the environmentally sensitive Texas coast, despite the Taiwan-based company's poor environmental reputation. Clements considered the issue in terms of economic development alone, a means of providing new jobs to a depressed area of the state. After being guaranteed $225 million in tax breaks and direct subsidies from Texas taxpayers, Formosa in 1988 agreed to proceed with a $1.5 billion expansion of its Calhoun County plant.[47]

Clements often bragged about his administration's role in Formosa's decision. His secretary of state, Jack Rains, had even taken a $1,543 taxpayer-paid trip to Taiwan to help sell company officials on the Texas location and later called his trip "probably one of the best investments in foreign travel ever made by this state."[48] Formosa already had a poor reputation among environmentalists in Louisiana before being courted to expand in Texas. And less than three years after accepting Texas' offer, the company was slapped with three major fines by state and federal regulatory agencies for environmental violations at its existing Texas plant. Some of the cited violations had occurred before 1988. The fines included the largest hazardous waste fine ever assessed by the Environmental Protection Agency, a $3.375 million penalty assessed in February 1991.[49]

Most state leaders believe economic development is crucial to Texas' future, now that the oil industry's glory days are history. Economic development can mean jobs and financial security for thousands of Texans. But most Texans, according to a survey by Rice University sociologist Stephen Klineberg, don't believe the environment should take a back seat to economic development. Klineberg's first "Texas Environmental Survey," conducted in the summer of 1990, found that 84 percent of 1,000 respondents favored stronger regulation of polluting industries and a large majority favored mandatory recycling.[50]

Under the 1991 law, the Texas Water Commission, Texas Air Control Board, and environmental functions of the Texas Department of Health were consolidated into the new Texas Natural Resources Conservation Commission. The Texas Department of Agriculture and the Structural Pest Control Board will continue to regulate pesticides, and the Texas Railroad Commission will continue to regulate oil, natural gas, and mining. Environmentalists were disappointed in the bill, which represented a victory for the more conservative House in a war of wills with the Senate, because it didn't require significant changes in what they considered inadequate agency practices and regulatory procedures.

Environmentalists and industry representatives alike, however, were pleased with another major environmental law enacted in 1991 to create an oil spill response and cleanup plan for the Texas coast. The new law imposed a 2-cents-per barrel tax on imported crude oil to feed a $25 million fund to pay for the state's costs in responding to spills and to provide compensation for damages. It made parties responsible for the accident primarily responsible for cleanup costs and made the General Land Office responsible for overseeing spill responses and cleanups. Previously the state had only a limited program handled by the Texas Water Commission. The same year, the legislature also imposed a four-month moratorium on new hazardous waste disposal permits and ordered agencies to strengthen their rules for granting the permits. It also put a $2 fee on the purchase prices of new car and truck tires and auto batteries to create a fund to encourage recycling.

## SUMMARY AND CONCLUSIONS

**1.** The political power necessary to shape policy is exercised through groups, and some groups or interests are more influential than others.

**2.** Setting public policy usually involves questions of costs and benefits. The ultimate political problem to resolve is who will benefit from specific policy decisions and who will pay the bill.

**3.** The legislature is primarily responsible for setting policy at the state level, but the government's separation of powers doctrine gives the judiciary important scrutiny over legislative action—or inaction. In recent years, consequently, there have been major federal and state court decisions forcing the legislature to make far-reaching changes in education, criminal justice, and mental health and mental retardation programs.

**4.** The "iron triangles" of state government—key legislators, their staffs, high-level bureaucrats and interest group lobbyists—are at the center of the policymaking process. They also can be part of larger "issue networks" that reflect the increased interdependence of state and local governments on the federal government and the heightened role of issue specialists.

**5.** The Texas legislature's budget-writing task is made increasingly difficult by heightened legal and political pressures for improved services, a two-year budget cycle, a changing economy, and outdated tax and budgetary structures.

**6.** The struggle for a sound public education system is a search for both quality in the classroom and equity in financing between school districts.

**7.** Even with a record prison construction program, Texas has been unable to build its way out of a criminal justice crisis. State officials are increasingly recognizing the importance of prevention—a better public education system and more drug abuse and alcoholism treatment programs. Inequities in criminal sentencing practices also have come under legislative scrutiny.

**8.** Texas historically has been stingy in spending on health and human services programs. This is a reflection of the individualistic political view that has long been dominant in the state.

**9.** Balancing economic growth with environmental protection is a goal that Texas continues to pursue with difficulty.


## KEY TERMS

Issue networks

Deficit financing

Dedicated funds

Regressive tax system

Sales tax

Franchise tax

Sin tax

Property tax

Income tax

Lottery

General obligation bonds

House Bill 72

Career ladder

No pass, no play

*Edgewood* v. *Kirby*

Permanent University Fund

*Ruiz* v. *Estelle*


## FURTHER READING

Anderson, James E., *Public Policymaking*, 2nd ed. New York: Holt, Rinehart and Winston, 1979.

Anderson, James E, David W. Brady, Charles S. Bullock, III, and Joseph Stewart, Jr., *Public Policy and Politics in America*, 2nd ed. Monterey, Calif.: Brooks/Cole Publishing Company, 1984.

Anton, Thomas J., *Federalism and Public Policy: How the System Works*. New York: Random House, 1989.

Armstrong, David, "Plastic Peril: Politicians Breed Pollution in Calhoun County," *The Texas Observer*, May 17,1991, pp. 4-7.

Campbell, Brett, "The Greening of the Legislature," *The Texas Observer*, May 17, 1991, pp. 15, 23-27.

Campbell, Brett, "Of Human Services: Who's Responsible for the DHS Mess?" *The Texas Observer*, November 9, 1990, pp. 4-9.

Champagne, Anthony, and Edward J. Harpham, eds., *Texas at the Crossroads*. College Station: Texas A&M University Press, 1987.

Cochran, Clarke E., Lawrence C. Mayer, T. R. Carr, and N. Joseph Cayer, *American Public Policy: An Introduction*, 2nd ed. New York: St. Martin's Press, 1986.

Cole, Richard L., and Delbert A. Taebel, *Texas Politics and Public Policy*. Orlando, FL: Harcourt Brace Jovanovich, 1987.

Cope, Glen, "Texas Constitutional Spending Limits: Reality versus Perception," *Public Affairs Comment*, 36 (Summer 1990), pp. 1-10.

Gerston, Larry N., *Making Public Policy: From Conflict to Resolution.* Glenview, Ill.: Scott, Foresman and Company, 1983.

Hamilton, Billy C., *Rethinking Texas Taxes*, 2 vols. Final Report of the Select Committee on Tax Equity, 71st Legislature, 1989.

Harper, Joellen M., "Financing Mental Health Care in Texas: Issues and Alternatives," *Public Affairs Comment* 36 (Spring 1990), pp. 1-12.

Heclo, Hugh, "Issue Networks and the Executive Establishment," in Anthony King, ed., *The New American Political System.* Washington, D.C.: American Enterprise Institute, 1978.

Henig, Jeffrey R., *Public Policy and Federalism.* New York: St. Martin's Press, 1985.

Henson, Scott, "Treasure Island: Corporate Pirates May Plunder South Padre," *The Texas Observer*, May 17, 1991, pp. 8, 12- 14.

Jones, Charles O., *An Introduction to the Study of Public Policy*, 2nd ed. North Scituate, Mass.: Duxbury Press, 1977.

Lineberry, Robert L., *American Public Policy.* New York: Harper & Row, 1977.

Lipari, Lisbeth, "Sharp Cuts," *The Texas Observer*, July 12, 1991, pp. 5-6, 23.

McCown, F. Scott, "Equity v. Adequacy: Excerpts from District Judge F. Scott McCown's *Edgewood* v. *Kirby* Opinion on School Finance," *The Texas Observer*, September 20, 1990, pp. 4-6.

Mitchell, Kathy, "Hazardous Oversight: Who's Minding the Store," *The Texas Observer*, June 14, 1991, pp. 4-8.

Riposa, Gerry, ed., *Texas Public Policy.* Dubuque, Iowa: Kendall/ Hunt, 1987.

Roberts, Elizabeth Travis, "Unhealthy Profits: What's Behind the Texas Insurance Crisis," *The Texas Observer*, February 22, 1991, pp. 12-13, 19.

Sharp, John, *Breaking the Hold: New Ways to Govern Texas: A Report from the Texas Performance Review*, 2 vols., Austin: Comptroller of Public Accounts, 1991.

Texas Comptroller of Public Accounts, "School Daze: Finding the Right Equation," *Fiscal Notes*, March, 1991, pp. 1-12.

Vines, Michael F., "Prisons and Politics: Why the System Isn't Working," *The Texas Observer*, January 11, 1991, pp. 6-10.

Wade, L. L., and R. L. Curry, Jr., *A Logic of Public Policy: Aspects of Political Economy.* Belmont, Calif.: Wadsworth Publishing Company, Inc., 1970.

Weiher, Gregory R., "Why Redistribution Reform Doesn't Work: State Education Reform Policy and Governmental Decentralization in Texas," *American Politics Quarterly*, 16 (April 1988), pp. 193-210.

Wong, Jennifer, "Lord of the Highways: The State Agency the Legislature Can't Control," *The Texas Observer*, April 5, 1991, pp. 11-12, 24.

## ENDNOTES

1. Lt. Governor Bob Bullock, January 31, 1991, responding to a reporter's question about how big a tax bill he believed the legislature would have to enact that year.
2. This section draws primarily from L. L. Wade and R. L. Curry, Jr., *A Logic of Public Policy: Aspects of Political Economy* (Belmont, Cal.: Wadsworth Publishing Company, Inc., 1970), chap. 1.
3. James Anderson, *Public Policy-Making*, 2nd ed. (New York: Holt, Rinehart and Winston, 1979), p. 3.
4. Ibid. See chapter one for an excellent introduction to the definitional issues and approaches to public policy analysis.
5. The following discussion is based on the general stages of the policy-making process developed by James E. Anderson, David W. Brady, Charles S. Bullock, III, and Joseph Stewart, Jr., *Public Policy and Politics in America*, 2nd ed. (Monterey, Cal.: Brooks/Cole Publishing Company, 1984; and Charles O. Jones, *An Introduction to the Study of Public Policy*, 2nd ed. (North Scituate, Mass.: Duxbury Press, 1977).
6. James Anderson, et al, *Public Policy and Politics in America*, p. 8.
7. Jones, *An Introduction to the Study of Public Policy*, pp. 138-139.
8. Ibid., p. 139.

9. Randall B. Ripley and Grace A. Franklin, *Congress, the Bureaucracy, and Public Policy*, 3rd edition (Homewood, Ill.: The Dorsey Press, 1984), p. 10.

10. Hugh Heclo, "Issue Networks and the Executive Establishment," in *The New American Political System*, ed. Anthony King (Washington, D.C.: American Enterprise Institute, 1978), p. 88. Much of this section is based on this article.

11. Ibid., p. 107.

12. Ibid., p. 104.

13. Texas Comptroller of Public Accounts, *Fiscal Notes*, April 1991.

14. *Houston Chronicle*, April 22, 1991.

15. Robert S. McIntyre, Michael P. Ettlinger, Douglas P. Kelly, and Elizabeth A. Fray, *A Far Cry from Fair*, CTJ'S Guide to State Tax Reform (Washington, D.C.: Citizens for Tax Justice, 1991), pp. 3-5.

16. *Houston Chronicle*, April 22, 1991.

17. Ibid.

18. Ibid.

19. *Houston Chronicle*, February 27, 1991.

20. *Houston Chronicle*, March 7, 1991.

21. *The Texas Poll*, April 21, 1991, conducted for Harte-Hanks Communications, Inc., by the Public Policy Resources Laboratory of Texas A & M University.

22. *Houston Chronicle*, March 7, 1991.

23. Executive order issued by Governor Ann Richards, March 6, 1991.

24. *Houston Chronicle*, April 12, 1991.

25. *Houston Chronicle*, June 30, 1991.

26. *Austin American-Statesman*, September 13, 1991.

27. *Houston Chronicle*, January 16, 1989.

28. Ibid.

29. *Fort Worth Star-Telegram*, March 24, 1991.

30. *Houston Chronicle*, October 3, 1989.

31. *Houston Chronicle*, August 19, 1990.

32. *Houston Chronicle*, February 27, 1991.

33. *Houston Chronicle*, August 18, 1991.

34. *Houston Chronicle*, August 27, 1991.

35. *Houston Post*, September 2, 1991.

36. *Houston Chronicle*, September 8, 1991.

37. Ibid.

38. Ibid.

39. Ibid.

40. U.S. Department of Commerce Bureau of the Census, State Government Finances in 1989.

41. Associated Press, as carried in the *Houston Chronicle*, March 30, 1991.

42. *Houston Chronicle*, March 17, 1991.

43. Phil Strickland letter to Governor Ann Richards and members of the legislature, July 18, 1991.

44. *Austin American-Statesman*, August 8, 1991.

45. *Houston Chronicle*, August 14, 1991.

46. *Houston Chronicle*, August 12, 1991.

47. *Houston Chronicle*, September 10, 1989.

48. Ibid.

49. *Houston Chronicle*, February 28, 1991.

50. *Houston Chronicle*, October 2, 1990.

# GLOSSARY

**Absentee (or early) voting** A period before the regularly scheduled election date during which voters are allowed to cast ballots. With recent changes in election law, a person does not have to offer a reason for voting absentee.

**Activists** A small segment of the population who are engaged in various political activities.

*Age of Indifference* A study published in 1990 by the Times Mirror Center for the People and the Press, which concluded that young people are paying less attention to what's going on in the world than their parents did at their age. These findings are particularly ironic and disturbing since they come during the middle of the so-called "information age," when information is so readily available.

**Agenda-setting** The process of groups organizing around issues and keeping pressure on elected officials to make policy changes. Also, a theory that the media's choice of which news events and issues to cover helps define what is important for the public to know. This expands into an agenda-building role by encouraging political action.

**Agriculture commissioner** An elected official responsible for administering laws and programs that benefit agriculture.

**Annexation** The authority of cities to add territory, subject to restrictions set by state law.

**Appellate jurisdiction** The authority of a court to review the decisions of lower courts to determine if the law was correctly interpreted and legal procedures were correctly followed.

**Appropriation** A legislative action authorizing the expenditure of money for a public program or purpose. A general appropriations bill approved by the legislature every two years is the state budget.

**At-large election** A system in which city council members or other officeholders are elected by voters in the entire city, school district or single-purpose district. Many of these election systems have been struck down by the federal courts or by the U.S. Justice Department under the Voting Rights Act as discriminatory against minorities.

**Attorney general** The state's chief legal officer. He or she represents the state in lawsuits and is responsible for enforcing the state's anti-trust, consumer protection and other civil laws. This elected officeholder has virtually no responsibility for criminal law enforcement.

**Bi-factionalism** The presence of two dominant factions organized around regional, economic, or ideological differences within a single political party. For much of the 20th century, Texas functioned as a one-party system with two dominant factions.

**Bicameral legislature** A lawmaking body, such as the Texas Legislature, that includes two chambers.

**Bifurcated court system** The existence of two courts at the highest level of the state judiciary. The Texas Supreme Court is the court of last resort in civil cases, and the Court of Criminal Appeals has the final authority to review criminal cases. Texas and Oklahoma are the only two states with such a system.

**Block grants** Federal grants of money to states and local governments for broad programs or services rather than narrowly defined programs. These grants give state and local governments more discretion over the use of the funds.

**Bureaucracy** The agencies of government and their employees responsible for carrying out policies and providing public services approved by elected officials.

**Calendar** The agenda or the list of bills to be considered by the House or the Senate on a given day.

**Campaign consultant** A professional expert who helps political candidates plan, organize and run their campaigns.

**Capital murder** Murder committed under certain circumstances for which the death penalty or life in prison must be imposed.

**Capitol Press Corps** Representatives of Texas newspapers, television and radio stations and wire services who are assigned to Austin full-time to report on state government and politics.

**Career ladder** A system for rewarding experienced teachers in the public schools with extra pay.

**Categorical grants-in-aid** Grants of federal money that can be spent only for specific programs or purposes. This is the source of most federal assistance to state and local governments.

**Caucus** A group of legislators who band together for common political or partisan goals or along ethnic or geographic lines.

**City commission** A form of city government in which elected commissioners collectively serve as a city's policy-making body and individually serve as administrative heads of different city departments. Although once popular, this form of government is rarely used in Texas now.

**City, general law** A city allowed to exercise only those powers specifically granted to it by the legislature. General law cities have fewer than 5,000 residents, and most cities in Texas are classified as general law cities.

**City charter** A document, defined or authorized by state law, under which a city operates. In home rule cities, local voters may choose among several forms of city government.

**City, home rule** A city with more than 5,000 population, which can adopt any form of government residents choose, provided it doesn't conflict with the state constitution or statutes. Home rule powers are formalized through local voters' adoption of a city charter spelling out how the city is to be governed.

**Civil War Constitution** The constitution adopted by Texans after the state seceded from the Union and joined the Confederacy in 1861.

**Civil lawsuit** A non-criminal legal dispute between two or more individuals, businesses, governments or other entities.

**Commissioners court** The principal policy-making body for county government. It sets the county tax rate and supervises expenditures.

**Committee, Calendars** A special procedural committee that schedules bills that already have been approved by other committees for floor debate in the House.

**Committee, conference** A panel of House members and senators appointed to work out a compromise on a bill if different versions of the legislation were passed by the House and the Senate.

**Committee** A group of legislators who review and hold public hearings on issues or bills they are assigned by the presiding officer. Committees normally specialize in bills by subject matter and are designated standing committees. A bill has to win committee approval before it can be considered by the full House or Senate. Most bills die in committees, which serve as a legislative screening process.

**Compact theory** The view that governments originated from the general agreement among and consent of members of the public to address common interests and needs.

**Comptroller of Public Accounts** The state's primary tax administrator and accounting officer. It is an elective position.

**Confederation** A system in which each member government is considered sovereign and the national government is limited to powers delegated to it by its member governments.

**Constable** An elected law enforcement officer assigned as an administrative officer in a justice of the peace precinct. He or she is responsible primarily for executing court judgments, serving subpoenas and delivering other legal documents. Constables also are authorized to patrol their precincts, make arrests and conduct criminal investigations.

**Constitution of 1845** The constitution under which Texas was admitted to the United States.

**Constitution of 1876** The Texas constitution adopted at the end of Reconstruction, while Texas was still a rural, frontier state. Amended many times since, it remains in effect today. It is a highly restrictive, anti-government document drafted by Texans reacting to the abuses of the Radical Reconstructionists and the oppressive administration of Gov. Edmund J. Davis. Tight restrictions placed on the governor, the legislature and other state officials inhibit the ability of state government to respond to the complex needs of what is now a growing, urban state.

**Constitution of 1866** The short lived constitution under which Texas sought to be readmitted to the Union after the Civil War and before the Radical Reconstructionists took control of Congress.

**Constitution of the Republic** The constitution adopted March 16, 1836 by Texas colonists declaring independence from Mexico and its military dictator, Santa Anna. It was the same charter under which Texas functioned as an independent republic for nine years.

**Constitution of Coahuila y Tejas** The first of seven constitutions under which Texas has been governed. Adopted in 1824 by the Republic of Mexico, it recognized Texas, then being colonized by Anglo settlers under Stephen F. Austin, as a Mexican state with Coahuila, its neighbor south of the Rio Grande.

**Constitutional convention of 1974** The last major attempt to write a new Texas constitution. Members of the legislature served as delegates and failed to overcome political differences and the influence of special interests.

**Cooperative federalism** Policies emphasizing cooperative efforts among the federal, state and local governments to address common problems and provide public services to the citizens.

**Cooptation** Influence over state regulatory boards by the industries they are supposed to regulate, often to the detriment of the general public.

**Council of governments** A council comprised of representatives of other governments in a defined region of the state. There are 24 of these regions in Texas, and these councils serve to encourage cooperation, coordination, and planning among local governments and to provide services to the participating governments.

**Council-manager government** A form of city government in which policy is set by an elected city council, which hires a professional city manager to head the daily administration of city government.

**County chair** The presiding officer of a political party's county executive committee. He or she is elected countywide by voters in the party primary.

**County auditor** An officer appointed by the district judges of the county. This person is primarily responsible for reviewing every bill and expenditure of a county to assure it is correct and legal. All counties with 10,000 or more residents are required to have an auditor, and smaller counties may have one if commissioners court chooses. In counties with more than 225,000 people, the auditor is also the budget officer who prepares the budget. Recent changes permit counties with 125,000 or more people to appoint a budget officer.

**County court-at-law, statutory** A court which exercises limited jurisdiction over criminal and/or civil cases. The jurisdiction of these courts varies from county to county. Drunken driving cases are the primary criminal cases tried before this court.

**County attorney** An elected official who is the chief legal officer of some counties. He or she also prosecutes lesser criminal offenses, primarily misdemeanors, in county courts.

**County court, constitutional** (see county judge.)

**County tax assessor-collector** An elected official who determines how much property tax is owed on the different pieces of property within a county and then collects the tax. This officeholder acts on the basis of property values determined by the county appraisal district and a tax rate set by county commissioners court.

**County executive committee** A panel responsible on the local level for the organization and management of a political party's primary election. It includes the party's county chair and each precinct chair.

**County treasurer** An elected officer who is responsible for receiving and disbursing county funds. The office's primary functions are now carried out by the county auditor, and the office has recently been eliminated in a number of counties.

**County judge** The presiding officer of a county commissioners court. This office also has some judicial authority, which is assumed by separate county courts-at-law in most urban counties.

**County clerk** The chief record-keeping officer of a county.

**Court of Appeals** An intermediate level court that reviews civil and criminal cases from the district courts.

**Court of Criminal Appeals** A nine-member court with final appellate jurisdiction over criminal cases.

**Dealignment** A view that the party system is breaking up and the electoral influence of political parties is being replaced by interest groups, the media and well-financed candidates who use their own media campaigns to dominate the nomination and election process.

**Dedicated funds** Constitutional or statutory requirements that restrict some state tax or fee revenues to spending on specific programs.

**Deficit financing** Borrowing money to meet operating expenses. It is prohibited by the Texas Constitution, which provides that state government operate on a pay-as-you-go basis.

**Delegated powers** These are powers specifically assigned to the national, or federal, government by the U.S. Constitution, including powers to tax, borrow and coin money, declare war and regulate interstate and foreign commerce.

**Denied powers** Powers that are denied to both the states and national government. The best-known restrictions are listed in the Bill of Rights.

**Dillon rule** A principle holding that local governments are creations of state government and their powers and responsibilities are defined by the state.

**District attorney** An elected official who prosecutes the more serious criminal offenses, usually felonies, before state district courts.

**District court** The primary trial court in Texas. It has jurisdiction over criminal felony cases and civil disputes involving $500 or more in damages.

**Economic diversification** The development of new and varied business activities. New businesses were encouraged to relocate or expand in Texas after the oil and gas industry, which had been the base of the state's economy, suffered a major recession in the 1980s.

*Edgewood* v. *Kirby* A lawsuit in which the Texas Supreme Court in 1989 declared the Texas school finance system unconstitutional because of wide disparities in property wealth and educational opportunities between school districts.

**Editorial autonomy** The freedom of a local newspaper or television station to set its own news policies independently of absentee owners who may run a chain of media outlets throughout the country.

**Election, general** An election for state, federal and county offices held in November of even-numbered years. The ballot includes nominees of the two major political parties plus other candidates who meet certain legal requirements.

**Election, local** An election for city council, the school board and certain other local offices. Most of these are non-partisan.

**Election, primary** An election in which the Democratic or Republican party chooses its nominees for public offices. In presidential election years, the primary also plays a key role in selecting Texas delegates to the parties' national nominating conventions.

**Election, rollback** An election in which local voters can nullify a property tax increase that exceeds 8 percent in a given year.

**Election, runoff** This is required if no candidate receives an absolute majority of the votes cast in a primary race. The runoff is between the two top vote-getters.

**Election, special** An election set by the legislature or called by the governor for a specific purpose, such as voting on constitutional amendments or filling a vacancy in a legislative office. Local governments can also call special elections.

**Elitism** The view that political power is primarily held by a few individuals who derive power from leadership positions in large business, civic or governmental institutions.

**Error, writ of** Primary means by which cases reach the Texas Supreme Court. Those seeking to have cases heard allege that the lower court ruled erroneously on points of law.

**Extradition** A process by which a person in one state can be returned to another state to face criminal charges.

**Extraterritorial jurisdiction** The power of an incorporated city to control development within nearby unincorporated areas.

**Fat cat** An individual who contributes a lot of money to political candidates.

**Federalism** A system that balances the power and sovereignty of state governments with the national government. Both the states and the national government derive their authority directly from the people, and the states have considerable autonomy within their areas of responsibility.

**Felony** A criminal offense that can be punished by imprisonment and/or a fine. This is a more serious offense than a misdemeanor.

**Filibuster** A procedure that allows a senator to speak against a bill for as long as he or she can stand and talk. It can become a formidable obstacle or threat against controversial bills near the end of a legislative session.

**Full faith and credit** A provision in the U.S. Constitution (Article IV, Section 1) that requires states to recognize civil judgments and official documents rendered by the courts of other states.

**General obligation bonds** A method of borrowing money to pay for new construction projects, such as prisons or mental hospitals. Interest on these bonds, which require voter approval in the form of constitutional amendments, are paid with tax revenue.

**Gerrymandering** The drawing of political districts in such a way as to reduce the effect of voting by members of an ethnic or political minority.

**Globalization of the economy** Increased interdependence in trade, manufacturing, and commerce as well as most other business activities between the United States and other countries.

**Governor E. J. Davis** The Reconstruction era governor of Texas who was alleged by his opponents and many historians as having been one of the most abusive governors in American history. After his election in 1869, he convinced a Radical majority in the legislature to impose a series of authoritarian laws, including measures to create an oppressive state police force and give the governor the power to declare martial law. He was defeated by Texas voters in 1873 but left office only after armed militia marched on the Capitol.

**Governor** The state's top executive officeholder.

**Grand jury** A panel that reviews evidence submitted by prosecutors to determine whether to indict, or charge, an individual with a criminal offense. A grand jury can hear witnesses, but all its meetings are in private.

**Grange, The** An organization formed in the late 19th century to improve the lot of farmers. Its influence in Texas after Reconstruction was felt in constitutional provisions limiting taxes and government spending and restricting banks, railroads and other big businesses.

**Grass roots** A term used to describe a wide range of political activity designed to organize and mobilize the electorate at the local level. While modern campaigns are increasingly dominated by the campaign consultants, such support can prove crucial for political candidates, particularly for those with limited financial resources.

**House Bill 72** A landmark school reform law enacted in 1984. Among other things, it reduced class sizes, required teachers to pass a literacy test to keep their jobs and imposed the no pass, no play rule, which restricts failing students from participating in extracurricular activities.

**Hyperpluralism** The rapid expansion of interest groups that serves to disrupt and potentially deadlock the policy-making process.

**Impeachment** A procedure by which the legislature can remove a governor or certain other public officials from office for misconduct. It is the first of two stages of the removal process and is essentially the political equivalent of an indictment.

**Implied powers** Although not specifically defined by the Constitution, these are powers assumed by the national government as necessary in carrying out its responsibilities.

**Independent school district** A specific form of special district that administers the public schools in a designated area. It is governed by an elected board of trustees empowered to levy local property taxes, establish local school policies, and employ a school superintendent as its chief administrator.

**Indictment** A written statement issued by a grand jury, charging a person or persons with a crime or crimes.

**Individualism** An attitude, rooted in classical liberal theory and reinforced by the frontier tradition, that citizens are capable of taking care of themselves with minimal governmental assistance.

**Individualistic subculture** A view that government should interfere as little as possible in the private activities of its citizens while assuring that adequate public facilities and a favorable business climate are available to permit individuals to pursue their self interests.

**Influence-peddling** The abuse of public office by elected or appointed officials who bend the rules or provide special treatment for certain individuals or groups in return for bribes or favors.

**Information age** A reference to the present, when modern technology has made it easier than ever before for people to be informed, despite indications that many young people are indifferent to public affairs. (See *Age of Indifference*.) The term also refers to the increased dominance of information technology and services in the American and world economy.

**Interest group** A group of people with common goals who are organized to seek political results they are unable to achieve by themselves.

**Interstate compacts** Formal, long-term cooperative agreements among the states dealing with common problems or issues and subject to approval of the U.S. Congress.

**Iron rule of oligarchy** A theory developed by Robert Michels, a European sociologist, that all organizations inevitably are dominated by a few individuals.

**Iron triangles** Relationships among the interest groups, the administrative agencies, and the legislative committees involved in drafting the laws and regulations affecting a particular area of the economy or a specific segment of the population.

**Issue networks** Term coined by political scientist Hugh Heclo to describe the complex institutional and political relationships in the policy-making process.

**Issue-attention cycle** A pattern in which public interest in an issue or problem is heightened by intensive media coverage. Media attention and public interest will wane after government takes steps to address their concerns, but most issues or problems are never permanently resolved. Another crisis, perhaps years later, will restart the cycle.

**Justice of the peace court** A low-ranking court with jurisdiction over minor civil disputes and criminal cases.

**Land commissioner** An elected official who manages the state's public lands and administers the Veterans Land Program, which provides low interest loans to veterans for the purchase of land and houses.

**Legislative norms** Unwritten rules of the legislature that define roles and behaviors of the legislators.

**Legislature** The lawmaking branch of state government. In Texas, it includes a 150-member House of Representatives and a 31-member Senate elected from districts throughout the state.

**Licensing** A key regulatory function of government that seeks to ensure that individuals and companies providing critical professional services to the public are properly trained or qualified.

**Lieutenant governor** The presiding officer of the Senate. This officeholder also becomes governor if the governor were to die, be incapacitated or removed from office.

**Limited government** The constitutional principle restricting governmental authority and spelling out personal rights.

**Lobbying** An effort, usually organized and using a variety of strategies and techniques, to influence the making of laws or public policy.

**Lottery** A form of gambling, conducted by many states, in which participants purchase tickets that offer an opportunity to cash in on a winning number. Voters legalized a state lottery in Texas in 1991.

**Mandamus, writ of** A court order directing a lower court or another public official to take a certain action.

**Mandates** Federal laws or regulations that require state or local governments to take certain actions, often at costs that the federal government doesn't reimburse. The state government also imposes mandates on local governments requiring compliance with state law.

**Matching funds** Money that states or local governments have to provide to qualify for certain federal grants.

**Mayor, weak** A form of city government in which the mayor shares authority with the city council and other elected officials but has little independent control over city policy or city administration.

**Mayor, strong** A form of city government that gives the mayor considerable power, including budgetary control and appointment and removal authority over city department heads.

**Media event** A staged event by an officeholder or political candidate that is designed to attract media, especially television, coverage.

**Media bias** A perception—sometimes real, sometimes imagined—that reporters and news organizations slant their news coverage to favor one side or the other in particular issues or disputes.

**Merit system** A personnel system where public employees are selected for government jobs through competitive examinations and the systematic evaluation of job performance.

**Merit selection** A proposal under which the governor would appoint state judges from lists of potential nominees recommended by committees of experts. Appointed judges would have to run later in retention elections to keep their seats but wouldn't have opponents on the ballot. Voters would simply decide whether a judge should remain in office or be replaced by another gubernatorial appointee.

**Metro government** Consolidation of city and county governments to avoid duplication of public services. This approach has been tried in several other parts of the country but so far has attracted little interest in Texas.

**Miranda ruling** A far-reaching decision of the U.S. Supreme Court that requires law enforcement officers to warn a criminal suspect of his right to remain silent and have an attorney present before questioning.

**Mischief of factions** Term coined by James Madison to describe the complex relationships among groups and interests within the American political system and the institutional arrangements that potentially balance the power of groups.

**Misdemeanor** A minor criminal offense punishable by a fine or a short sentence in the county jail.

**Moralistic subculture** A view that government's primary responsibility is to promote the public welfare and should actively use its authority and power to improve the social and economic well-being of its citizens.

**Municipal court** A low-ranking court that hears cases involving city ordinances and primarily handles traffic tickets. It is a major revenue raiser for most cities.

**Myths** Stories, narratives or phrases used to describe past events, explain their significance and help provide an understanding of a society's culture, its political history and institutional arrangements.

**Negative TV ads** Television commercials in which political candidates attack their opponents, sometimes over a legitimate issue, but more often over an alleged flaw in their opponent's character or ability to hold office. Many such ads are deliberately misleading or outright false.

**New federalism** A term used to describe recent changes in federal-state relationships. Used primarily by conservative presidents, it suggests a devolution or return of power to the states and a decreased role of the federal government in domestic policy.

**No pass, no play** Prohibits students who fail any course from participating in school athletics and other extracurricular activities for six weeks.

**Nolo contendere** A plea of no contest to a criminal charge.

**Ombudsman** A special assistant to an elected official or designated employee in a state agency who handles citizen complaints about government.

**One-party system** The domination of elections and governmental processes by a single party, which may be split into different ideological, economic, or regional factions. In Texas, the phrase is use to describe the period from the late 1870s to the late 1970s when the Democratic party claimed virtually all elected, partisan offices.

**Open Meetings-Open Records acts** Laws that require state and local governmental bodies to conduct most of their actions in public and maintain records for public inspection.

**Original jurisdiction** The authority of a court to try or resolve a civil lawsuit or a criminal prosecution being heard for the first time.

**Pack journalism** The tendency of news organizations to cover the same elements of major stories and issues and of reporters to swarm key figures when major news is breaking.

**Parole** The early release of an inmate from prison, subject to certain conditions.

**Pay as you go** A constitutional prohibition against state government borrowing money for its operating budget.

**Penal Code** A body of law that defines most criminal offenses and sets a range of punishments that can be assessed.

**Permanent University Fund** A land- and mineral-rich endowment that benefits the University of Texas and Texas A&M University systems, particularly the flagship universities in Austin and College Station.

**Petit jury** A panel of citizens that hears evidence in a civil lawsuit or a criminal prosecution and decides the outcome by issuing a verdict.

**Platform** A set of principles or positions on various issues adopted by a political party at its state or national convention.

**Plea bargain** A procedure that allows a person charged with a crime to negotiate a guilty plea with prosecutors in exchange for a lighter sentence than he would expect to receive if convicted in a trial.

**Plural executive** A fragmented system of authority under which most statewide, executive officeholders are elected independently of the governor. This arrangement, which is used in Texas, places severe limitations on the governor's power.

**Pluralism** Theories holding that a diversity of groups—and people—are instrumental in the policy-making process, and no one group is able to dominate the decisions of government.

**Political culture** A widely shared set of views, attitudes, beliefs and customs of a people as to how their government should be organized and run.

**Political patronage** The hiring of government employees on the basis of personal friendships or favors rather than ability or merit.

**Political party** A group that seeks to elect public officeholders under its own name.

**Political socialization** The process which begins in early childhood whereby a person assimilates the beliefs, attitudes and behaviors of society and acquires views toward the political system and government.

**Political action committee** Often referred to as a PAC, this is a committee representing a specific interest group or including employees of a specific company that raises money from its members for distribution to selected officeholders and political candidates.

**Poll tax** A tax that Texas and some other states used to require people to pay before allowing them to vote. The purpose was to discourage minorities and poor whites from participating in the political process. The tax was declared unconstitutional in the 1960s.

**Popular sovereignty** The constitutional principle of self-government; the belief that the people control their government and governments are subject to limitations and constraints.

**Population density** The number of residents living within the boundaries of a city, county or state in relationship to the land area. It is a significant factor in determining the level of local public services.

**Precinct** A specific, local voting area created by county commissioners court. The state election code outlines detailed requirements for drawing up these election units.

**Precinct chair** A local officer in a political party who presides over the precinct convention and serves on the party's county executive committee. Voters in each precinct elect a chair in the party's primary election.

**Precinct convention** A meeting held by a political party in each precinct on the same day as the party primary. In presidential election years, the precinct conventions and the primaries are the first steps in the selection of delegates to the major parties' national nominating conventions.

**Preemptions** Federal laws that preempt the authority or powers of state and local governments.

**Privatization** Government contracting with private companies to provide some public services.

**Privileges and immunities** The right of a resident of one state to be protected by the laws and afforded the legal opportunities in any other state he or she visits. Certain exceptions, however, have been allowed by the courts, including the right of states to charge non-residents higher college tuition or higher hunting and fishing license fees.

**Probation** A procedure under which a convicted criminal isn't sent to prison if he promises to behave himself and meet certain conditions, such as restrictions on where he travels and with whom he associates.

**Prosecution** The conduct of legal proceedings against an individual charged with a crime.

**Public opinion polling** The scientific sampling of people's attitudes toward business products, public issues, public officeholders or political candidates. It has become a key ingredient of statewide political campaigns and is usually conducted by telephone using a representative sample of voters.

**Public interest groups** Groups that are primarily concerned with consumer or environmental protection, the promotion of strong ethical standards for public officials or increased funding for health and human services programs. Since they often are poorly funded, grass-roots, volunteer efforts are crucial to their success.

**Radical right** An ultraconservative political faction that draws considerable support from fundamentalist religious groups and economic conservatives.

**Radical Reconstructionists** The group of Republicans who took control of Congress in 1866 and imposed hated military governments on the former Confederate states after the Civil War.

**Railroad Commission** A three-member, elected body that regulates intrastate trucking and bus service and oil and natural gas production in Texas.

**Reading, third** Final presentation of a bill before the full House or Senate.

**Reading, second** Initial debate by the full House or Senate on a bill that has been approved by a committee.

**Reading, first** The introduction of a bill in the House or the Senate and its referral to a committee by the presiding officer.

**Realignment** A major shift in political party support or identification which usually occurs around a critical election. In Texas, this was a gradual transformation from a one-party system dominated by Democrats to a two-party system in which Republicans became competitive in elections.

**Reconstruction Constitution** Drafted in 1869, this constitution centralized power in state government while weakening local governments. It didn't reflect the sentiments of most Texans, but it conformed to the wishes of the Radical Reconstructionists.

**Record vote** A vote taken in the House or the Senate of which a permanent record is kept, listing how individual legislators voted. By contrast, there are voice votes where legislators simply voice ayes or nays on an issue.

**Regressive tax system** A tax system that imposes a disproportionately heavier burden on low income people than on the more affluent.

**Reserved powers** Powers given state governments by the Tenth Amendment. These are powers not delegated to the national government nor otherwise prohibited to the states by the Constitution.

**Revenue sharing** A program begun under President Nixon and later repealed in which state and local governments received federal aid that could be used for virtually any purpose the recipient government wanted.

**Revolving door** The practice of former members of state boards and commissions or key employees of agencies leaving state government for more lucrative jobs with the industries they used to regulate. It raises questions of undue industry influence over regulatory agencies.

***Ruiz* v. *Estelle*** A lawsuit in which a federal judge in 1980 declared the Texas prison system unconstitutional and ordered sweeping, expensive reforms.

**Secretary of State** Administers state election laws, grants charters to corporations and processes the extradition of prisoners to other states. This officeholder is appointed by the governor.

**Senatorial courtesy** An unwritten policy that permits a senator to block the confirmation of a gubernatorial appointee who lives in the senator's district.

**Separation of powers** The division of authority among three distinct branches of government—the legislative, the executive and the judicial—which serve as checks and balances on each other's power.

**Session, regular** This is the 140-day period in odd-numbered years in which the legislature meets and can consider and pass laws on any issue or subject.

**Session, special** A legislative session that can be called at any other time by the governor. It is limited to 30 days' duration and can consider only subjects or issues designated by the governor.

**Sharpstown stock fraud scandal** After rocking state government in 1971 and 1972, it helped produce some far-reaching legislative and political changes. It involved the passage of banking legislation sought by Houston financier Frank Sharp and quick profits that some state officials made on stock purchased in an insurance company owned by Sharp with unsecured loans from Sharp's Sharpstown State Bank.

**Sheriff** An elected official who is the chief law enforcement officer of a county. In urban areas, his or her jurisdiction usually is limited to the unincorporated areas of a county, while local police departments have jurisdiction over incorporated cities.

**Single-issue groups** Single purpose or highly ideological groups that promote a single issue or cause with only limited regard for the views or interests of other groups. They often are reluctant to compromise.

**Single-member district election** A system in which a legislator, city council member or other public official is elected from a specific, geographic area.

**Sound bite** A short, quotable phrase by a public official or political candidate that may sound good on television or radio but lacks depth and is often meaningless.

**Speaker** The presiding officer of the House of Representatives.

**Special district** Units of local government created by the state to perform specific functions not met by cities or counties, including the provision of public services to unincorporated areas.

**Spin** The presentation of information in the best possible light for a public official or political candidate. It usually is provided by a press secretary, campaign consultant or other individual representing the officeholder or candidate.

**Staggered terms** A requirement that members of state boards and commissions appointed by the governor serve terms that begin on different dates. This is to assure that a board maintains a level of experience by guarding against situations where all board members leave office at the same time.

**State chair and vice chair** The two top state leaders of a political party, one of whom must be a woman. They are selected every two years by delegates to the party's state convention.

**State executive committee** The statewide governing board of a political party. It includes a man and a woman elected by party members from each of the 31 state senatorial districts and the state chair and vice chair, who are selected by delegates to the party's biennial state convention.

**State convention** A meeting held in June of even-numbered years by each of the two major political parties. Delegates to this convention elect the party's state leadership and adopt a party platform. In presidential election years, it selects the delegates to the party's national nominating convention.

**State treasurer** The custodian of state funds. Funds administered by this office are placed in financial institutions until they are needed to pay the state's bills. It is an elected office.

**State Board of Education** An elected panel that oversees the administration of public education in Texas.

**Subcommittee** A few members of a larger committee appointed to review legislation and make recommendations to the committee on the disposition of a bill.

**Suffrage** The right to vote.

**Sunset** The process under which most state agencies have to be periodically reviewed and re-created by the legislature or go out of business.

**Supremacy clause** A provision of the U.S. Constitution that says federal law prevails in conflicts between the powers of the states and the national government.

**Supreme Court, Texas** A nine-member court with final appellate jurisdiction over civil lawsuits.

**Tag** A rule that allows an individual senator to postpone a committee hearing on any bill for at least 48 hours, a delay that can be fatal to a bill during the closing days of a legislative session.

**Tax, property** A tax on homes, businesses and certain other forms of property that is the main source of revenue for local governments. The tax is based on the assessed value of the property.

**Tax, income** A tax based on a corporation's or an individual's income. Texas has a hybrid corporate income tax but is one of only a few states without a personal income tax.

**Tax, sales** A tax charged as a set percentage of most retail purchases and many services. It is the main source of tax revenue for state government and an important source of revenue for many cities and metropolitan transit authorities.

**Tax, sin** A common nickname for a tax on tobacco or alcoholic beverages.

**Tax, franchise** The state's major business tax. It is applied only to corporations and, until changed by the legislature in 1991, was based on a business' assets. Now it is a hybrid corporate income tax that is based on a corporation's income or assets, whichever would produce the highest payment to the state.

**The Establishment** In the days of one-party, Democratic politics in Texas, it was a loosely knit coalition of Anglo businessmen, oilmen, bankers and lawyers who controlled state policy making through the dominant, conservative wing of the Democratic party.

**Third party** A minor political party. There have been many in Texas over the years, but none has had significant success on a statewide level.

**Ticket splitters** Voters who divide their votes among candidates of more than one political party in the same election.

**Tort reform** Changes in state law to put limits on personal injury lawsuits and damage judgments entered by the courts. These changes have been advocated by businesses, professional associations, cities and insurance companies that are defendants in most major personal injury lawsuits. A tort is a wrongful act over which a damage lawsuit can be brought.

**Traditionalistic subculture** A view that political power should be concentrated in the hands of a few elite citizens who belong to established families or influential social groups. Public policy basically serves the interests of this small group.

**Transnational regionalism** The expanding economic and social interdependence of South Texas and Mexico.

**Two-party system** A political system that has two dominant parties, such as that of the United States.

**Two-thirds rule** A rule under which the Texas Senate has traditionally operated that requires approval of at least two- thirds of senators before a bill can be debated on the Senate floor. It allows a minority of senators to block controversial legislation.

**Unitary system** A system in which ultimate power is vested in a central or national government and local governments have only those powers granted them by the central government. This principle describes the relationship between the state and local governments in Texas.

**Urbanization** The process by which a predominantly rural society or area becomes urban.

**Veto** The power of the governor to reject, or kill, a bill passed by the legislature.

**Veto, line item** The power of the governor to reject certain parts of an appropriations, or spending, bill without killing the entire measure.

**Voting Rights Act** A federal law designed to protect the voting rights of minorities by requiring the Justice Department's approval of changes in political districts and certain other electoral procedures. The act, as amended, has eliminated most of the more restrictive state laws that limited minority political participation.

**Whistleblower** A government employee who publicly complains about wrongdoing or unethical conduct within a government agency.

**White primary** A series of state laws and party rules that denied African-Americans the right to vote in the Democratic primary in Texas in the first half of the 20th century.

# INDEX